SPAIN RODRIGUEZ

MY LIFE & TIMES

compiled and edited by
Patrick Rosenkranz

FANTAGRAPHICS BOOKS
SEATTLE, WASHINGTON

Editor: Patrick Rosenkranz

Designer: Chelsea Wirtz

Assistant Editor: RJ Casey

Production: Paul Baresh

Promotion: Jacq Cohen

Associate Publisher: Eric Reynolds

Publisher: Gary Groth

Fantagraphics Books, Inc.
7563 Lake City Way NE
Seattle, WA 98115
www.fantagraphics.com

ISBN: 978-1-68396-381-3
Library of Congress Control Number: 2020937733
First Printing: 2020
Printed in Korea

ACKNOWLEDGMENTS

The author would like to acknowledge the assistance of the following individuals for helping him tell the story of this remarkable underground cartoonist: Dominic Albanese, Monte Beauchamp, Glenn Bray, Jo Ellen Bray, Susie Bright, M.K. Brown, Paul Buhle, Edward Cardoni, Hope Hoetzer-Cook, Al Cooper, Robert Crumb, Kim Deitch, Phoebe Gloeckner, Justin Green, Bruce Jackson, Jay Kinney, Paul Mavrides, Carl Mildenberger, Hal Robbins, Cynthia Rodriguez-Badendyck, Nora Rodriguez, Crispin Rosenkranz, Joel Schechter, Gilbert Shelton, Ron Turner, Robert and Suzanne Williams, Janet Underwood, Thunder Watso, Ken Weaver, and Maxine Weaver. Very special thanks go to Spain's widow, Susan Stern, for granting access to his artwork and personal photos, his studio and archives, and for her diligence and encouragement. It was pleasure to work with her and my honor to present the artist's life and art for posterity.

CONTENTS

SPAIN RODRIGUEZ: REVOLUTIONARY COMIX ARTIST, SOCIAL ACTIVIST, AND OUTLAW BIKER

This is the third in a series of books about one of the underground's greatest artists, Manuel "Spain" Rodriguez. In *My Life & Times*, Spain trains his eye on himself, drawing from the pivotal moments of his life—cruising with his teen pals, patronizing Buffalo jazz clubs, and eventually becoming a respected community elder in San Francisco's Mission District. This volume collects Spain's most candid comic stories from publications like *Rip Off Comix*, *Blab!*, and *Prime Cuts*, including his personal account of the 1968 Democratic National Convention protest.

Manuel Rodriguez's real life was as exciting as the adventures he drew for *Zap Comix*, *Insect Fear*, and the other radical publications he contributed to. Raised in the industrial city of Buffalo, New York, he made his bones with the Italian and Irish neighborhood kids by forcefully declaring his Spanish ancestry was as good as, if not better. That's when he got the nickname Spain, which he kept all his life. He went to art school, came home to work in a factory, and joined the Road Vulture Motorcycle Club in 1961.

He helped organize anti-war protests, drew covers for the first underground newspaper in Buffalo, and rode and rumbled with his biker comrades. It wasn't long before he moved to New York City and began working for a major player in the counterculture press, the *East Village Other*.

He gave writer credit for his *EVO* strips to an imaginary wordsmith, and alias, Algernon Backwash—a shadowy figure, never quoted or photographed, but who "wrote stories" for Spain year after year, never flagging or running out of ideas.

Spain's reputation grew when he moved to San Francisco in 1969 and became a charter member in the underground comix revolution. He launched new comic titles like *Subvert* and joined Robert Crumb, Gilbert Shelton, and other prominent artists to produce *Zap Comix*. This series was a major influence in the movement that changed comics forever.

He lived the rest of his life in San Francisco, and never lost his zeal for social activism and political action. He was a poster artist for the San Francisco Mime Troupe and a well-known figure in the Mission District, where he taught children how to draw comics at the Mission Center and painted murals and street art. He was prolific and profane, unable to resist a blank surface or an opportunity to make an artistic impact. Spain drew flyers, posters, comic strips, and produced one of the internet's first webcomics, *Dark Hotel* for Salon.com. He also designed film and stage sets, created editorial cartoons and magazine illustrations, and was a maestro of pornographic art, declaring himself a "crude dude in a lewd mood."

Spain Rodriguez died on November 28, 2012, at home with his family, from prostate cancer complications. He was given a lavish send off at the Brava Theater the following March to a packed house of friends and fans. His widow, Susan Stern, is producing a feature-length documentary about his life and work, titled *Bad Attitude: The Art of Spain Rodriguez*.

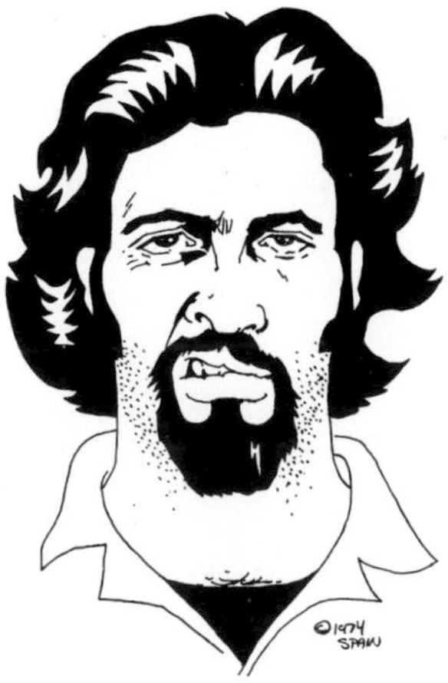
©1974 SPAIN

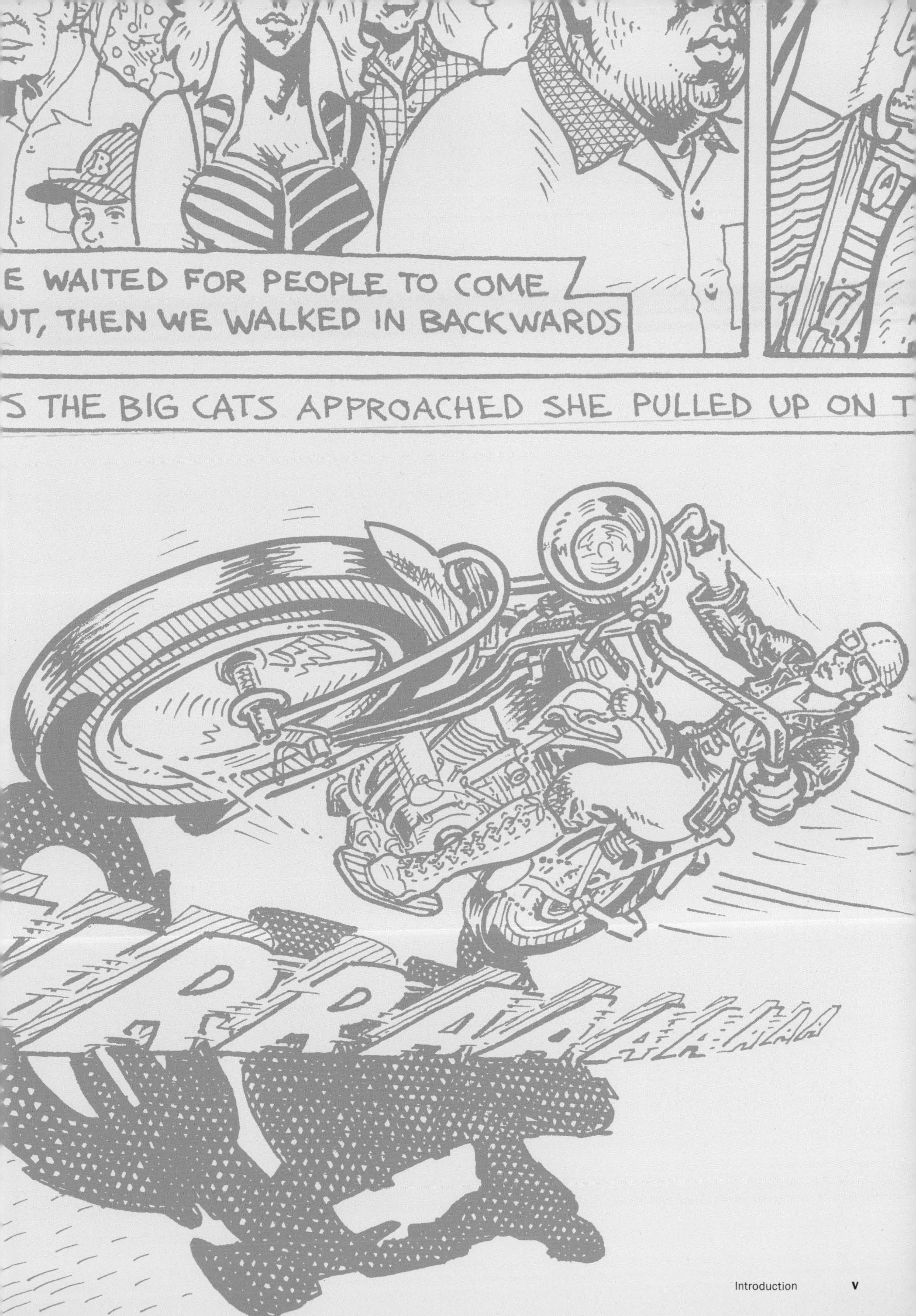
E WAITED FOR PEOPLE TO COME
UT, THEN WE WALKED IN BACKWARDS
S THE BIG CATS APPROACHED SHE PULLED UP ON T

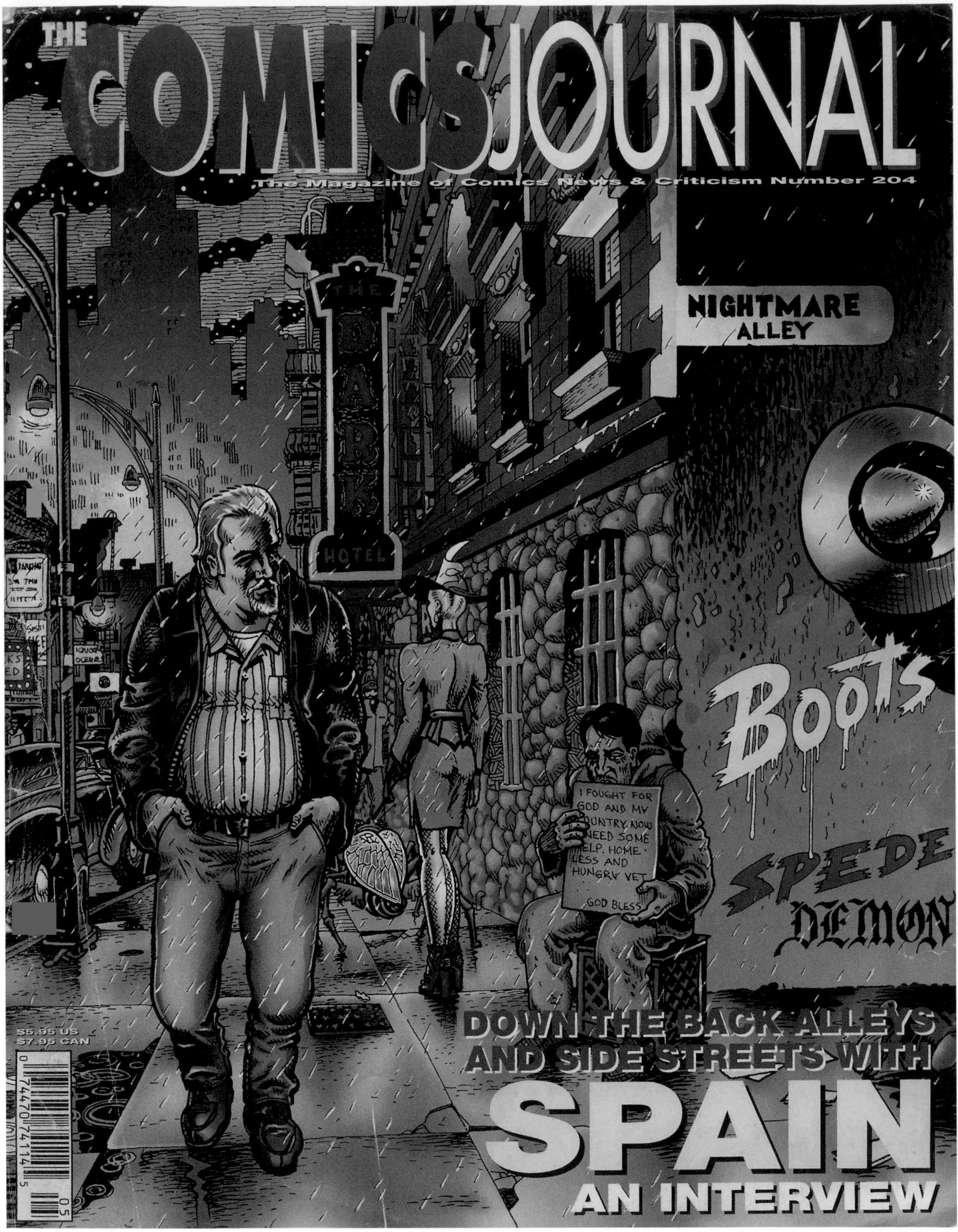
THE COMICS JOURNAL
The Magazine of Comics News & Criticism Number 204
THE DARK HOTEL
NIGHTMARE ALLEY
I FOUGHT FOR
GOD AND MY
LESS AND
HUNGRY VET
GOD BLESS
Boots
SPEDE
DEMON
$5.95 US
$7.95 CAN
DOWN THE BACK ALLEYS
AND SIDE STREETS WITH
SPAIN
AN INTERVIEW

ABOVE: The graffiti on Spain's cover for *The Comics Journal* #204 in 1998 highlights many of his graphic novels and serials, including *The Dark Hotel*, *Nightmare Alley*, *Boots*, and *Spede Demon.*

OPPOSITE: Spain at home, circa 1995.

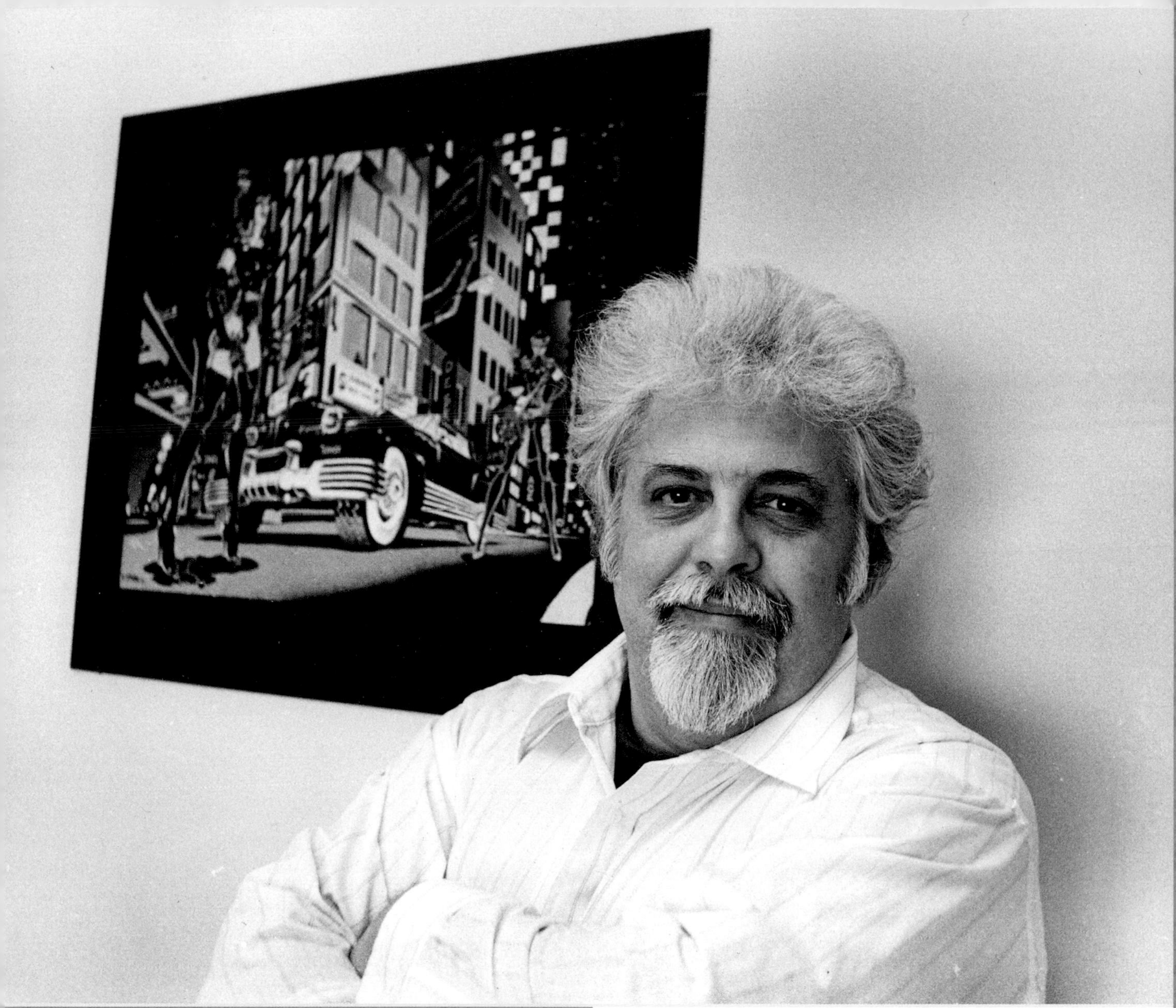

FORTY YEARS IN THE MISSION DISTRICT

PATRICK ROSENKRANZ

The Rise and Fall of the Comix Movement

Coming from New York City in 1969, San Francisco looked pretty clean and safe to Spain Rodriguez, with its wide palm-lined avenues, gaily painted Victorian houses, and vistas of San Francisco Bay from atop its many hills; a far cry from the dark, dirty streets of the Lower East Side. When people warned him some neighborhoods were unsafe, he chortled to himself. He'd seen much worse in the Big Apple, and he also came of age in Buffalo, which he fondly recalled as "the city of no illusions," "the mecca of reckless youth."

Almost immediately, he was busy on several new comic projects in the anything-goes atmosphere of the rapidly expanding underground comix movement. He started a new anthology titled *Insect Fear* and produced two issues in 1970. His sole editorial guideline specified that there must be insects crawling on the walls somewhere in the story. He drew stories for three issues of *San Francisco Comic Book*, published by Gary Arlington, the proprietor of one of the earliest comic book emporiums in America, which quickly became ground zero for comix creators

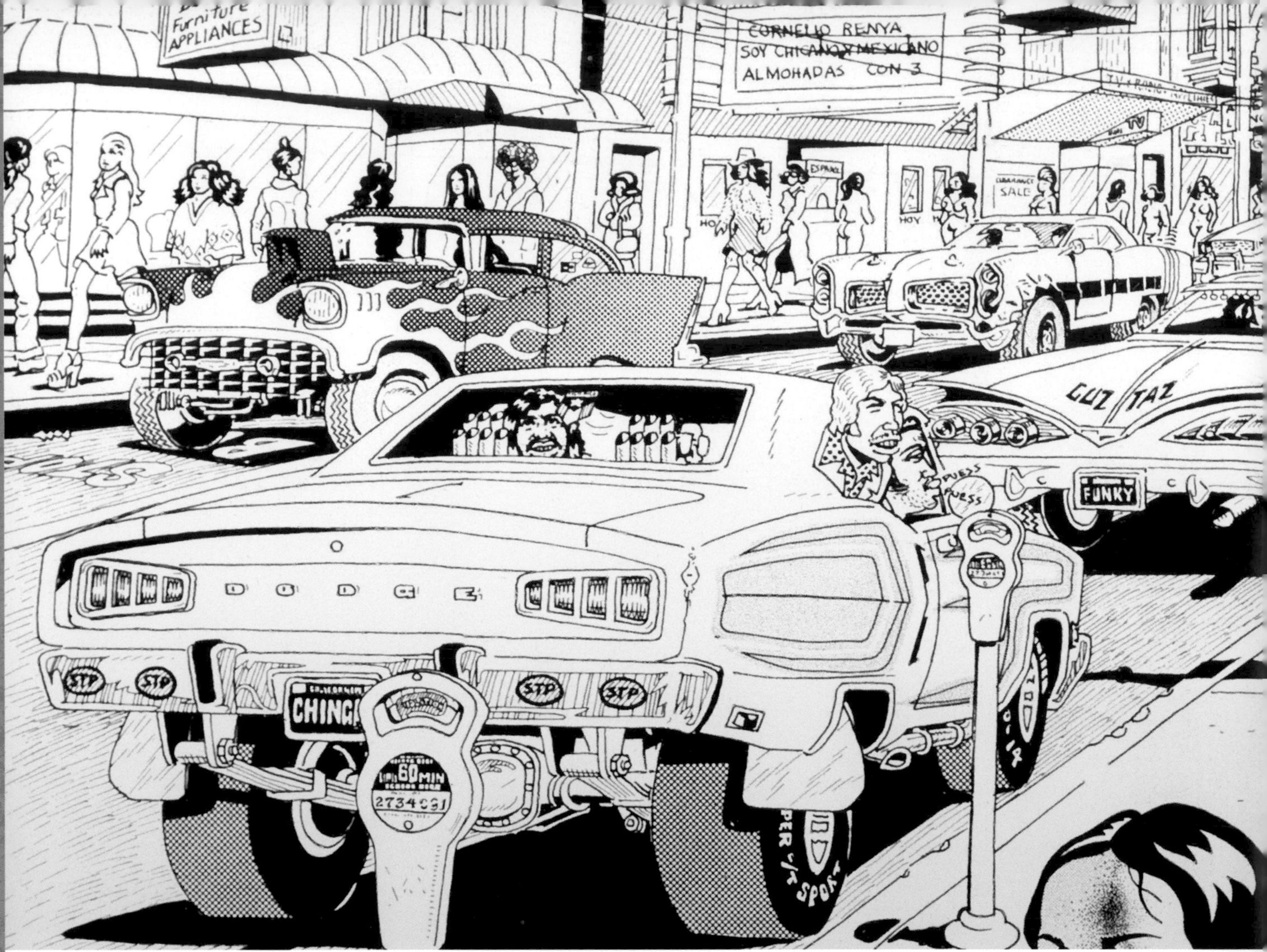
Furniture APPLIANCES
ALMOHADAS CON 3
SALE
FUNKY
D O D G E

and fans. That fall, Rip Off Press published *Subvert Comics*, which continued the Trashman saga begun in the *East Village Other*. A tabloid compilation of those strips, *The Collected Trashman*, had been published by the *Berkeley Barb* a year earlier, and whetted California comix readers' appetites for more tales of their favorite counterculture guerrilla.

Many other cartoonists showed up in San Francisco that year, including Justin Green, Bill Griffith, Kim Deitch, Trina Robbins, Roger Brand, Jack Jackson, S. Clay Wilson, Art Spiegelman, Jim Osborne, Willy Mendes, Jay Kinney, and Willy Murphy. They all gravitated toward the low-rent districts of the city including the Mission District, home of the San Francisco Comic Book Company. It was an ethnically diverse neighborhood, back when that was considered a bad thing to some, but for counterculture artists it meant the living was easy and gentrification was decades away.

"A lot of the artists were living within a few blocks of each other in the Mission District," said Jay Kinney. "Rip Off Press was a bunch of crazed Texans who had moved to San Francisco to be part of the comic scene, most notably Gilbert Shelton. There was the great camaraderie of deciding, 'OK, I've been working all day on this strip,' and then taking the page that you were working on over to your friend living three blocks away and having him critique it, or having her give her reaction. So, I think that really fed the movement from that sense of we're all in sort of close proximity to each other. It really made for a lot of momentum and a lot of energy. But eventually that began to break apart, because different factions began forming. There was in-fighting. You had different notions of what underground comix ought to be about. Ultimately, that was kind of a fatal development in the movement. But until that really came to the fore, there was a strong sense of brotherhood."

For forty-three years, Spain Rodriguez made San Francisco his home. He became an active member of his community, allying with activists and other artists, participating in radical politics and theater, getting involved in the Latino art movement, and teaching, while continuing to demonstrate complete freedom of expression in his own artwork. He was known far and wide as a *Zap* cartoonist, a star of the underground comic book that started it all. Landmarks of San Francisco were often featured in his comic stories, especially those starring Trashman and Big Bitch, who appeared in familiar urban neighborhoods, nightclubs, movie theaters, and dives.

Spain reportedly painted the first official mural in the Mission District; he was an iconic poster artist for dozens of San Francisco Mime Troupe productions; an arts educator for twenty years, teaching his hard-learned "tips and tricks" to scores of

TOP: "An Average Day on Mission Street," from *Arcade* #2, 1975.

OPPOSITE: *Zap* artists Robert Williams, S. Clay Wilson, Victor Moscoso, and Spain Rodriguez gather together for a jam session in 1994. Photo by Lorraine Chamberlain.

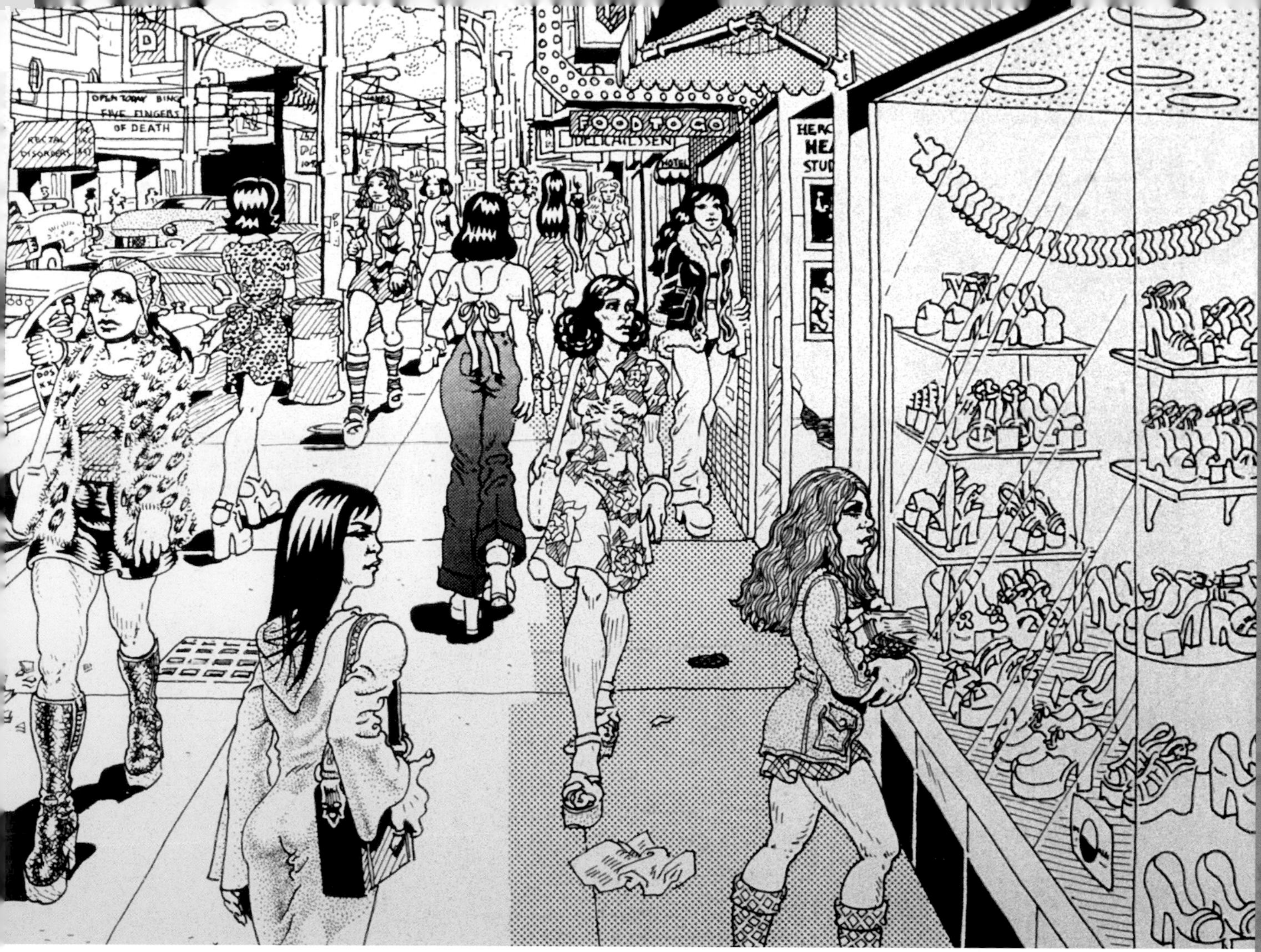
FIVE FINGERS
OF DEATH
FOOD TO GO
DELICATESSEN

children and adults; a co-creator with Bob Callahan of one of the first online comic strips, *The Dark Hotel*; and a proud husband, father, and solid citizen, living a life full of work that inspired the many people he interacted with during his lifetime. An energetically packed house turned out for his memorial service at the Brava Theater in March, 2013, five months after his death at 72 of cancer.

He couldn't complete a final assignment, but he asked fellow cartoonist Jay Kinney to finish it and meet the deadline for him—a story called "Modicut and the Yiddish Bohemians." Kinney agreed out of respect for his friend's sixty-year artistic legacy and tried to do his best to represent Spain's artistic style, using similar tools and techniques.

"I didn't see Spain as 'ambitious' or very concerned with reputation, competition, or how the world was treating him financially. He calmly went on with the work he loved to do, and that's what he talked about."

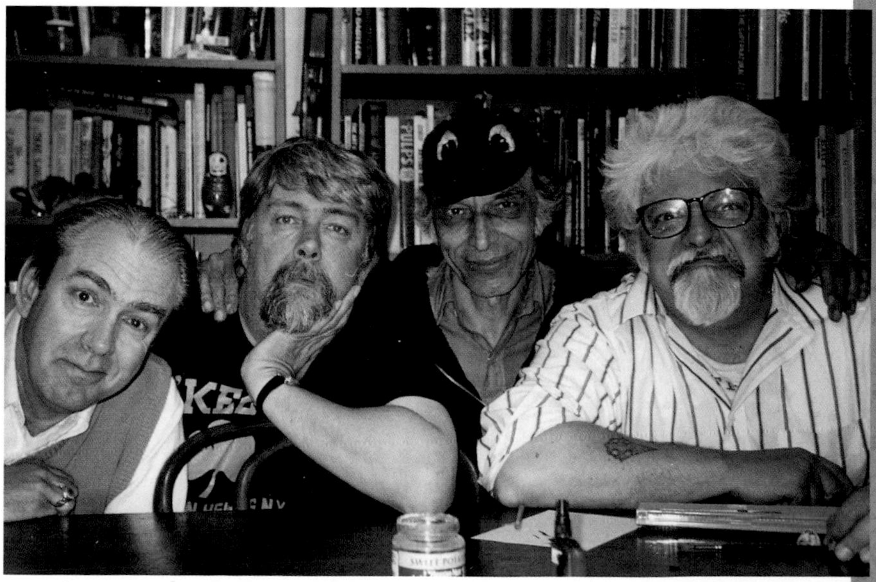

During the early 1970s, underground comix were a hot commodity. Most popular titles like *Skull* and *Slow Death Funnies* often sold 20,000 or even 40,000 copies. Some super-sellers like *Zap Comix*, *Furry Freak Brothers*, and *Young Lust* sold hundreds of thousands. Making the rent was easier when regular royalty checks came from Print Mint and other underground publishers, but by the middle of the '70s that formerly red-hot enthusiasm had chilled and the boom wasn't coming back. Before long they were burning comic books in the woodstove at Rip Off Press to keep warm in the winter.

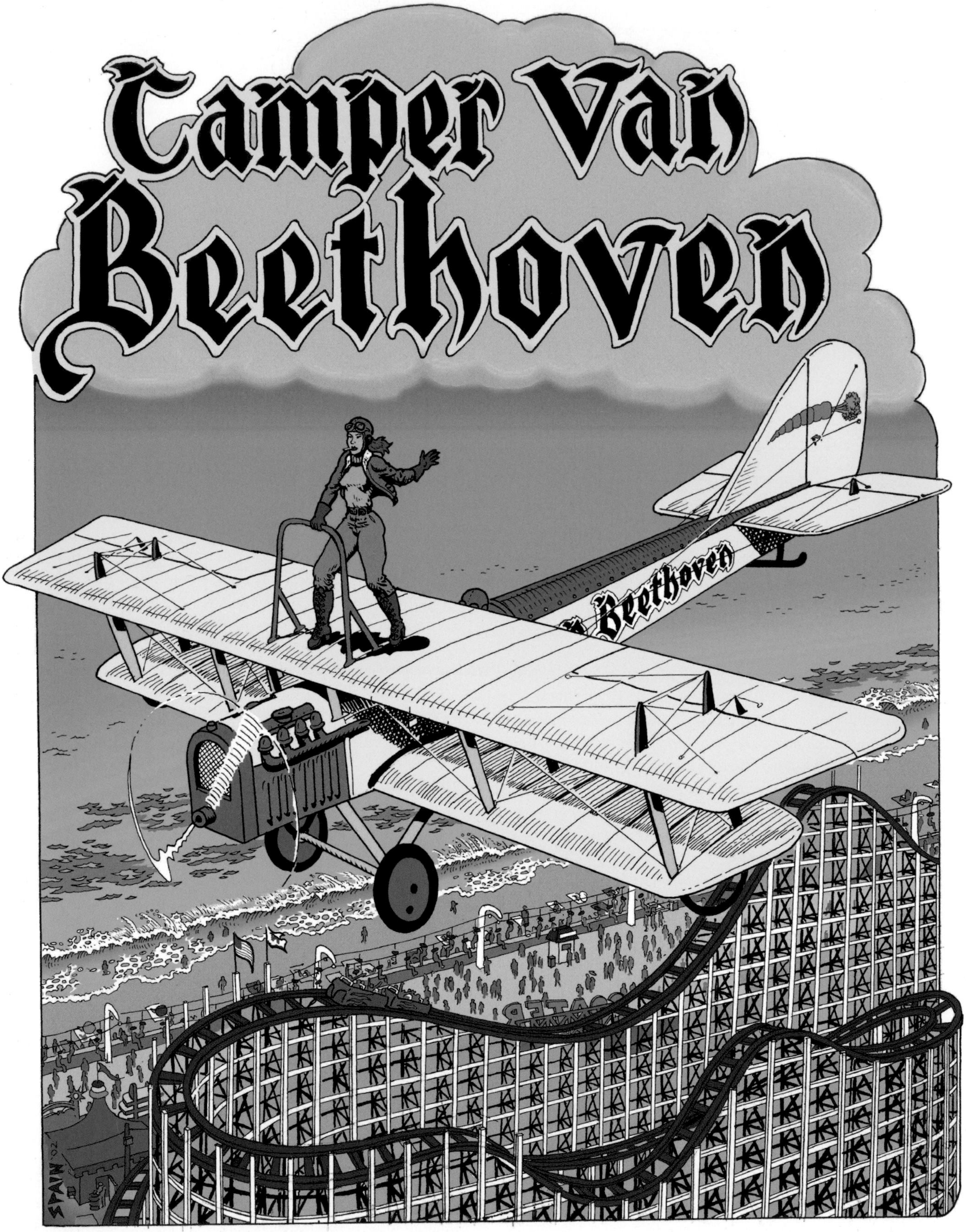
Camper Van Beethoven
Beethoven
SPAIN '02

ABOVE: Artwork for Camper Van Beethoven's *Greatest Hits Played Faster*, 2002.

OPPOSITE TOP: Original art for Frank Zappa's *Beat the Boots!* limited edition box set from 1991.

OPPOSITE BOTTOM: Concert flyer for Steve Earle, 2005.

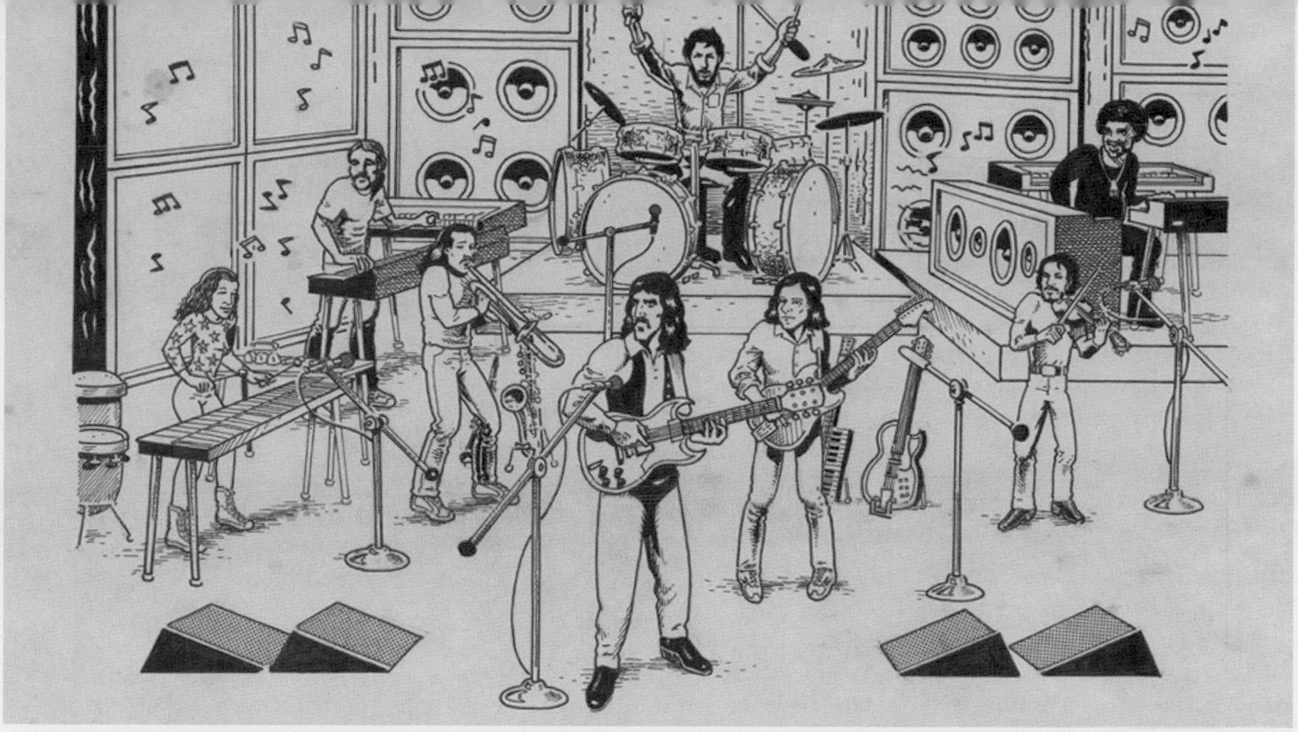

Art Spiegelman and Bill Griffith proposed *Arcade*, a comic magazine that would appear on newsstands next to *National Lampoon* and *The New Yorker*, and provide access to a new readership. In a last noble effort, everyone rallied around *Arcade* as a life raft to save their movement. Spiegelman and Griffith imposed tougher editorial guidelines than was usual for this group of independent artists, and many cartoonists did some of their finest work for the publication. Their quarterly production schedule taxed everyone involved, including the Print Mint, which went broke paying the bills on this expensive venture. *Arcade* never did get much newsstand display; no new distribution channels formed outside the underground model of head shops and mail-order catalogs; and no one was raking in dough. After seven issues, artists, editors, and publishers had enough. They needed to find other work.

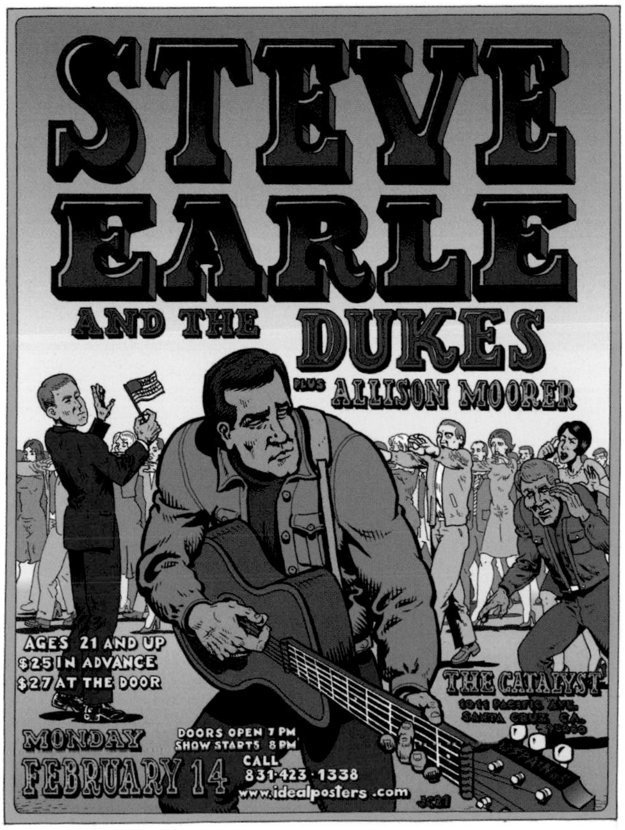
STEVE
EARLE
AND THE
DUKES
ALLISON MOORER
AGES 21 AND UP
$25 IN ADVANCE
$27 AT THE DOOR
THE CATALYST
MONDAY
FEBRUARY 14
DOORS OPEN 7 PM
SHOW STARTS 8 PM
CALL
831·423·1338
www.idealposters .com

No longer able to rely on the few but proud underground publishers to provide a living wage, many cartoonists were forced to look farther afield for paying work and often found fans sitting behind art directors' desks. Slick magazines began to recruit from the underground, including *Playboy*, *National Lampoon*, *Coq*, *Cavalier*, *Apple Pie*, *High Times*, *Heavy Metal*, and *Gallery*. Book publishers such as Bellerophon Books, Troubador, And/Or, and Belier Press also tapped this unique talent pool of cartoonists.

Spain managed to make ends meet through freelancing work after *Arcade* folded, said his girlfriend at the time, Maxine Weaver. Spain always seemed to have some personal or commercial project in progress, and didn't spend much time going out looking for work, she recalled. "Spain didn't talk about *Arcade* or the overall comix scene, where it was going, etcetera," she said. "I don't know how he went about finding work. I think that instead work came to him. I didn't see Spain as 'ambitious' or very concerned with reputation, competition, or how the world was treating him financially. He calmly went on with the work he loved to do, and that's what he talked about."

When some of the excesses of the 1960s led to psychedelic casualties among his friends and colleagues, Spain took a good look at his own drink and drug habits and questioned whether it was having any effect on his work. His doctor helped him decide to be sober.

"He stopped drinking in 1974 because it made his arthritis worse," said Weaver. "Stopping definitely helped. He was also told to cut way back on red meat for the same reason, which made him much more furious. Shortly after the doctor told him no red meat, we went on a camping trip and ate the most elegant non-red-meat meals possible, grilling lobster and Asian-spice-marinated chicken on the hibachi. Later he went back to red meat and hated the idea of going without it, which I think he saw as un-masculine and a breach of freedom, but he never went back to alcohol. I don't know how his friends felt about his not drinking, but Spain was not somebody other people tried to pressure, so they surely accepted his decision without argument."

The seven samurai of *Zap Comix* did some of their best comic work for their own signature publication, but Spain didn't like waiting so long between issues. *Zap* #7 came out in 1974, *Zap* #8 in 1975. It was three years before *Zap* #9 came together, and four years after that for *Zap* #10 in 1982. In the meantime, Spain began drawing historical documentaries for *Anarchy Comics*, and contributed work to other anthology titles like *San Francisco Comic Book* and *Young Lust*. He drew complete stories for nine issues of *Weirdo* and three of *Weird Smut*. *Gallery* and *Hustler* commissioned him to illustrate articles about Vietnam MIAs, CIA subvert operations, and political chicanery in Africa. Sex tabloid *Screw* appreciated his facility with sexy comics and commissioned him to draw dozens of covers featuring exotic women in chic fashions and settings.

"Spain worked for *Screw* magazine for the money and because he liked drawing pictures of naked women and because he probably had a lot of editorial freedom," said his wife Susan Stern. "I don't know that anyone actually exercised control over him. He drew images that were consistent with the kind of images he liked to draw. He liked to draw beautiful women. He liked to draw long-legged women, I'd say, with medium-sized breasts and cool clothes and shoes on. He got to draw a lot of those for *Screw*."

His work also appeared in fourteen issues of a slick girlie magazine, *Fling*, between 1979 and 1986, but he didn't like publisher Arv Miller's constant demands for changes in his art, including his nagging to "draw the tits bigger."

"That was very much work for hire," said Stern. "He was illustrating other people's stories. He was actually working for a very dominating editor. I don't see the *Fling* work as representing his sexual expression. There's really some icky stuff in *Fling*. A weird obsession with medical procedures, and, of course really huge breasts."

Spain was often asked to draw flyers to advertise political events, which he did pro bono many times. Though his musical preferences tended toward doo-wop and 1950s rock and roll, he also was recruited to graphically promote bands, in the Bay Area and beyond. He drew concert posters and album covers for a number of musicians, including Frank Zappa, Steve Earle, and Buddy Blue.

"He did this poster for a band called The Dadas back in the late 1970s," said his fellow cartoonist Paul Mavrides. "Naomi Ruth Eisenberg of Dan Hicks and His Hot Licks was their singer, so Spain did this surreal or Dadaistic drawing of the band performing and it looks like they're in some bombed-out war zone farmhouse with chunks of wall missing and there's all these strange characters ... One in bondage gear and a Wally Wood alien. It's so dense and there's smoke drawn in front of the band that you almost don't take notice that it's all taking place on the moon, and there's this landscape with craters off in the distance and it's just really nicely done, and it doesn't seem forced. He threw all this stuff in it and it didn't seem forced or false to pile it on like that. He found the solution to playing with these things. And it seemed innate too. It wasn't like he pondered and pondered and thought about what he was doing. It was quick and poured out of his moving hand."

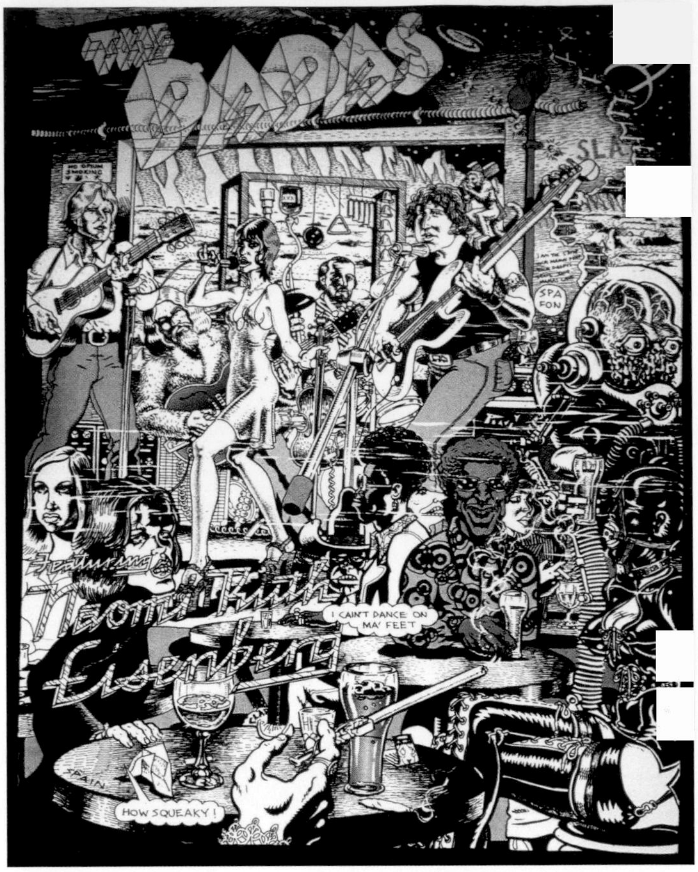
I CAN'T DANCE ON MA' FEET
HOW SQUEAKY!
SPAIN

The San Francisco Mime Troupe

His association with the San Francisco Mime Troupe began around 1971 when Spain and then-girlfriend Linda Post designed a "cranky," said Andrea Snow, a long-time Mime Troupe actor who lived in the same house with Spain on Coso Avenue. The "cranky" was a freestanding frame holding a roll of paper with a series of drawings. Two people would crank the roll as they pulled it across the stage while telling a story.

"It was like a paper movie," said Snow. "I think the first one had something to do with GIs and the war in Vietnam." In those days, as today, the Troupe performed in parks around the city, using a small portable stage.

"The Mime Troupe staged especially mobile shows," added Snow. "The stage is mainly this little portable *commedia dell'arte* stage, a little postage-stamp stage and a backdrop painted on canvas. People make their exits around the corners of the backdrop."

The original troupe began in 1959 and came to define the term "guerrilla theater." In 1963, they were denied a permit to perform in San Francisco city parks by the Recreation and Parks Commission on grounds of obscenity, but that ruling was overturned in court. In their subsequent *Minstrel Show, Or Civil Rights in a Cracker Barrel*, a racially mixed group of actors in blackface and whiteface perverted a historically racist form of entertainment to attack racial prejudice. During the years of active anti-Vietnam War protest the Mime Troupe began touring at many college campuses across the United States. They performed Bertolt Brecht's *The Mother* in Mexico City in 1974, in

ABOVE: A 1976 poster for the San Francisco band The Dadas.

OPPOSITE: Spain's first poster for The San Francisco Mime Troupe, 1974.

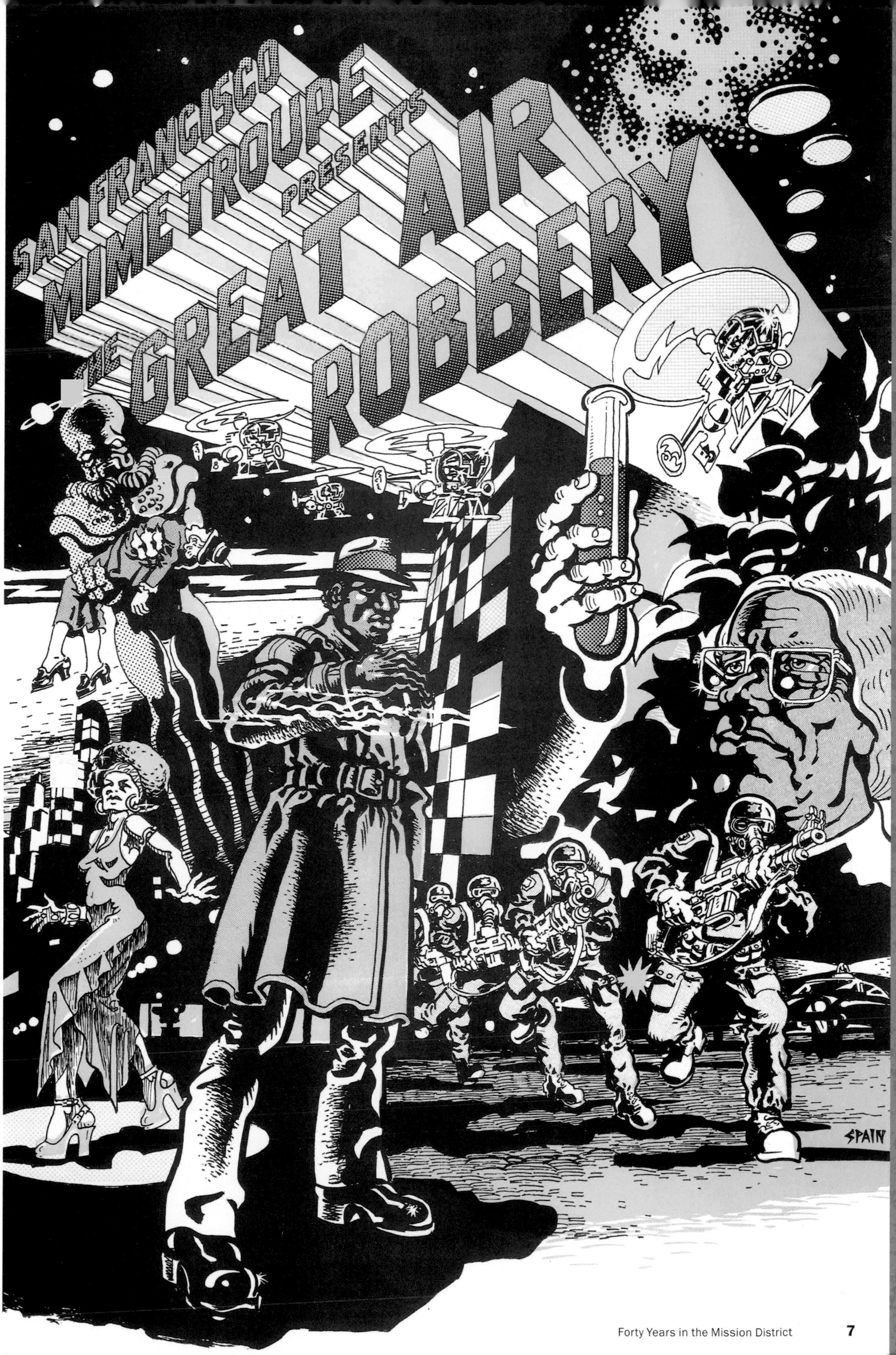
SAN FRANCISCO
MIME TROUPE
PRESENTS
THE
GREAT AIR
ROBBERY
SPAIN

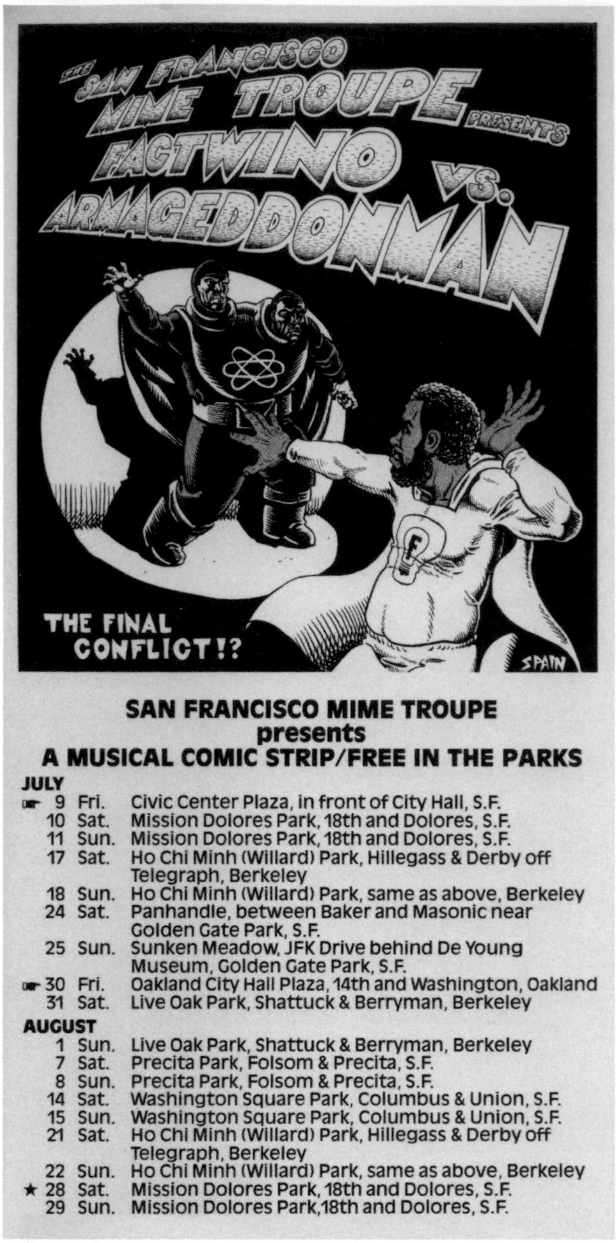
THE SAN FRANCISCO MIME TROUPE PRESENTS
FACTWINO VS. ARMAGEDDONMAN
THE FINAL CONFLICT!?
SPAIN
SAN FRANCISCO MIME TROUPE
presents
A MUSICAL COMIC STRIP/FREE IN THE PARKS
JULY
☞ 9 Fri. Civic Center Plaza, in front of City Hall, S.F.
10 Sat. Mission Dolores Park, 18th and Dolores, S.F.
11 Sun. Mission Dolores Park, 18th and Dolores, S.F.
17 Sat. Ho Chi Minh (Willard) Park, Hillegass & Derby off Telegraph, Berkeley
18 Sun. Ho Chi Minh (Willard) Park, same as above, Berkeley
24 Sat. Panhandle, between Baker and Masonic near Golden Gate Park, S.F.
25 Sun. Sunken Meadow, JFK Drive behind De Young Museum, Golden Gate Park, S.F.
☞ 30 Fri. Oakland City Hall Plaza, 14th and Washington, Oakland
31 Sat. Live Oak Park, Shattuck & Berryman, Berkeley
AUGUST
1 Sun. Live Oak Park, Shattuck & Berryman, Berkeley
7 Sat. Precita Park, Folsom & Precita, S.F.
8 Sun. Precita Park, Folsom & Precita, S.F.
14 Sat. Washington Square Park, Columbus & Union, S.F.
15 Sun. Washington Square Park, Columbus & Union, S.F.
21 Sat. Ho Chi Minh (Willard) Park, Hillegass & Derby off Telegraph, Berkeley
22 Sun. Ho Chi Minh (Willard) Park, same as above, Berkeley
★ 28 Sat. Mission Dolores Park, 18th and Dolores, S.F.
29 Sun. Mission Dolores Park,18th and Dolores, S.F.

celebration with the world people's theater movement. That same year the troupe won an Obie Award for *The Dragon Lady's Revenge*, with Andrea Snow in the title role.

Spain drew his first poster for the group in 1974 for a production called *The Great Air Robbery*. Whether it actually increased public interest or boosted ticket sales is ultimately unknowable, but it definitely went over big with the cast and crew. They wanted to work with him again. In 1977, Spain was recruited to design scenery for the production of *Hotel Universe*.

His next collaboration with the group came in 1980 when they first staged *Fact Person*, a superhero of information, who was resurrected and revisited several times over the next few years, and eventually became *Factwino: The Opera*. In addition to posters and program illustrations, Spain drew *Factwino* comic strips that ran in the *San Francisco Bay Guardian* advertising the shows. (See page 42.)

Principal composer Bruce Barthol thinks he might have encouraged Spain's connection with the Mime Troupe. "I was in the Troupe from 1976 to 2009. For a good part of it, Spain and I lived in the same apartment building on Coso. We also had a mutual interest in the Spanish Civil War. Spain was always a Red of some sort. I met him through Andrea Snow, who I had known at Berkeley during the Free Speech Movement."

This particular revolutionary cartoonist and these radical performers had a lot in common, said Snow. "He loved the Mime Troupe and he was really good at it. I think it was just a good fit. He understood what the Mime Troupe did. He was political and the Mime Troupe loved his work. The Mime Troupe could teach capitalism and imperialism and racism and those were all things Spain was curious about, and thoughtful about. Maybe not the feminism part, I don't know."

"I ended up living with a bunch of people who were really involved in political protests, and got to know people from the San Francisco Mime Troupe," recalled Spain in a 1998 *Comics Journal* interview. "So yeah, that kind of political ferment was really building up. The whole thing about the anti-war movement, it had stops and starts and periods of discouragement, then it would pull itself up by the bootstraps. Because the war was so horrible that even if you got discouraged, you knew that they're still sending off people like yourself that get killed, really for nothing. The documents that have come out show they even knew that the war couldn't be won, but kept sending American youth into this meat grinder."

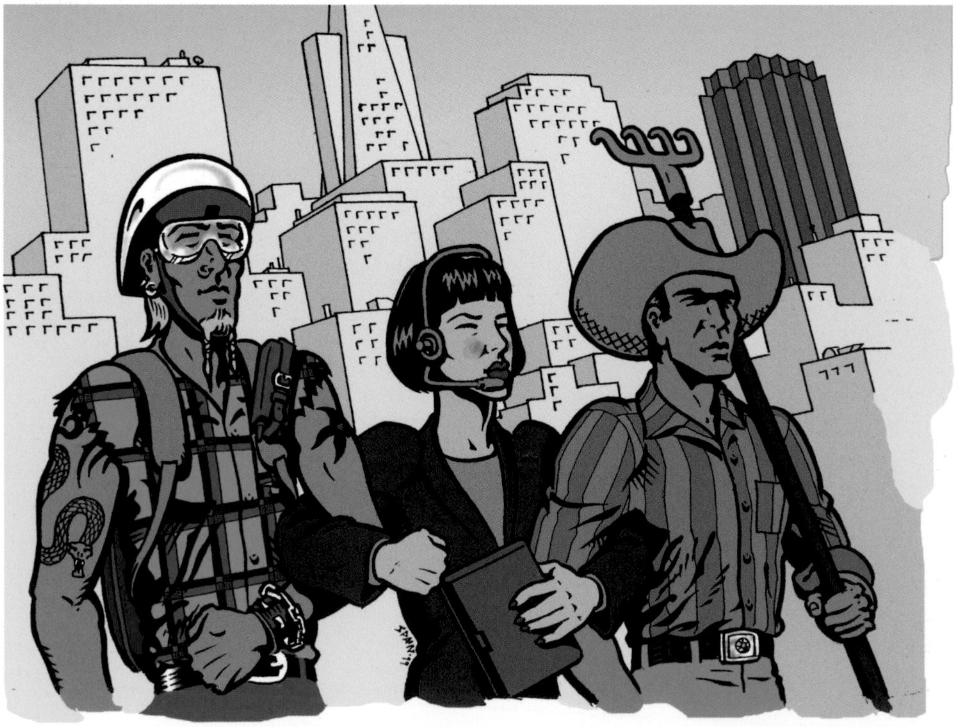

ABOVE: A 1982 flyer for a Mime Troupe production.
LEFT: A 1999 illustration for the *San Francisco Bay Guardian* that accompanies an article titled "Take Back May Day."
OPPOSITE: A postcard featuring the York Theatre, one of a series done for Galería de la Raza's Studio 24 store in the mid-1970s.

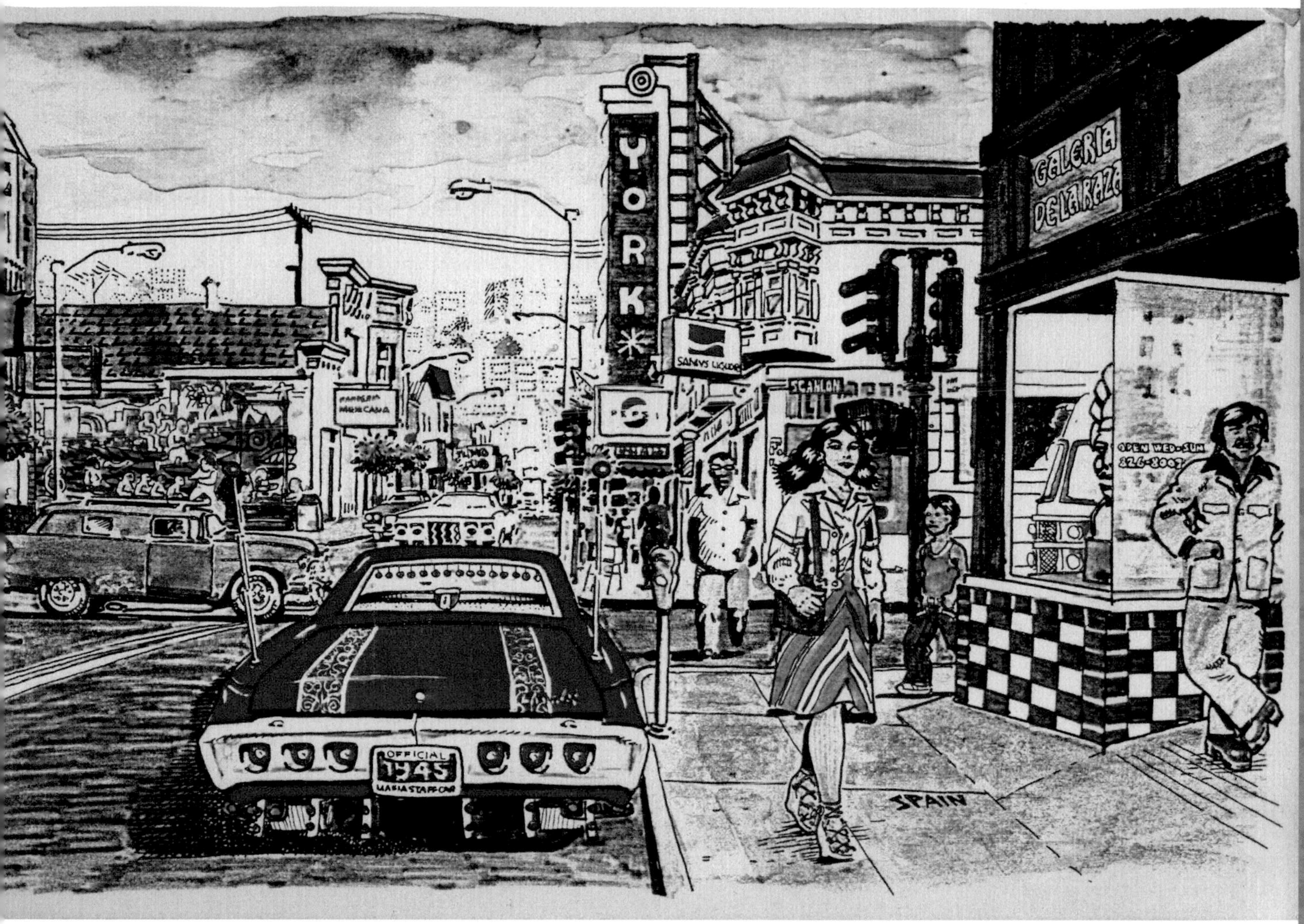
YORK
GALERIA DE LA RAZA
SCANLON
OFFICIAL
1945
SPAIN

“His style fit what the troupe was doing,” said Barthol. “He was also very easy to work with. He was trying to fulfill the task at hand, basically, like any good worker. Often, he would be doing a poster and the show would change, or some element he was going to put in had to come out and he was very cooperative about that stuff. He was there to do the job and he was going to do the job. He understood what we were trying to do and what the poster should do. His style linked with the Mime Troupe. That’s my opinion. There was something about his representational, almost neo-Soviet kind of style that fit the shows and the topics.”

“He believed in the little guy,” said Snow. “He hated the rich.”

“Spain was a working-class kid and his family didn’t sing the songs of the Republic or anything, but there was just the knowledge that rich people were evil, basically,” agreed Barthol. “I think he had very strong positions but he saw his position in the world as kind of serving the movement in a broad way.”

That included action, not just art. “The Nazis were going to have a white workers’ day parade on Haight Street in San Francisco which is galling on nineteen different levels, right?” said Barthol. “So, I walked downstairs, knocked on the door and yelled through the door, ‘Hey Spain, Nazis are marching on Haight Street!’ Spain said, ‘Just a minute.’ He came to the door and off we went.”

Over the next 30 years, Spain drew dozens of posters for the San Francisco Mime Troupe, from *Revenger Rat Meets the Merchant of Death* to *1600 Transylvania Avenue* to *Open Conspiracy to Right the Boat*, as well as their 40th and their 50th Anniversary shows in 1999 and 2009, right up to his final commission *2012 – The Musical*. Other artists supplied Mime Troupe posters as well, but Spain became graphically associated with them and his new posters were avidly collected by fans. “I always urged that we use him for our posters,” said Barthol. “I know that was my constant refrain. When we didn’t, we often regretted it.”

“Spain and I met in 1977, but got together in 1979, and Nora was born in 1989,” said Susan Stern. “So, the ’80s was the time that we were together before we had a child, so it was really a fun time.” Spain and his wife attended many of the Mime Troupe productions and treasured their long relationship with the troupe as it evolved and grew.

“He was very involved with the San Francisco Mime Troupe in the 1980s,” Stern said, and he always welcomed new commissions from them. “There were a lot of fun parties that had to do with the Mime Troupe. Spain drew posters and scenery for the Mime Troupe. We hung out with those people. We were young, single people in the ’80s and San Francisco was a really fun place to be and I was a journalist. I worked for the *Oakland Tribune*. There were a lot of fun parties with the *Oakland Tribune* and other people I knew in the media, so we hung out in these media circles. There were still a lot of underground comix parties in the ’80s. Rip Off still had parties in the 1980s. Last Gasp had parties in the 1980s.”

Stern appeared as the heroine of one of Spain’s stories, “Susan

Strom, Girl Reporter" that was published in *Rip Off Comix* #16 in 1987. The story centers on Stern's work for the *Oakland Tribune* newspaper, but ends up revealing Spain's ability to appreciate, not compete with, his wife.

As the strip opens, the young reporter Strom (serving as a stand-in for Stern), has been assigned an inane feature story on a dog obedience school. But her luck changes when she's teamed with another investigative reporter to break a series of stories revealing Bay Area ties to the Iran-Contra scandal.

"The Reagan administration was illegally selling arms to Iran and then using the proceeds to illegally fund the right-wing 'Contras,' the paramilitaries fighting the socialist government in Nicaragua," said Stern. "We found out that aid to the Contras was going through the Oakland Airport, and the financial mastermind of the whole Iran Contra scandal was living in the Bay Area suburbs. We tried to confront him—but he was gone."

While Susan was having that adventure, Spain depicts himself sweeping the kitchen floor and cooking dinner. "Susan is more useful to society than I am," the cartoon Spain says. His tongue is, no doubt, firmly planted in cheek and yet there seems also no doubt that Spain is reveling in his partner's triumph. When it's her turn to cook, she takes him out for Chinese food, and they walk arm-in-arm, equal partners framed by the lights of San Francisco's Diamond Heights.

Galería de la Raza and the Mission Cultural Center

"What most people don't know about Spain was that he was part of the Latino art movement of the 1970s." said Stern. One of the centers of the movement was the San Francisco Mission District, particularly the Galería de la Raza, founded by artists René Yañez, Ralph Maradiaga, and others.

"Spain and I both lived in the Mission or on the Mission District/Bernal Heights border before and after we were together, and continued to live there throughout his life," said Stern. "I think it was the Mission District, rather than San Francisco as a whole, that was Spain's third home—after Buffalo and the Lower East Side."

His new turf provided long-lasting artistic inspiration for him, she declared, and his record of local culture and landmarks remains a memorial to a bygone era. "He did many, many drawings in his sketchbooks, both published and unpublished of the Mission District—of its architecture, of its people, of its women, of its *gatos*, its cars and its low-riders, of its culture. This is some of his greatest artwork and his greatest contribution to culture because that San Francisco Mission District is now being gentrified almost out of existence. He was an opponent of that gentrification. He was also a great teacher and mentor."

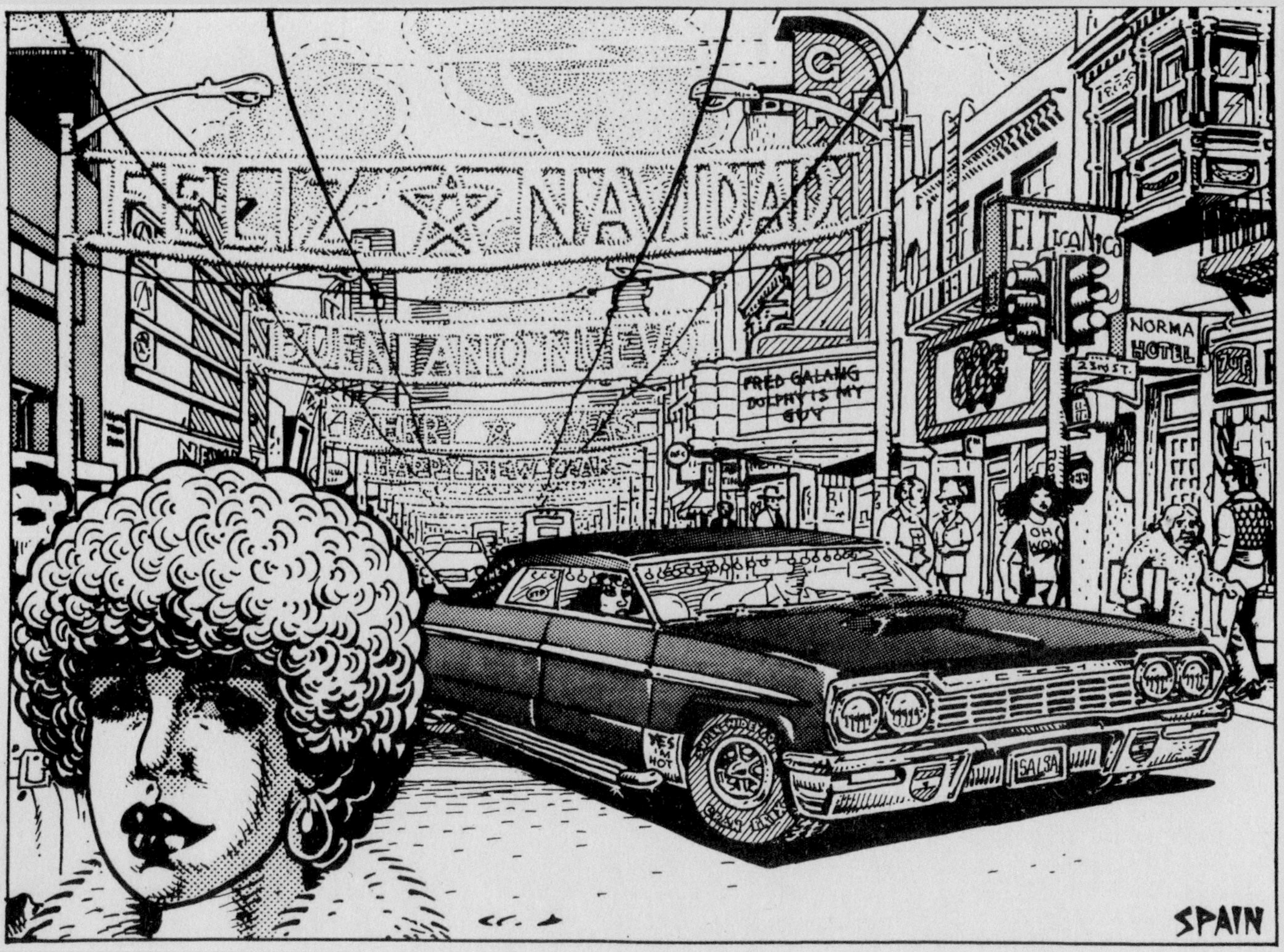
FELIZ NAVIDAD
NORMA
HOTEL
23rd ST.
FRED GALANG
DOLPHY IS MY
GUY
YES
I'M
HOT
SALSA
SPAIN

For her documentary, *Bad Attitude: The Art of Spain Rodriguez*, Stern interviewed René Yañez and his ex-wife Yolanda Lopez, both seminal artists in the Latino art movement.

"In 1969, there was a group that René belonged to that eventually became Galería de la Raza," said Lopez. "But, in 1970, I was actually hunted down by Graciela Carrillo and Patricia Rodriguez to be in their first women's show. I had never heard of the Galería and the idea of a women's show was very exciting to me. They recruited me to be part of the exhibit. I have to give René a lot of credit along with Ralph Maradiaga and the other men who were founders of the Galería because I think all of a sudden there was a sense of cohesiveness that never existed before. It was very exciting to me and it changed my whole mindset."

"I met Spain at Gary Arlington's comic book shop," said Yañez. "We met and he was kind of curious because I said, 'I'm Chicano.' He said, 'Is that a Spaniard with an attitude?' We started bantering back and forth. Through him, I met Robert Crumb, S. Clay Wilson, and other people."

"In the Galería, René and others created a space where differences could be discussed," said Stern. "I remember a lot of joking around between Spain and René. I think largely through the greatness of spirit of the late René Yañez, the Latino art movement and the underground comix movement had some moments together in San Francisco."

"By '72 we had moved to 24th and Bryant, which was a neighborhood in transition," said Yañez. "The German people, the Italians were moving out. There were a lot of empty houses, empty storefronts. There were a lot of artists in the storefronts that were really cheap to rent, $75, $100 a month for a storefront. It was just teeming with artists. There was also Carlos Santana's music. There were murals going up, poetry, Alejandro Murguía, Roberto Vargas. Everything was teeming all at the same time. So, it was that mix. We did workshops. We did outreach. People from the neighborhood came and did critiques of the exhibits."

At the time, the Bay Area subway system, BART, was just getting started, and the Mission Street was being torn up to build stations. Mom-and-pop businesses were being destroyed for a transit system designed to whisk suburbanites past the Mission into the downtown financial district.

Yañez came up with a plan to try to stake out the character of the Mission in the face of what would become the first wave of gentrification: murals. He would get artists to make murals to define the Mission.

"I was working for the Neighborhood Arts Program," explained Yañez. "I had a budget to commission people to do murals. Spain was actually the first artist to do a mural in the Mission. After that Robert Crumb did one."

"Murals are a gas," said Spain in a 1998 interview. "I like murals, but it's pretty time consuming." It took him nearly six months to do his part of a mural at Horizons Unlimited, an employment placement group for young people. Two other local artists did the prep work and prepared four large panels for Spain to fill in with cityscapes and portraits of kids. Meanwhile, down the street at 17th and Valencia, Robert Crumb knocked his mural out quickly, said Spain. It was larger than his, covering all three floors of the building's front with large graphics saying "Mission Rebels in Action Inc." up one side and down the other. He also painted one large comic panel on the right side of the

OPPOSITE: Postcard drawn for the Galería de la Raza, circa 1975.

ABOVE: Spain and his daughter Nora, 1989. Photo by Susan Stern.

bottom floor showing people from the organization with raised fists, and revolutionary slogans in speech balloons above them.

"I met Spain in a show that we were in together called, 'In Progress,' which was about 1981," said Lopez. "All the pieces were four-feet by eight-feet. He did one of his great statuesque goddesses there, you know, which represented the Mission. It was a very good experience."

"It was a very popular exhibit," said Yañez. "The idea was to invite artists to paint 'in progress' in front of the public and as people were coming in they would engage the public. It was also getting to know each other, people from different backgrounds. They talked about identity and what they were doing." Spain's artistic skills helped many of the other participants, he added. "Spain knew a lot of shortcuts. He was really fast. He knew perspective and some people admired that. Later, we had a couple of workshops on perspective because he was really good at perspective. It was a good thing he was there. He got to meet a lot of people. It was a pretty good exhibit."

"Spain felt there was a lot of romanticism in the Latino art of the time," recalled Stern. "A lot of exploration of indigenous mythology, of the Virgin of Guadeloupe, glorious rural scenes, agriculture. The Native American brave holding his slain woman in his arms on all the taqueria calendars and Spain, with his hard-edged contemporary urbanism, was very critical of all that."

"I introduced him to some people that I thought were good artists and they got into discussions," said Yañez. "He didn't like the folk artists or people that didn't use perspective, or if they were too romantic, or attached to certain imagery, Latino or Chicano imagery. He had certain definite opinions. He would get into discussions with other artists whose work he didn't like and they would say, 'Oh man, you're just a gringo. You went to art school. And you have this art school perspective. I didn't go to art school. I couldn't afford it.' They would get into fights and then he would say, 'Well, you should have worked harder.' Those were discussions about identity, about quality of work, about technique, about all these different levels of art. It wasn't like, I'm better than you. It attached nuances, in discussing each other's work about the technique of using ink or painting. You know, one artist told him, 'Art only comes out of a brush.' And Spain told him, 'You can shove that brush up your ass.' Things like that."

Spain's work was wildly popular in underground comix, and the very nature of the artistic revolution that the comix movement pioneered and engendered in other art forms meant breaking all the rules and alarming people to make their point. Sex and violence, long suppressed in all forms of expression became a starting point for storylines in the underground press. Some cartoonists took taboo-busting to a further extreme than others and these iconoclasts attracted the most criticism from those who would censor comics. However, many people enjoyed seeing what Spain or S. Clay Wilson or Robert Crumb would come up with next. There was a constant competition between underground cartoonist to outdo their previous outrages.

"At one point, I did object to some of the violence that I was seeing because I didn't think it was necessary to the story to have so much violence. He would say, 'René, sex and violence, they sell. I'm an underground comic book artist. What do you expect? Goody-two-shoes? This is the reality of it.' He had a definite perspective on what made his underground comic books popular, what made him popular. Being controversial in a way made him popular because he never apologized after being lectured, he'd still continue. I rather admire that but, you know, I did question the violence because it wasn't furthering the storyline. It just seemed gratuitous in its use. He had certain things in his comic books that were right on and I consider them genius. I really appreciated what he was doing and some of the other stories I didn't. You know, I picked and chose. As a curator, I loved art from comic books to museum art and I still like ephemeral street art stickers and graffiti. I put it all on the same level. If it's good, if it's got that swing, it means a thing. I just gravitate towards things that excite me and part of Spain's work really excited me, even though I challenged him, I still liked the work.

"One of the justifications that he had when people threw sexism at him, you know, you're exploiting women, he would say, 'Well, they're strong women that have guns and they stand up and have character. They're not weaklings. They stand up.' 'Well how come the woman have to be so violent and kill so many people?' He's, 'Well, I want to show how strong they are.' To him it counterbalanced any accusations of being sexist because the women were strong and they could stand up for themselves and kill a man just as well.

"Spain never did apologize. People called him sexist but it was OK with him," said Yañez." "He had a strong point of view. I mean, he was around women from the Mime Troupe, from the Galería, they questioned him. He would just patiently listen and go, 'Oh, well that's the way it goes, you know.' He wasn't going to apologize or retract or redo. He had a vision. I respected him because it was at a time where it was very difficult. Underground comic book artist Robert Crumb was also being criticized for drawing women with big butts and things like that, and sadomasochism. There were a whole group of underground comic books artists holding the line saying, 'This is where we are and we're not going to apologize for it,' which, you know, I thought was fair. Not politically correct, but it was a strong point of view."

It was also during this period that Spain and Susan traveled several times to both Mexico and Spain. "In Mexico, we sought out the murals of the great Spanish muralists. We even went into the stairway of the Electrical Workers Union to see the David Siqueiros mural there," said Stern. "Of course, we went to all the museums and great Mayan and Aztec cities.

"We studied Spanish in Spain with our daughter Nora, and Spain made sure we saw a bullfight. I know that bullfighting is considered cruelty to animals by some, but I have to say, I appreciated the skill of one matador we saw who killed the bull with a single surgical blow. The crowd applauded him—and turned their backs on the matador who was abusing a bull. In that case, the other matadors quickly put the bull to death."

In 1977, a group of community activists formed the Mission

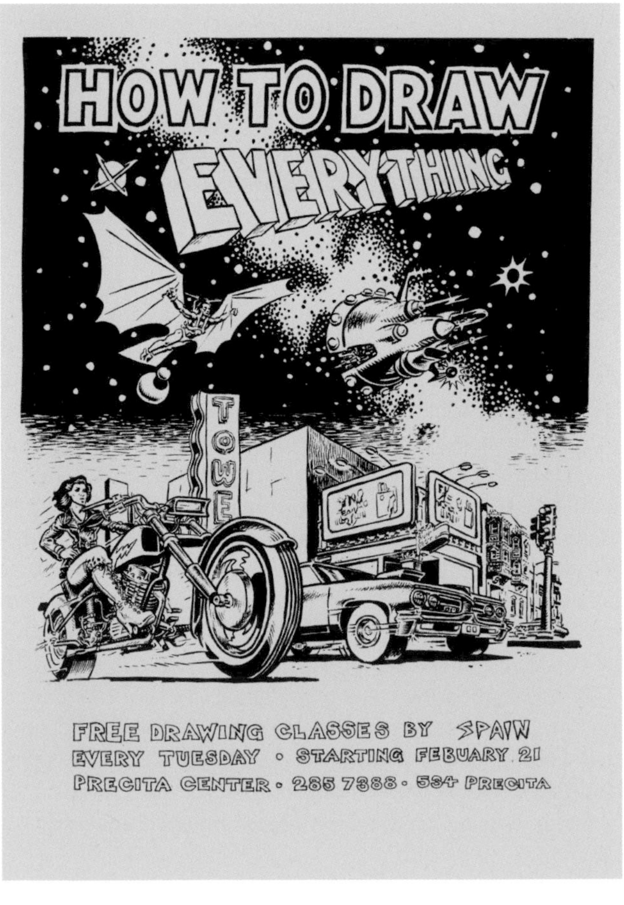
HOW TO DRAW
EVERYTHING
FREE DRAWING CLASSES BY SPAIN
EVERY TUESDAY • STARTING FEBUARY 21
PRECITA CENTER • 285 7388 • 534 PRECITA

LEFT: Poster for one of Spain's free art classes, circa 1985.

OPPOSITE: A 2002 pen and ink drawing done for the San Francisco strip club O'Farrell Theatre, owned by the Mitchell Brothers.

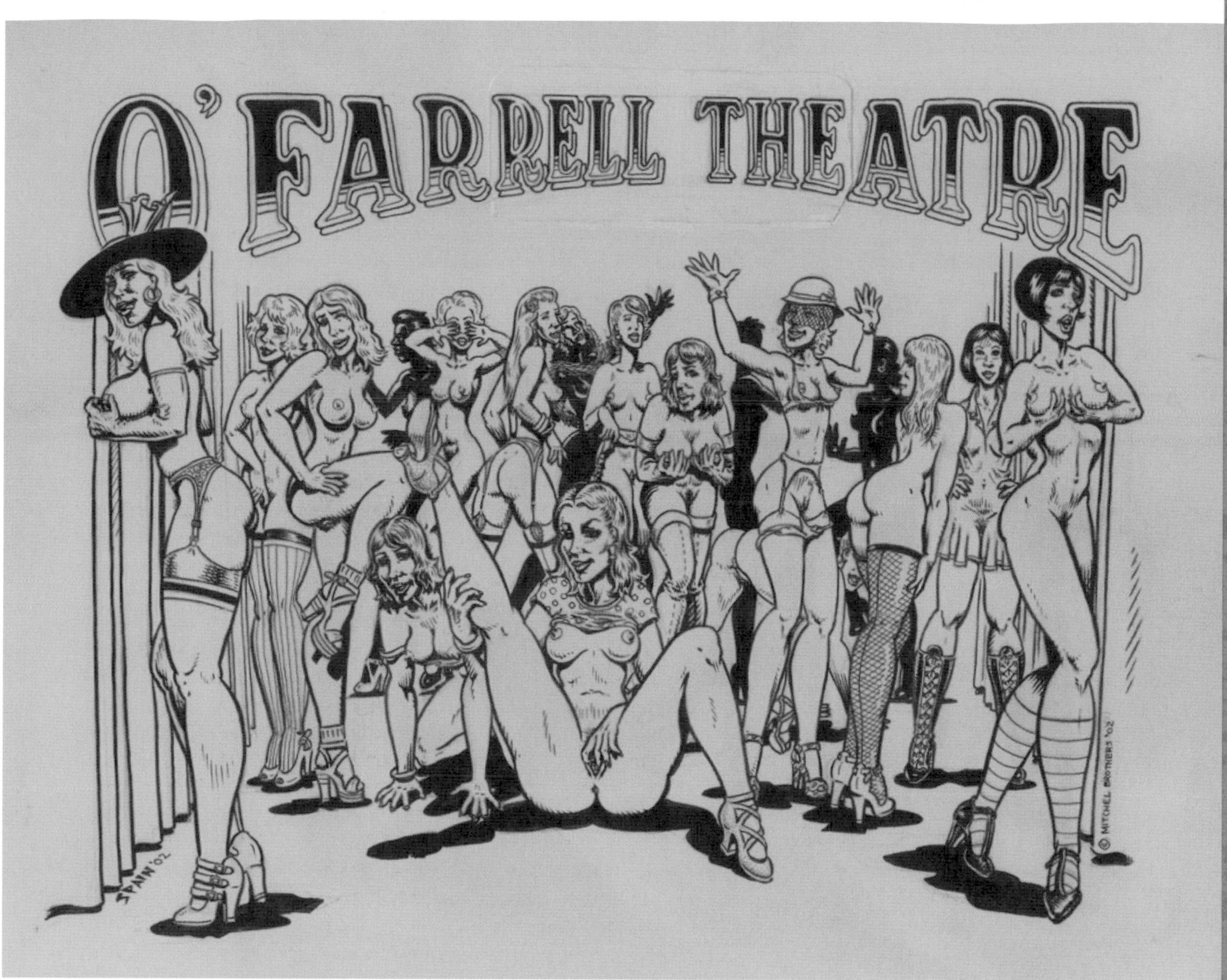
O'FARRELL THEATRE
SPAIN '02
© MITCHELL BROTHERS '02

Cultural Center for Latino Arts and acquired a former furniture store at 2868 Mission Street. They built performance spaces, galleries, classrooms, and dance studios, and became a major neighborhood center for the arts.

Spain taught drawing classes at the Mission Cultural Center for more than a decade, to both children and adults. "Every so often someone would come up to me and say my kid likes comics. Show him your stuff," said Spain. "I developed these little techniques where you could take something simple, like a cube, and show how you can use that to do various ways of drawing. The first time I taught was at the Galería de la Raza. At some point, I realized what a big task it was to break down everything that I knew. First, somebody got me to write a grant proposal to the California Arts Council. They said we like your proposal but we have a bunch of questions. I found out the problem was that I had done work for [the owners of the strip club O'Farrell Theatre] the Mitchell Brothers. They didn't know if they wanted someone like me teaching kids. When the Mitchell Brothers found out, they offered a grant to the Mission Cultural Center to let me teach the kids. The Mission Cultural Center felt that they couldn't not accept. Later on, they got a grant for me to teach a class for the summer, it might have been the summer of 1991, and they just kept me there for another five years. I would teach once a week, every Saturday. We put out a book. The title that the kids came up with was *Enemy Blade*."

Yañez and Lopez's son, Rio, took drawing lessons from Spain at the Mission Cultural Center for several years. "I really felt like I got to know Spain in the late '80s and early '90s when I started taking drawing classes from him. Saturday mornings I would take my little sketch pad and walk down to the Mission Cultural Center on Mission Street and Spain would just, you know, he'd sit there with a giant pad of paper and he was always about perspective. He would try and teach us how you draw buildings in perspective and three-point perspective, two-point perspective. 'Here is your horizon line.' It was almost Zen the way he would talk about perspective. It was great on Saturday mornings spending three, four hours drawing with Spain. It was probably one of the most influential kinds of experiences of my life as an artist. I did it for four years straight."

"I had some great kids," Spain said. "I had kids who couldn't draw a straight line with a ruler and you had to show them stuff. Some did great stuff. I had tons of kids who came in and out of the class. Some stayed for a while. When I had enough good

"He wasn't going to apologize or retract or redo. He had a vision."

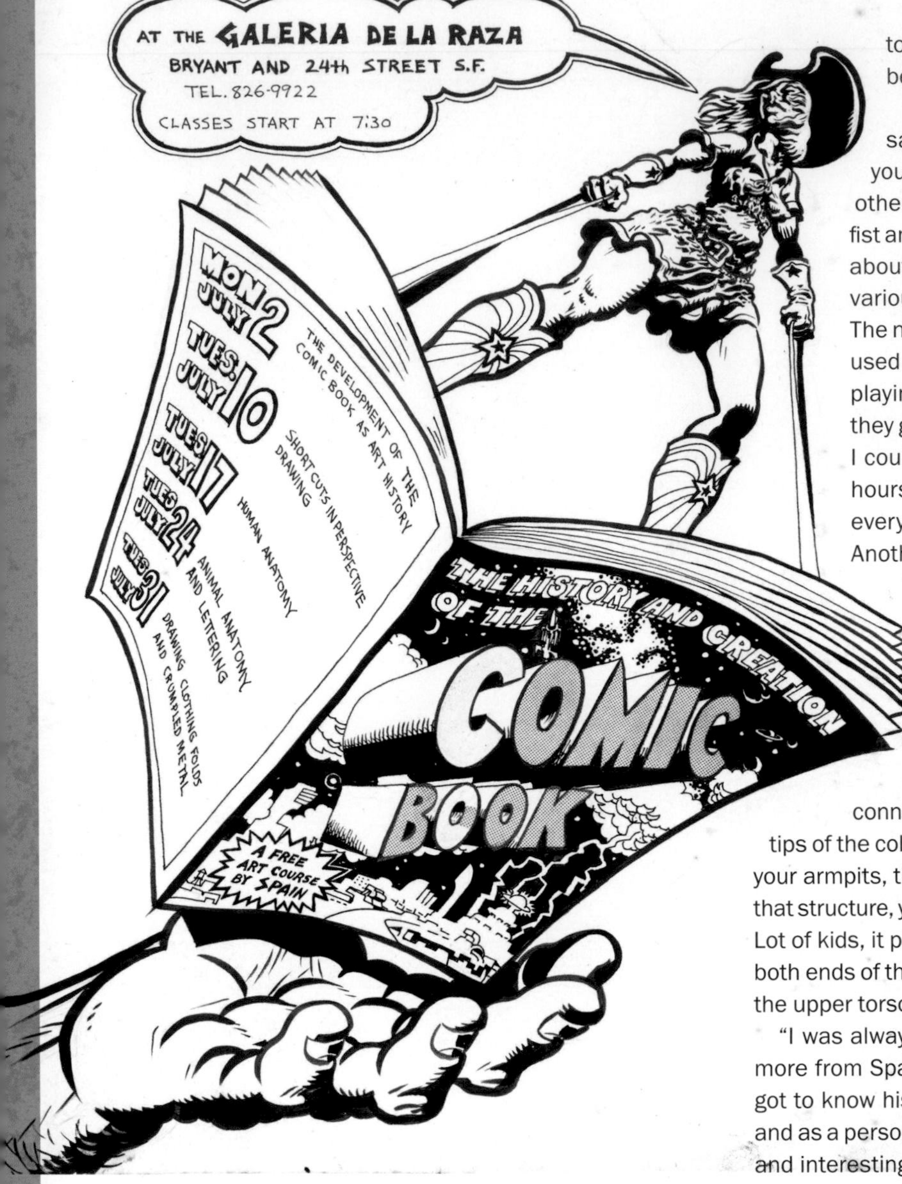
AT THE GALERIA DE LA RAZA
BRYANT AND 24th STREET S.F.
TEL. 826-9922
CLASSES START AT 7:30
MON JULY 2
THE DEVELOPMENT OF THE COMIC BOOK AS ART HISTORY
TUES. JULY 10
SHORT CUTS IN PERSPECTIVE DRAWING
TUES JULY 17
HUMAN ANATOMY
TUES JULY 24
ANIMAL ANATOMY AND LETTERING
TUES JULY 31
DRAWING CLOTHING FOLDS AND CRUMPLED METAL
THE HISTORY AND CREATION OF THE
COMIC BOOK
A FREE ART COURSE BY SPAIN

stuff, I would Xerox it and make it into a book."

"It was a very interesting time to be a student of his, because this was in the early '90s and kind of at the height of the popularity and explosion of Image comic books," said Rio Yañez.

"The technical work that Spain did was kind of working against the grain of what all the kids were really excited about. This was the era of Rob Liefeld and Todd McFarlane, extreme and super-stylized artwork in comics and very bad writing. So, everyone wanted to draw very exaggerated figures and very exaggerated poses and you know, Spain was kind of like this old Kung-Fu master. He would teach us how to lay things out in a way that was very technically sound. He talked to us about perspective, and tricks to achieve it. For example, I learned that most adult bodies are the height of eight of their respective heads. He also taught us how to draw really great guns. That was also really exciting. He knew all the technical details and he'd say, 'Oh, well if you want to do it like a World War II era German rifle it would be like this.'"

"You have this discipline problem in teaching," said Spain. "It's really dealing with the mob, so you have to try to get them on your side and, on the other hand, you have to control things with an iron fist and you have to keep them intrigued. In one class, about two-thirds of the students got up and left, on various pretexts, so they could watch a soccer game. The next lesson I had them draw a soccer field, which used perspective. It combined everything. It had guys playing soccer and I showed them getting smaller as they got further away. What I would do is use any trick I could come up with to hold their attention for two hours. What I found was that you have to break down everything you know into the simplest, clearest form. Another lesson I had was in drawing a bank robbery. They all enjoyed it. I got to show them how to draw a building, with columns, using perspective, and guys running out of the bank."

There was also the Spain Rodriguez Five-Point Plan. "I have a five-point system which is the way muscles connect in the upper body, which you use a lot," he explained. "First is the connection between the neck and the chest; then the tips of the collarbone where your shoulders pivot up; and then your armpits, that begin your biceps and pectorals. If you have that structure, you already have much of the upper body. It works. Lot of kids, it piques their interest. Those five points—the neck, both ends of the collarbones, and the armpits frame and define the upper torso."

"I was always kind of in awe that I kept learning more and more from Spain," said Rio Yañez. "The more I read his work, got to know his work, the more I learned about him as a man and as a person, I think it just made him all the more fascinating and interesting to me."

Being 10 or 11 years old meant there was a lot that he couldn't quite wrap his head around, though. "I would go to the Mission Cultural Center and I was his student. He would be there and we'd draw together, we'd talk. Then, I'd go home and I'd root through my dad's comics and sure enough there was Big Bitch getting eaten out and he'd draw these veiny penises. It was like, 'That's Spain. Spain drew that,' you know, and it kind of blew my mind. Then, my mom bought me a copy of *My True Story*, one of his autobiographical comics. I read all these stories about how he joined a motorcycle gang and he was involved in all these brawls. You know, all the things he did."

"I was the education director at the Mission Cultural Center," said Lopez, "and Rio would come in after school when Spain was teaching there. I dropped in on the class because I was a little bit apprehensive, to tell you the truth, because of his imagery. But then I saw what happened in the class: He talked about drawing panels, and cartoons, and beginning to look at the whole

TOP: Flyer advertising Spain's class, The History and Creation of the Comic Book, circa 1987.

OPPOSITE TOP LEFT: Un Poco Loco Carnaval poster, donated to the Urban School of San Francisco to promote an annual fundraiser, 2004.

OPPOSITE TOP RIGHT: "A Streetcar Named Displacement," from the *San Francisco Bay Guardian*, 1998.

OPPOSITE BOTTOM: Blue Flame was part of a series of color Xerox postcards done for the Galería de la Raza, circa 1975.

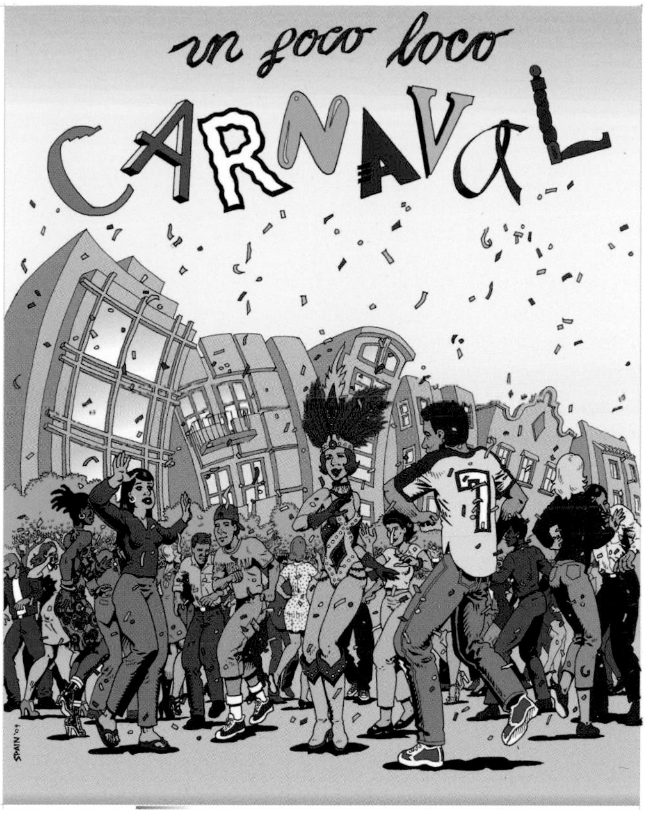
un foco loco
CARNAVAL

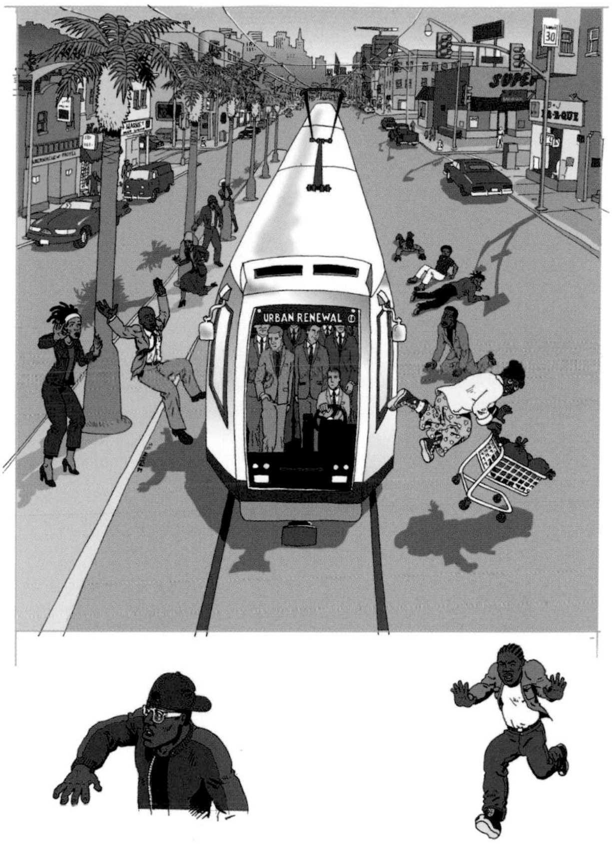
URBAN RENEWAL

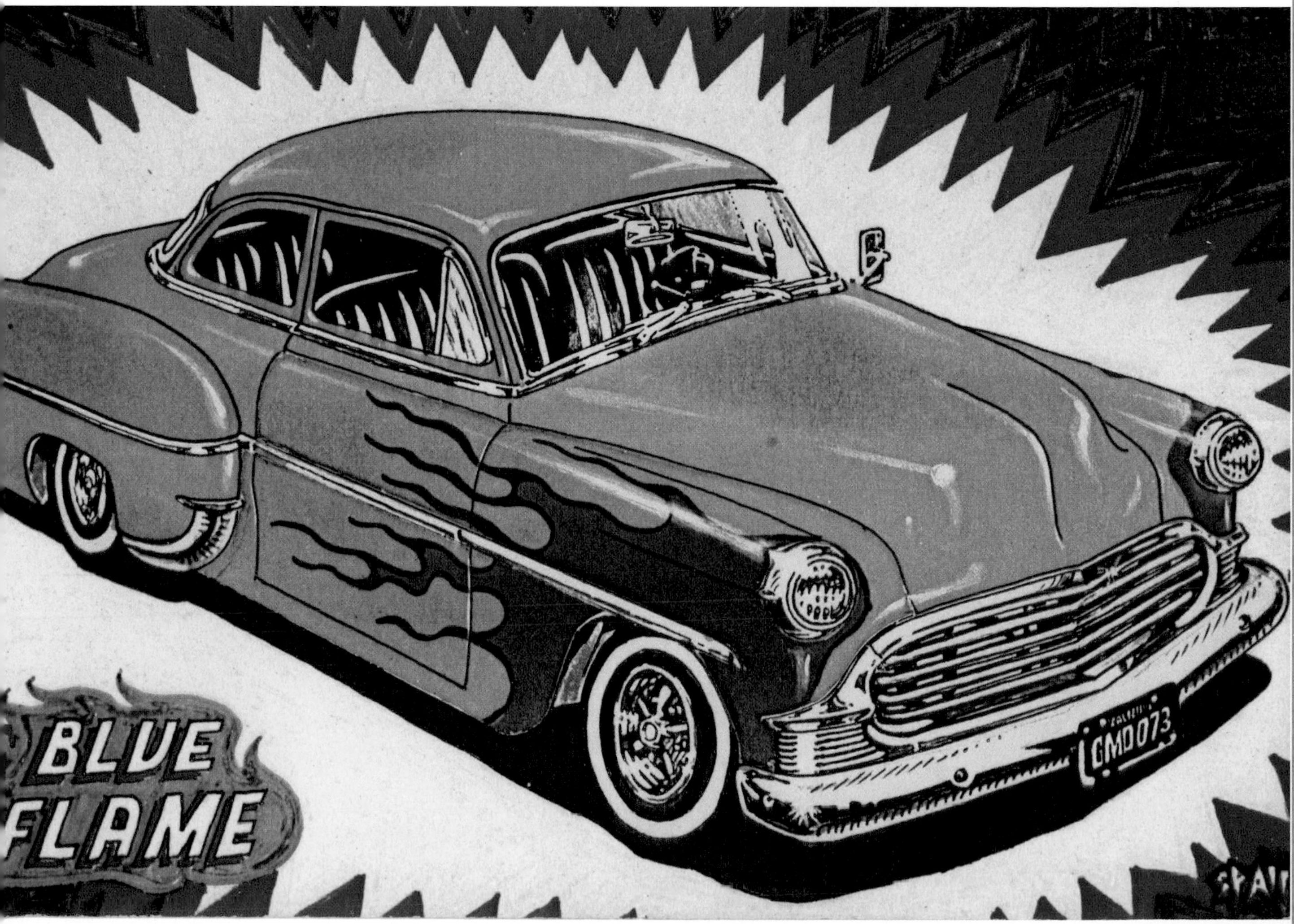
BLUE
FLAME
GMD073

page, and overlapping imagery, going outside the squares or the frames, which I thought was really important and not many artists would even talk about that. I said, 'Well, he's all right.' I felt like he was really talking about the technique of drawing."

Most of the kids there had no idea about his work outside of class, said Rio. "They didn't know who Trashman was. They hadn't read any of his comics, but shortly after the class started, there was this buzz about him and all the neighborhood kids were really excited because of the way he drew cars. A lot of kids would go there just to watch Spain draw. Some of us would be there with our sketchbooks and he'd teach us how to layout comic pages in the class and some kids would be there just to watch him draw his examples. We were all really fortunate to have Spain there. He brought his knowledge of warfare and that technical sense. He was kind of excited to share that with the kids that showed up. He had students that were there to learn but he also had just a whole audience of kids that just took so much excitement and joy in just watching him draw."

"Teaching kids was some sort of karmic comeuppance," said Spain. "I had all these young boys from 8 to about 12, and they'd just love to bust your chops. I would do my best to answer any question they would throw at me. I would just answer them as straight as I could. Even if they were being a wise guy. I mean, at some point, you might just have to say, 'Everybody in this class knows that that's not a serious question, and you know it, too, and so you're just taking up time in the class when we could be doing something that's cool.' But that was a rare occasion. I still basically sympathize with those kids. I see them as kids who were just like me. At some point, you might have to clamp down. They tend to get a little too bloody-minded. One time I showed them how to draw action in a sequence of panels. A car coming down the street, and they'd say, 'Put a cat in it so it can run over it.' OK, so I would draw a run-over cat. 'Oh, put a baby in there.' 'Guys, now you're going too far.'"

Spain's daughter Nora also attended some of his drawing classes at the Mission Cultural Center, but she remembered being younger than all the rest of his students. "I don't know how many of those classes I sat in the back of. It was like a form of childcare," she said. "I don't know if I ever went to one class from beginning to end but it was like whenever he was teaching and taking care of me, I would sit back there. I remember that they had an age requirement and I definitely started going when I was too young, but I remember it was a big deal. Maybe I was six, maybe I was eight. I was just a little bit too young to be taking his classes but because I was his daughter they let it slide. I remember I liked impressing the older kids because I had already learned all this stuff so I was pretty good for a little kid, so I liked showing off a little bit."

"There's a middle school in the Mission District and it's got portraits of 'neighborhood heroes' on a mural on the side of the building. Spain is one of them."

"Spain was pretty analytical in doing comix in a way that I think a lot of other cartoonists weren't," said Jay Kinney. "He just loved that stuff. That's why he enjoyed doing the comic class at the Mission Cultural Center where he'd teach how to draw comics to kids. It's like he was passing along the tricks that he had to come up with or learned and a lot of that was perspective and a cool way to draw cars and whatnot. And that was it. He really enjoyed drawing. I think that's what kept him going. It was a pleasure to him. You sensed that enjoyment in his art."

"He was very good at giving tips and advice about drawing," said Robert Crumb. "He showed me stuff about perspective and anatomy that was very helpful. He was very clear about the formula for achieving correct perspective—the vanishing point, the horizon line, and all that stuff. He knew the tricks to make it look correct. Sometimes you don't have to be absolutely correct because people can believe certain illusions. For example, if you draw a large head in the foreground, if you look at it logically, it seems that it can't be right. A large head in the foreground and people, drawn smaller, in the background, would not be in the same line of vision. But that's an illusion you can get away with. You had to have certain key rules of thumb about anatomy that I didn't know. Maybe he did pick it up in art school. I never went to art school."

"He was a good teacher," agreed Paul Mavrides, who substitute

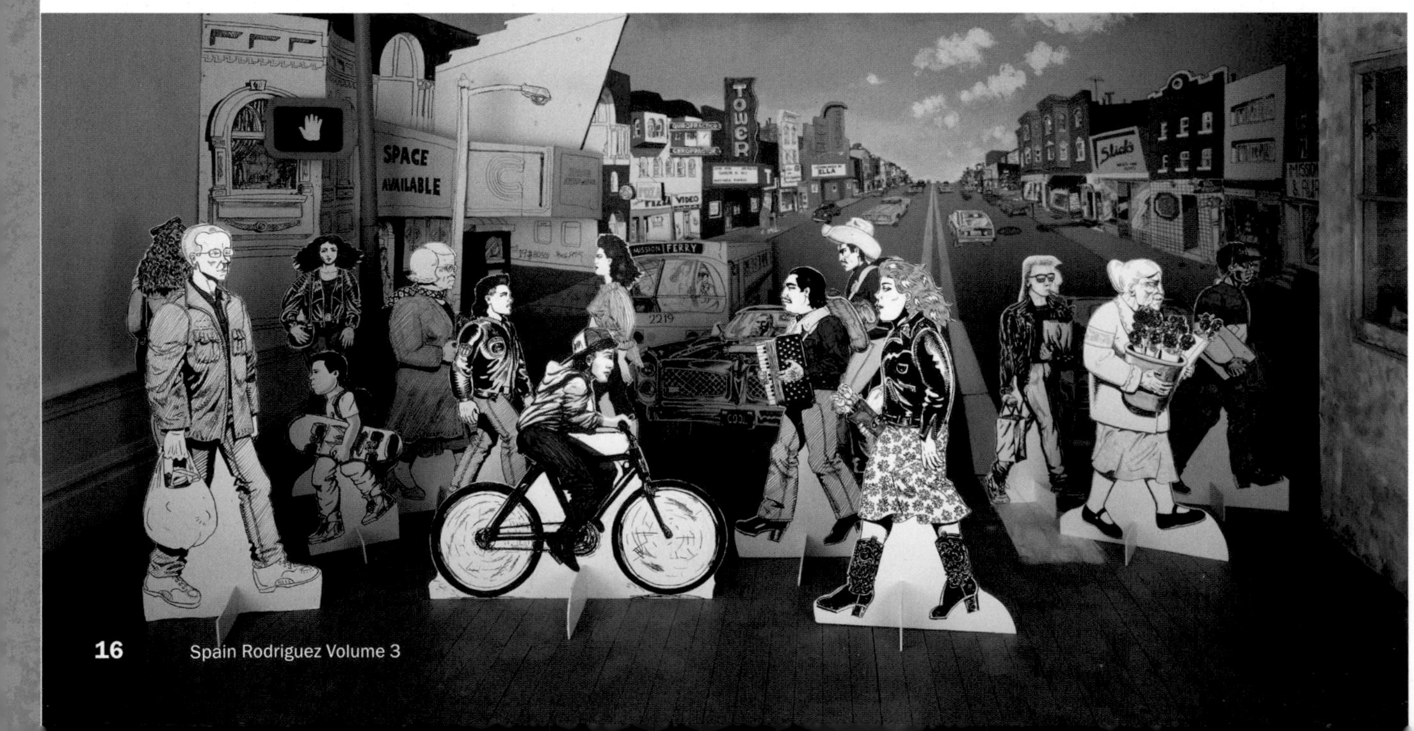
SPACE
AVAILABLE
TOWER
MISSION FERRY
2219

SPAIN RODRIGUEZ

taught for Spain a few times. "He talked to the students, not down to them. He'd engage them. He would pay attention to what they were doing. He encouraged them and he'd tailor his lesson to different people, depending on what they were there to do. In his cartooning class, some of the kids who showed up just wanted to learn to design tattoos. Others really wanted to do comics. Some didn't want to be there at all. Some parents made them come, but they all liked him pretty much. There's a middle school in the Mission District and it's got portraits of 'neighborhood heroes' on a mural on the side of the building. Spain is one of them. You don't get that for drawing comic books by yourself about motorcycle gangs. You get that because you're engaged with your community and you do things to help people."

"There was a time in San Francisco when you could see Spain's murals all over the place in the heart of the Mission," said Kinney. "That's one of the contributions that he made to the city and he helped the whole mural movement get off the ground in its early days. People come from all over the world to check them out. His murals were around for many years and were part of the feel of the Mission. I think that his portrayals of Mission Street, of the older movie theater marquees and the streetlights, the palm

trees, the sleazy bars ... when I think of the Mission, at least as it was, it's rapidly evolving away from that, but when I think of Spain's portrayals of the Mission, he's in my mind as the quintessential Mission District artist."

Some of Spain's old pals from the underground liked to razz him about his politics as he became more successful in his career. "If you'd walk the streets with him in San Francisco, the poor on the street immediately identified him and called out his name," said fellow *Zap* artist Robert Williams. "I remember we used to walk through a park when we were going to his house, and the homeless in the park would always yell for him and cheer for him and then after he got married and had a house, that changed things a little bit. Then we would walk through the park and again people would cheer for Spain, and Spain would whisper to me, 'You know that asshole could be working.' I'd say 'What do you mean? You've got your house. You could put two or three of those people up in your living room'... joking with him you know. He didn't say anything. He knew what the fuck I was saying. I was saying, buddy let's see that communist charity now that you've got a fucking house. Drag some of these clowns home."

"I was out walking with Spain and [S. Clay] Wilson one time and one or the other of them went up to this homeless guy and pulled art supplies out of their bag and gave them to the homeless guy," recalled Paul Mavrides. "From knowing him, they knew the guy liked to draw so they went out and got him pencils and paper and stuff."

His wife Susan shines a different light on the situation. "I think Spain knew lots of homeless people because, unfortunately, they were people who grew up as children here in Bernal Heights

---

OPPOSITE: Mission District Cutouts, a mural with cardboard cutouts, done at Intersection for the Arts Gallery, June 1989, with work by Mauricio Vazquez and Lucius Wong. Photo by Wolfgang Dietze.

TOP: Spain next to his portrait in the Mission Heroes mural at Buena Vista Horace Mann K-8 Community School, 2012. Photo by Marshal Potter.

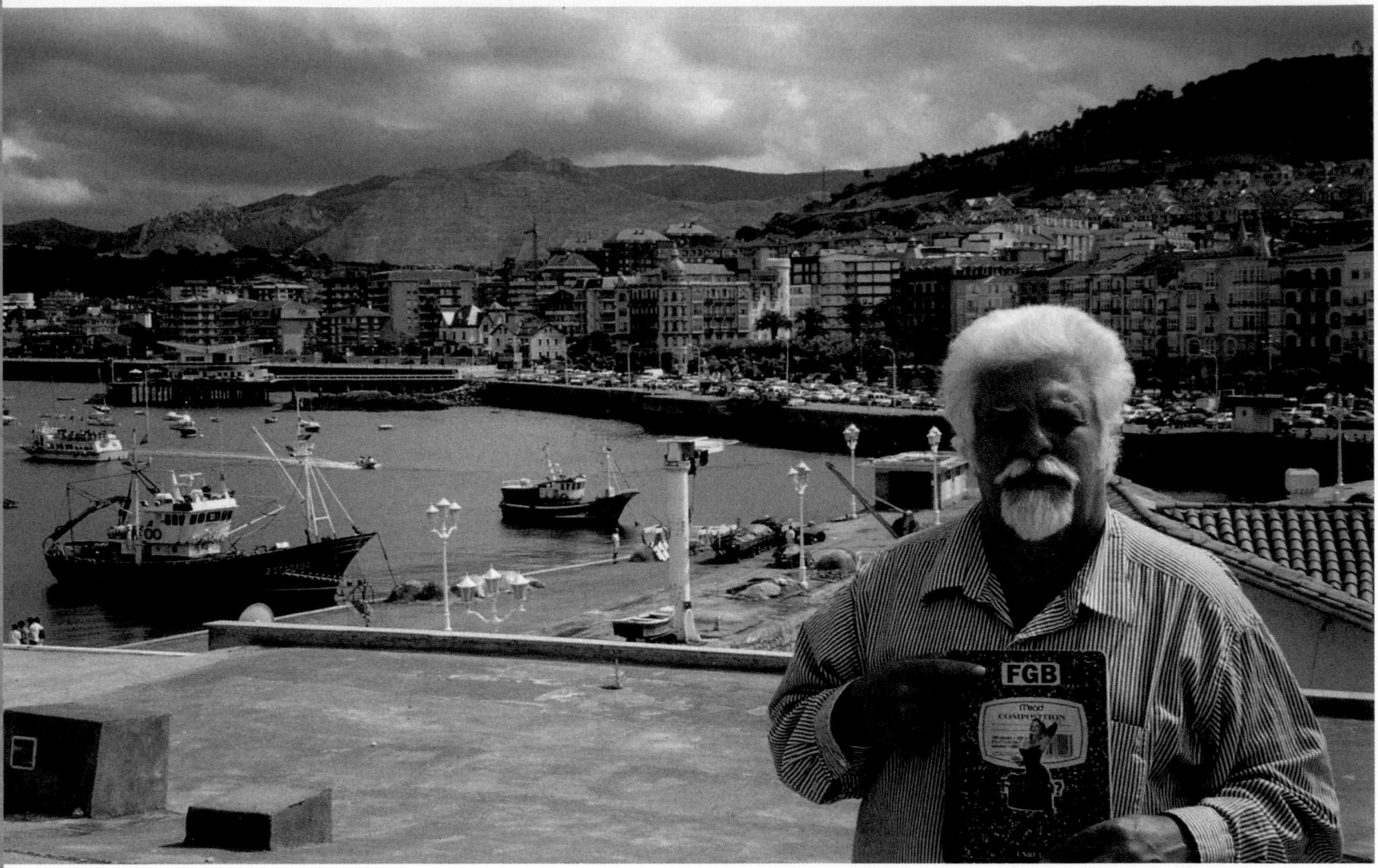
FGB

and some of them, because of alcoholism and drug abuse, ended up on the streets. While he had been living in Bernal Heights, he and other people were very involved with youth in various ways, in various programs with youth, so he actually did know these people. He would give money to people on the street. But he didn't have any illusions about who he could help and who he couldn't."

"There was a group in San Francisco called the Holy Order of MANS, and there was a guy named Sufi Sam in Precita Park who had these Sufi sessions in the morning," recalled Spain's friend Dominic Albanese. "Sam asked me and a couple of my biker buddies to please stop these young toughs in Precita Park from harassing the Sufi dancers. And I told Spain about this, and he said, 'We're going to straighten those guys out.' And we did. We went there one morning, and these guys came, and Spain put up his hand and he said, 'These people are now under the protection of us. If you do this again, you'll deal with us.' And he wasn't the kind of guy who sold wolf tickets. If he told you he was going to punch you, you got punched. There were no ifs or buts about it."

For Spain being a community elder added new responsibilities to his life, which he was willing to accept, but he wasn't about to forget his own rebellious attitude from back when he was a kid. As both a respected member of his community and "the world's oldest juvenile delinquent," he had to find new ways to harmonize his contrasting views.

"I just had a dislike for the established order that I still have today," he said in 1998. "It hasn't changed. And it's funny, my kid goes to school, and I understand that she needs an education, and I try to do my best to foster a respect for learning, and she certainly has a good attitude towards school, but my attitude

"Spain believed not so much in hope but in struggle. He thought the thing to do is to keep fighting injustice, even if you didn't see big changes in your lifetime."

TOP: Spain with a sketchbook in Santander, Spain, 2005. Photo by Susan Stern.

BELOW: A small sampling of Spain's toy soldier collection.

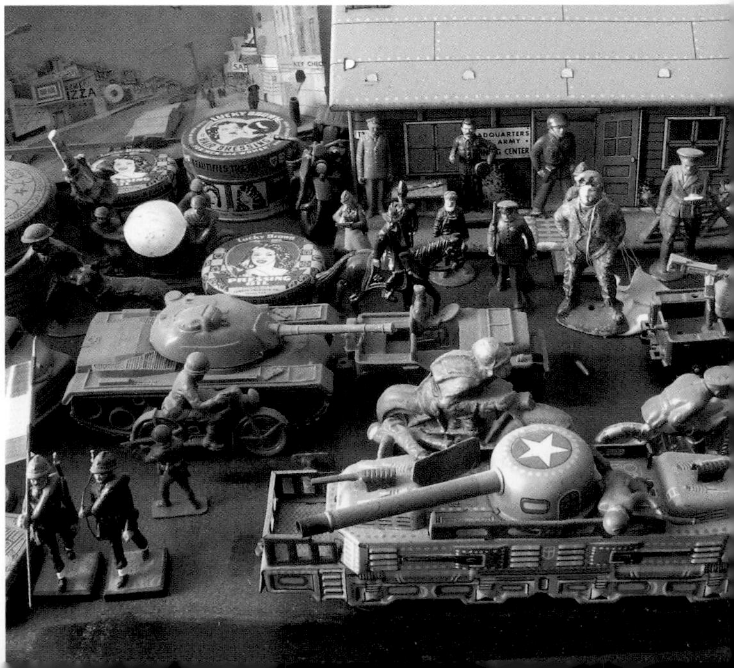

hasn't changed, man. What I try to do is to encourage a good attitude toward learning about the world in all of its diverse aspects. This is what's necessary, not only to survive and prosper, but to have a fulfilling life. My real attitude to official authority is the same as it has always been. San Francisco tends to be more progressive than lot of places, so Nora's exposed to a lot of good progressive ideas: feminism, peace activism, things like that. She has an attitude that girls can do anything, which is a good thing. So often I'll tease her and say, 'No, girls can't do that sort of stuff.' And of course, she just completely rejects it."

"Spain's politics were not unchanging," said Stern. "Yet he remained committed to core values. A core value that he was committed to was that income inequality, as we call it now, in his day we called it 'the class struggle,' is central to what is wrong with the world. It's central to injustice. He thought it was the most central contradiction. I think he voted Socialist the first time he ever voted and he certainly actively worked for political justice all of his life. He was part of one of the first demonstrations against the war in Vietnam in 1964. He and I went to many demonstrations against the war in Central America and the war in Iraq, so he was active in politics and he called himself a Marxist.

"I would not say that Spain had a utopian vision for the future but I would say he had an optimistic vision of the future. Spain believed not so much in hope but in struggle. He thought the thing to do is to keep fighting injustice, even if you didn't see big changes in your lifetime."

"It's heartbreaking to me that people don't vote," said Stern. "Spain and I would work every election. We would walk door to door for candidates and for propositions. We would try to get out the vote. In San Francisco, that means climbing up and down hills and climbing up and down lots of stairs to people's doors. I remember going out one year when he was already very sick. It was a hot day in the Mission District. We ran into some guy coming out of his apartment who brushed us off. He said he was too busy to vote. And I thought: 'Here's this old man, dying of cancer, and he's walking around trying to get out the vote—and you can't even be bothered to vote?' I think Spain is an inspiring figure. Both as an artist and as a person."

After Spain's death in 2012, Stern began making a documentary film about him and sorting, indexing, and preserving his

work and effects. It's a big job with an emotional toll, but Stern said she feels she has to do it. "Now that I'm going through all his work, I see how politically committed he was. I see that everything he did, from small paid political jobs to a ton of work he must have done for free for every progressive political party under the sun—spot illustrations, banners, logos—and there's just box after box after box of it.

"I think Spain was a great artist," she said. "I think that underground comix was a seminal artistic and literary movement. I think it needs to be preserved."

Spain's studio and its contents have now been organized and preserved. His original artwork is cataloged and scanned and entered into a database, and tucked away, cushioned with tissue paper in archival boxes. His Road Vulture Motorcycle Club's leather jacket is wrapped and stored and the silkscreened T-shirts from their many reunions are laundered and packed away for posterity. Legions of his model soldiers parade in formation on shelves and dresser tops and in glass cases, protecting the house and guarding his ashes. An oversized 1942 map shows the progress of the Crimean war.

His reference books remain: *Jane's Fighting Aircraft of World War II, Historical Facts of World War II, Combat Arms, Modern Helicopters, Warplanes, America in the Air War, Soviet Airpower, Warplanes, Fighters, The Third Reich, Architecture of Air Power,* and more. His favorite framed comic pages by EC-era artists—Wally Wood, "Ghastly" Graham Ingels, Jack Davis, Johnny Craig—still hang on the walls. He didn't actually draw in that room; he preferred the dining-room table, but his tools and supplies are stored there, many worn down to small bits from long and frugal use—pencil stubs, bits of erasers, well-worn pens and brushes. The comics he loved and read for insights are stored in boxes—mostly action adventures like *Blackhawk* and *Frontline Combat.* Photos and drawings by Spain and many others, correspondence, documents, flyers, and posters decorate the rest of the wall space, mapping out Spain's journey through his life—geographical, historical, and spiritual. He kept everything—his earliest toy soldiers, nearly empty ink bottles, sketchbooks, photo albums, Strathmore scraps, and letters from the "Disciples of Spain." His collection of *Playboys* and other men's magazines, which he referred to as his "reference files" are mostly gone, except for the ones containing his work. You can see the floor now, which was a rarity when Spain used piles to keep track of ongoing projects. It has the air of a shrine, to a modest man, not a saint, but a dedicated artist, who used what he had to say what he had to say. A place devoted to work, that not surprisingly, gave birth to many remarkable works of art.

MISSION REBELS

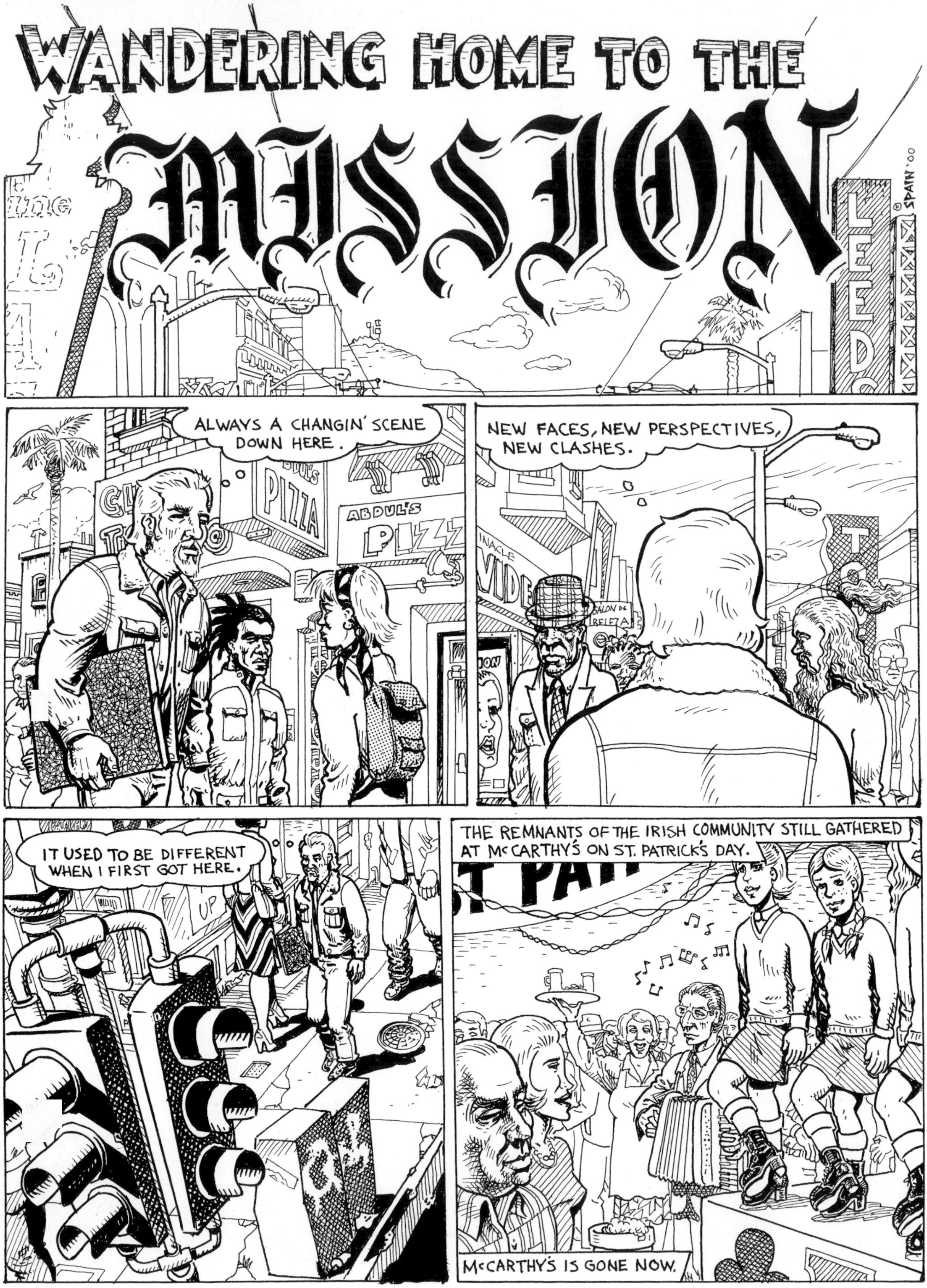
WANDERING HOME TO THE
MISSION
© SPAIN '00
ALWAYS A CHANGIN' SCENE DOWN HERE.
NEW FACES, NEW PERSPECTIVES, NEW CLASHES.
IT USED TO BE DIFFERENT WHEN I FIRST GOT HERE.
THE REMNANTS OF THE IRISH COMMUNITY STILL GATHERED AT McCARTHY'S ON ST. PATRICK'S DAY.
McCARTHY'S IS GONE NOW.

P. 20–21 from *Zap* #16, 2016

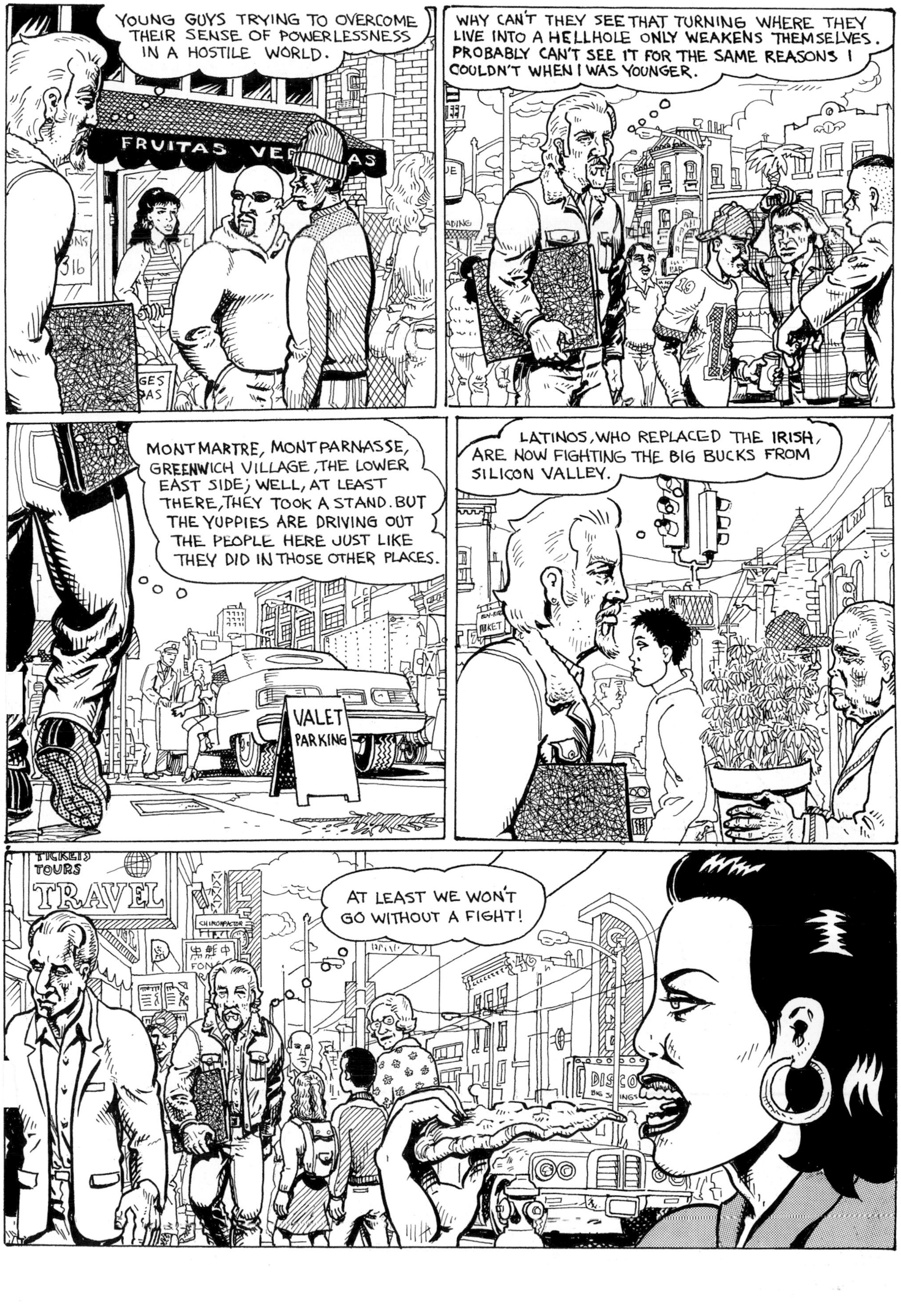
YOUNG GUYS TRYING TO OVERCOME THEIR SENSE OF POWERLESSNESS IN A HOSTILE WORLD.
WHY CAN'T THEY SEE THAT TURNING WHERE THEY LIVE INTO A HELLHOLE ONLY WEAKENS THEMSELVES. PROBABLY CAN'T SEE IT FOR THE SAME REASONS I COULDN'T WHEN I WAS YOUNGER.
MONTMARTRE, MONTPARNASSE, GREENWICH VILLAGE, THE LOWER EAST SIDE; WELL, AT LEAST THERE, THEY TOOK A STAND. BUT THE YUPPIES ARE DRIVING OUT THE PEOPLE HERE JUST LIKE THEY DID IN THOSE OTHER PLACES.
VALET PARKING
LATINOS, WHO REPLACED THE IRISH, ARE NOW FIGHTING THE BIG BUCKS FROM SILICON VALLEY.
TOURS
TRAVEL
AT LEAST WE WON'T GO WITHOUT A FIGHT!

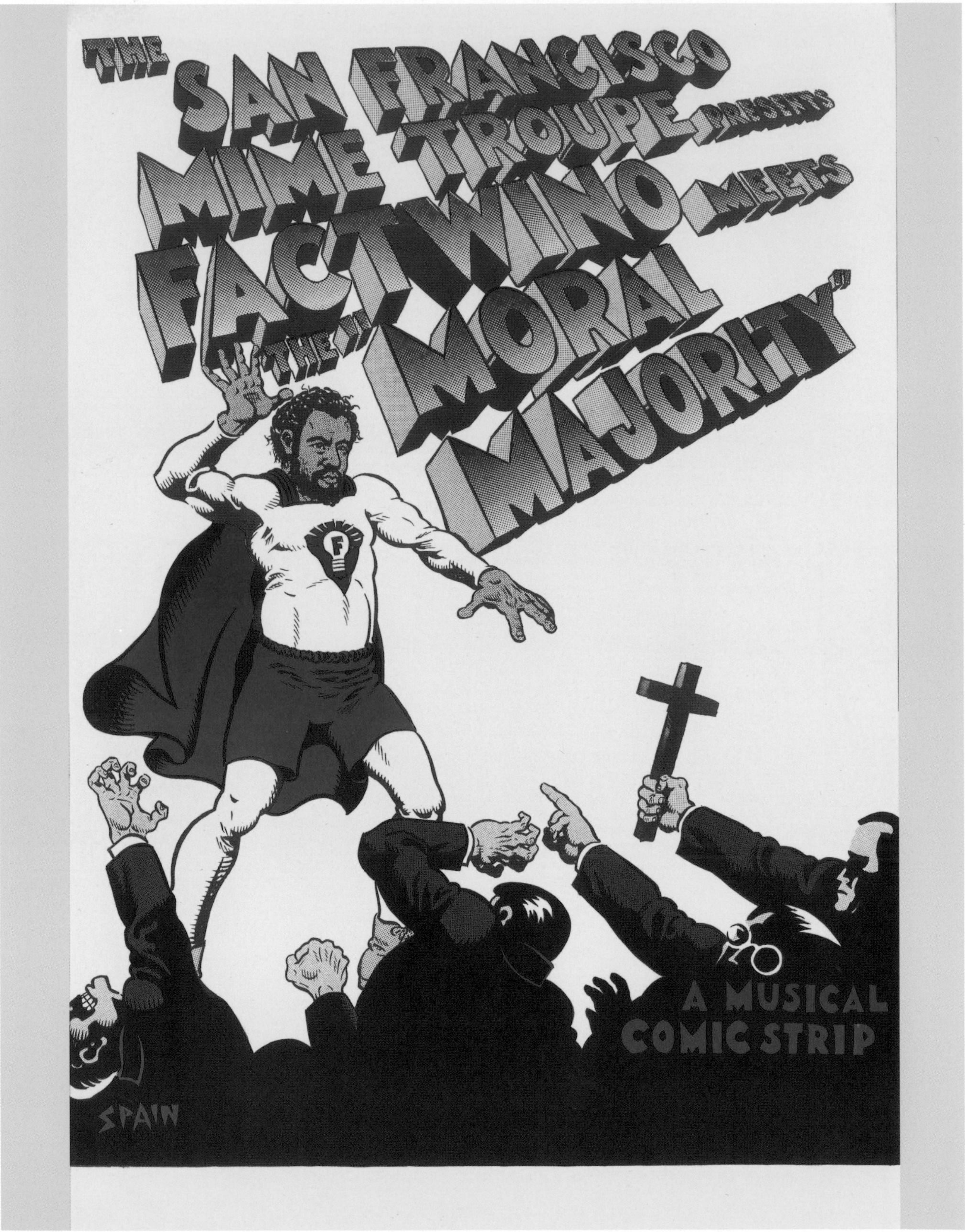
THE SAN FRANCISCO MIME TROUPE PRESENTS
FACTWINO MEETS "THE MORAL MAJORITY"
A MUSICAL COMIC STRIP
SPAIN

P. 22–40 San Francisco Mime Troupe posters, 1985–2012

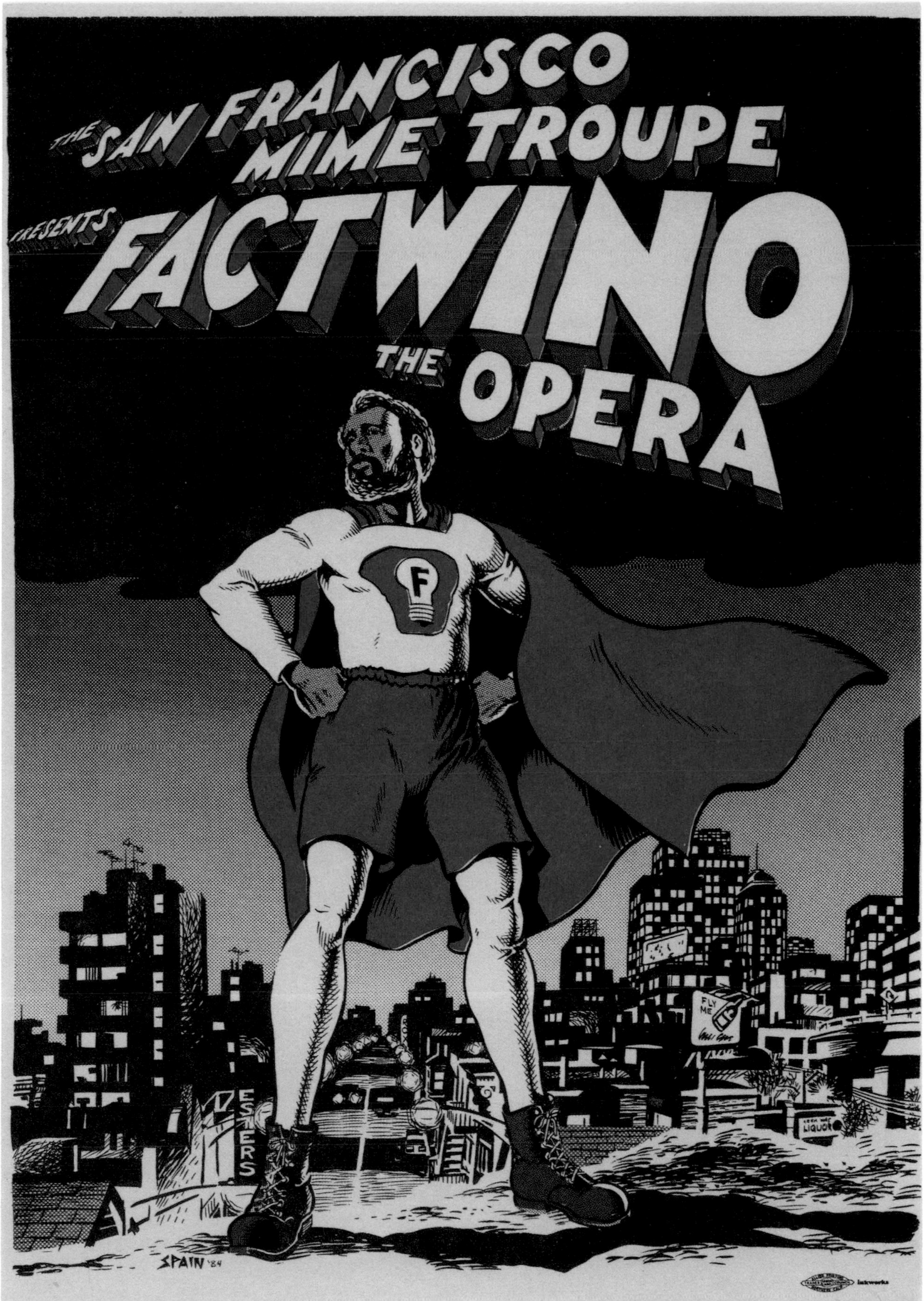
THE SAN FRANCISCO MIME TROUPE
PRESENTS FACTWINO
THE OPERA
FLY ME
LIQUOR
SPAIN '84

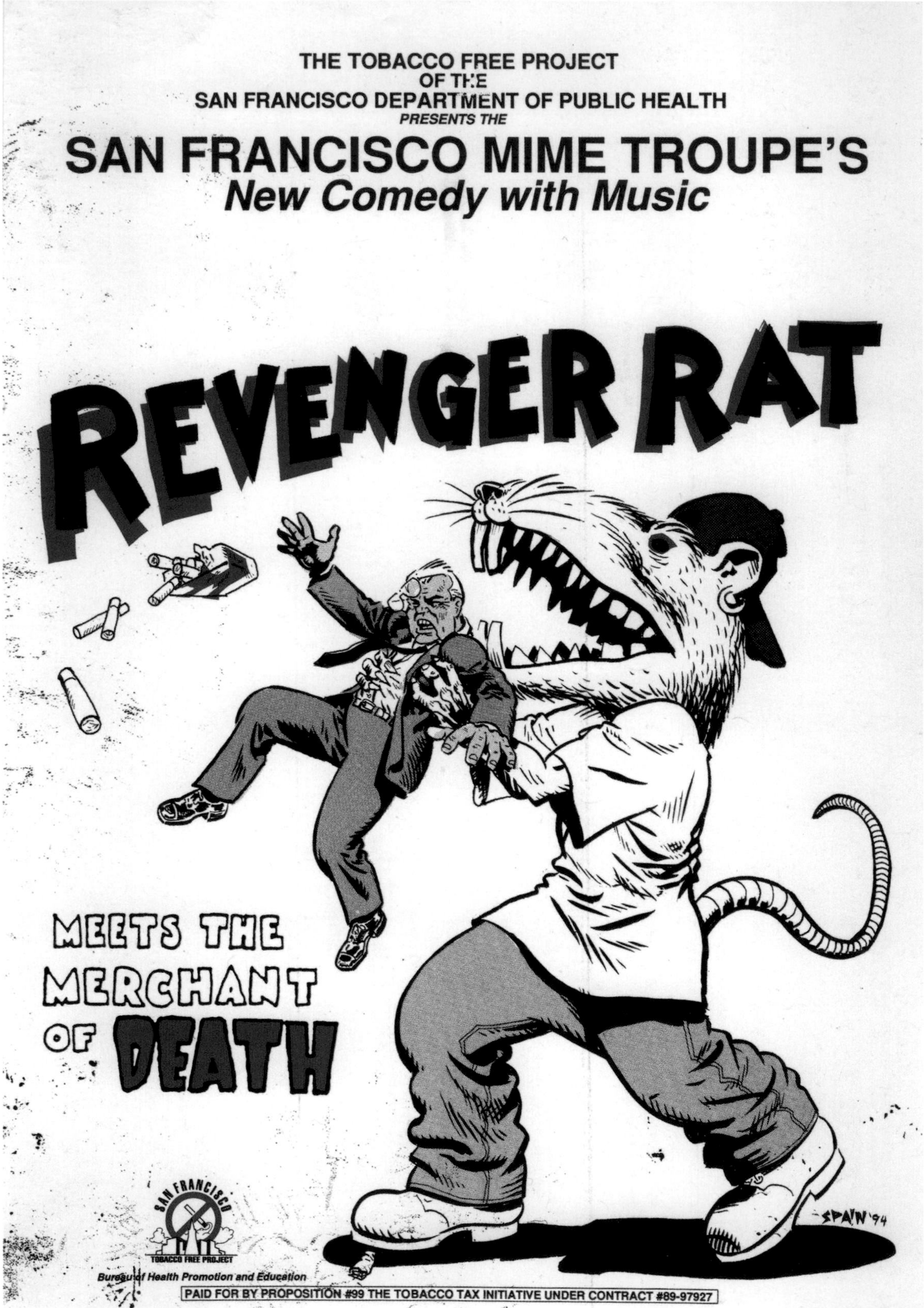
THE TOBACCO FREE PROJECT
OF THE
SAN FRANCISCO DEPARTMENT OF PUBLIC HEALTH
PRESENTS THE
SAN FRANCISCO MIME TROUPE'S
New Comedy with Music
REVENGER RAT
MEETS THE
MERCHANT
OF DEATH
SPAIN '94
SAN FRANCISCO
TOBACCO FREE PROJECT
Bureau of Health Promotion and Education
PAID FOR BY PROPOSITION #99 THE TOBACCO TAX INITIATIVE UNDER CONTRACT #89-97927

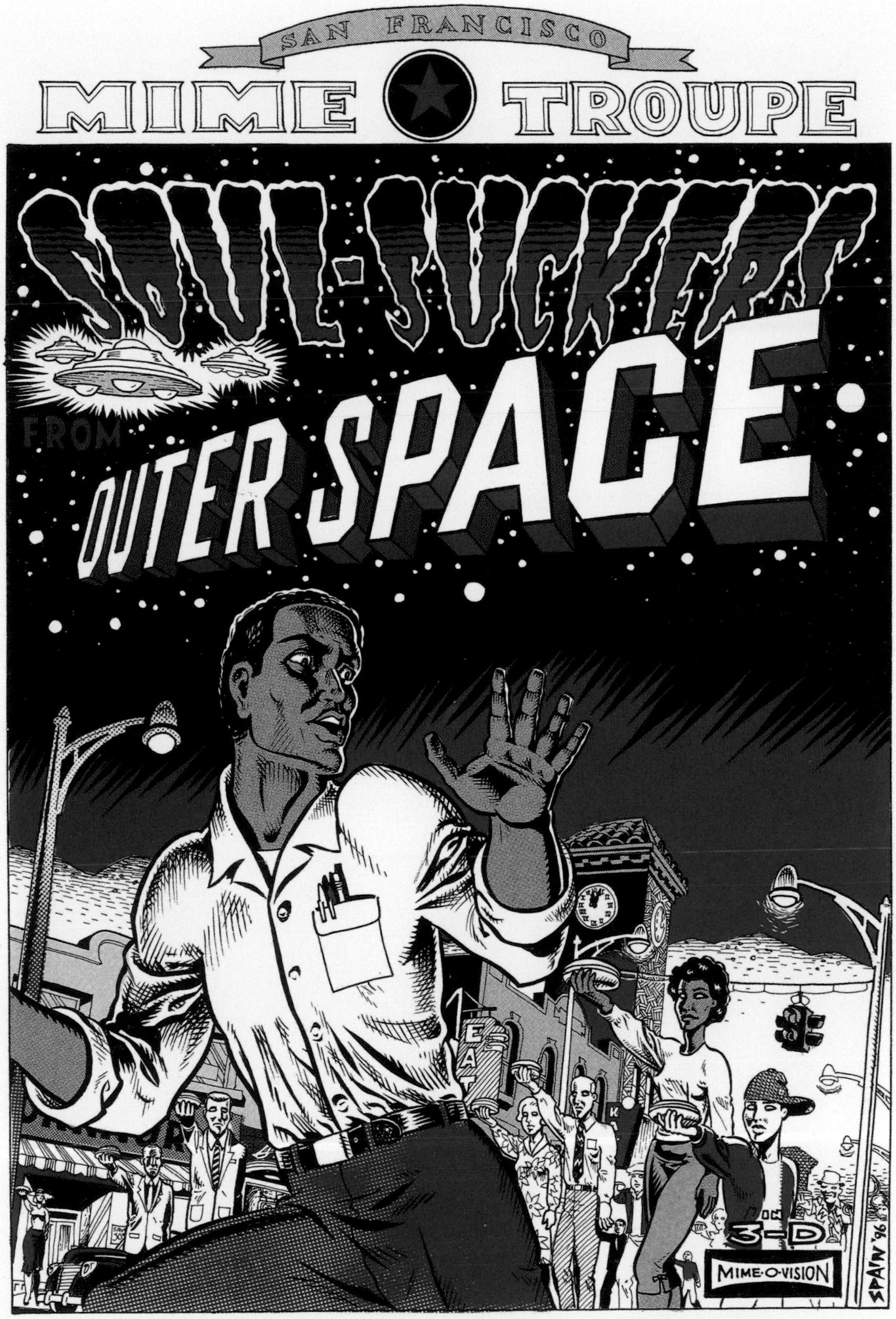
SAN FRANCISCO
MIME TROUPE
SOUL-SUCKERS
FROM
OUTER SPACE
EAT
3-D
MIME-O-VISION
SPAIN '96
FREE IN THE PARKS
JULY 4 TO AUGUST 4
Call 415-285-1720 For Information

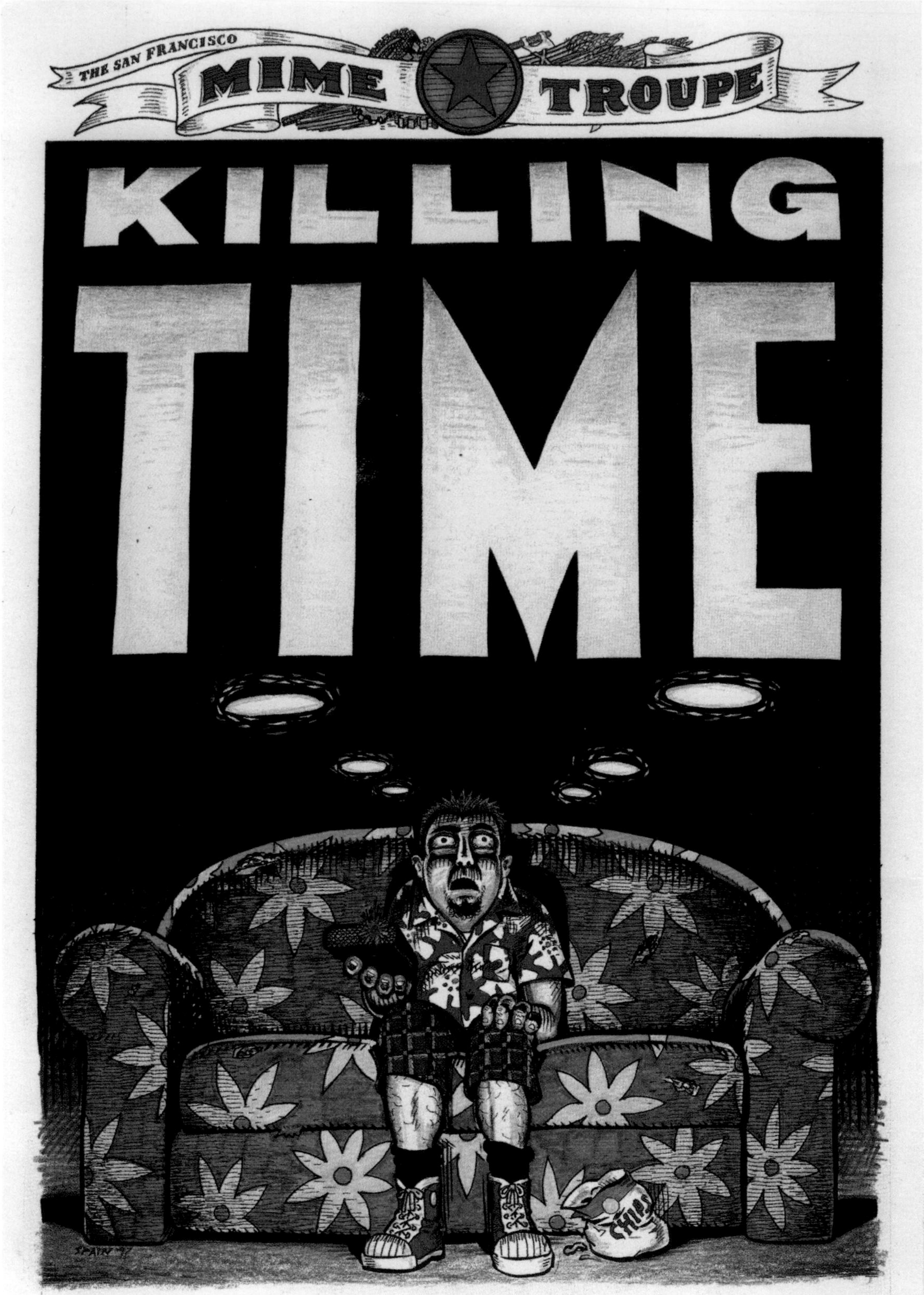
THE SAN FRANCISCO
MIME TROUPE
KILLING
TIME
CHIPS
35th SEASON
FREE PARK SHOWS!

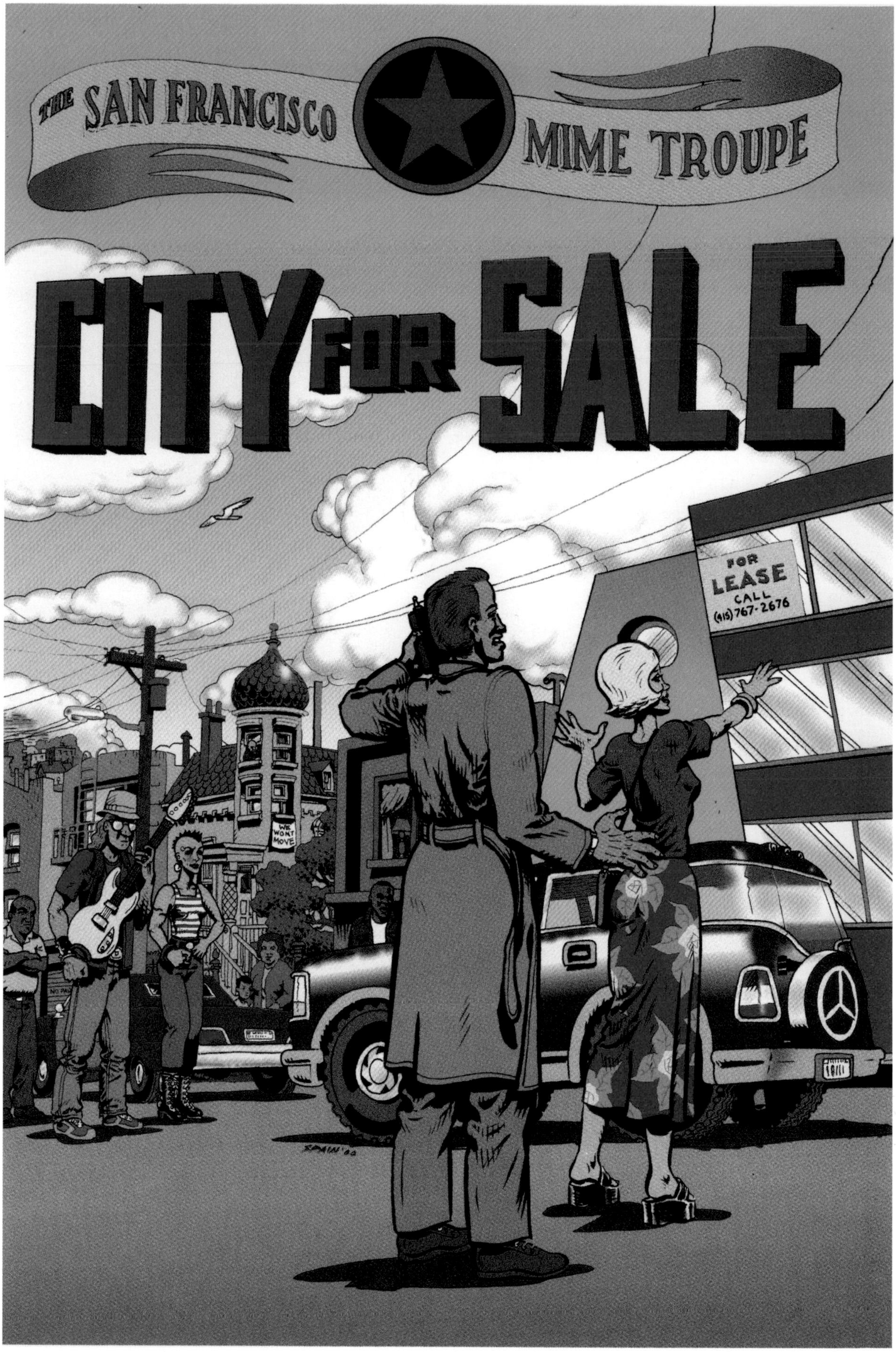
THE SAN FRANCISCO MIME TROUPE
CITY FOR SALE
FOR LEASE
CALL
(415) 767-2676
WE WONT MOVE
SPAIN '00

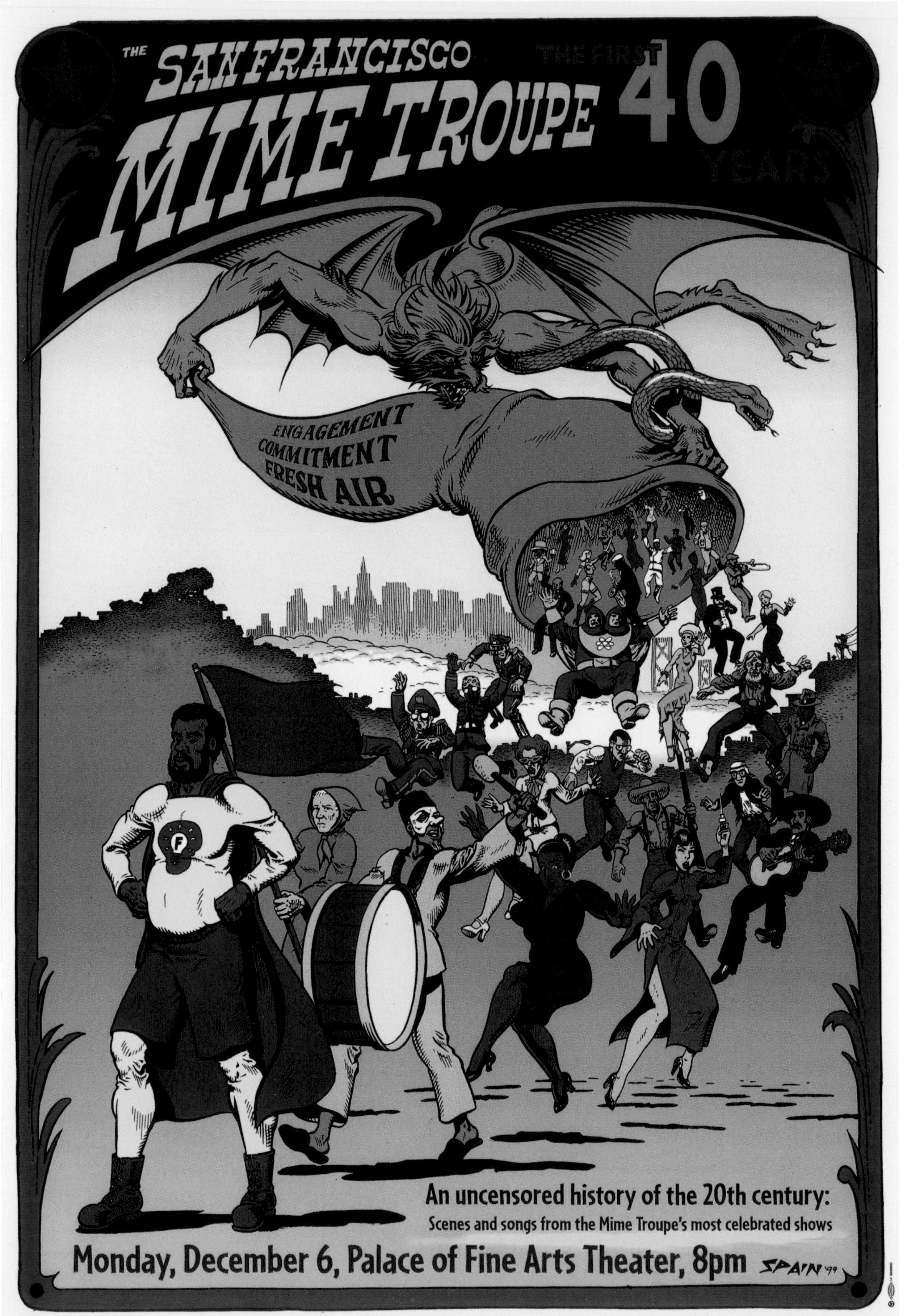
THE SAN FRANCISCO
MIME TROUPE
THE FIRST 40 YEARS
ENGAGEMENT
COMMITMENT
FRESH AIR
An uncensored history of the 20th century:
Scenes and songs from the Mime Troupe's most celebrated shows
Monday, December 6, Palace of Fine Arts Theater, 8pm
SPAIN '99
Tickets at City Lights and Modern Times Bookstores, San Francisco and Cody's Books, Berkeley • Info: SFMT at 415/285-1717 or www.sfmt.org

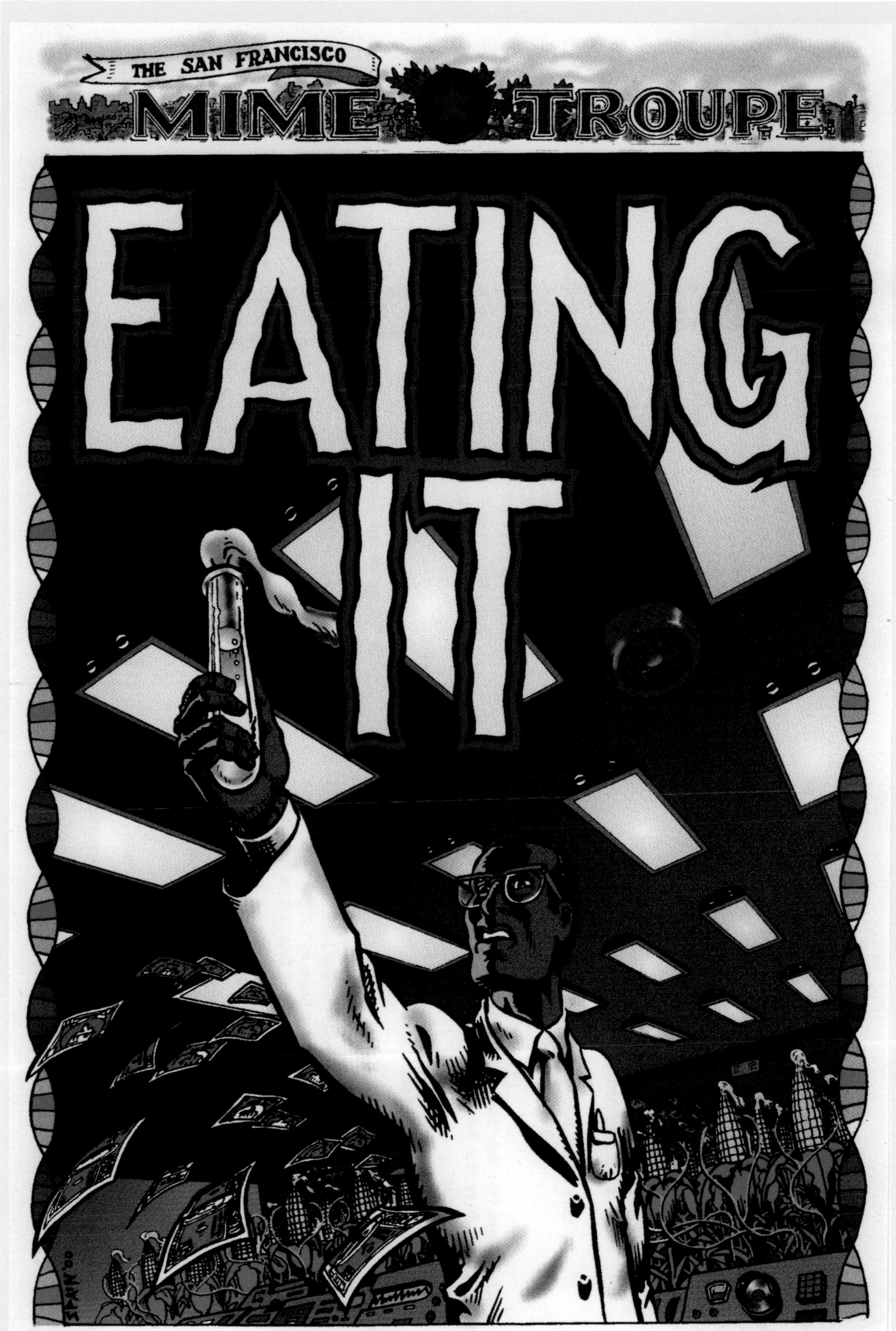
THE SAN FRANCISCO
MIME TROUPE
EATING
IT
FREE IN THE PARK
July 1st to Labor Day, 2000 Call 415/285-1717 for information

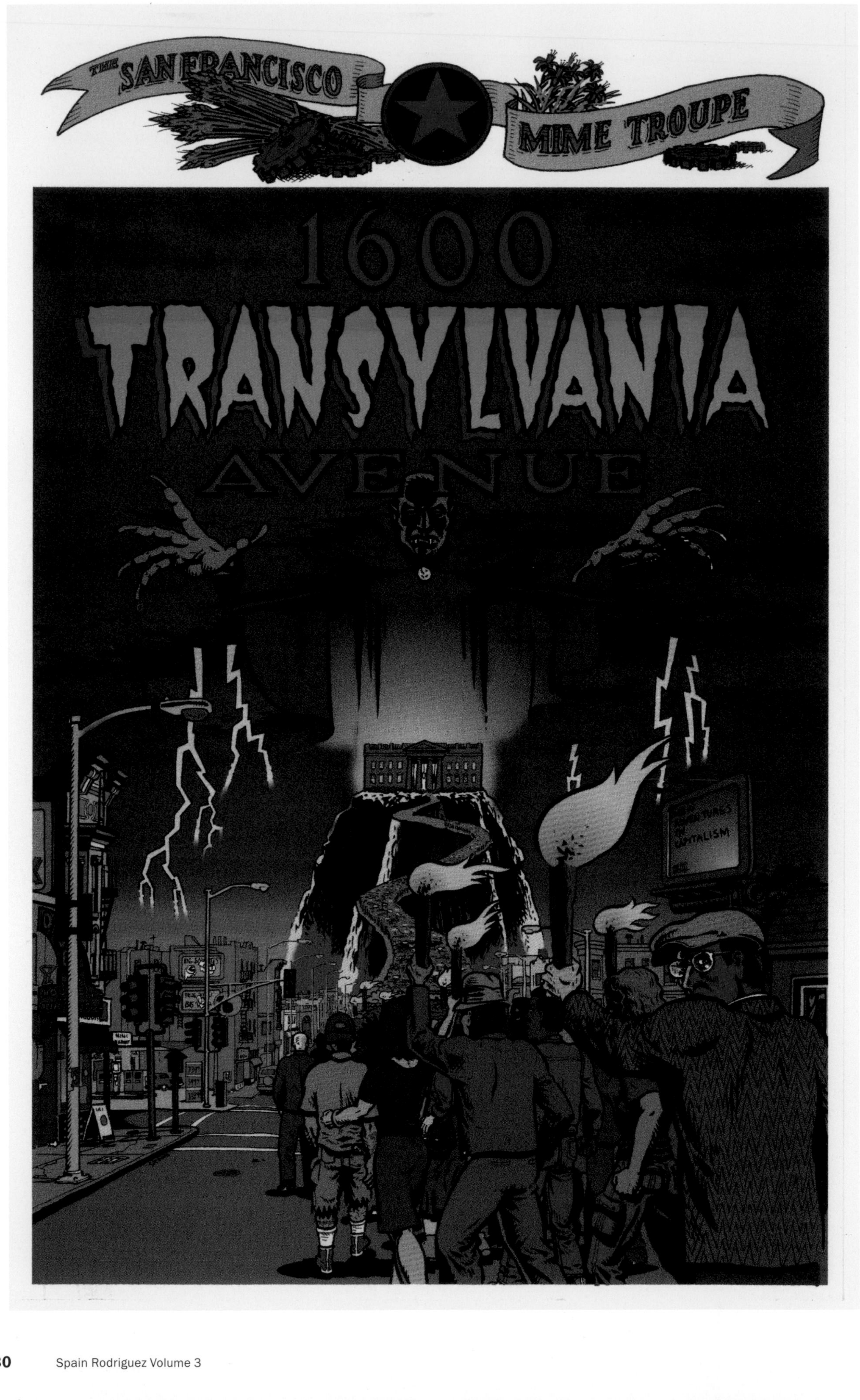
THE SAN FRANCISCO
MIME TROUPE
1600
TRANSYLVANIA
AVENUE

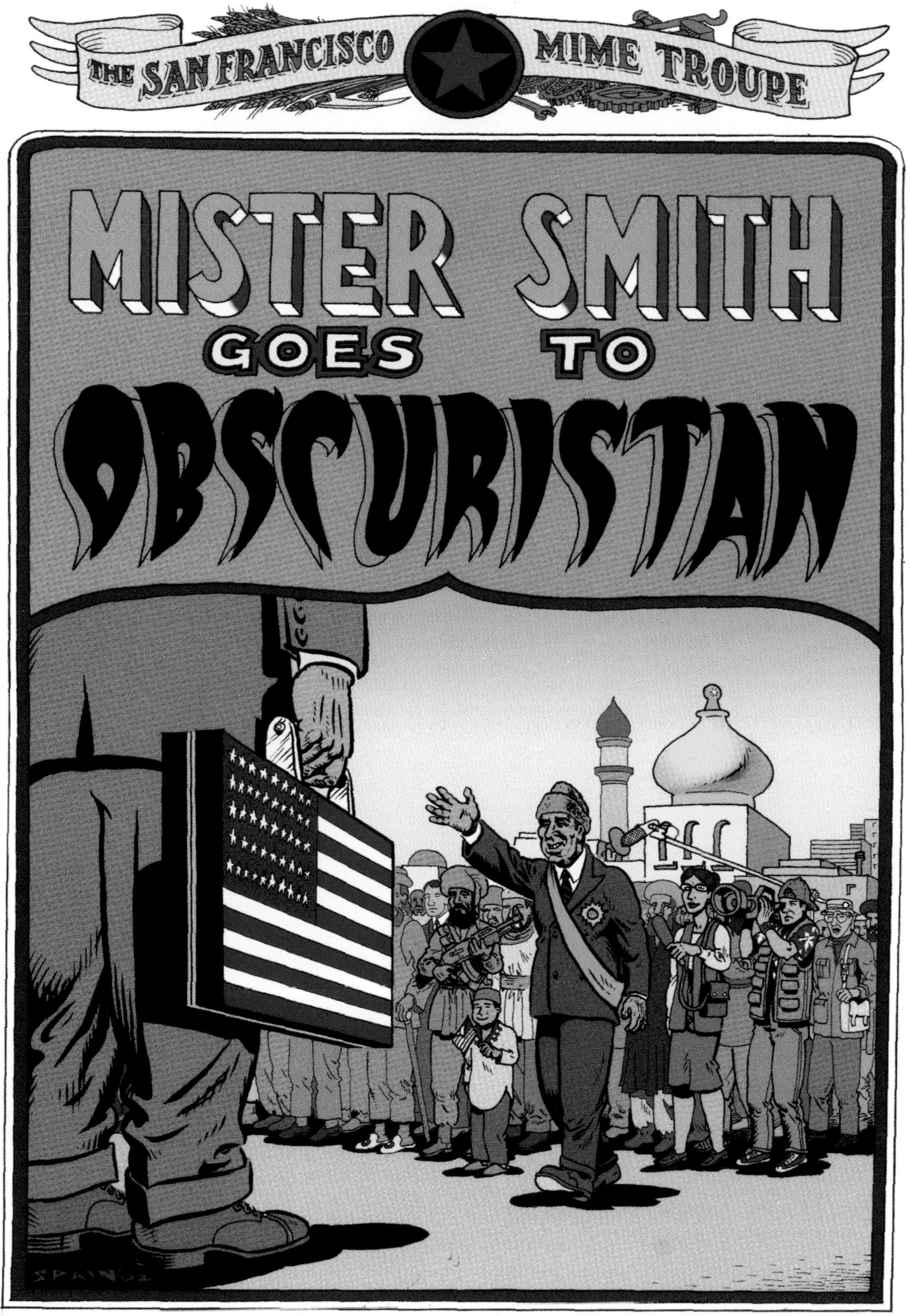
THE SAN FRANCISCO MIME TROUPE
MISTER SMITH
GOES TO
OBSCURISTAN

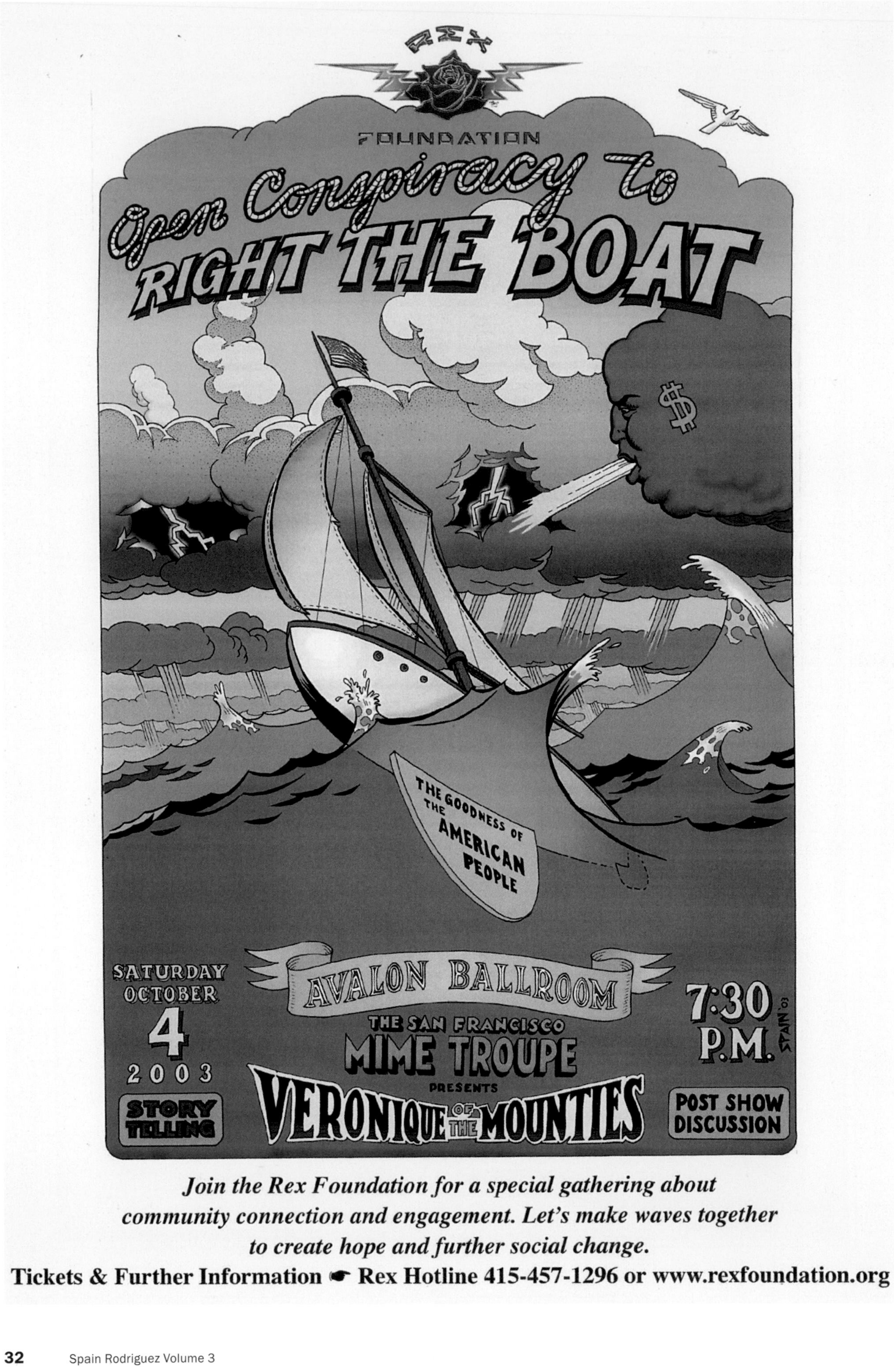
REX
FOUNDATION
Open Conspiracy to
RIGHT THE BOAT
$
THE GOODNESS OF THE AMERICAN PEOPLE
SATURDAY
OCTOBER
4
2003
STORY TELLING
AVALON BALLROOM
THE SAN FRANCISCO
MIME TROUPE
PRESENTS
VERONIQUE OF THE MOUNTIES
7:30
P.M.
POST SHOW DISCUSSION
Join the Rex Foundation for a special gathering about
community connection and engagement. Let's make waves together
to create hope and further social change.
Tickets & Further Information ☛ Rex Hotline 415-457-1296 or www.rexfoundation.org

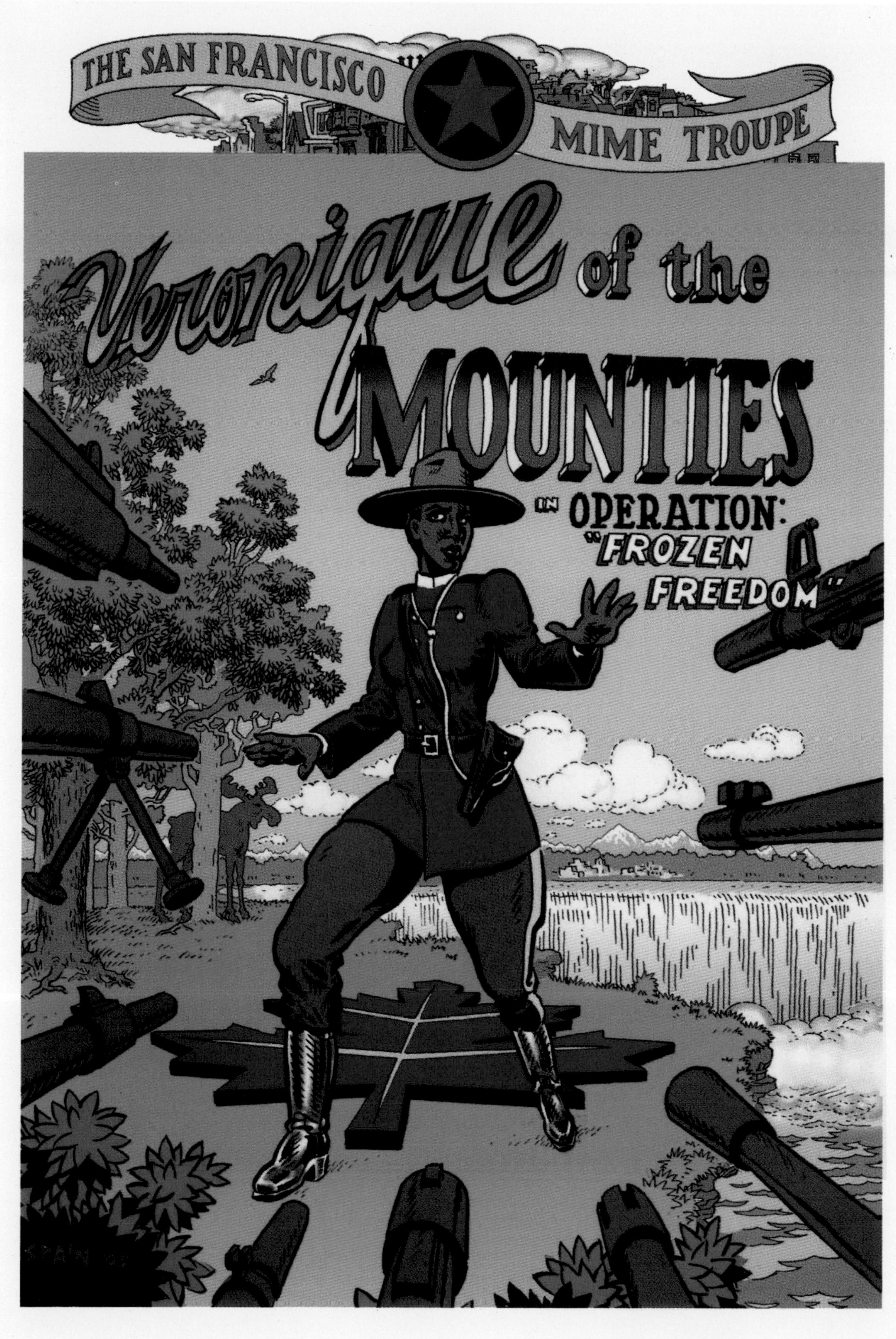
THE SAN FRANCISCO
MIME TROUPE
Veronique of the
MOUNTIES
IN OPERATION:
"FROZEN
FREEDOM"

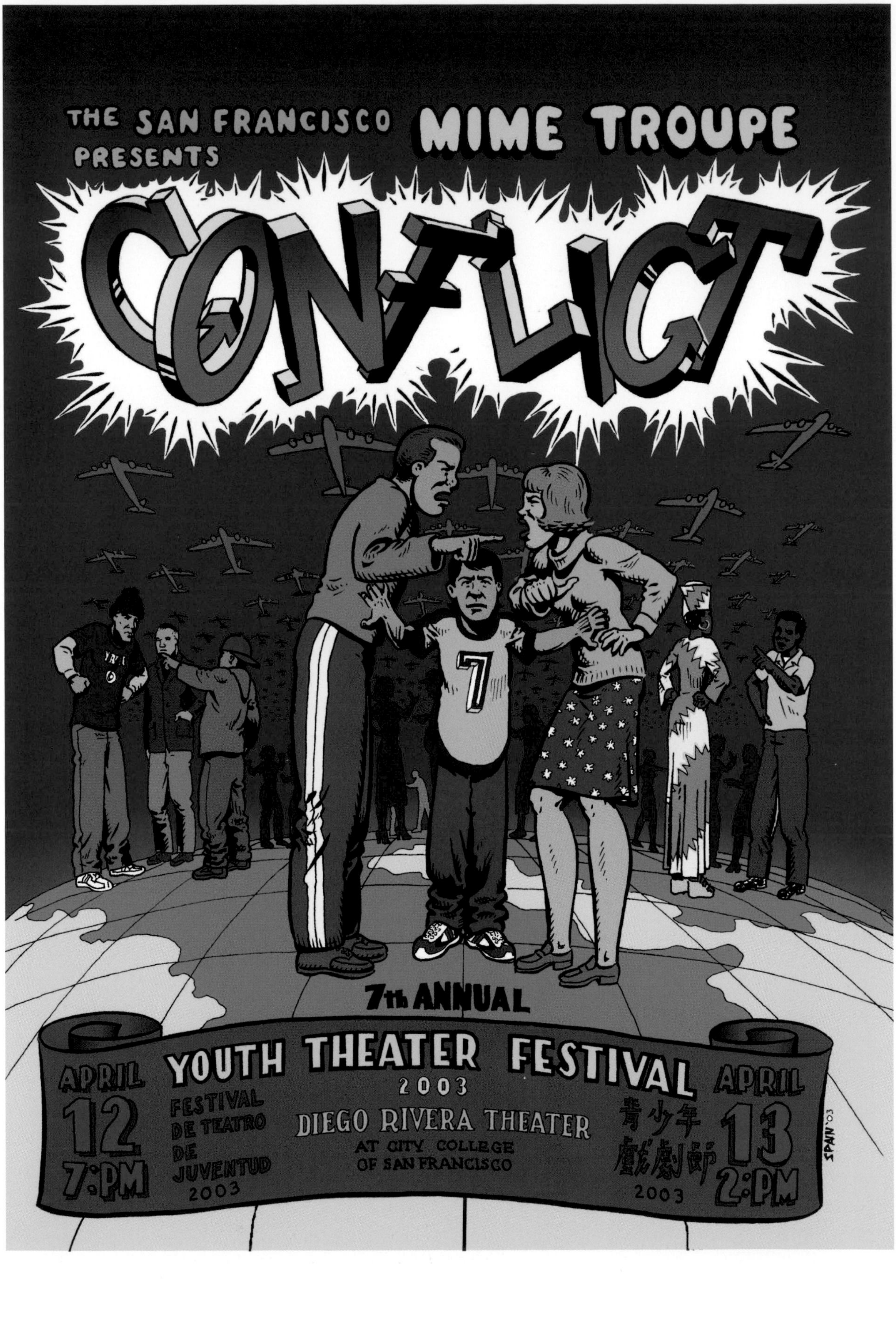
THE SAN FRANCISCO MIME TROUPE
PRESENTS
CONFLICT
7
7th ANNUAL
YOUTH THEATER FESTIVAL
2003
APRIL
12
7:PM
FESTIVAL
DE TEATRO
DE
JUVENTUD
2003
DIEGO RIVERA THEATER
AT CITY COLLEGE
OF SAN FRANCISCO
青少年
戲劇節
2003
APRIL
13
2:PM
SPAIN '03

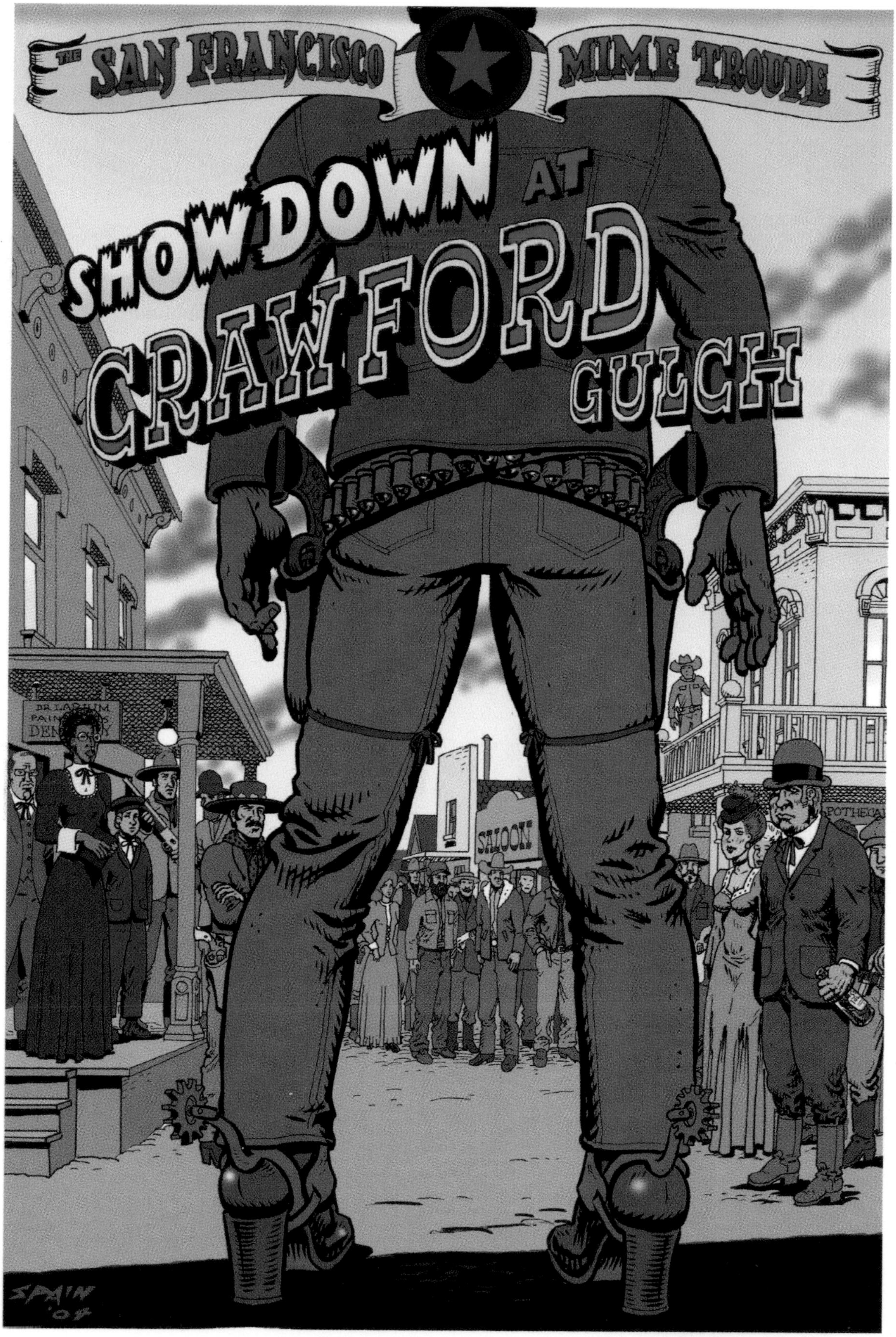
THE SAN FRANCISCO
MIME TROUPE
SHOWDOWN AT
CRAWFORD
GULCH
SALOON

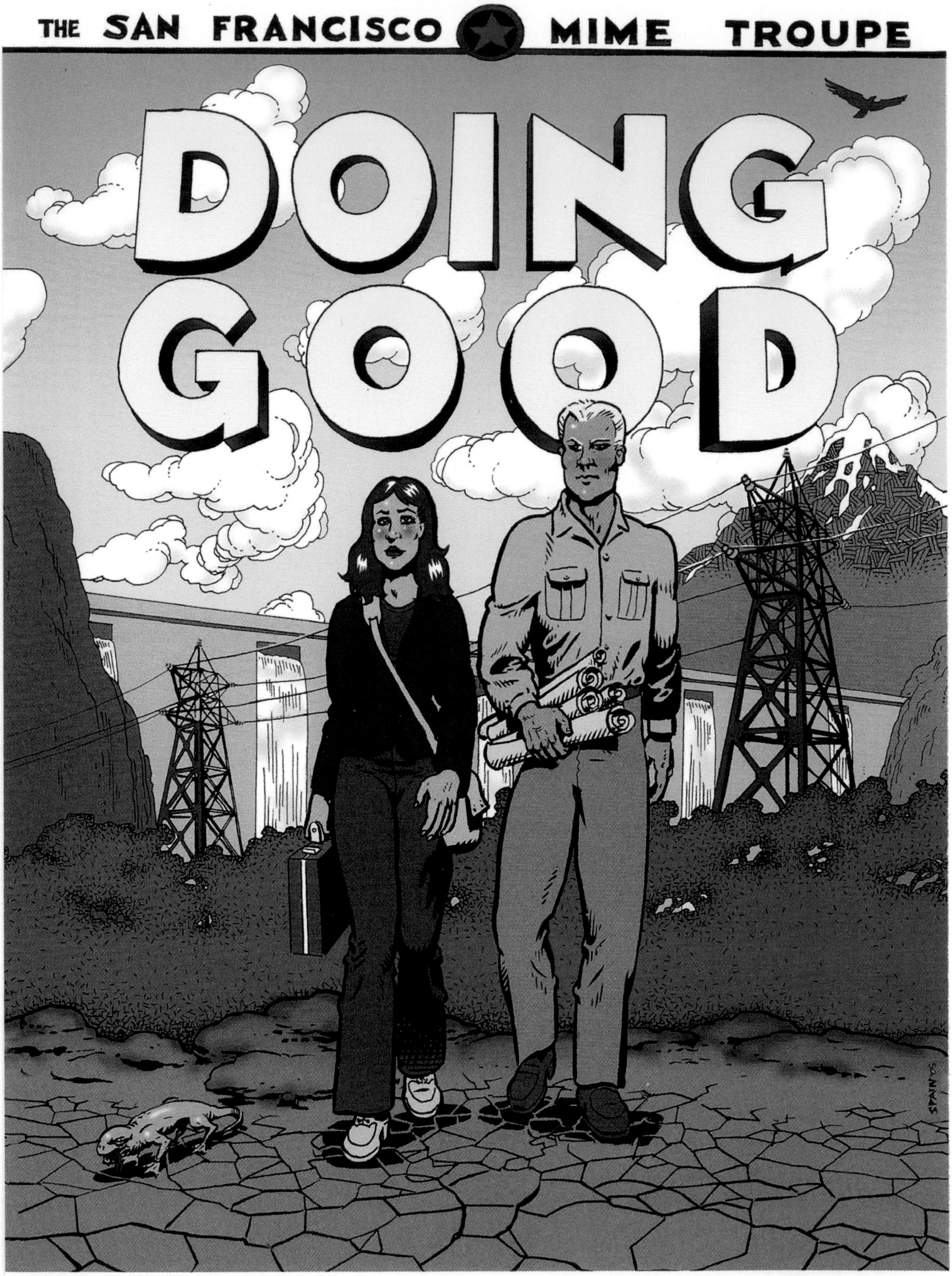
THE SAN FRANCISCO MIME TROUPE
DOING GOOD
SPAIN '05

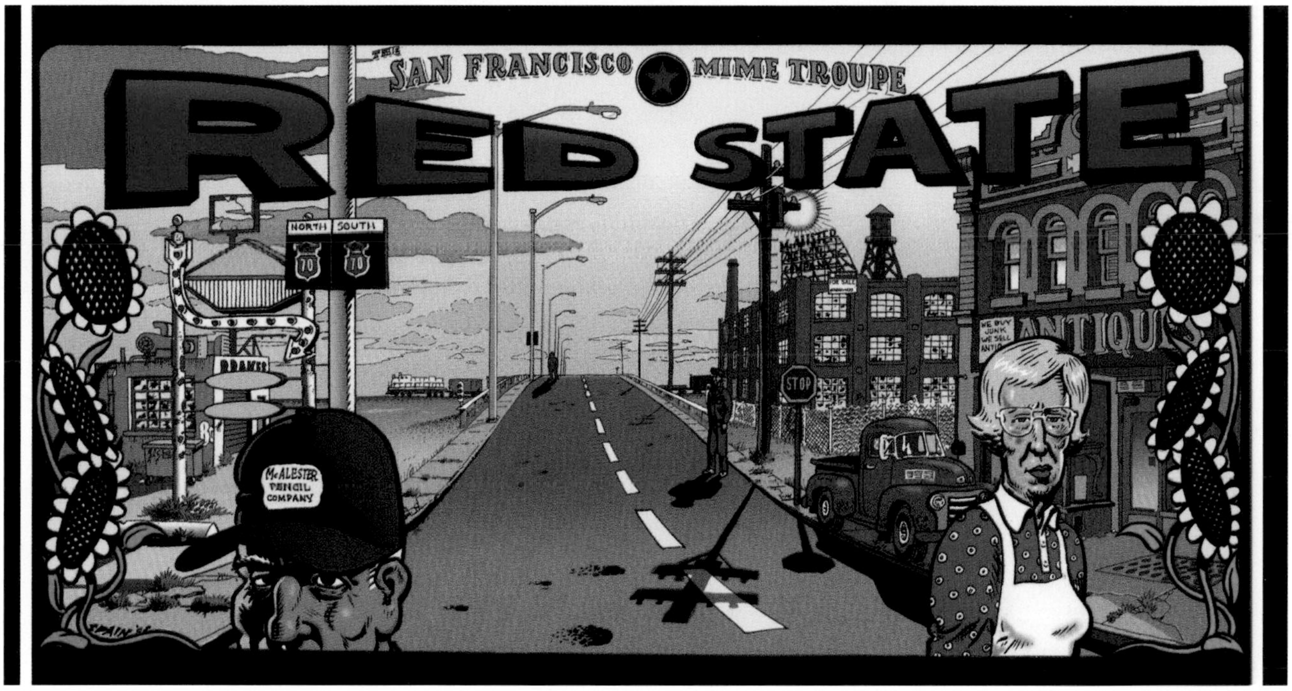
THE SAN FRANCISCO MIME TROUPE
RED STATE
NORTH SOUTH
70 70
McALESTER PENCIL COMPANY
STOP
ANTIQU

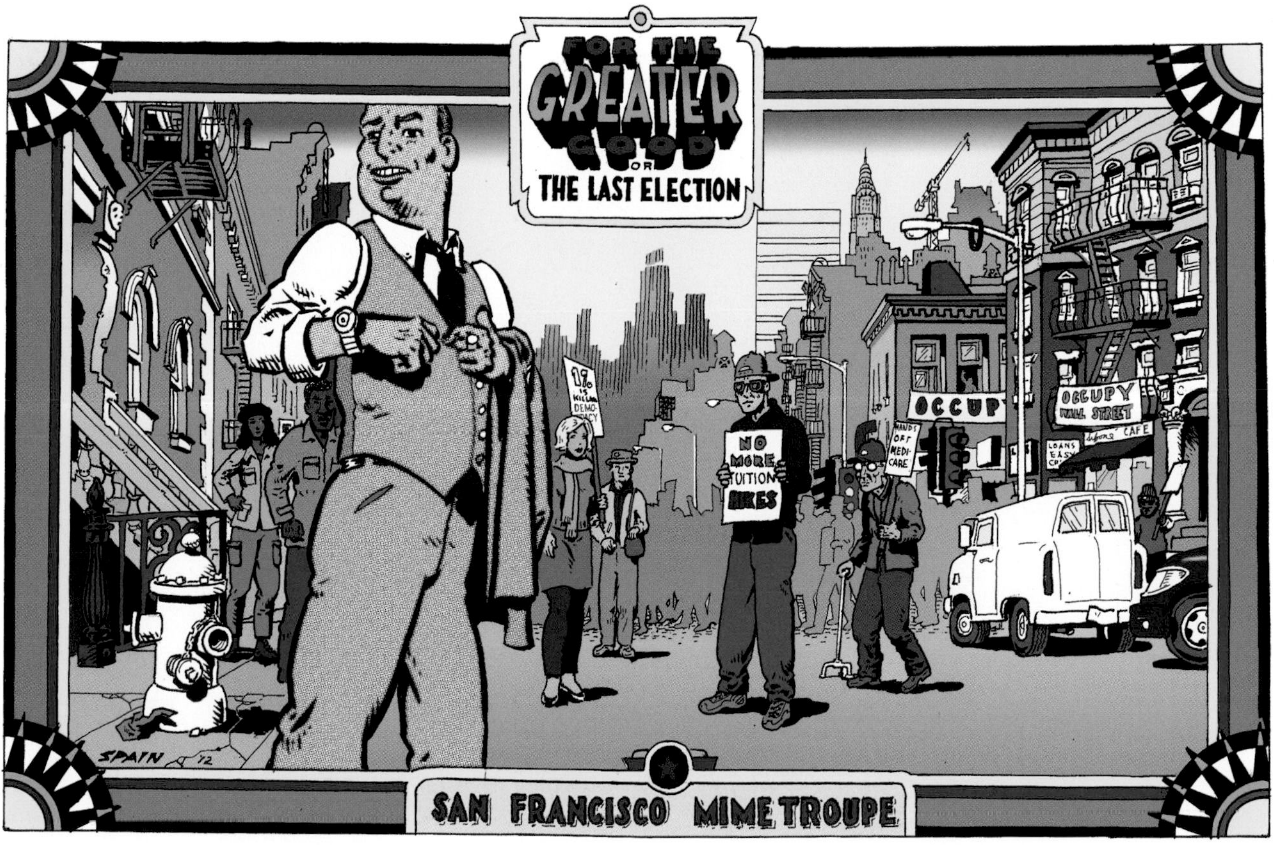
FOR THE GREATER GOOD
OR
THE LAST ELECTION
NO MORE TUITION HIKES
OCCUPY
OCCUPY WALL STREET
CAFE
SPAIN
SAN FRANCISCO MIME TROUPE

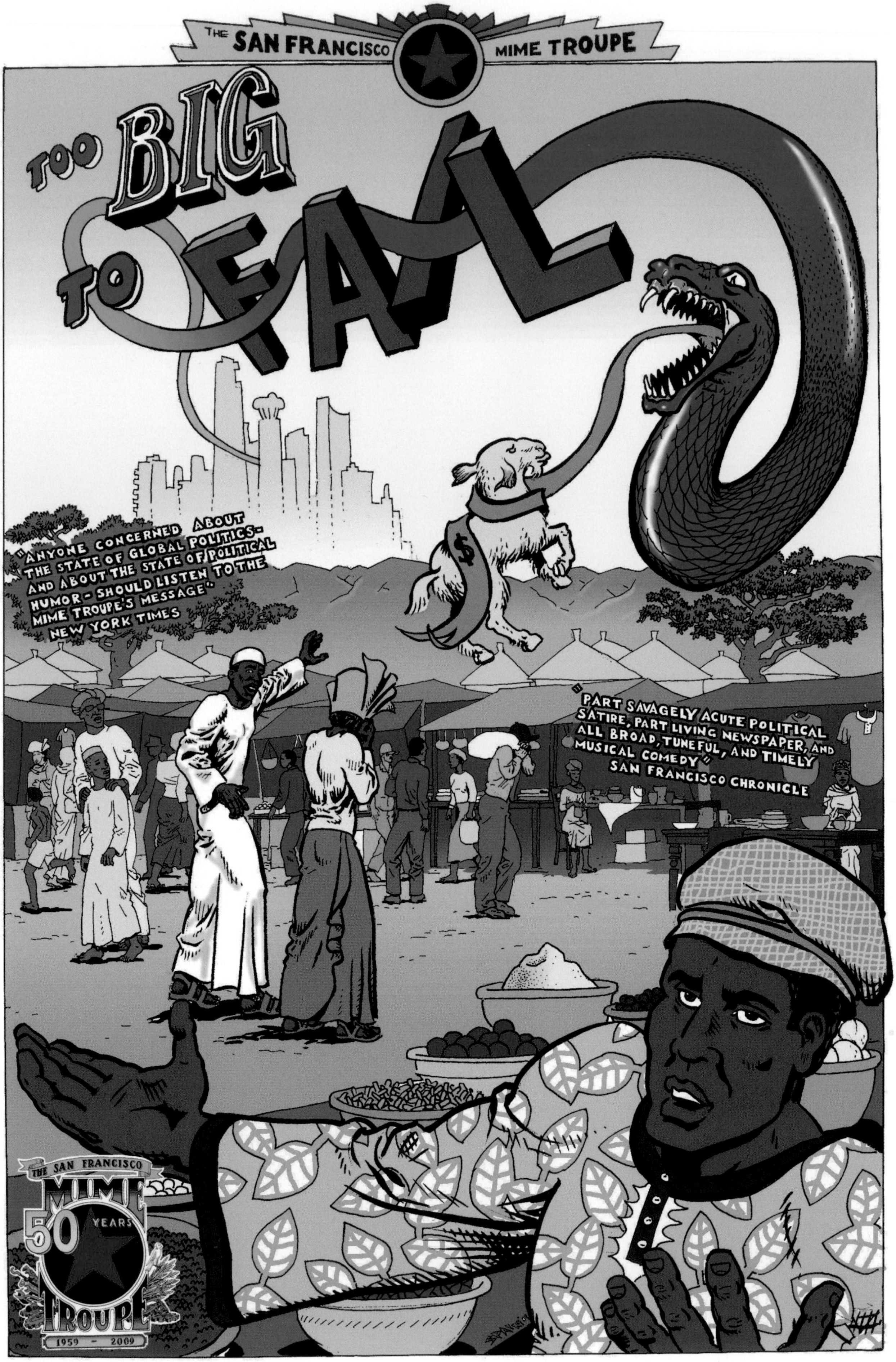
THE SAN FRANCISCO MIME TROUPE
TOO BIG TO FAIL
"ANYONE CONCERNED ABOUT THE STATE OF GLOBAL POLITICS- AND ABOUT THE STATE OF POLITICAL HUMOR - SHOULD LISTEN TO THE MIME TROUPE'S MESSAGE".
NEW YORK TIMES
"PART SAVAGELY ACUTE POLITICAL SATIRE, PART LIVING NEWSPAPER, AND ALL BROAD, TUNEFUL, AND TIMELY MUSICAL COMEDY"
SAN FRANCISCO CHRONICLE
THE SAN FRANCISCO MIME TROUPE
50 YEARS
1959 - 2009

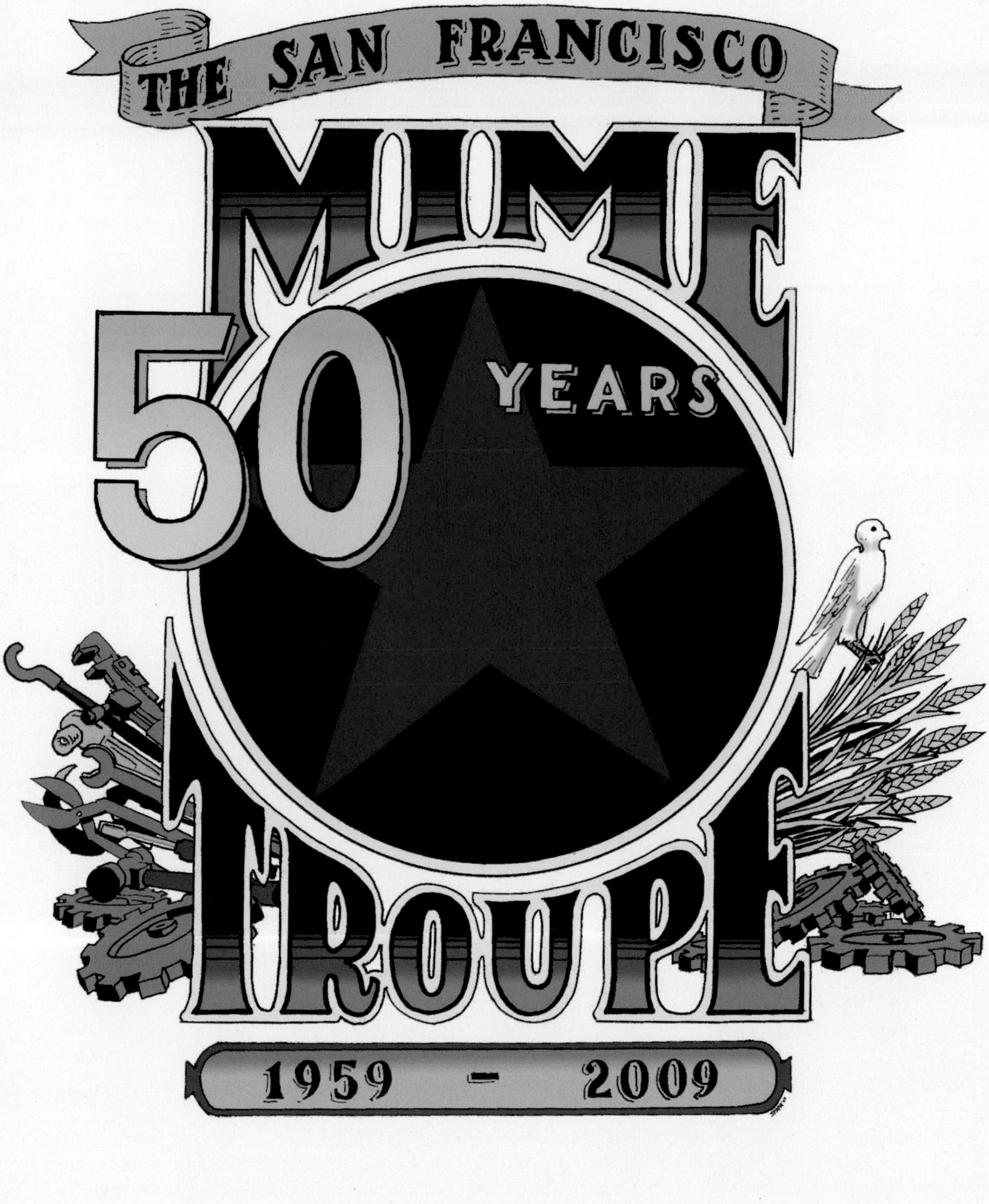
THE SAN FRANCISCO
MIME
50 YEARS
TROUPE
1959 – 2009

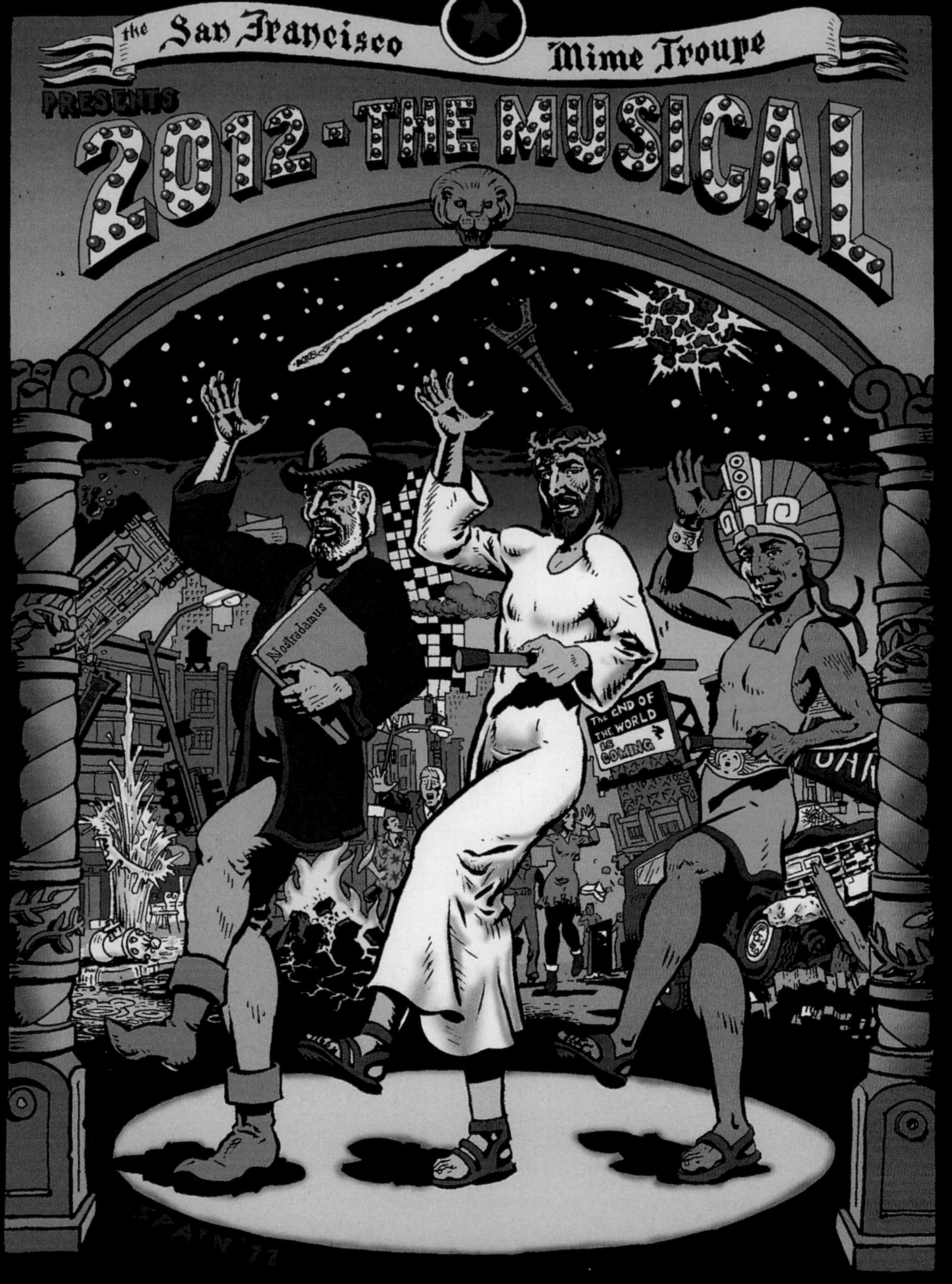
the San Francisco Mime Troupe
PRESENTS
2012 - THE MUSICAL
Nostradamus
The END OF THE WORLD IS COMING
SPAIN '11

A small political theater company — Theater BAM! — finds itself at a crossroads: should they keep telling the stories they feel can change the world (and starve while telling them), or feed at the corporate trough, and be a mouthpiece for The Man? Tough decision! But before having to make it, they are offered an artistic commission that may save the company; all they have to do is create a new play, "2012 — The Musical!" But is it political? Is it in line with the company's mission? What's the true purpose of this ridiculous production, and who's really bankrolling the thing? Find out the answers to these questions and more in this lively, skewering satire of corporate funding and the art of mass distraction.

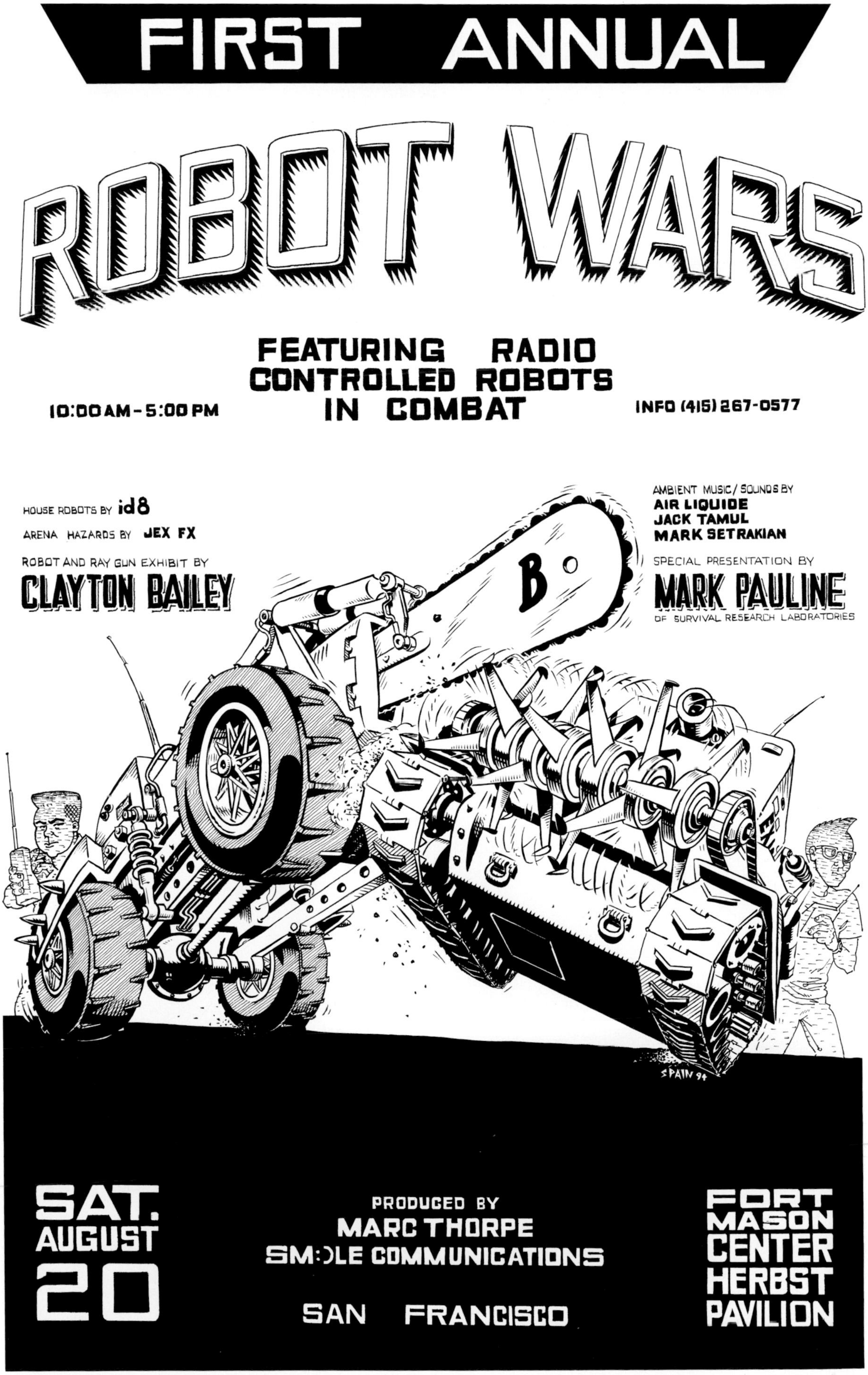
FIRST ANNUAL
ROBOT WARS
FEATURING RADIO CONTROLLED ROBOTS IN COMBAT
10:00AM-5:00PM
INFO (415) 267-0577
HOUSE ROBOTS BY id8
ARENA HAZARDS BY JEX FX
ROBOT AND RAY GUN EXHIBIT BY
CLAYTON BAILEY
AMBIENT MUSIC/SOUNDS BY
AIR LIQUIDE
JACK TAMUL
MARK SETRAKIAN
SPECIAL PRESENTATION BY
MARK PAULINE
OF SURVIVAL RESEARCH LABORATORIES
B
SPAIN 94
SAT. AUGUST 20
PRODUCED BY
MARC THORPE
SM:)LE COMMUNICATIONS
SAN FRANCISCO
FORT MASON CENTER HERBST PAVILION

Robot Wars poster, 1994

FACTWINO VS. ARMAGEDDONMAN — SF MIME TROUPE/SPAIN

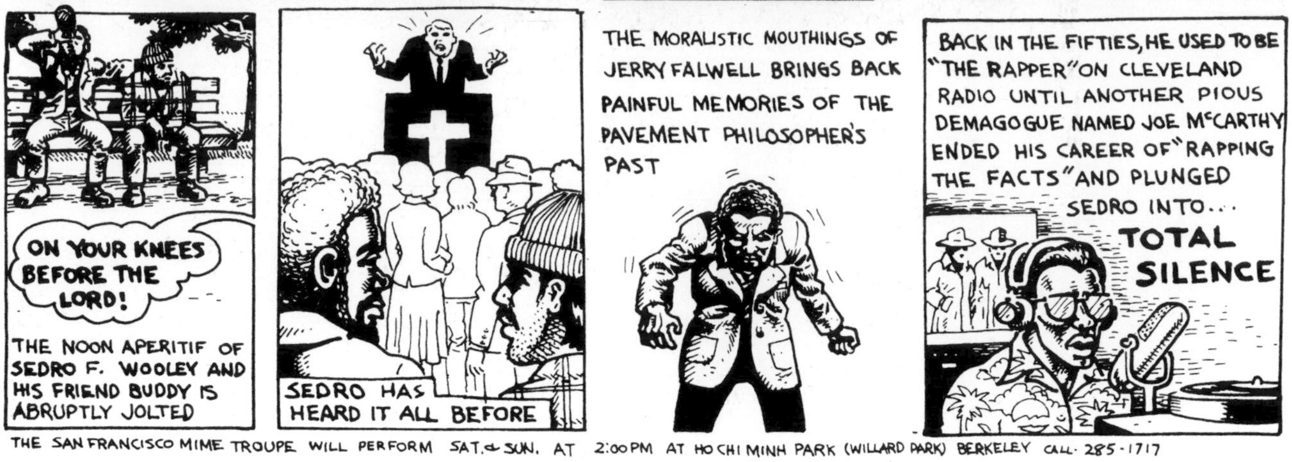
ON YOUR KNEES BEFORE THE LORD!
THE NOON APERITIF OF SEDRO F. WOOLEY AND HIS FRIEND BUDDY IS ABRUPTLY JOLTED
SEDRO HAS HEARD IT ALL BEFORE
THE MORALISTIC MOUTHINGS OF JERRY FALWELL BRINGS BACK PAINFUL MEMORIES OF THE PAVEMENT PHILOSOPHER'S PAST
BACK IN THE FIFTIES, HE USED TO BE "THE RAPPER" ON CLEVELAND RADIO UNTIL ANOTHER PIOUS DEMAGOGUE NAMED JOE McCARTHY ENDED HIS CAREER OF "RAPPING THE FACTS" AND PLUNGED SEDRO INTO...
TOTAL SILENCE
THE SAN FRANCISCO MIME TROUPE WILL PERFORM SAT. & SUN. AT 2:00PM AT HO CHI MINH PARK (WILLARD PARK) BERKELEY CALL 285-1717

FACTWINO VS. ARMAGEDDONMAN — SPAIN

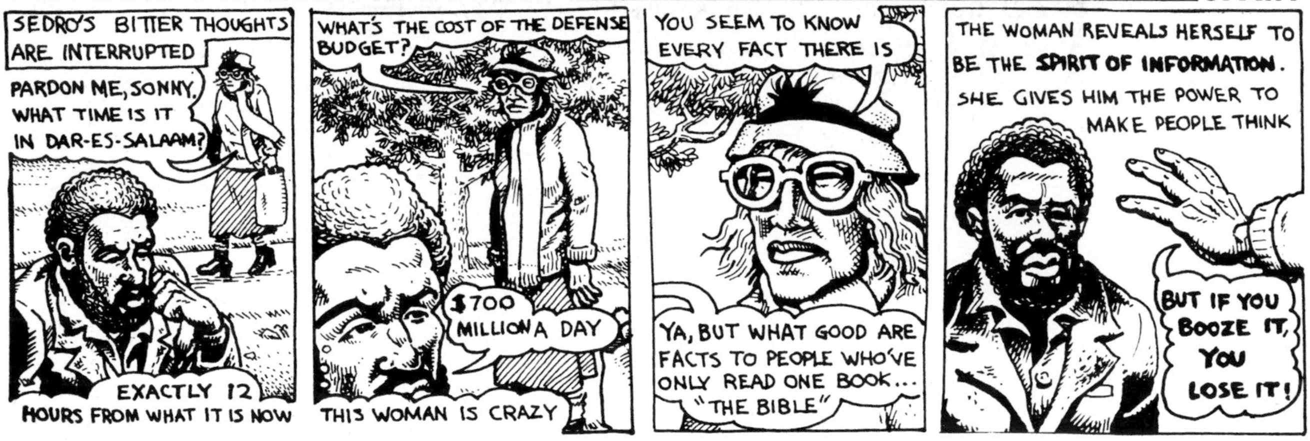
SEDRO'S BITTER THOUGHTS ARE INTERRUPTED
PARDON ME, SONNY, WHAT TIME IS IT IN DAR-ES-SALAAM?
EXACTLY 12 HOURS FROM WHAT IT IS NOW
WHAT'S THE COST OF THE DEFENSE BUDGET?
$700 MILLION A DAY
THIS WOMAN IS CRAZY
YOU SEEM TO KNOW EVERY FACT THERE IS
YA, BUT WHAT GOOD ARE FACTS TO PEOPLE WHO'VE ONLY READ ONE BOOK... "THE BIBLE"
THE WOMAN REVEALS HERSELF TO BE THE SPIRIT OF INFORMATION. SHE GIVES HIM THE POWER TO MAKE PEOPLE THINK
BUT IF YOU BOOZE IT, YOU LOSE IT!

FACTWINO VS. ARMAGEDDONMAN — SPAIN

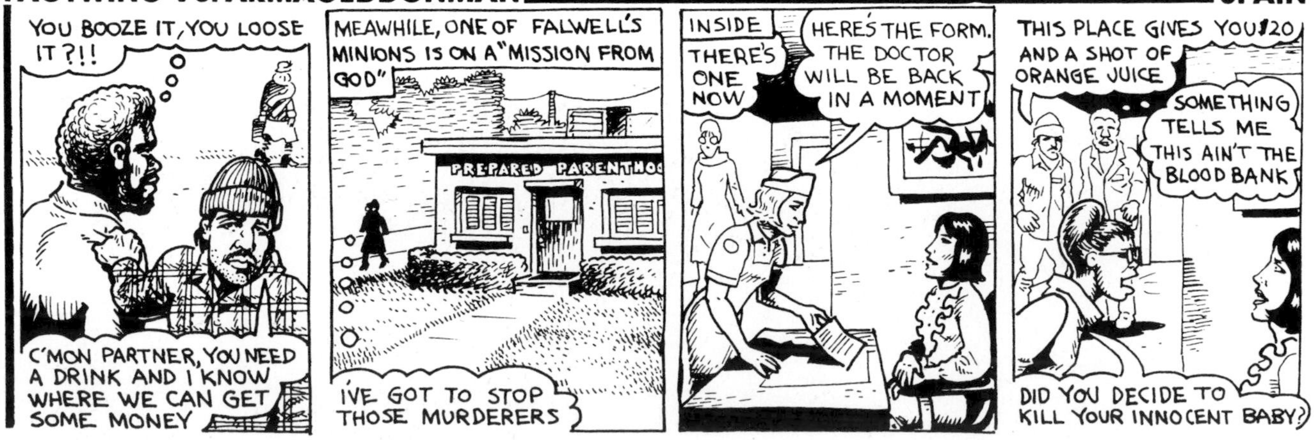
YOU BOOZE IT, YOU LOOSE IT?!!
C'MON PARTNER, YOU NEED A DRINK AND I KNOW WHERE WE CAN GET SOME MONEY
MEAWHILE, ONE OF FALWELL'S MINIONS IS ON A "MISSION FROM GOD"
PREPARED PARENTHOO
I'VE GOT TO STOP THOSE MURDERERS
INSIDE THERE'S ONE NOW
HERE'S THE FORM. THE DOCTOR WILL BE BACK IN A MOMENT
THIS PLACE GIVES YOU $20 AND A SHOT OF ORANGE JUICE
SOMETHING TELLS ME THIS AIN'T THE BLOOD BANK
DID YOU DECIDE TO KILL YOUR INNOCENT BABY?

P. 42–45 *Factwino vs. Armageddonman* from the *San Francisco Bay Guardian*, 1982

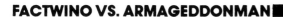

FACTWINO VS. ARMAGEDDONMAN SPAIN

BUDDY, LOOKING FOR A BLOOD BANK, HAS MISTAKENLY LED SEDRO TO A PREPARED PARENTHOOD CLINIC PENETRATED BY ONE OF FALWELL'S DEVOTEES

YOU WOULDN'T BE IN THIS MESS IF WE HAD PRAYERS IN SCHOOL INSTEAD OF SEX EDUCATION

BUT I ALREADY HAVE ONE KID. IF I HAVE ANOTHER ONE, I'LL HAVE TO GO BACK ON WELFARE

SUDDENLY

!?

SEDRO, NOW "FACTWINO," ZAPS THE WOMAN. SHE NOW STARTS THINKING BUT IF ABORTION WERE OUTLAWED, HOW MANY WOMEN WOULD DIE FROM BACK ALLEY ABORTIONS? WHAT ABOUT THEIR "RIGHT TO LIFE"?

FACTWINO VS. ARMAGEDDONMAN SPAIN

HEY SEDRO, WHERE DID YOU GET THOSE CRAZY DRAWERS?

THE REALIZATION OF HIS MISSION SUDDENLY DAWNS ON SEDRO

C'MON PARTNER, LET'S GET A DRINK

IF YOU BOOZE IT, YOU LOSE IT

I CAN'T, BUDDY!

WE'VE GOT WORK TO DO

CHRISTIAN FAMILY CRUSADE

REV. JER FALWE

NEGRI I MISS

FACTWINO VS. ARMAGEDDONMAN SPAIN

SEDRO AND BUDDY ARRIVE AT THE "CRUSADE RALLY"

THE REVEREND JERRY COULDN'T MAKE IT TODAY BUT I WANT YOU TO KNOW THAT WE ARE ALL FILLED WITH LOVE!

REDUCE CORPORATE TAXES

NO FUNDING FOR ABORTION OR SCHOOL LUNCHES

PLUNDER OUR NATURAL RESOURCES GODS COMING BACK SOON ANYWAY

MORE NUKES FOR JESUS

WE ARE FULL OF IT!

LOOKS LIKE I GOT MY WORK CUT OUT FOR ME!

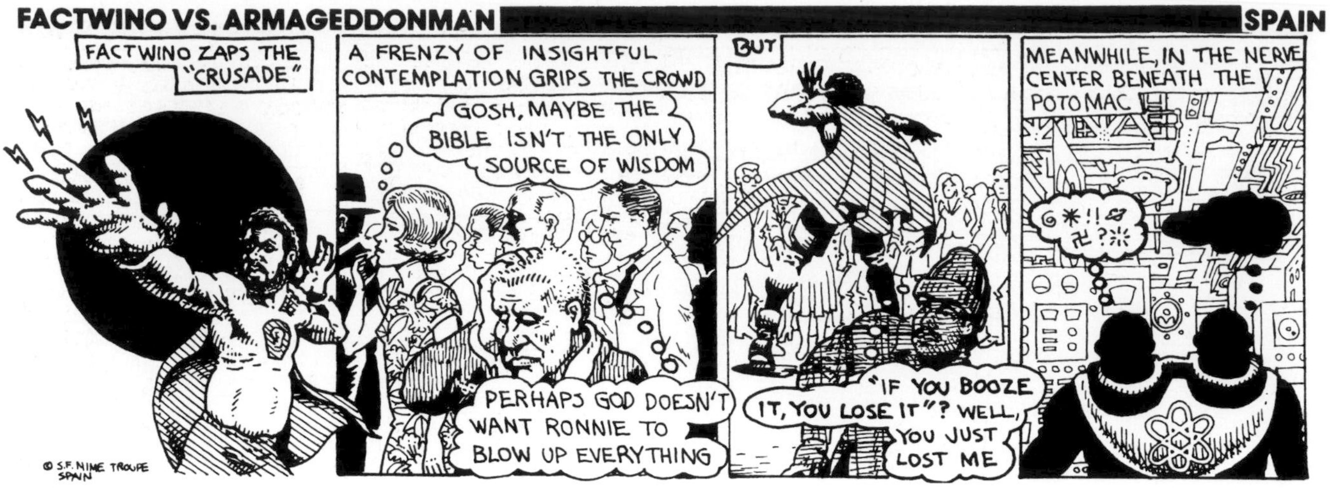
FACTWINO VS. ARMAGEDDONMAN
SPAIN
FACTWINO ZAPS THE "CRUSADE"
© S.F. MIME TROUPE SPAIN
A FRENZY OF INSIGHTFUL CONTEMPLATION GRIPS THE CROWD
GOSH, MAYBE THE BIBLE ISN'T THE ONLY SOURCE OF WISDOM
PERHAPS GOD DOESN'T WANT RONNIE TO BLOW UP EVERYTHING
BUT
"IF YOU BOOZE IT, YOU LOSE IT"? WELL, YOU JUST LOST ME
MEANWHILE, IN THE NERVE CENTER BENEATH THE POTOMAC

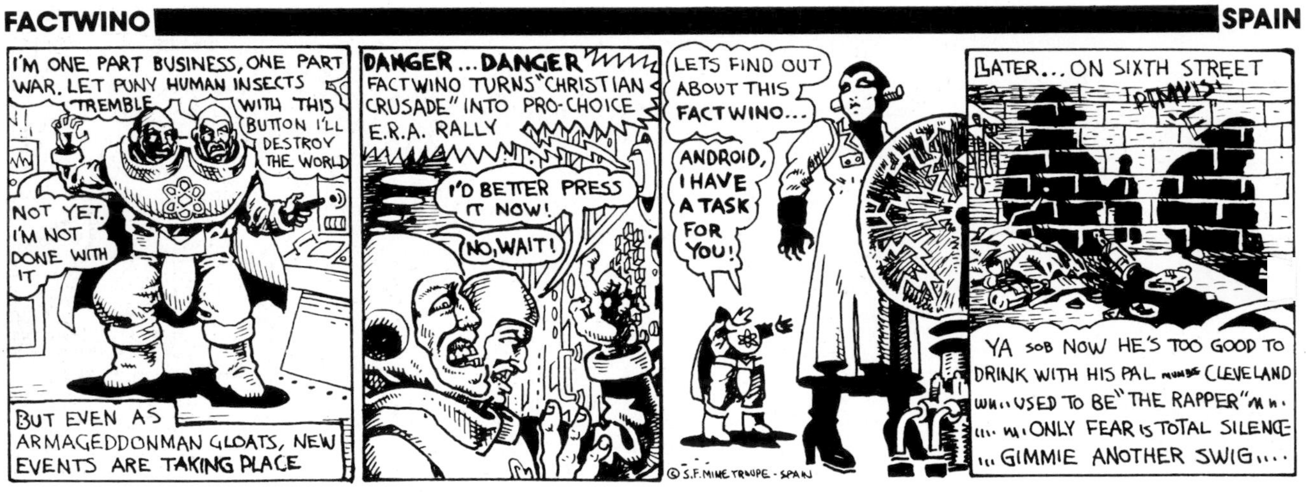
FACTWINO
SPAIN
I'M ONE PART BUSINESS, ONE PART WAR. LET PUNY HUMAN INSECTS TREMBLE
WITH THIS BUTTON I'LL DESTROY THE WORLD
NOT YET. I'M NOT DONE WITH IT
BUT EVEN AS ARMAGEDDONMAN GLOATS, NEW EVENTS ARE TAKING PLACE
DANGER... DANGER
FACTWINO TURNS "CHRISTIAN CRUSADE" INTO PRO-CHOICE E.R.A. RALLY
I'D BETTER PRESS IT NOW!
NO, WAIT!
LETS FIND OUT ABOUT THIS FACTWINO...
ANDROID, I HAVE A TASK FOR YOU!
© S.F. MIME TROUPE - SPAIN
LATER... ON SIXTH STREET
YA SOB NOW HE'S TOO GOOD TO DRINK WITH HIS PAL CLEVELAND ... USED TO BE "THE RAPPER" ... ONLY FEAR IS TOTAL SILENCE ... GIMMIE ANOTHER SWIG....

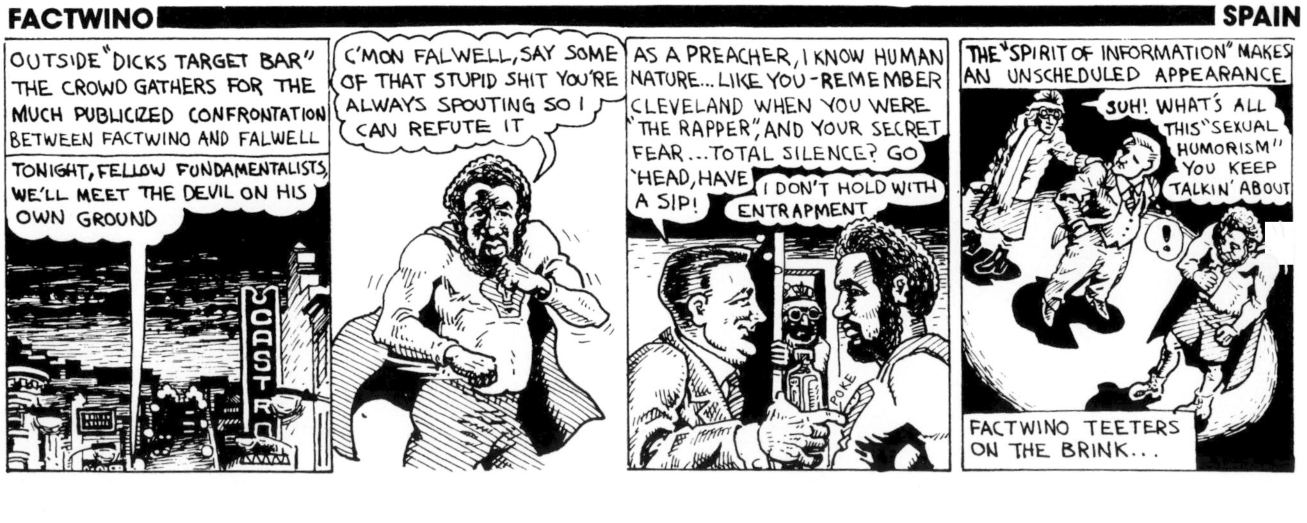
FACTWINO
SPAIN
OUTSIDE "DICKS TARGET BAR" THE CROWD GATHERS FOR THE MUCH PUBLICIZED CONFRONTATION BETWEEN FACTWINO AND FALWELL
TONIGHT, FELLOW FUNDAMENTALISTS, WE'LL MEET THE DEVIL ON HIS OWN GROUND
CASTRO
C'MON FALWELL, SAY SOME OF THAT STUPID SHIT YOU'RE ALWAYS SPOUTING SO I CAN REFUTE IT
AS A PREACHER, I KNOW HUMAN NATURE... LIKE YOU - REMEMBER CLEVELAND WHEN YOU WERE "THE RAPPER", AND YOUR SECRET FEAR... TOTAL SILENCE? GO 'HEAD, HAVE A SIP!
I DON'T HOLD WITH ENTRAPMENT
POKE
THE "SPIRIT OF INFORMATION" MAKES AN UNSCHEDULED APPEARANCE
SUH! WHAT'S ALL THIS "SEXUAL HUMORISM" YOU KEEP TALKIN' ABOUT
!
FACTWINO TEETERS ON THE BRINK...

FACTWINO — **SPAIN**

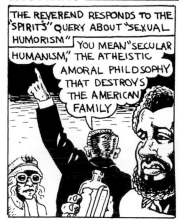

THE REVEREND RESPONDS TO THE "SPIRITS" QUERY ABOUT "SEXUAL HUMORISM"
YOU MEAN "SECULAR HUMANISM," THE ATHEISTIC
AMORAL PHILOSOPHY THAT DESTROYS THE AMERICAN FAMILY
AND UNDERMINES THE GREAT CHRISTIAN PRINCIPLES UPON WHICH THIS COUNTRY WAS BUILT
THEN AGAIN, GEORGE WASHINGTON SAID, "THE GOVERNMENT OF THE UNITED STATES IS NOT IN ANY SENSE FOUNDED ON THE CHRISTIAN RELIGION"
AFTER HIS CONFRONTATION WITH FACTWINO, JERRY FALWELL QUICKLY DISAPPEARS. HE IS LAST SEEN ON THE STREETS OF LAS VEGAS, RAVING:
CASINO
AYNE EWTON
WHERE'S BO DEREK?

FACTWINO — **SPAIN**

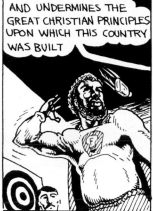

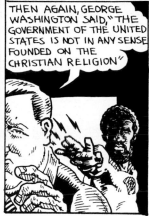

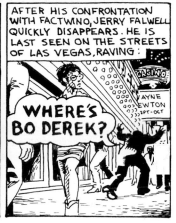

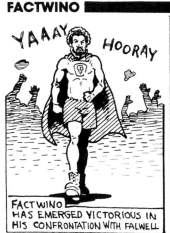

YAAAY
HOORAY
FACTWINO HAS EMERGED VICTORIOUS IN HIS CONFRONTATION WITH FALWELL
BUT LATER, AS FACTWINO RETURNS FROM THE LIBRARY
PARTIAL LOBOTOMY RAY
HEY BUDDY, I JUST GOT THESE BOOKS AND..
THEN...
BUDDY, HELP ME!
TRACTOR BEAM
BUDDY, HELP ME
WASN'T THERE SOMEONE ELSE HERE?
WILL FACTWINO BE FORGOTTEN?

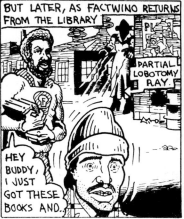

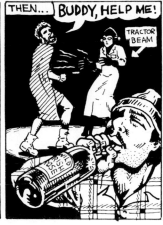

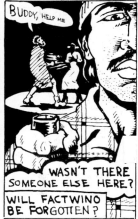

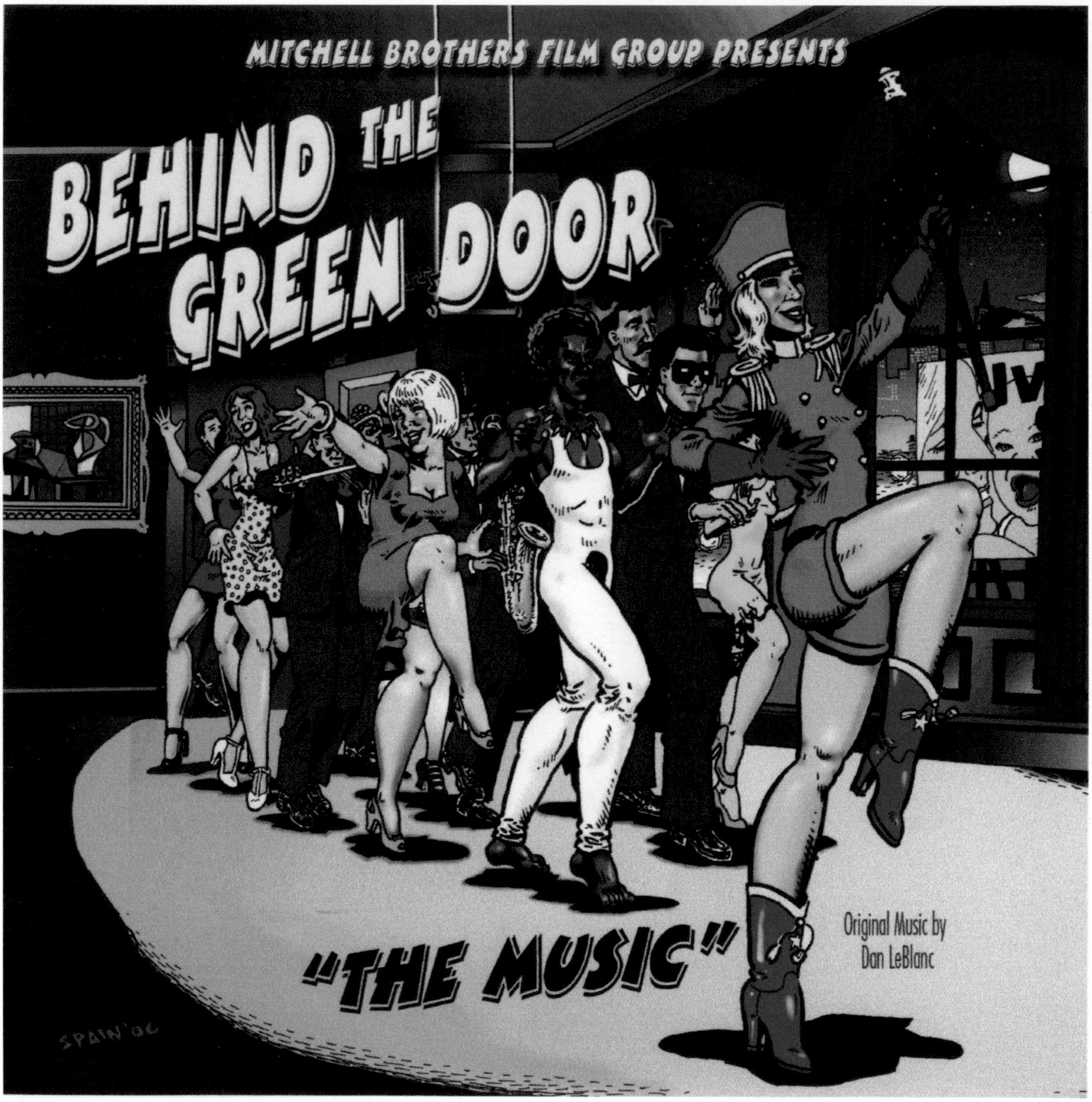
MITCHELL BROTHERS FILM GROUP PRESENTS
BEHIND THE GREEN DOOR
"THE MUSIC"
Original Music by
Dan LeBlanc
SPAIN '06

Poster art advertising the soundtrack album for the Mitchell Brothers film, *Behind the Green Door*, 2006

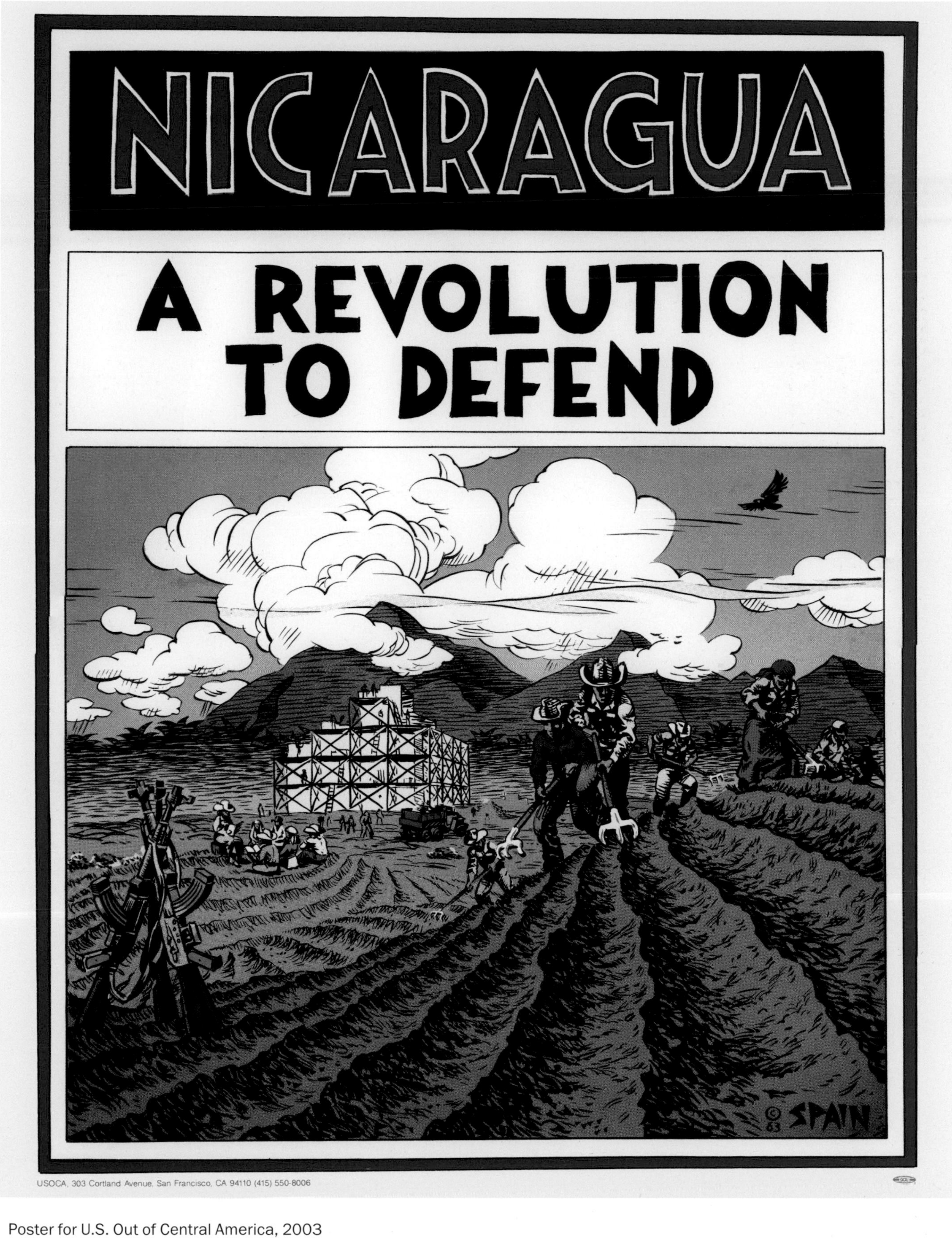
NICARAGUA
A REVOLUTION
TO DEFEND
© 83 SPAIN
USOCA, 303 Cortland Avenue, San Francisco, CA 94110 (415) 550-8006

Poster for U.S. Out of Central America, 2003

FANTASY COVERS

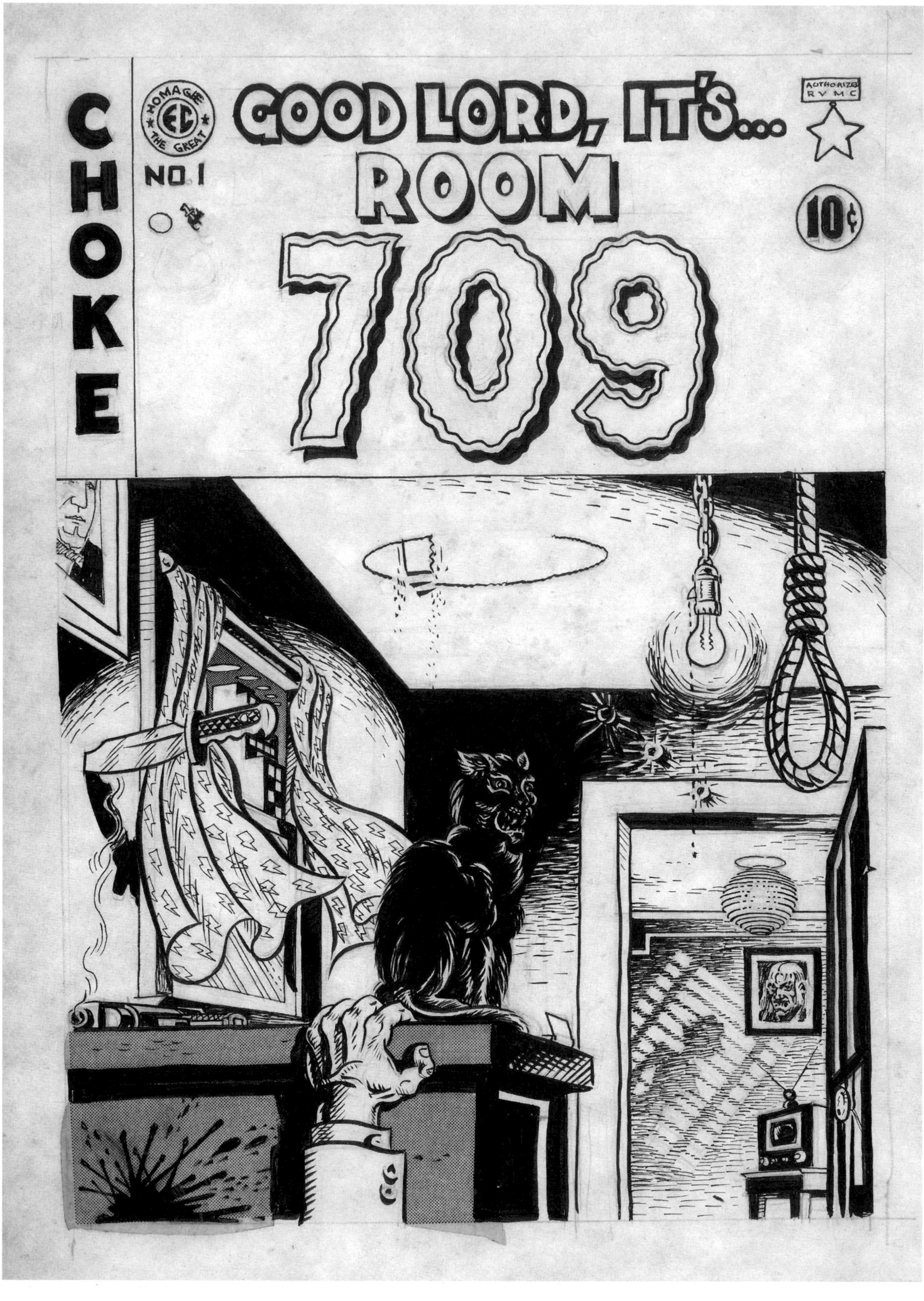

CHOKE
HOMAGE EC THE GREAT
NO. 1
GOOD LORD, IT'S...
ROOM
709
AUTHORIZED RVMC
10¢

P. 48–58 Unpublished comic book covers created as private commissions. Special thanks to the Glenn Bray Archives.

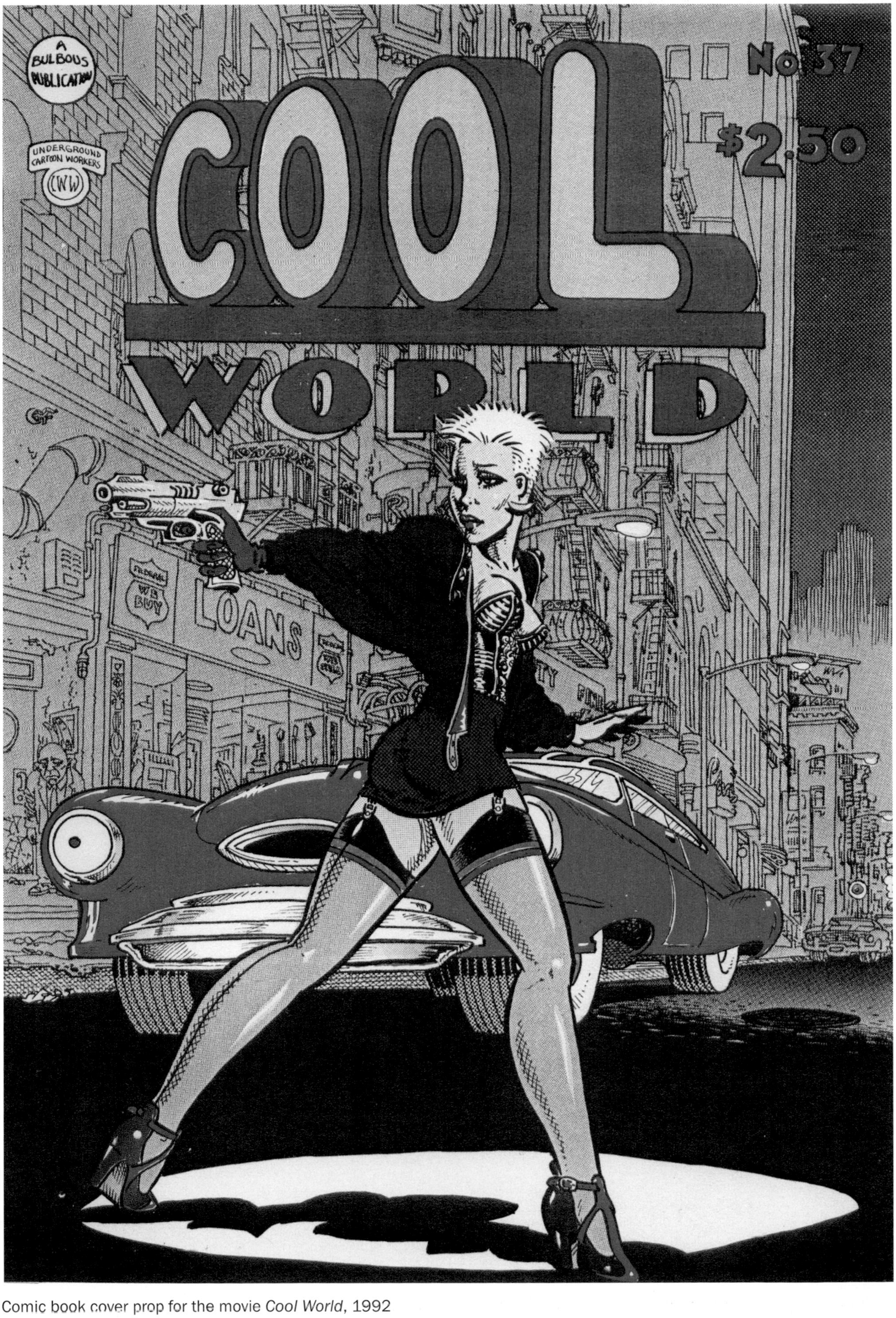
A BULBOUS PUBLICATION
UNDERGROUND CARTOON WORKERS
CWW
No. 37
$2.50
COOL
WORLD
LOANS
WE BUY
Comic book cover prop for the movie *Cool World*, 1992

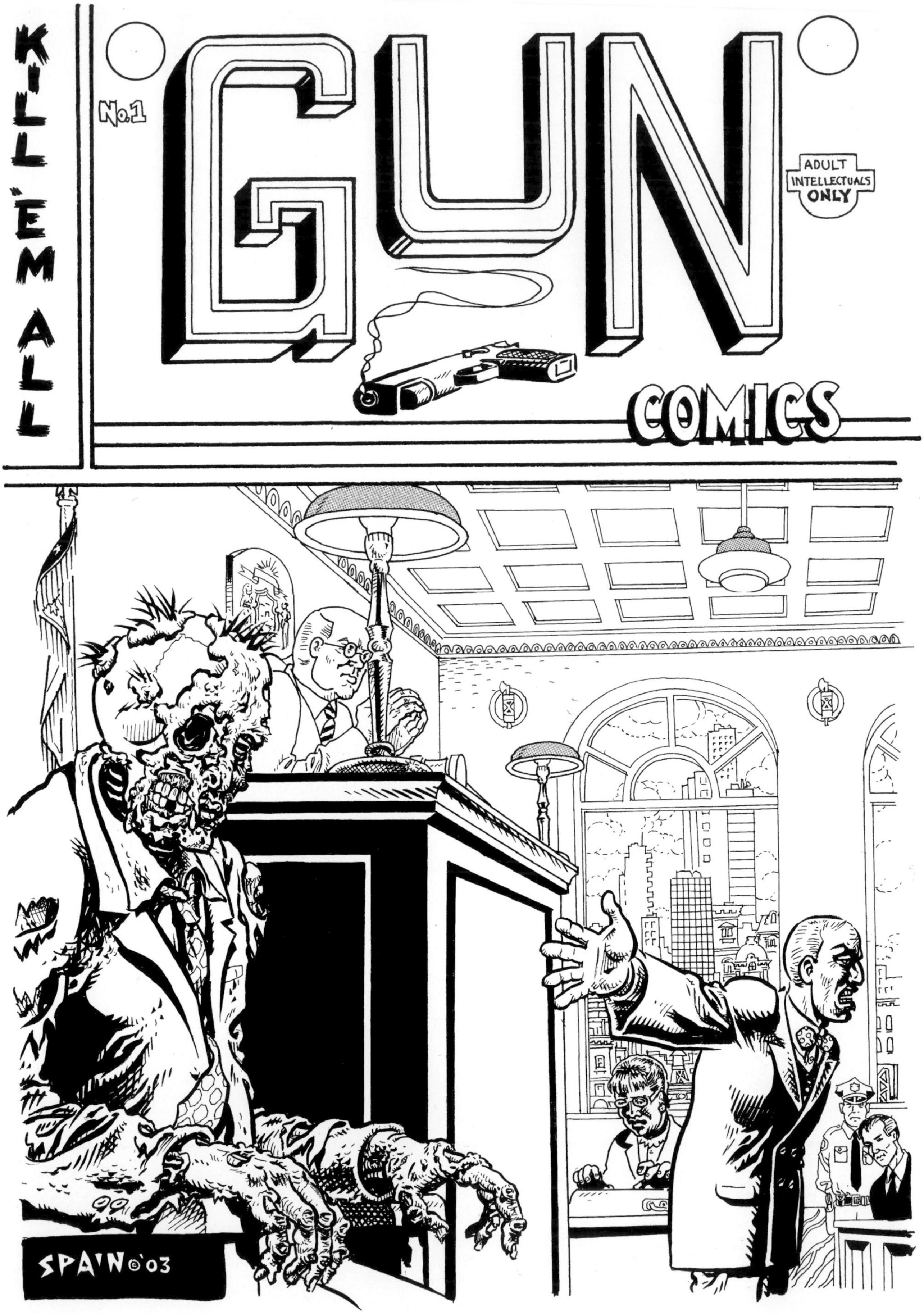
KILL 'EM ALL
No.1
GUN
ADULT INTELLECTUALS ONLY
COMICS
SPAIN © '03

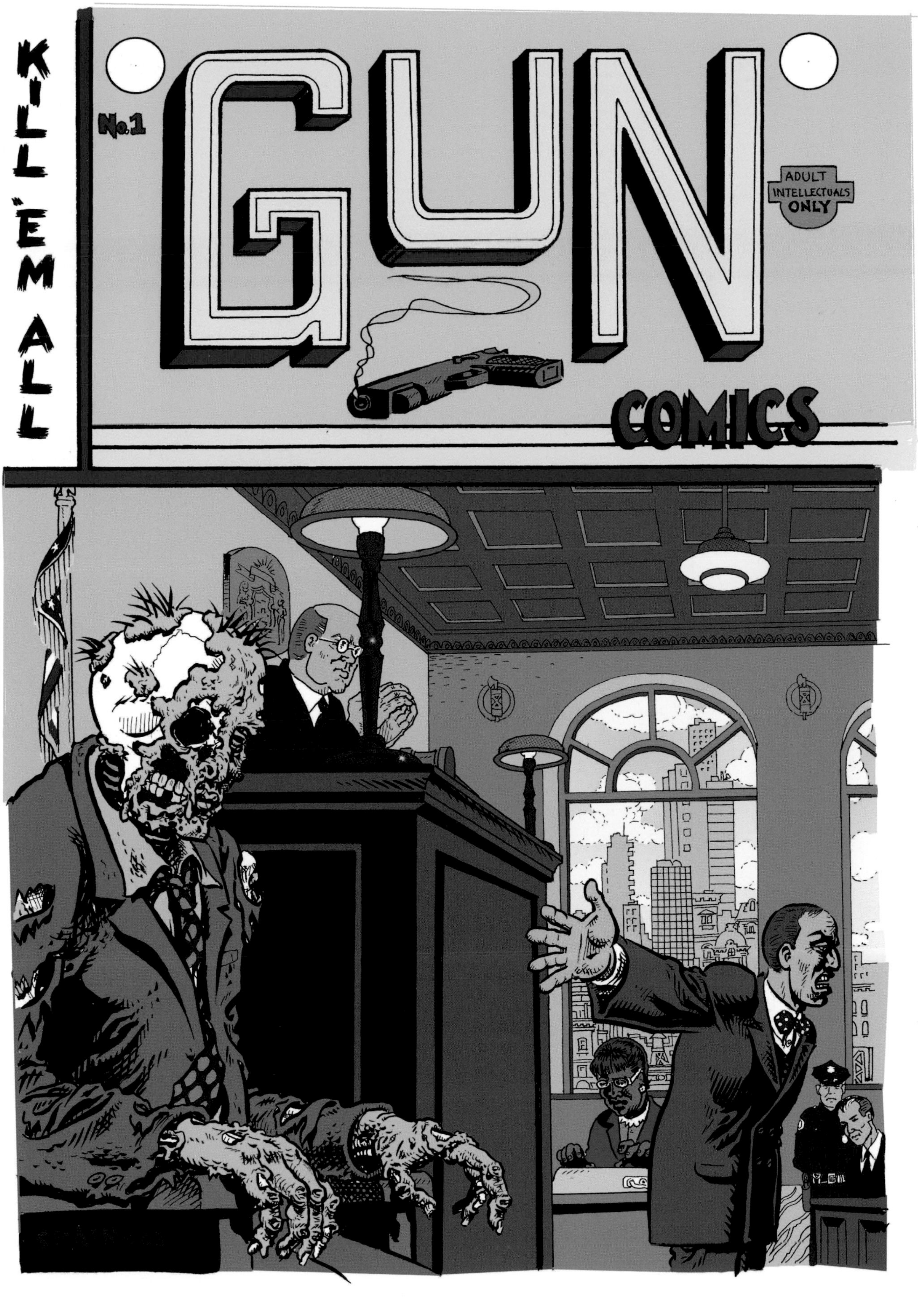
KILL 'EM ALL
No.1
GUN
ADULT INTELLECTUALS ONLY
COMICS

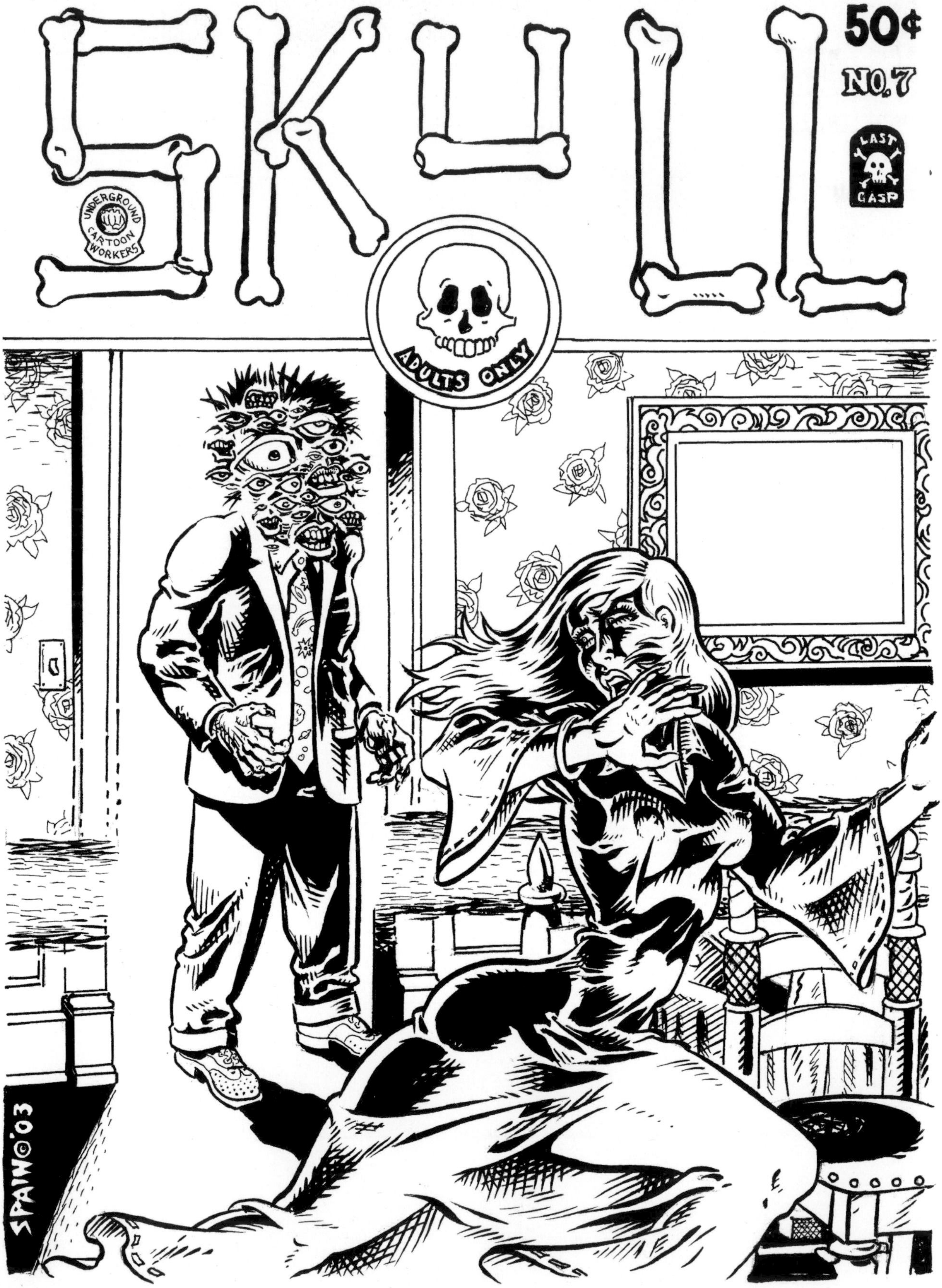
SKULL
50¢
NO.7
LAST GASP
UNDERGROUND CARTOON WORKERS
ADULTS ONLY
SPAIN©'03

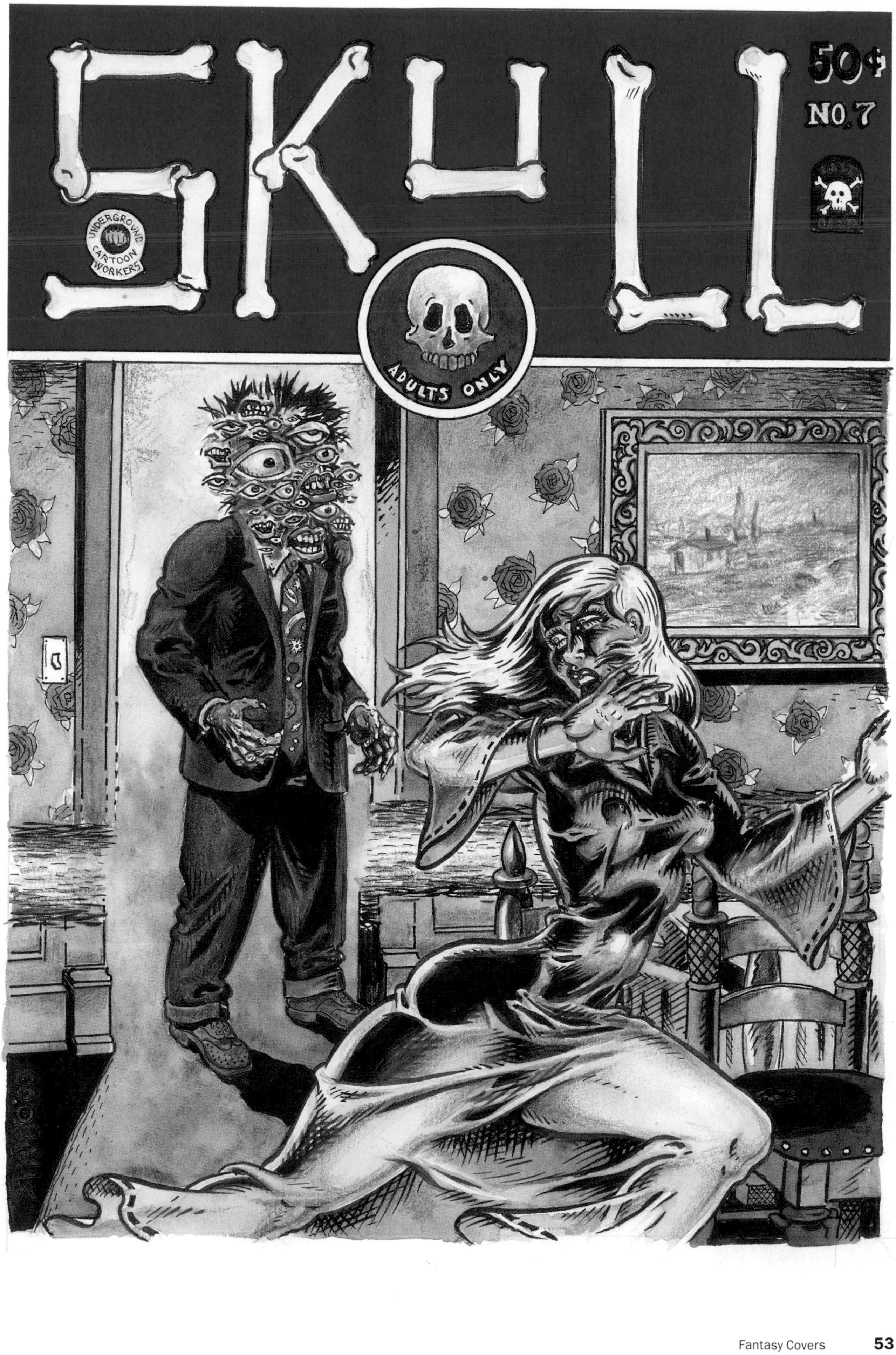
SKULL
50¢
NO.7
UNDERGROUND CARTOON WORKERS
ADULTS ONLY

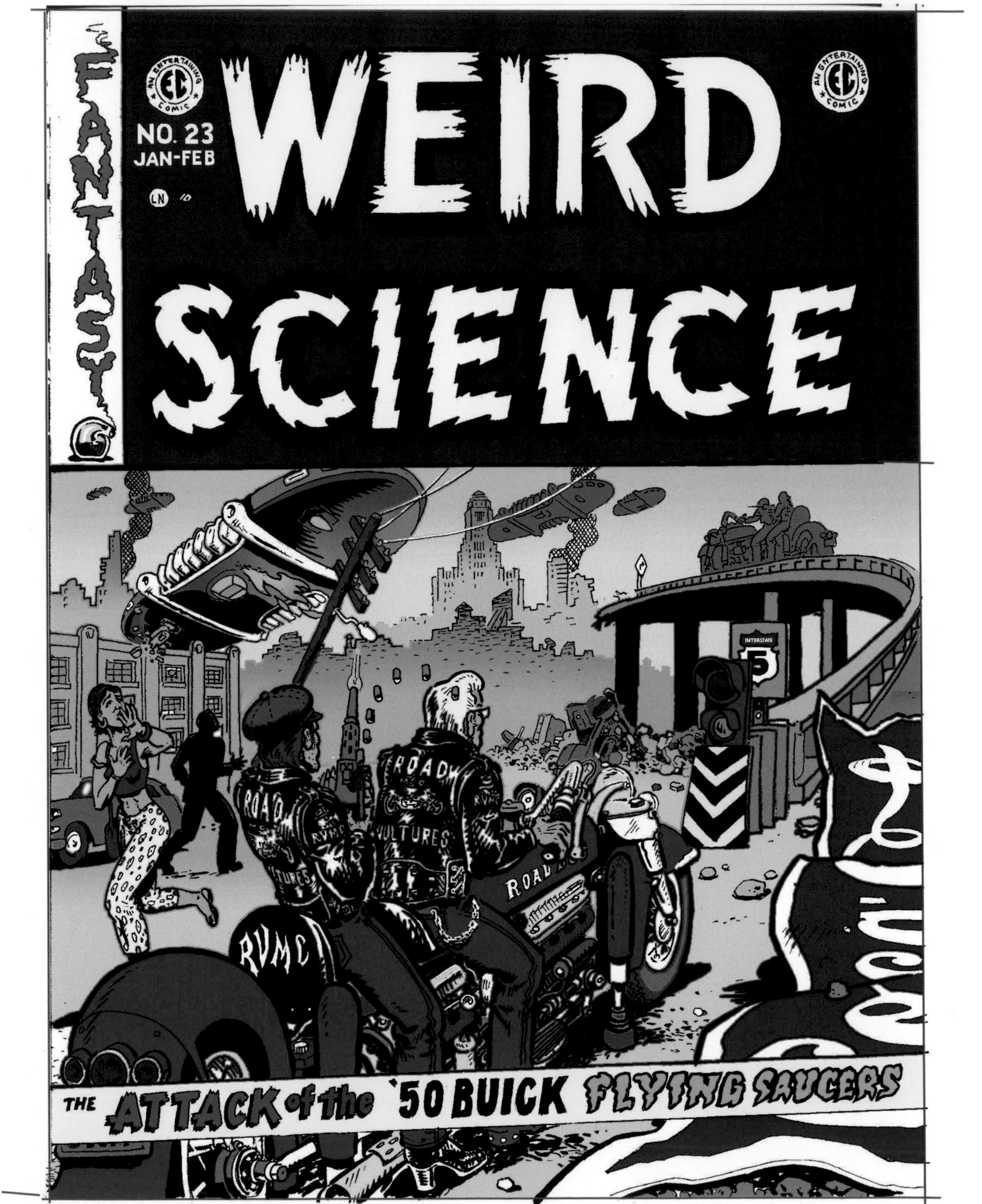
FANTASY
AN ENTERTAINING EC COMIC
NO. 23
JAN-FEB
WEIRD SCIENCE
INTERSTATE 5
ROAD
ROAD VULTURES
RVMC
THE ATTACK of the '50 BUICK FLYING SAUCERS

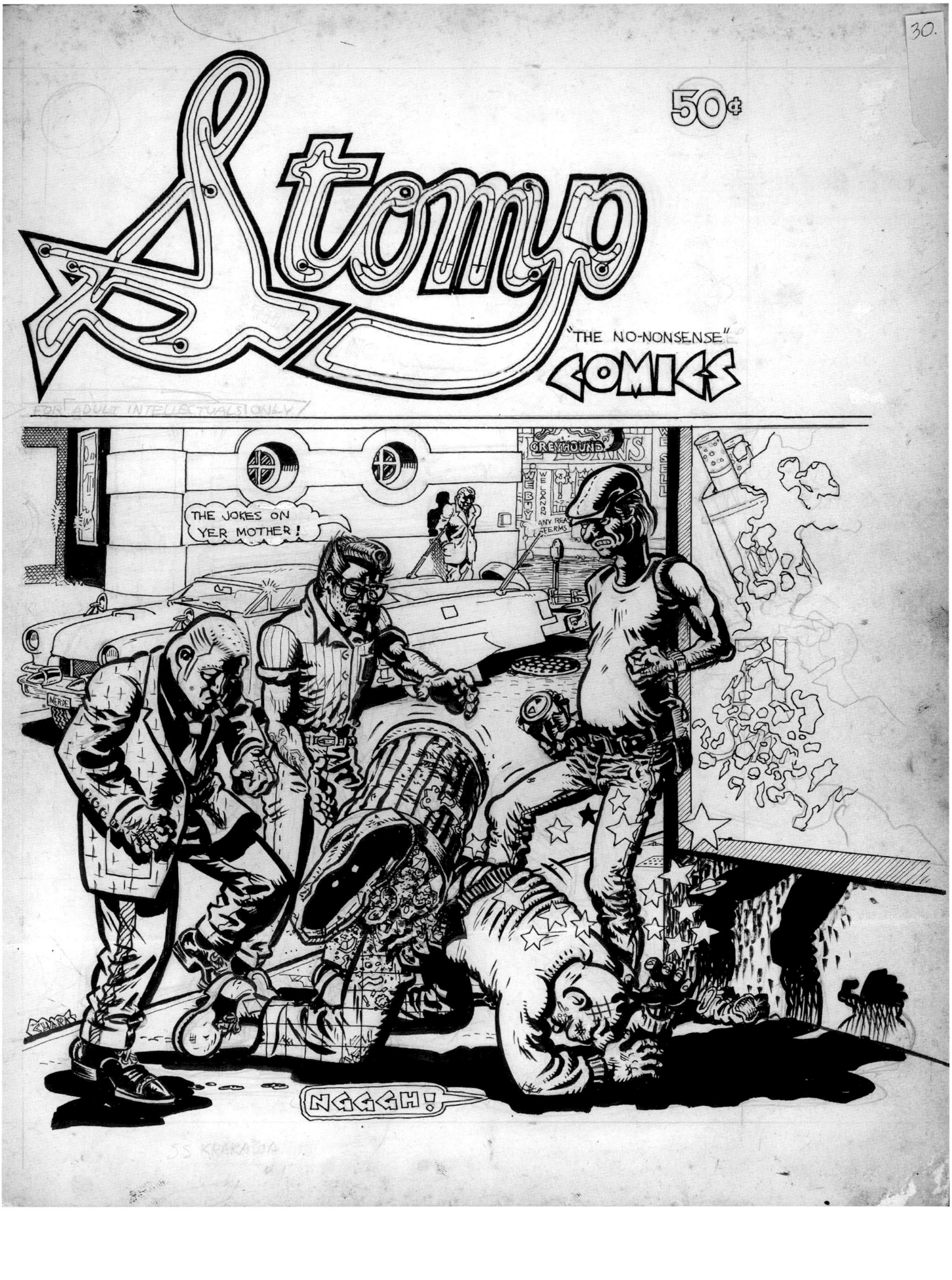
30.
50¢
Stomp
"THE NO-NONSENSE"
COMICS
FOR ADULT INTELLECTUALS ONLY
GREYHOUND
WE BUY
WE LOAN ON ANY REAL TERMS
THE JOKES ON YER MOTHER!
NGGGH!

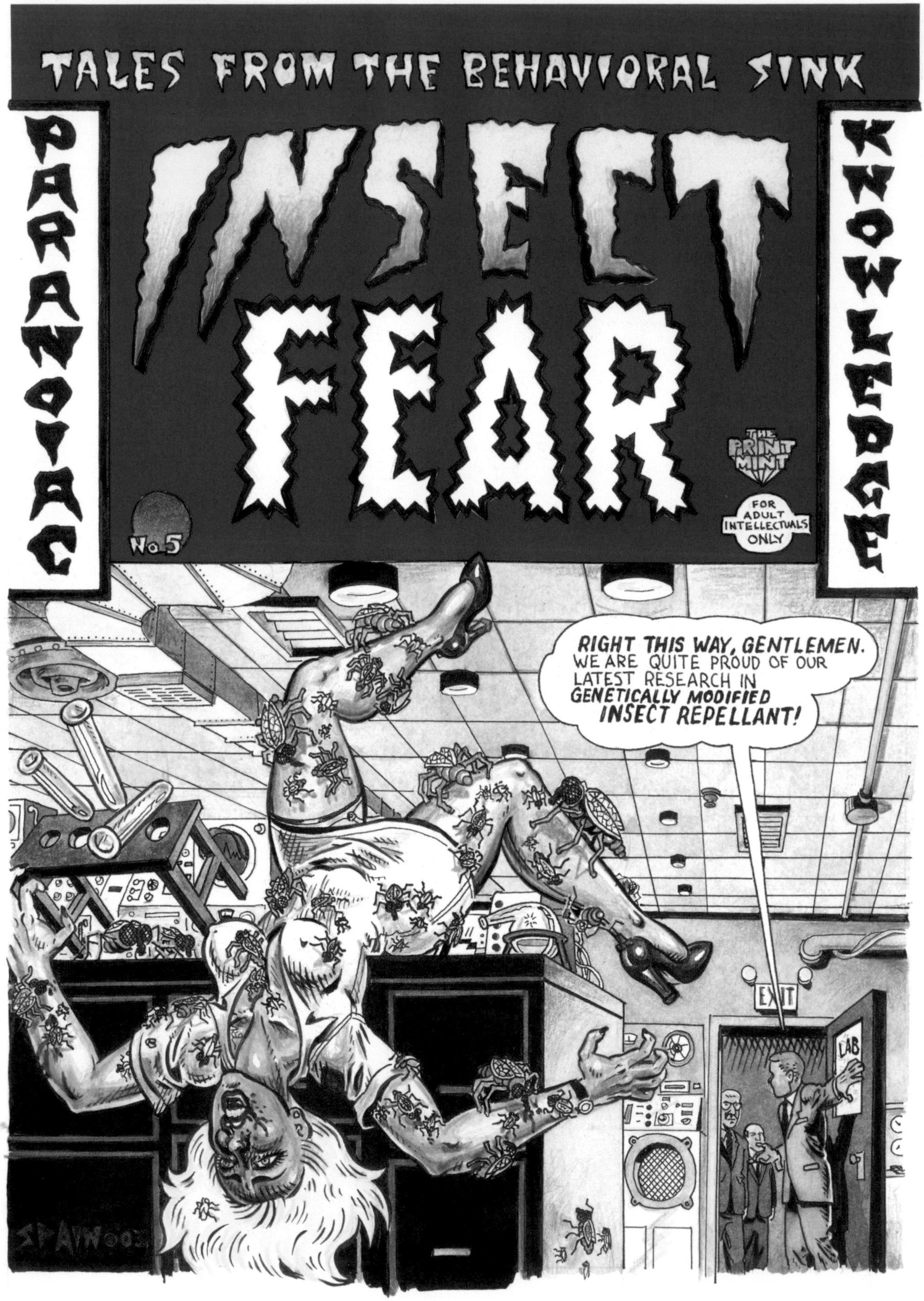
TALES FROM THE BEHAVIORAL SINK
PARANOIAC
KNOWLEDGE
INSECT FEAR
No 5
THE PRINT MINT
FOR ADULT INTELLECTUALS ONLY
RIGHT THIS WAY, GENTLEMEN. WE ARE QUITE PROUD OF OUR LATEST RESEARCH IN GENETICALLY MODIFIED INSECT REPELLANT!
EXIT
LAB

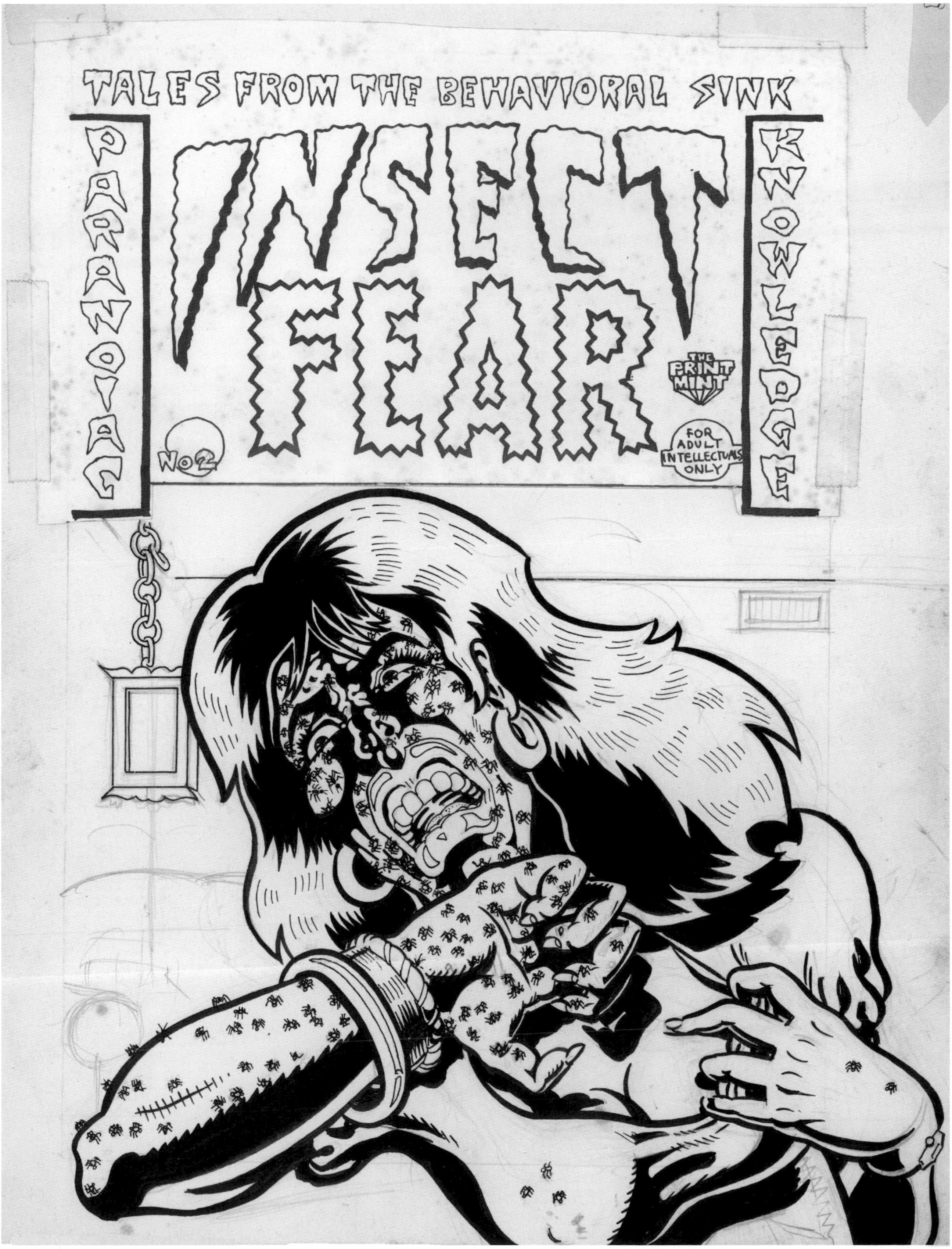

TALES FROM THE BEHAVIORAL SINK
PARANOIAC
INSECT FEAR
KNOWLEDGE
THE PRINT MINT
No 2
FOR ADULT INTELLECTUALS ONLY

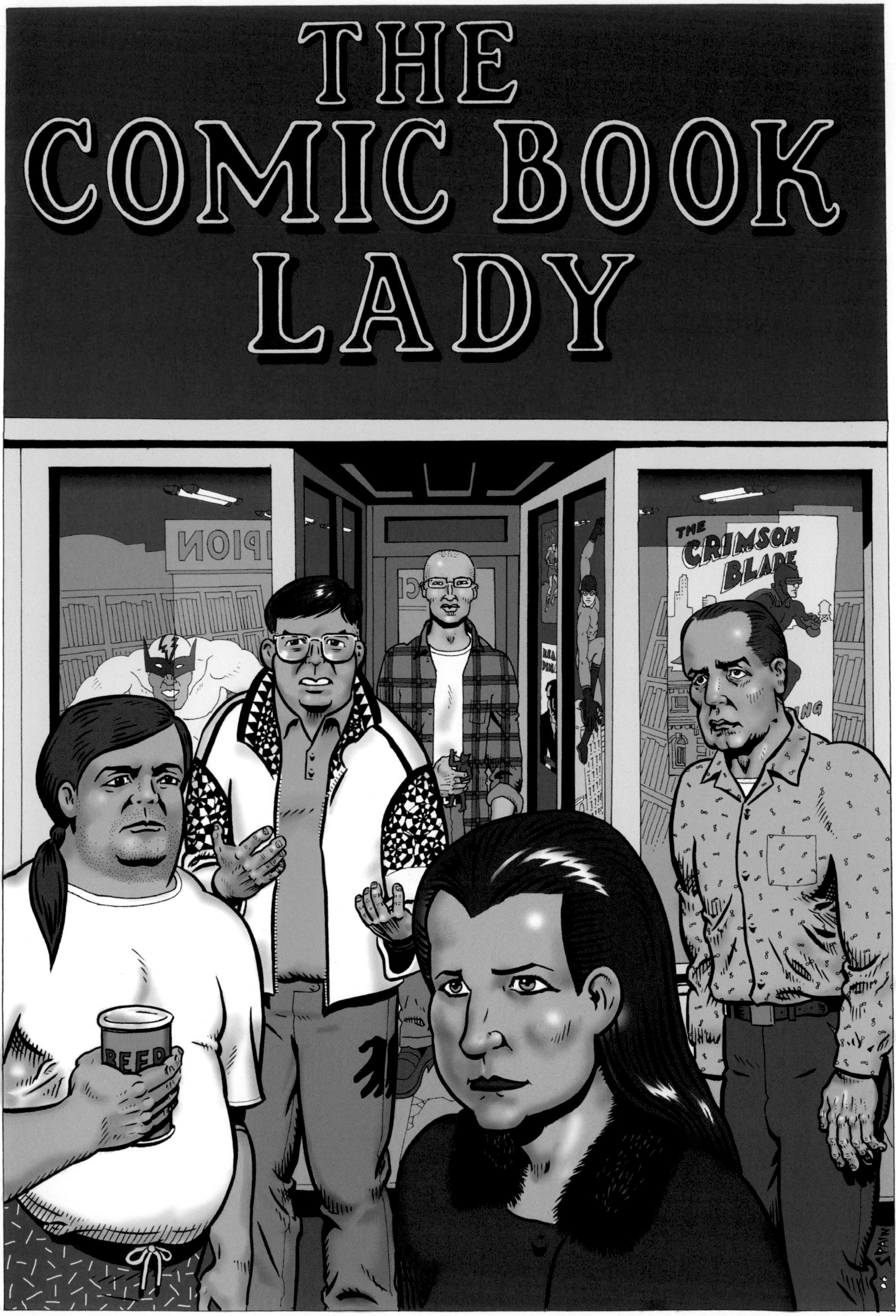
THE COMIC BOOK LADY
THE CRIMSON BLADE
BEER
SPAIN

Poster for the indie movie *The Comic Book Lady*, 2008

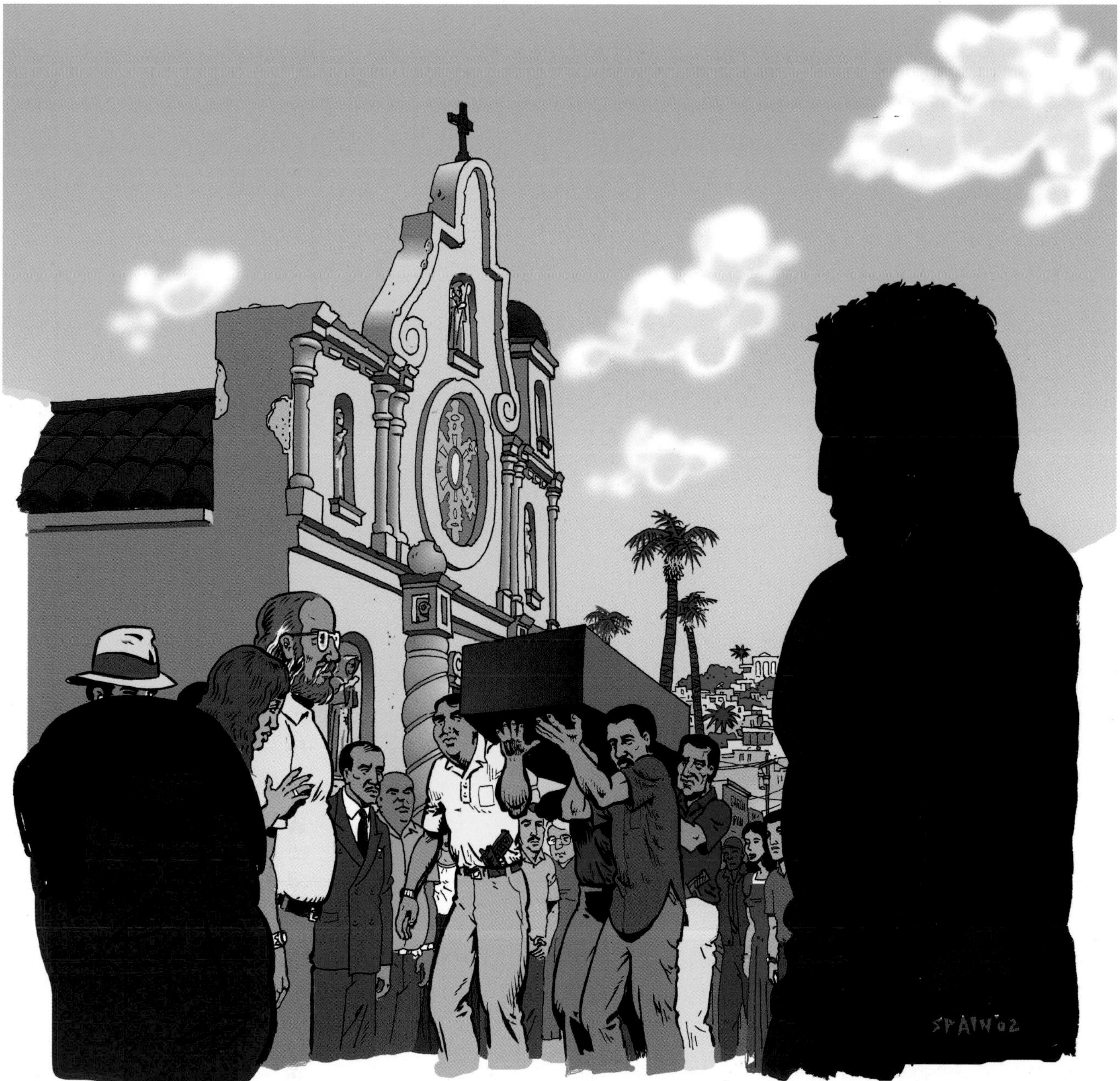
SPAIN '02

Illustration from *LA Weekly*, Vol. 25, No. 2, 2002

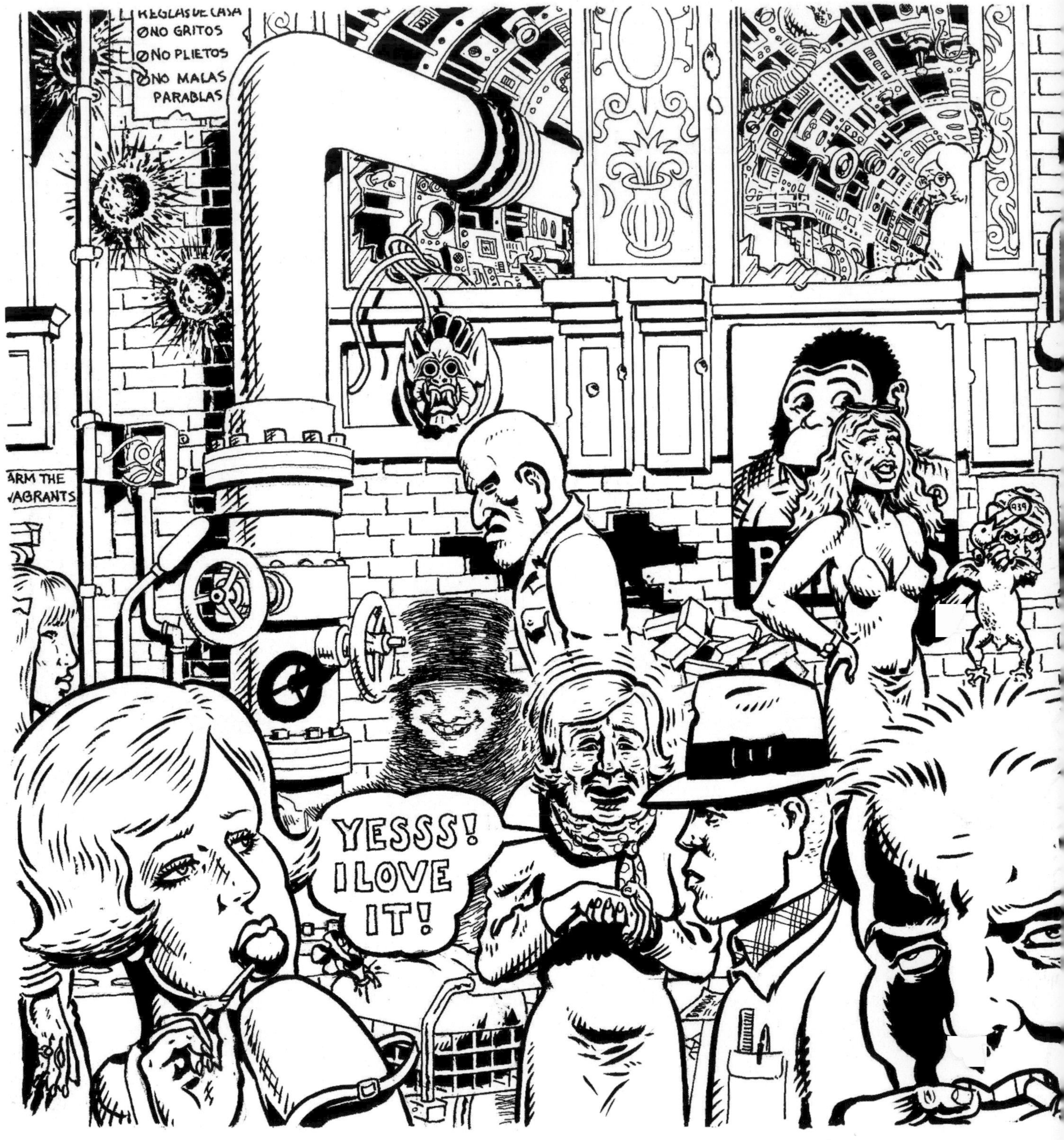
REGLAS DE CASA
ØNO GRITOS
ØNO PLIETOS
ØNO MALAS PARABLAS
ARM THE VAGRANTS
YESSS! I LOVE IT!

P. 60–63 From *Blab World* #1, 2010

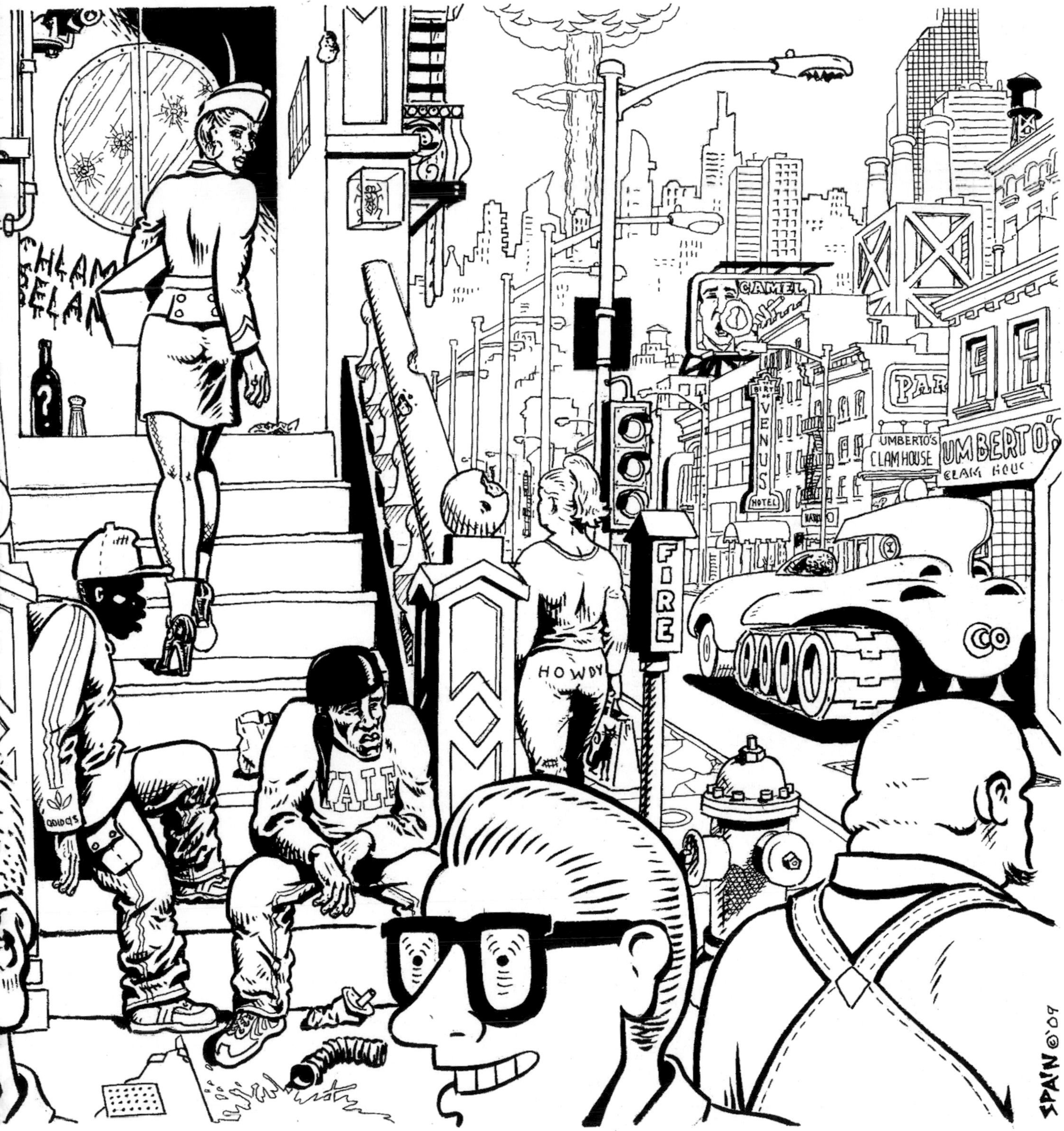
CHLAM
BELAN
CAMEL
VENUS
HOTEL
PAR
UMBERTO'S
CLAM HOUSE
UMBERTO'S
FIRE
HOWDY
ALE
SPAIN ©'09

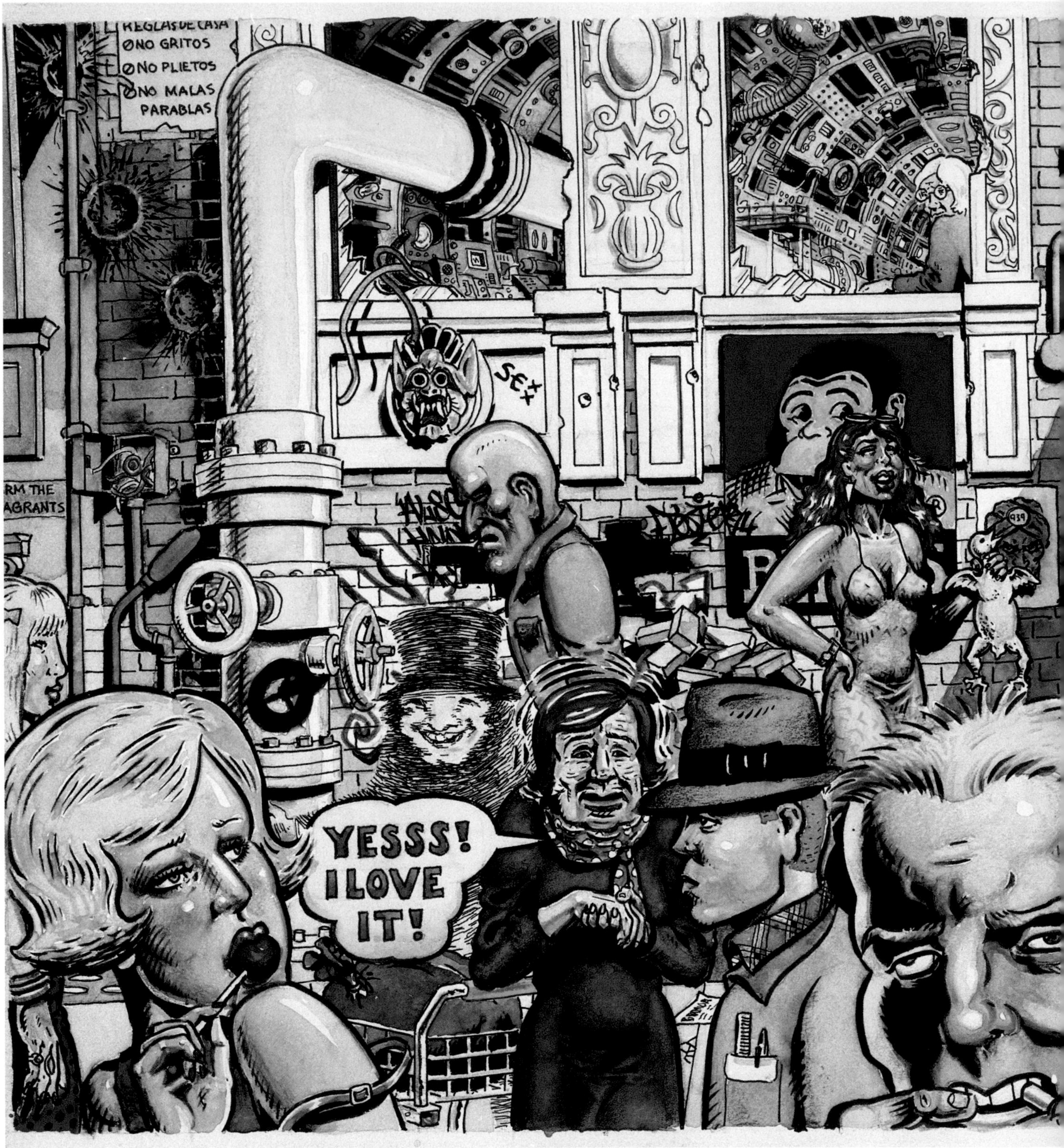
REGLAS DE CASA
NO GRITOS
NO PLIETOS
NO MALAS PARABLAS
SEX
RM THE
AGRANTS
YESSS! I LOVE IT!

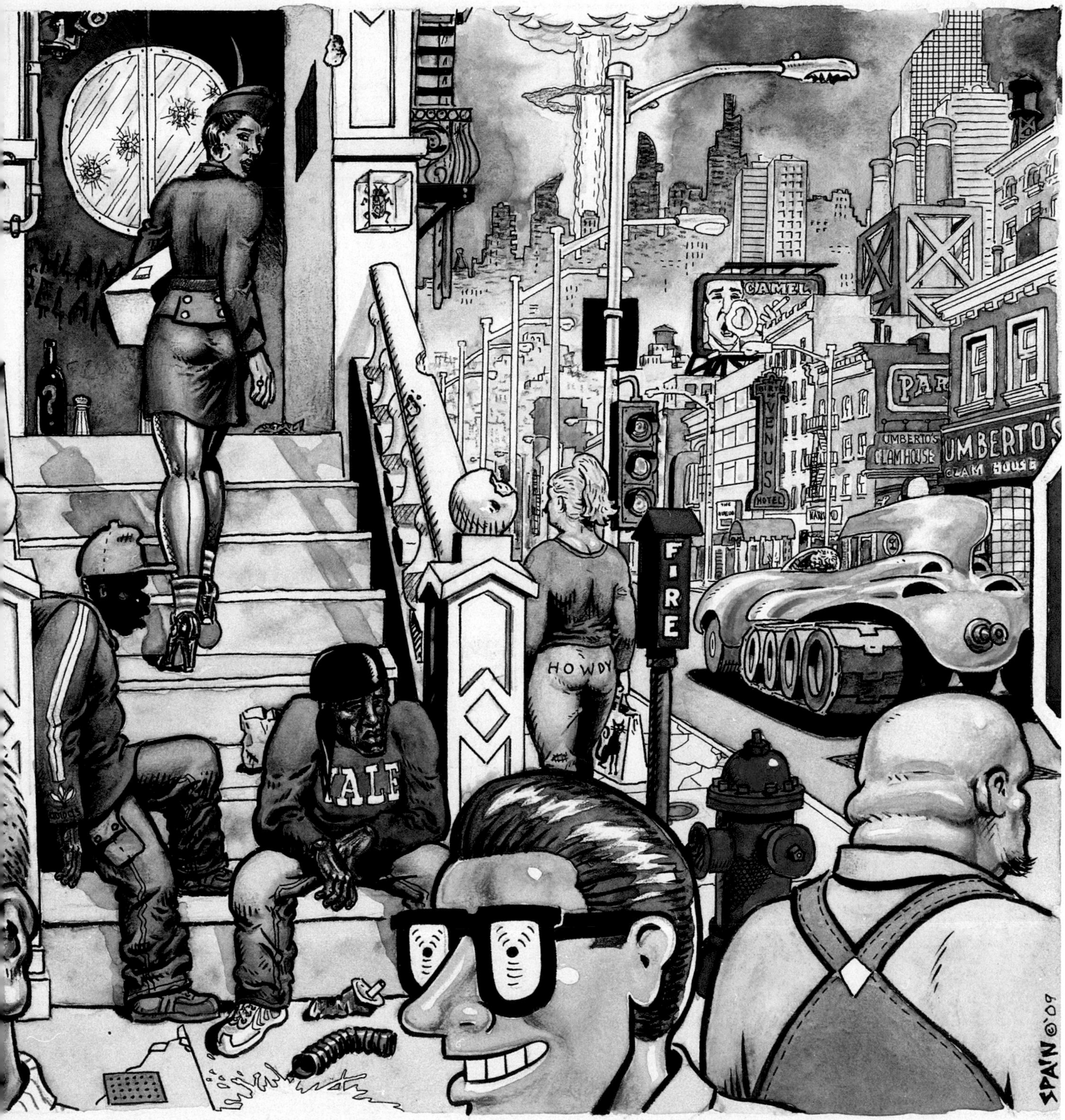
CAMEL
VENUS
HOTEL
UMBERTO'S
CLAM HOUSE
UMBERTO'S
CLAM HOUSE
FIRE
HOWDY
YALE
SPAIN ©'09

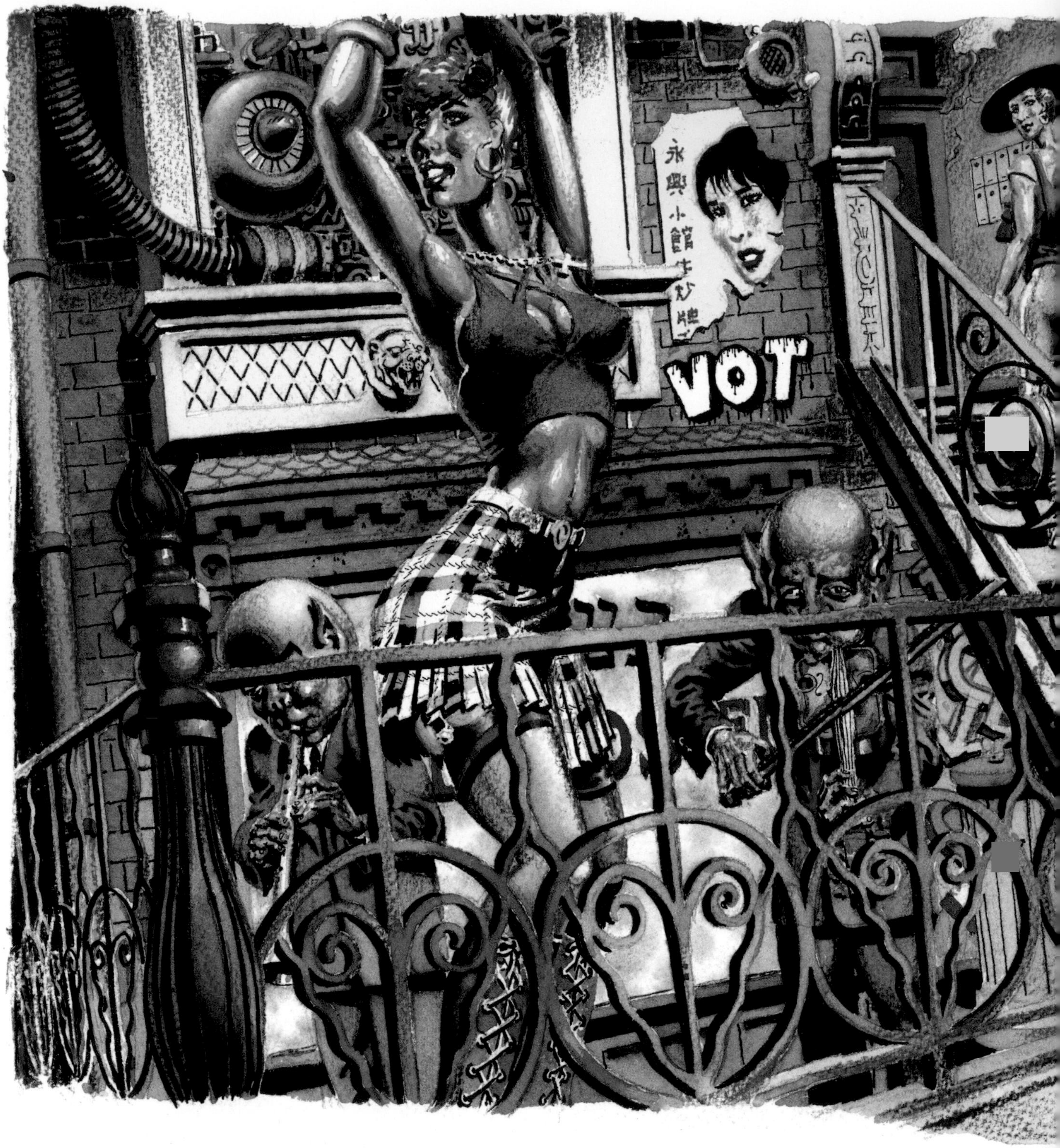
永興小館
VOT

P. 64–65: Unpublished illustration done for *Zap Comix*, 2008

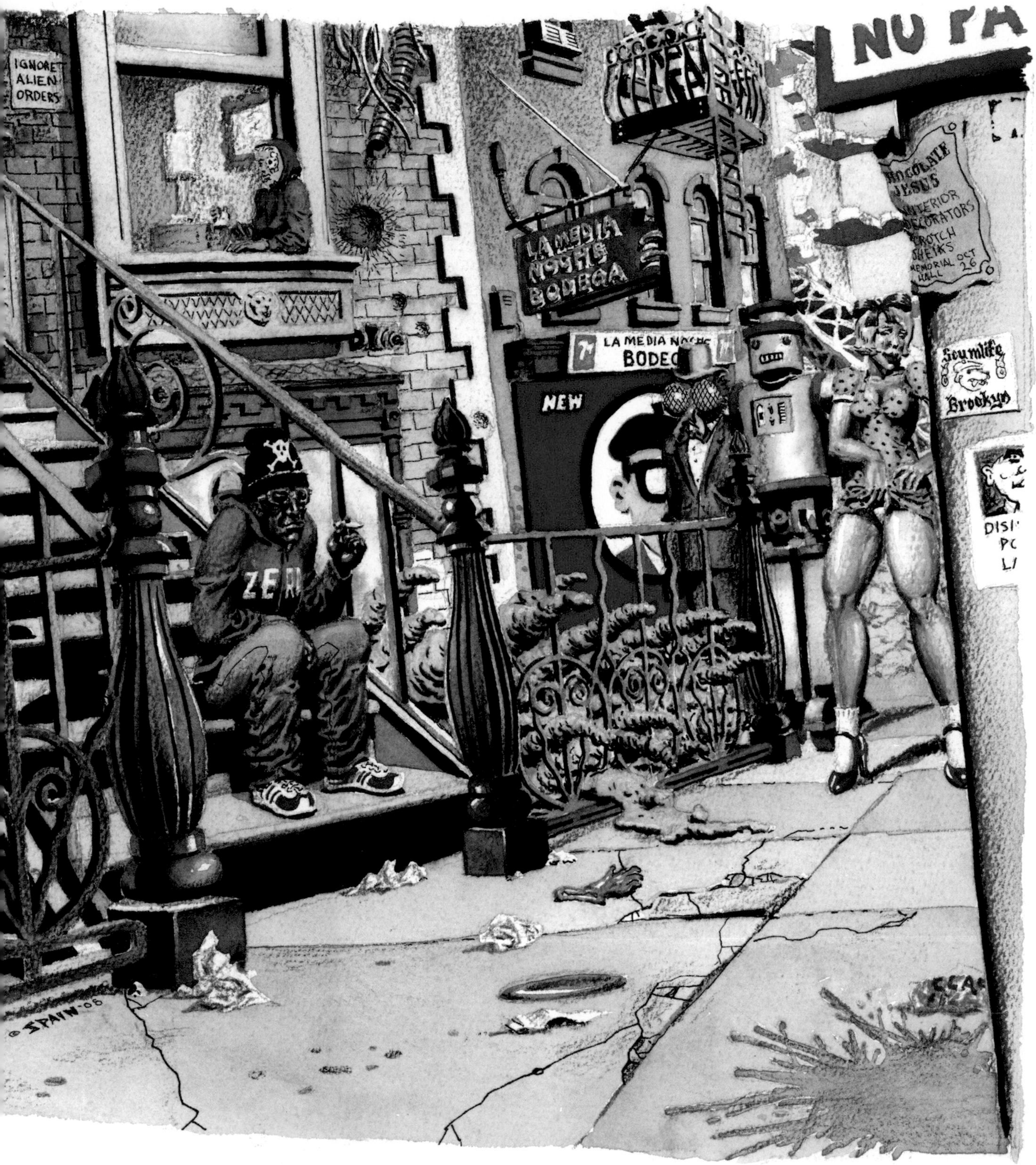
IGNORE ALIEN ORDERS
LA MEDIA NOCHE BODEGA
NEW
INTERIOR DECORATORS
MEMORIAL HALL
© SPAIN '08

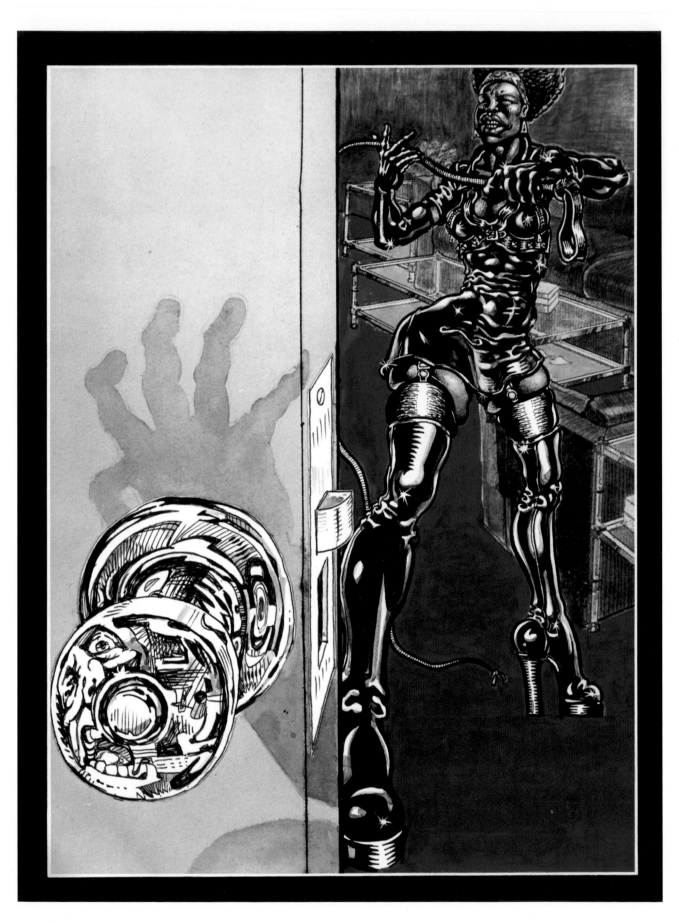

From "Spain Rodriguez: The True Story," in *Juxtapoz* magazine, Spring 1996

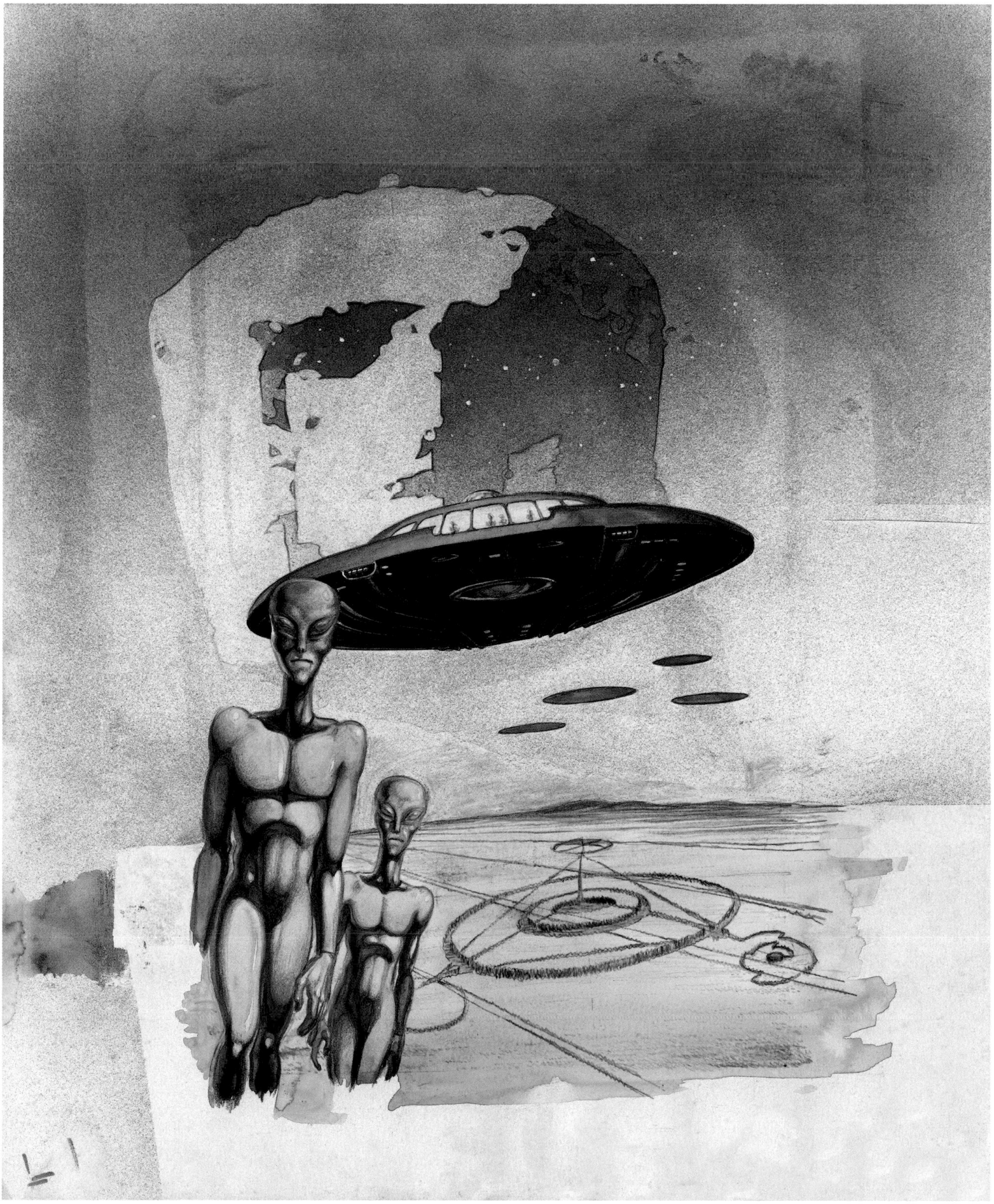

Cover illustration for Bob Frissell's *Nothing in This Book is True, But It's Exactly How Things Are*, 1994

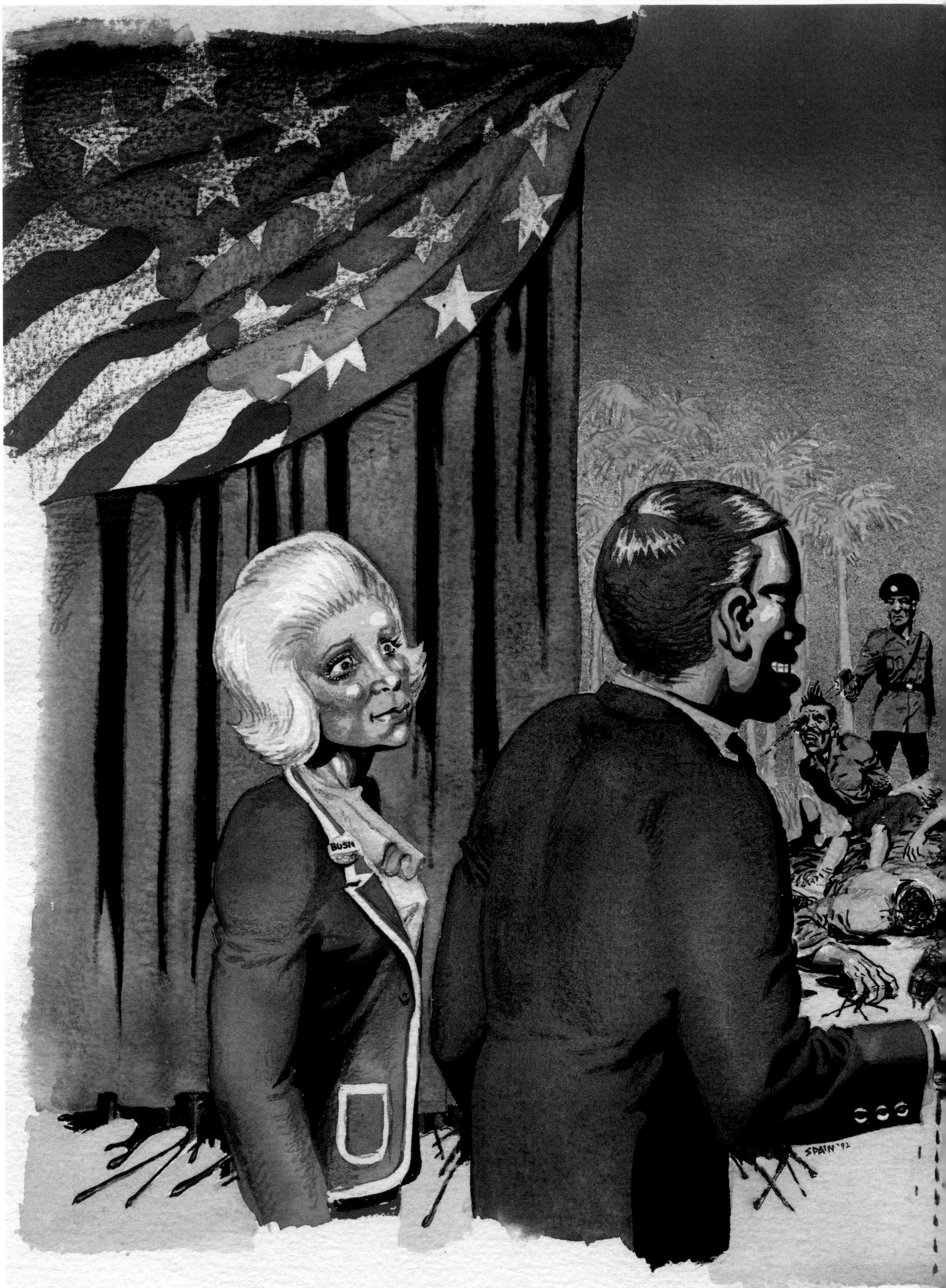
BUSH
SPAIN '92

P. 68–69: From *Hustler* magazine, 1992

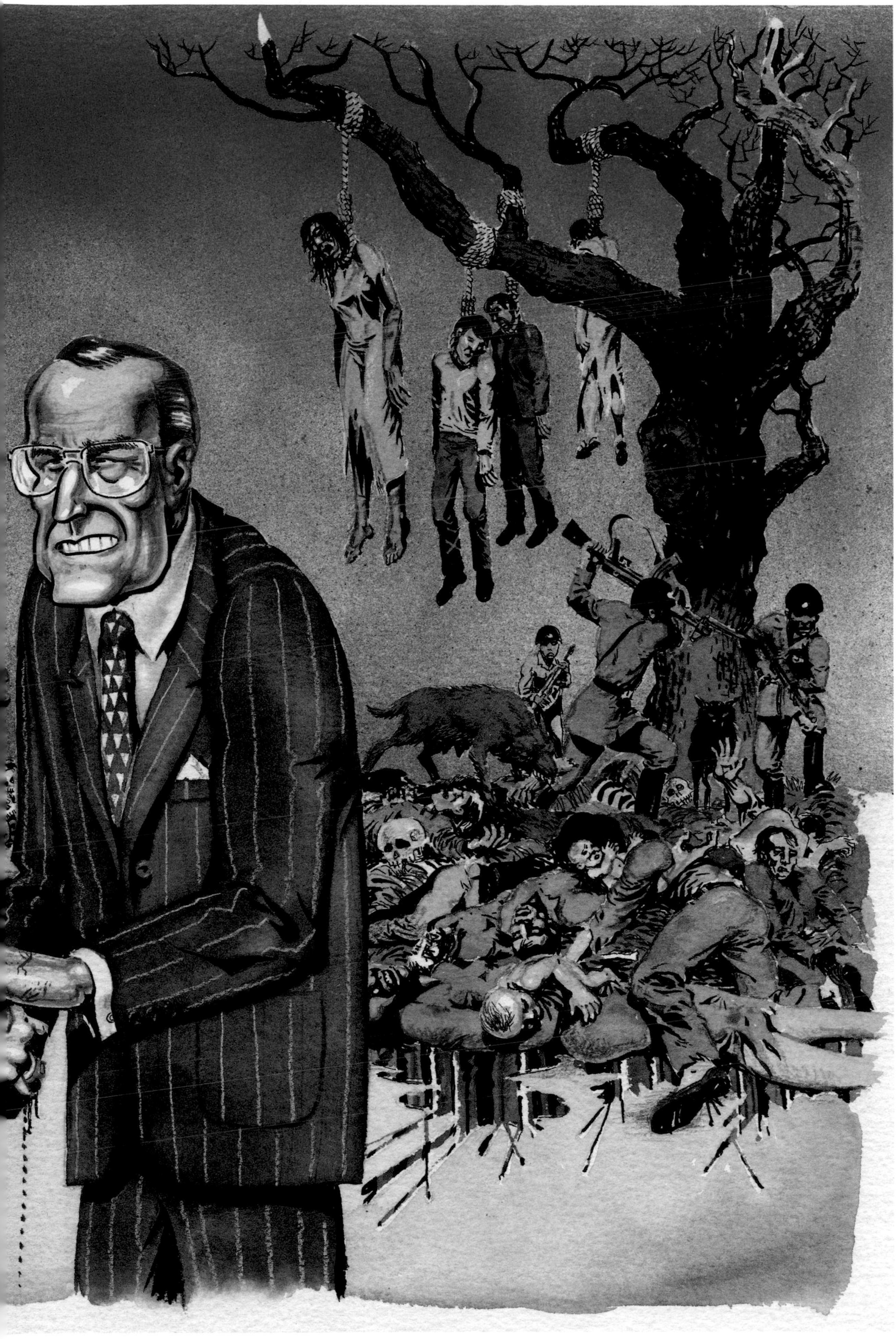

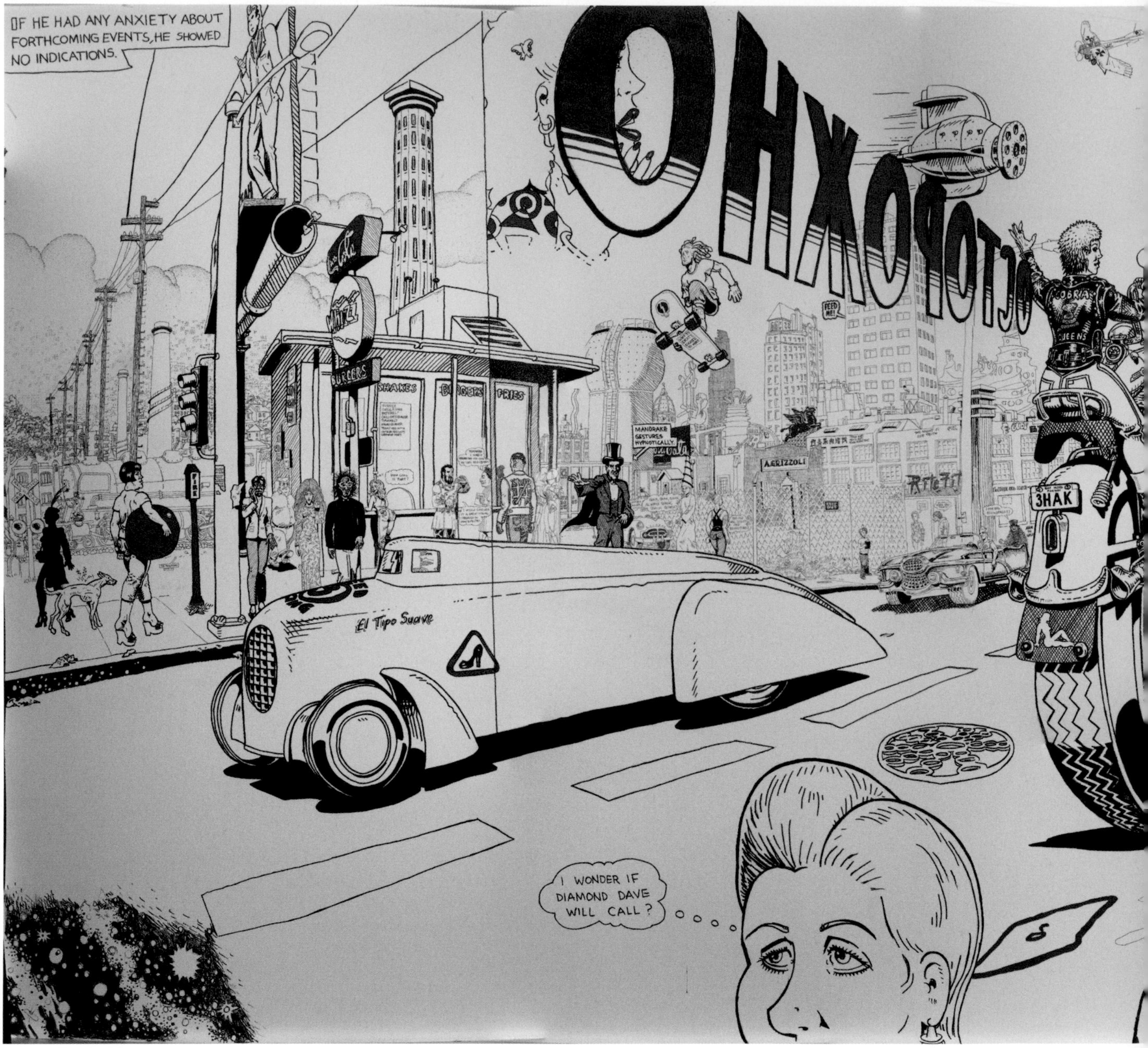
IF HE HAD ANY ANXIETY ABOUT FORTHCOMING EVENTS, HE SHOWED NO INDICATIONS.
ОКТОРОЖНО
BURGERS
SHAKES
BURGERS FRIES
MANDRAKE GESTURES HYPNOTICALLY
A. RIZZOLI
FEED ME!
3HAK
El Tipo Suave
I WONDER IF DIAMOND DAVE WILL CALL?

P. 70–71: Wall mural painted over several years in Spain's home

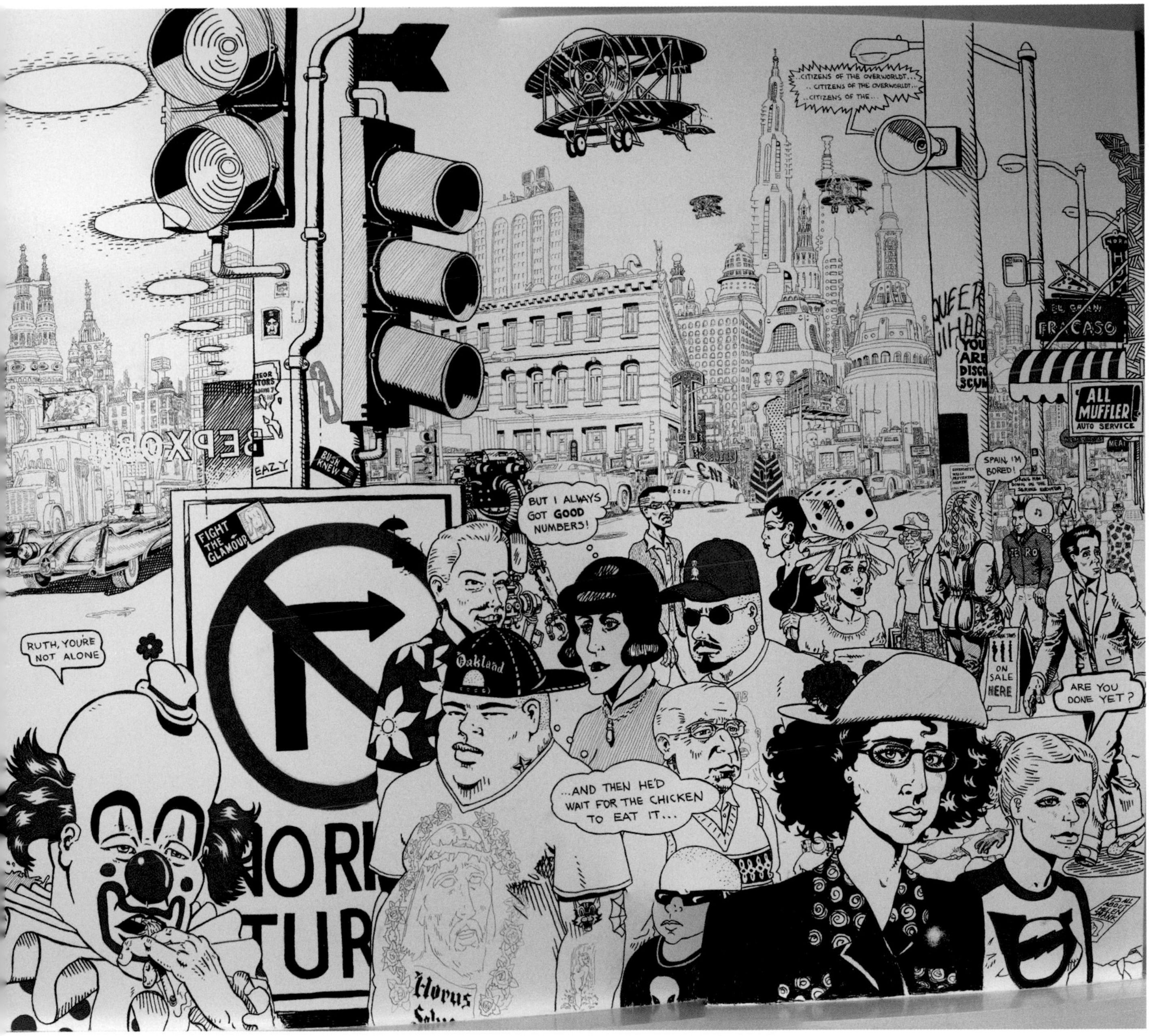

CITIZENS OF THE OVERWORLD!... ...CITIZENS OF THE OVERWORLD!... ...CITIZENS OF THE...
QUEER JIHAD
YOU ARE DISCO SCUM
FRACASO
ALL MUFFLER AUTO SERVICE
SPAIN, I'M BORED!
BUT I ALWAYS GOT GOOD NUMBERS!
FIGHT THE GLAMOUR
BUSH KNEW
EAZY
Modelo
RUTH, YOU'RE NOT ALONE
Oakland
...AND THEN HE'D WAIT FOR THE CHICKEN TO EAT IT...
ON SALE HERE
ARE YOU DONE YET?
NO R TUR
Horus

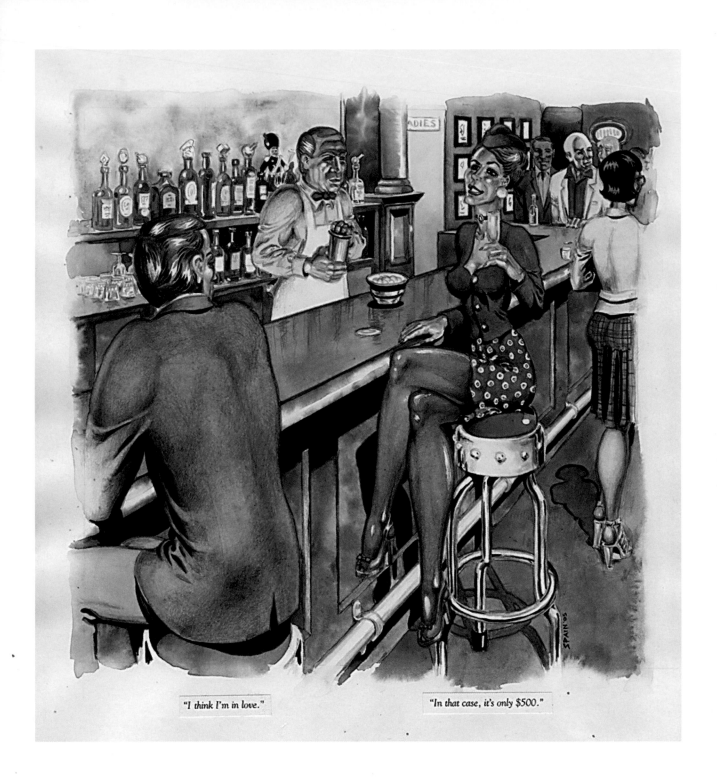

"I think I'm in love."

"In that case, it's only $500."

From *Blab!* #16, 2005

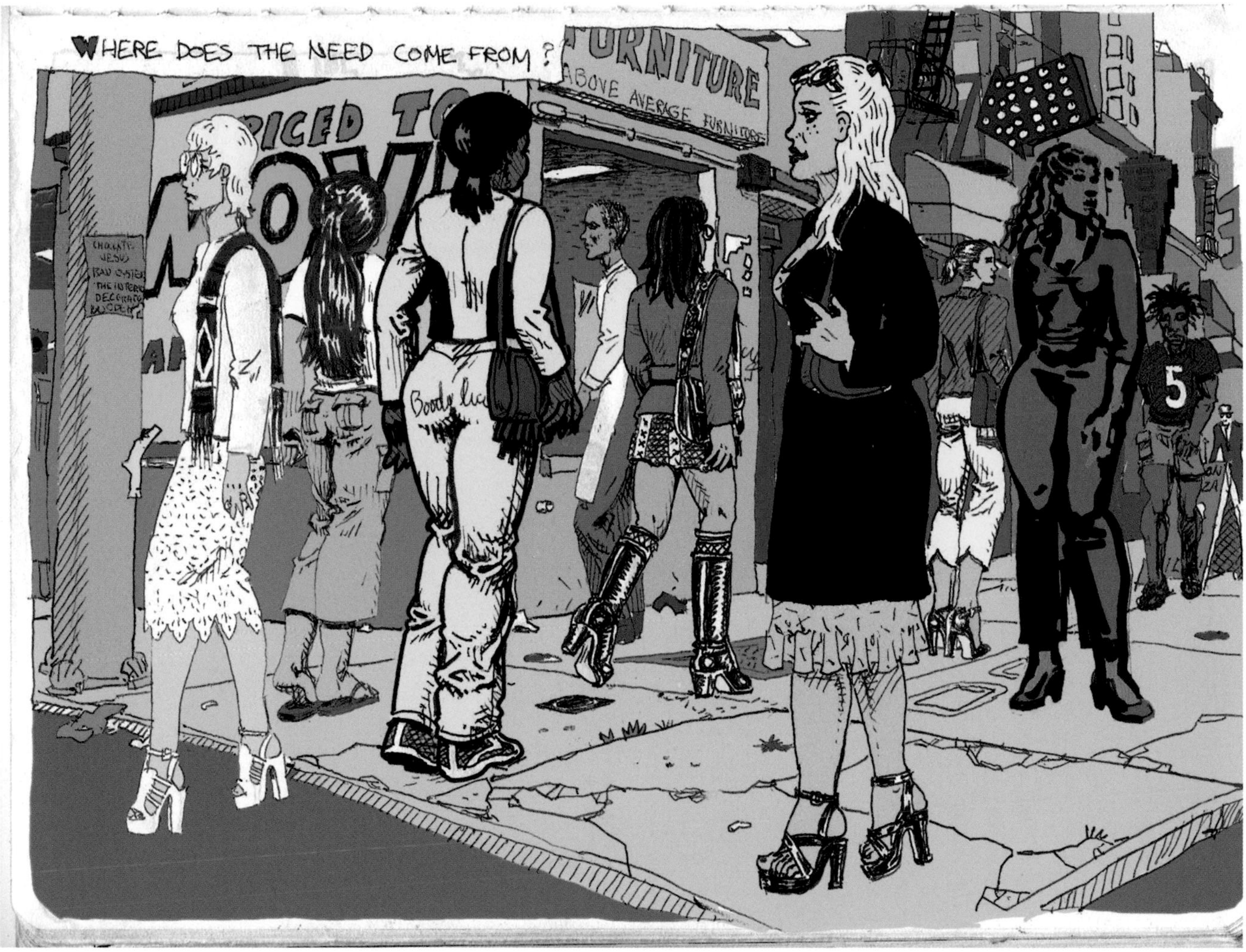
WHERE DOES THE NEED COME FROM ?
FURNITURE
ABOVE AVERAGE
5

Cover illustration for *Fourteen Hills: The San Francisco State University Review*, 2005

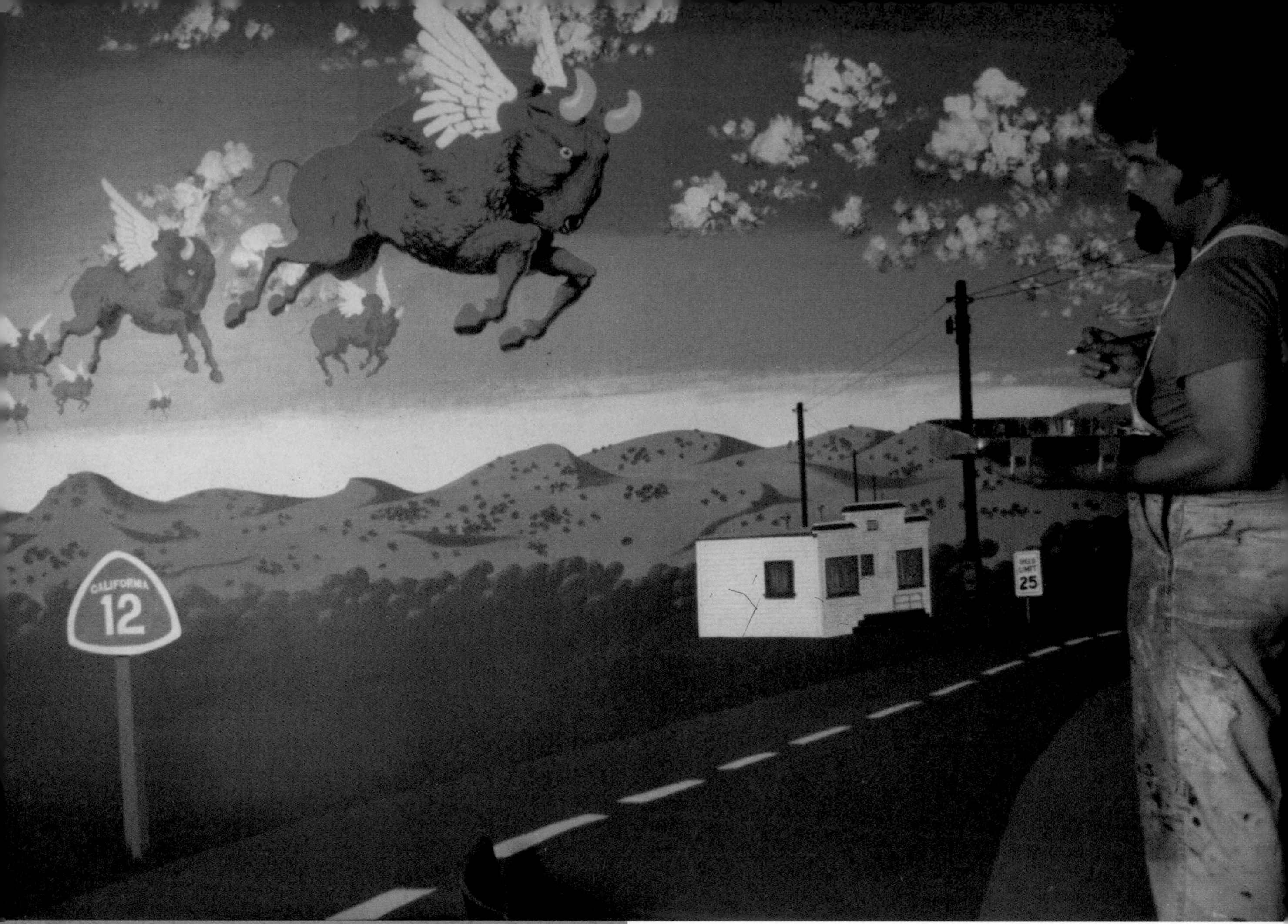
CALIFORNIA
12
25

WORKING METHODS

PATRICK ROSENKRANZ

TOP: Spain creating a mural at the Buffalo Wings Café in Sonoma, California, circa 1981.

OPPOSITE: One of Spain's last unfinished pages, 2012.

Spain's ways and means of designing comic pages were idiosyncratic, especially on longer stories, where he might begin in the middle or even the end. He didn't always use the best drawing paper and he hoarded scraps of Strathmore board. He wore his pencils and erasers down to nubs and cleaned his brushes on slivers of soap. He saw himself as a long-distance runner who could turn out comic stories for many years. He studied narratives in print, on TV, on stage, seeking raw material to spin into his own gold. Even dumb network sitcoms could provide a plot device or starting point that he might borrow for himself.

He drew incessantly in sketchbooks wherever he was—and did graffiti on walls all over the world. In later years, he drew his comics on a drawing board propped against the dining-room table, but in earlier years, he put his paper on a broken Ouija board, and drew in an old easy chair in front of the TV.

"The first thing that I noticed, and I had to gradually respect, was that he loved to work in front of the television," said former girlfriend Maxine Weaver. "The work he was doing was like fine stitchery, he had already done the imagination work and then he was refining the lines in the hatching and all that and he loved to work in front of the television. I always say that I became a serious reader while I was going with Spain to get away from the television because he would have it on by the hour and he was in a kind of trance-like state."

"Yeah, Spain liked to sit home and draw and watch TV," said fellow *Zap* artist Robert Crumb. "He'd sit in front of the TV and

DUE TO THE ULTRA-SENSITIVE NATURE OF THIS AGENCY, IT'S IMPERATIVE THAT OUR WORK REMAIN SECRET. THAT WORK IS NOW IN GRAVE DANGER OF EXPOSURE. YOU GENTLEMEN, BECAUSE OF YOUR PROVEN DEDICATION HAVE BEEN CHOSEN TO SEE THAT THIS DOESN'T HAPPEN

LATER

THE ONGOING CLAMOR FOR CRADLE TO THE GRAVE SECURITY...

DECISION MAKING BEING TAKEN OUT OF THE HANDS OF CORPORATE MANAGEMENT BY ECOLOGY AND JOB SAFETY REGULATIONS

SQUARE HACK

TOTALLY

AGAINST THIS, THE AGENCY WAGES ITS SECRET WAR. NOW SOME BLEEDING HEART WANTS TO BLOW THE WHISTLE

BRDRM

DUMPF

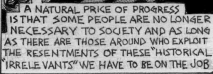

A NATURAL PRICE OF PROGRESS IS THAT SOME PEOPLE ARE NO LONGER NECESSARY TO SOCIETY AND AS LONG AS THERE ARE THOSE AROUND WHO EXPLOIT THE RESENTMENTS OF THESE "HISTORICAL IRRELEVANTS" WE HAVE TO BE ON THE JOB

TO PROTECT THE PEOPLE FROM ... BIG GOVERNMENT

AGAINST THIS
THE AGENCY WAGES
ITS SECRET WAR. THEN
SOME BLEEDING HEART
WANTS TO BLOW THE
WHIST

COAT

A NATURAL PRICE OF PROGRESS IS THAT
SOME PEOPLE ARE NO LONGER NECESSARY
TO SOCIETY AND AS LONG AS THERE ARE
THOSE AROUND WHO EXPLOIT THE
RESENTMENTS OF THESE HISTORICAL
IRRELEVANTS WE HAVE TO BE ON
THE JOBS

FACE

THE VERY NATURE
OF OUR FREE MARKET
SOCIETY IS IMPERILED 100%
ITS A HORROR STORY

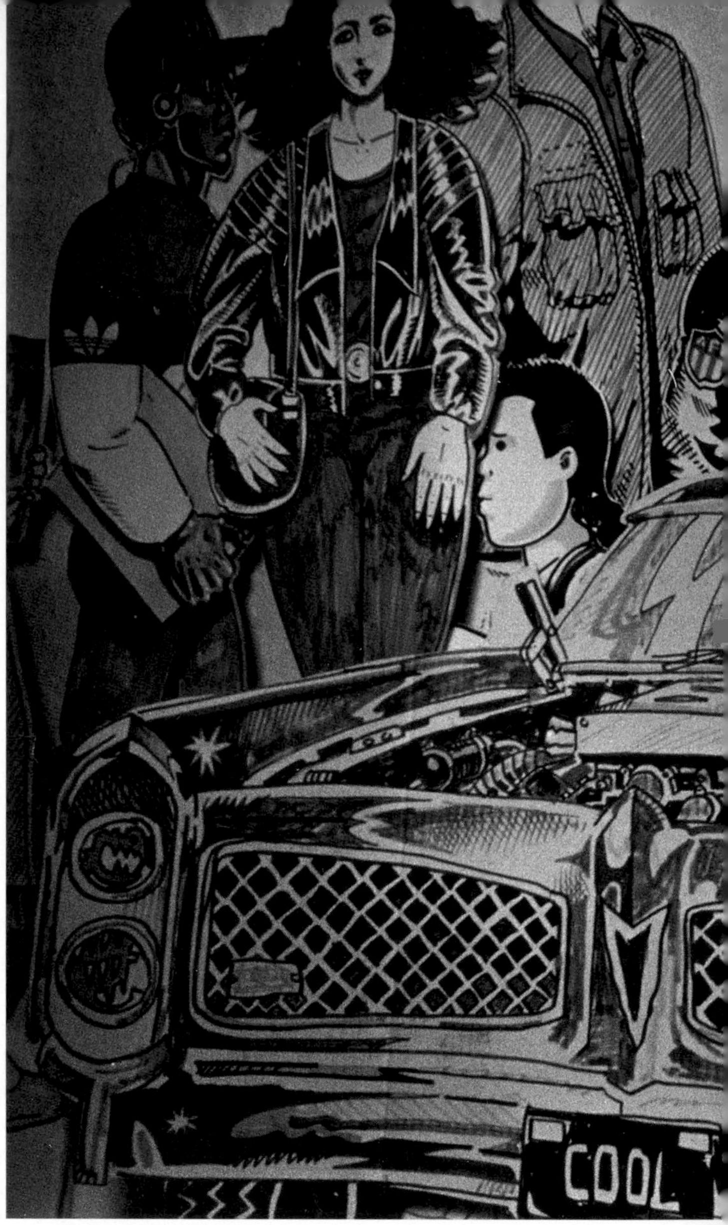
COOL

RIGHT: Spain with his Mission District Cutouts, June 1989. Photo by Wolfgang Dietze.

he had a board to draw on while he watched TV. He was always working. He worked in these funky situations like that. He didn't like formal situations for drawing. He never had a drawing table that I ever saw. He worked on his dining-room table on Harrison Street. When he was on Coso Avenue for like nine years, he sat on this funky caved-in couch in front of the TV and drew."

"He also was the most serious artist of all, of probably anyone I've ever met in my life, because he worked all the time," said Aline Kominsky-Crumb. "That was an incredible role model to me. I had a job, and I came home and I worked on my comics at night. I said, 'Spain just works all the time.' He also didn't talk about himself that much. He just focused on the work. He was for me a really important role model."

"It took Spain a long time to do certain strips, as I remember, and he was such a perfectionist," said Last Gasp publisher Ron Turner. "He'd have to design entire pages and then panels and where the word balloons would go, and the lettering, he would struggle with it. I think he was more like the slow and steady wins the race, but Spain was definitely in the long-term race. I don't know if this is true, but I think he was one of those guys who actually started at the end. He got a good sense of the end period, and then he constructed it all to get there, like building a maze backwards, but I'm not sure he did, but I kind of sensed that."

"The way Spain worked was he would sort of jump around in the strip, doing the things he felt were the most fun to do initially, or the juiciest," said cartoonist Jay Kinney, who co-created several comic strips with Spain. "He'd do a panel and skip two panels and do part of another panel and then jump ahead and do another part of a panel so there were holes throughout the strip that I had to fill in."

"You'd see these pages spread out on this kitchen table or dining-room table and there would be a panel here, a panel there, sketched in or even inked, and then a lot of blank space," described Crumb. "Maybe they were the key action panels or something ... the key panels in the narrative and the others would materialize around them gradually ... very intuitive that way. There were never any scripts around."

"I remember visiting him once in the '70s while he was working on a very long story," said Art Spiegelman. "He had piles of pages strewn all around the room. Some were ruled out and partially lettered, some boards were only lightly penciled with intense rendering on only one or two scattered panels, some almost empty with just a car or a torso randomly inked. I was baffled and asked if he always worked that haphazardly since I'd have blown a fuse trying to get anything done that way. He said he figured as long as he kept his hand moving it would all get done eventually."

"He had a great ability to spot blacks," said Kinney. "By which I mean black shadow and the use of chiaroscuro ... the interplay of black and white on the page. He was great at that. I think he had a good combination of use of brush and of pen. He really worked hard on composition and was always pushing himself on having changes of angle from panel to panel. He referred to these things as tricks. I remember him mentioning on the *Che* graphic history, he used up all his graphic tricks in the course of doing that book."

"He was an enormously hard worker," agreed fellow *Zap* artist Robert Williams. "Anytime he had an idle moment, he was drawing. Anytime we'd go into public he'd be drawing something on the wall, a wall that wasn't his, a wall that wasn't meant to be drawn on. I remember for one of the *Zap* comic promotions, I think at Hidey Ho in '85, we went to a punk rock radio station. We were in there being interviewed and while they weren't looking, he started drawing all over their fucking walls and blew their minds. They were real upset over that. He had half a fucking mural done before they got him stopped."

"Spain was very skilled at his craft," said the painter Suzanne Williams. "When he was drawing, he penciled some of his stuff and some he didn't. I once saw him draw a truck that was crashing. This was at Baby Tattooville. Bob Self was the publisher of Baby Tattoo Books. He put on this event at the Mission Inn every year. The year Bob and I were invited as paid guests, Spain was too. I saw him drawing a truck, crashing upside down, and he drew it

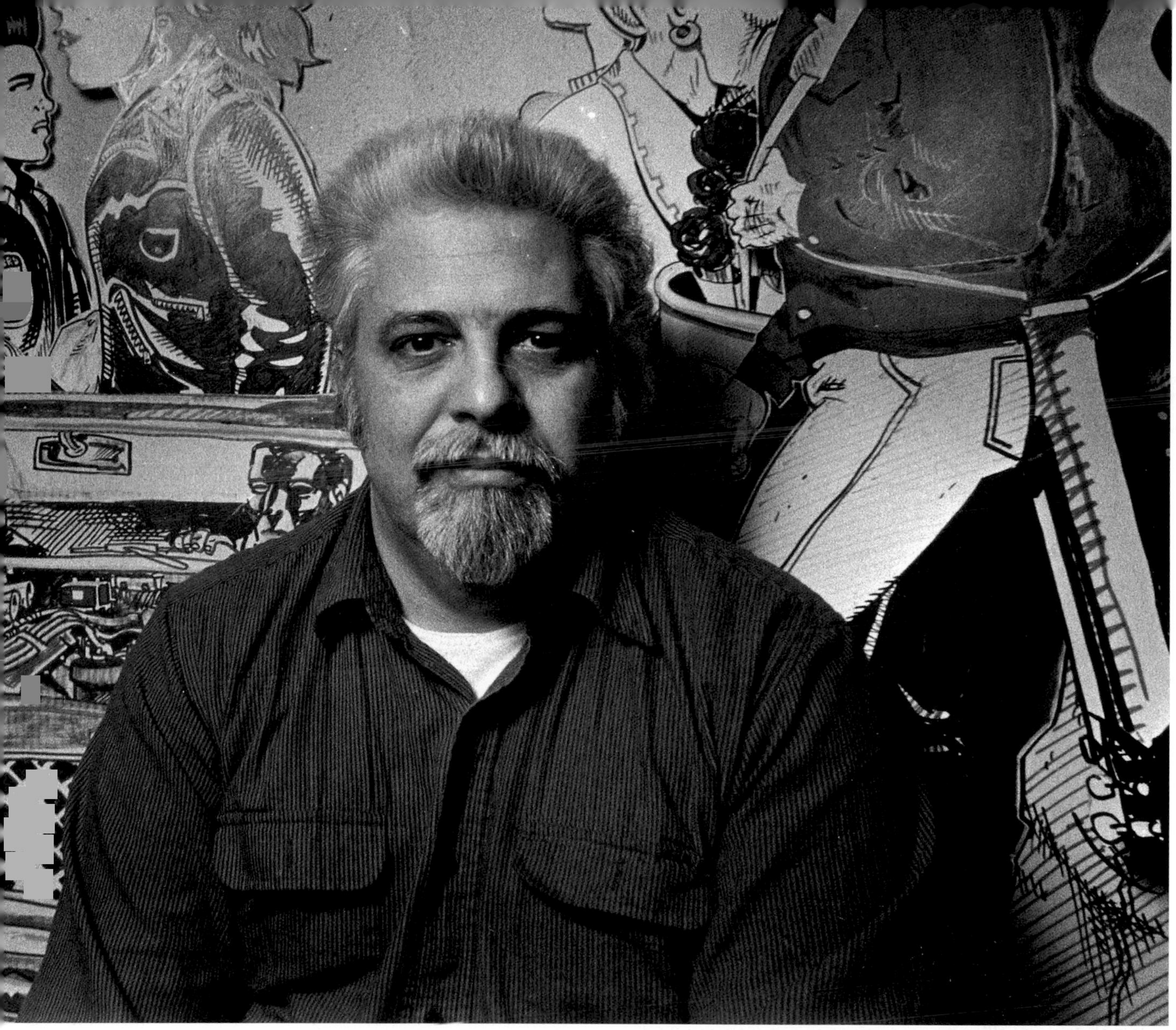

upside down. He didn't turn the thing around. It was pretty amazing. I think he did a little penciling and then inked it in, but not much penciling, considering what he was doing."

Ken Weaver, formerly of the Fugs once asked him, "How do you figure this out without mapping it all out like the old classical art in the Renaissance? They had lines going all over the place for the figures and the ones in the back and everything. He said, 'I don't know, I just imagine what it is that I want to draw and how it's gonna fit in the frame, and then I just copy it,' which sounds impossible to me."

"Spain was cosmic that way," said fellow cartoonist Kim Deitch. "Plus, the way he drew. I've seen it in a few people, but not many, where it's just like you feel like it was all in his head, and he was just tracing around the outline he could already see right in front of him. Crumb's like that maybe even to a larger degree. Spain practically didn't have to pencil sometimes. He could just sit there and do, do, do, which is so far from the way I draw. I've gotta get it all planned out and trace over something and fuss with it forever. For Spain, it just sort of came out. Like automatic writing or something."

"He must have had a remarkably involved mind to do those cityscapes with those fire escapes hanging on the outside," avowed Robert Williams. "Each building had neoclassic cornices

"He didn't like formal situations for drawing. He never had a drawing table that I ever saw."

and ledges and stuff. That takes a real fundamental understanding of perspective ... getting the windows right and working around the fire escapes. His signage and everything is just remarkable. He just did it time after time after time. Let me tell you something else he did. He would do the same picture over and over again until he could do it almost without an under sketch. What he would do is he would do a three-quarter angle of a motorcycle coming at you and that was very, very difficult because you've got the extended forks and the ellipses of the wheels and the sitting of the driver ... he did that so many times that in front of a crowd ... he could go up with nothing on that drawing board or canvas, and just start knocking that thing out and leave room for

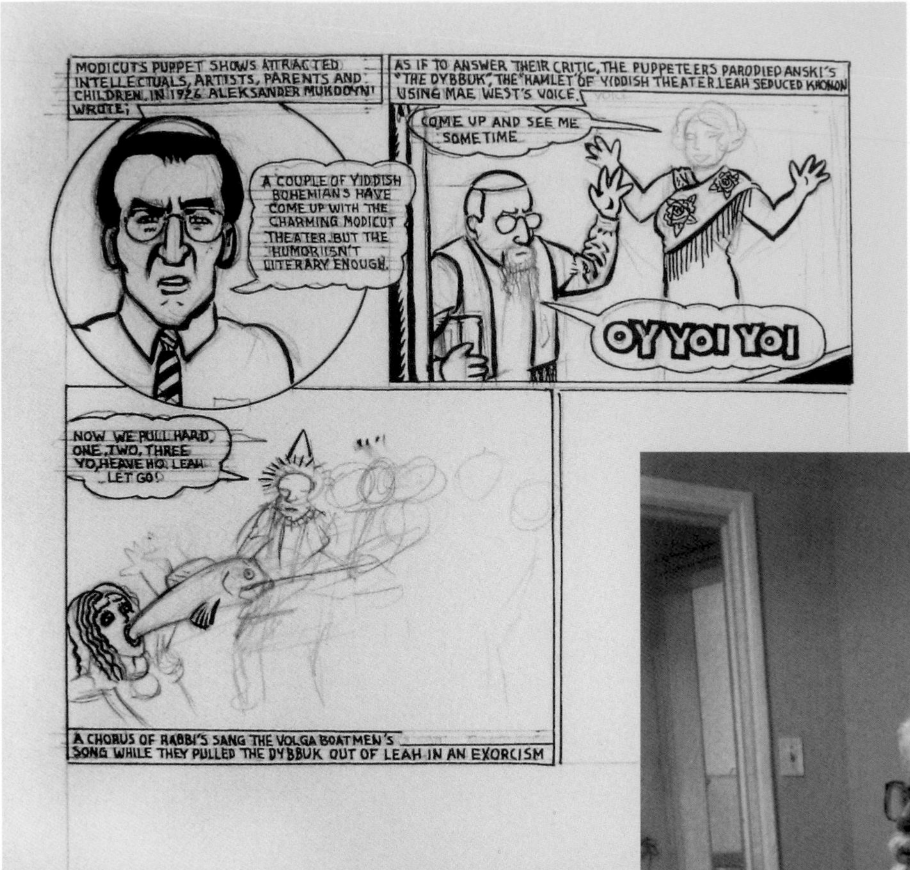
MODICUTS PUPPET SHOWS ATTRACTED INTELLECTUALS, ARTISTS, PARENTS AND CHILDREN. IN 1926 ALEKSANDER MUKDOYNI WROTE;
A COUPLE OF YIDDISH BOHEMIANS HAVE COME UP WITH THE CHARMING MODICUT THEATER. BUT THE HUMOR ISN'T LITERARY ENOUGH.
AS IF TO ANSWER THEIR CRITIC, THE PUPPETEERS PARODIED ANSKI'S "THE DYBBUK", THE "HAMLET" OF YIDDISH THEATER. LEAH SEDUCED KHONON USING MAE WEST'S VOICE.
COME UP AND SEE ME SOMETIME
OY YOI YOI
NOW WE PULL HARD, ONE, TWO, THREE YO, HEAVE HO. LEAH LET GO!
A CHORUS OF RABBI'S SANG THE VOLGA BOATMEN'S SONG WHILE THEY PULLED THE DYBBUK OUT OF LEAH IN AN EXORCISM

> **"He said he figured as long as he kept his hand moving it would all get done eventually."**

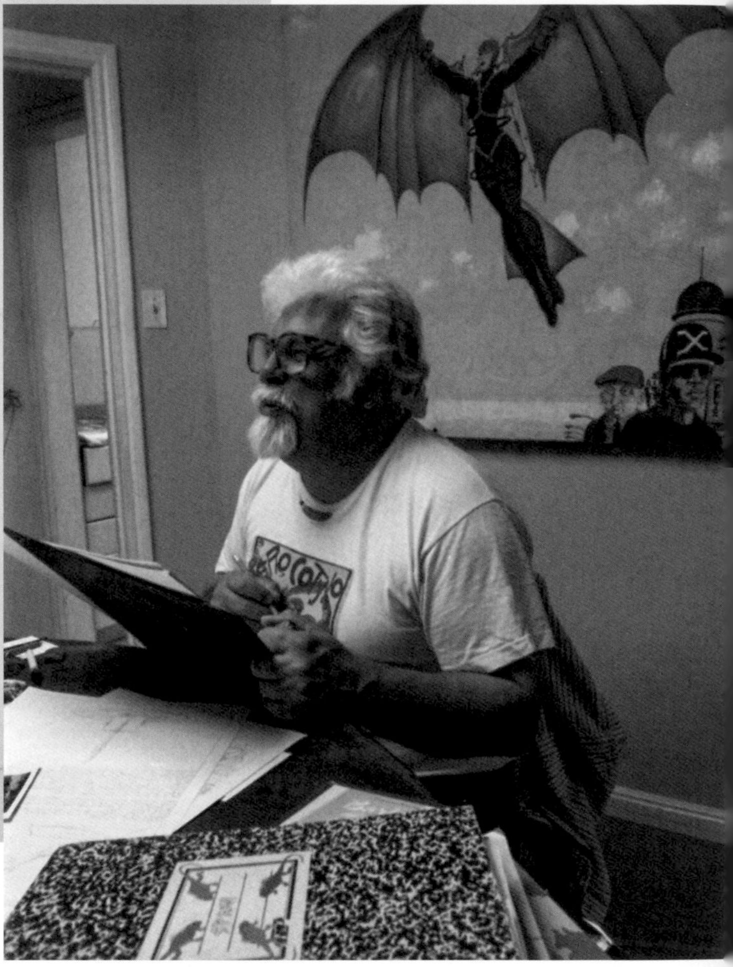
ROCOCO

TOP LEFT: Unfinished page from "Modicut and the Yiddish Bohemians." Spain asked fellow cartoonist Jay Kinney to finish the story for publication after his death.

ABOVE: Spain at his drawing board, 1998. Photo by Patrick Rosenkranz.

the ellipses of the wheels and forks without crossing it. It looked amazing. Like god's hand ... like a printing machine. It was just remarkable the way he could do that."

"There was quiescence about him when he was working because he was really blessed with and then cultivated the gift of concentration and persistence," said Maxine Weaver. "His sketchbooks were my favorite things he did, because in his stories he would often impose this kind of rigorous ideology about power struggles and the bad and the good. In the sketchbooks, he drew what he saw and he wrote what he heard and they were wonderful. They were so often funny and beautiful and even the way he would fill a page with little bits, the whole page would be beautiful in the way they came together."

"It's what he did... his mountain of work," said colleague Paul Mavrides. "He drew and drew. While he was asleep, he was drawing. He appreciated art. He promoted it. Like many a great artist he was interested in a lot of things. It's the rare person who does great work and is so singularly devoted that they don't pay attention to anything else. Most people... their vision or their curiosity or intellectual awareness just naturally keeps them influenced and interested in things outside of what they do."

SKETCHBOOK ART

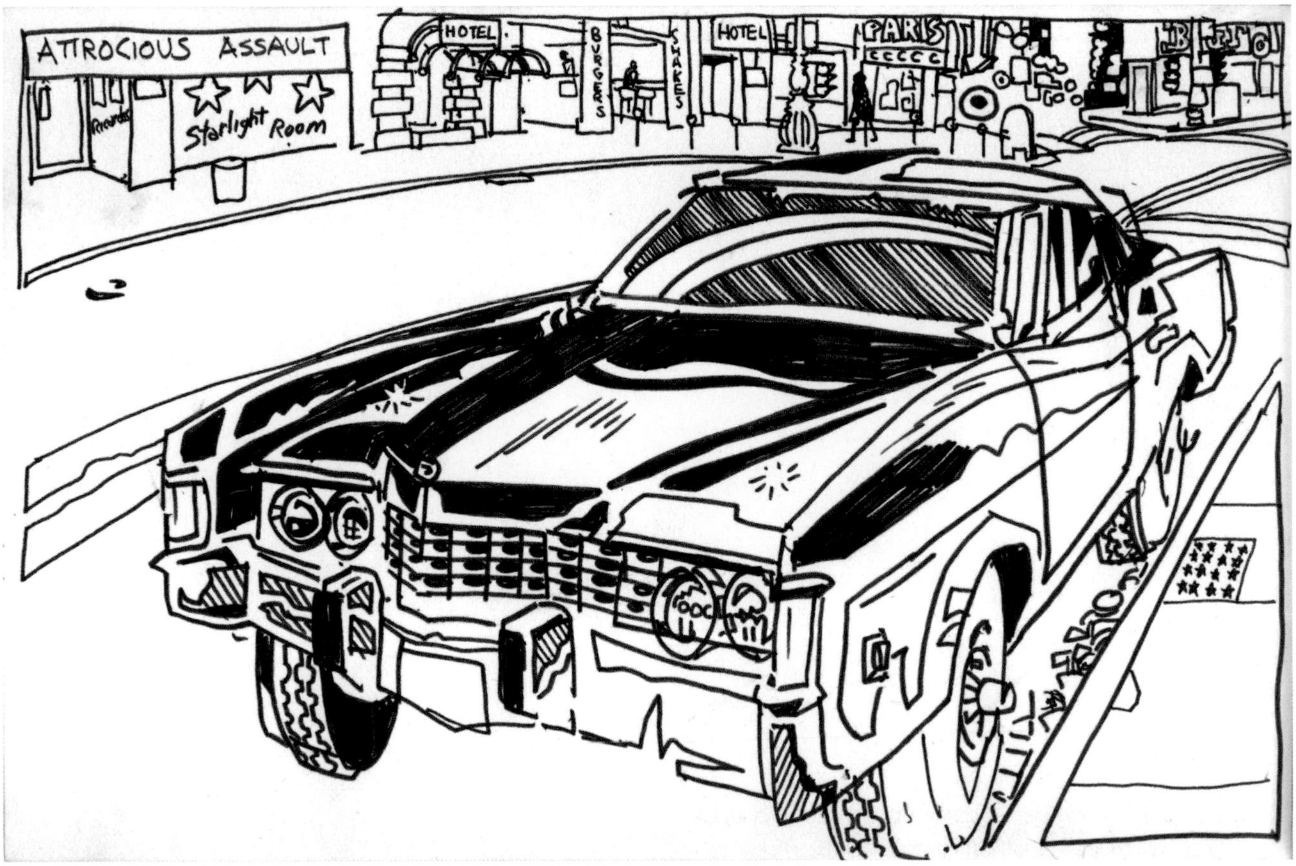
ATTROCIOUS ASSAULT
Starlight Room
HOTEL
BURGERS
SHAKES
HOTEL
PARIS

P. 79–132 Previously unpublished sketchbook pages

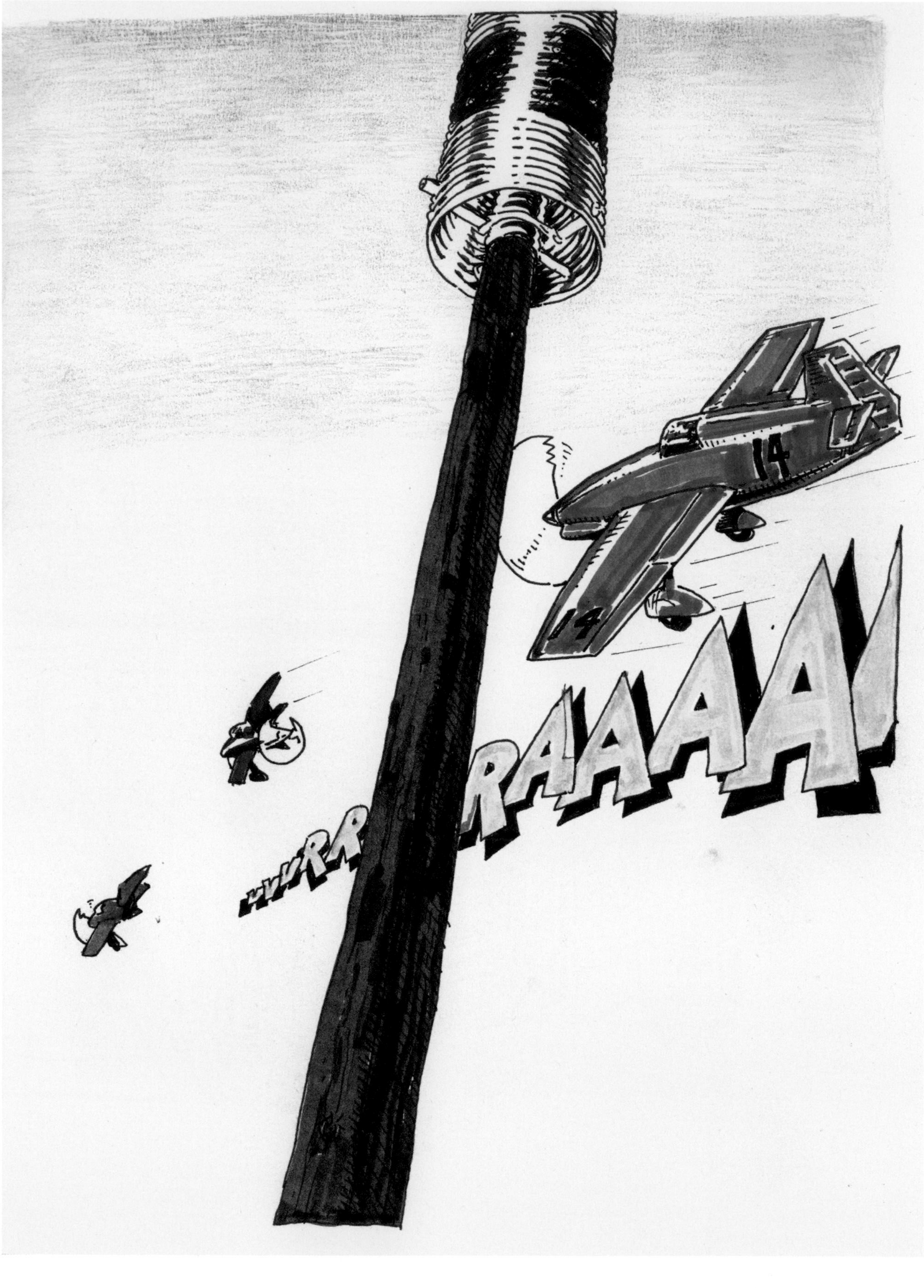
vvvRRRAAAAA

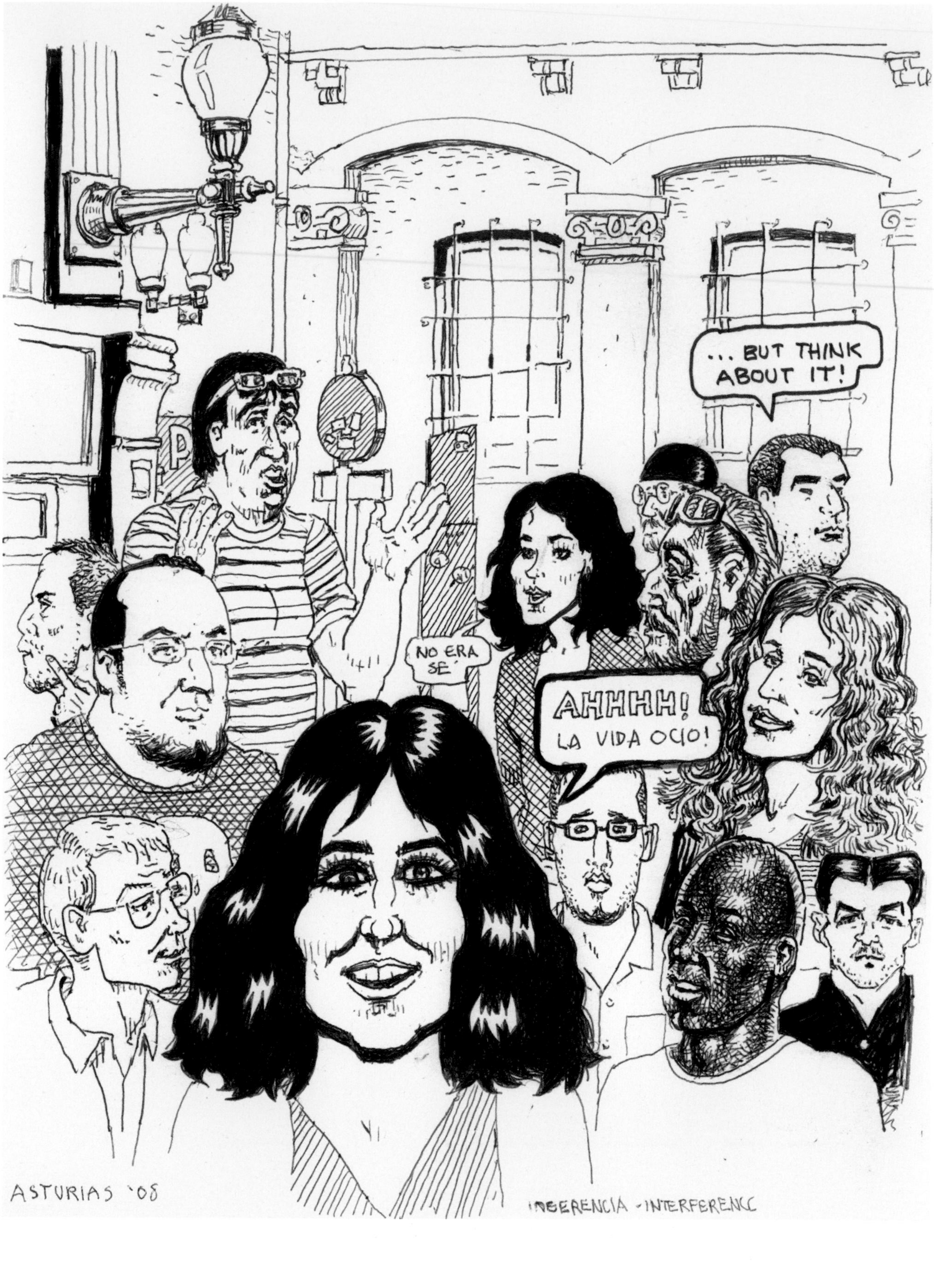
... BUT THINK ABOUT IT!
NO ERA SE´
AHHHH! LA VIDA OCIO!
ASTURIAS '08
INGERENCIA - INTERFERENCC

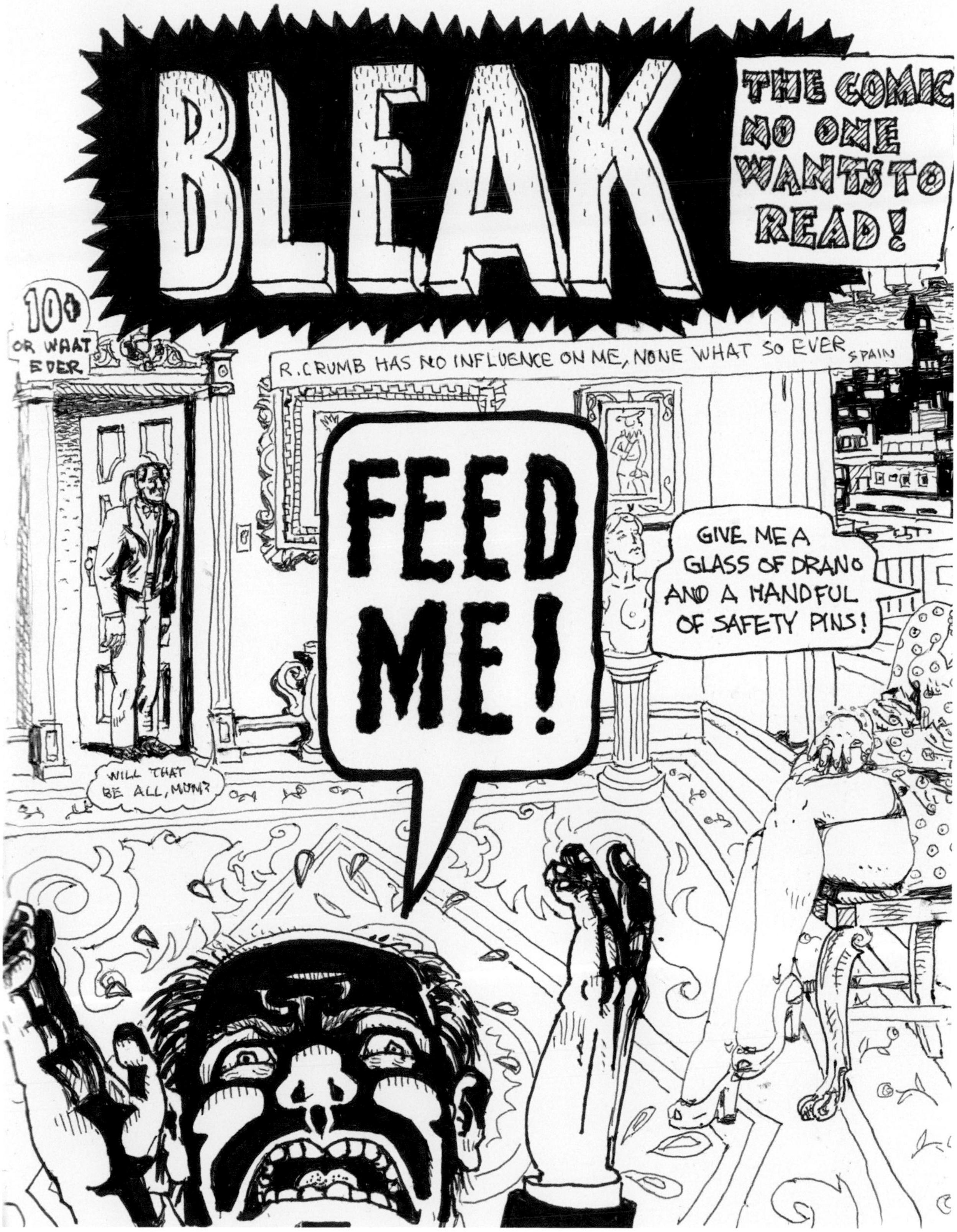
BLEAK
THE COMIC NO ONE WANTS TO READ!
10¢ OR WHAT EVER
R. CRUMB HAS NO INFLUENCE ON ME, NONE WHAT SO EVER SPAIN
FEED ME!
GIVE ME A GLASS OF DRANO AND A HANDFUL OF SAFETY PINS!
WILL THAT BE ALL, MUM?

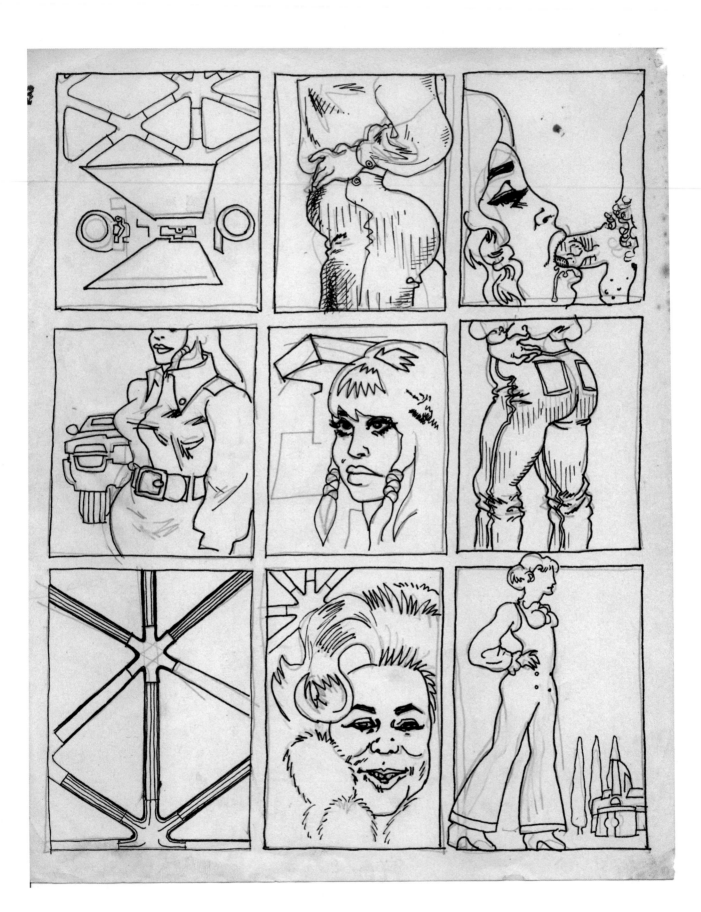

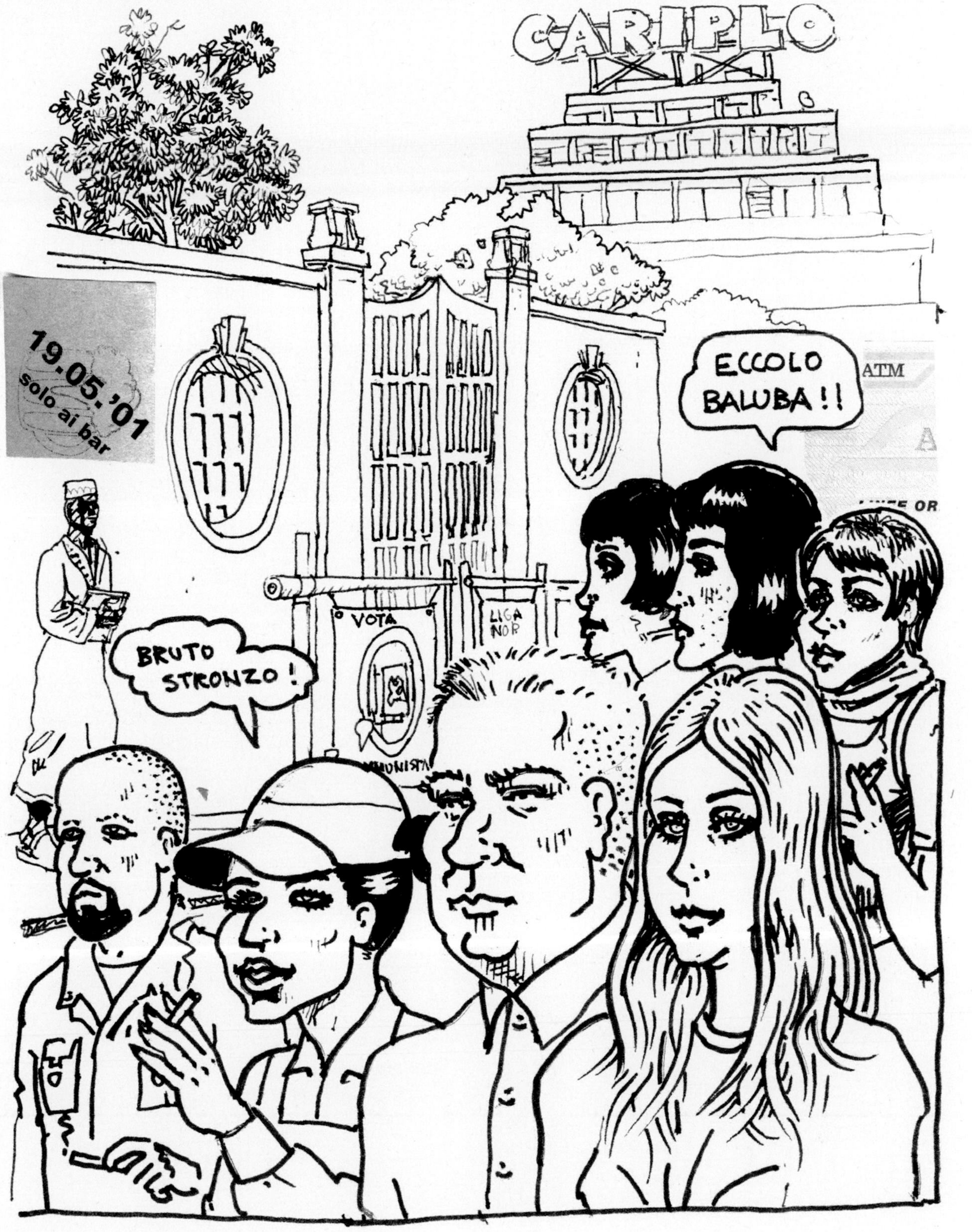
CARIPLO
19.05.'01
solo ai bar
ECCOLO BALUBA!!
ATM
VOTA
LIGA NOR
BRUTO STRONZO!

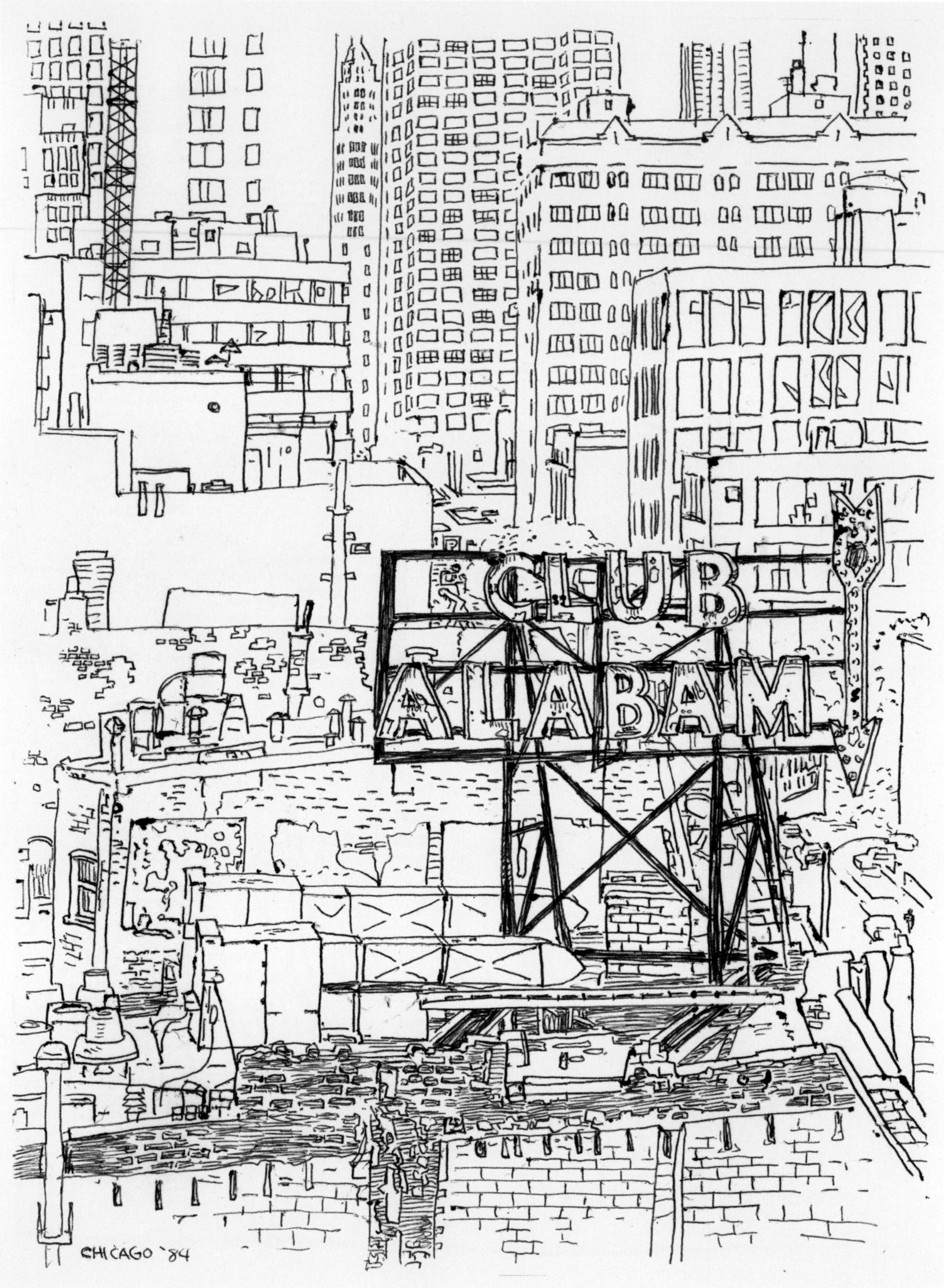
CLUB
ALABAM
CHICAGO '84

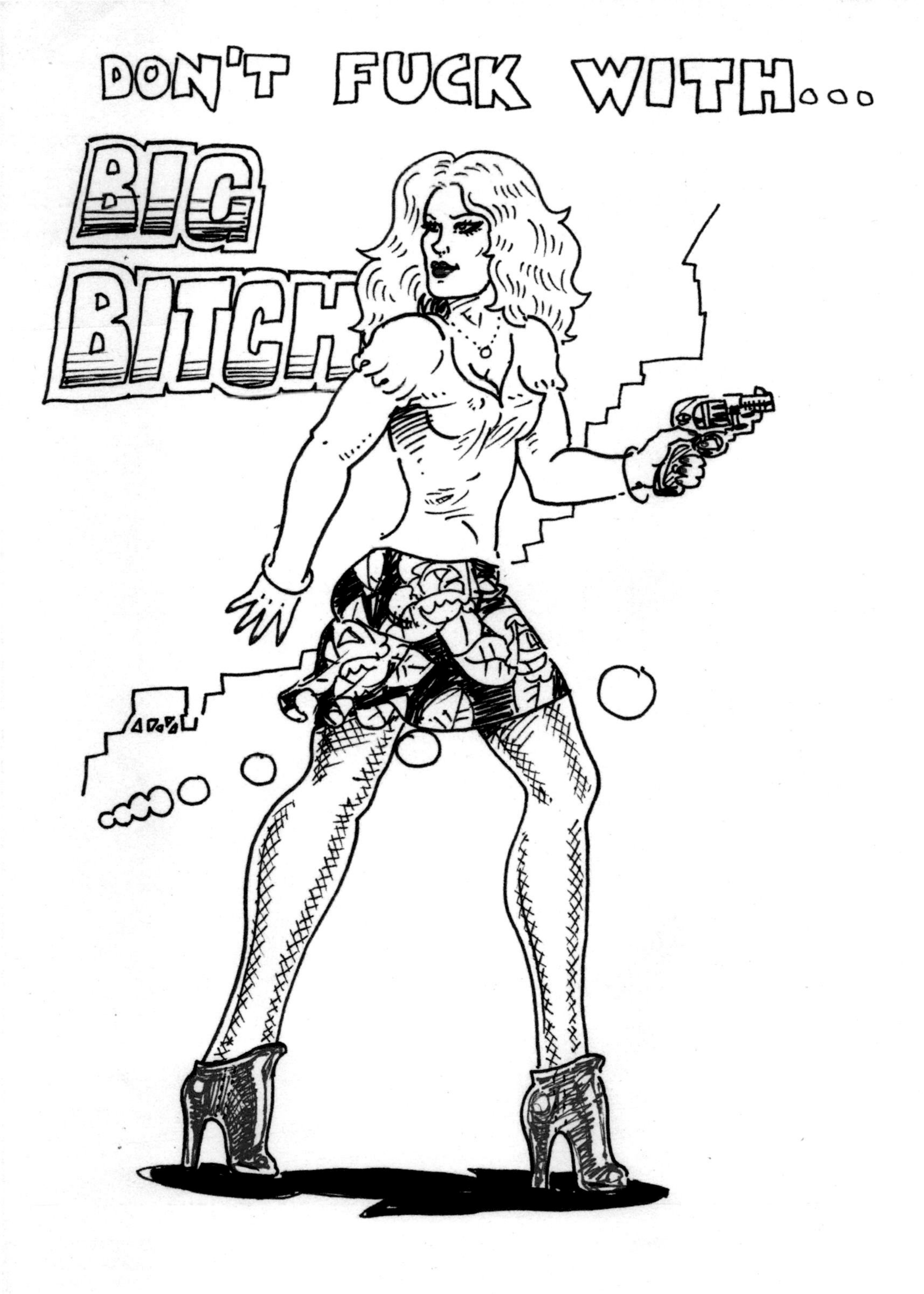
DON'T FUCK WITH...
BIG BITCH

DREAM 8-10

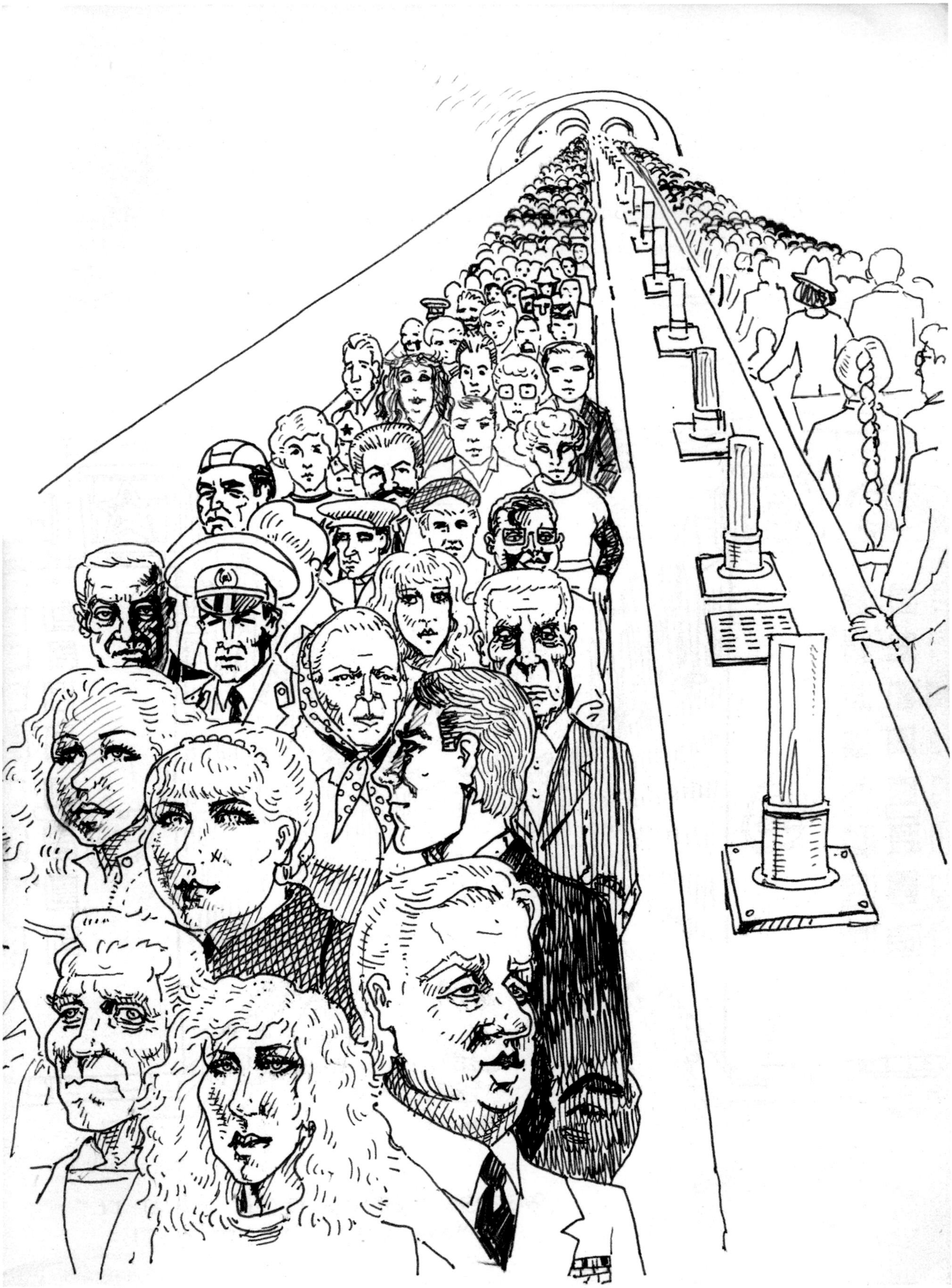

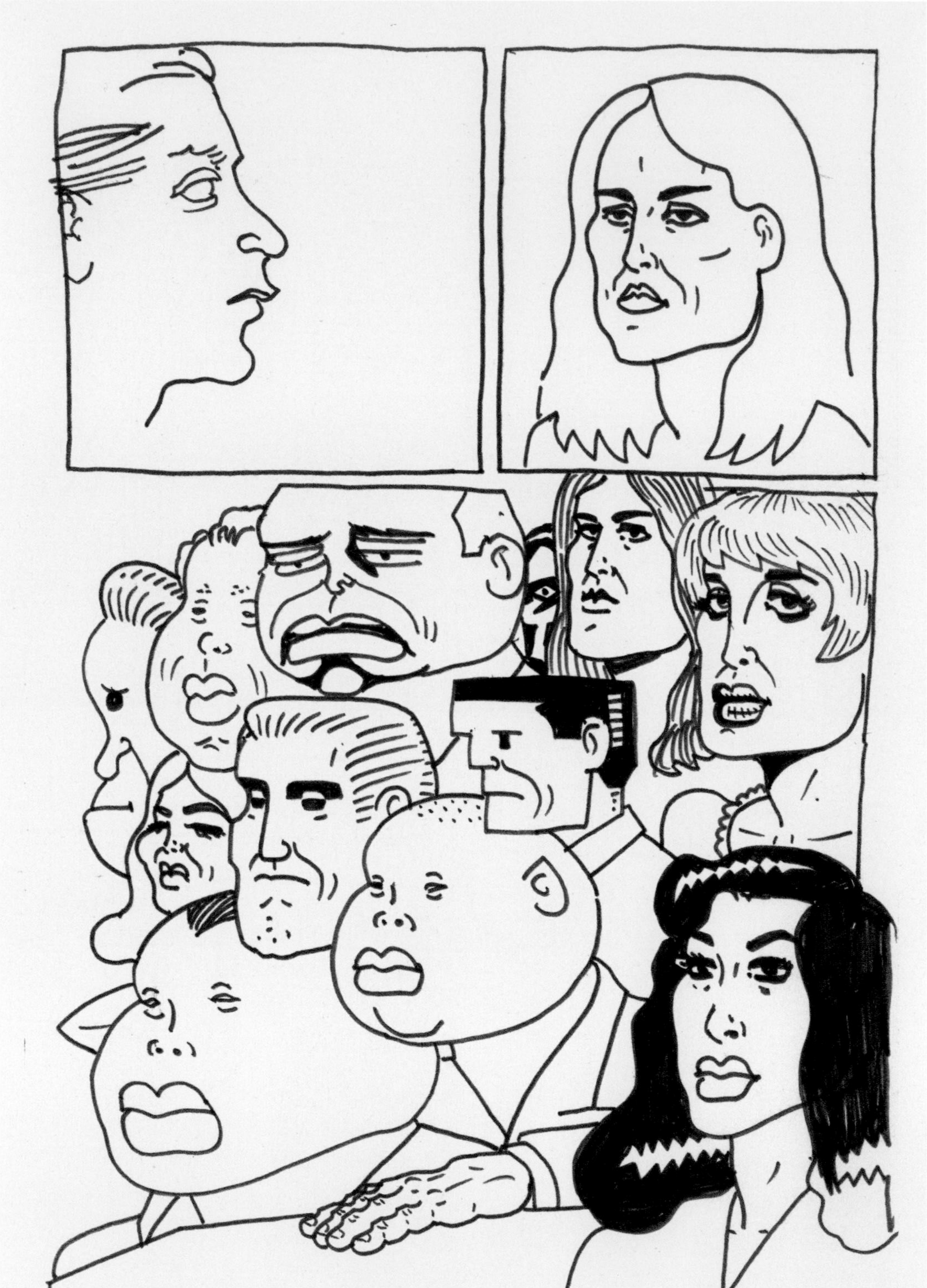

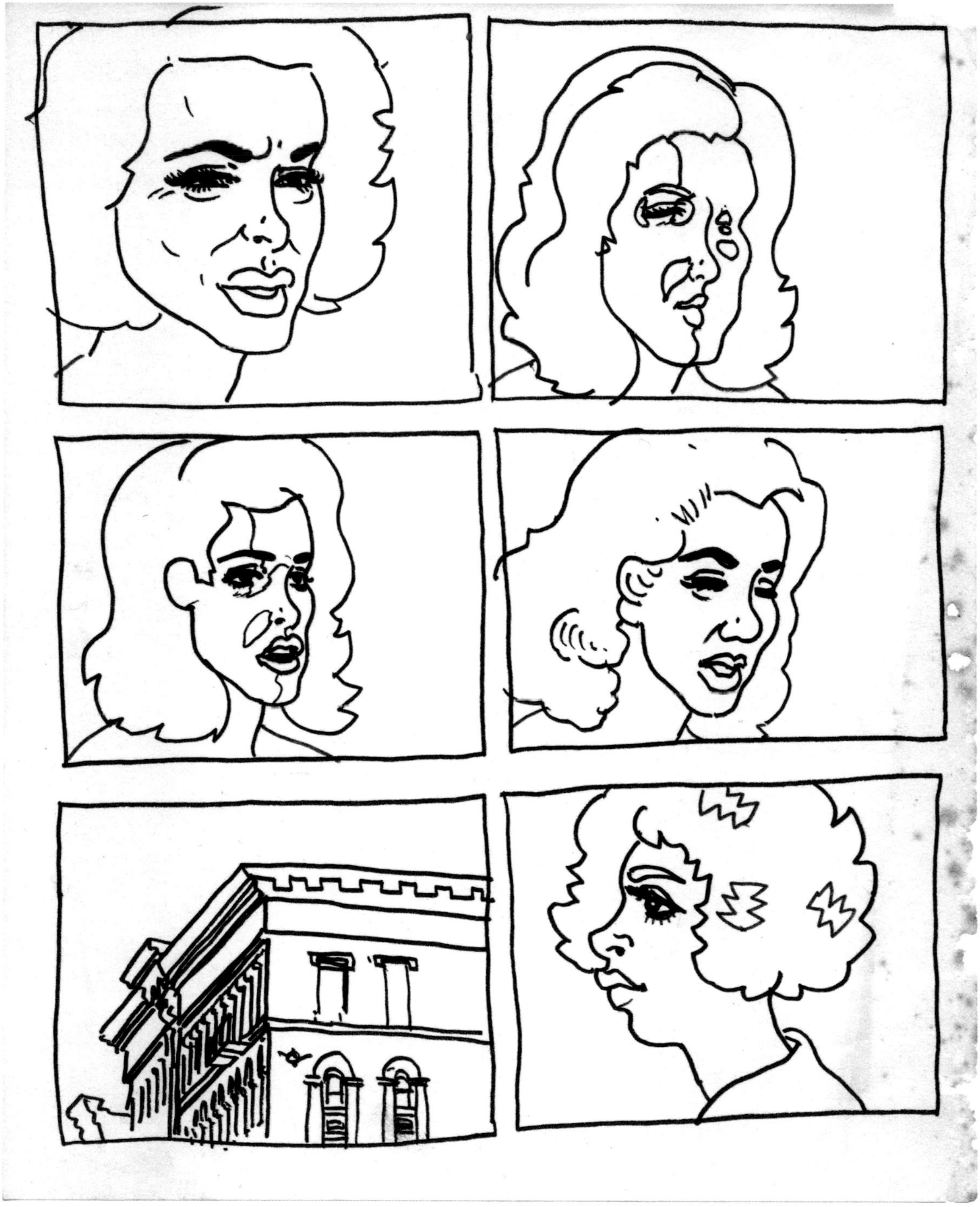

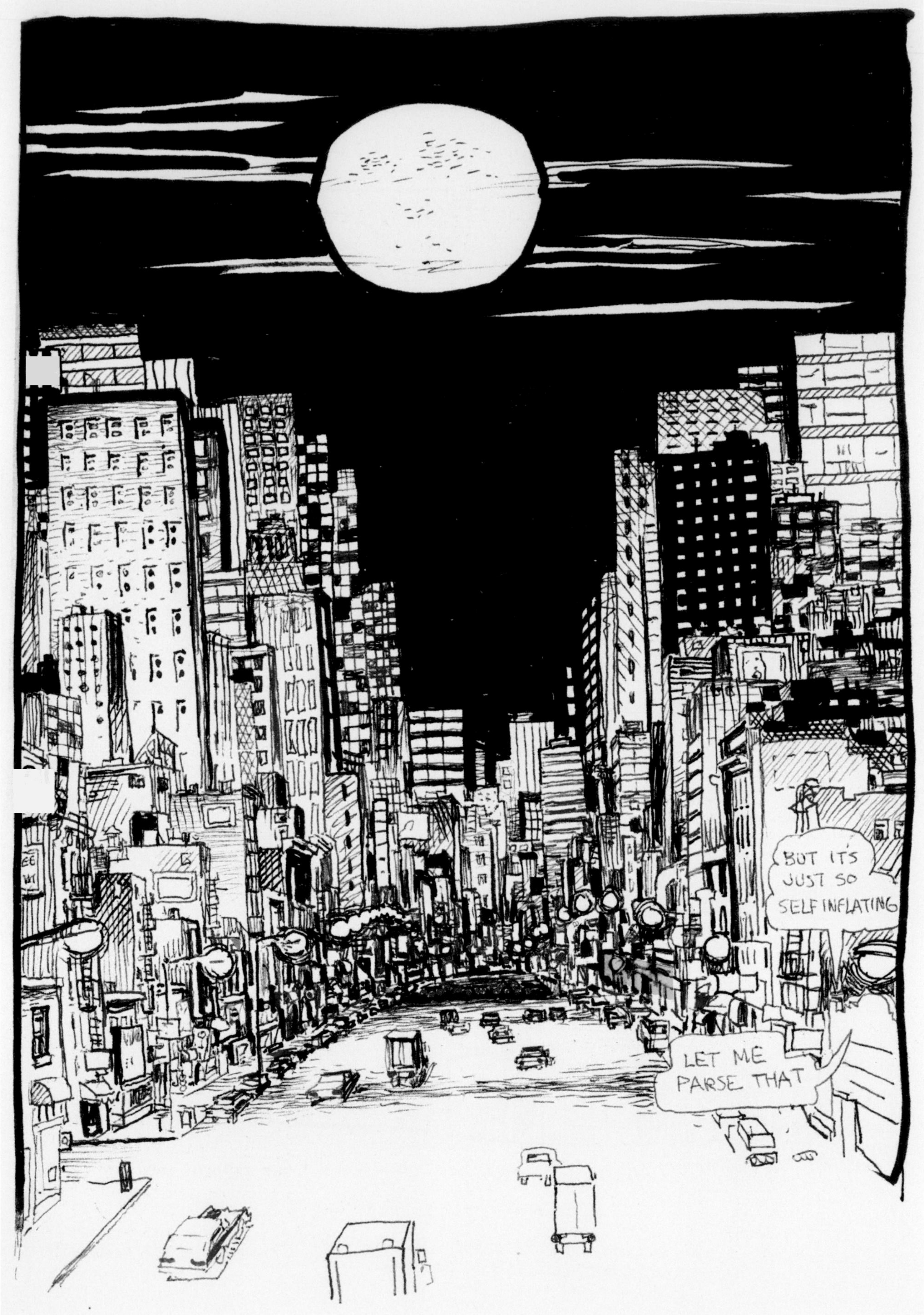
BUT IT'S JUST SO SELF INFLATING
LET ME PARSE THAT

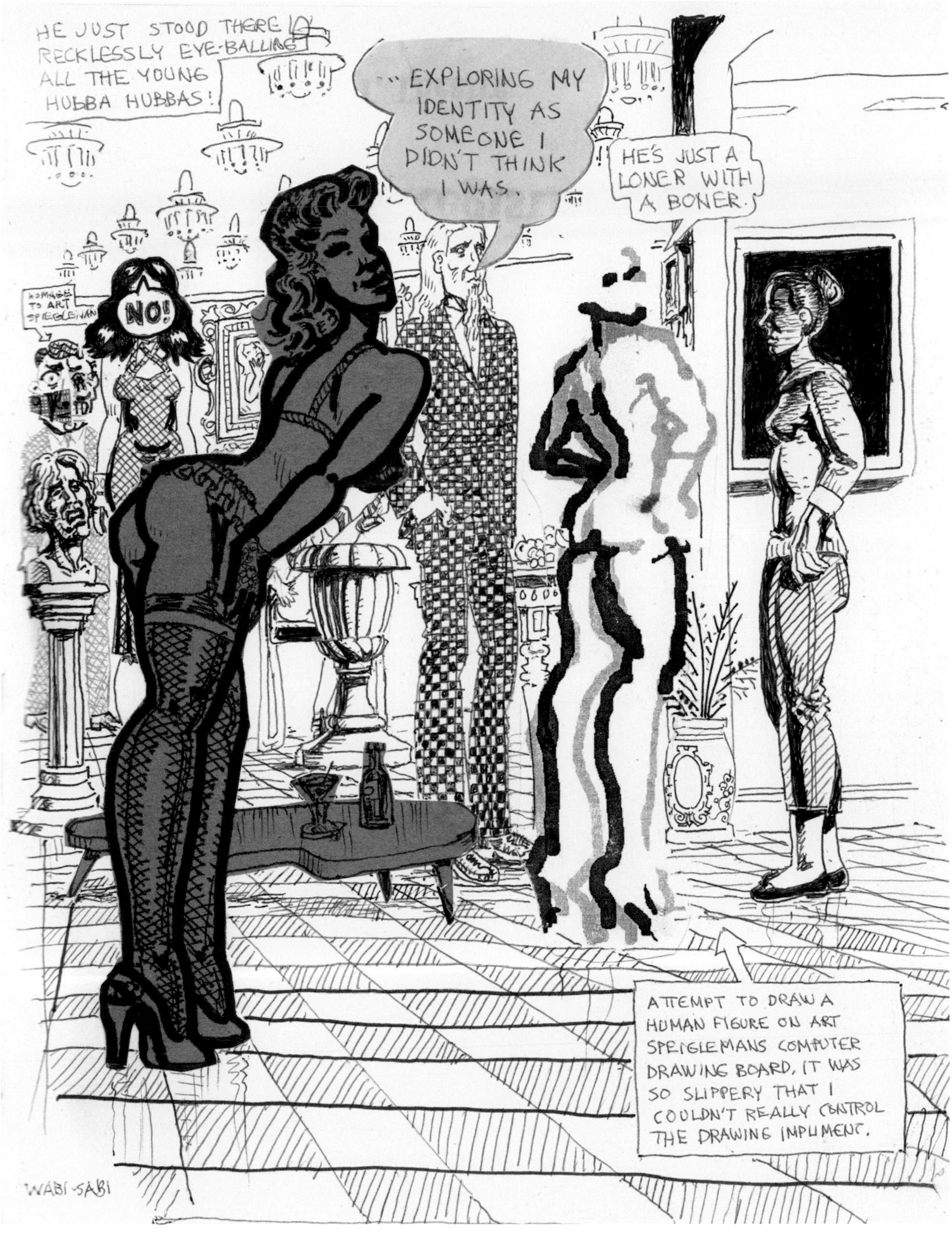
HE JUST STOOD THERE RECKLESSLY EYE-BALLING ALL THE YOUNG HUBBA HUBBAS!
..EXPLORING MY IDENTITY AS SOMEONE I DIDN'T THINK I WAS.
HE'S JUST A LONER WITH A BONER.
HOMAGE TO ART SPEIGLEMAN
NO!
ATTEMPT TO DRAW A HUMAN FIGURE ON ART SPEIGLEMANS COMPUTER DRAWING BOARD, IT WAS SO SLIPPERY THAT I COULDN'T REALLY CONTROL THE DRAWING IMPLIMENT.
WABI-SABI

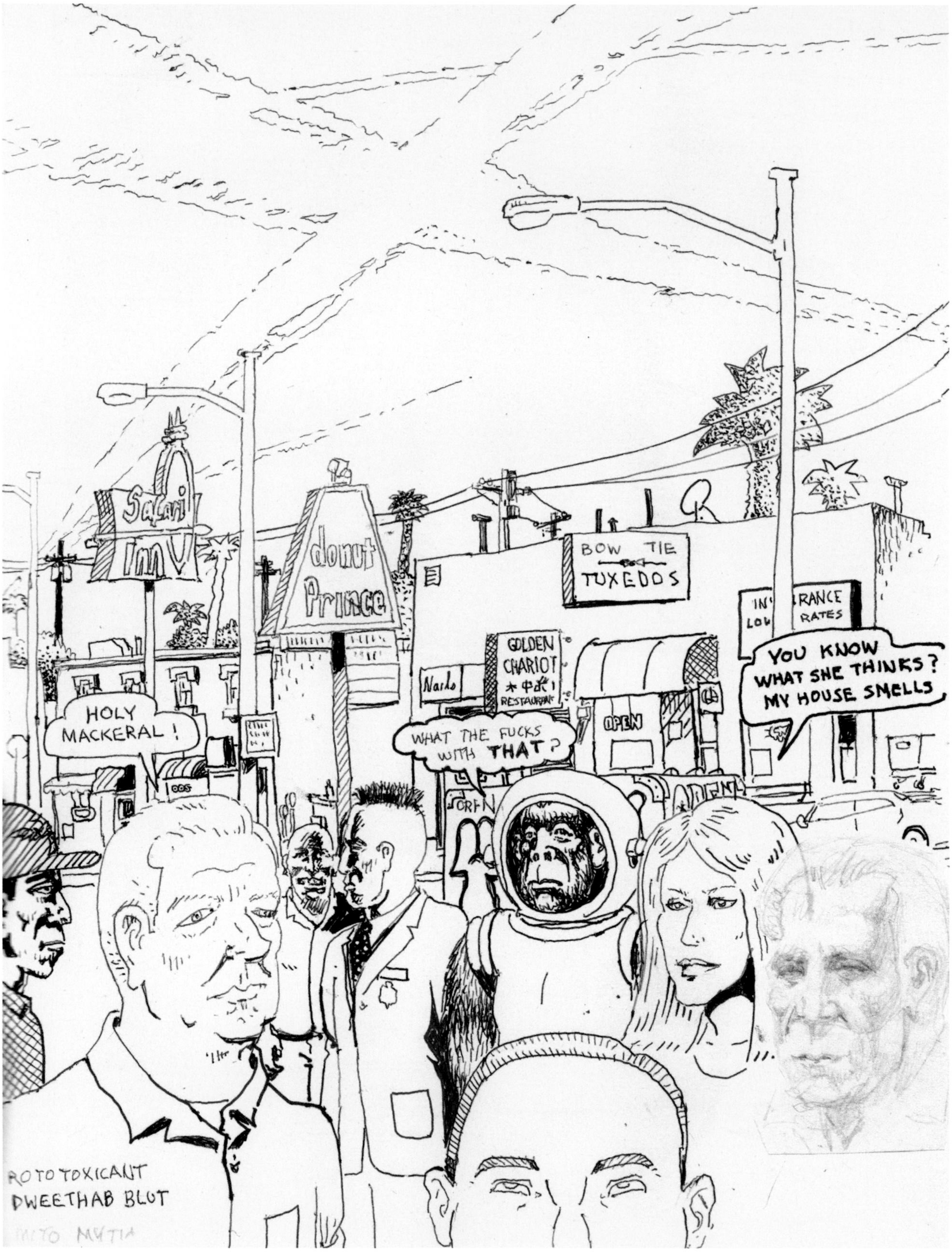

Safari Inn
donut Prince
BOW TIE TUXEDOS
GOLDEN CHARIOT RESTAURANT
OPEN
HOLY MACKERAL !
WHAT THE FUCKS WITH THAT?
YOU KNOW WHAT SHE THINKS? MY HOUSE SMELLS
ROTOTOXICANT
DWEETHAB BLUT

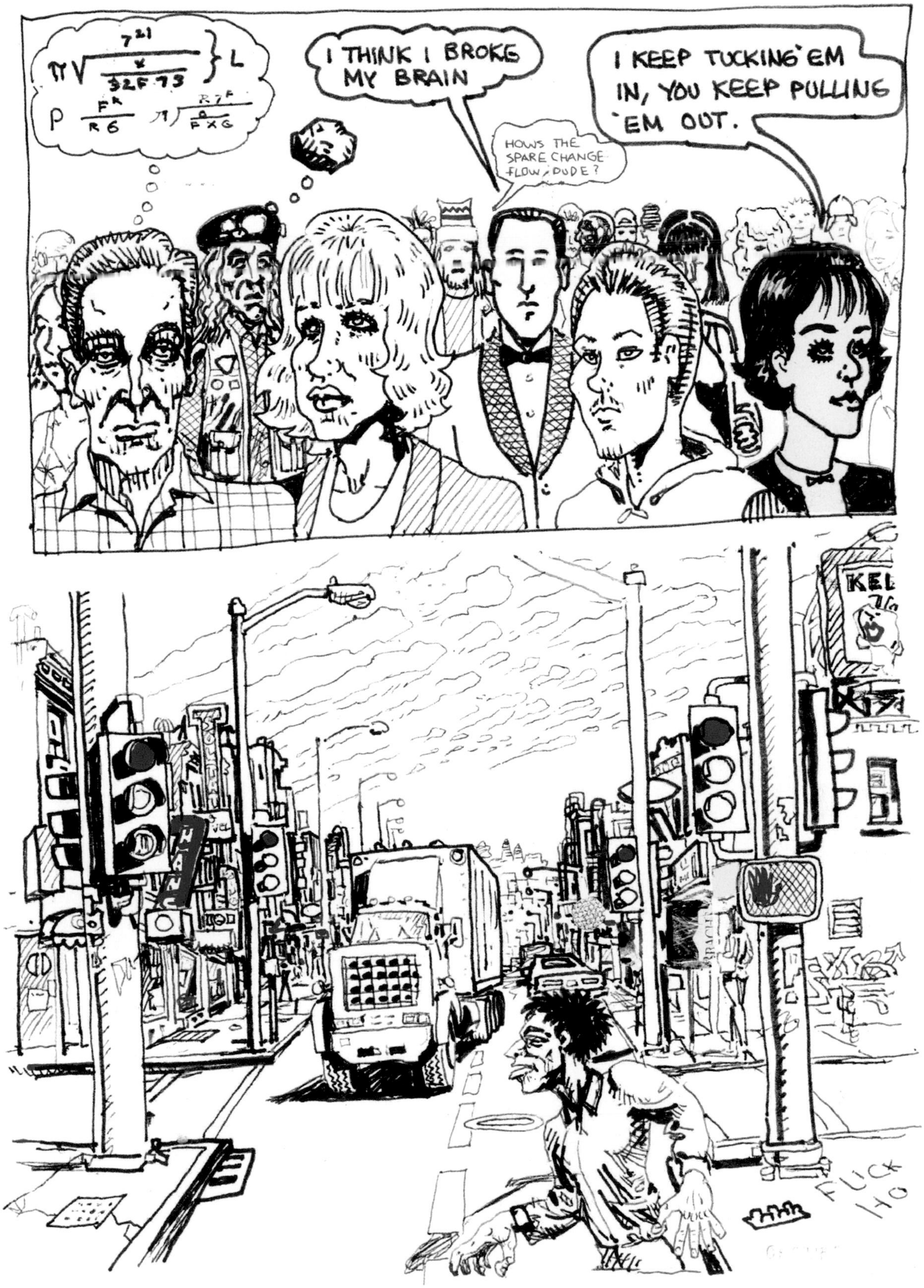
I THINK I BROKE MY BRAIN
HOWS THE SPARE CHANGE FLOW, DUDE?
I KEEP TUCKING 'EM IN, YOU KEEP PULLING 'EM OUT.

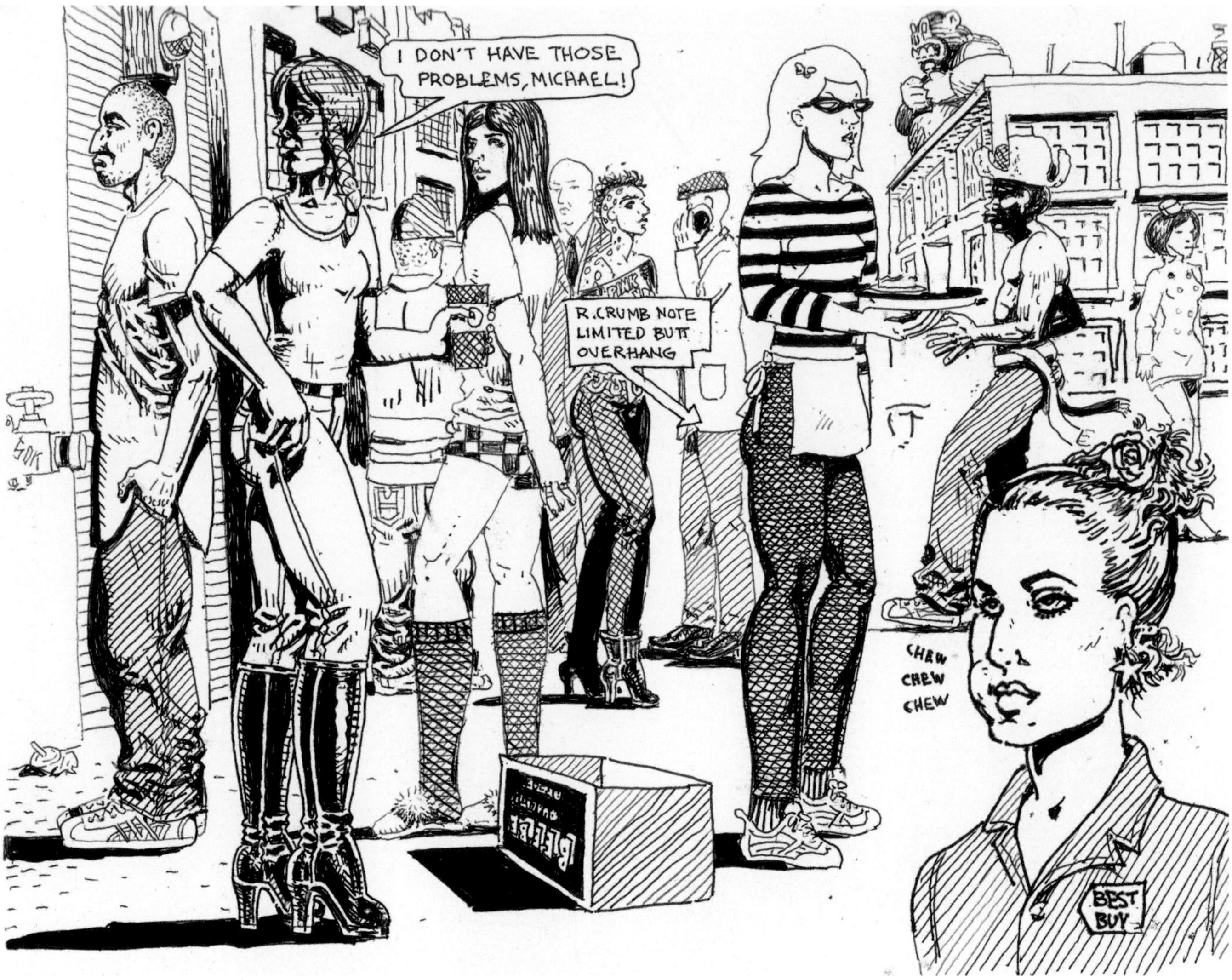
I DON'T HAVE THOSE PROBLEMS, MICHAEL!
R.CRUMB NOTE LIMITED BUTT OVERHANG
CHEW CHEW CHEW
BEST BUY

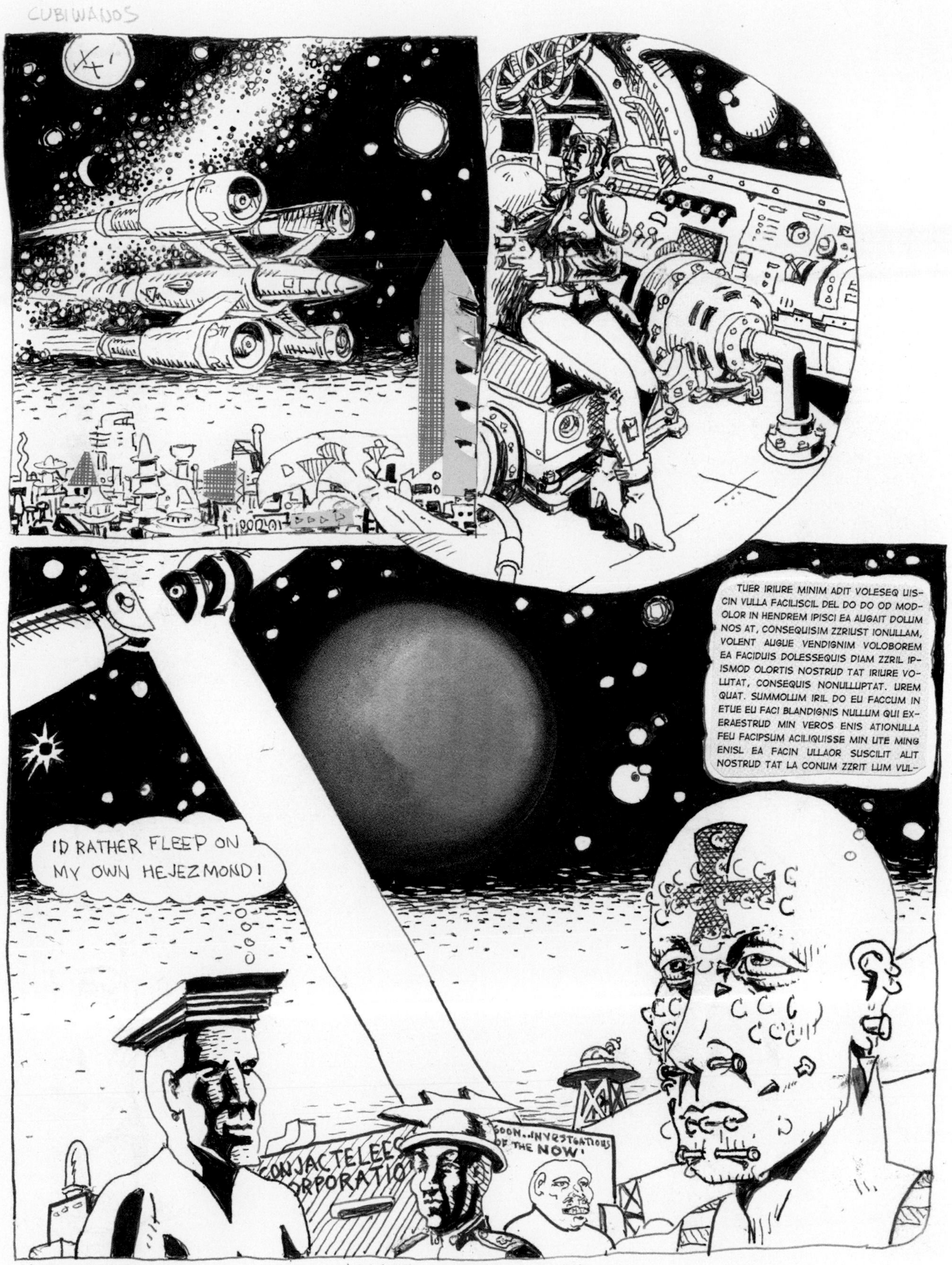
CUBIWANOS
TUER IRIURE MINIM ADIT VOLESEQ UISCIN VULLA FACILISCIL DEL DO DO OD MODOLOR IN HENDREM IPISCI EA AUGAIT DOLUM NOS AT, CONSEQUISIM ZZRIUST IONULLAM, VOLENT AUGUE VENDIGNIM VOLOBOREM EA FACIDUIS DOLESSEQUIS DIAM ZZRIL IPISMOD OLORTIS NOSTRUD TAT IRIURE VOLUTAT, CONSEQUIS NONULLUPTAT. UREM QUAT. SUMMOLUM IRIL DO EU FACCUM IN ETUE EU FACI BLANDIGNIS NULLUM QUI EXERAESTRUD MIN VEROS ENIS ATIONULLA FEU FACIPSUM ACILIQUISSE MIN UTE MING ENISL EA FACIN ULLAOR SUSCILIT ALIT NOSTRUD TAT LA CONUM ZZRIT LUM VUL-
ID RATHER FLEEP ON MY OWN HEJEZMOND!
SOON.. INVESTIGATIONS OF THE NOW!
NEATHBAUM FATAK HYMAN JAPLOOTI ADRIAN GOOLAN

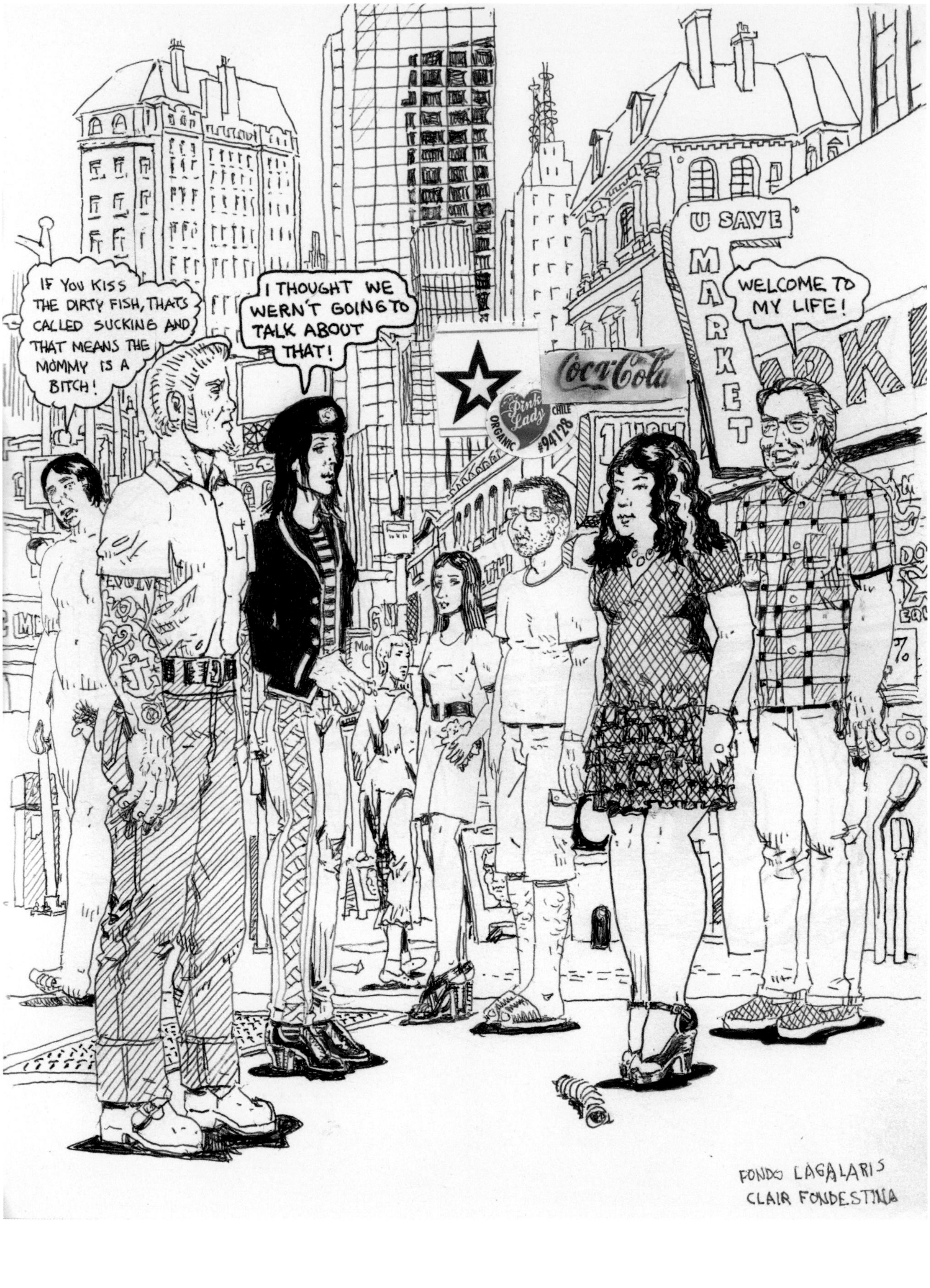
IF YOU KISS THE DIRTY FISH, THAT'S CALLED SUCKING AND THAT MEANS THE MOMMY IS A BITCH!
I THOUGHT WE WERN'T GOING TO TALK ABOUT THAT!
WELCOME TO MY LIFE!
U SAVE
MARKET
Coca-Cola
Pink Lady
ORGANIC
CHILE
#94128
FONDO LAGALARIS
CLAIR FONDESTINA

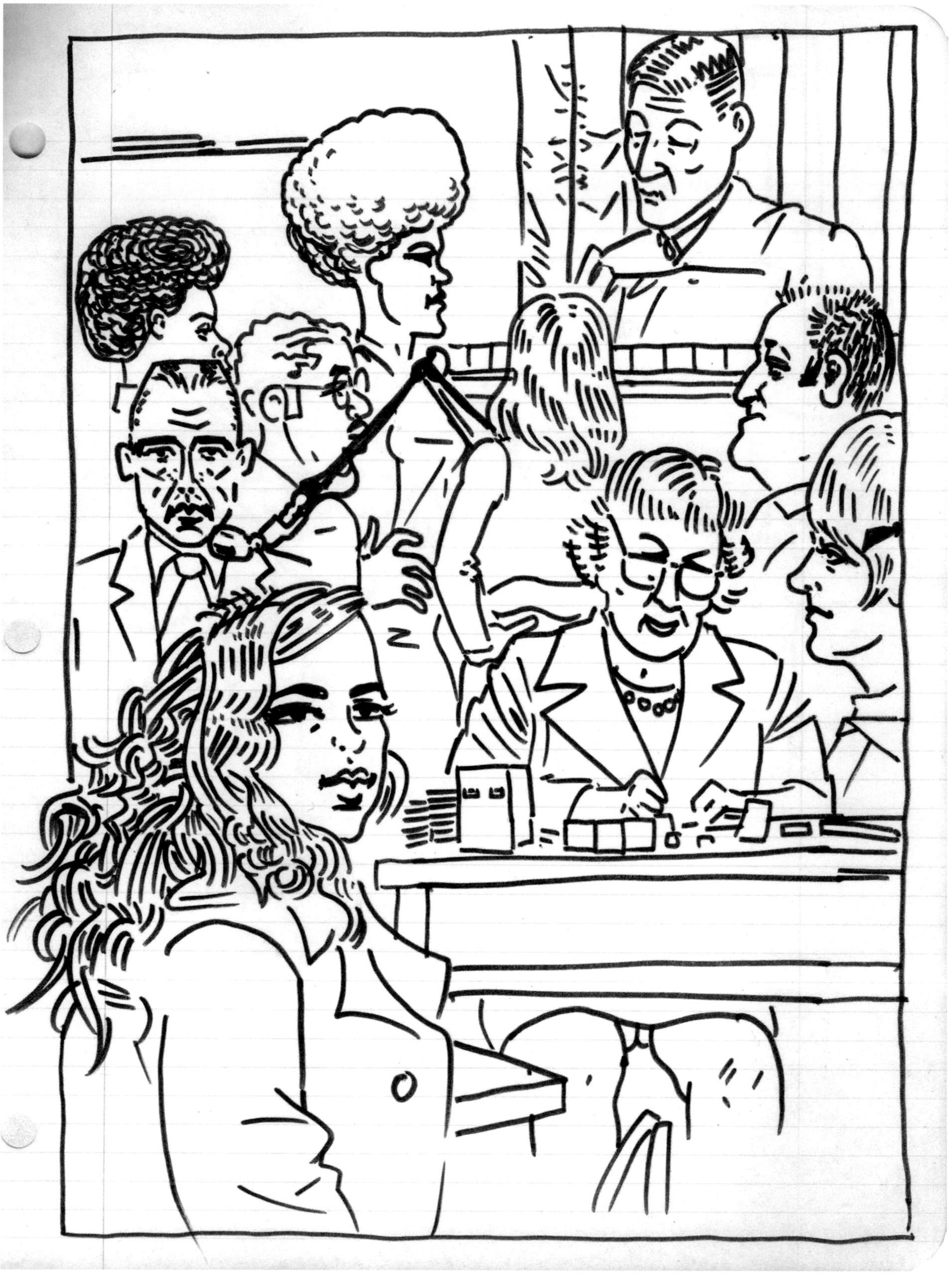

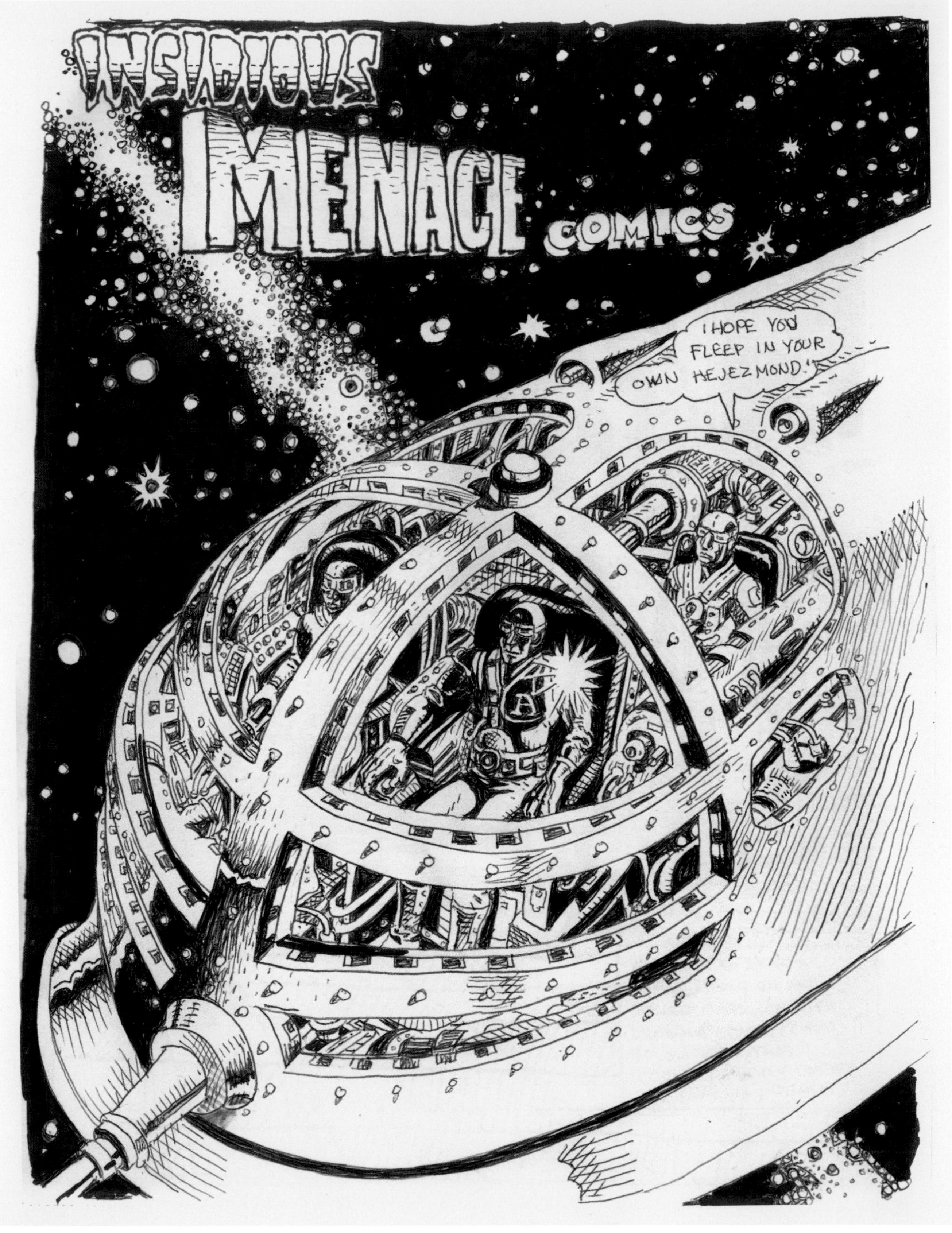
INSIDIOUS
MENACE COMICS
I HOPE YOU FLEEP IN YOUR OWN HEJEZMOND!

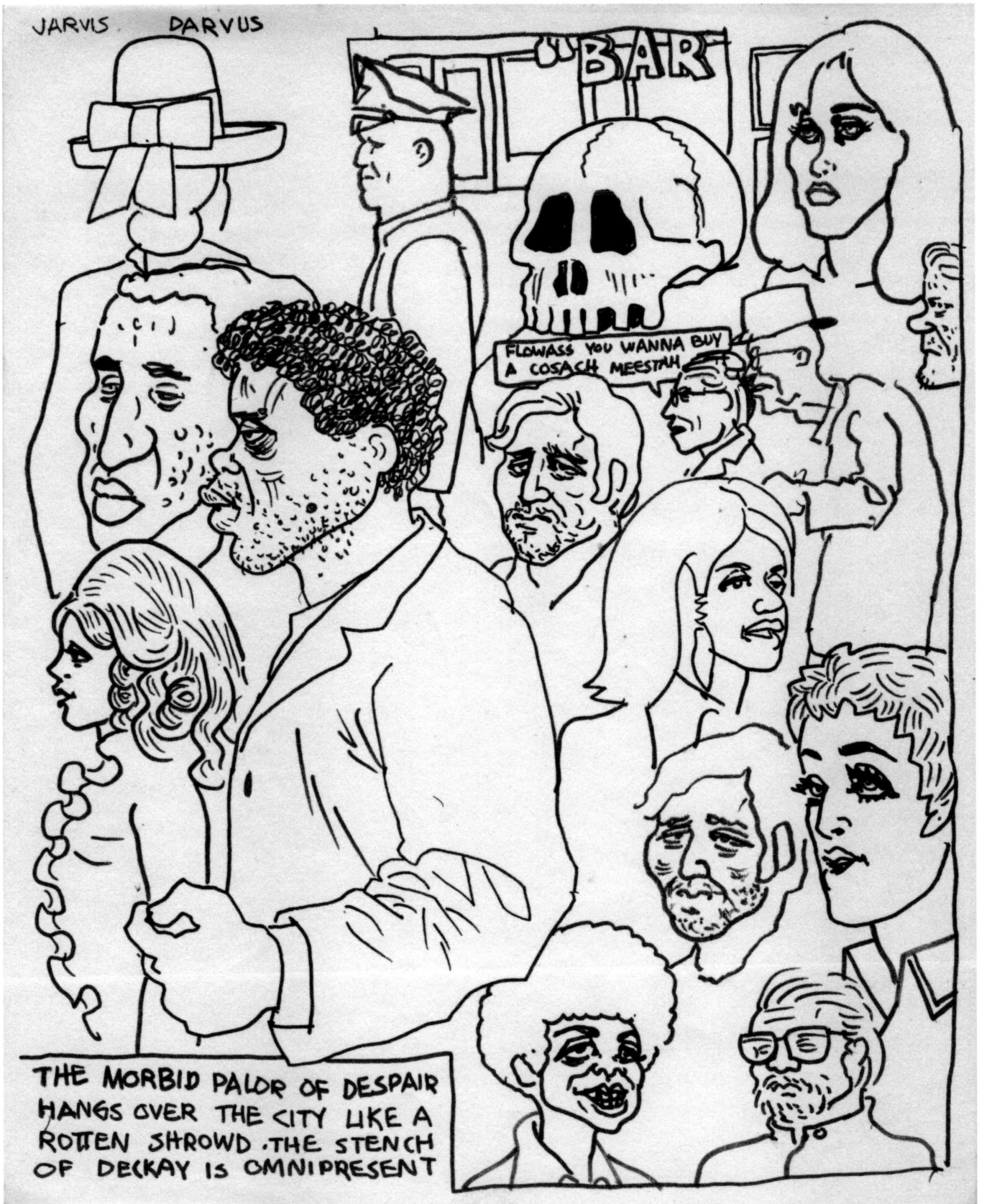
JARVIS DARVUS
BAR
FLOWASS YOU WANNA BUY A COSACH MEESTAH
THE MORBID PALOR OF DESPAIR HANGS OVER THE CITY LIKE A ROTTEN SHROWD. THE STENCH OF DECKAY IS OMNIPRESENT

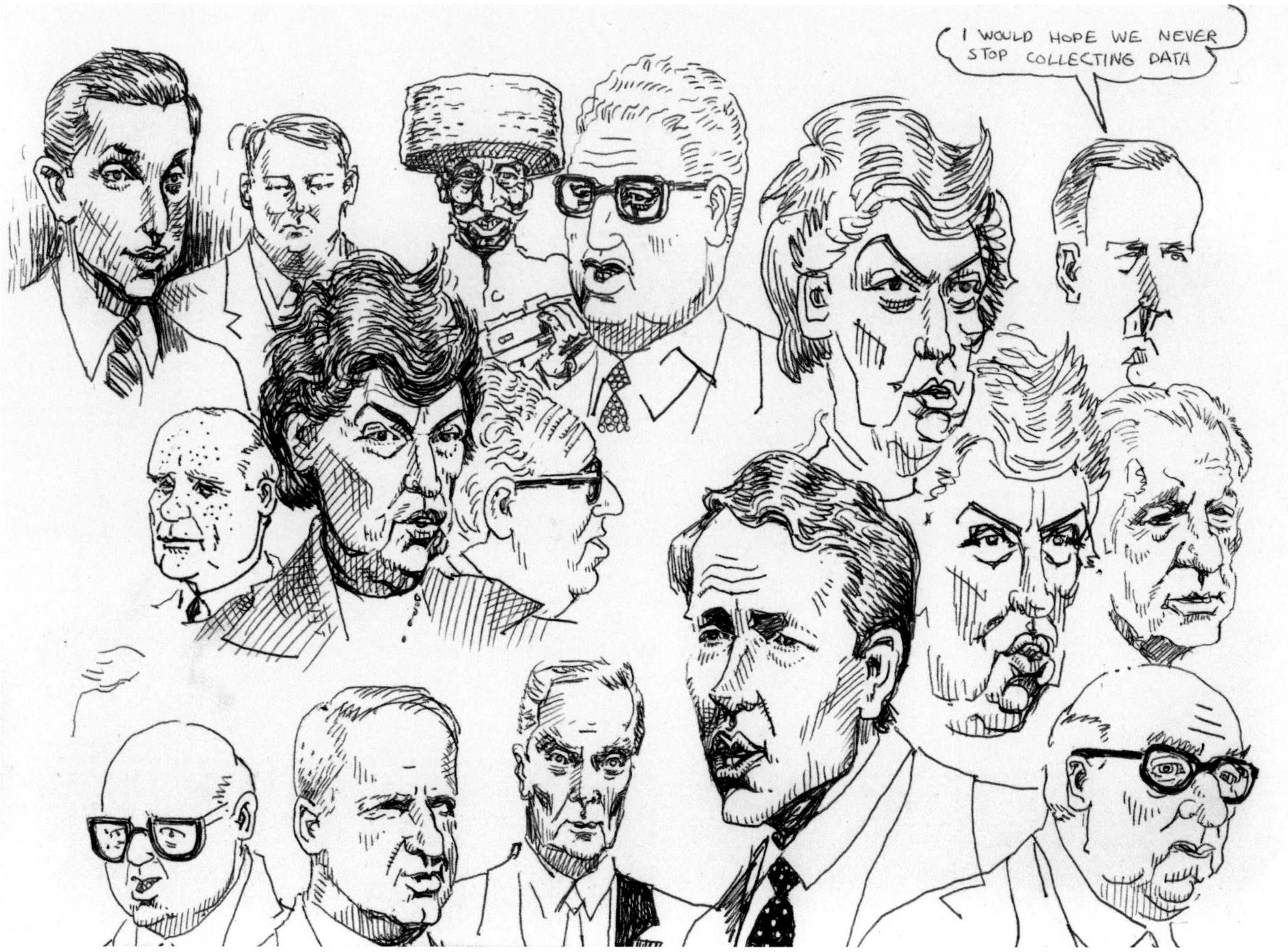
I WOULD HOPE WE NEVER STOP COLLECTING DATA

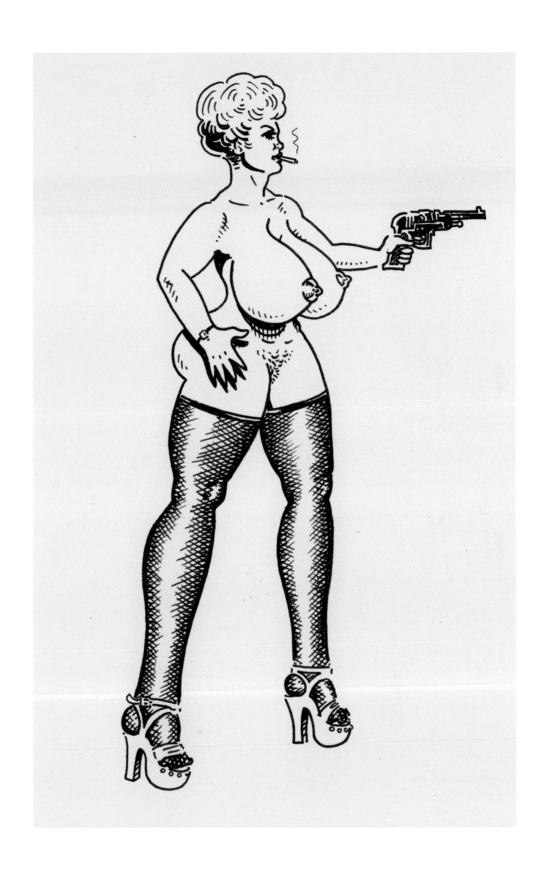

LENINGRAD

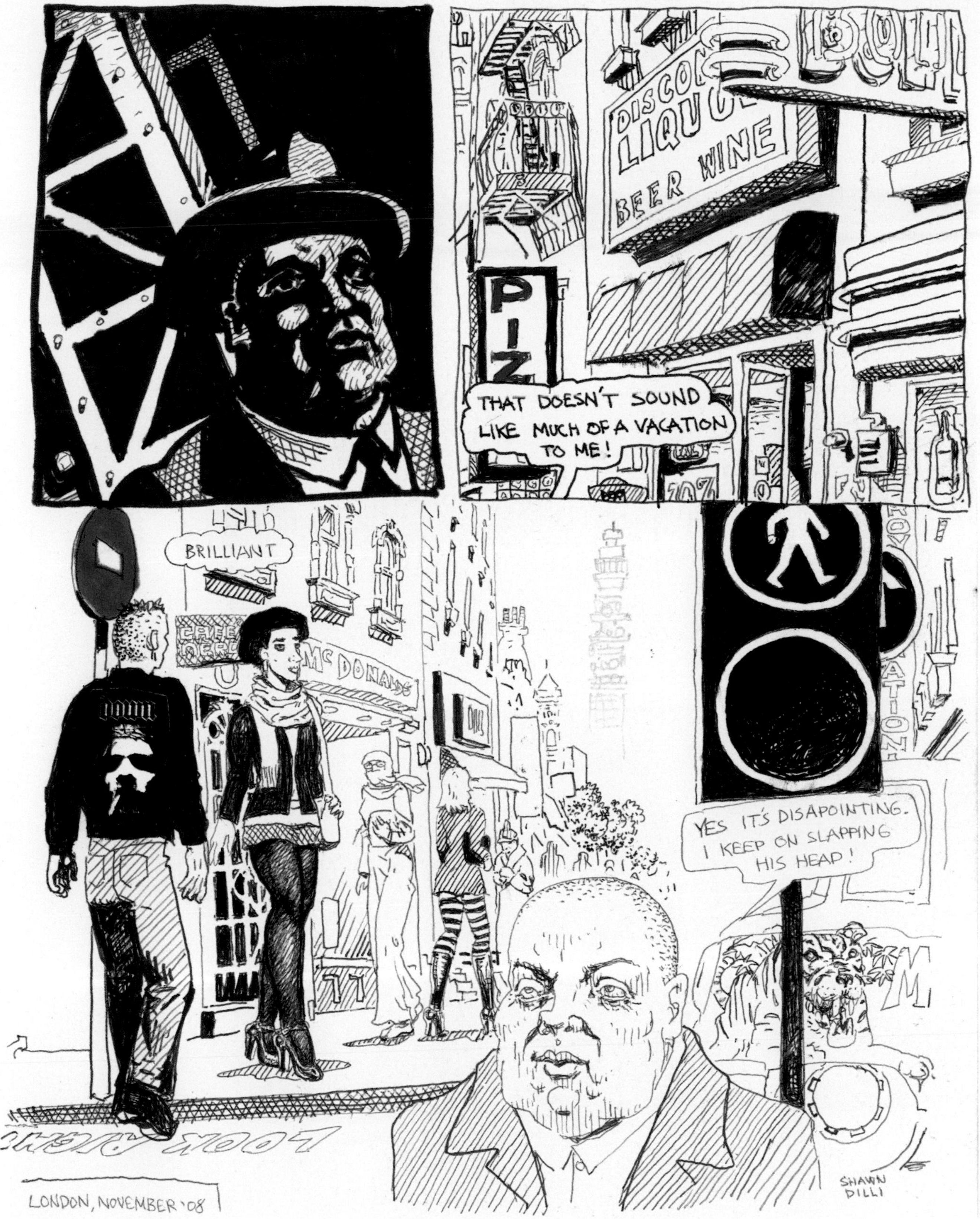

THAT DOESN'T SOUND LIKE MUCH OF A VACATION TO ME!
BRILLIANT
YES IT'S DISAPOINTING. I KEEP ON SLAPPING HIS HEAD!
LONDON, NOVEMBER '08
SHAWN DILLI

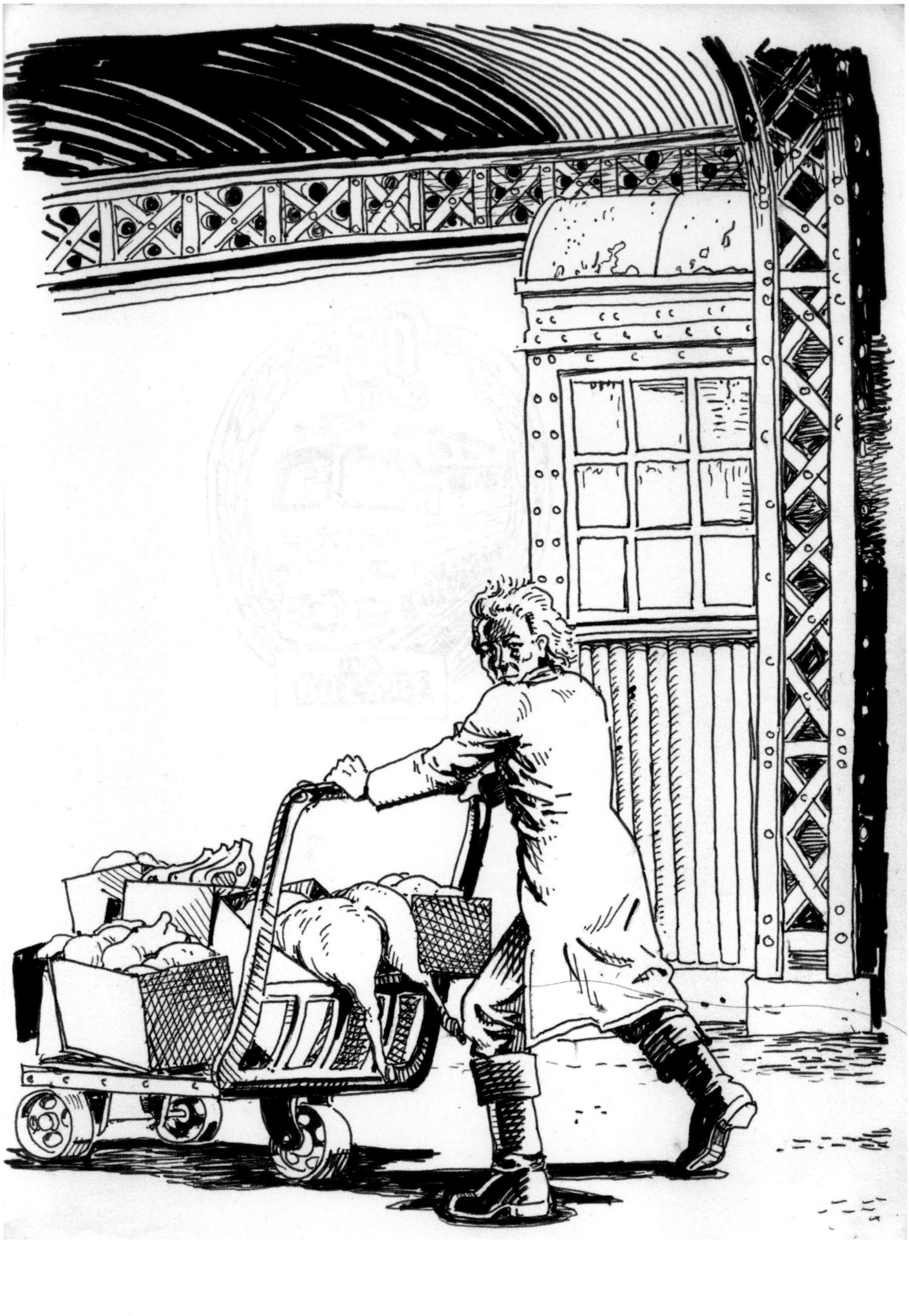

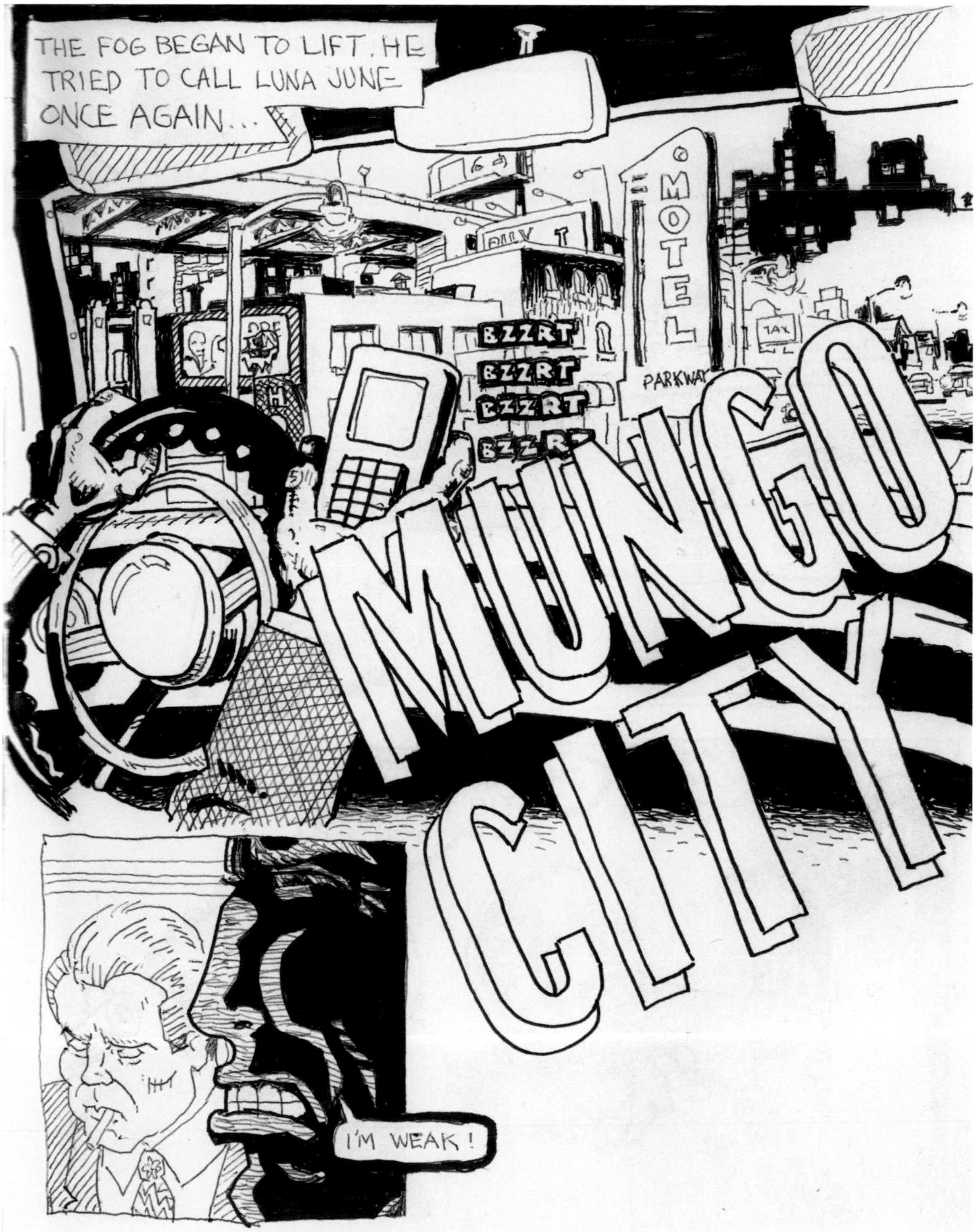
THE FOG BEGAN TO LIFT. HE TRIED TO CALL LUNA JUNE ONCE AGAIN...
MOTEL
PARKWAY
BZZRT
BZZRT
BZZRT
MUNGO CITY
I'M WEAK!

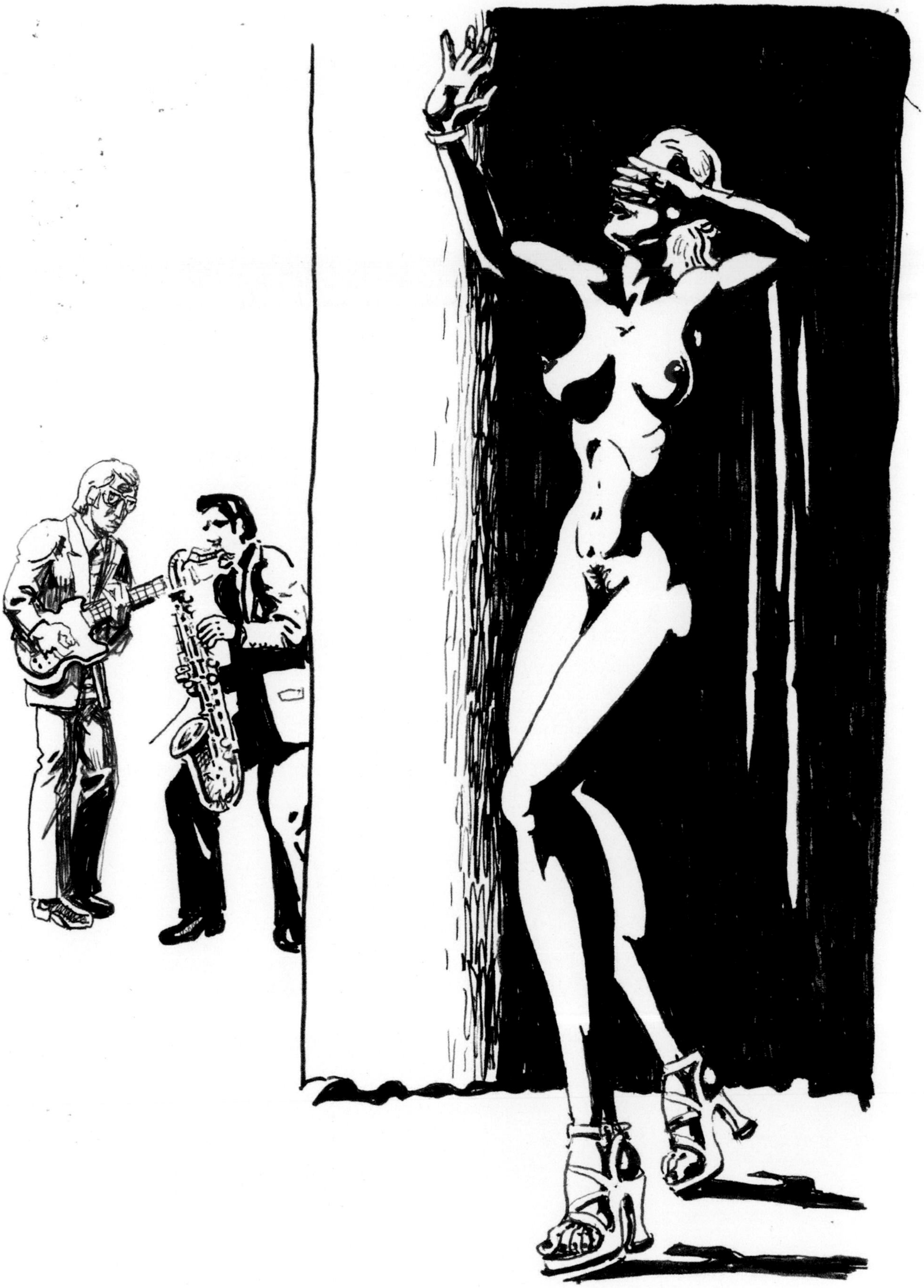

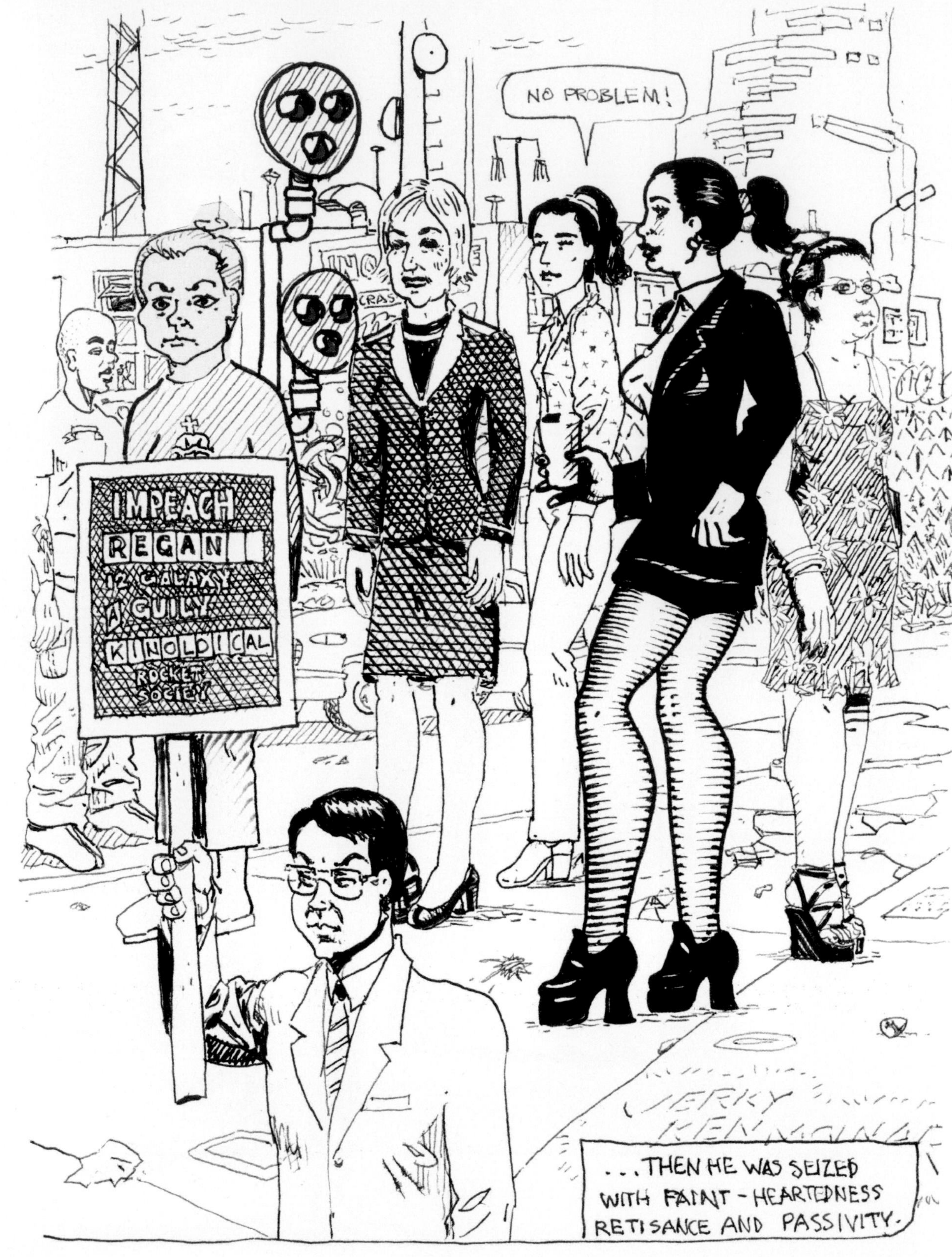
NO PROBLEM!
IMPEACH REGAN 12 GALAXY A GUILY KINOLDICAL ROCKET SOCIETY
...THEN HE WAS SEIZED WITH FAINT-HEARTEDNESS RETISANCE AND PASSIVITY.

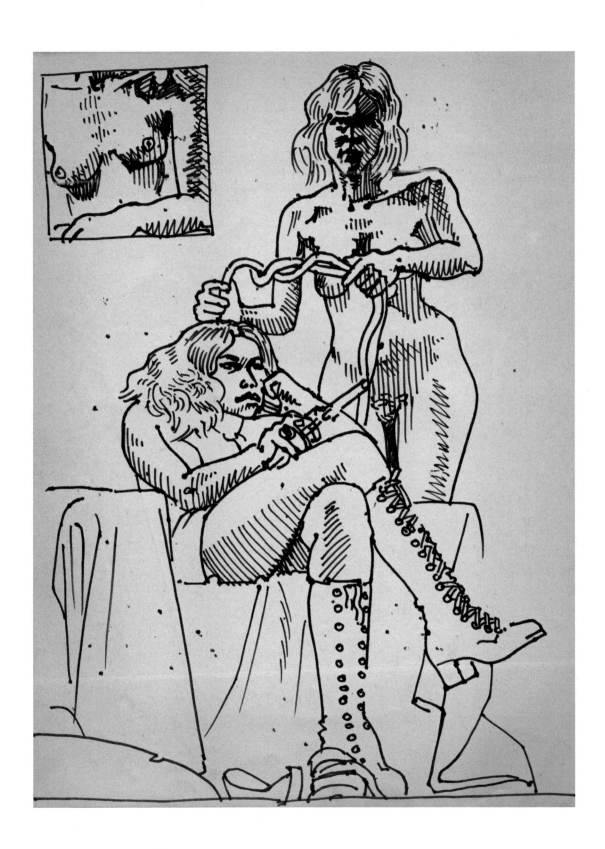

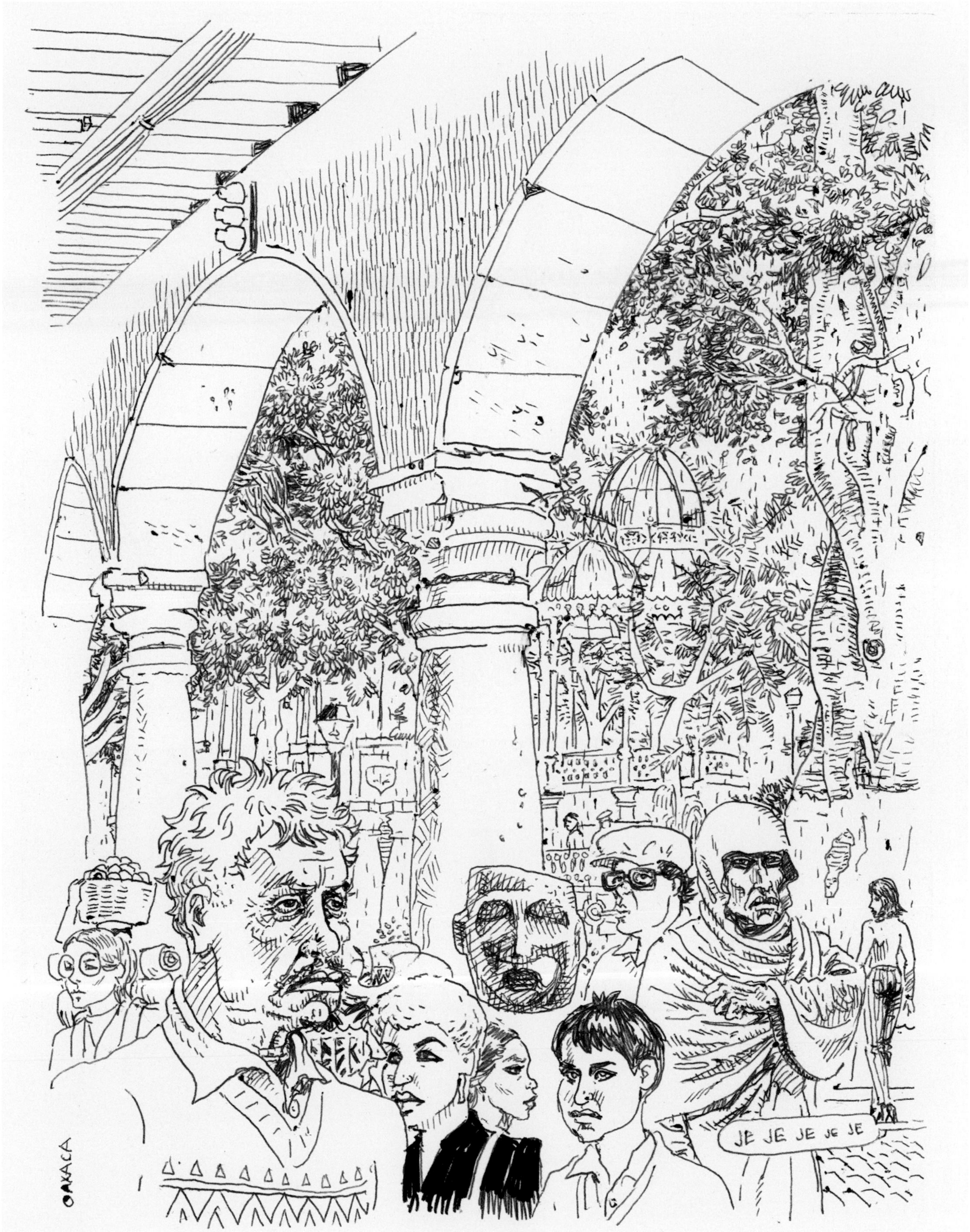
OAXACA
JE JE JE JE JE

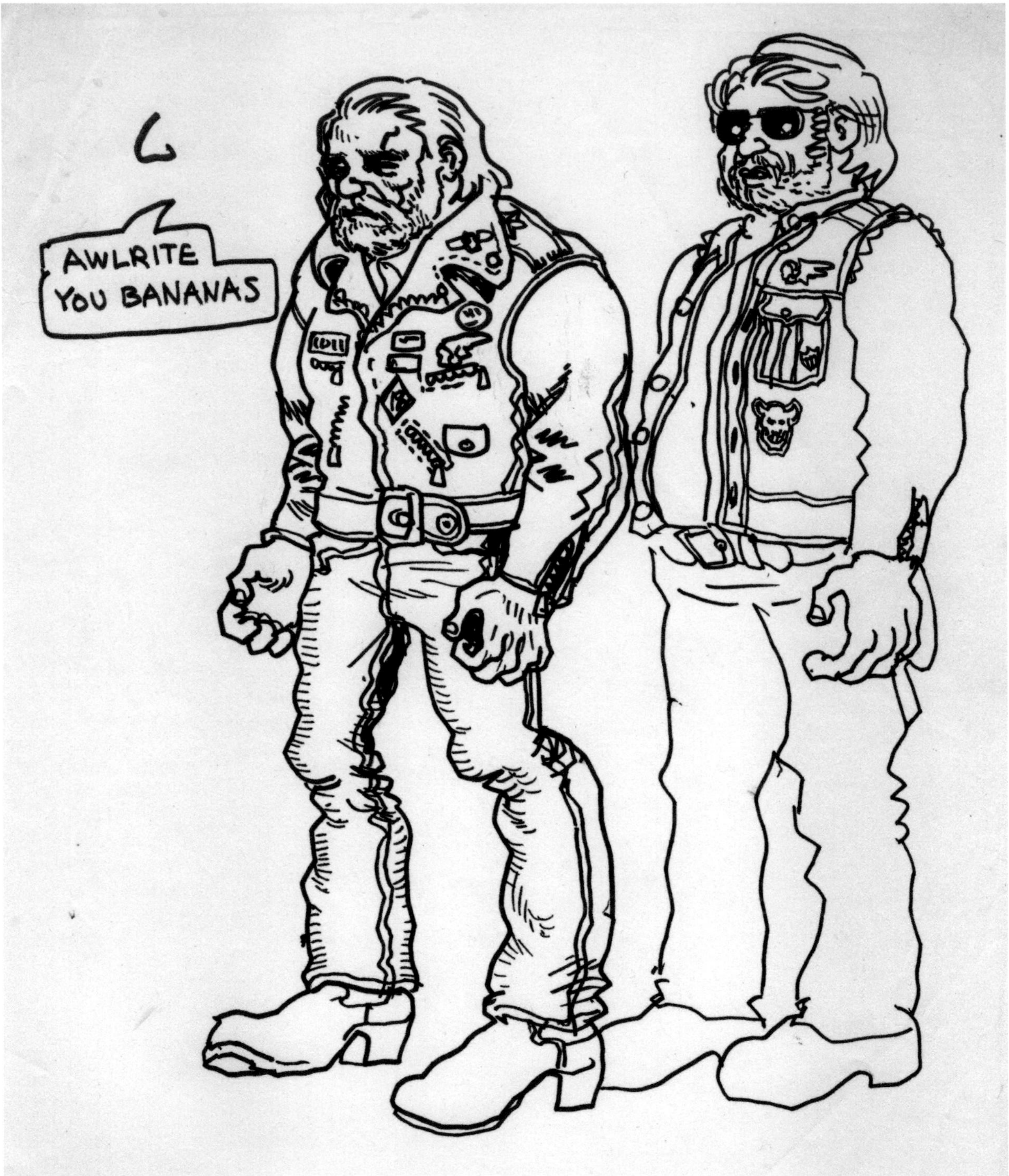
AWLRITE YOU BANANAS

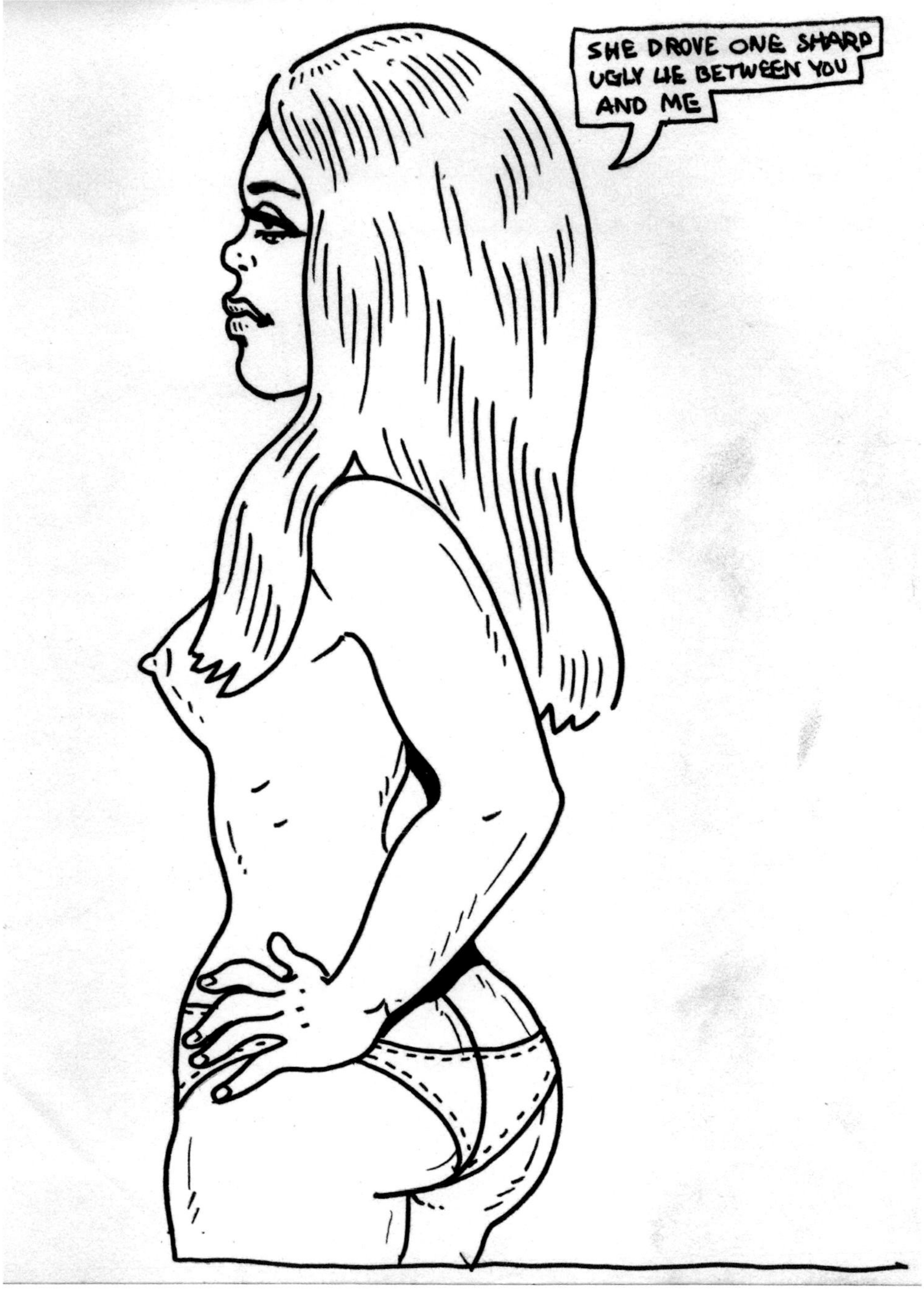
SHE DROVE ONE SHARD UGLY LIE BETWEEN YOU AND ME

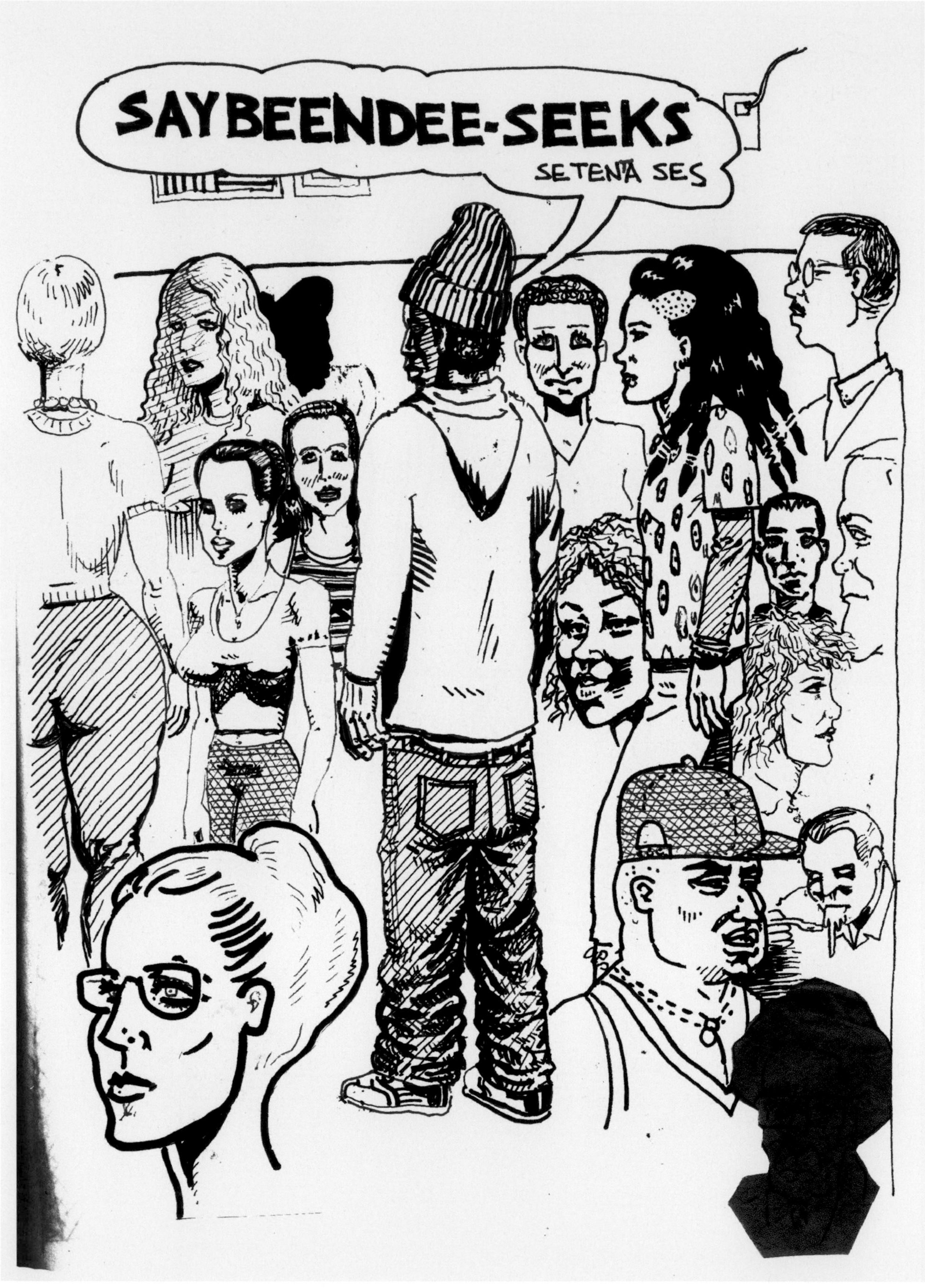
SAYBEENDEE-SEEKS
SETENTA SES

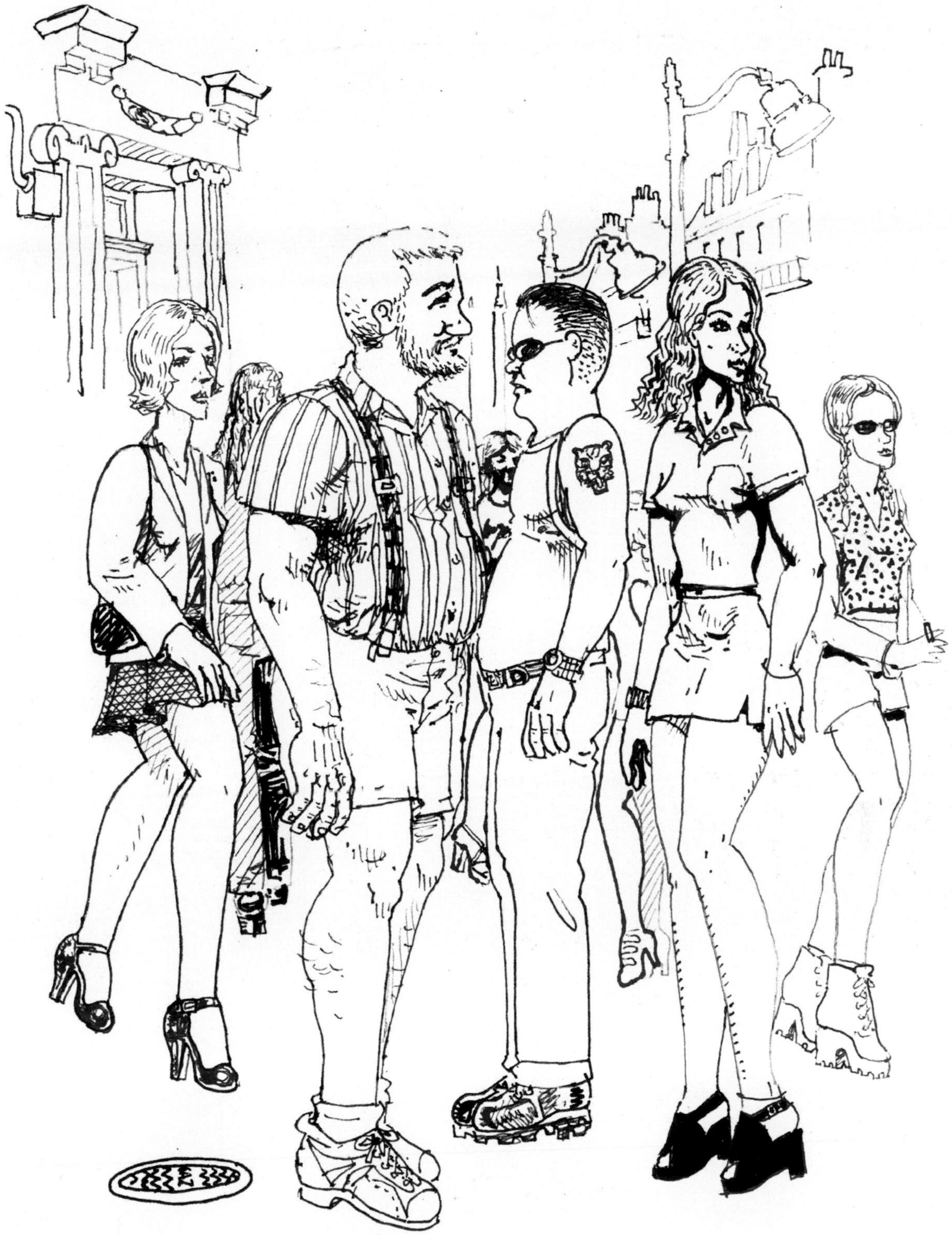

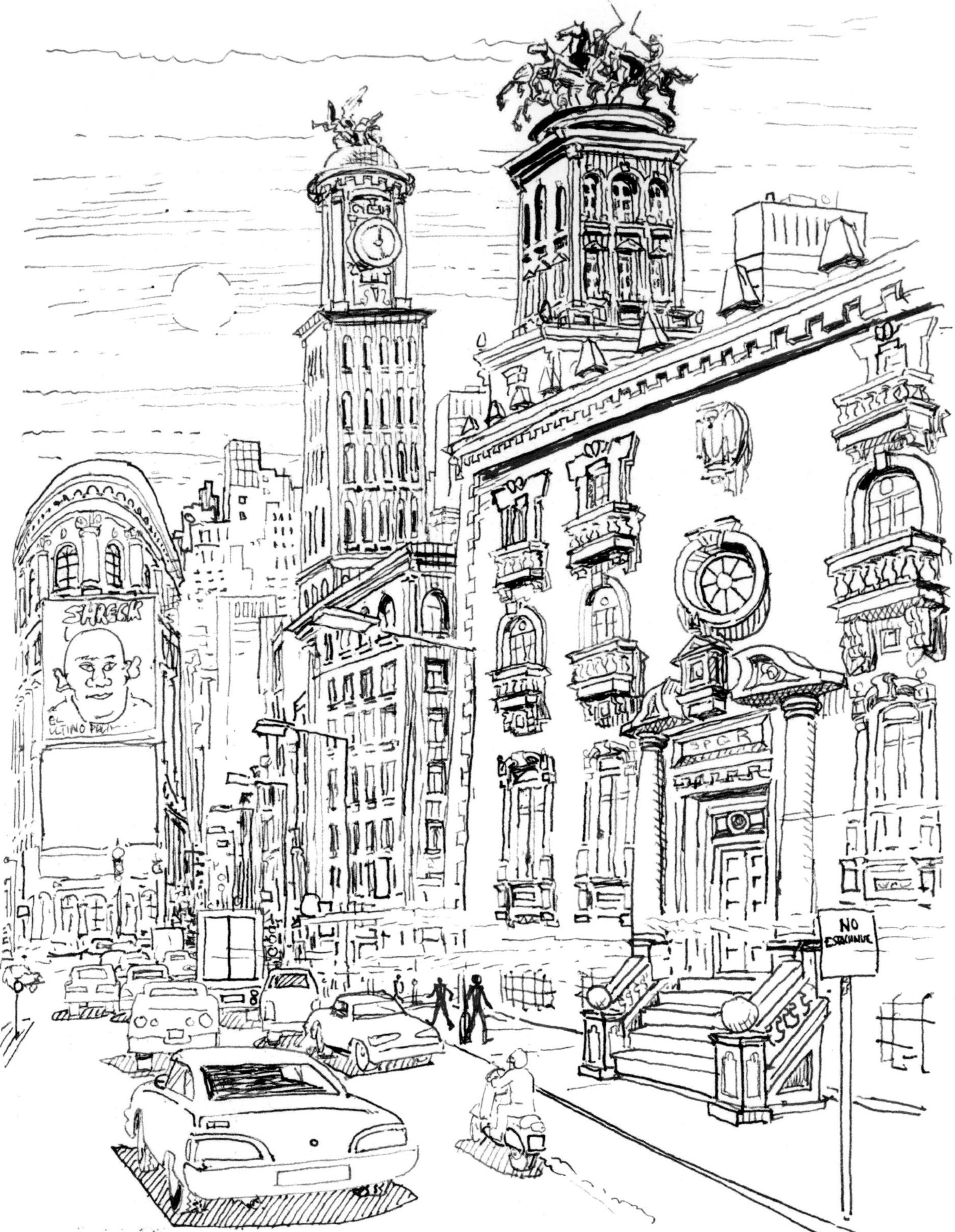
SHRESK
NO

MADRID

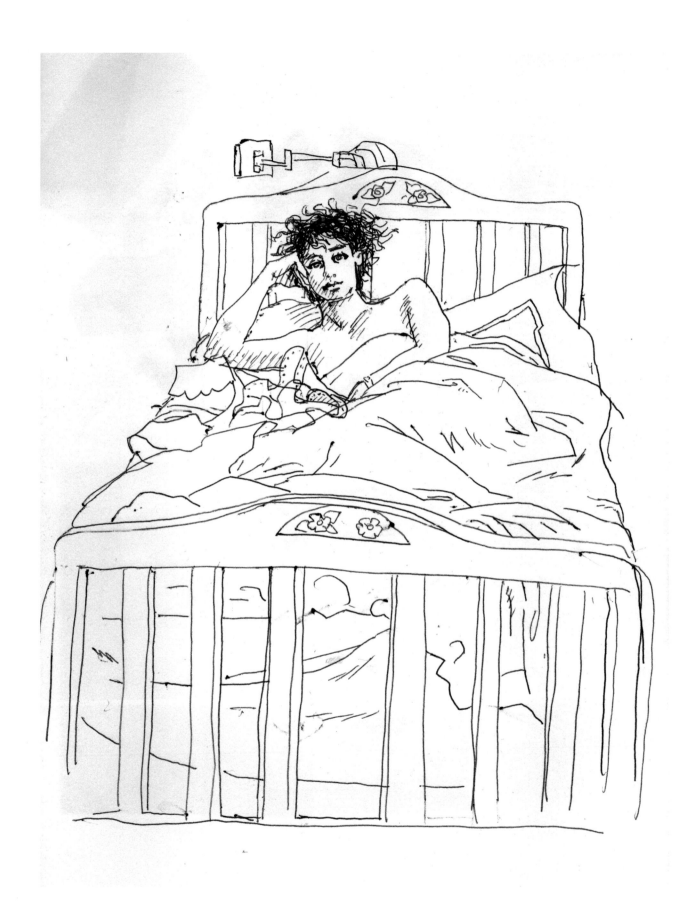

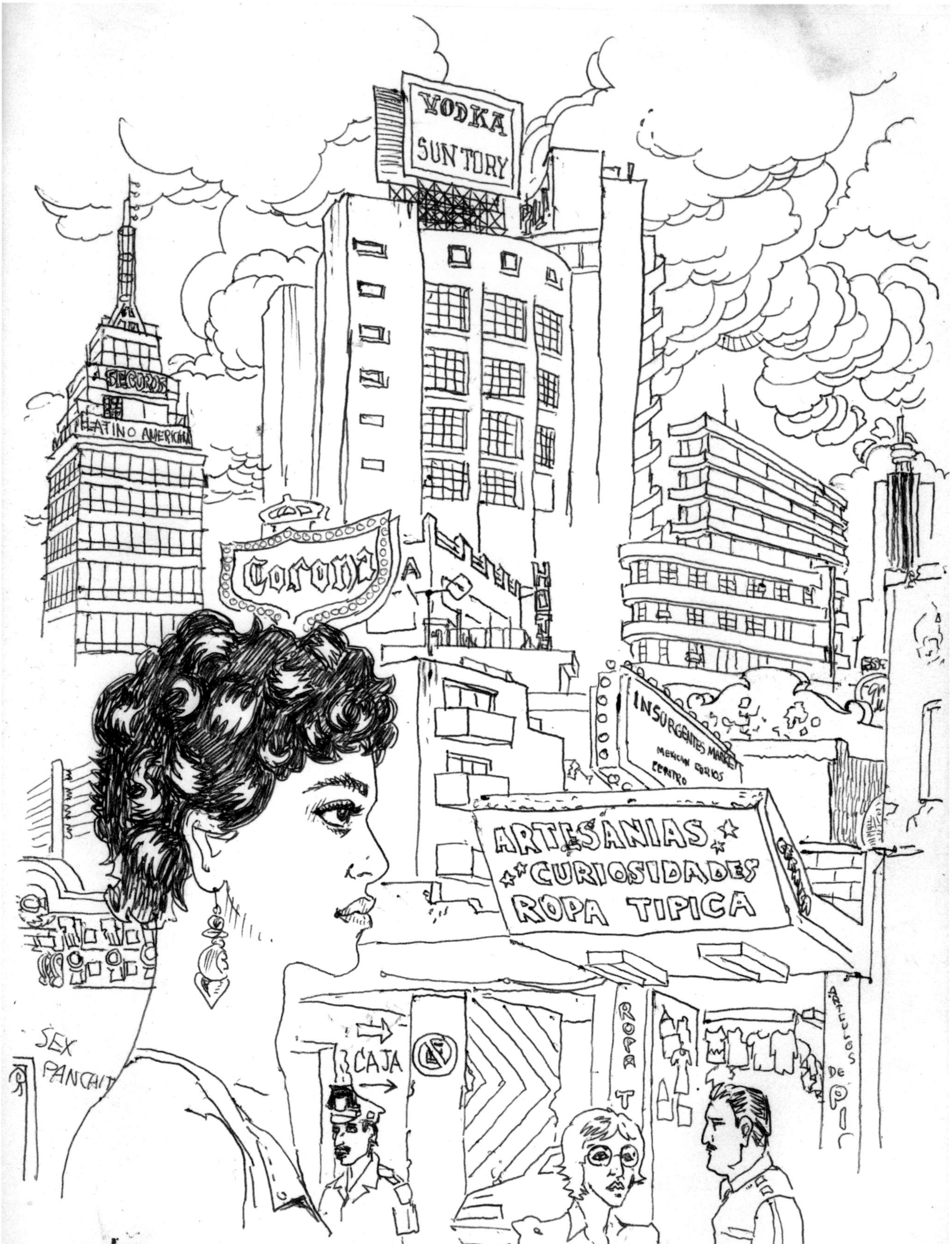
VODKA
SUNTORY
SEGUROS
LATINO AMERICANA
Corona
INSURGENTES MARKET
MEXICAN CURIOS
CENTRO
ARTESANIAS
CURIOSIDADES
ROPA TIPICA
CAJA
SEX
ROPA

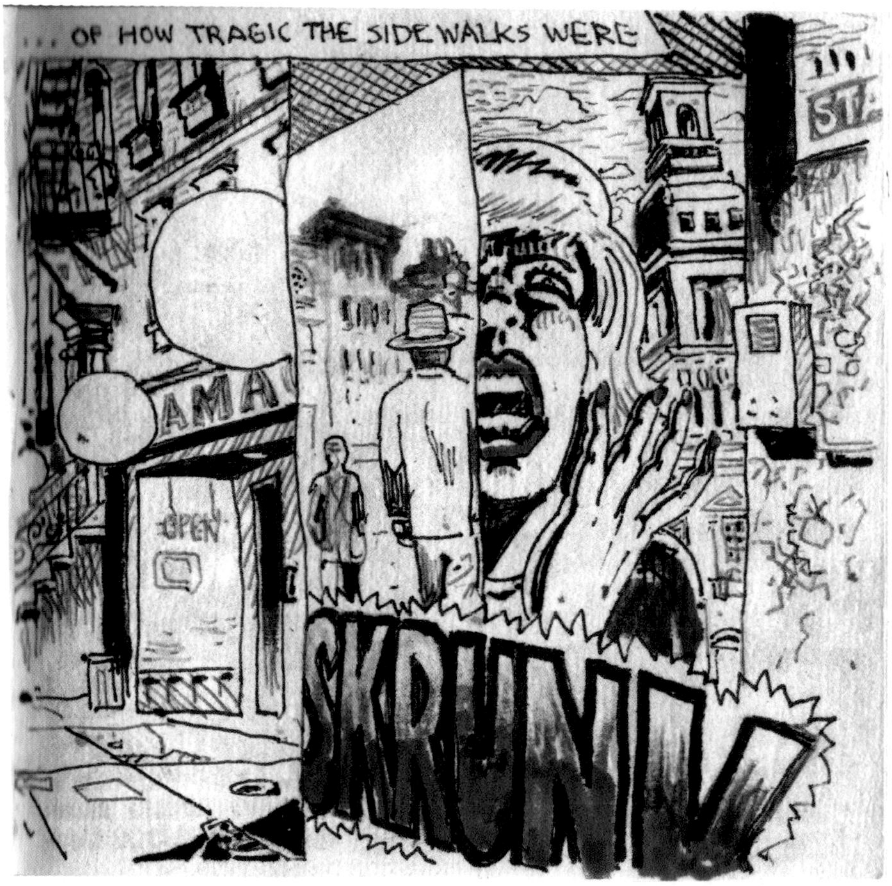
... OF HOW TRAGIC THE SIDEWALKS WERE
AMA
OPEN
SKRUNK

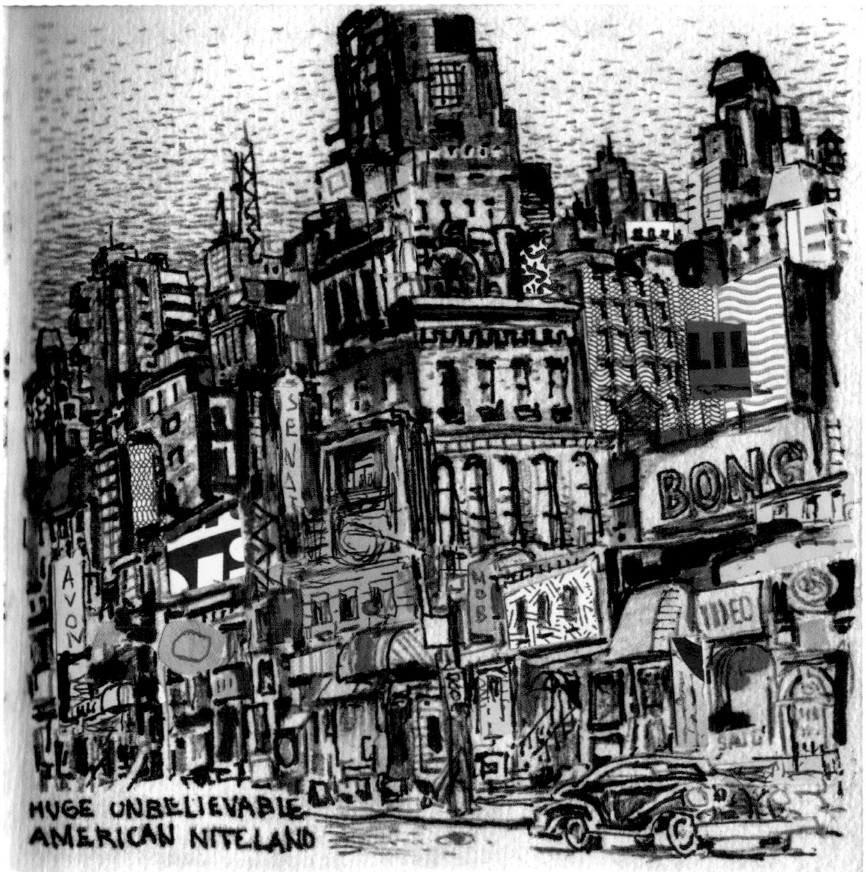
BONG
AVON
HUGE UNBELIEVABLE
AMERICAN NITELAND

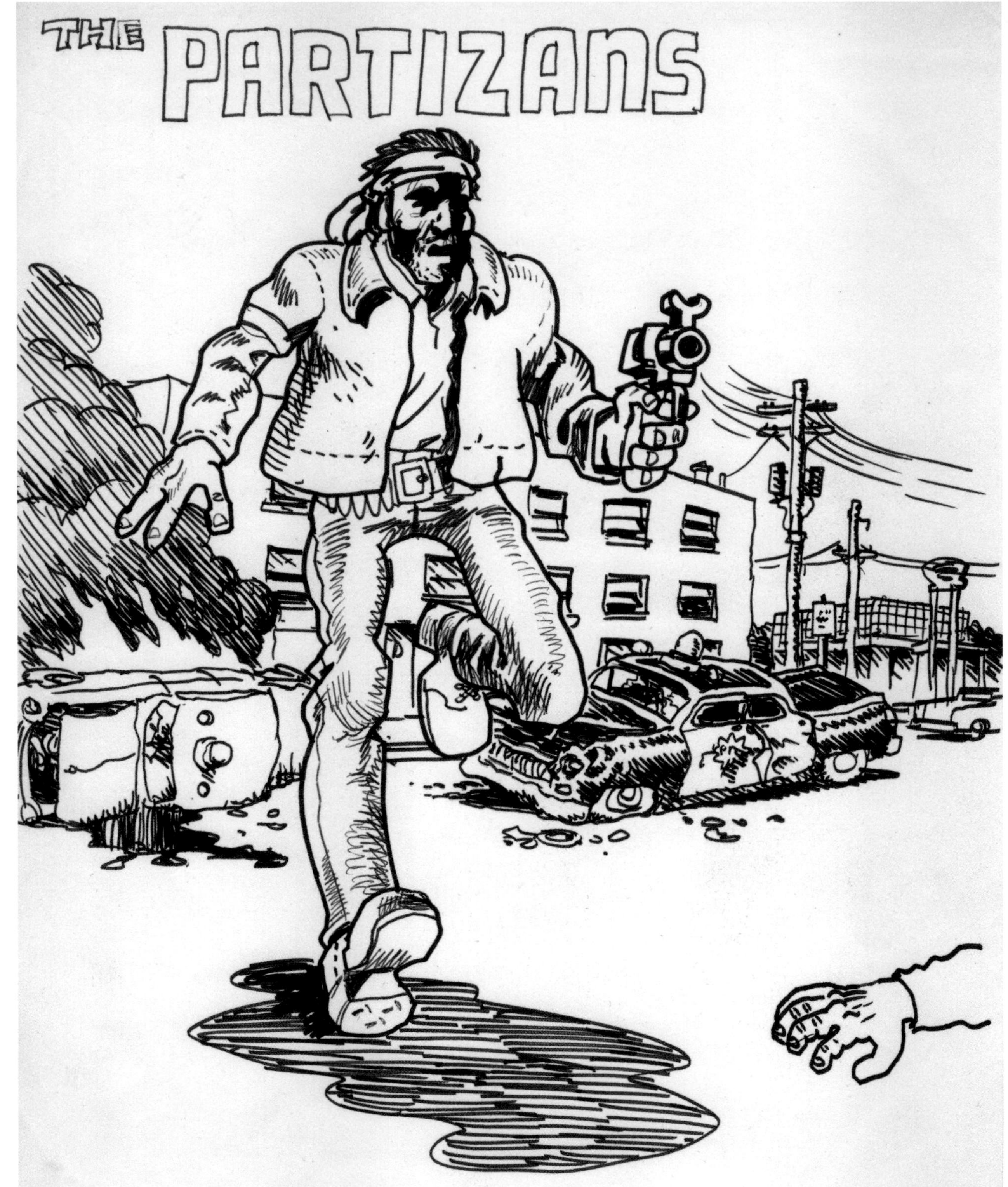
THE PARTIZANS

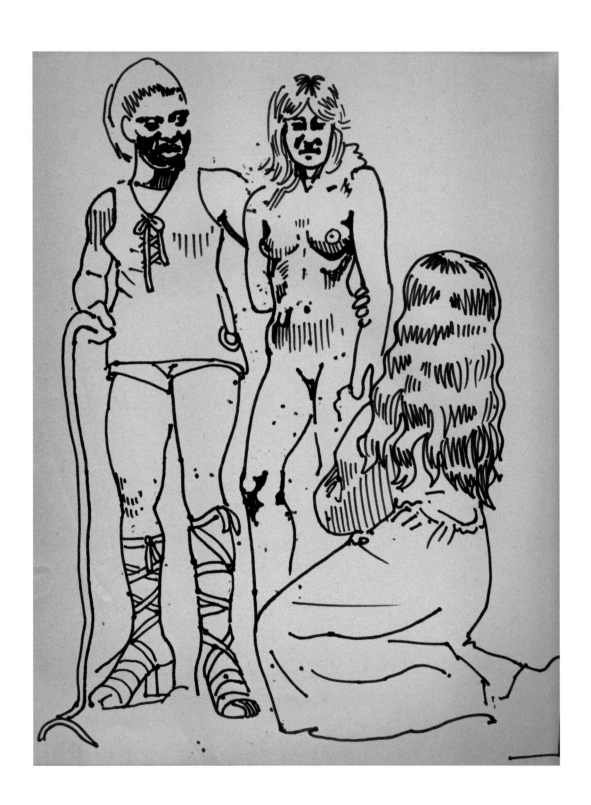

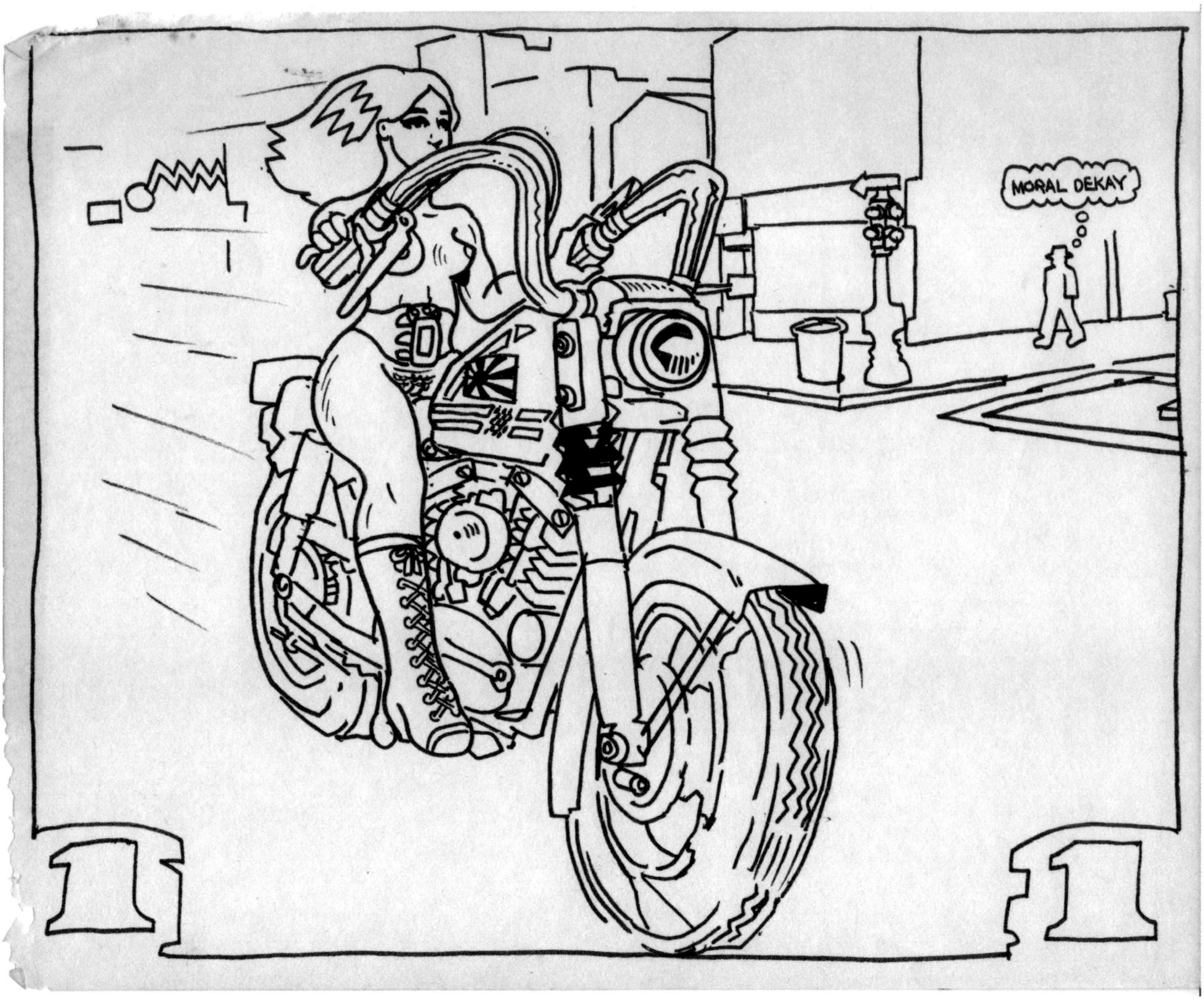
MORAL DEKAY
1
1

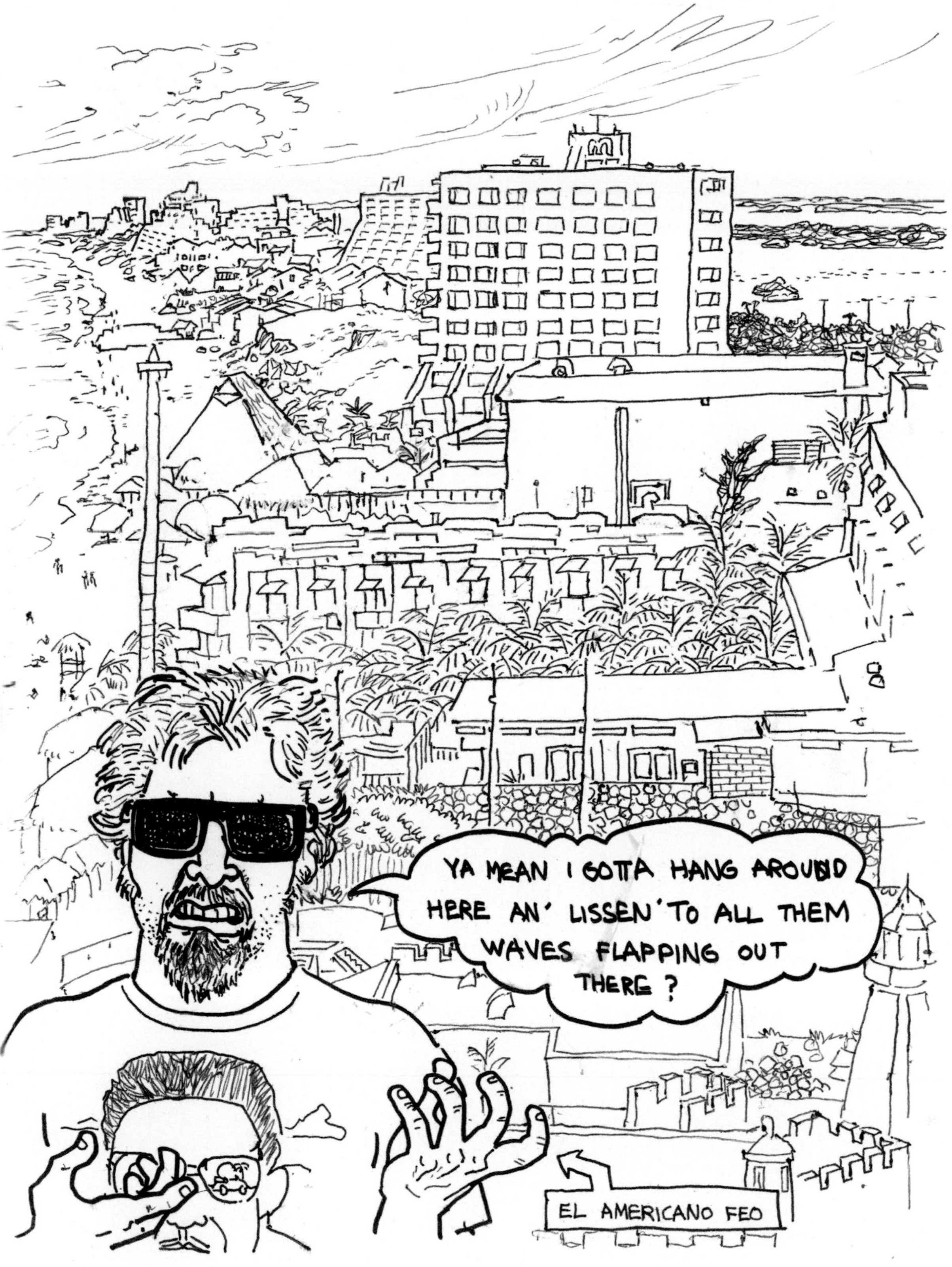
YA MEAN I GOTTA HANG AROUND HERE AN' LISSEN' TO ALL THEM WAVES FLAPPING OUT THERE?
EL AMERICANO FEO

YOU MEASURE QUESTION AND COMPARE EVERYTHING
DOES IT MAKE ANYDIFFERENCE?
ITMITE 100 YEARS FROM NOW
ITS ALL GONE WITH THE WIIND CANCELED
FINI
SORRY THAT TUNE DOESNT END UP ON DO
HES BEEN HERE I CAN FEEL IT
DONT YOU FEEL THE NEED TO BE PUNISHED
CUNT BITCH
BUT WILLIE I DIDN T MEAN IT
SOCK STENCH
funnies

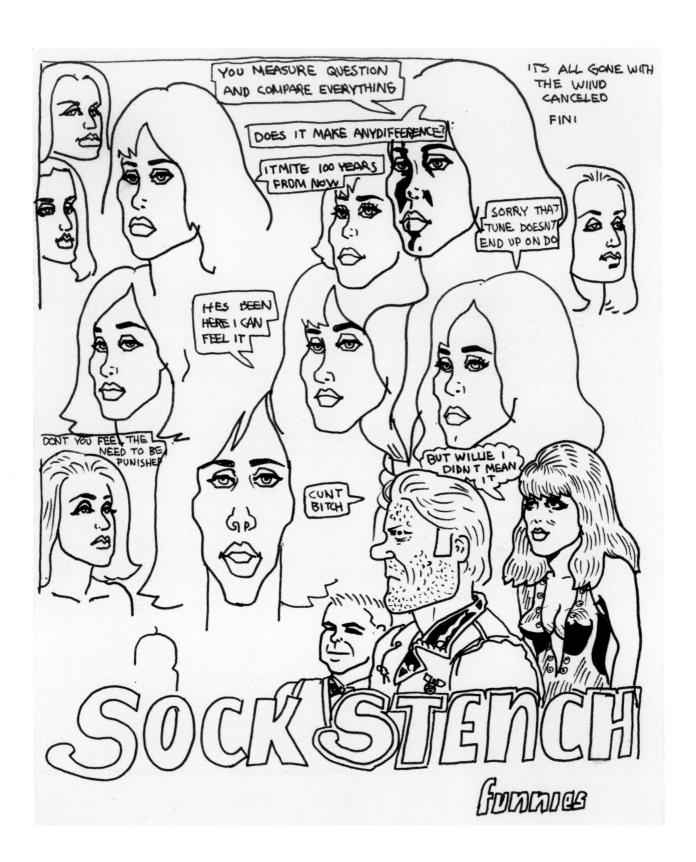

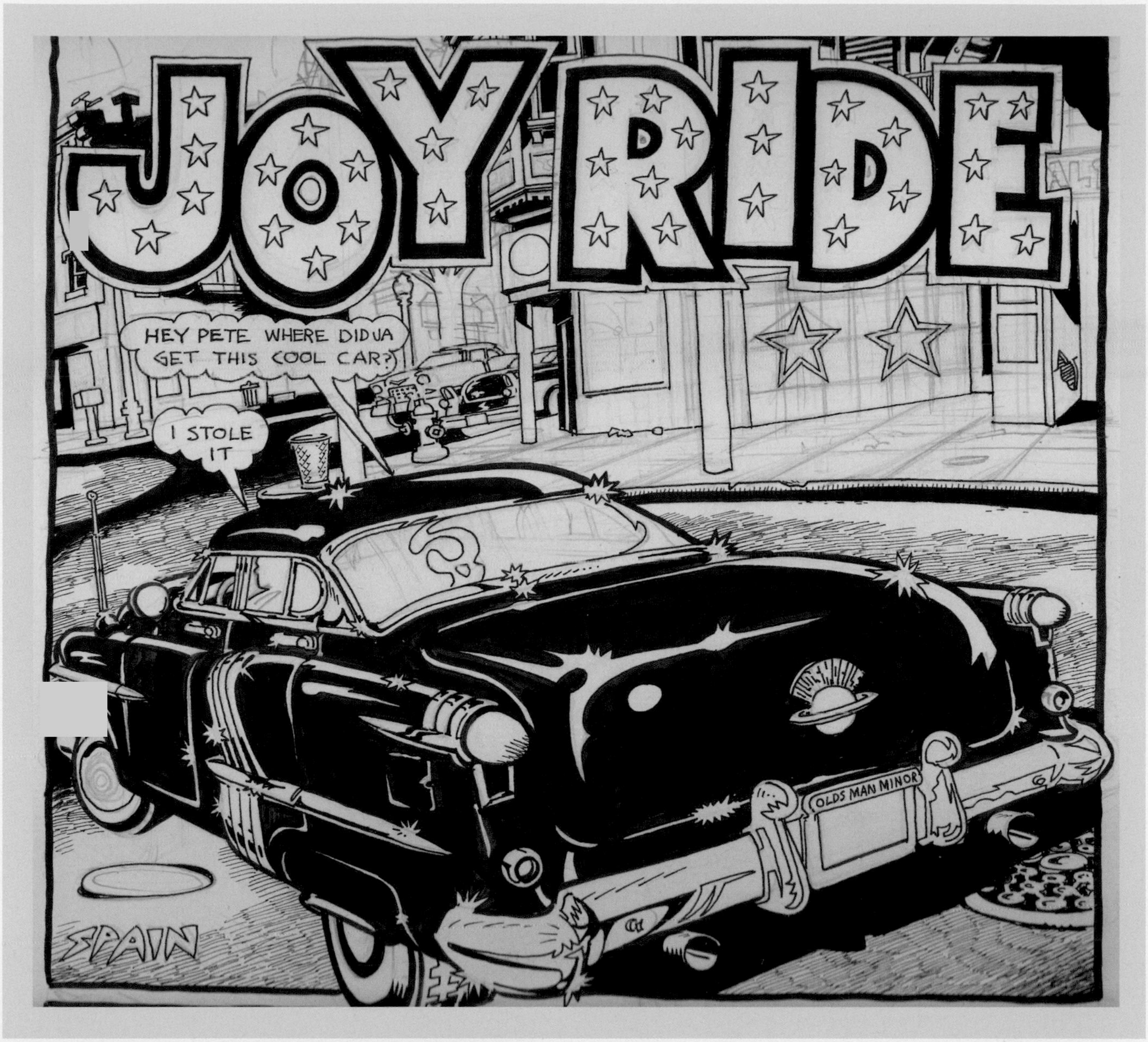
JOY RIDE
HEY PETE WHERE DIDJA GET THIS COOL CAR?
I STOLE IT
OLDS MAN MINOR
SPAIN

BLAB! TELLS ALL

PATRICK ROSENKRANZ

TOP: Panel from an unfinished and unpublished comic, circa early 1970s.

Spain Rodriguez drew six comic stories about his adventures riding with the Road Vultures Motorcycle Club for *Zap Comix* between 1973 and 2014. They were set in the mid-1960s when he returned to Buffalo from art school, a few years before he left his home town to work in the counterculture press in New York City. These memoirs were exuberant tales of young adults looking for identity and excitement and exercising their personal freedoms. They didn't look for trouble, according to Spain, but they were ready for it when it inevitably appeared. The Vultures came out on top in "Hard-Ass Friday Nite," "Fissure's Jacket," and "Mickey's Meatwagon"—still on their feet at the end of the barroom brawls and sexual escapades, and living to fight another day.

During the 1980s, Spain moved into new personal territory with a series of autobiographical stories of his life as a teenager. In his Road Vulture stories, Spain always played a minor character in the plot, if he appeared at all. When he began drawing tales

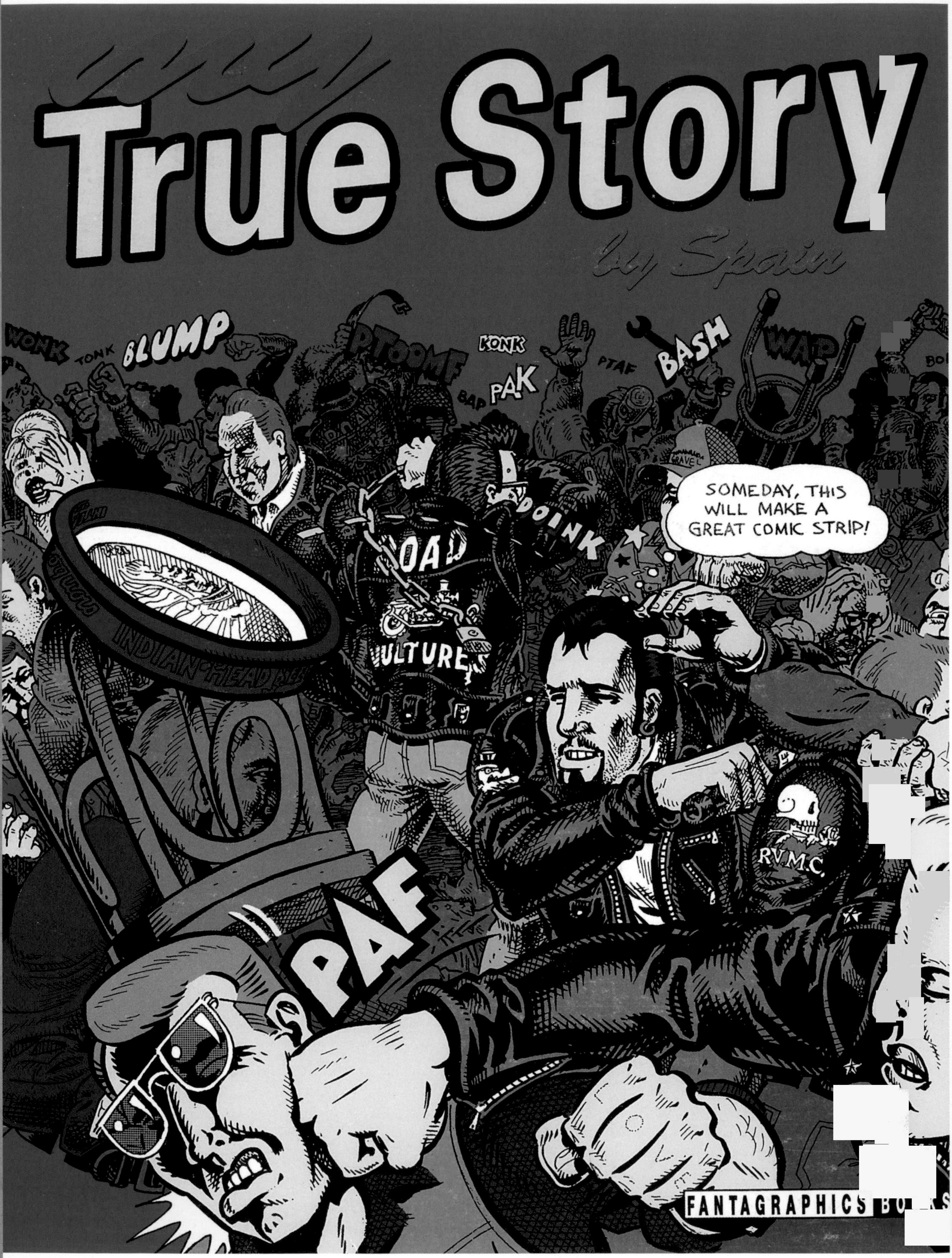
True Story
by Spain
WONK
TONK
BLUMP
PTOOMF
KONK
BAP
PAK
PTAF
BASH
WAP
DOINK
SOMEDAY, THIS WILL MAKE A GREAT COMIC STRIP!
PAF
FANTAGRAPHICS

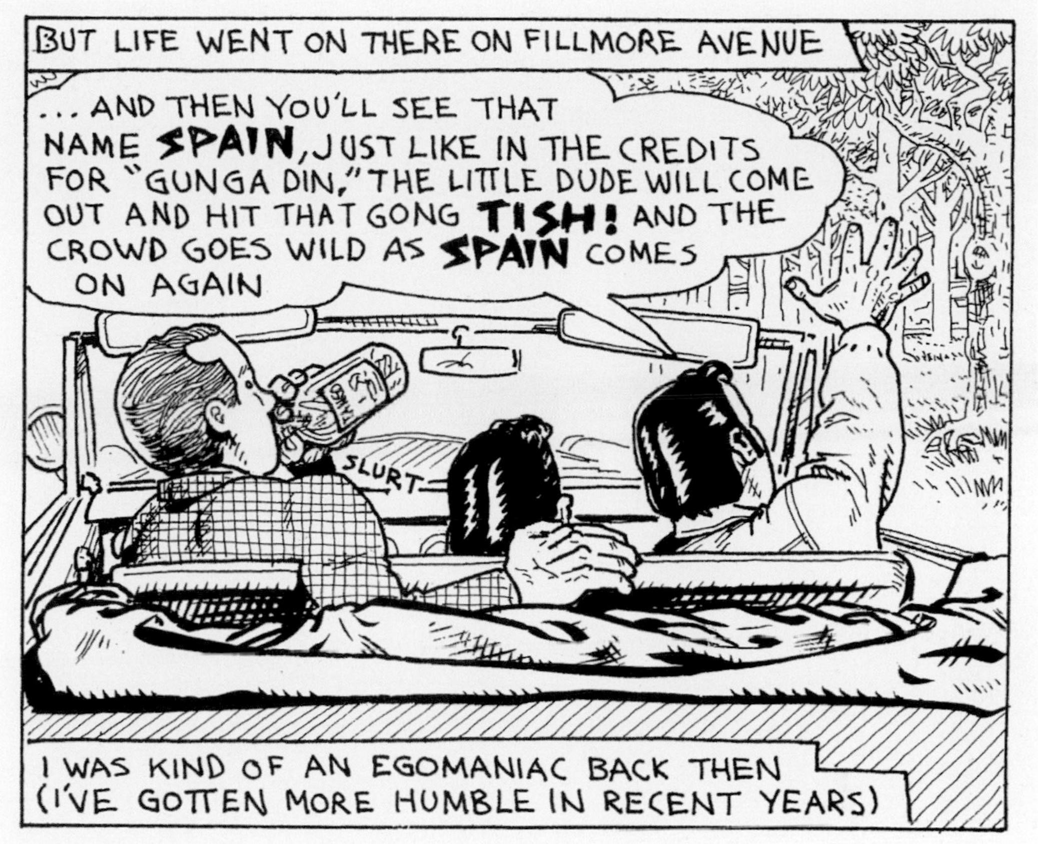
BUT LIFE WENT ON THERE ON FILLMORE AVENUE
... AND THEN YOU'LL SEE THAT NAME SPAIN, JUST LIKE IN THE CREDITS FOR "GUNGA DIN," THE LITTLE DUDE WILL COME OUT AND HIT THAT GONG TISH! AND THE CROWD GOES WILD AS SPAIN COMES ON AGAIN
SLURT
I WAS KIND OF AN EGOMANIAC BACK THEN (I'VE GOTTEN MORE HUMBLE IN RECENT YEARS)

OPPOSITE: The cover to *My True Story*, 1994.

ABOVE: From "Cruisin' with the Hound" in *Blab!* #8, 1995.

of Fred Tooté and Tex and the Buffalonians of his youth, he was often the lead character in the strip.

Spain drew vivid portraits of his reckless young adventures, depicting his first blowjob in the shadow of St. Francis de Sales Church, scarfing down Watt's famous Bar-B-Que pork sandwiches, hopping fences to get into carnivals for free, and finding a dead man in a house on Wakefield Street. He recalled bawdy times at hot spots and nightclubs where hoodlums and hooligans brawled over women and perceived insults. "They were all there," he wrote in his story "Down at the Kitty Kat." "The pimps, the fags, the whores, the curious, the alcoholic, the weird of the late '50s, blues lovers, Canadian bikers, thrill seekers, junkies, insomniacs, hepcats." He identified peculiar experiences that paved his path to becoming an underground cartoonist. He resurrected local heroes like radio DJ The Hound who broadcasted "the new sound going down" all over the Northeast, and Ron Radetsky, the "Michelangelo of the lavatory wall" who drew pornographic pictures nightly at the Western Electric plant. The neon-lit territory he cruised with his buddies Tex and Tooté featured landmarks he remembered so well: The Mansion House Lounge, the Bowl-O-Drome, Horowitz Pharmacy, The Paris Bar and Grill, The Deco 28, Heat Appliance, Vernor's Delicatessen, the Sunoco station, and Dellwood Dances, among others. The restaurants and bars, the cars, the clothes, and the blocks of storefronts are true to life, or to a life that once was. "I have that kind of memory," Spain described. "I'm always observing things and checking things out and looking at what people are wearing. I have notebooks upon notebooks."

"I'm always observing things and checking things out and looking at what people are wearing. I have notebooks upon notebooks."

Fifteen of these accounts appeared in Monte Beauchamp's *Blab!* art magazine, starting with its premier issue in 1986, and continuing through *Blab World* #1 in 2010. Four others appeared in *The Comics Journal Special Editions* and several more were published in his paperback collections *My True Story* and *Cruisin' With the Hound*.

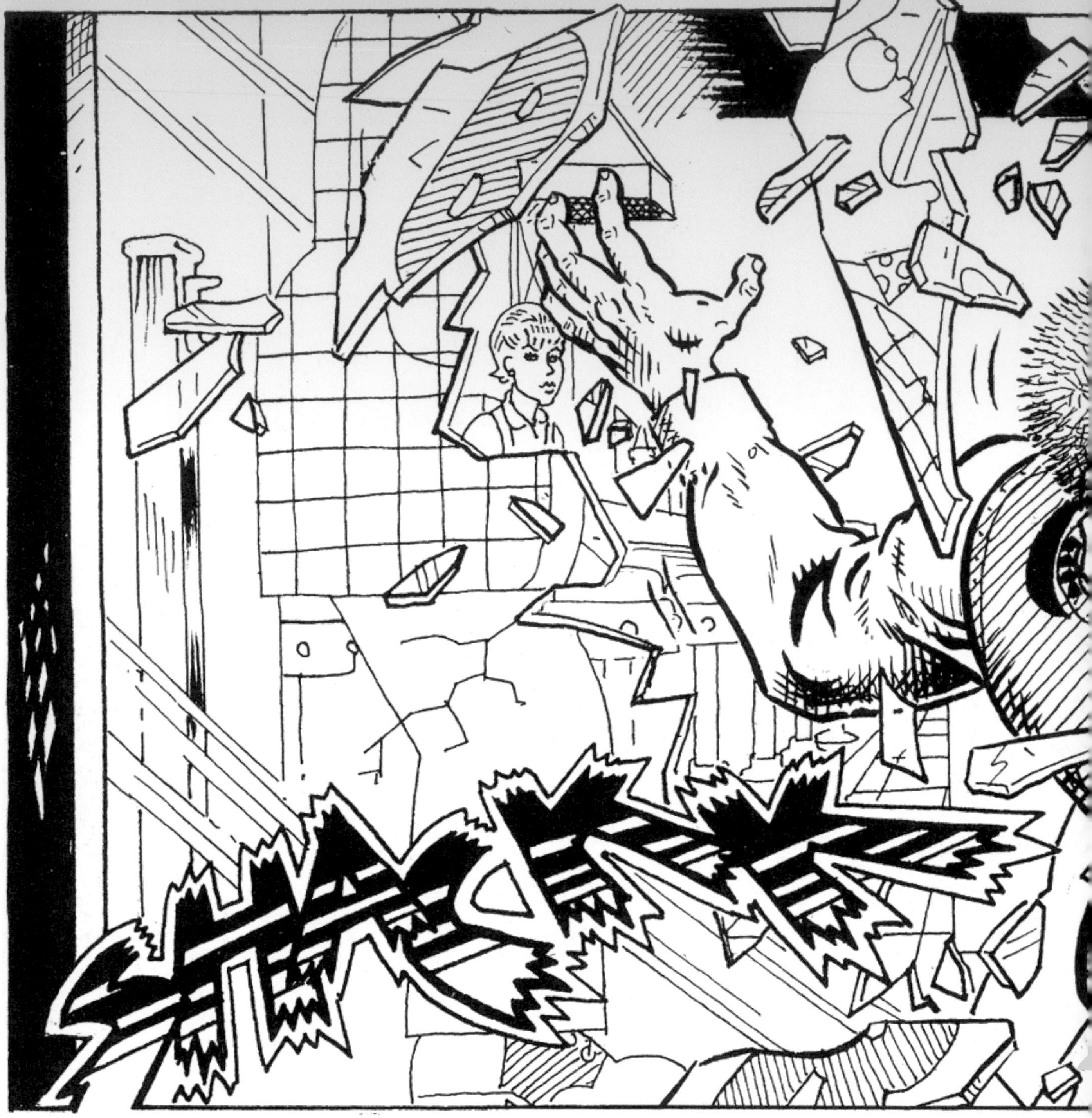

"*Blab!* was conceived as a one-shot fanzine comprised of essays by the counter-culture cartoonists of the '60s 'blabbing' about the monumental influence that *Mad*, *Tales from the Crypt*, and the rest of the EC Comics line of the '50s had on their work," said editor Monte Beauchamp. "Being that Spain was a contributor to *Zap*, the title that spearheaded the underground comic book revolution, and that EC had a monumental impact on his style, it was essential he be included in that first collection of memoirs."

The second issue continued the question of EC's effect on younger cartoonists. The third issue, published under the Kitchen Sink imprint, included a series of testimonials that recognized the influence of Robert Crumb's comix. Spain said that Crumb's first appearance in the underground newspaper *Yarrowstalks* sent a lot of cartoonists into a deep, personal crisis, when they compared their work to his, but not him. "Although I liked Crumb's stuff a lot, I didn't see him as a personal rival."

"I think a recurring theme was the folly of humans."

Spain wrote about buying his first EC comic book, a used copy of *Weird Science*, and its impact on his life. "Needless to say, it had a profound affect on me. Afterwards, I was hooked." The subsequent campaign against comics in the 1950s as an alleged cause of juvenile delinquency, and the formation of the Comics Code Authority, actually shocked him. "It was a severe

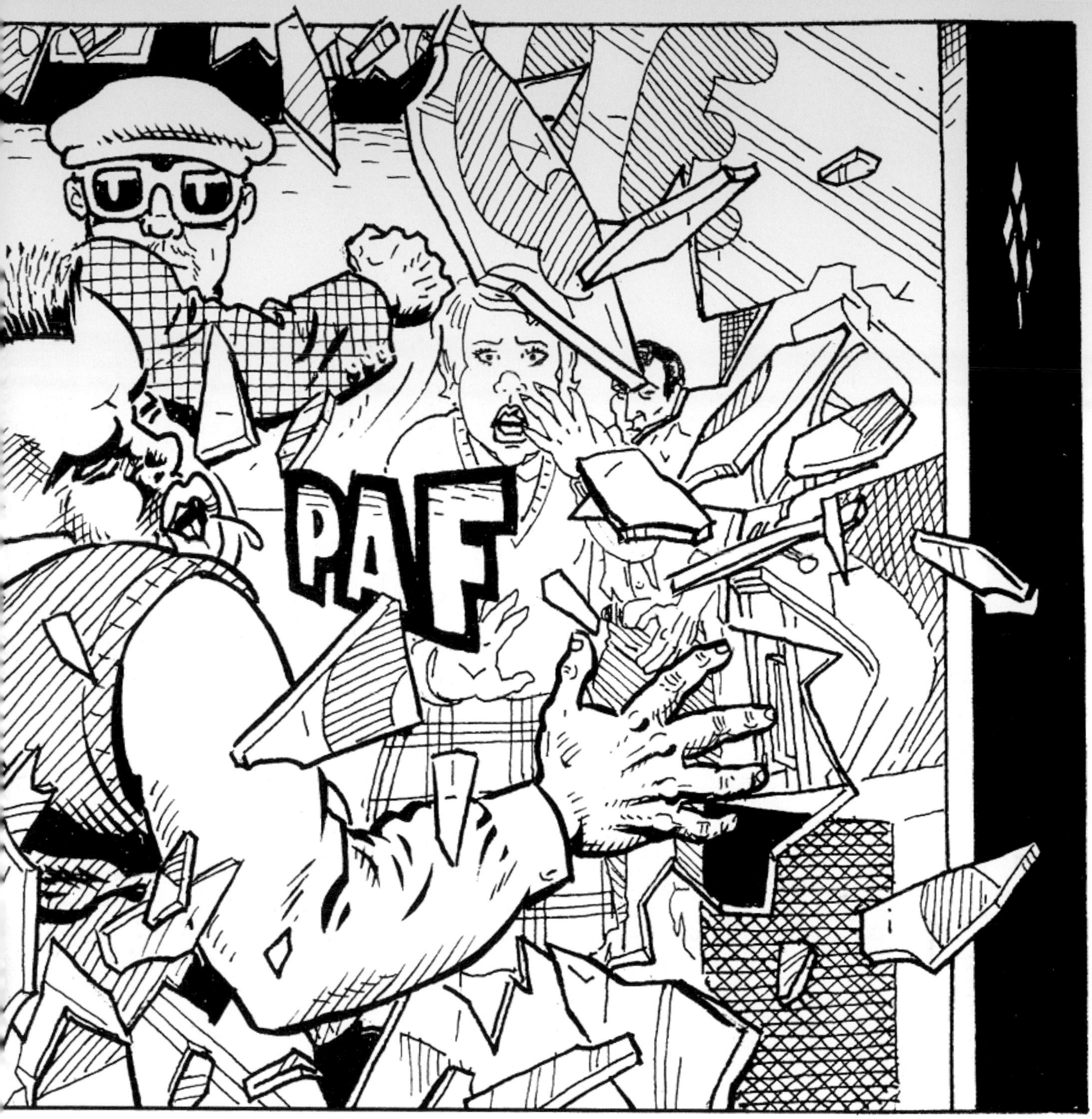
PAF

blow to my youthful idealism. I never thought something like this could happen in America."

"*Blab!* was never intended to be a continuing series, but due to all the fan mail that poured in, along with a handful of very positive reviews, I decided to self-publish a second issue, which appeared in late spring 1987," said Beauchamp. "At that summer's Chicago Comic Con, I gave Denis Kitchen (of Kitchen Sink Press) a copy. As he began flipping through it, he offered me a publishing deal to transform *Blab!* from a fanzine into a full-fledged comics anthology, which I readily agreed to. And from there, I reached out to Spain to become a regular contributor."

"I queried him if there were any incidents related to the untimely demise of EC Comics—the witch hunts, comic book burnings, etc.—that he might like to cover for his first *Blab!* story, which led to us talking about Fred Tooté, who would see people on the street and describe them as being drawn in the style of an EC artist—say, Wally Wood or Jack Davis, for example. After Spain finished telling me the tale about Tooté and a crusty old street hag called the 'Egg Lady,' I knew we had found our story. And Spain delivered *big* time; it was aces all the way. When I phoned to thank him for his superb story, we discussed the possibilities for *Blab!* #4, which led to another tale about his offbeat friend—'Fred Tooté Rides.'"

"For *Blab!* #5, I assigned the theme of crime and Spain had yet another story from the days of his youth about two cats who robbed banks using a bazooka," said Beauchamp. "And then for the alcohol-themed issue of *Blab!* #6 we decided on yet

ABOVE: From "The Fighting Poets" in *Blab!* #9, 1997.

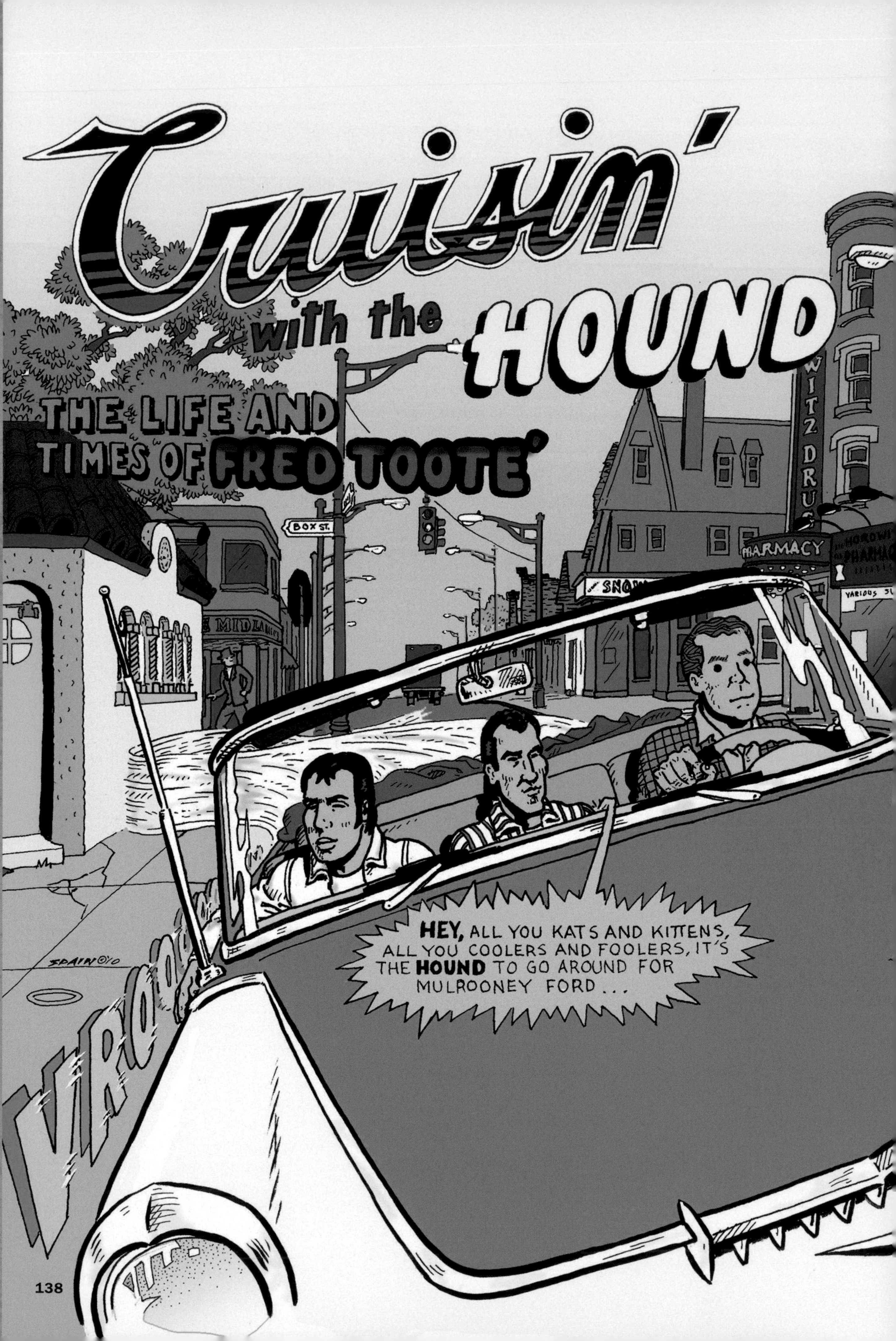

Cruisin' with the HOUND
THE LIFE AND TIMES OF FRED TOOTE'
BOX ST.
PHARMACY
HEY, ALL YOU KATS AND KITTENS, ALL YOU COOLERS AND FOOLERS, IT'S THE HOUND TO GO AROUND FOR MULROONEY FORD...
SPAIN ©'10

another story from the days of his youth, "Down at the Kitty Kat." Does comic book characterization get any better than this? That prostitute Spain consorts with delivers the heat. Spain so knocked it out of the ballpark with that one. And from there, we kept his string of autobiographical stories going. They fit in perfectly with the title *Blab!*"

Spain contributed stories about Buffalo to every subsequent issue of *Blab!* His last contribution, "High Smile Guy in a Low Smile Zone" in *Blab!* #17 told of Spain's five years working in the Western Electric factory.

"When we got ready to develop each issue of *Blab!* I would give Spain a call," explained Beauchamp. "We'd talk about a series of story possibilities and then I would select the one I liked, then ask how many pages he thought he might need ... and from there he'd go off and create the story. I never requested to see pencils; I didn't want to get in the way of the energy of the work. After the originals were delivered, I would always discover typos. And there were several situations in which I requested panels be redrawn; and Spain was good about that. He never gave me any art-itude about it."

Spain always said he had a lot more stories to tell, but he just ran out of time. He presented his rebellious youth as a series of adventures that sometimes he wasn't fully equipped to handle, but he relied on his instincts to guide him.

"I think a recurring theme was the folly of humans," said Jay Kinney. "I think a lot of the Road Vulture stories and his stories of being a teenager in Buffalo had this sense of irony. There's this foolish stuff mixed up with heroic stuff, all meshed together. Sometime he had a political point but often it was more that you can have a wonderful glorious moment in the middle of utter stupidity and insanity."

"One of my main motivations for autobiographical comics is that I won't have to tell these stories any more, especially stories about Fred Tooté," said Spain in 2012. "I'm in touch with Tex, the small guy who hung out with us. Fred died, as he predicted, a hideous death. He fell asleep with a lit cigarette in a drunken state and burned himself up."

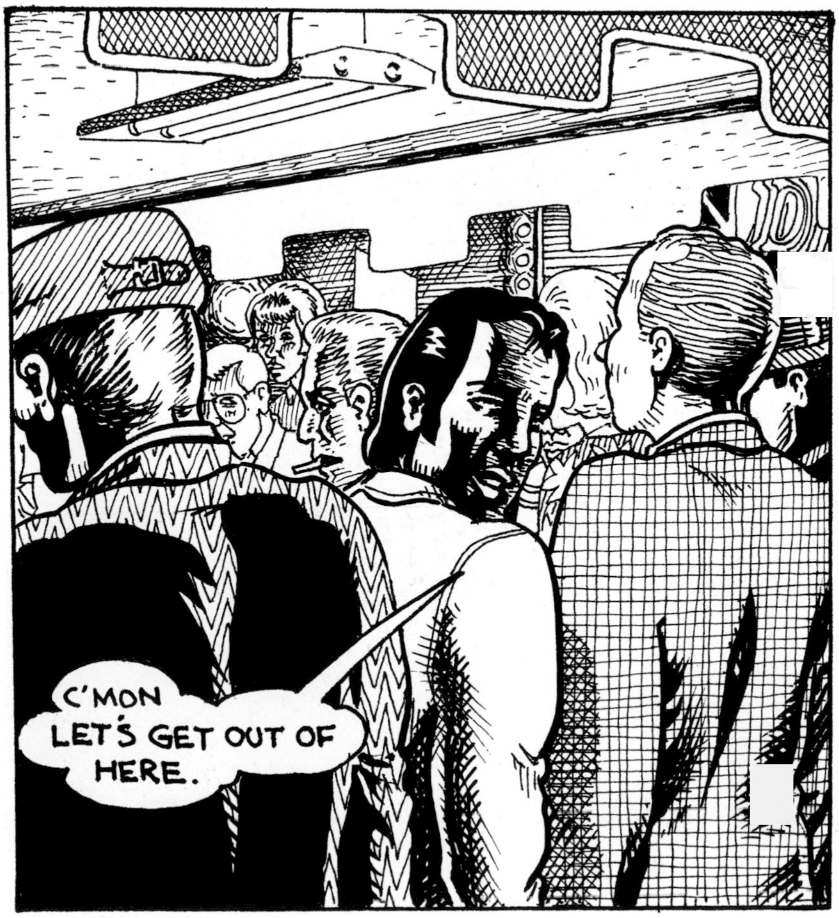
C'MON LET'S GET OUT OF HERE.

OPPOSITE: Cover to *Cruisin' with the Hound*, 2012.
RIGHT: From "Carney" in *Blab!* #10, 1998.

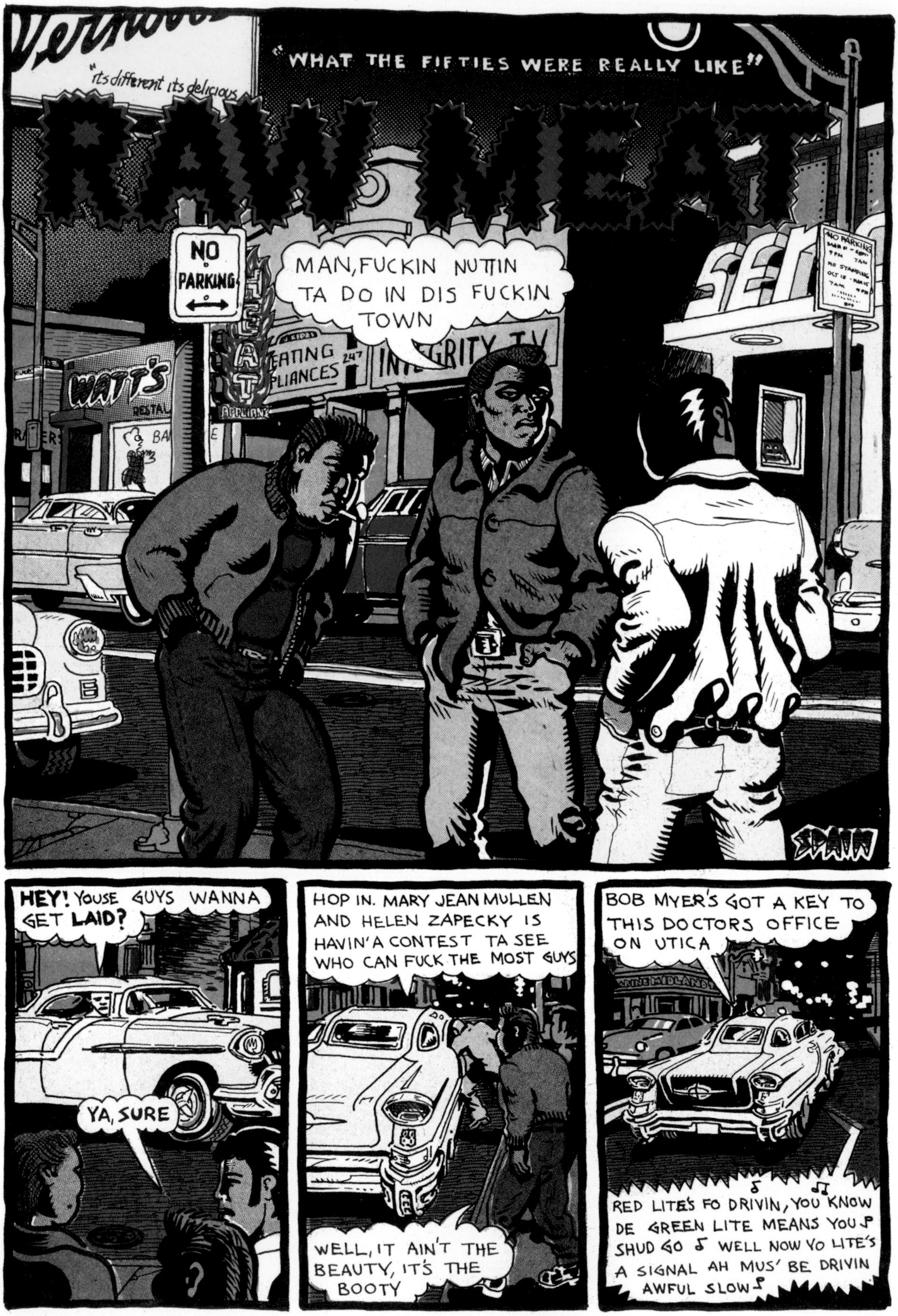
"WHAT THE FIFTIES WERE REALLY LIKE"
RAW MEAT
"its different its delicious"
NO PARKING
MAN, FUCKIN NUTTIN TA DO IN DIS FUCKIN TOWN
SPAIN
HEY! YOUSE GUYS WANNA GET LAID?
YA, SURE
HOP IN. MARY JEAN MULLEN AND HELEN ZAPECKY IS HAVIN' A CONTEST TA SEE WHO CAN FUCK THE MOST GUYS
WELL, IT AIN'T THE BEAUTY, IT'S THE BOOTY
BOB MYER'S GOT A KEY TO THIS DOCTORS OFFICE ON UTICA
RED LITE'S FO DRIVIN, YOU KNOW DE GREEN LITE MEANS YOU SHUD GO WELL NOW YO LITE'S A SIGNAL AH MUS' BE DRIVIN AWFUL SLOW

P. 140–143 from *Young Lust* #4, 1974

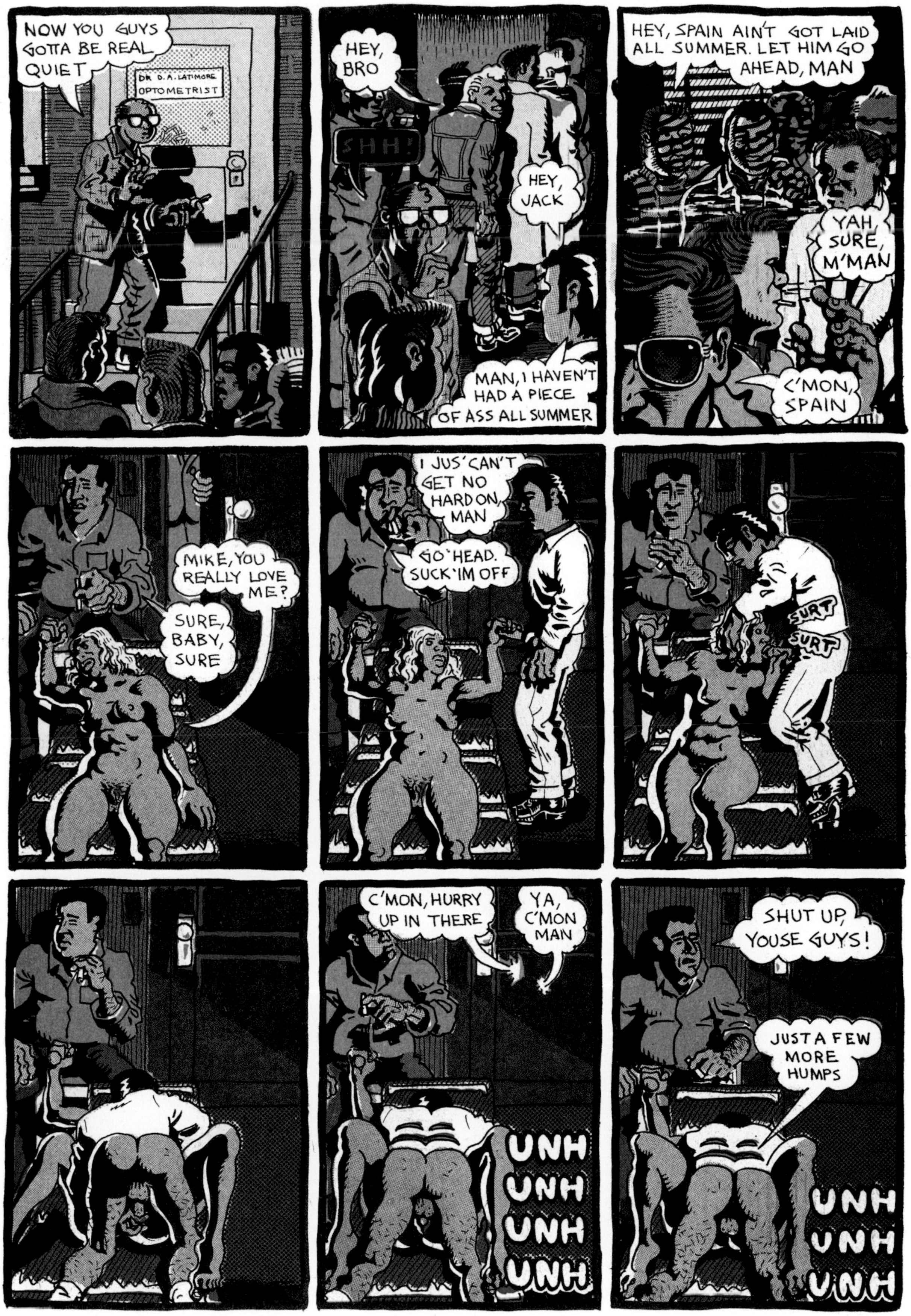
NOW YOU GUYS GOTTA BE REAL QUIET
DR. D. A. LATIMORE OPTOMETRIST
HEY, BRO
SHH!
HEY, JACK
MAN, I HAVEN'T HAD A PIECE OF ASS ALL SUMMER
HEY, SPAIN AIN'T GOT LAID ALL SUMMER. LET HIM GO AHEAD, MAN
YAH, SURE, M'MAN
C'MON, SPAIN
MIKE, YOU REALLY LOVE ME?
SURE, BABY, SURE
I JUS' CAN'T GET NO HARD ON, MAN
GO' HEAD. SUCK 'IM OFF
SURT
SURT
C'MON, HURRY UP IN THERE
YA, C'MON MAN
UNH
UNH
UNH
UNH
SHUT UP, YOUSE GUYS!
JUST A FEW MORE HUMPS
UNH
UNH
UNH

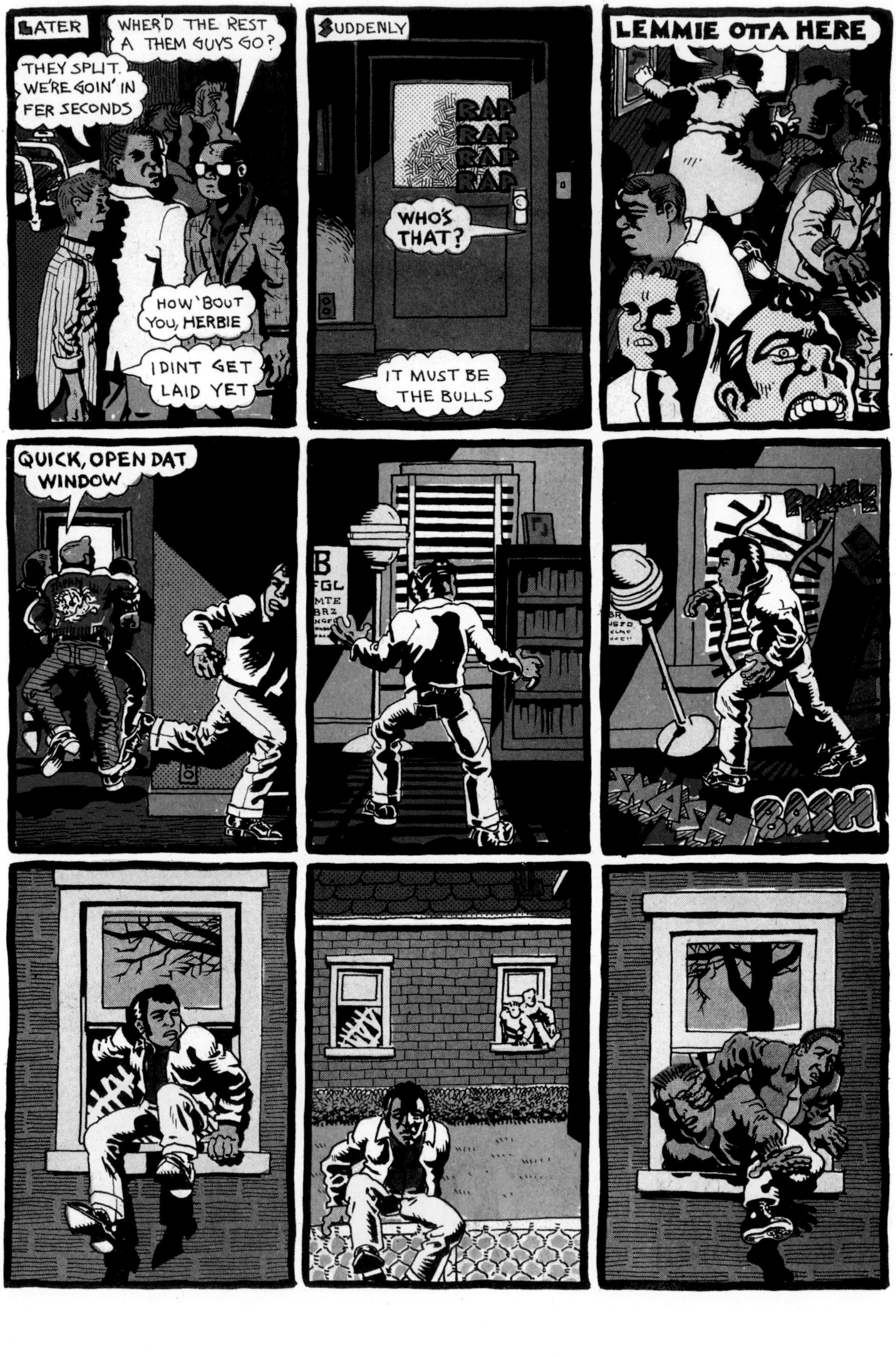
LATER
WHER'D THE REST A THEM GUYS GO?
THEY SPLIT. WE'RE GOIN' IN FER SECONDS
HOW 'BOUT YOU, HERBIE
I DINT GET LAID YET
SUDDENLY
RAP RAP RAP RAP
WHO'S THAT?
IT MUST BE THE BULLS
LEMMIE OTTA HERE
QUICK, OPEN DAT WINDOW
BASH

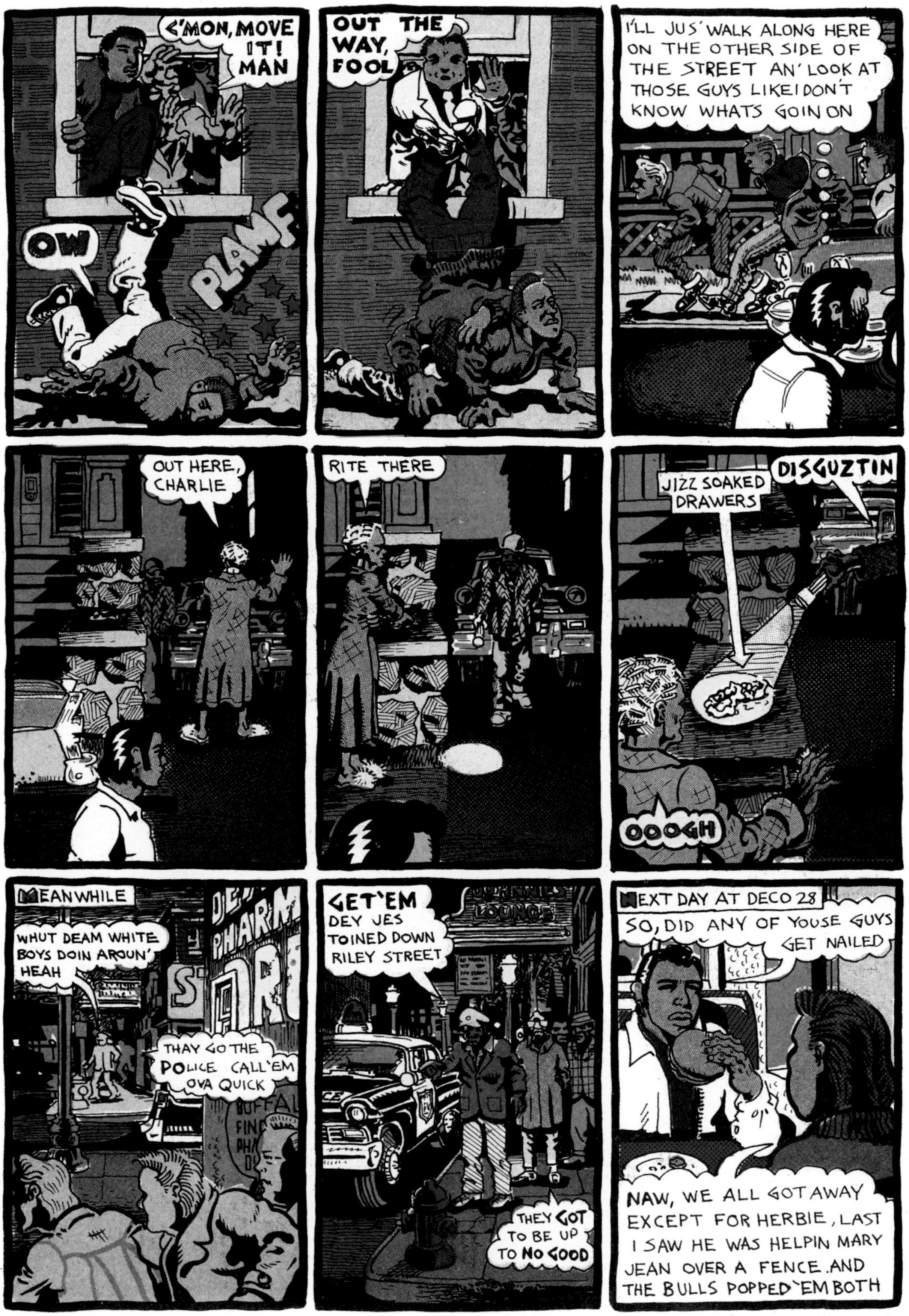
C'MON, MOVE IT! MAN
OW
PLAMF
OUT THE WAY, FOOL
I'LL JUS' WALK ALONG HERE ON THE OTHER SIDE OF THE STREET AN' LOOK AT THOSE GUYS LIKE I DON'T KNOW WHATS GOIN ON
OUT HERE, CHARLIE
RITE THERE
JIZZ SOAKED DRAWERS
DISGUZTIN
OOOGH
MEANWHILE
WHUT DEAM WHITE BOYS DOIN AROUN' HEAH
THAY GO THE POLICE CALL'EM OVA QUICK
GET'EM DEY JES TOINED DOWN RILEY STREET
THEY GOT TO BE UP TO NO GOOD
NEXT DAY AT DECO 28
SO, DID ANY OF YOUSE GUYS GET NAILED
NAW, WE ALL GOT AWAY EXCEPT FOR HERBIE, LAST I SAW HE WAS HELPIN MARY JEAN OVER A FENCE. AND THE BULLS POPPED 'EM BOTH

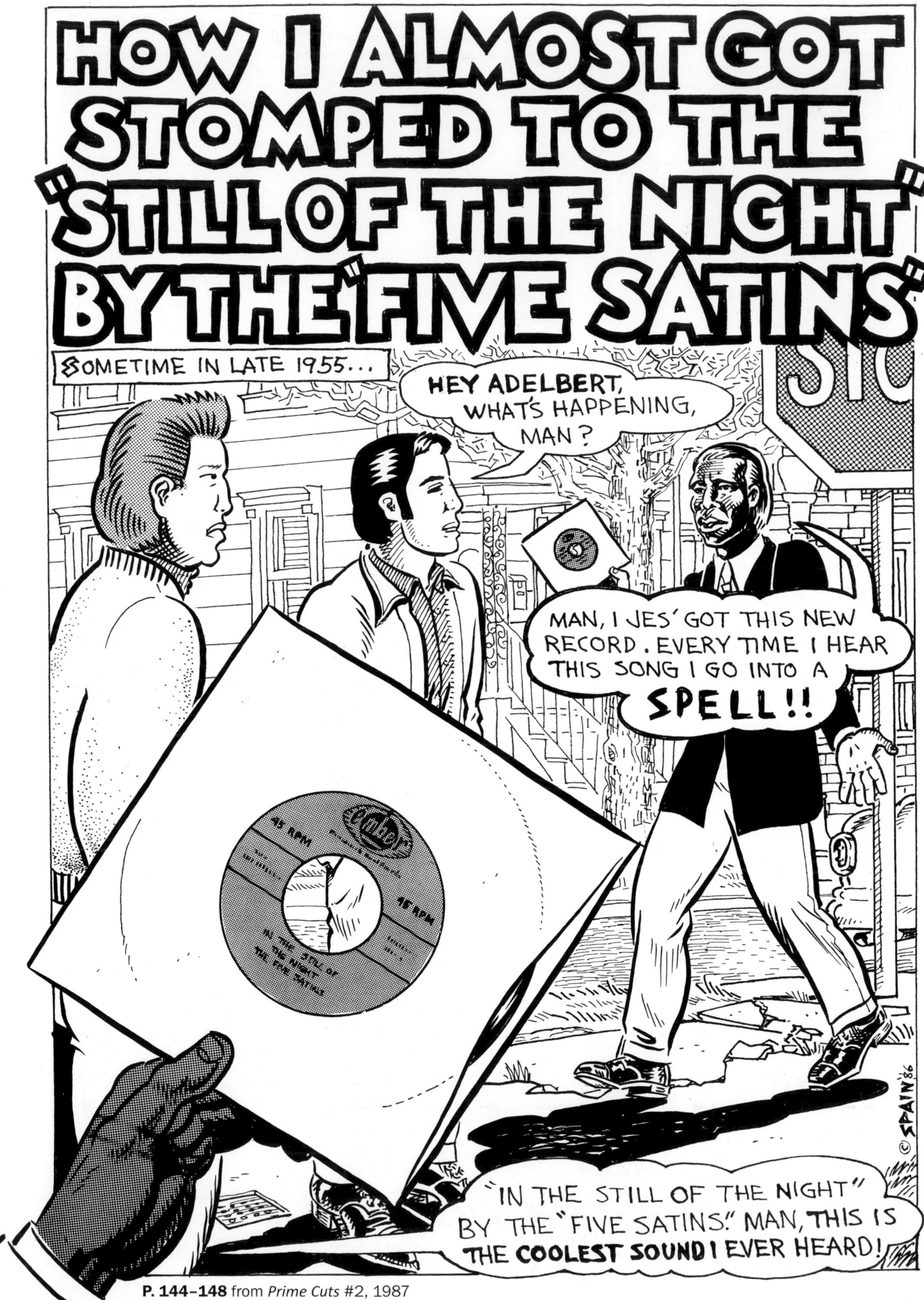
HOW I ALMOST GOT STOMPED TO THE "STILL OF THE NIGHT" BY THE "FIVE SATINS"
SOMETIME IN LATE 1955...
HEY ADELBERT, WHAT'S HAPPENING, MAN?
MAN, I JES' GOT THIS NEW RECORD. EVERY TIME I HEAR THIS SONG I GO INTO A SPELL!!
"IN THE STILL OF THE NIGHT" BY THE "FIVE SATINS." MAN, THIS IS THE COOLEST SOUND I EVER HEARD!
© SPAIN '86

P. 144–148 from *Prime Cuts* #2, 1987

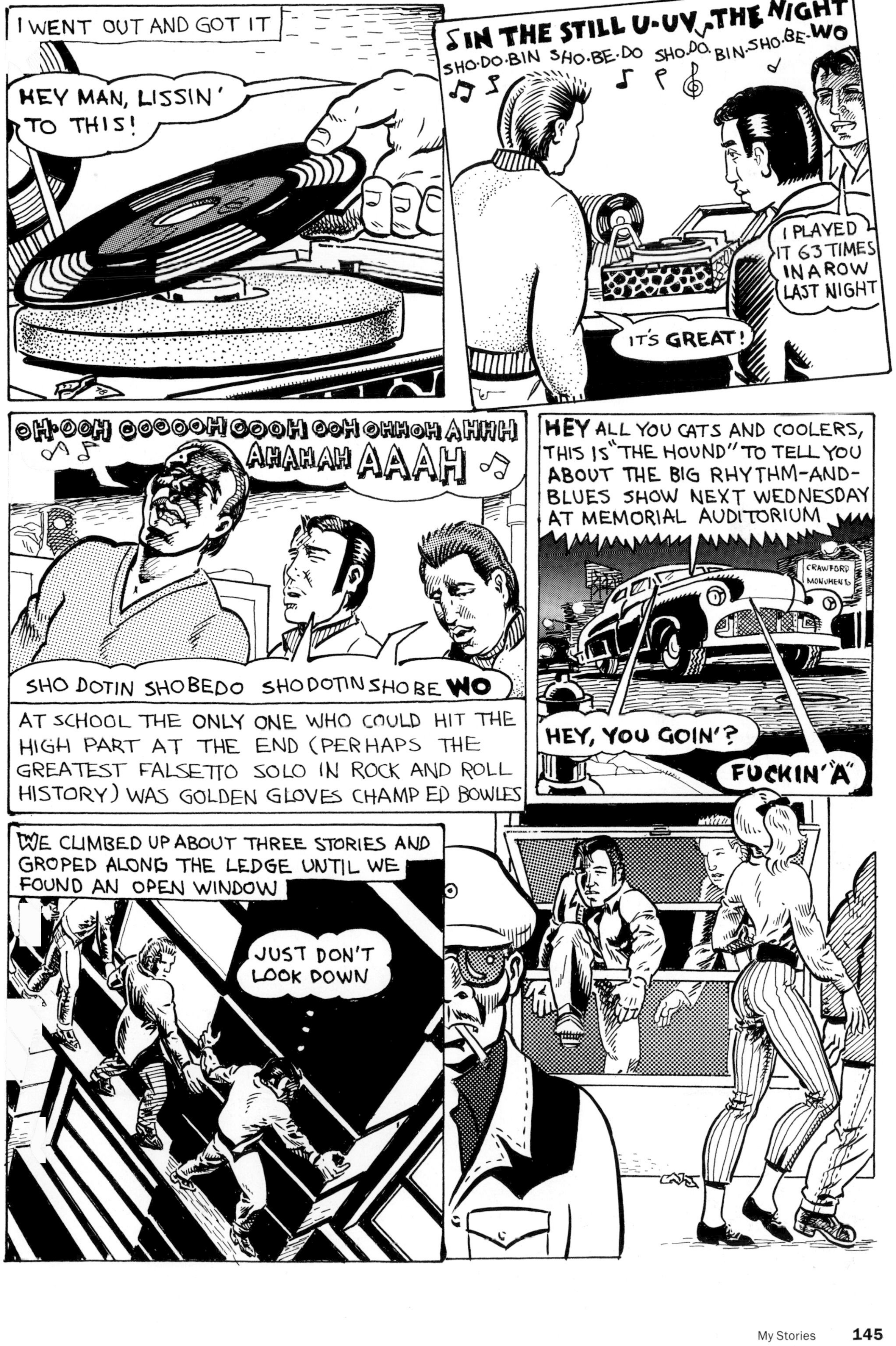
I WENT OUT AND GOT IT
HEY MAN, LISSIN' TO THIS!
IN THE STILL U-UV THE NIGHT
SHO-DO-BIN SHO-BE-DO SHO-DO BIN-SHO-BE-WO
I PLAYED IT 63 TIMES IN A ROW LAST NIGHT
IT'S GREAT!
OH-OOH OOOOOH OOOH OOH OHHOH AHHH AHAHAH AAAH
SHO DOTIN SHOBEDO SHODOTIN SHOBE WO
AT SCHOOL THE ONLY ONE WHO COULD HIT THE HIGH PART AT THE END (PERHAPS THE GREATEST FALSETTO SOLO IN ROCK AND ROLL HISTORY) WAS GOLDEN GLOVES CHAMP ED BOWLES
HEY ALL YOU CATS AND COOLERS, THIS IS "THE HOUND" TO TELL YOU ABOUT THE BIG RHYTHM-AND-BLUES SHOW NEXT WEDNESDAY AT MEMORIAL AUDITORIUM
CRAWFORD MONUMENTS
HEY, YOU GOIN'?
FUCKIN' "A"
WE CLIMBED UP ABOUT THREE STORIES AND GROPED ALONG THE LEDGE UNTIL WE FOUND AN OPEN WINDOW
JUST DON'T LOOK DOWN

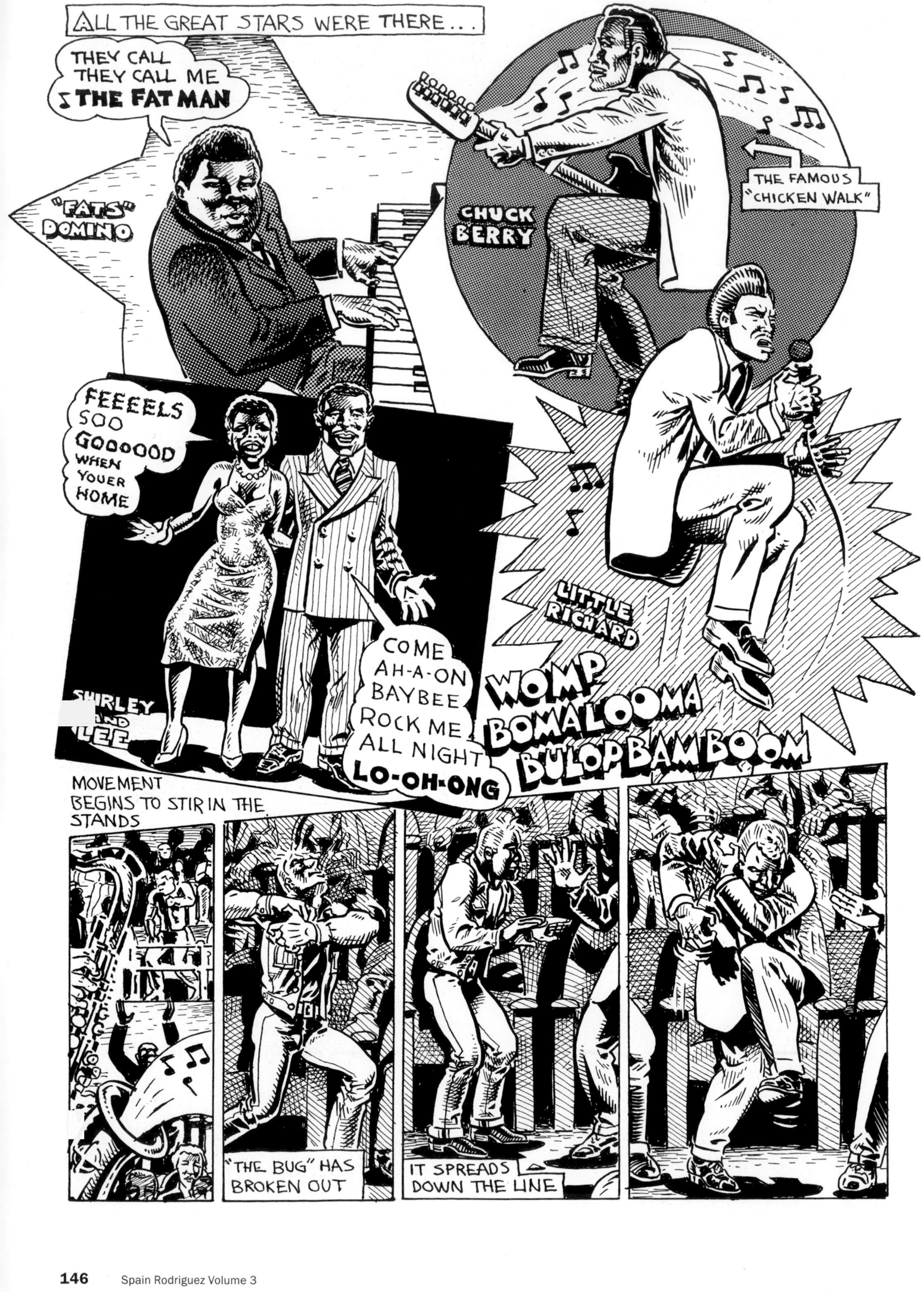
ALL THE GREAT STARS WERE THERE...
THEY CALL THEY CALL ME THE FAT MAN
"FATS" DOMINO
CHUCK BERRY
THE FAMOUS "CHICKEN WALK"
FEEEELS SOO GOOOOOD WHEN YOUER HOME
COME AH-A-ON BAYBEE ROCK ME ALL NIGHT LO-OH-ONG
SHIRLEY
LEE
LITTLE RICHARD
WOMP BOMALOOMA BULOPBAMBOOM
MOVEMENT BEGINS TO STIR IN THE STANDS
"THE BUG" HAS BROKEN OUT
IT SPREADS DOWN THE LINE

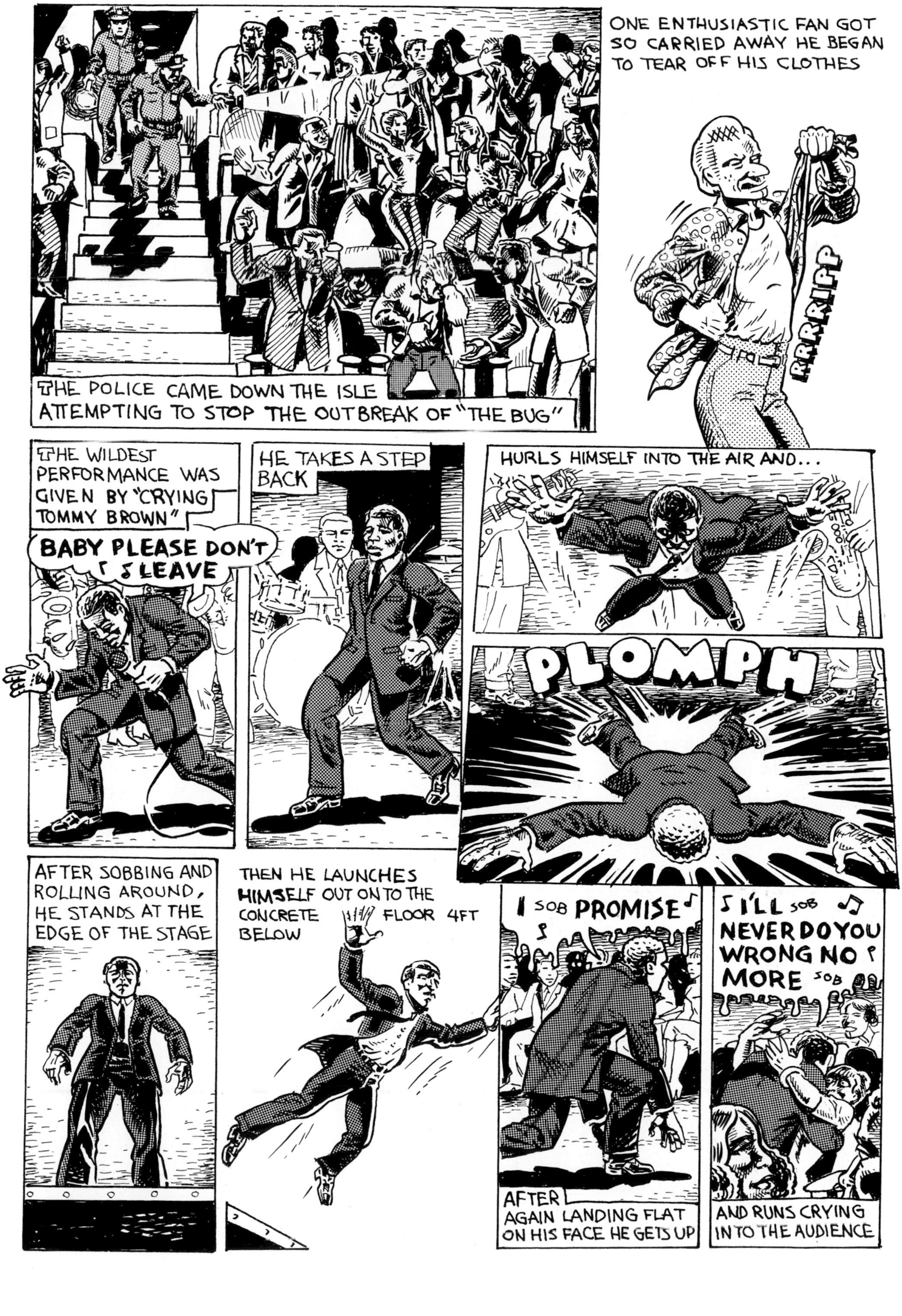

THE POLICE CAME DOWN THE ISLE ATTEMPTING TO STOP THE OUTBREAK OF "THE BUG"
ONE ENTHUSIASTIC FAN GOT SO CARRIED AWAY HE BEGAN TO TEAR OFF HIS CLOTHES
RRRRIPP
THE WILDEST PERFORMANCE WAS GIVEN BY "CRYING TOMMY BROWN"
BABY PLEASE DON'T LEAVE
HE TAKES A STEP BACK
HURLS HIMSELF INTO THE AIR AND...
PLOMPH
AFTER SOBBING AND ROLLING AROUND, HE STANDS AT THE EDGE OF THE STAGE
THEN HE LAUNCHES HIMSELF OUT ON TO THE CONCRETE FLOOR 4FT BELOW
SOB PROMISE
AFTER AGAIN LANDING FLAT ON HIS FACE HE GETS UP
I'LL SOB NEVER DO YOU WRONG NO MORE SOB
AND RUNS CRYING INTO THE AUDIENCE

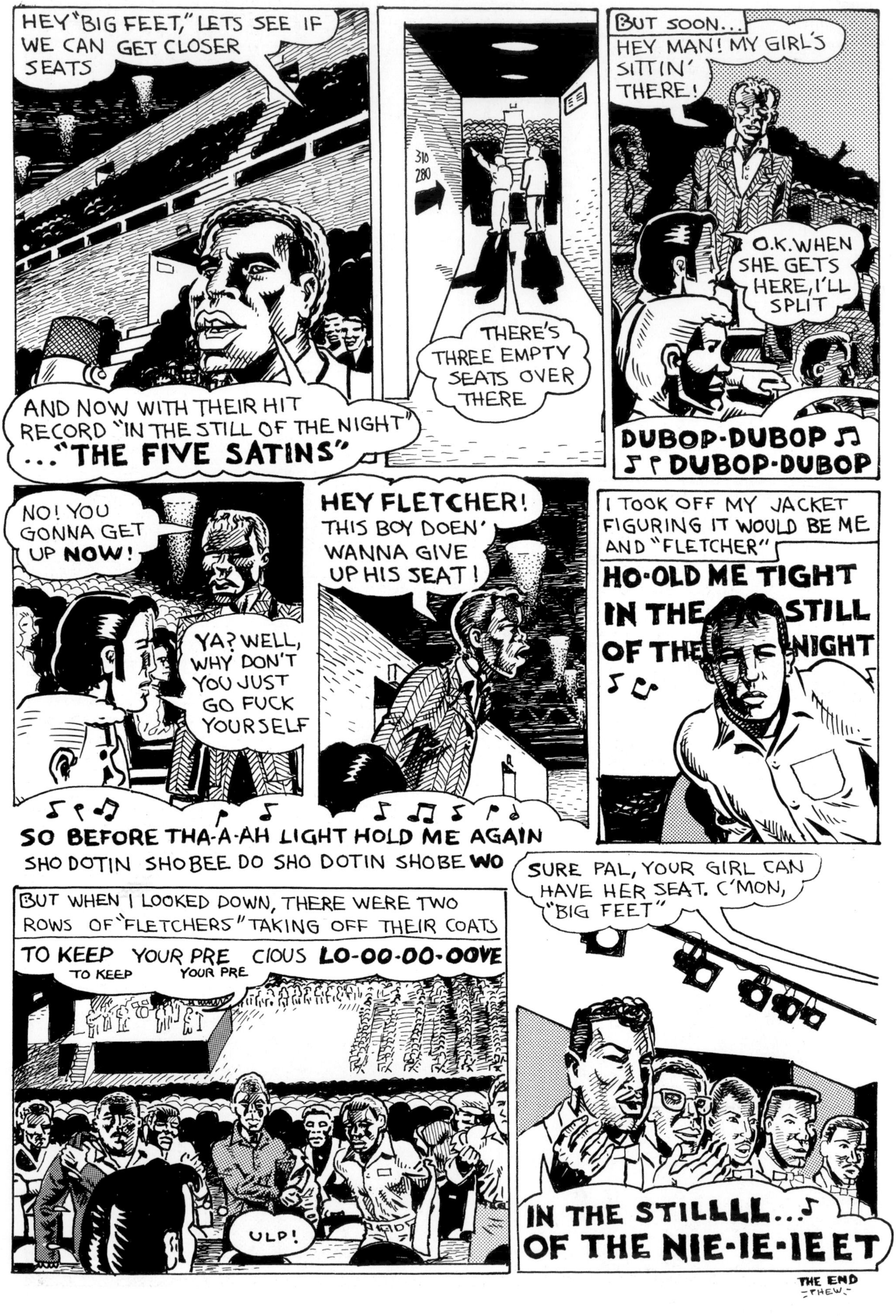
HEY "BIG FEET," LETS SEE IF WE CAN GET CLOSER SEATS
AND NOW WITH THEIR HIT RECORD "IN THE STILL OF THE NIGHT" ..."THE FIVE SATINS"
310
280
THERE'S THREE EMPTY SEATS OVER THERE
BUT SOON...
HEY MAN! MY GIRL'S SITTIN' THERE!
O.K. WHEN SHE GETS HERE, I'LL SPLIT
DUBOP-DUBOP DUBOP-DUBOP
NO! YOU GONNA GET UP NOW!
YA? WELL, WHY DON'T YOU JUST GO FUCK YOURSELF
HEY FLETCHER! THIS BOY DOEN' WANNA GIVE UP HIS SEAT!
I TOOK OFF MY JACKET FIGURING IT WOULD BE ME AND "FLETCHER"
HO-OLD ME TIGHT IN THE STILL OF THE NIGHT
SO BEFORE THA-A-AH LIGHT HOLD ME AGAIN
SHO DOTIN SHOBEE DO SHO DOTIN SHOBE WO
BUT WHEN I LOOKED DOWN, THERE WERE TWO ROWS OF "FLETCHERS" TAKING OFF THEIR COATS
TO KEEP YOUR PRE CIOUS LO-OO-OO-OOVE
TO KEEP YOUR PRE
ULP!
SURE PAL, YOUR GIRL CAN HAVE HER SEAT. C'MON, "BIG FEET"
IN THE STILLLL... OF THE NIE-IE-IE ET
THE END
PHEW

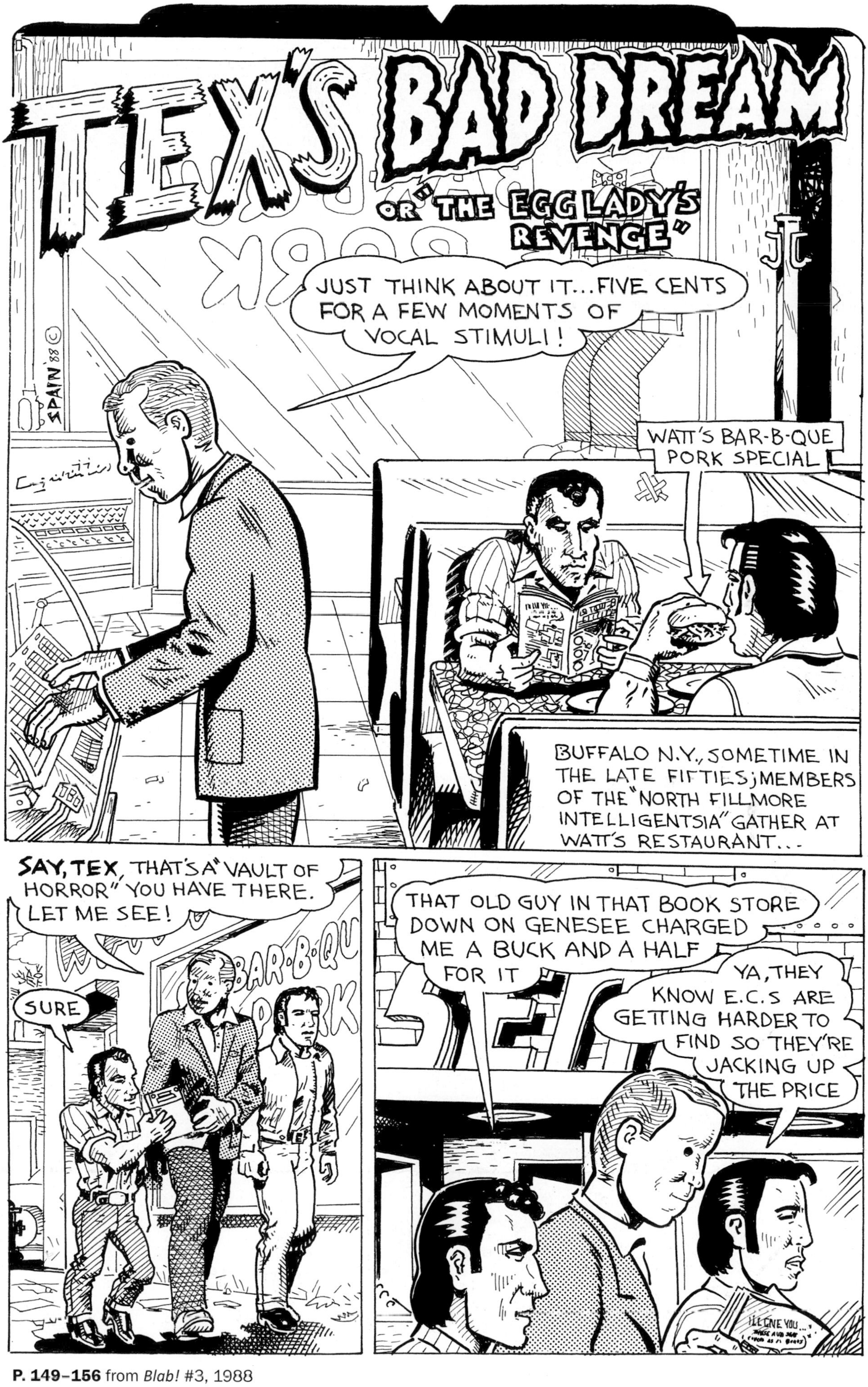
TEX'S BAD DREAM
OR "THE EGG LADY'S REVENGE"
SPAIN '88 ©
JUST THINK ABOUT IT...FIVE CENTS FOR A FEW MOMENTS OF VOCAL STIMULI!
WATT'S BAR-B-QUE PORK SPECIAL
BUFFALO N.Y., SOMETIME IN THE LATE FIFTIES; MEMBERS OF THE "NORTH FILLMORE INTELLIGENTSIA" GATHER AT WATT'S RESTAURANT...
SAY, TEX, THAT'S A "VAULT OF HORROR" YOU HAVE THERE. LET ME SEE!
SURE
BAR-B-QU
PORK
THAT OLD GUY IN THAT BOOK STORE DOWN ON GENESEE CHARGED ME A BUCK AND A HALF FOR IT
YA, THEY KNOW E.C.S ARE GETTING HARDER TO FIND SO THEY'RE JACKING UP THE PRICE

P. 149–156 from *Blab!* #3, 1988

FRED TOOTE' (TOO-TAY') HAD A SHARP EYE FOR PEOPLE'S FACES THAT MIGHT HAVE BEEN DRAWN BY E.C. ARTISTS

ACROSS THE STREET... JACK KAMEN!

SURE ENOUGH!

SUDDENLY TEX STOPS AND CALLS OUT...

OH EGG LADY

NOW THE TIME HAS ARRIVED FOR THE HAIR COMBING RITUAL AT THE FRONT WINDOW OF LOUIE'S LUNCHEONETTE

LOUIE'S LUNCHEONETTE

IT'S GETTING GOOD IN THE BACK

THIS WAS TAKEN AS A PERSONAL AFFRONT BY LOUIE WHO DIDN'T HAVE MUCH HAIR TO COMB

A WHILE BACK WE WERE ALL PALS

WHAT CAN I GET YOU GUYS?

LOUIE LIKED TO TEASE TEX ABOUT HIS HEIGHT
HEY TEX, I CAN'T SEEM TO REACH THIS LIGHT SOCKET. C'MERE, MAYBE YOU CAN DO IT
BUFFALO BISONS
THATS O.K. LOUIE, WITH ALL THE LIGHT REFLECTING OFF THAT DOME OF YOURS YOU DON'T NEED A BULB
REST ROOMS
THIS WENT ON FOR MONTHS UNTIL...
HEY TEX! THIS MEAT CLEAVER'S PRETTY SHARP. I'LL BET I COULD CUT YOU DOWN TO THE LEVEL OF MY CROTCH, THEN YOU COULD DO SOMETHING USEFUL
I DON'T THINK SO, LOUIE!
MUMBLE MUTTER IT'S NOT FUN ANYMORE MUTTER MUMBLE.... MUTTER JUST NOT FUN
THINGS WERE JUST NEVER THE SAME AFTERWARDS
WE TOOK OUR BUSINESS DOWN TO DECO 28
BOX

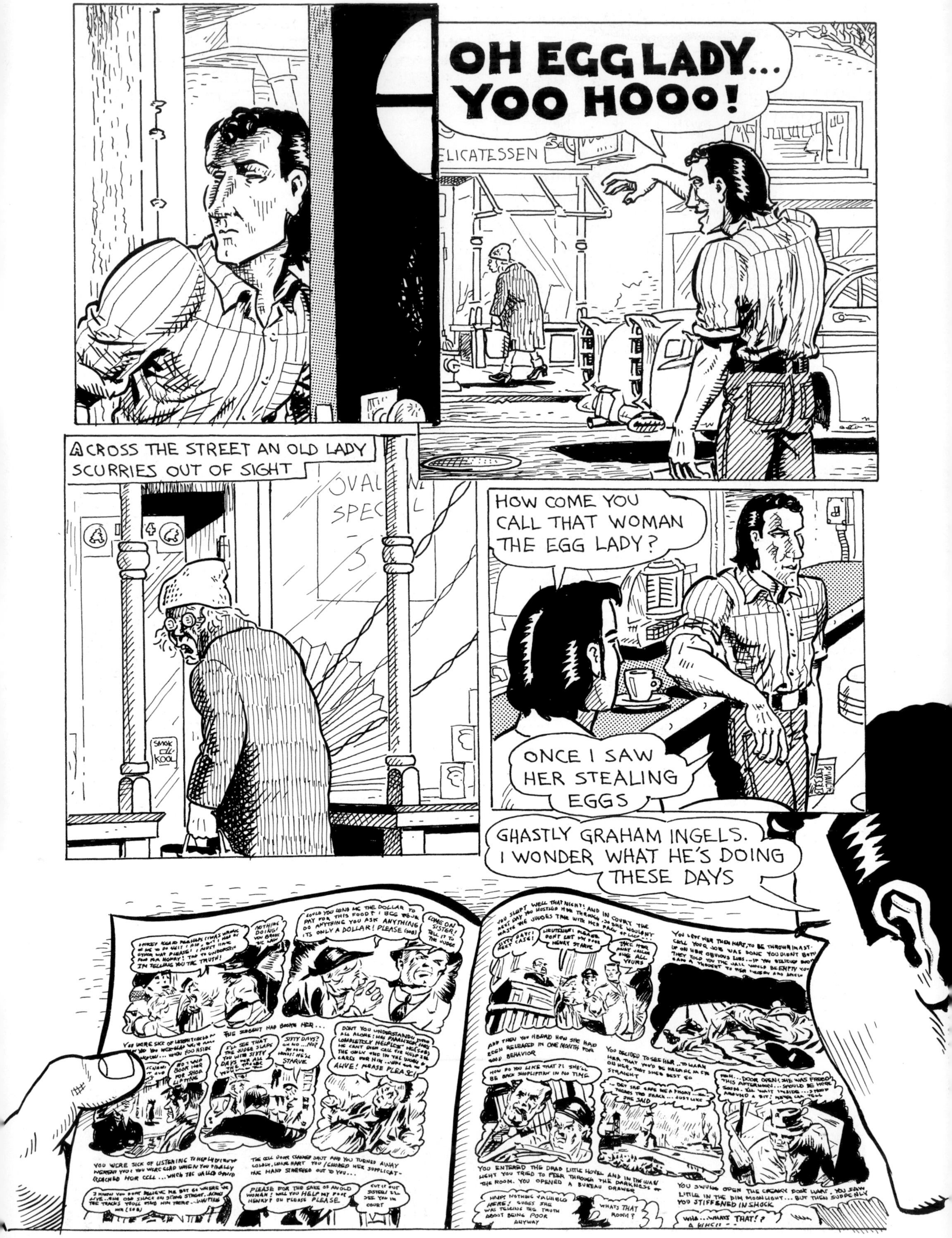
OH EGG LADY... YOO HOOO!
ELICATESSEN
ACROSS THE STREET AN OLD LADY SCURRIES OUT OF SIGHT
HOW COME YOU CALL THAT WOMAN THE EGG LADY?
ONCE I SAW HER STEALING EGGS
GHASTLY GRAHAM INGELS. I WONDER WHAT HE'S DOING THESE DAYS

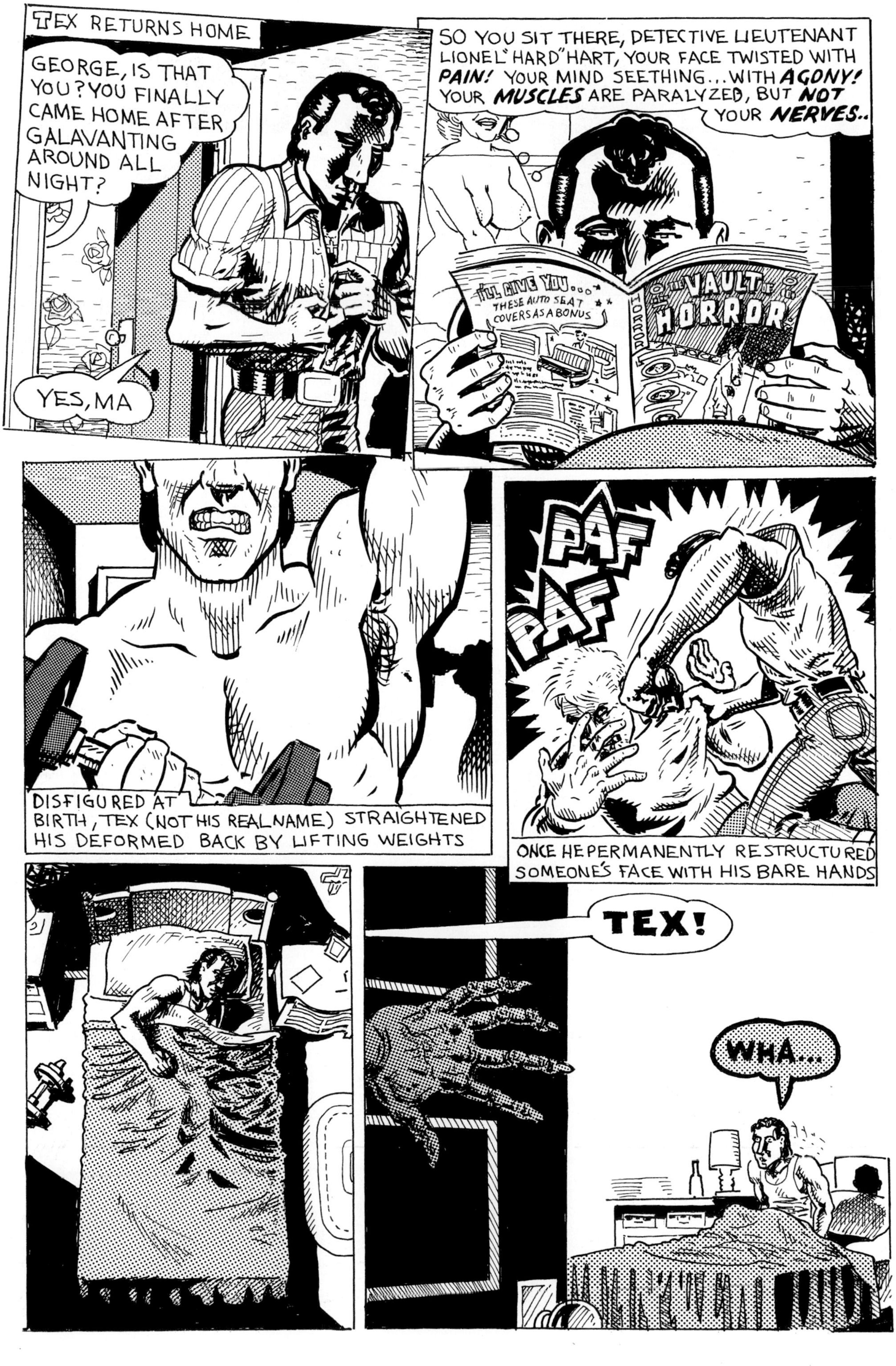
TEX RETURNS HOME
GEORGE, IS THAT YOU? YOU FINALLY CAME HOME AFTER GALAVANTING AROUND ALL NIGHT?
YES, MA
SO YOU SIT THERE, DETECTIVE LIEUTENANT LIONEL "HARD" HART, YOUR FACE TWISTED WITH PAIN! YOUR MIND SEETHING... WITH AGONY! YOUR MUSCLES ARE PARALYZED, BUT NOT YOUR NERVES..
I'LL GIVE YOU...
THESE AUTO SEAT COVERS AS A BONUS
THE VAULT OF HORROR
HORROR
DISFIGURED AT BIRTH, TEX (NOT HIS REAL NAME) STRAIGHTENED HIS DEFORMED BACK BY LIFTING WEIGHTS
PAF
PAF
ONCE HE PERMANENTLY RESTRUCTURED SOMEONE'S FACE WITH HIS BARE HANDS
TEX!
WHA...

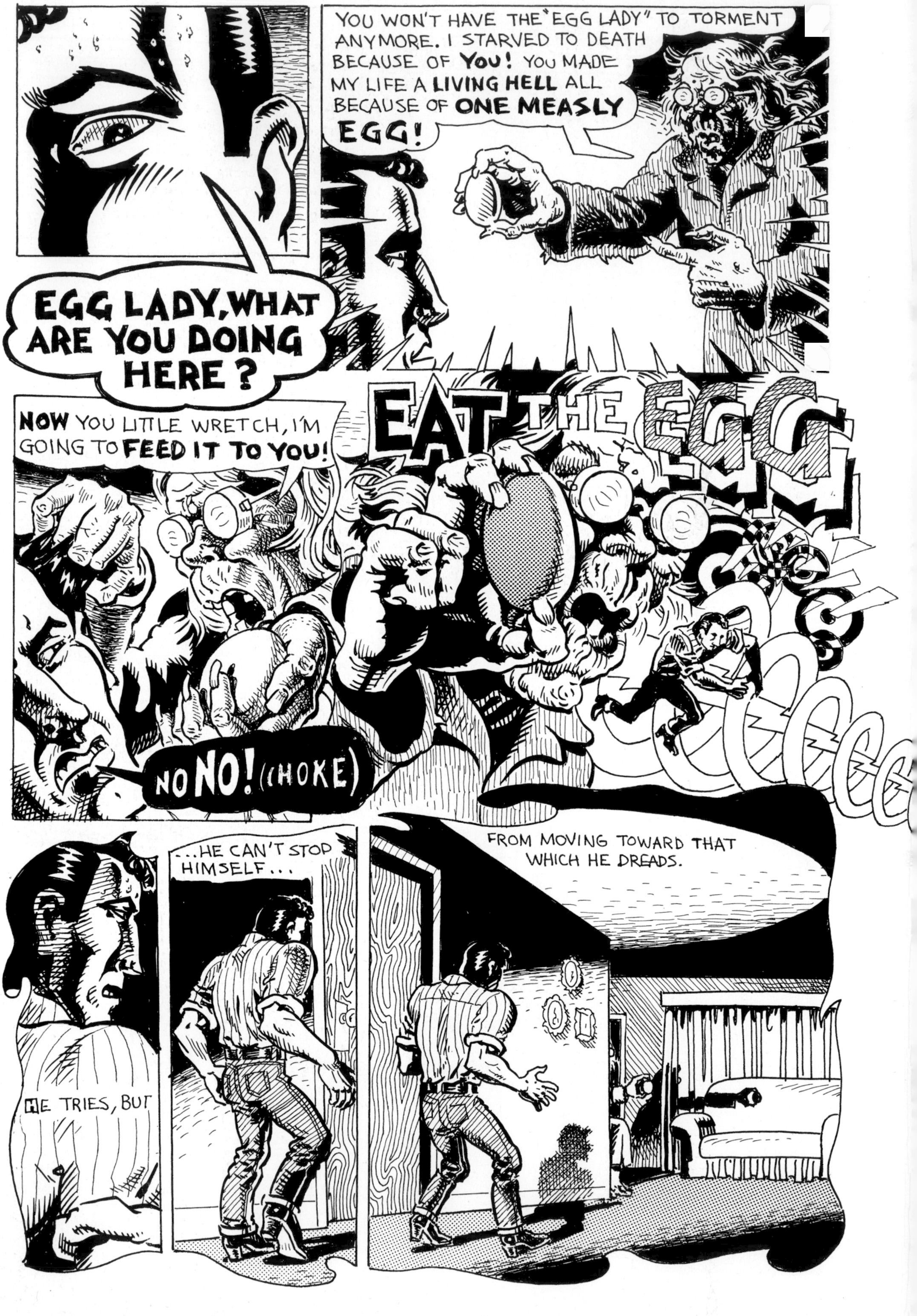

YOU WON'T HAVE THE "EGG LADY" TO TORMENT ANYMORE. I STARVED TO DEATH BECAUSE OF YOU! YOU MADE MY LIFE A LIVING HELL ALL BECAUSE OF ONE MEASLY EGG!
EGG LADY, WHAT ARE YOU DOING HERE?
NOW YOU LITTLE WRETCH, I'M GOING TO FEED IT TO YOU!
EAT THE EGG
NO NO! (CHOKE)
HE TRIES, BUT
...HE CAN'T STOP HIMSELF...
FROM MOVING TOWARD THAT WHICH HE DREADS.

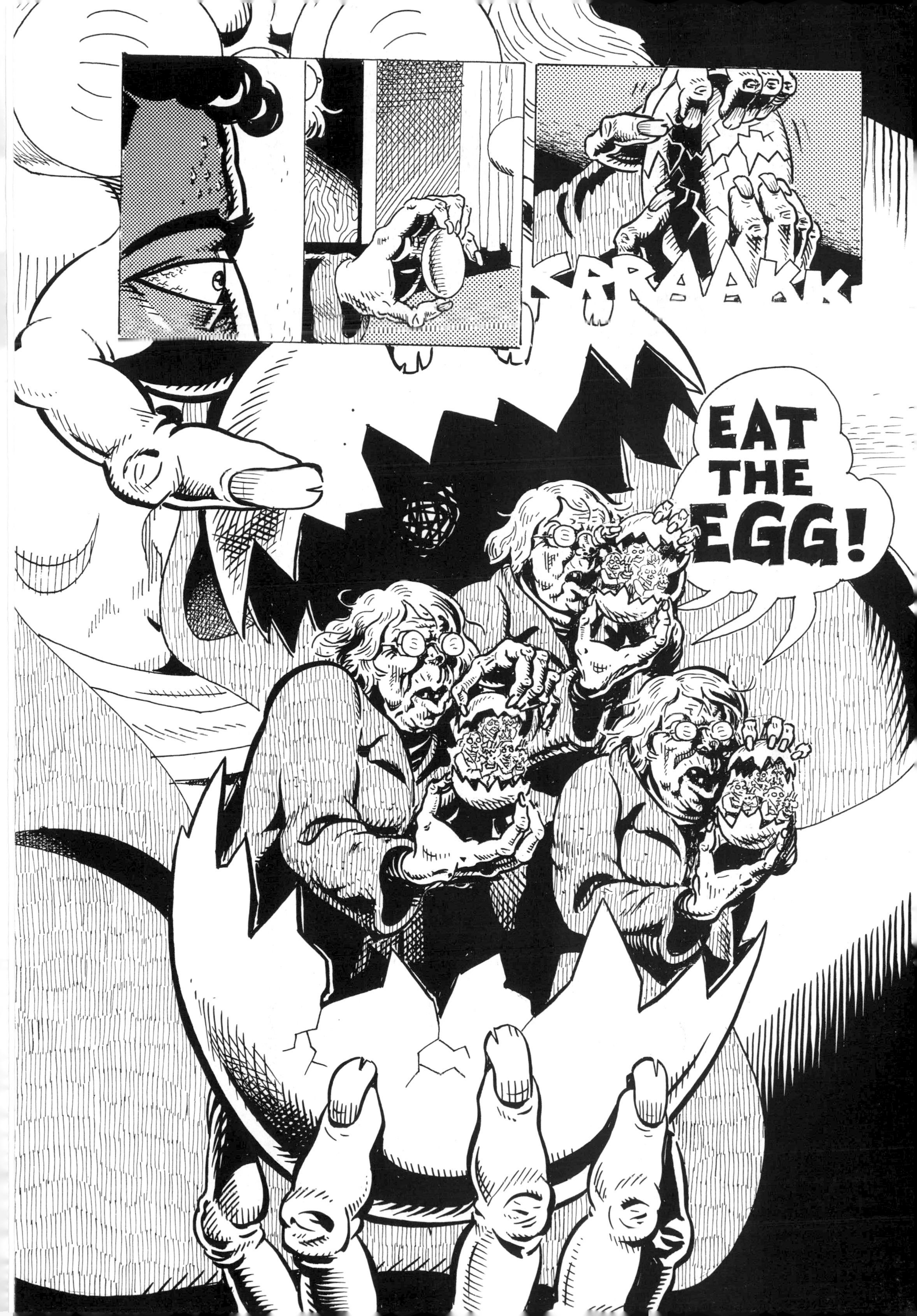
KRAAAKK
EAT THE EGG!

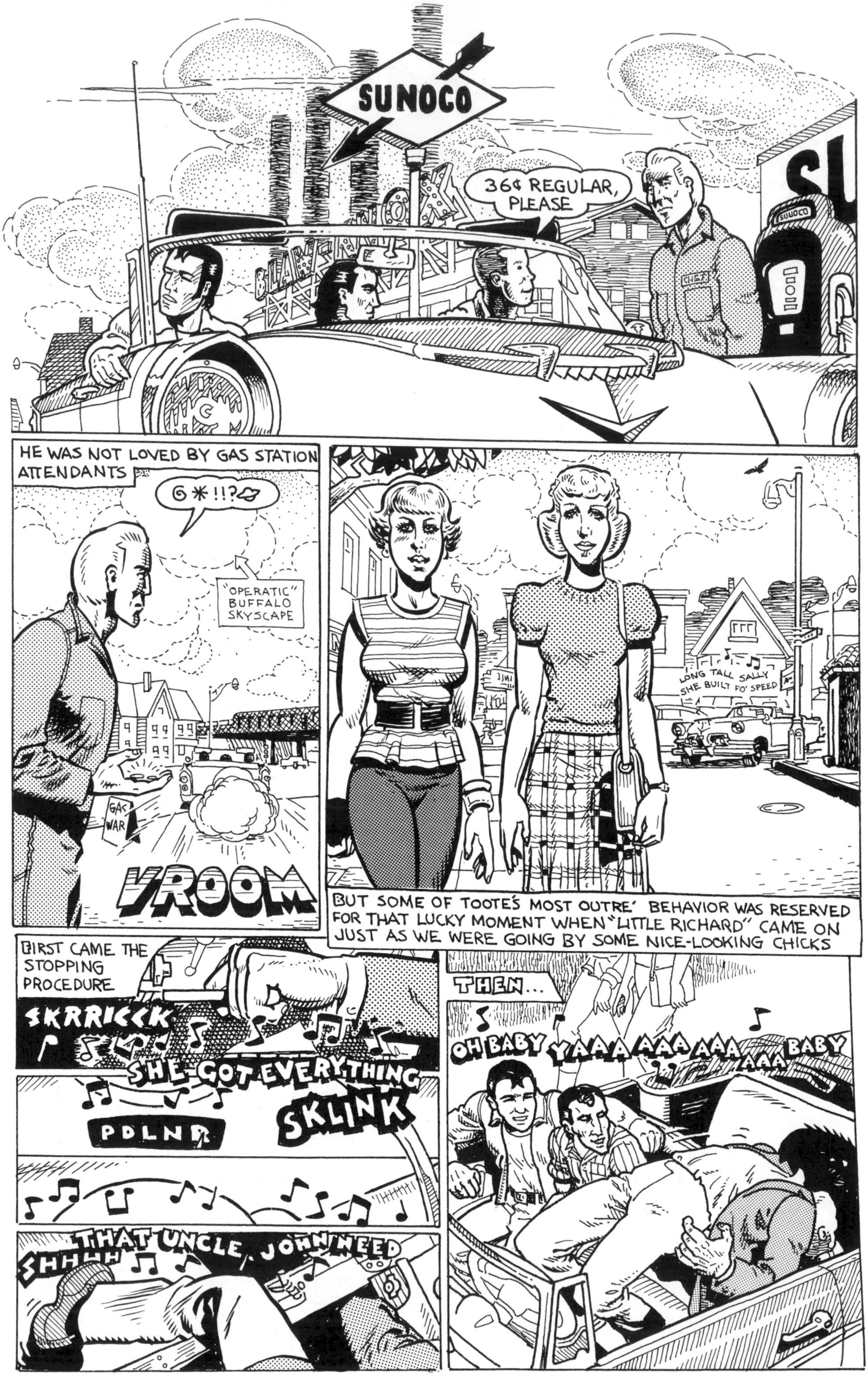
SUNOCO
36¢ REGULAR, PLEASE
HE WAS NOT LOVED BY GAS STATION ATTENDANTS
"OPERATIC" BUFFALO SKYSCAPE
GAS WAR
VROOM
LONG TALL SALLY SHE BUILT FO' SPEED
BUT SOME OF TOOTE'S MOST OUTRE' BEHAVIOR WAS RESERVED FOR THAT LUCKY MOMENT WHEN "LITTLE RICHARD" CAME ON JUST AS WE WERE GOING BY SOME NICE-LOOKING CHICKS
FIRST CAME THE STOPPING PROCEDURE
SKRRICCK
SHE GOT EVERYTHING
SKLINK
PDLNR
SHHHH THAT UNCLE JOHN NEED
THEN...
OH BABY YAAA AAA AAA AAA BABY

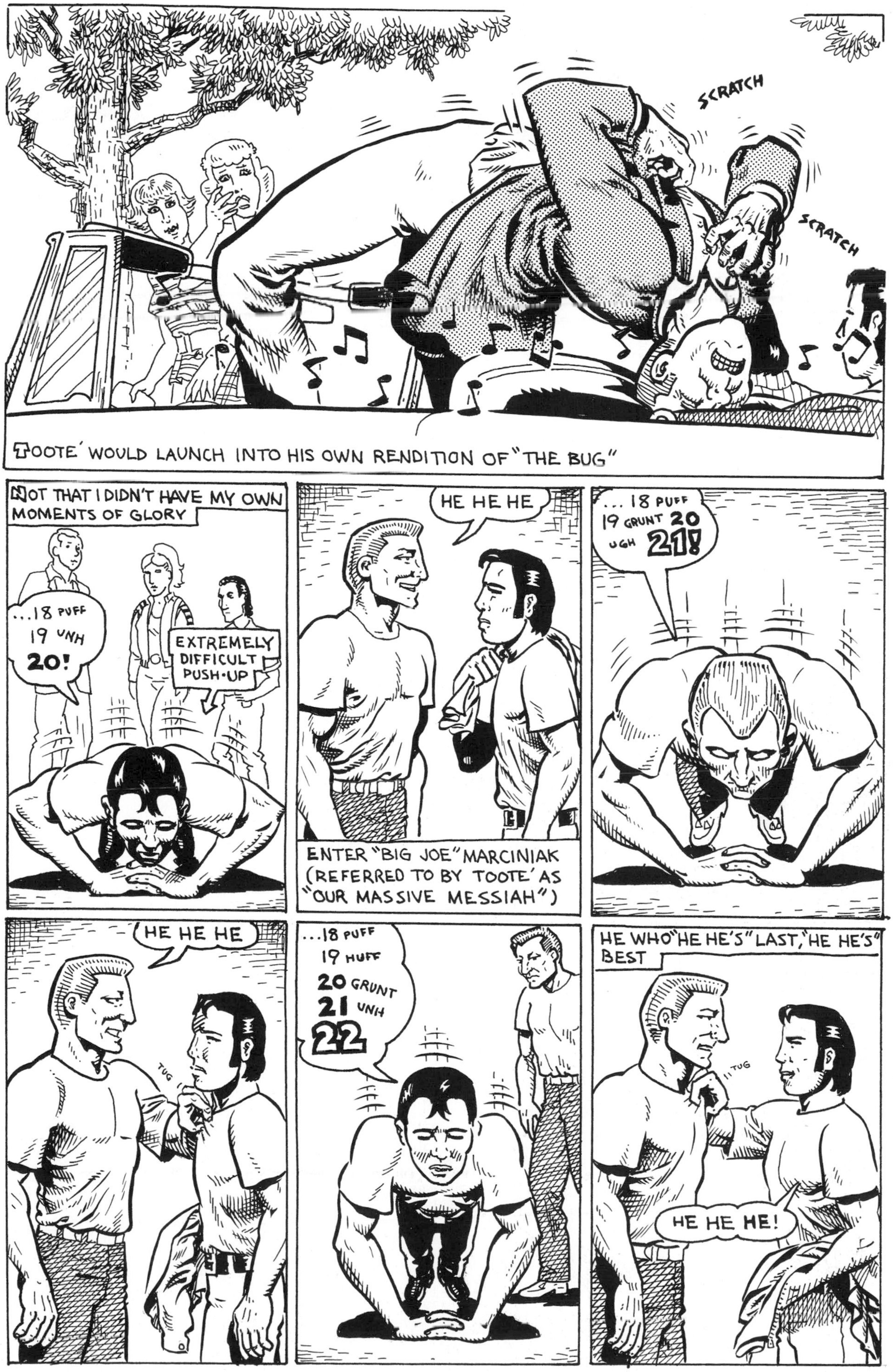
SCRATCH
SCRATCH
TOOTE' WOULD LAUNCH INTO HIS OWN RENDITION OF "THE BUG"
NOT THAT I DIDN'T HAVE MY OWN MOMENTS OF GLORY
...18 PUFF 19 UNH 20!
EXTREMELY DIFFICULT PUSH-UP
HE HE HE
ENTER "BIG JOE" MARCINIAK (REFERRED TO BY TOOTE' AS "OUR MASSIVE MESSIAH")
...18 PUFF 19 GRUNT 20 UGH 21!
HE HE HE
TUG
...18 PUFF 19 HUFF 20 GRUNT 21 UNH 22
HE WHO "HE HE'S" LAST, "HE HE'S" BEST
TUG
HE HE HE!

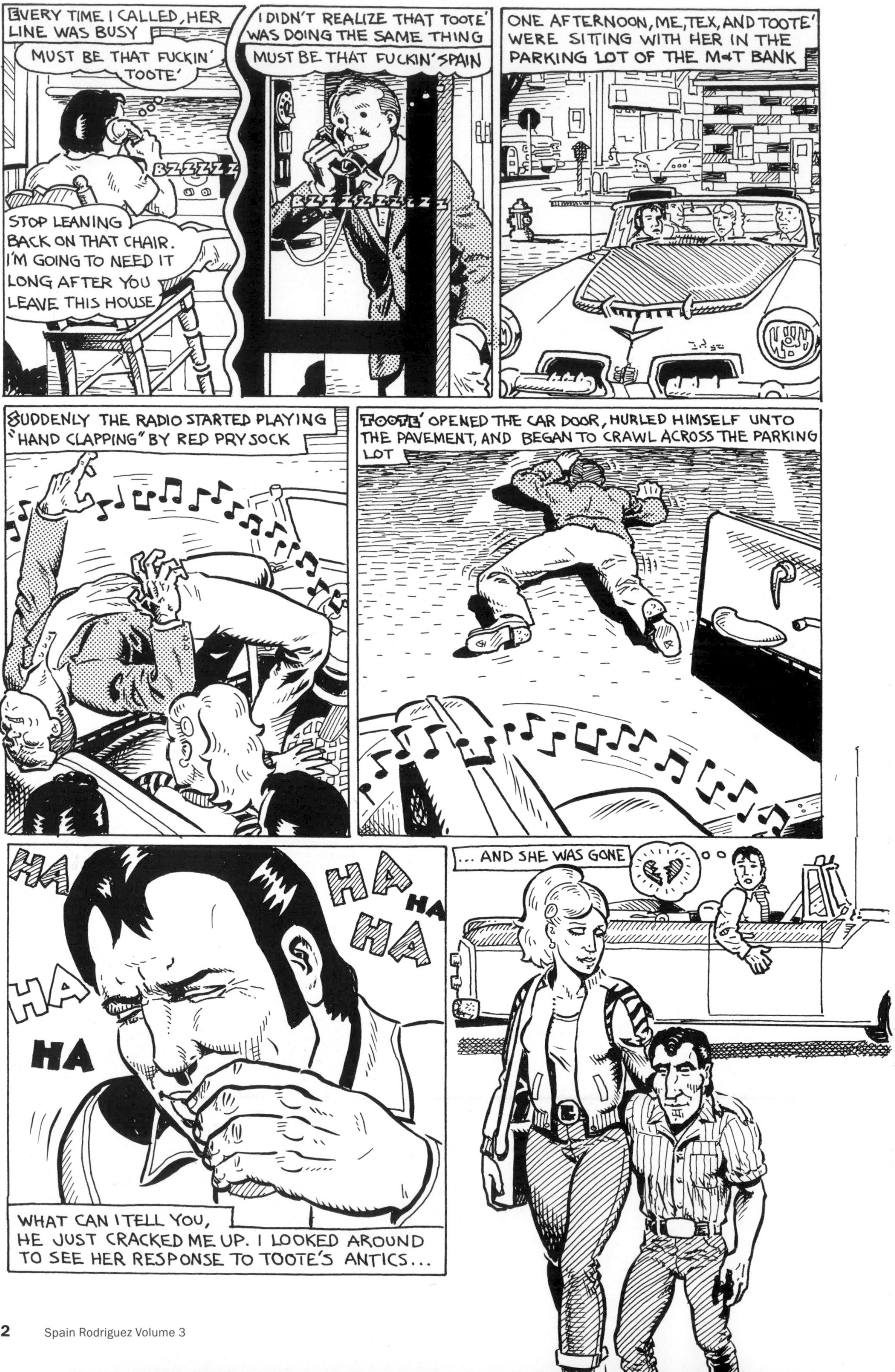
EVERY TIME I CALLED, HER LINE WAS BUSY
MUST BE THAT FUCKIN' TOOTE'
BZZZZZ
STOP LEANING BACK ON THAT CHAIR. I'M GOING TO NEED IT LONG AFTER YOU LEAVE THIS HOUSE
I DIDN'T REALIZE THAT TOOTE' WAS DOING THE SAME THING
MUST BE THAT FUCKIN' SPAIN
ONE AFTERNOON, ME, TEX, AND TOOTE' WERE SITTING WITH HER IN THE PARKING LOT OF THE M&T BANK
SUDDENLY THE RADIO STARTED PLAYING "HAND CLAPPING" BY RED PRYSOCK
TOOTE' OPENED THE CAR DOOR, HURLED HIMSELF UNTO THE PAVEMENT, AND BEGAN TO CRAWL ACROSS THE PARKING LOT
HA HA HA HA HA HA
WHAT CAN I TELL YOU, HE JUST CRACKED ME UP. I LOOKED AROUND TO SEE HER RESPONSE TO TOOTE'S ANTICS...
... AND SHE WAS GONE

AY TEX! WHAT'S HAPPENING, MAN?
1960.. BUFFALO N.Y.
DID YOU SEE ALL THIS ABOUT THESE TWO GUYS?
COURIER EXPRESS
WILCOXSON AND NUSSBAUM
BUFFALO PEACE BRIDGE CANADA
TAK TAK TAK TAK
MIDLAND
SPAIN '90

P. 163–169 from *Blab!* #5, 1990

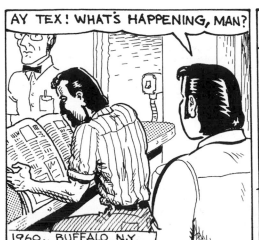

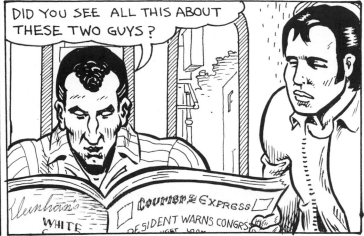

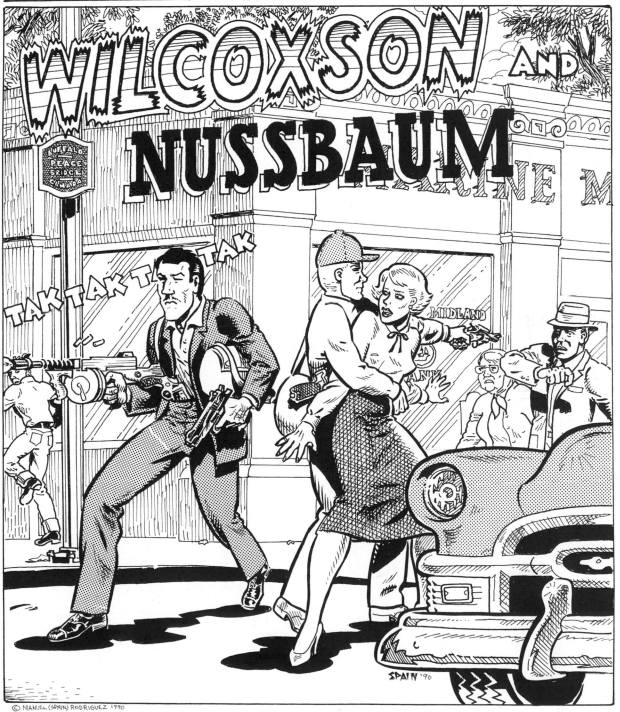

I HEARD ONE OF THEM CAME FROM AROUND HERE. I DON'T KNOW WHICH ONE
Edna's HOUSE of Beauty
THERE'S TOOTE'! WONDER WHAT HE'S UP TO
RROWITZ
LOW COST
1.39
HEY FRED! WHAT THE FUCK ARE YOU DOING?
I'M SURE THAT IF I CONCENTRATE HARD ENOUGH, I'LL BE ABLE TO FLY
SOME MIGHT HAVE CONCLUDED THAT TOOTE' WAS QUITE MAD
TOOTE'S PAD
SNOW WHITE
I GOTTA GO UP TO MY HOUSE AND GET SOMETHING
TOOTE'S BROTHER, VEZAY, HAD A DOCTORATE OF DIVINITY AND RARELY WORKED
YA, NUSSBAUM WENT TO EAST* WHEN I WAS THERE, I REMEMBER...
*EAST HIGH SCHOOL
... THE PRINCIPAL BAWLING HIM OUT ABOUT SOMETHING

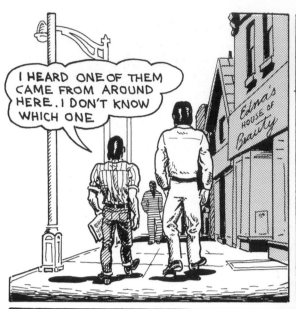

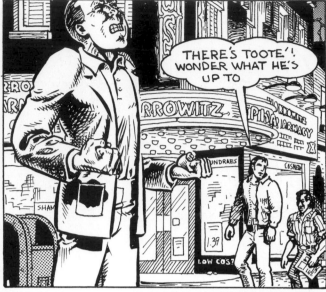

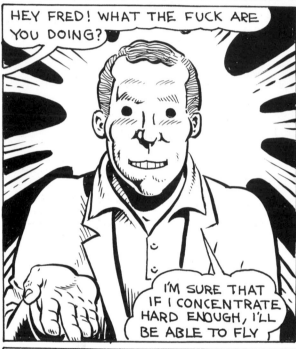

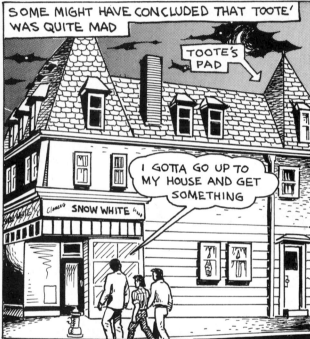

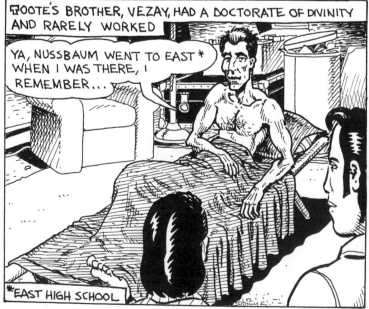

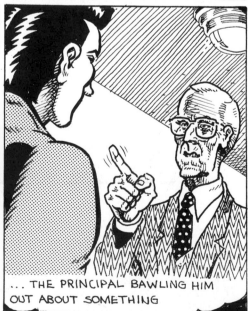

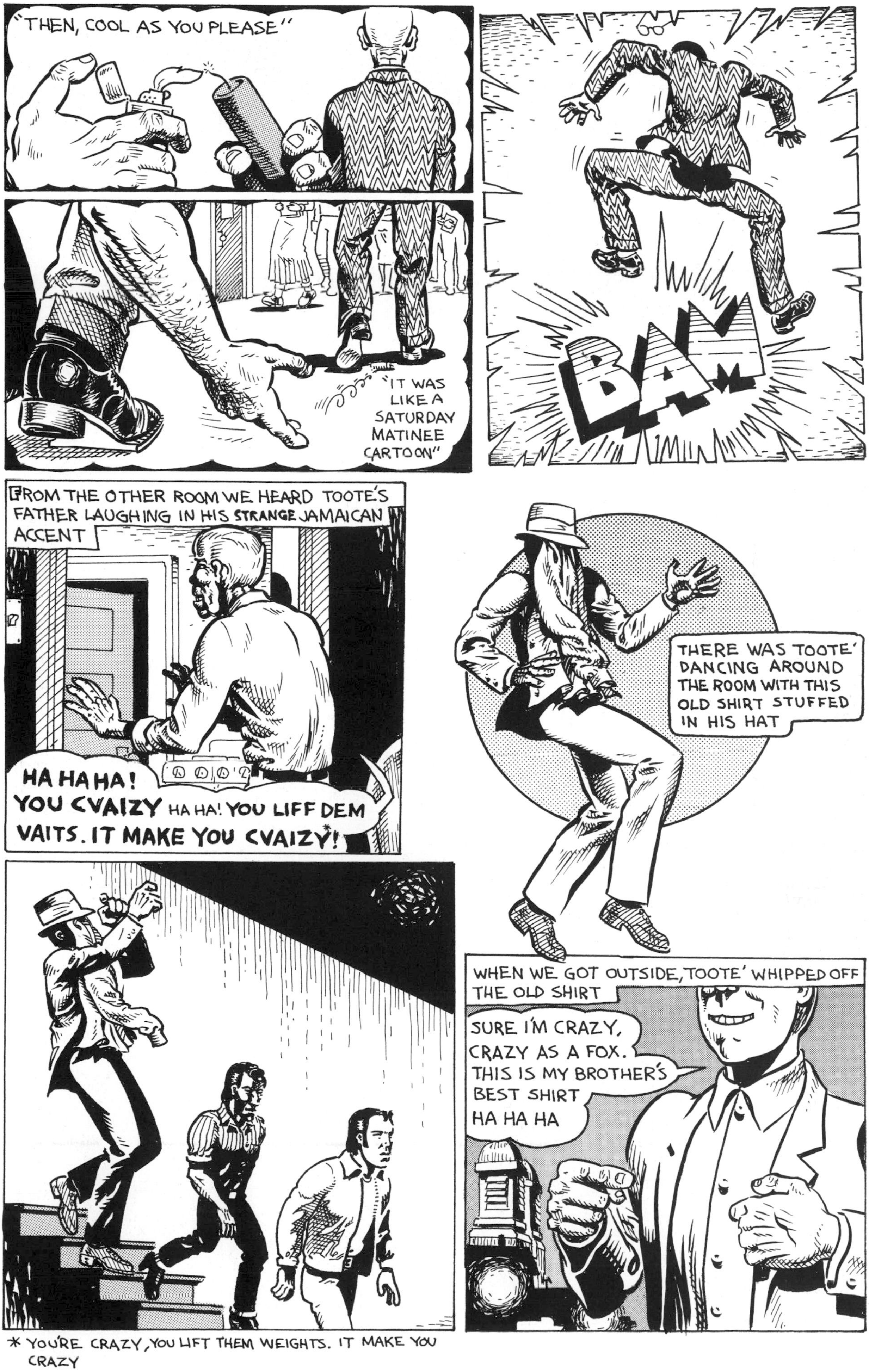
"THEN, COOL AS YOU PLEASE"
"IT WAS LIKE A SATURDAY MATINEE CARTOON"
BAM
FROM THE OTHER ROOM WE HEARD TOOTE'S FATHER LAUGHING IN HIS STRANGE JAMAICAN ACCENT
HA HA HA! YOU CVAIZY HA HA! YOU LIFF DEM VAITS. IT MAKE YOU CVAIZY*!
THERE WAS TOOTE' DANCING AROUND THE ROOM WITH THIS OLD SHIRT STUFFED IN HIS HAT
WHEN WE GOT OUTSIDE, TOOTE' WHIPPED OFF THE OLD SHIRT
SURE I'M CRAZY, CRAZY AS A FOX. THIS IS MY BROTHER'S BEST SHIRT HA HA HA
* YOU'RE CRAZY, YOU LIFT THEM WEIGHTS. IT MAKE YOU CRAZY

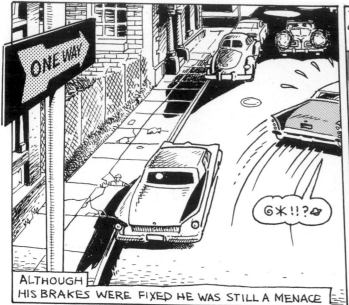

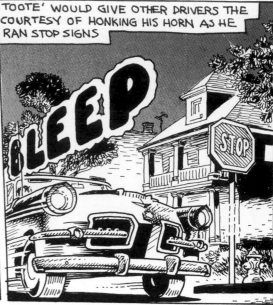

ONE WAY
G*!!?
ALTHOUGH HIS BRAKES WERE FIXED HE WAS STILL A MENACE
TOOTE' WOULD GIVE OTHER DRIVERS THE COURTESY OF HONKING HIS HORN AS HE RAN STOP SIGNS
BLEEP
STOP
BUT SOMEHOW WE ALWAYS GOT THERE
MILLER
ROOM
DELLWOOD DANCES
DELLWOOD DANCES
TEXAS RED HOTS
BURGERS
SHAKES
7up
I COULD NEVER QUITE FIGURE OUT HOW TO DANCE TO THAT PART OF "THE BOOK OF LOVE" WHERE THEY RECITE ALL THE CHAPTERS. BUT I DIDN'T HAVE TO WORRY ABOUT DANCING
WELL I WONDER WONDER WHO BO DOO DOO WHO! WHO WROTE THE BOOK OF LOVE
CHAPTER ONE SEZ YOU LOVE'ERR YOU LOVE ERR
WITH ALL YOUR HEART CHAPTER TWO YOU TELL ERR YOU'RE NEVER, NEVER, NEVER, NEVER, NEVER GONNA PART
DID YA HEAR ABOUT THOSE TWO GUYS WHO ROBBED THAT BANK ON THE EAST SIDE?
YA! ONE OF THOSE GUYS COMES FROM MY NEIGHBORHOOD
EVERYONE WAS TALKING ABOUT WILCOXSON AND NUSSBAUM

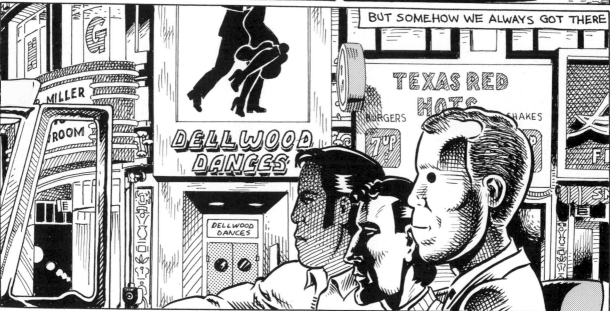

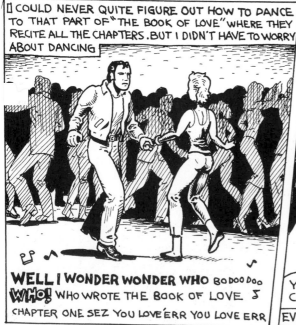

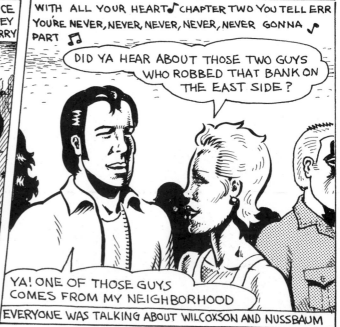

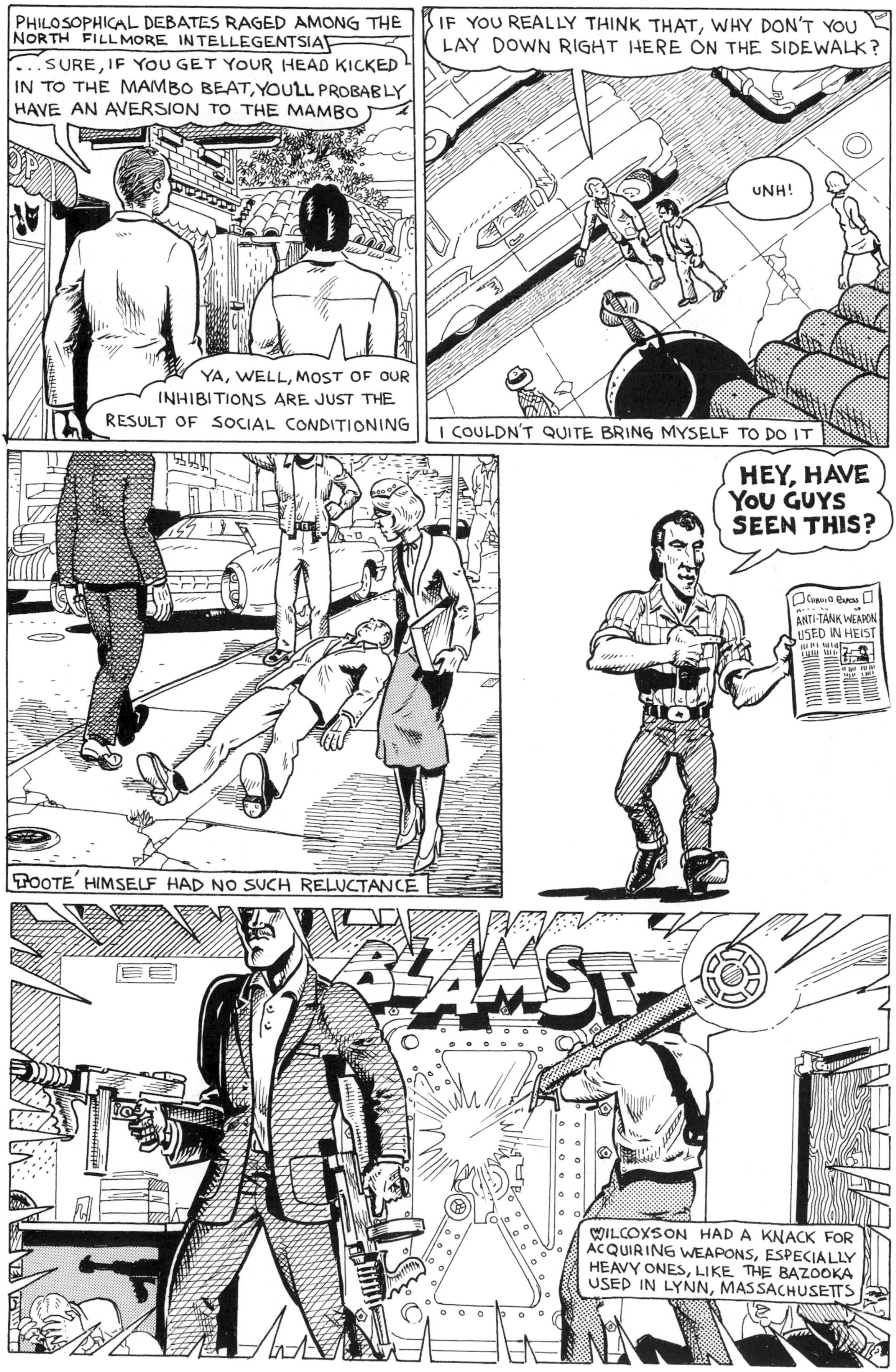
PHILOSOPHICAL DEBATES RAGED AMONG THE NORTH FILLMORE INTELLEGENTSIA
. . . SURE, IF YOU GET YOUR HEAD KICKED IN TO THE MAMBO BEAT, YOU'LL PROBABLY HAVE AN AVERSION TO THE MAMBO
YA, WELL, MOST OF OUR INHIBITIONS ARE JUST THE RESULT OF SOCIAL CONDITIONING
IF YOU REALLY THINK THAT, WHY DON'T YOU LAY DOWN RIGHT HERE ON THE SIDEWALK?
UNH!
I COULDN'T QUITE BRING MYSELF TO DO IT
DOOTE' HIMSELF HAD NO SUCH RELUCTANCE
HEY, HAVE YOU GUYS SEEN THIS?
ANTI-TANK WEAPON USED IN HEIST
BLAMST
WILCOXSON HAD A KNACK FOR ACQUIRING WEAPONS, ESPECIALLY HEAVY ONES, LIKE THE BAZOOKA USED IN LYNN, MASSACHUSETTS

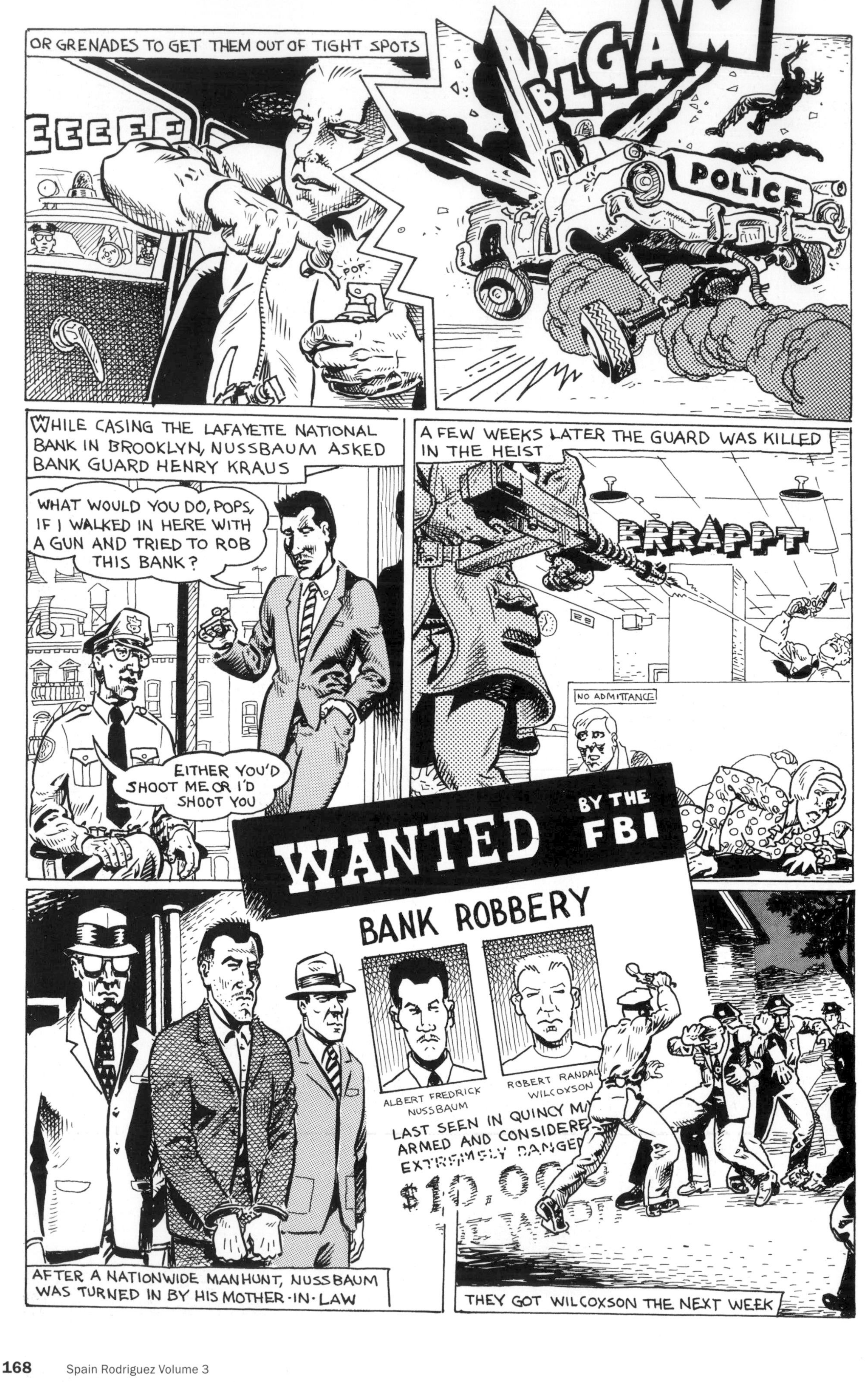
OR GRENADES TO GET THEM OUT OF TIGHT SPOTS
EEEEE
POP
VBLGAM
POLICE
WHILE CASING THE LAFAYETTE NATIONAL BANK IN BROOKLYN, NUSSBAUM ASKED BANK GUARD HENRY KRAUS
WHAT WOULD YOU DO, POPS, IF I WALKED IN HERE WITH A GUN AND TRIED TO ROB THIS BANK?
EITHER YOU'D SHOOT ME OR I'D SHOOT YOU
A FEW WEEKS LATER THE GUARD WAS KILLED IN THE HEIST
BRRAPPT
NO ADMITTANCE
WANTED BY THE FBI
BANK ROBBERY
ALBERT FREDRICK NUSSBAUM
ROBERT RANDAL WILCOXSON
LAST SEEN IN QUINCY MA
ARMED AND CONSIDERE
AFTER A NATIONWIDE MANHUNT, NUSSBAUM WAS TURNED IN BY HIS MOTHER-IN-LAW
THEY GOT WILCOXSON THE NEXT WEEK

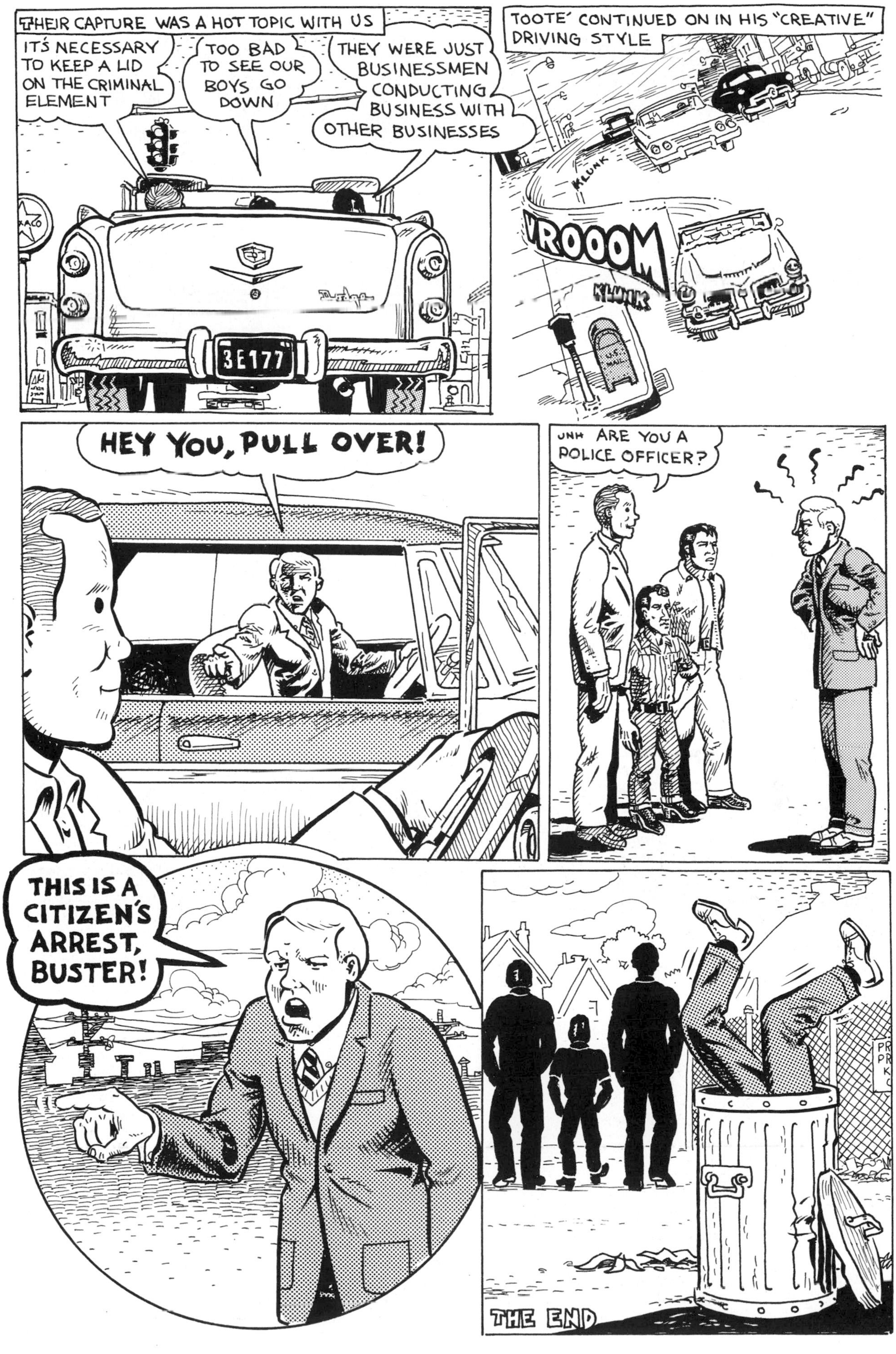
THEIR CAPTURE WAS A HOT TOPIC WITH US
IT'S NECESSARY TO KEEP A LID ON THE CRIMINAL ELEMENT
TOO BAD TO SEE OUR BOYS GO DOWN
THEY WERE JUST BUSINESSMEN CONDUCTING BUSINESS WITH OTHER BUSINESSES
3E177
TOOTE' CONTINUED ON IN HIS "CREATIVE" DRIVING STYLE
KLUNK
VROOOM
KLUNK
HEY YOU, PULL OVER!
UNH ARE YOU A POLICE OFFICER?
THIS IS A CITIZEN'S ARREST, BUSTER!
THE END

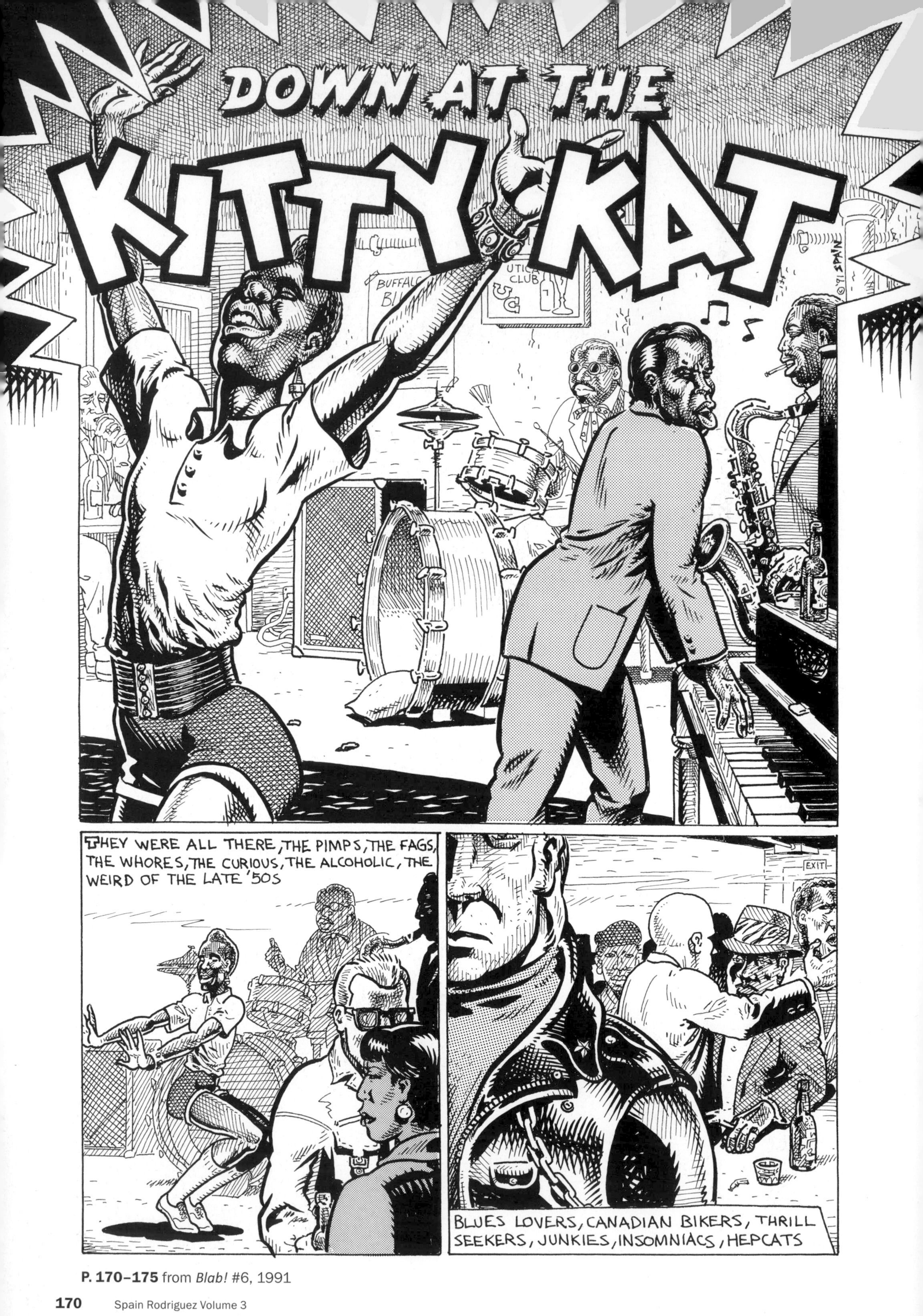
DOWN AT THE
KITTY KAT
©'91 SPAIN
THEY WERE ALL THERE, THE PIMPS, THE FAGS, THE WHORES, THE CURIOUS, THE ALCOHOLIC, THE WEIRD OF THE LATE '50S
EXIT
BLUES LOVERS, CANADIAN BIKERS, THRILL SEEKERS, JUNKIES, INSOMNIACS, HEPCATS

P. 170–175 from *Blab!* #6, 1991

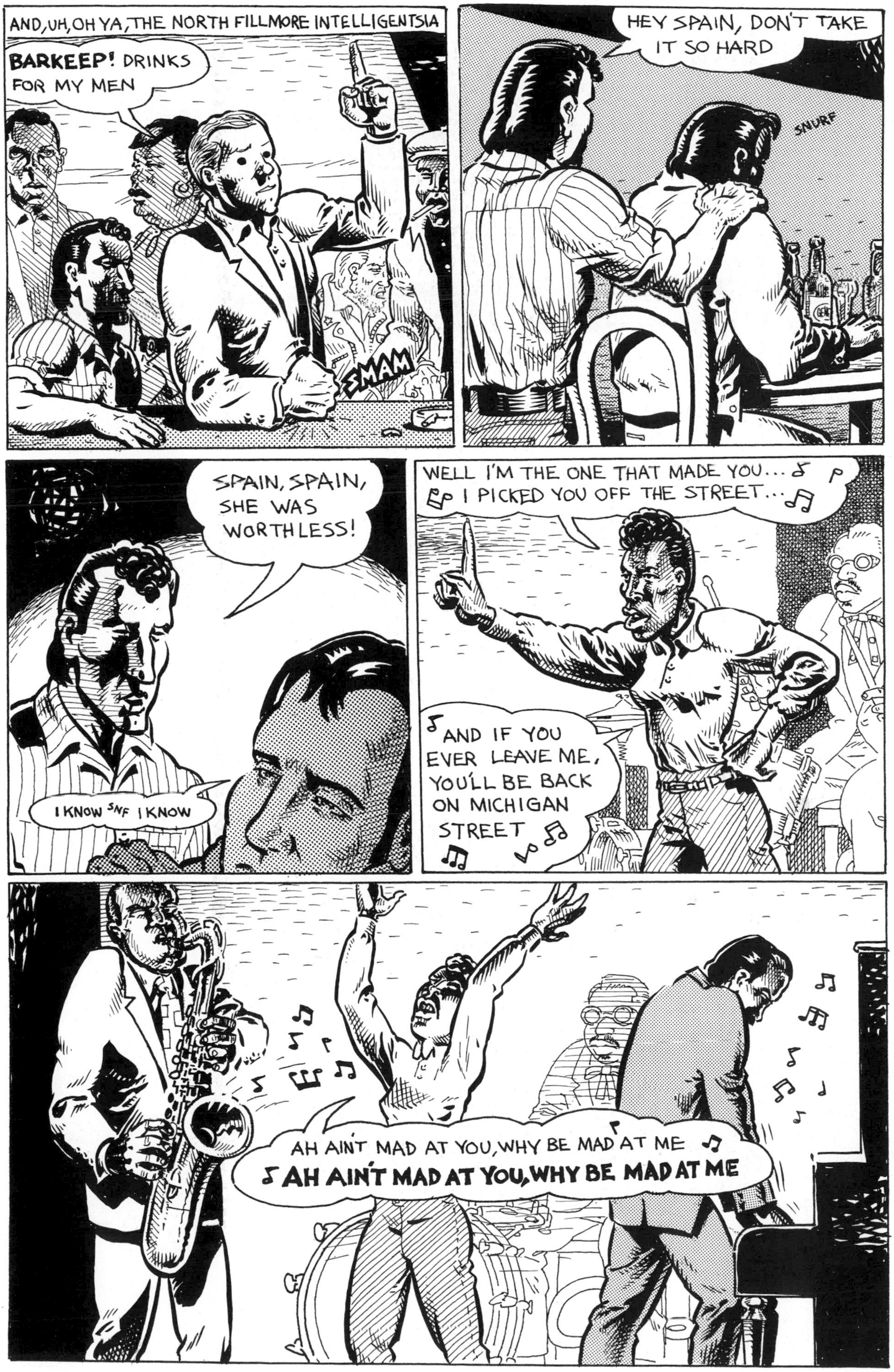
AND, UH, OH YA, THE NORTH FILLMORE INTELLIGENTSIA
BARKEEP! DRINKS FOR MY MEN
SMAM
HEY SPAIN, DON'T TAKE IT SO HARD
SNURF
SPAIN, SPAIN, SHE WAS WORTHLESS!
I KNOW SNF I KNOW
WELL I'M THE ONE THAT MADE YOU... I PICKED YOU OFF THE STREET...
AND IF YOU EVER LEAVE ME, YOU'LL BE BACK ON MICHIGAN STREET
AH AIN'T MAD AT YOU, WHY BE MAD AT ME
AH AIN'T MAD AT YOU, WHY BE MAD AT ME

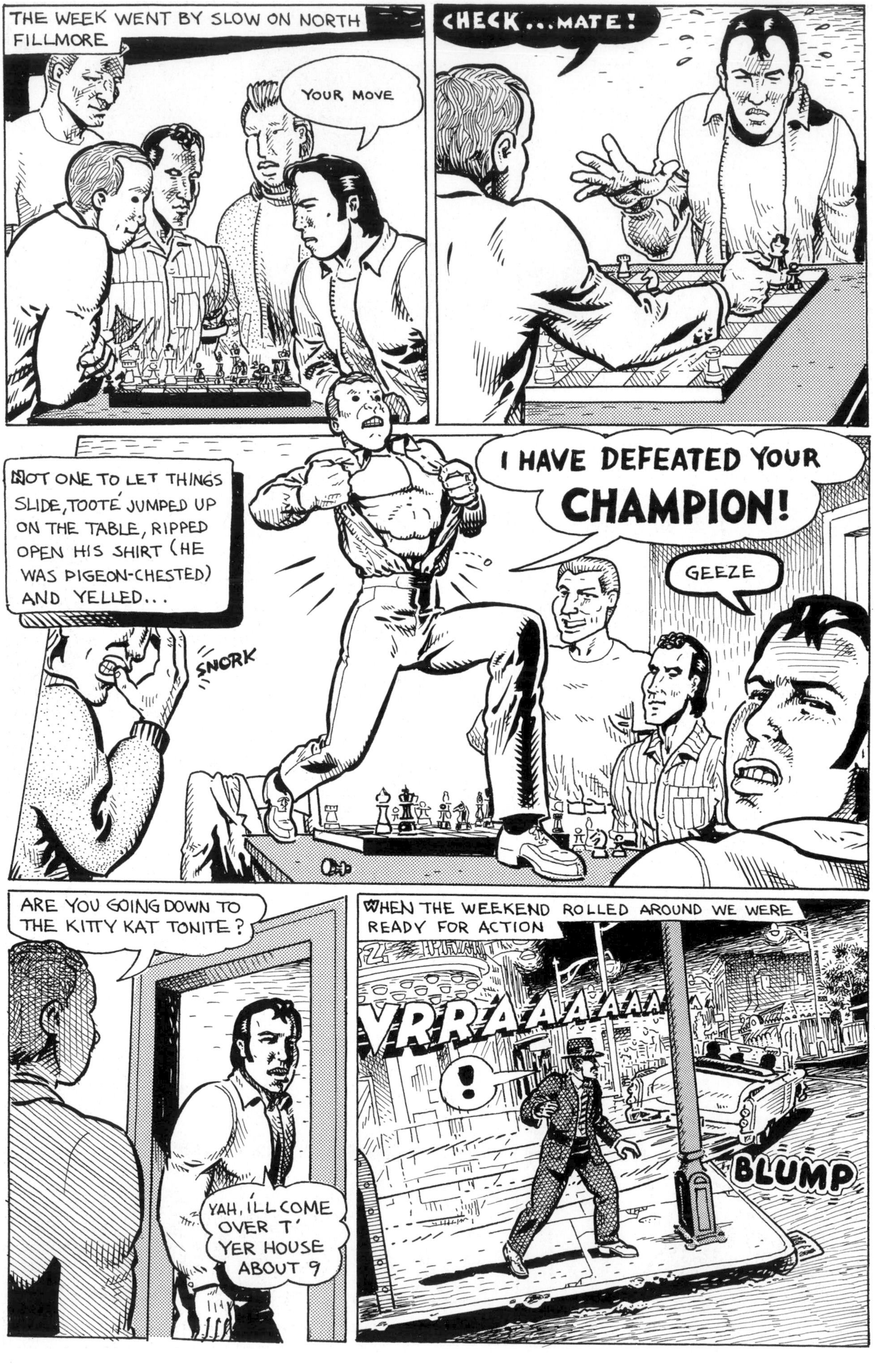

THE WEEK WENT BY SLOW ON NORTH FILLMORE
YOUR MOVE
CHECK...MATE!
NOT ONE TO LET THINGS SLIDE, TOOTÉ JUMPED UP ON THE TABLE, RIPPED OPEN HIS SHIRT (HE WAS PIGEON-CHESTED) AND YELLED...
I HAVE DEFEATED YOUR CHAMPION!
GEEZE
SNORK
ARE YOU GOING DOWN TO THE KITTY KAT TONITE?
YAH, I'LL COME OVER T' YER HOUSE ABOUT 9
WHEN THE WEEKEND ROLLED AROUND WE WERE READY FOR ACTION
VRRAAAAAAA
!
BLUMP

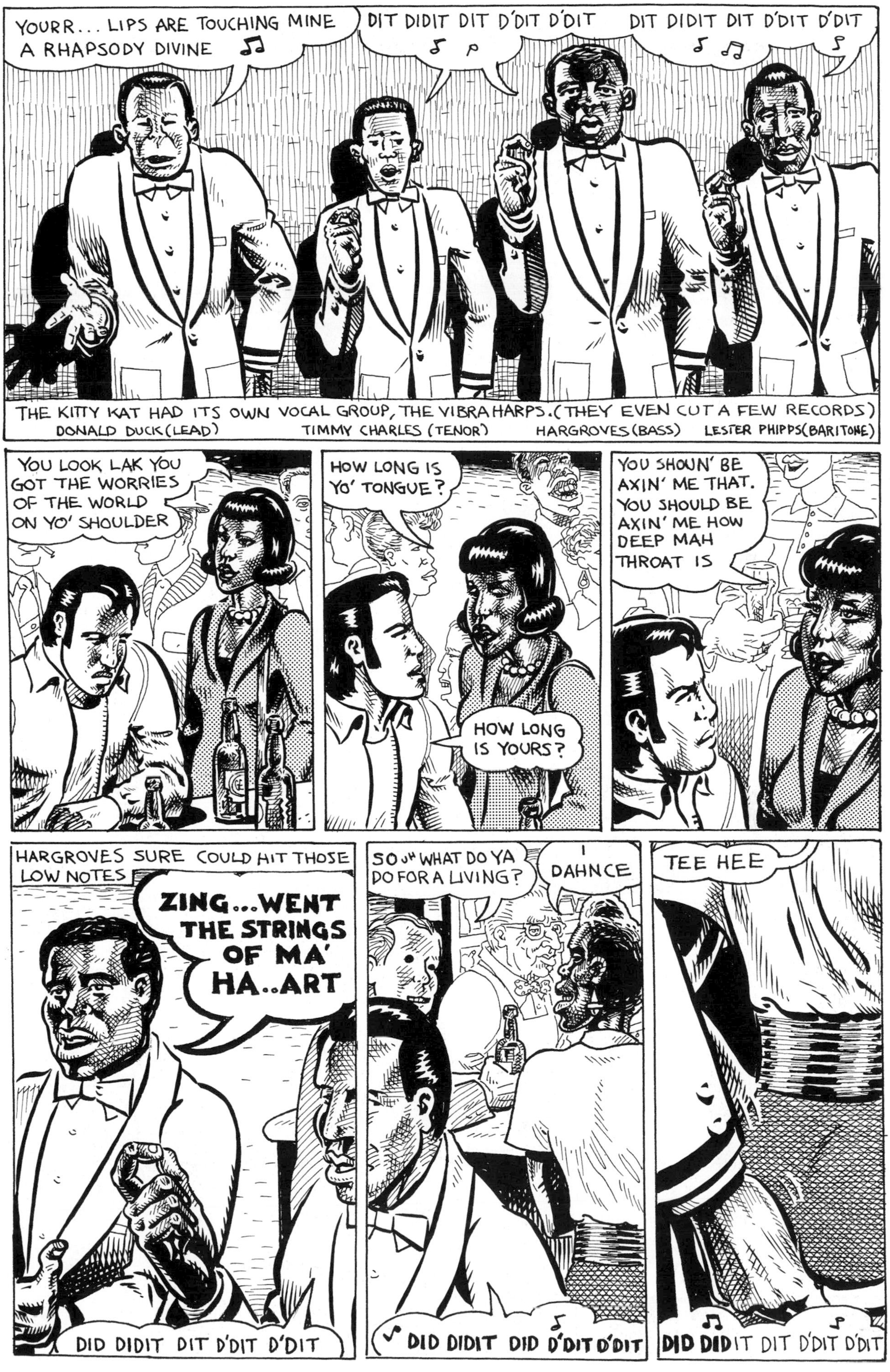

YOURR... LIPS ARE TOUCHING MINE
A RHAPSODY DIVINE
DIT DIDIT DIT D'DIT D'DIT
DIT DIDIT DIT D'DIT D'DIT
THE KITTY KAT HAD ITS OWN VOCAL GROUP, THE VIBRAHARPS. (THEY EVEN CUT A FEW RECORDS)
DONALD DUCK (LEAD)
TIMMY CHARLES (TENOR)
HARGROVES (BASS)
LESTER PHIPPS (BARITONE)
YOU LOOK LAK YOU GOT THE WORRIES OF THE WORLD ON YO' SHOULDER
HOW LONG IS YO' TONGUE?
HOW LONG IS YOURS?
YOU SHOUN' BE AXIN' ME THAT. YOU SHOULD BE AXIN' ME HOW DEEP MAH THROAT IS
HARGROVES SURE COULD HIT THOSE LOW NOTES
ZING...WENT THE STRINGS OF MA' HA..ART
DID DIDIT DIT D'DIT D'DIT
SO UH WHAT DO YA DO FOR A LIVING?
I DAHNCE
DID DIDIT DID D'DIT D'DIT
TEE HEE
DID DIDIT DIT D'DIT D'DIT

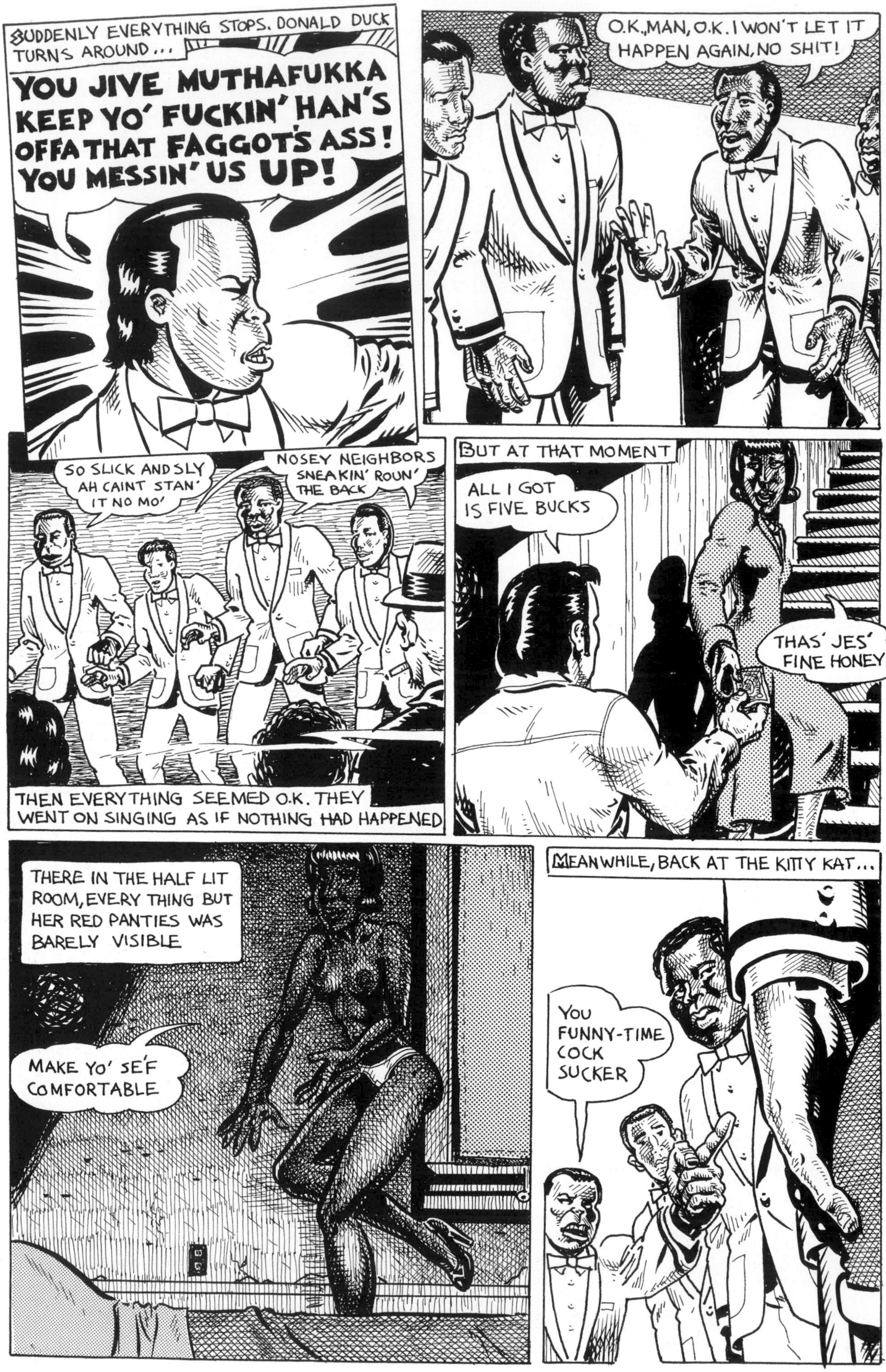
SUDDENLY EVERYTHING STOPS. DONALD DUCK TURNS AROUND...
YOU JIVE MUTHAFUKKA KEEP YO' FUCKIN' HAN'S OFFA THAT FAGGOT'S ASS! YOU MESSIN' US UP!
O.K., MAN, O.K. I WON'T LET IT HAPPEN AGAIN, NO SHIT!
SO SLICK AND SLY AH CAINT STAN' IT NO MO'
NOSEY NEIGHBORS SNEAKIN' ROUN' THE BACK
THEN EVERYTHING SEEMED O.K. THEY WENT ON SINGING AS IF NOTHING HAD HAPPENED
BUT AT THAT MOMENT
ALL I GOT IS FIVE BUCKS
THAS' JES' FINE HONEY
THERE IN THE HALF LIT ROOM, EVERY THING BUT HER RED PANTIES WAS BARELY VISIBLE
MAKE YO' SE'F COMFORTABLE
MEANWHILE, BACK AT THE KITTY KAT...
YOU FUNNY-TIME COCK SUCKER

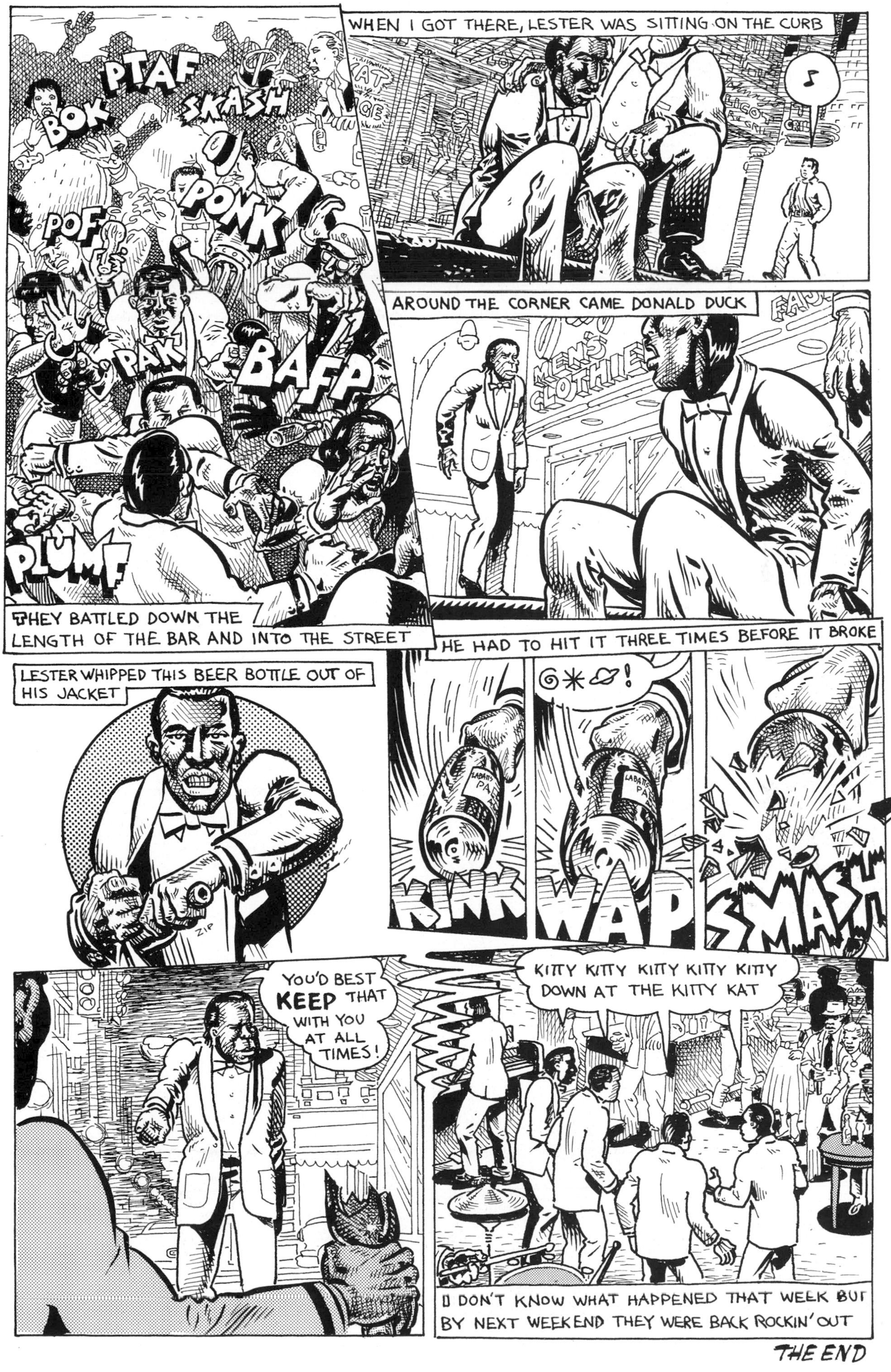
BOK
PTAF
SKASH
PONK
POF
PAK
BAFP
PLÜMF
THEY BATTLED DOWN THE LENGTH OF THE BAR AND INTO THE STREET
WHEN I GOT THERE, LESTER WAS SITTING ON THE CURB
AROUND THE CORNER CAME DONALD DUCK
MEN'S CLOTHIER
LESTER WHIPPED THIS BEER BOTTLE OUT OF HIS JACKET
ZIP
HE HAD TO HIT IT THREE TIMES BEFORE IT BROKE
KINK
WAP
SMASH
YOU'D BEST KEEP THAT WITH YOU AT ALL TIMES!
KITTY KITTY KITTY KITTY KITTY DOWN AT THE KITTY KAT
I DON'T KNOW WHAT HAPPENED THAT WEEK BUT BY NEXT WEEKEND THEY WERE BACK ROCKIN' OUT
THE END

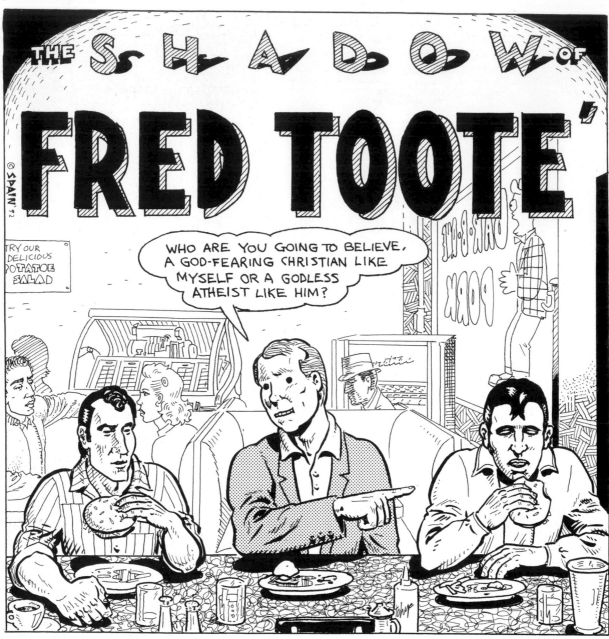

THE SHADOW OF FRED TOOTE'

WHO ARE YOU GOING TO BELIEVE, A GOD-FEARING CHRISTIAN LIKE MYSELF OR A GODLESS ATHEIST LIKE HIM?

TRY OUR DELICIOUS POTATOE SALAD

AY! FUCK "GOD" UP THE ASS

THE NORTH FILLMORE INTELLEGENTSIA ENGAGE IN PHILOSOPHICAL BANTER WHILE CONSUMING WATT'S BAR-B-QUE PORK SPECIALS

IF THERE'S NO GOD WHY WOULDN'T I GO OUT AND KILL SOMEONE?

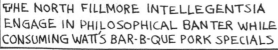

P. 176–181 from *Blab!* #7, 1992

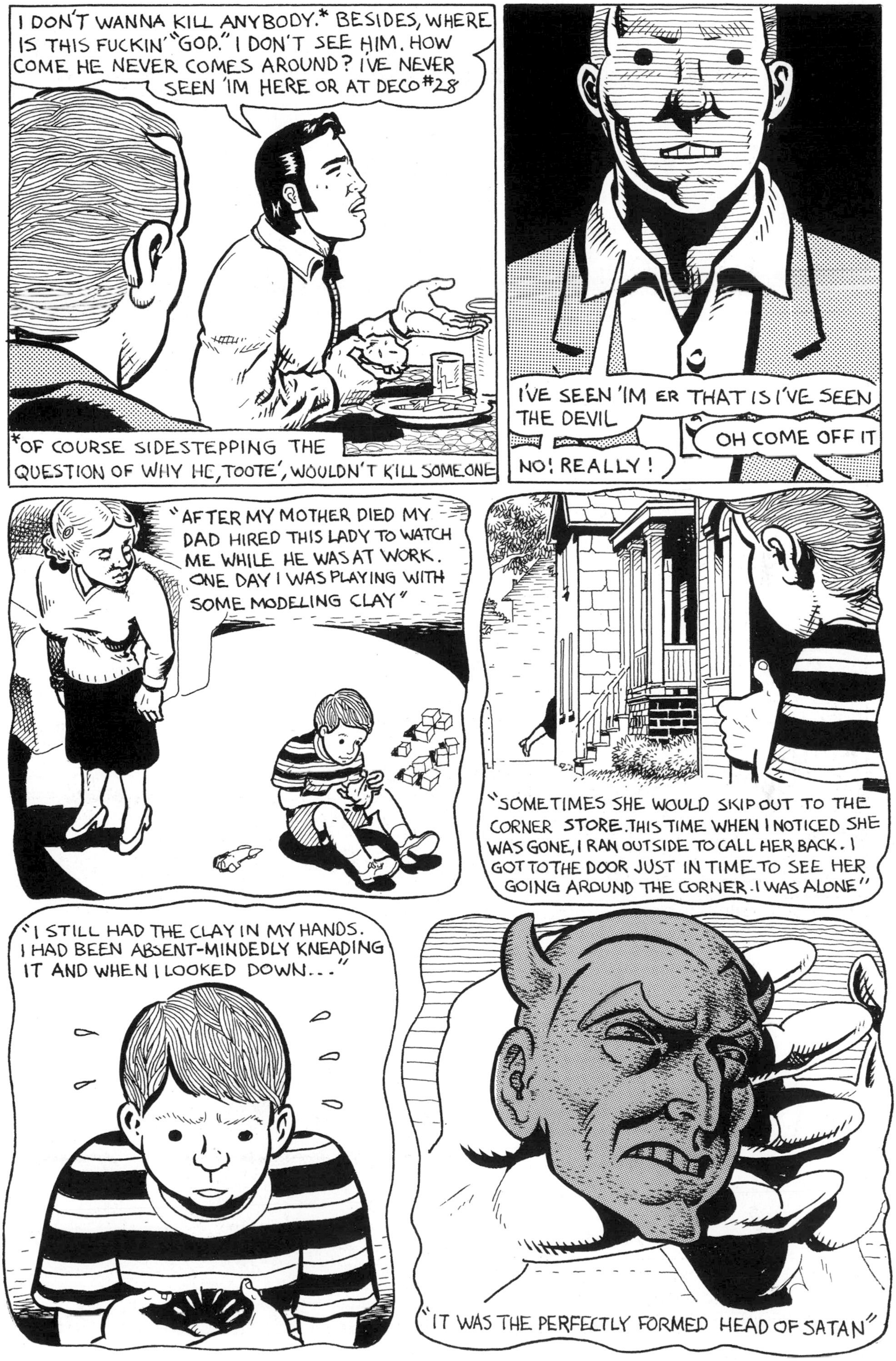
I DON'T WANNA KILL ANYBODY.* BESIDES, WHERE IS THIS FUCKIN' "GOD." I DON'T SEE HIM. HOW COME HE NEVER COMES AROUND? I'VE NEVER SEEN 'IM HERE OR AT DECO #28
*OF COURSE SIDESTEPPING THE QUESTION OF WHY HE, TOOTE', WOULDN'T KILL SOMEONE
I'VE SEEN 'IM ER THAT IS I'VE SEEN THE DEVIL
OH COME OFF IT
NO! REALLY!
"AFTER MY MOTHER DIED MY DAD HIRED THIS LADY TO WATCH ME WHILE HE WAS AT WORK. ONE DAY I WAS PLAYING WITH SOME MODELING CLAY"
"SOMETIMES SHE WOULD SKIP OUT TO THE CORNER STORE. THIS TIME WHEN I NOTICED SHE WAS GONE, I RAN OUTSIDE TO CALL HER BACK. I GOT TO THE DOOR JUST IN TIME TO SEE HER GOING AROUND THE CORNER. I WAS ALONE"
"I STILL HAD THE CLAY IN MY HANDS. I HAD BEEN ABSENT-MINDEDLY KNEADING IT AND WHEN I LOOKED DOWN..."
"IT WAS THE PERFECTLY FORMED HEAD OF SATAN"

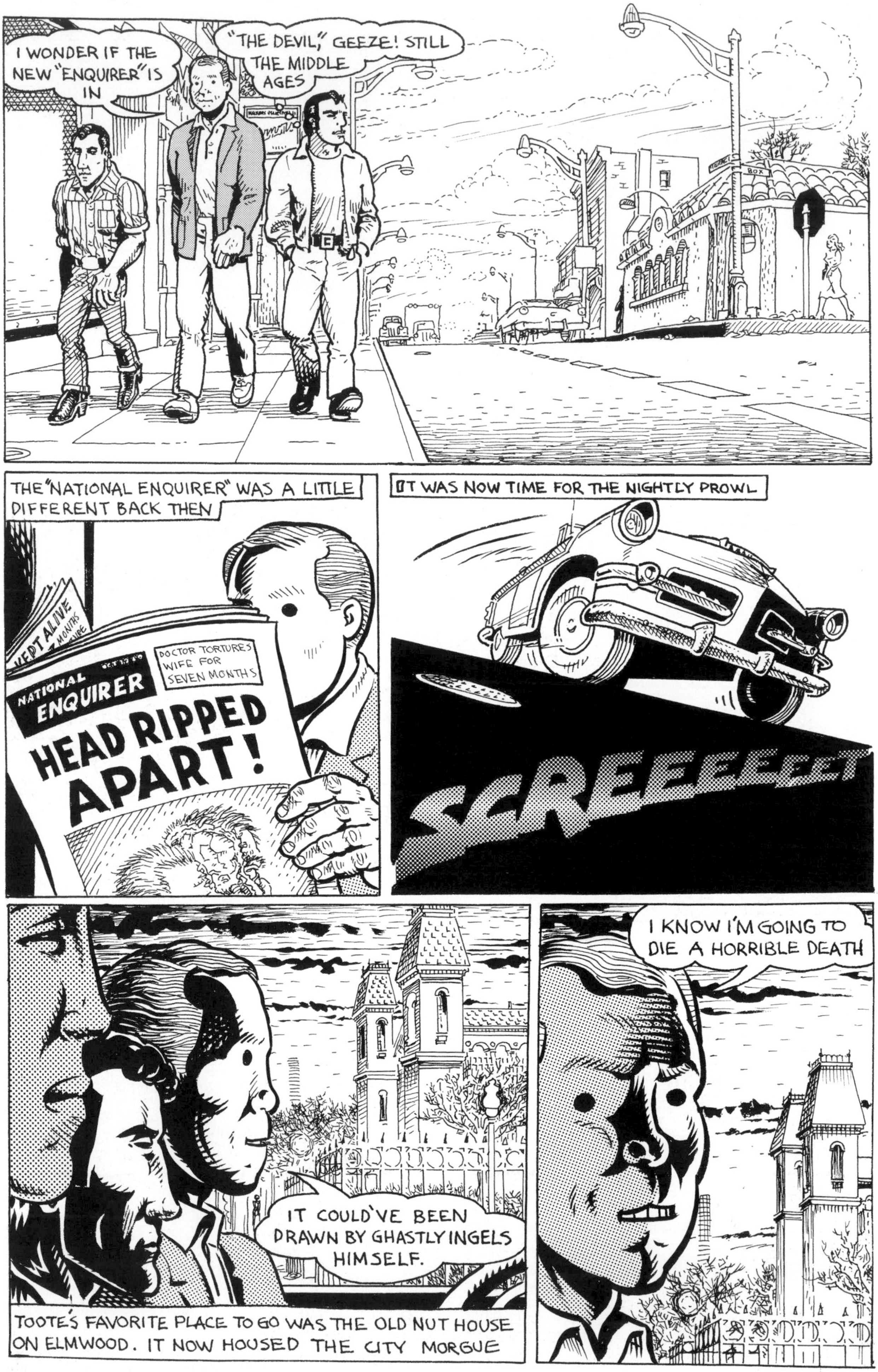
I WONDER IF THE NEW "ENQUIRER" IS IN
"THE DEVIL," GEEZE! STILL THE MIDDLE AGES
THE "NATIONAL ENQUIRER" WAS A LITTLE DIFFERENT BACK THEN
NATIONAL ENQUIRER
DOCTOR TORTURES WIFE FOR SEVEN MONTHS
HEAD RIPPED APART!
IT WAS NOW TIME FOR THE NIGHTLY PROWL
SCREEEEEEEE
IT COULD'VE BEEN DRAWN BY GHASTLY INGELS HIMSELF.
TOOTE'S FAVORITE PLACE TO GO WAS THE OLD NUT HOUSE ON ELMWOOD. IT NOW HOUSED THE CITY MORGUE
I KNOW I'M GOING TO DIE A HORRIBLE DEATH

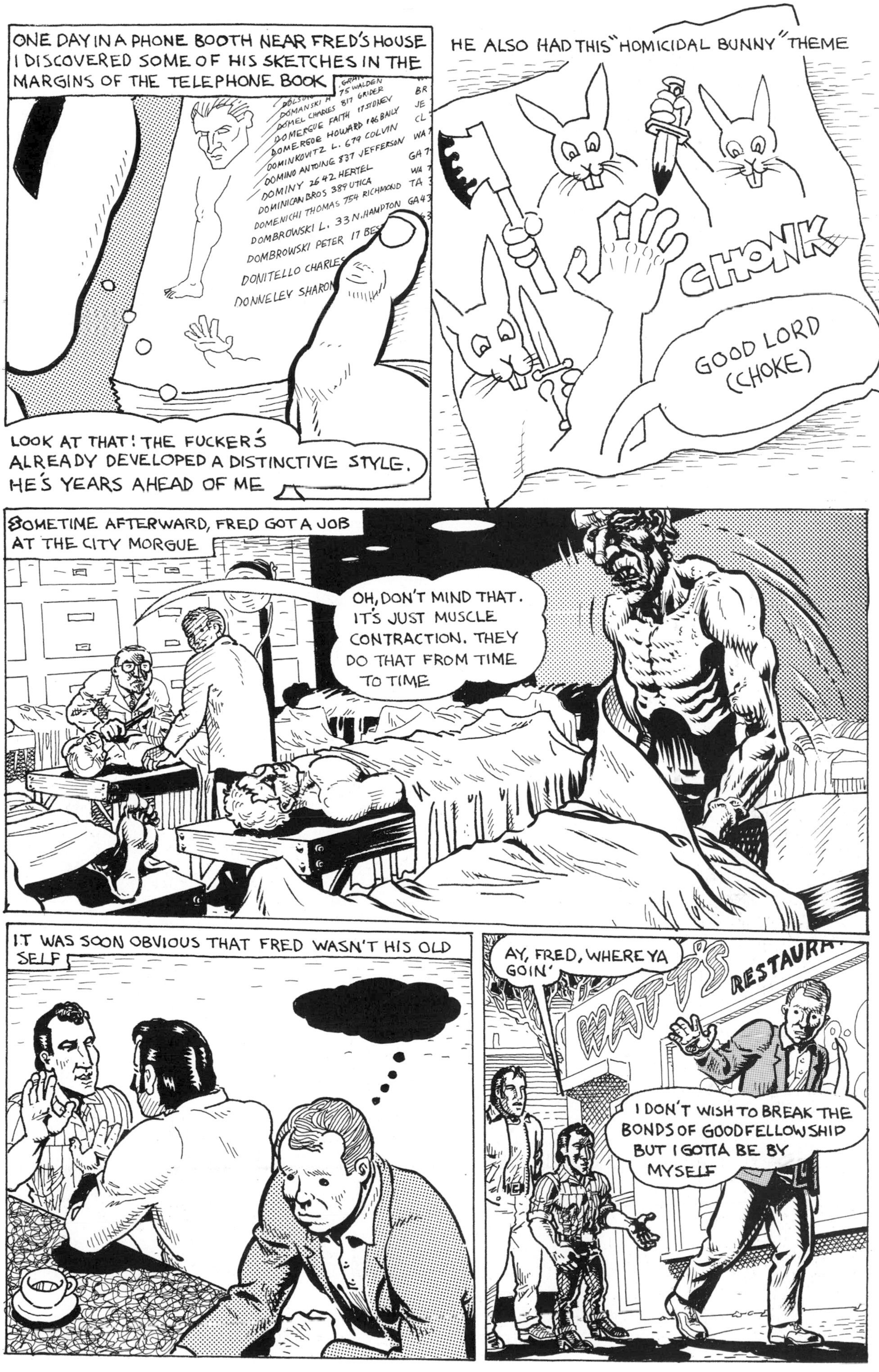

ONE DAY IN A PHONE BOOTH NEAR FRED'S HOUSE I DISCOVERED SOME OF HIS SKETCHES IN THE MARGINS OF THE TELEPHONE BOOK
LOOK AT THAT! THE FUCKER'S ALREADY DEVELOPED A DISTINCTIVE STYLE. HE'S YEARS AHEAD OF ME
HE ALSO HAD THIS "HOMICIDAL BUNNY" THEME
CHONK
GOOD LORD (CHOKE)
SOMETIME AFTERWARD, FRED GOT A JOB AT THE CITY MORGUE
OH, DON'T MIND THAT. IT'S JUST MUSCLE CONTRACTION. THEY DO THAT FROM TIME TO TIME
IT WAS SOON OBVIOUS THAT FRED WASN'T HIS OLD SELF
AY, FRED, WHERE YA GOIN'
WATT'S RESTAURA
I DON'T WISH TO BREAK THE BONDS OF GOODFELLOWSHIP BUT I GOTTA BE BY MYSELF

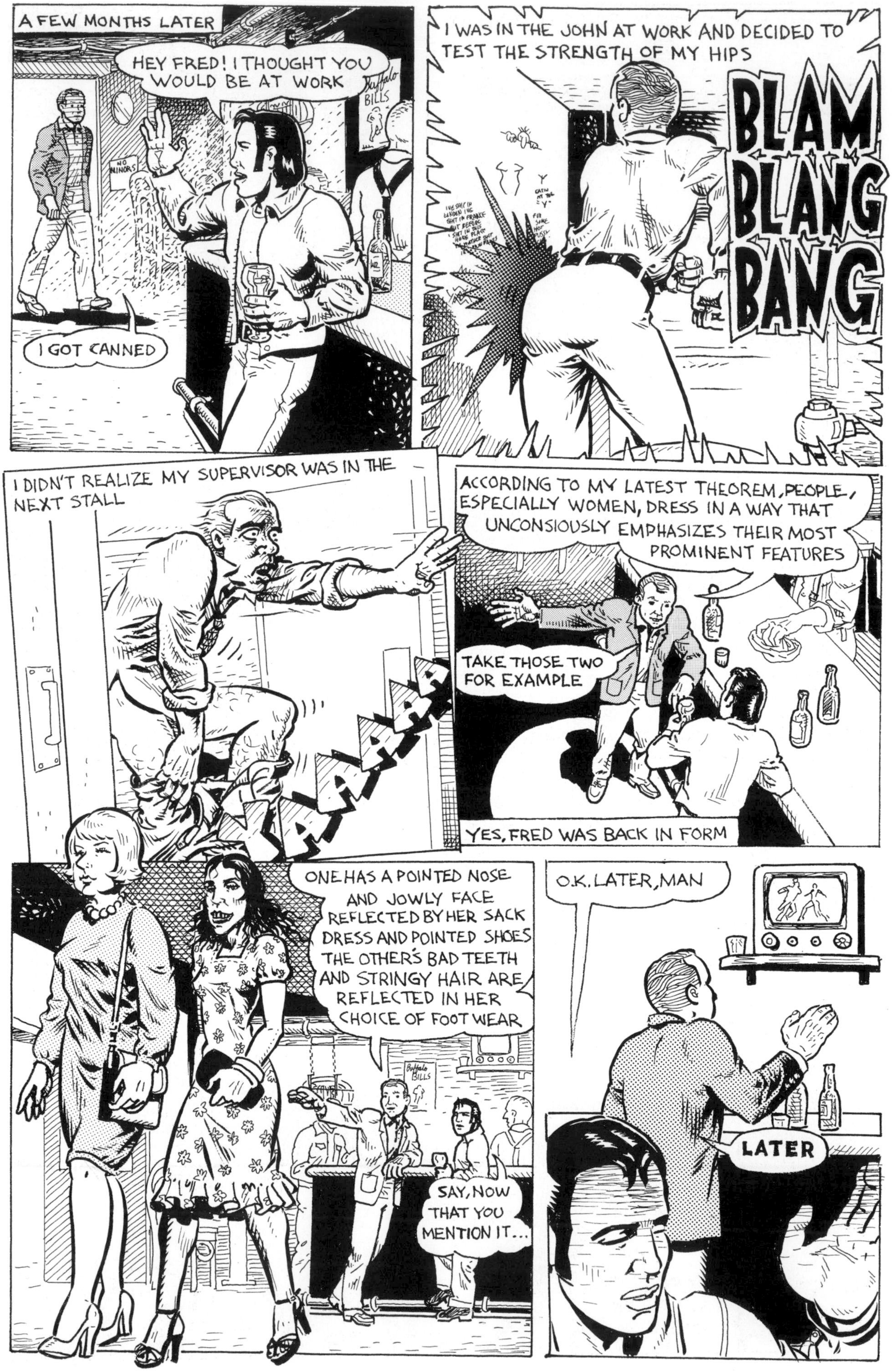
A FEW MONTHS LATER
HEY FRED! I THOUGHT YOU WOULD BE AT WORK
I GOT CANNED
I WAS IN THE JOHN AT WORK AND DECIDED TO TEST THE STRENGTH OF MY HIPS
BLAM BLANG BANG
I DIDN'T REALIZE MY SUPERVISOR WAS IN THE NEXT STALL
ACCORDING TO MY LATEST THEOREM, PEOPLE, ESPECIALLY WOMEN, DRESS IN A WAY THAT UNCONSIOUSLY EMPHASIZES THEIR MOST PROMINENT FEATURES
TAKE THOSE TWO FOR EXAMPLE
YES, FRED WAS BACK IN FORM
ONE HAS A POINTED NOSE AND JOWLY FACE REFLECTED BY HER SACK DRESS AND POINTED SHOES THE OTHER'S BAD TEETH AND STRINGY HAIR ARE REFLECTED IN HER CHOICE OF FOOT WEAR
SAY, NOW THAT YOU MENTION IT...
O.K. LATER, MAN
LATER

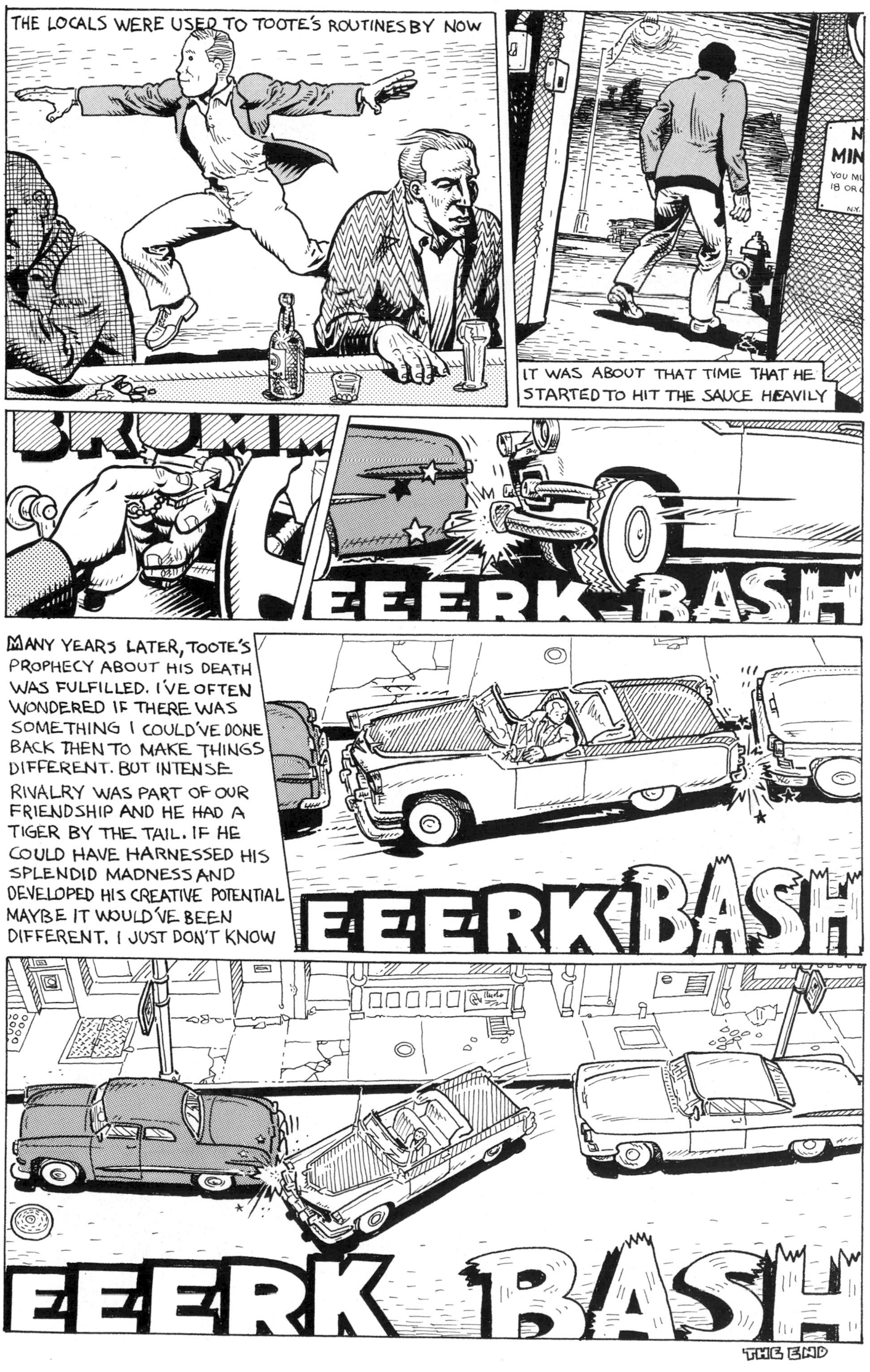
THE LOCALS WERE USED TO TOOTE'S ROUTINES BY NOW
IT WAS ABOUT THAT TIME THAT HE STARTED TO HIT THE SAUCE HEAVILY
BRUMM
EEERK BASH
MANY YEARS LATER, TOOTE'S PROPHECY ABOUT HIS DEATH WAS FULFILLED. I'VE OFTEN WONDERED IF THERE WAS SOMETHING I COULD'VE DONE BACK THEN TO MAKE THINGS DIFFERENT. BUT INTENSE RIVALRY WAS PART OF OUR FRIENDSHIP AND HE HAD A TIGER BY THE TAIL. IF HE COULD HAVE HARNESSED HIS SPLENDID MADNESS AND DEVELOPED HIS CREATIVE POTENTIAL MAYBE IT WOULD'VE BEEN DIFFERENT. I JUST DON'T KNOW
EEERK BASH
EEERK BASH
THE END

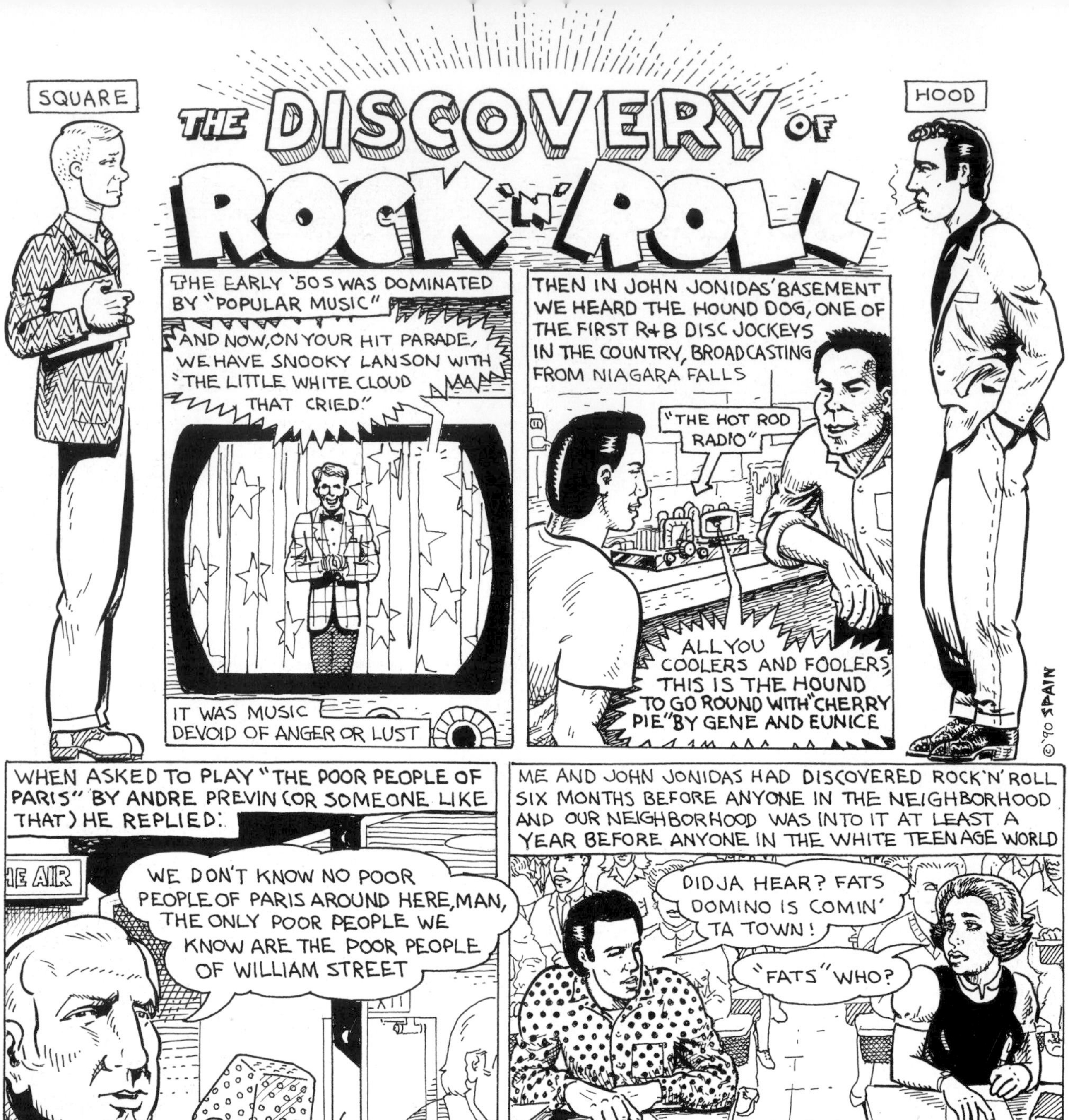

SQUARE
THE DISCOVERY OF ROCK'N'ROLL
HOOD
THE EARLY '50S WAS DOMINATED BY "POPULAR MUSIC"
AND NOW, ON YOUR HIT PARADE, WE HAVE SNOOKY LANSON WITH "THE LITTLE WHITE CLOUD THAT CRIED."
IT WAS MUSIC DEVOID OF ANGER OR LUST
THEN IN JOHN JONIDAS' BASEMENT WE HEARD THE HOUND DOG, ONE OF THE FIRST R&B DISC JOCKEYS IN THE COUNTRY, BROADCASTING FROM NIAGARA FALLS
"THE HOT ROD RADIO"
ALL YOU COOLERS AND FOOLERS, THIS IS THE HOUND TO GO ROUND WITH "CHERRY PIE" BY GENE AND EUNICE
©'90 SPAIN
WHEN ASKED TO PLAY "THE POOR PEOPLE OF PARIS" BY ANDRE PREVIN (OR SOMEONE LIKE THAT) HE REPLIED:
HE AIR
WE DON'T KNOW NO POOR PEOPLE OF PARIS AROUND HERE, MAN, THE ONLY POOR PEOPLE WE KNOW ARE THE POOR PEOPLE OF WILLIAM STREET
ME AND JOHN JONIDAS HAD DISCOVERED ROCK'N'ROLL SIX MONTHS BEFORE ANYONE IN THE NEIGHBORHOOD AND OUR NEIGHBORHOOD WAS INTO IT AT LEAST A YEAR BEFORE ANYONE IN THE WHITE TEENAGE WORLD
DIDJA HEAR? FATS DOMINO IS COMIN' TA TOWN!
"FATS" WHO?
NOT LONG AFTER, THE WHOLE NATION WAS ROCKIN' OUT, AND NOT TOO LONG AFTER THAT, THE WORLD
FRANK SINATRA FELT CALLED UPON TO COMMENT...
MY ONLY SORROW IS THE UNRELENTING INSISTENCE OF RECORDING AND MOTION PICTURE COMPANIES UPON PURVEYING THE MOST BRUTAL, UGLY, DEGENERATE, VICIOUS FORM OF EXPRESSION IT HAS BEEN MY MISFORTUNE TO HEAR. NATURALLY I REFER TO THE BULK OF ROCK'N'ROLL. IT FOSTERS ALMOST TOTALLY NEGATIVE AND DESTRUCTIVE REACTIONS IN YOUNG PEOPLE. IT SMELLS PHONY AND FALSE. IT IS SUNG, PLAYED, AND WRITTEN FOR THE MOST PART BY CRETINOUS GOONS AND BY MEANS OF ITS ALMOST IMBECILLIC REITERATIONS AND SLY-LEWD-IN PLAIN FACT DIRTY LYRICS IT MANAGES TO BE THE MARTIAL MUSIC OF EVERY SIDEBURNED DELINQUENT ON THE FACE OF THE EARTH. THIS RANCID APHRODISIAC I DEPORE..
THANX, FRANK. WE KNOW HOW OFFENDED YOU ARE BY ANY BUT THE MOST UPRIGHT OF CITIZENS

P. 182–186 from *My True Story*, 1994

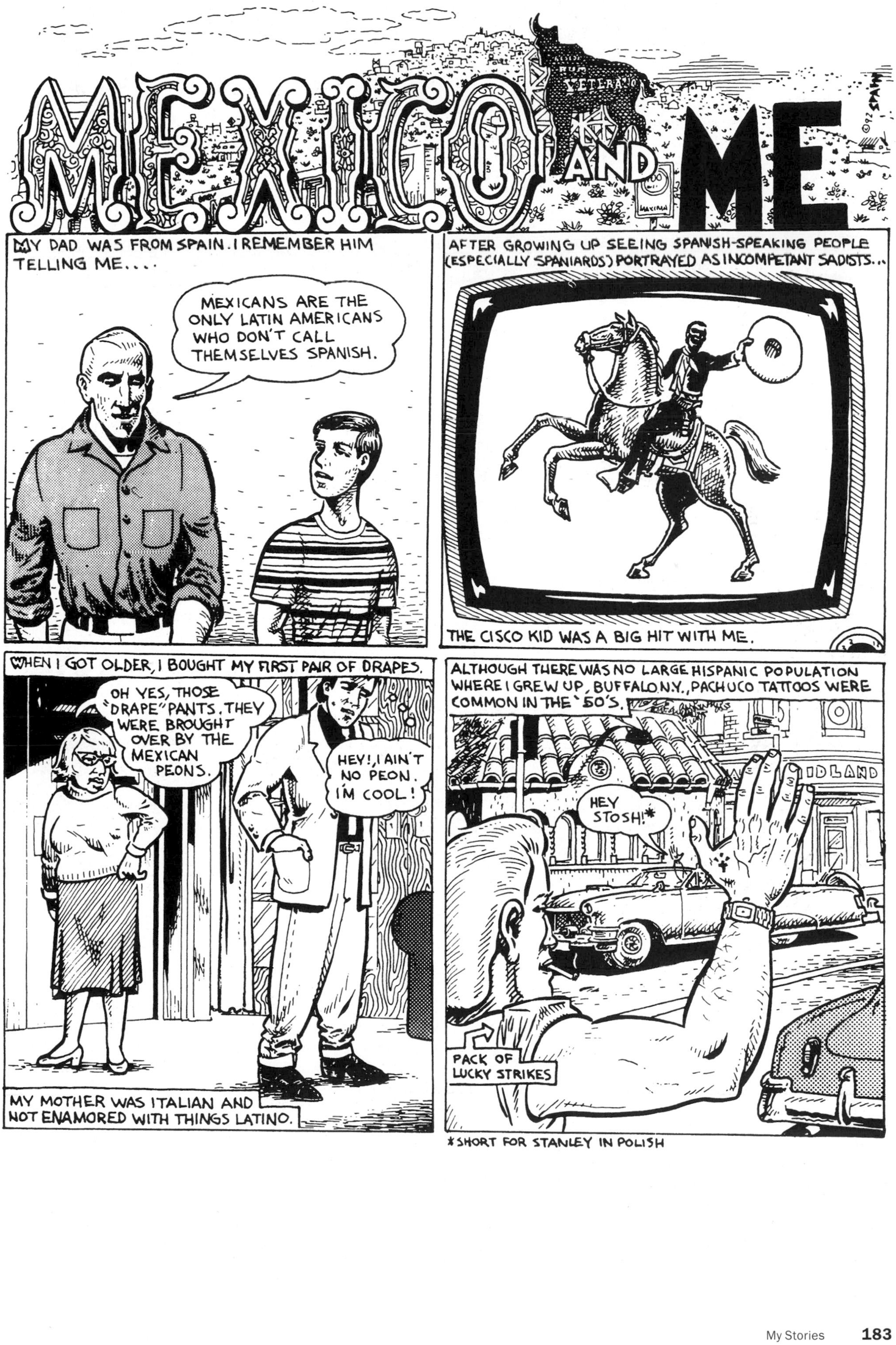
MEXICO AND ME
©92 SPAIN
MY DAD WAS FROM SPAIN. I REMEMBER HIM TELLING ME...
MEXICANS ARE THE ONLY LATIN AMERICANS WHO DON'T CALL THEMSELVES SPANISH.
AFTER GROWING UP SEEING SPANISH-SPEAKING PEOPLE (ESPECIALLY SPANIARDS) PORTRAYED AS INCOMPETANT SADISTS...
THE CISCO KID WAS A BIG HIT WITH ME.
WHEN I GOT OLDER, I BOUGHT MY FIRST PAIR OF DRAPES.
OH YES, THOSE "DRAPE" PANTS. THEY WERE BROUGHT OVER BY THE MEXICAN PEONS.
HEY!, I AIN'T NO PEON. I'M COOL!
MY MOTHER WAS ITALIAN AND NOT ENAMORED WITH THINGS LATINO.
ALTHOUGH THERE WAS NO LARGE HISPANIC POPULATION WHERE I GREW UP, BUFFALO N.Y., PACHUCO TATTOOS WERE COMMON IN THE '50'S.
HEY STOSH!*
PACK OF LUCKY STRIKES
*SHORT FOR STANLEY IN POLISH

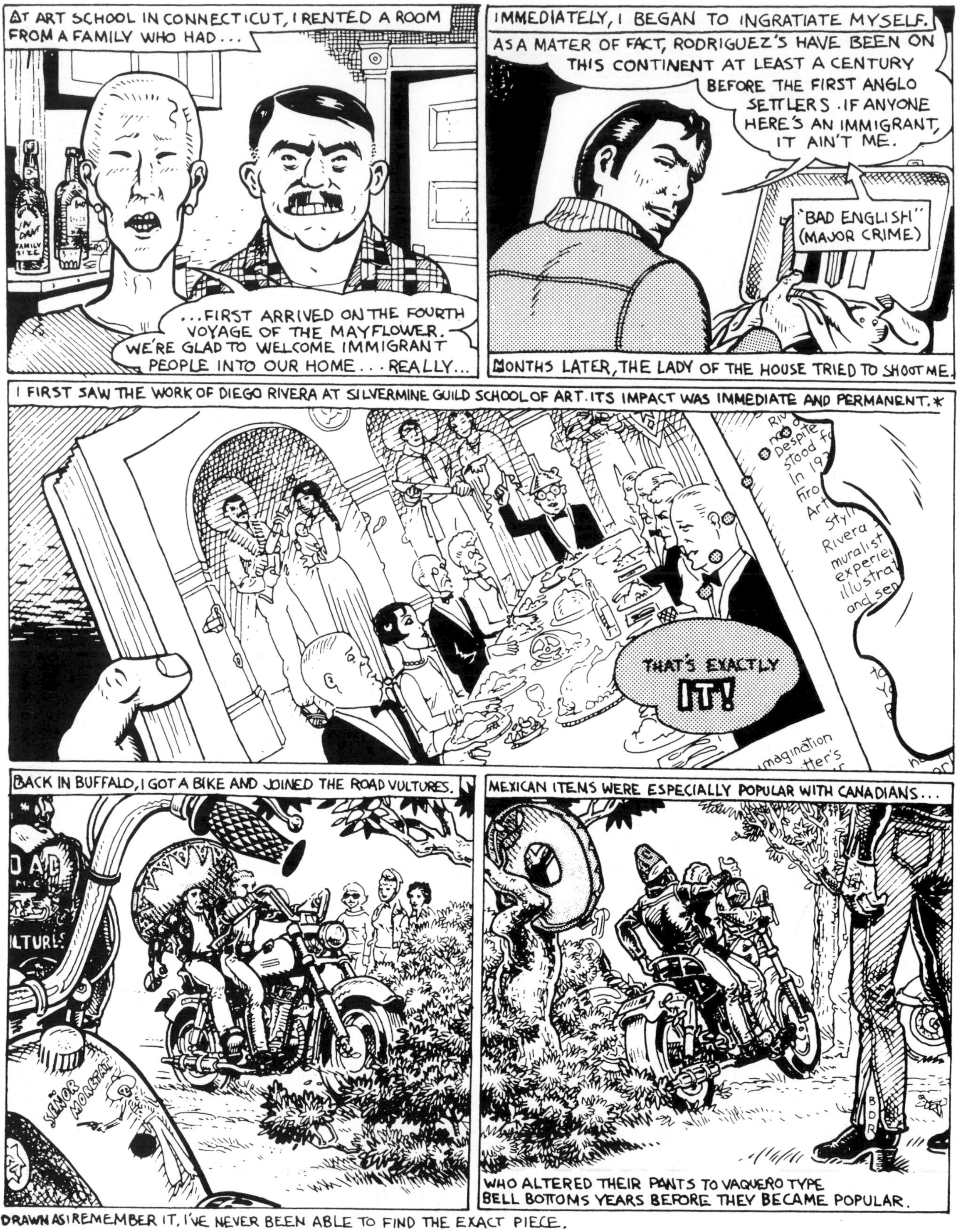
AT ART SCHOOL IN CONNECTICUT, I RENTED A ROOM FROM A FAMILY WHO HAD...
...FIRST ARRIVED ON THE FOURTH VOYAGE OF THE MAYFLOWER. WE'RE GLAD TO WELCOME IMMIGRANT PEOPLE INTO OUR HOME... REALLY...
IMMEDIATELY, I BEGAN TO INGRATIATE MYSELF.
AS A MATER OF FACT, RODRIGUEZ'S HAVE BEEN ON THIS CONTINENT AT LEAST A CENTURY BEFORE THE FIRST ANGLO SETTLERS. IF ANYONE HERE'S AN IMMIGRANT, IT AIN'T ME.
"BAD ENGLISH" (MAJOR CRIME)
MONTHS LATER, THE LADY OF THE HOUSE TRIED TO SHOOT ME.
I FIRST SAW THE WORK OF DIEGO RIVERA AT SILVERMINE GUILD SCHOOL OF ART. ITS IMPACT WAS IMMEDIATE AND PERMANENT.*
THAT'S EXACTLY IT!
BACK IN BUFFALO, I GOT A BIKE AND JOINED THE ROAD VULTURES.
MEXICAN ITEMS WERE ESPECIALLY POPULAR WITH CANADIANS...
WHO ALTERED THEIR PANTS TO VAQUERO TYPE BELL BOTTOMS YEARS BEFORE THEY BECAME POPULAR.

* DRAWN AS I REMEMBER IT, I'VE NEVER BEEN ABLE TO FIND THE EXACT PIECE.

I DIDN'T GET DOWN TO MEXICO UNTIL THE MID-EIGHTIES. WHAT I SAW AMAZED ME.

JEEZE, LOOK AT THAT!

AT THE RUFINO TAMAYO MUSEUM IN OAXACA, THE DIVERSITY AND REFINEMENT OF THE ORIGINAL CULTURE WAS FURTHER REVEALED.

COLONIAL ARCHITECTURE SEEMED LIKE AN ATTEMPT TO VIE FOR THE ALLEGIANCE OF A VISUALLY SOPHISTICATED AUDIENCE.

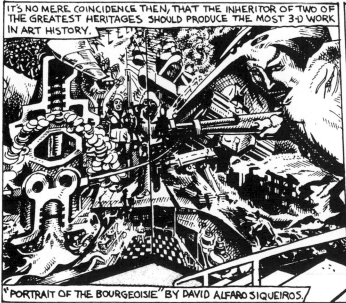

IT'S NO MERE COINCIDENCE THEN, THAT THE INHERITOR OF TWO OF THE GREATEST HERITAGES SHOULD PRODUCE THE MOST 3-D WORK IN ART HISTORY.

"PORTRAIT OF THE BOURGEOISIE" BY DAVID ALFARO SIQUEIROS.

500 YEARS AGO COLUMBUS DISCOVERED AMERICA FOR EUROPE AND THE REST OF THE WORLD, AND THE REST OF THE WORLD FOR AMERICA.

WHAT A KIND, GENEROUS, AND PEACEFUL PEOPLE!

DESTRUCTION OF CODICES LIKE THE BURNING OF THE LIBRARY AT UXMUL HAVE TRAGICALLY DIMINISHED OUR COLLECTIVE KNOWLEDGE AND RANKS WITH THE DESTRUCTION OF THE LIBRARY OF ALEXANDRIA AS AN ACT OF CRIMINAL IGNORANCE, AND YET...

IDEAL FOR RAPE, PLUNDER, EXPLOITATION, AND MURDER!

SOME HAVE ARGUED THAT NATIVE PEOPLES WOULD HAVE BEEN BETTER OFF WITHOUT THIS KNOWLEDGE.

SPAIN HAD DEFEATED THE HEMISPHERE'S BEST WARRIORS. AFTERWARD, SPANIARDS SUCH AS BARTOLOMÉ DE LAS CASAS DENOUNCED THE ABUSE OF INDIANS BY COLONISTS. THE SPANISH GOVERNMENT TRIED TO STOP SLAVERY WHILE OTHER EUROPEAN POWERS ENRICHED THEMSELVES ON IT. NATIVE PEOPLES HAD PRACTICED NOT ONLY SLAVERY BUT CUSTOMS MORE GRIM...

WHEN CORTEZ FIRST CAME TO THE AZTEC CAPITAL, MOCTEZUMA LED HIM TO A SACRIFICIAL CHAMBER.

CORTEZ PLACED A STATUE ON THE IDOL.

'THE VIRGIN MARY'

THESE ARE NOT GODS BUT DEMONS. WORSHIP HER. SHE WILL PROTECT YOU.

MOCTEZUMA REMOVED THE STATUE.

THESE ARE OUR GODS. THEY HAVE GIVEN US VICTORY IN BATTLE AND SUCESSFUL HARVESTS.

WE WILL NOT DISCUSS THIS AGAIN.

IT'S NOT HARD TO SEE WHY THE "BLESSED VIRGIN" EVENTUALLY WON OUT.

THE END

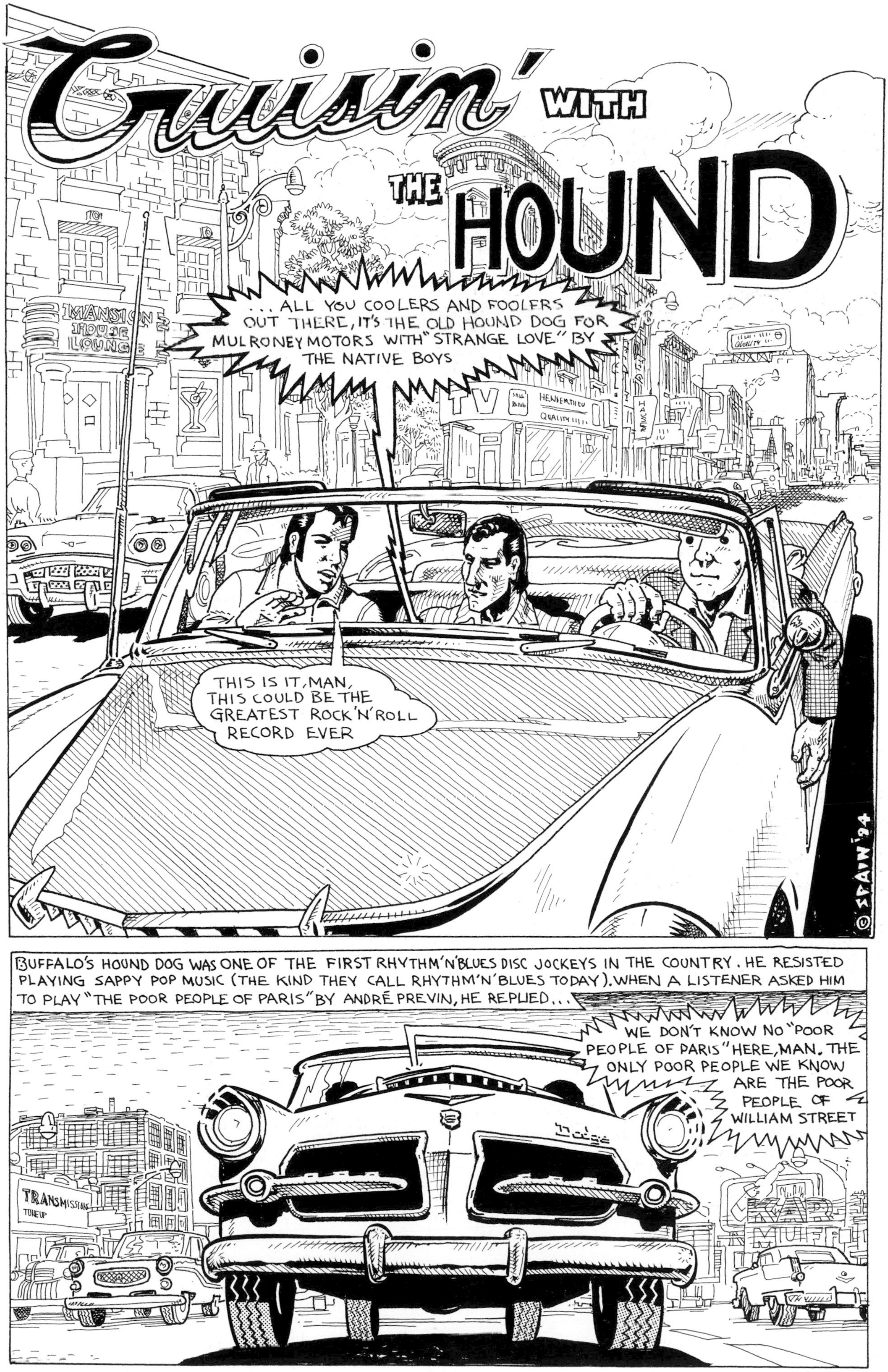
Cruisin' with the HOUND
MANSION HOUSE LOUNGE
...ALL YOU COOLERS AND FOOLERS OUT THERE, IT'S THE OLD HOUND DOG FOR MULRONEY MOTORS WITH "STRANGE LOVE" BY THE NATIVE BOYS
TV
THIS IS IT, MAN, THIS COULD BE THE GREATEST ROCK'N'ROLL RECORD EVER
© SPAIN '94
BUFFALO'S HOUND DOG WAS ONE OF THE FIRST RHYTHM'N'BLUES DISC JOCKEYS IN THE COUNTRY. HE RESISTED PLAYING SAPPY POP MUSIC (THE KIND THEY CALL RHYTHM'N'BLUES TODAY). WHEN A LISTENER ASKED HIM TO PLAY "THE POOR PEOPLE OF PARIS" BY ANDRÉ PREVIN, HE REPLIED...
WE DON'T KNOW NO "POOR PEOPLE OF PARIS" HERE, MAN. THE ONLY POOR PEOPLE WE KNOW ARE THE POOR PEOPLE OF WILLIAM STREET
TRANSMISSION TUNE UP

P. 187–192 from *Blab!* #8, 1995

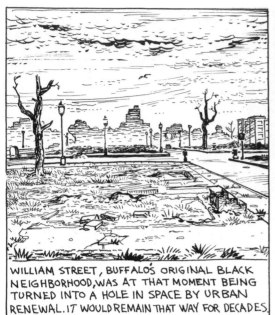

WILLIAM STREET, BUFFALO'S ORIGINAL BLACK NEIGHBORHOOD, WAS AT THAT MOMENT BEING TURNED INTO A HOLE IN SPACE BY URBAN RENEWAL. IT WOULD REMAIN THAT WAY FOR DECADES.

I COULD CARRY A TUNE PRETTY GOOD

PUTIN'N'TAIN, PUTIN'N'TAIN
ASK ME AGAIN AND I'LL TELL YOU THE SAME

NOW WE'RE GOIN' STEADY AND
I FOUND OUT HER REAL NAME IS BETTY

BUT THE GUY WHO REALLY HAD IT DOWN WAS JOCKO REESE

HEY, MAN, DO "IN THE CHAPEL OF DREAMS"

"IN THE CHAPEL OF DREAMS"? YOU MUST BE OUT OF YOUR TOILET!

IT NEVER TOOK MUCH TO TALK HIM INTO IT

IN THE CHAPEL OF...

DRE-E-E-E-EE-EE-EEMS

EVERY DREAM WILL COME TRUE

HIS VOICE HAD AMAZING RANGE. HE WOULD HIT EACH NOTE, INCLUDING THE INSTRUMENTAL, PERFECTLY

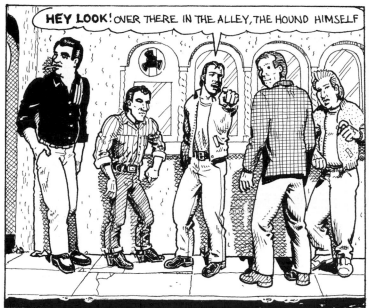

HEY LOOK! OVER THERE IN THE ALLEY, THE HOUND HIMSELF

SURE ENOUGH, IT WAS HIM HOBBLING DOWN TOWARD THE APARTMENTS IN BACK OF MOLNAR'S

OH YAH! HE VISITS CHUCKIE'S MOM

YOU MIGHT SAY WE'RE "MORE THAN FRIENDS"

ONE NIGHT OUT IN FRONT OF CHUCKIE'S HOUSE

HEY YOU GUYS! IT'S THE HOUND

BAD DAY FOR OLD DADDY HOUND

DON'T HAND ME THAT SHIT ABOUT STANDIN' UNDER THAT AWNING TO GET OUT OF THE RAIN

BAP

I'M SURE THAT THE HOUND WAS GREATLY EMBARRASSED TO BE SEEN IN THE BACK OF A COP CAR BUT TO US IT WAS FURTHER EVIDENCE OF COMMON EXPERIENCE

BUT LIFE WENT ON THERE ON FILLMORE AVENUE

... AND THEN YOU'LL SEE THAT NAME **SPAIN**, JUST LIKE IN THE CREDITS FOR "GUNGA DIN," THE LITTLE DUDE WILL COME OUT AND HIT THAT GONG **TISH!** AND THE CROWD GOES WILD AS **SPAIN** COMES ON AGAIN

SLURT

I WAS KIND OF AN EGOMANIAC BACK THEN (I'VE GOTTEN MORE HUMBLE IN RECENT YEARS)

HEY, IT'S STARTING TO RAIN

THE TOP OF TOOTE'S CONVERTIBLE WAS BUSTED SO WE HAD TO HOLD A BLANKET OVER OUR HEADS

FLAWAP FLAWAP

SEE YOU GUYS LATER

BY THE TIME WE DROPPED OFF TEX, THE BLANKET WAS SOAKED

SOON THE RAIN LET UP

SAY, THERE GOES ANITA AND JUDY

A CERTAIN LITTLE MAMA GONNA JUMP AND SHOUT, WHEN THAT ELDORADO ROLLS UP AND I COME JUMPIN' OUT

TOOTE' INVITED THEM TO JOIN US. THEY WERE GAME

I'LL BET HE'S LOOKING AT MY TITS

ANITA WAS A BIT PLUMP BUT STILL NOT TOO BAD

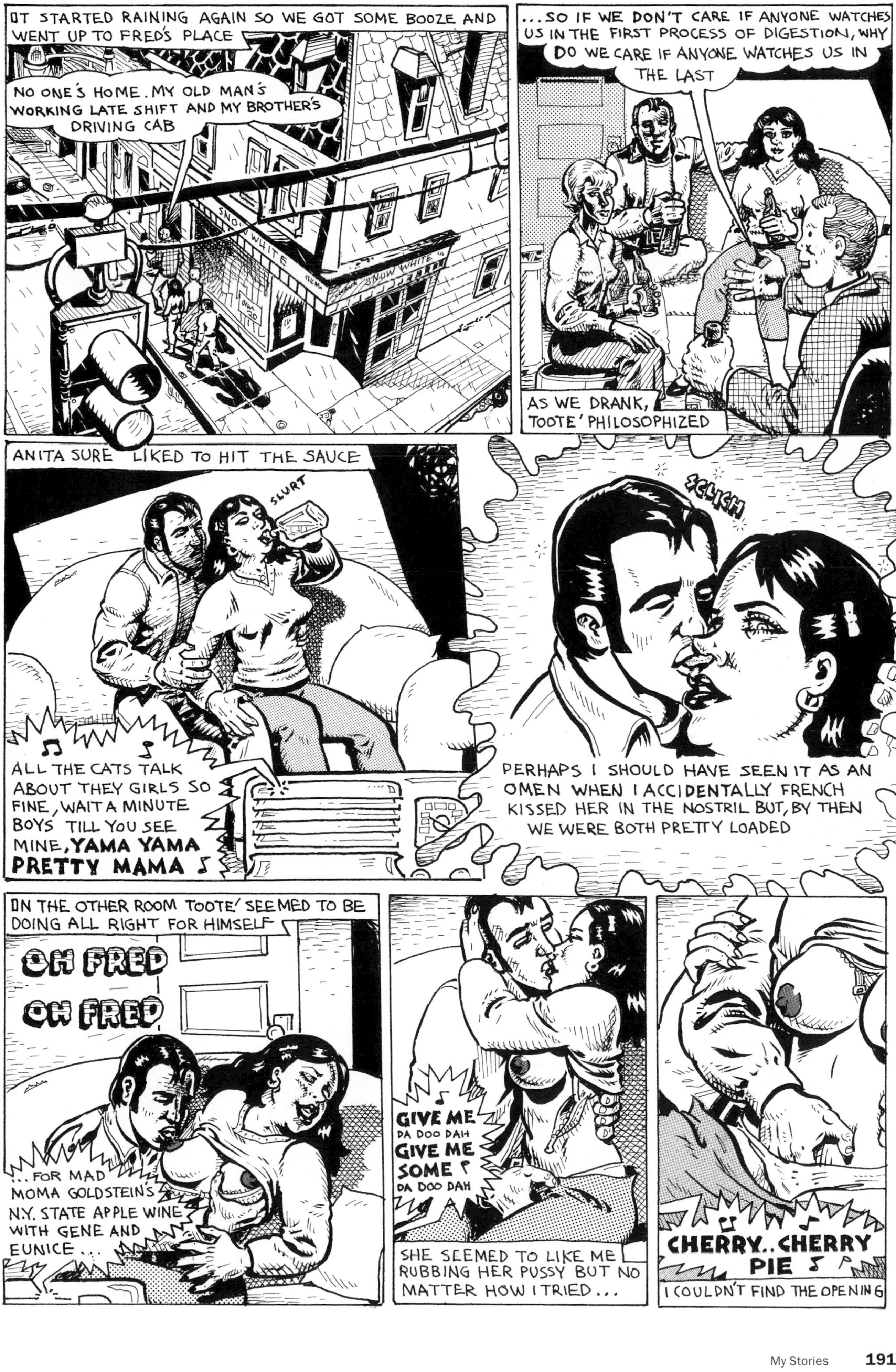
IT STARTED RAINING AGAIN SO WE GOT SOME BOOZE AND WENT UP TO FRED'S PLACE
NO ONE'S HOME. MY OLD MAN'S WORKING LATE SHIFT AND MY BROTHER'S DRIVING CAB
SNOW WHITE
...SO IF WE DON'T CARE IF ANYONE WATCHES US IN THE FIRST PROCESS OF DIGESTION, WHY DO WE CARE IF ANYONE WATCHES US IN THE LAST
AS WE DRANK, TOOTE' PHILOSOPHIZED
ANITA SURE LIKED TO HIT THE SAUCE
SLURT
ALL THE CATS TALK ABOUT THEY GIRLS SO FINE, WAIT A MINUTE BOYS TILL YOU SEE MINE, YAMA YAMA PRETTY MAMA
SCLICH
PERHAPS I SHOULD HAVE SEEN IT AS AN OMEN WHEN I ACCIDENTALLY FRENCH KISSED HER IN THE NOSTRIL BUT, BY THEN WE WERE BOTH PRETTY LOADED
IN THE OTHER ROOM TOOTE' SEEMED TO BE DOING ALL RIGHT FOR HIMSELF
OH FRED
OH FRED
...FOR MAD MOMA GOLDSTEIN'S N.Y. STATE APPLE WINE WITH GENE AND EUNICE...
GIVE ME DA DOO DAH GIVE ME SOME DA DOO DAH
SHE SEEMED TO LIKE ME RUBBING HER PUSSY BUT NO MATTER HOW I TRIED...
CHERRY.. CHERRY PIE
I COULDN'T FIND THE OPENING

AS I ATTEMPTED VAINLY TO GET HER PANTS OFF ONLY THE HOUND UNDERSTOOD MY PLIGHT
MOMA SAID THERE'D BE DAYS LIKE THIS THERE'D BE DAY'S LIKE THIS MAH MAMA SAID MAMA SAID MAMA SAID
N-NO
THEN SUDDENLY SHE GOT UP
I'M A BAD GIRL HIC... I'M A BAD GIRL
SHE PASSED OUT ACROSS A CHAIR REVEALING "IT"
ZZZZZ
IT OCCURRED TO ME TO CONTINUE TO TRY TO FIND HER SNAPPER BUT I THOUGHT IT WAS BEST NOT TO
I SAW HER ONCE MORE. WE WENT BOWLING. SHE BEAT ME 146 TO 63
IT WAS REAL SQUARE BACK THEN. ONCE, WHEN THE HOUND DROPPED IN AT DECO 28, AN OLD TIMER, SEEING HIS GOATEE AND SIDEBURNS, ASKED...
HEY, MISTER! IS THERE A CENTENNIAL GOING ON AROUND HERE SOMEWHERE
HAMBURG SPECIAL 50¢
THE HOUND WAS HEARD TO SAY
THEY'LL NEVER UNDERSTAND, WILL THEY, MAN?
THE END

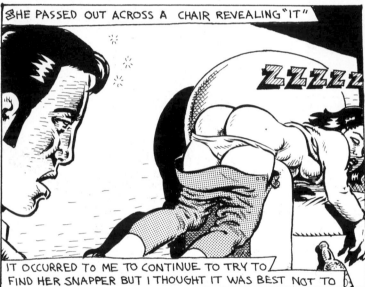

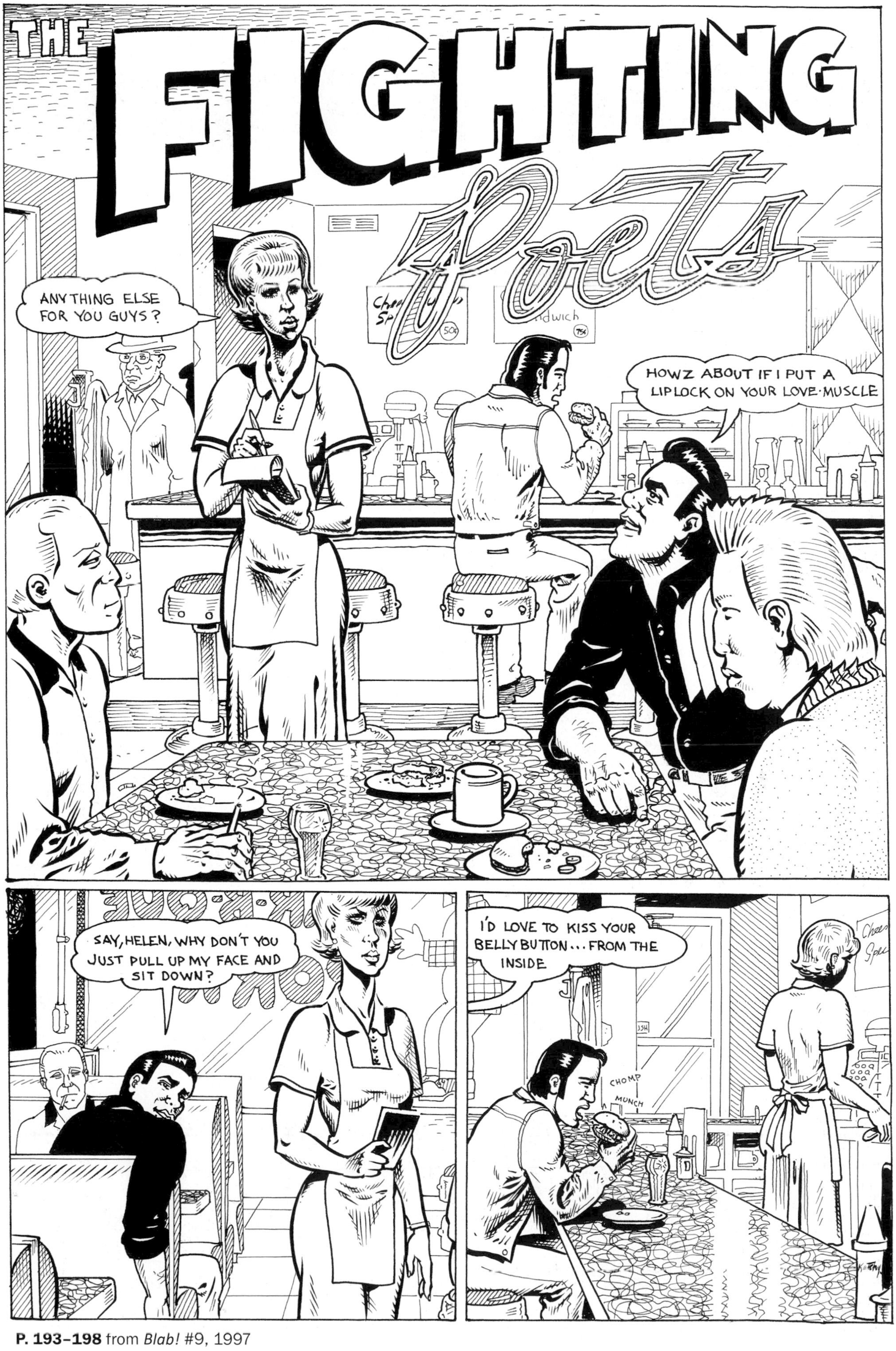
THE FIGHTING Poets
ANYTHING ELSE FOR YOU GUYS?
HOWZ ABOUT IF I PUT A LIPLOCK ON YOUR LOVE-MUSCLE
SAY, HELEN, WHY DON'T YOU JUST PULL UP MY FACE AND SIT DOWN?
I'D LOVE TO KISS YOUR BELLY BUTTON... FROM THE INSIDE
CHOMP
MUNCH

P. 193–198 from *Blab!* #9, 1997

SAY, JOCKO... WHY DON'T YOU JUST **SHUT, THE FUCK, UP**

THINGS GOT REAL QUIET THERE AT WATT'S RESTAURANT (WITH IT'S FAMOUS BAR-B-QUE PORK SANDWICHES)

I DON'T KNOW QUITE WHAT GOT INTO ME, BUT AFTER ALL, HER NAME WAS HELEN

HELEN, THY BEAUTY IS TO ME LIKE THOSE NICEAN BARKS OF YORE...

MY RECITATION, HOWEVER, WAS RUDELY INTERRUPTED

... WHICH GENTLY O'ER A PERFUMED SEA THE WEARY WAYWORN WAND...

DOINK

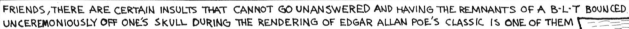

FRIENDS, THERE ARE CERTAIN INSULTS THAT CANNOT GO UNANSWERED AND HAVING THE REMNANTS OF A B-L-T BOUNCED UNCEREMONIOUSLY OFF ONE'S SKULL DURING THE RENDERING OF EDGAR ALLAN POE'S CLASSIC IS ONE OF THEM

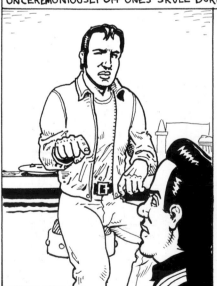

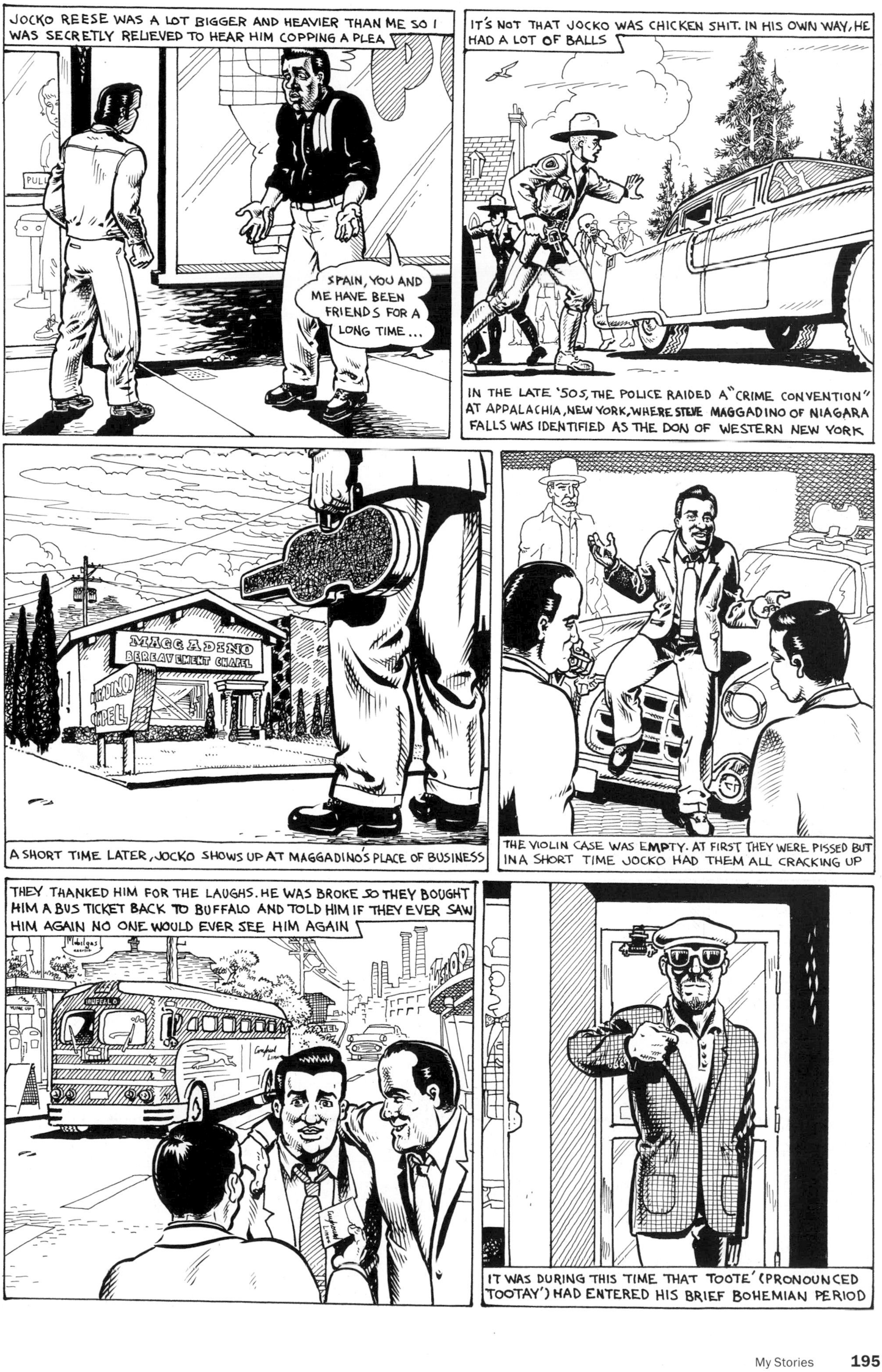
JOCKO REESE WAS A LOT BIGGER AND HEAVIER THAN ME SO I WAS SECRETLY RELIEVED TO HEAR HIM COPPING A PLEA
PULL
SPAIN, YOU AND ME HAVE BEEN FRIENDS FOR A LONG TIME...
IT'S NOT THAT JOCKO WAS CHICKEN SHIT. IN HIS OWN WAY, HE HAD A LOT OF BALLS
IN THE LATE '50S, THE POLICE RAIDED A "CRIME CONVENTION" AT APPALACHIA, NEW YORK, WHERE STEVE MAGGADINO OF NIAGARA FALLS WAS IDENTIFIED AS THE DON OF WESTERN NEW YORK
MAGGADINO
BEREAVEMENT CHAPEL
A SHORT TIME LATER, JOCKO SHOWS UP AT MAGGADINO'S PLACE OF BUSINESS
THE VIOLIN CASE WAS EMPTY. AT FIRST THEY WERE PISSED BUT IN A SHORT TIME JOCKO HAD THEM ALL CRACKING UP
THEY THANKED HIM FOR THE LAUGHS. HE WAS BROKE SO THEY BOUGHT HIM A BUS TICKET BACK TO BUFFALO AND TOLD HIM IF THEY EVER SAW HIM AGAIN NO ONE WOULD EVER SEE HIM AGAIN
BUFFALO
IT WAS DURING THIS TIME THAT TOOTE' (PRONOUNCED TOOTAY') HAD ENTERED HIS BRIEF BOHEMIAN PERIOD

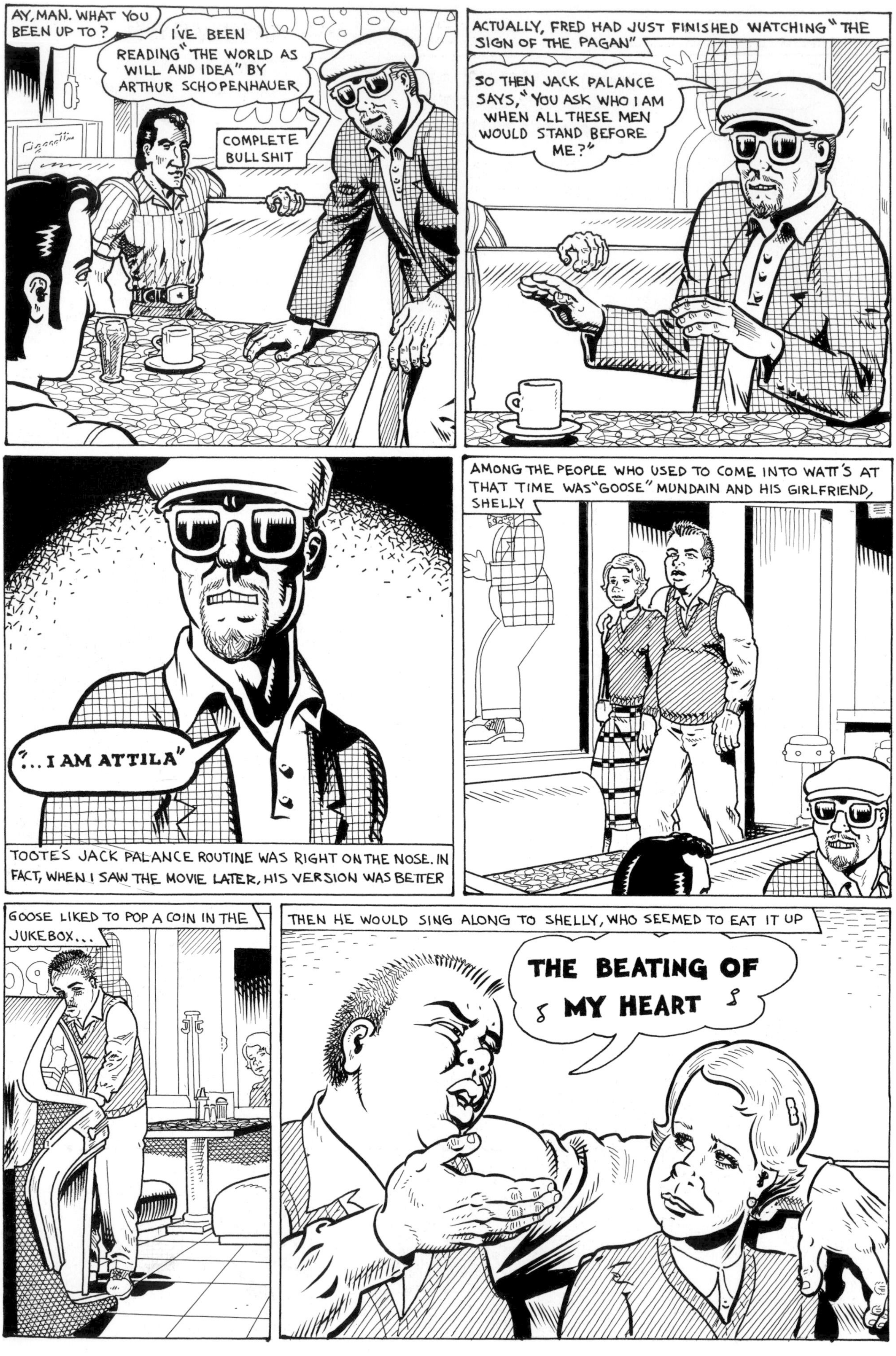
AY, MAN. WHAT YOU BEEN UP TO?
I'VE BEEN READING "THE WORLD AS WILL AND IDEA" BY ARTHUR SCHOPENHAUER
COMPLETE BULLSHIT
ACTUALLY, FRED HAD JUST FINISHED WATCHING "THE SIGN OF THE PAGAN"
SO THEN JACK PALANCE SAYS, "YOU ASK WHO I AM WHEN ALL THESE MEN WOULD STAND BEFORE ME?"
"... I AM ATTILA"
TOOTE'S JACK PALANCE ROUTINE WAS RIGHT ON THE NOSE. IN FACT, WHEN I SAW THE MOVIE LATER, HIS VERSION WAS BETTER
AMONG THE PEOPLE WHO USED TO COME INTO WATT'S AT THAT TIME WAS "GOOSE" MUNDAIN AND HIS GIRLFRIEND, SHELLY
GOOSE LIKED TO POP A COIN IN THE JUKEBOX...
THEN HE WOULD SING ALONG TO SHELLY, WHO SEEMED TO EAT IT UP
THE BEATING OF MY HEART

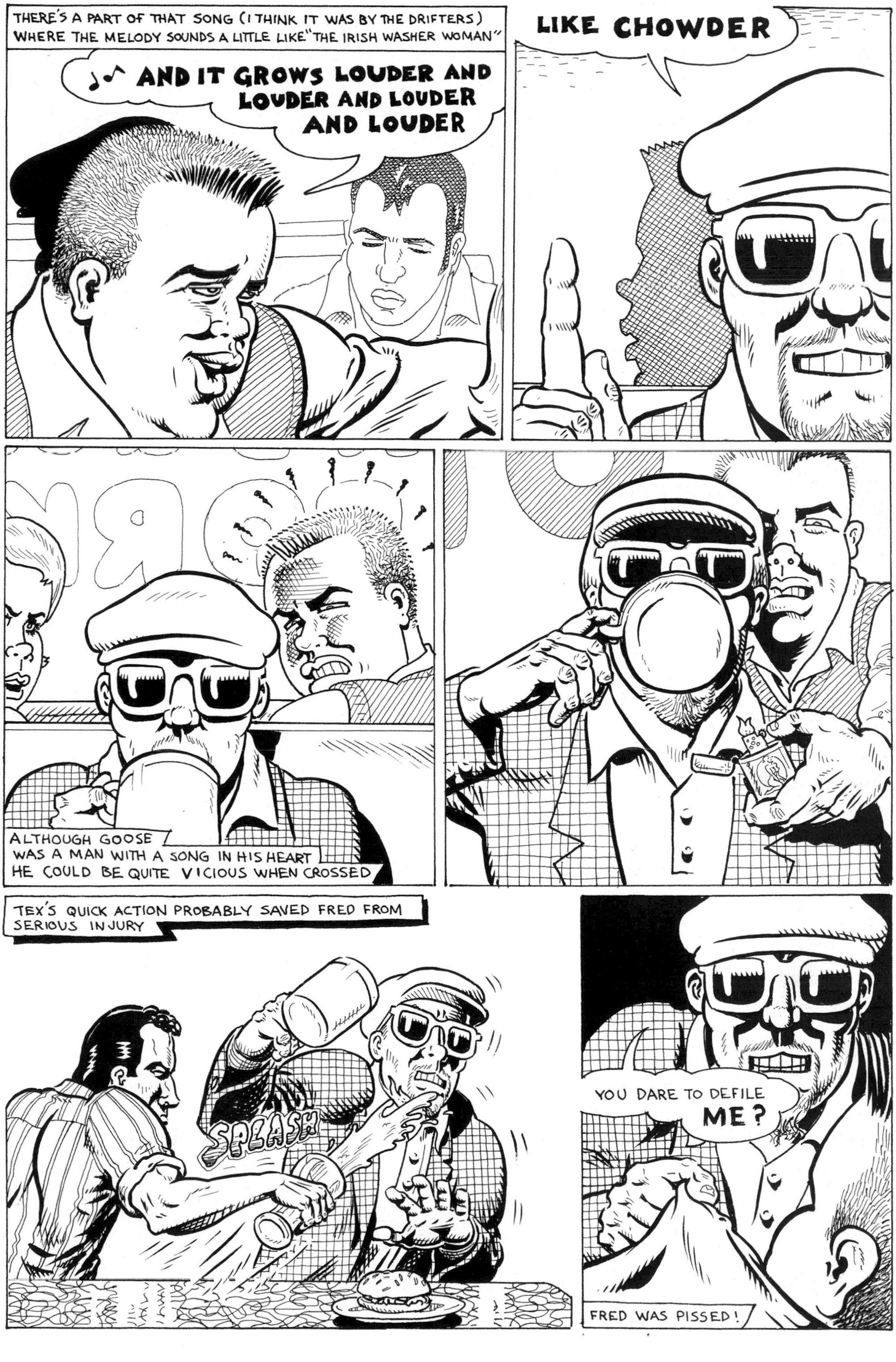
THERE'S A PART OF THAT SONG (I THINK IT WAS BY THE DRIFTERS) WHERE THE MELODY SOUNDS A LITTLE LIKE "THE IRISH WASHER WOMAN"
♪♪ AND IT GROWS LOUDER AND LOUDER AND LOUDER AND LOUDER
LIKE CHOWDER
ALTHOUGH GOOSE WAS A MAN WITH A SONG IN HIS HEART HE COULD BE QUITE VICIOUS WHEN CROSSED
TEX'S QUICK ACTION PROBABLY SAVED FRED FROM SERIOUS INJURY
SPLASH
YOU DARE TO DEFILE ME?
FRED WAS PISSED!

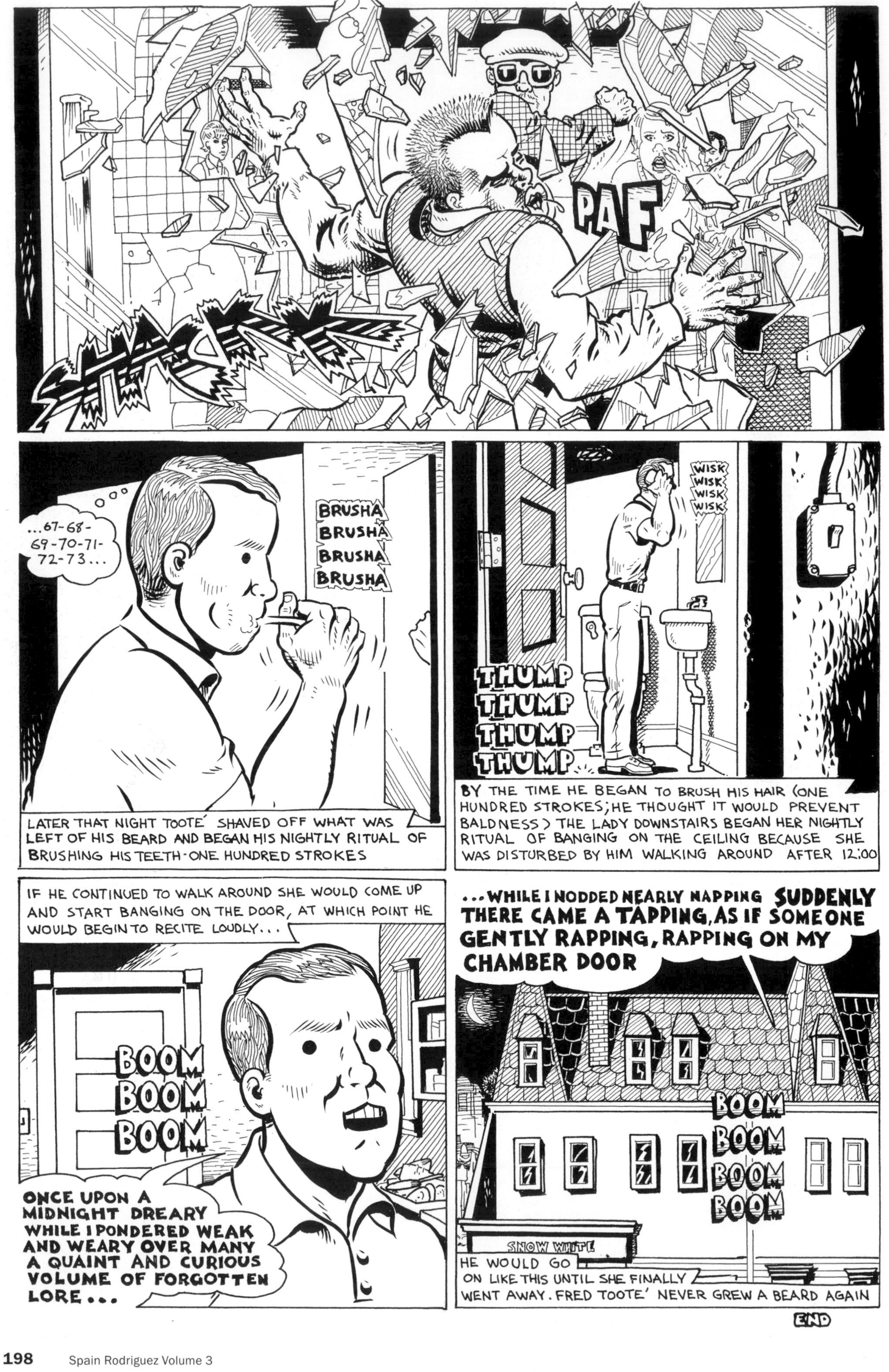
PAF
...67-68-69-70-71-72-73...
BRUSHA BRUSHA BRUSHA BRUSHA
LATER THAT NIGHT TOOTE' SHAVED OFF WHAT WAS LEFT OF HIS BEARD AND BEGAN HIS NIGHTLY RITUAL OF BRUSHING HIS TEETH-ONE HUNDRED STROKES
WISK WISK WISK WISK
THUMP THUMP THUMP THUMP
BY THE TIME HE BEGAN TO BRUSH HIS HAIR (ONE HUNDRED STROKES; HE THOUGHT IT WOULD PREVENT BALDNESS) THE LADY DOWNSTAIRS BEGAN HER NIGHTLY RITUAL OF BANGING ON THE CEILING BECAUSE SHE WAS DISTURBED BY HIM WALKING AROUND AFTER 12:00
IF HE CONTINUED TO WALK AROUND SHE WOULD COME UP AND START BANGING ON THE DOOR, AT WHICH POINT HE WOULD BEGIN TO RECITE LOUDLY...
BOOM BOOM BOOM
ONCE UPON A MIDNIGHT DREARY WHILE I PONDERED WEAK AND WEARY OVER MANY A QUAINT AND CURIOUS VOLUME OF FORGOTTEN LORE...
...WHILE I NODDED NEARLY NAPPING SUDDENLY THERE CAME A TAPPING, AS IF SOMEONE GENTLY RAPPING, RAPPING ON MY CHAMBER DOOR
BOOM BOOM BOOM BOOM
SNOW WHITE
HE WOULD GO ON LIKE THIS UNTIL SHE FINALLY WENT AWAY. FRED TOOTE' NEVER GREW A BEARD AGAIN
END

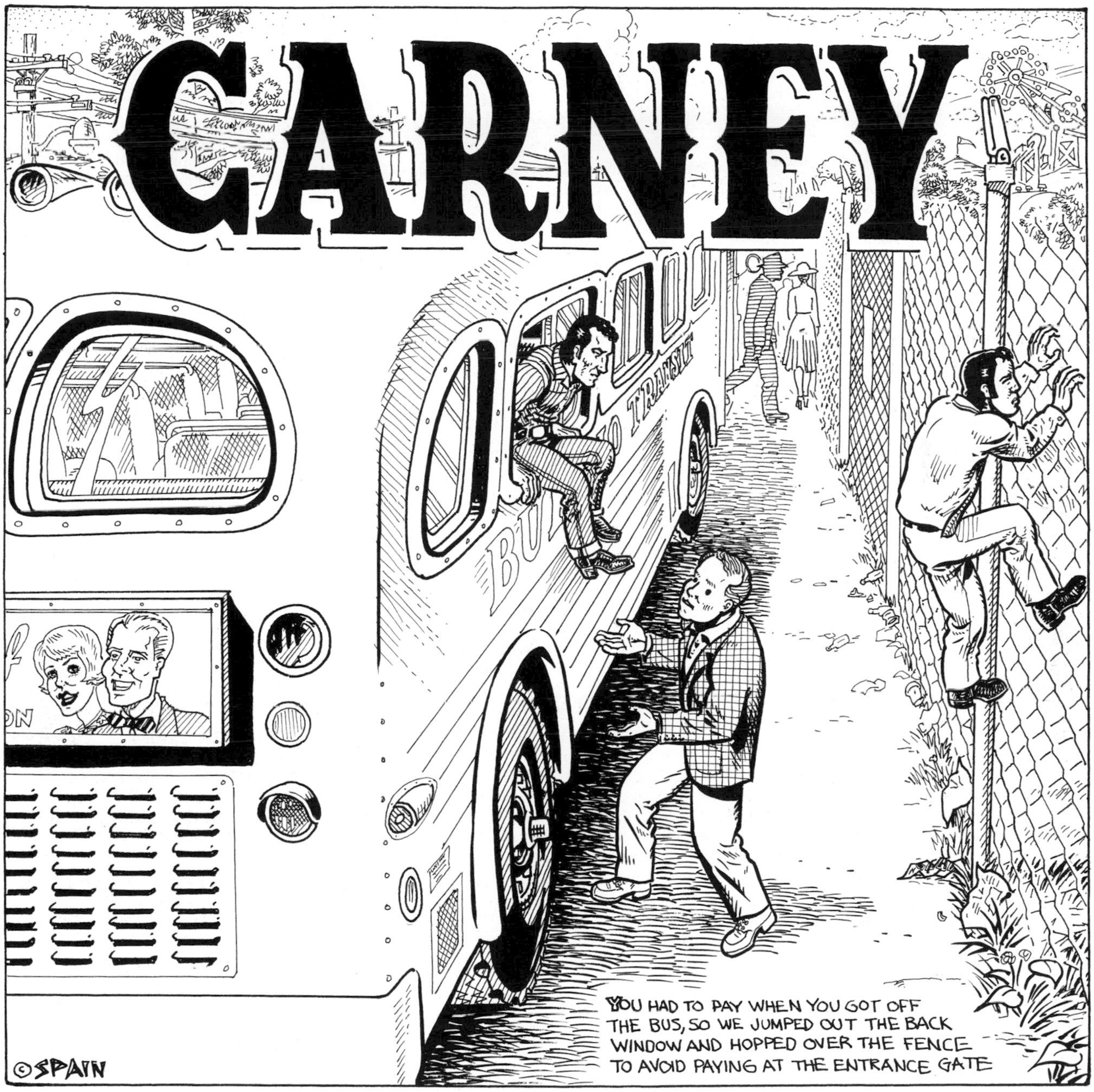
CARNEY
BUFFALO TRANSIT
YOU HAD TO PAY WHEN YOU GOT OFF THE BUS, SO WE JUMPED OUT THE BACK WINDOW AND HOPPED OVER THE FENCE TO AVOID PAYING AT THE ENTRANCE GATE
©SPAIN

P. 199–207 from *Blab!* #10, 1998

WE QUICKLY GOT LOST IN THE CROWD. THE IDEA WAS TO SEE HOW LITTLE WE COULD GET AWAY WITH SPENDING, SO WE IMMEDIATELY HEADED FOR THE FREE STUFF
THE SOY BURGERS WERE FREE, BUT INGRATE THAT I WAS...
MAN, THIS SHIT GETS MORE FETID EVERY YEAR
VEGETARIA
A HEATHY WAY TO EAT
PTOOEY
WIMPY WOULD HAVE BEEN PROUD
OVER AT THE HOG EXHIBIT, SOME FARMER WAS LASCIVIOUSLY STROKING THE PIG'S UNDERSIDE WITH A CHROME-TIPPED POLE
SQORNK
THE PIG SEEMED TO BE GOING FOR IT.
I NOTICED YOU WERE GETTING A LITTLE HOT WHEN THEY WERE STROKING THAT PIG'S BALLS, SPAIN
NO, THAT'S JUST MY DICK IN ITS NORMAL STATE. PERHAPS YOU'D LIKE TO GET DOWN ON YOUR KNEES SO YOU CAN MONITOR MY DONG MORE CLOSELY

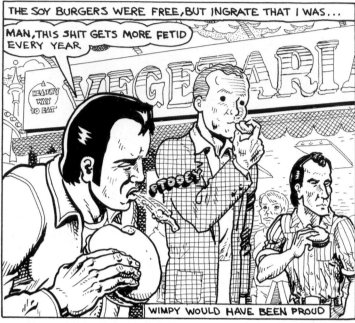

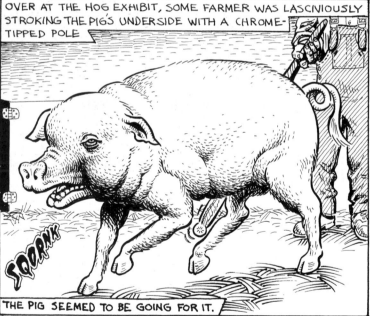

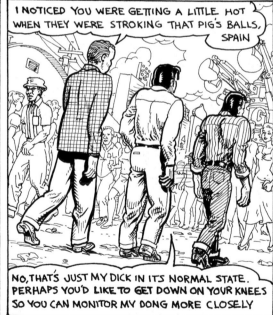

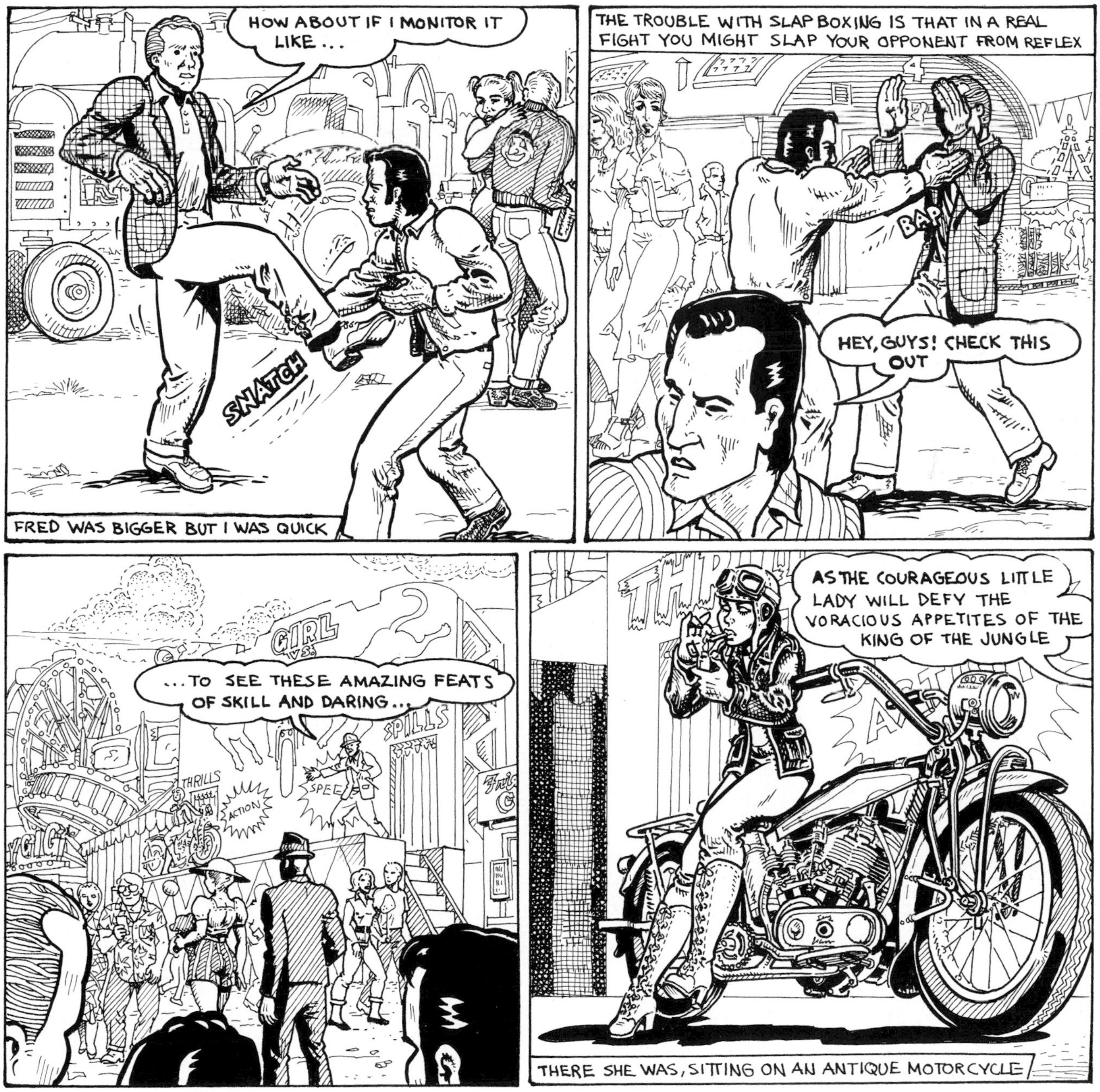

HOW ABOUT IF I MONITOR IT LIKE...
SNATCH
FRED WAS BIGGER BUT I WAS QUICK
THE TROUBLE WITH SLAP BOXING IS THAT IN A REAL FIGHT YOU MIGHT SLAP YOUR OPPONENT FROM REFLEX
BAP
HEY, GUYS! CHECK THIS OUT
...TO SEE THESE AMAZING FEATS OF SKILL AND DARING...
GIRL VS.
SPILLS
THRILLS
ACTION
AS THE COURAGEOUS LITTLE LADY WILL DEFY THE VORACIOUS APPETITES OF THE KING OF THE JUNGLE
THERE SHE WAS, SITTING ON AN ANTIQUE MOTORCYCLE

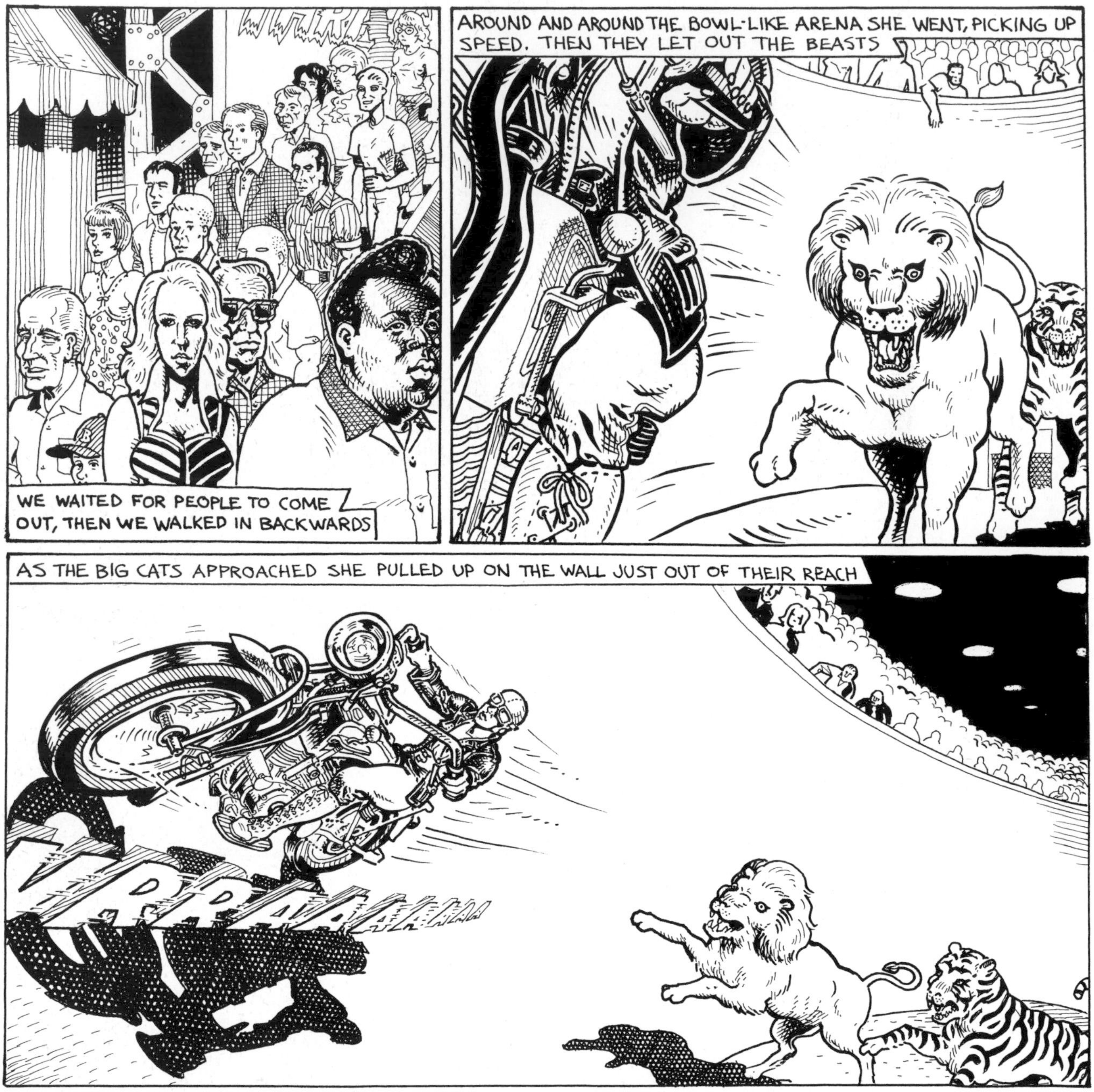
WE WAITED FOR PEOPLE TO COME OUT, THEN WE WALKED IN BACKWARDS
AROUND AND AROUND THE BOWL-LIKE ARENA SHE WENT, PICKING UP SPEED. THEN THEY LET OUT THE BEASTS
AS THE BIG CATS APPROACHED SHE PULLED UP ON THE WALL JUST OUT OF THEIR REACH

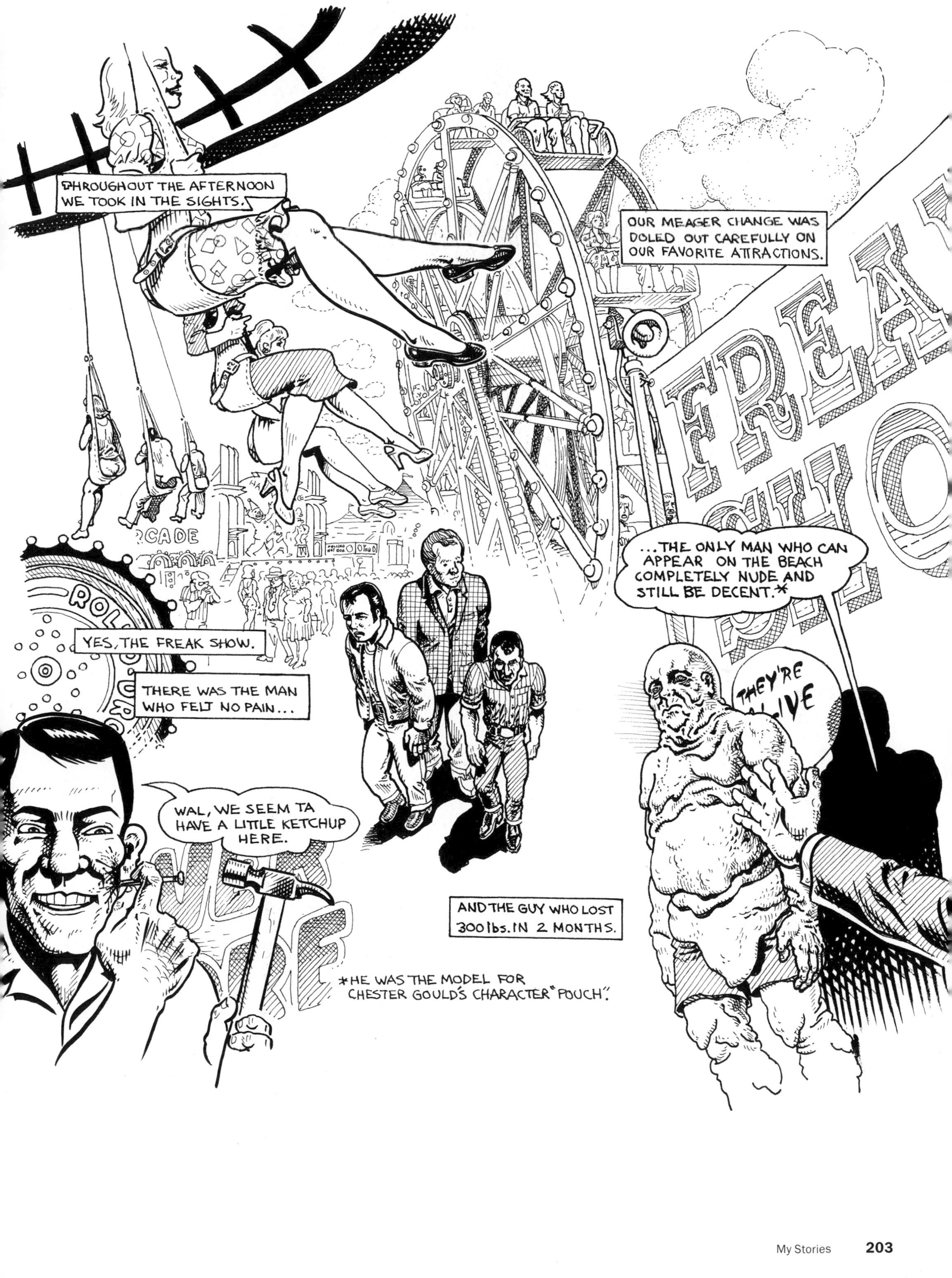
THROUGHOUT THE AFTERNOON WE TOOK IN THE SIGHTS.
OUR MEAGER CHANGE WAS DOLED OUT CAREFULLY ON OUR FAVORITE ATTRACTIONS.
ARCADE
YES, THE FREAK SHOW.
THERE WAS THE MAN WHO FELT NO PAIN...
WAL, WE SEEM TA HAVE A LITTLE KETCHUP HERE.
AND THE GUY WHO LOST 300 lbs. IN 2 MONTHS.
...THE ONLY MAN WHO CAN APPEAR ON THE BEACH COMPLETELY NUDE AND STILL BE DECENT.*
*HE WAS THE MODEL FOR CHESTER GOULD'S CHARACTER "POUCH".

BUT THE WEIRDEST OF ALL WAS THE HERMAPHRODITE. FOR AN EXTRA QUARTER YOU WENT INTO A TENT WITH A CURTAIN THAT DIVIDED THE MEN FROM THE WOMEN

OVER THE YEARS I'VE HAD TWO HUSBANDS AND ONE WIFE

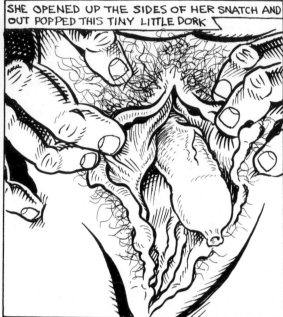

SHE OPENED UP THE SIDES OF HER SNATCH AND OUT POPPED THIS TINY LITTLE DORK

GIRLS GALORE

NEXT, WE CHECKED OUT THE GIRLIE SHOW

I HAD FOND MEMORIES OF THE OLD STRIP QUEENS LIKE RITA CORTEZ AND PAGAN JONES FROM WHEN I WAS YOUNGER AND COULD GET INTO CARNY BURLESQUE SHOWS WITHOUT PROOF OF AGE

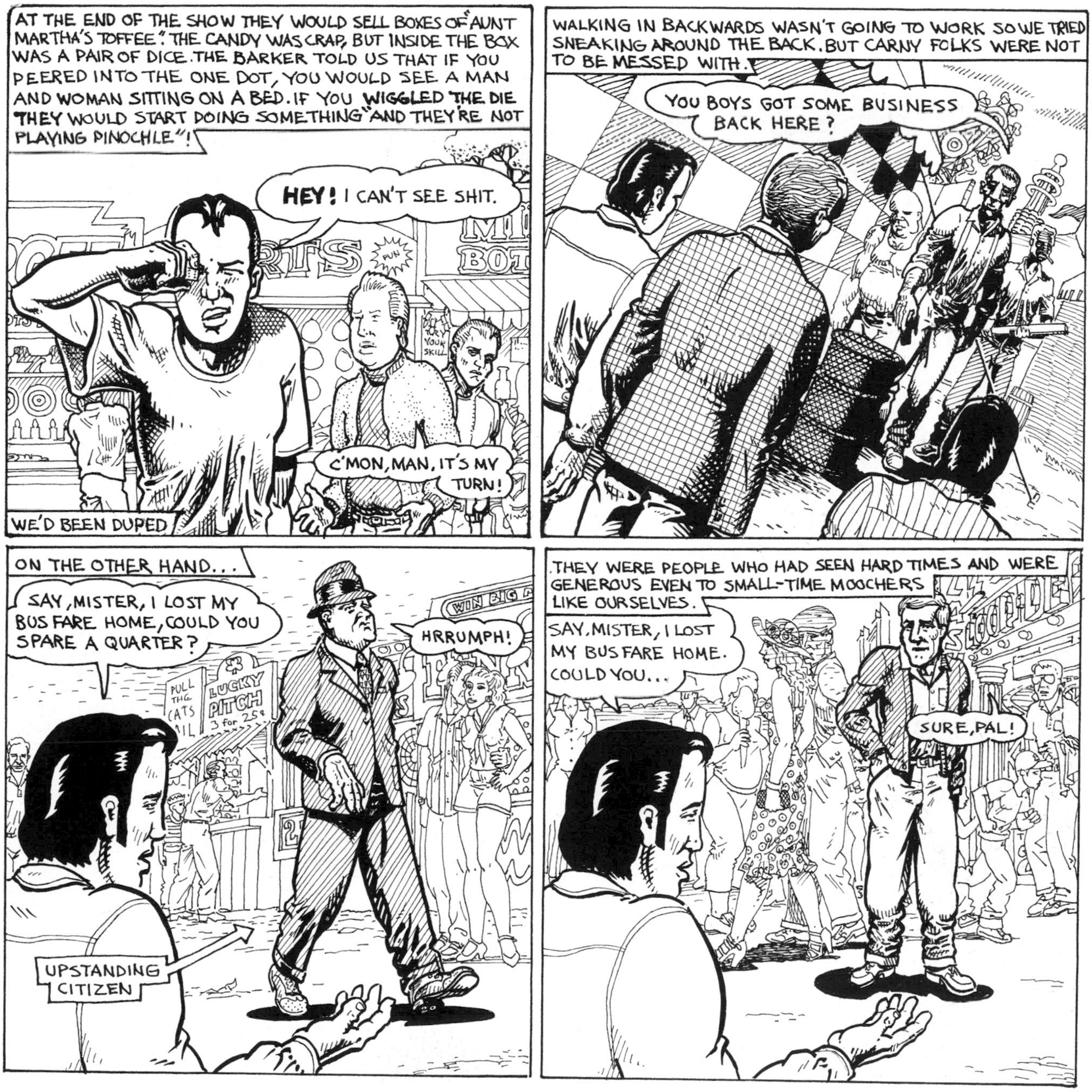
AT THE END OF THE SHOW THEY WOULD SELL BOXES OF "AUNT MARTHA'S TOFFEE". THE CANDY WAS CRAP, BUT INSIDE THE BOX WAS A PAIR OF DICE. THE BARKER TOLD US THAT IF YOU PEERED INTO THE ONE DOT, YOU WOULD SEE A MAN AND WOMAN SITTING ON A BED. IF YOU WIGGLED THE DIE THEY WOULD START DOING SOMETHING "AND THEY'RE NOT PLAYING PINOCHLE"!
HEY! I CAN'T SEE SHIT.
C'MON, MAN, IT'S MY TURN!
WE'D BEEN DUPED
WALKING IN BACKWARDS WASN'T GOING TO WORK SO WE TRIED SNEAKING AROUND THE BACK. BUT CARNY FOLKS WERE NOT TO BE MESSED WITH.
YOU BOYS GOT SOME BUSINESS BACK HERE?
ON THE OTHER HAND...
SAY, MISTER, I LOST MY BUS FARE HOME, COULD YOU SPARE A QUARTER?
HRRUMPH!
LUCKY PITCH 3 for 25¢
UPSTANDING CITIZEN
THEY WERE PEOPLE WHO HAD SEEN HARD TIMES AND WERE GENEROUS EVEN TO SMALL-TIME MOOCHERS LIKE OURSELVES.
SAY, MISTER, I LOST MY BUS FARE HOME. COULD YOU...
SURE, PAL!

WE WAITED IN ANTICIPATION FOR THE WOMEN. BUT FIRST WE HAD TO SIT THROUGH SOME CORNBALL COMEDIAN

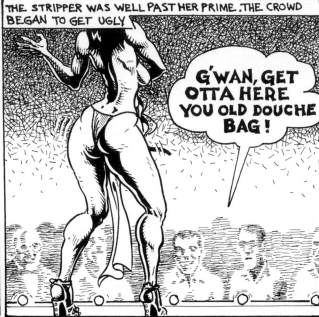

THE STRIPPER WAS WELL PAST HER PRIME. THE CROWD BEGAN TO GET UGLY

G'WAN, GET OTTA HERE YOU OLD DOUCHE BAG!

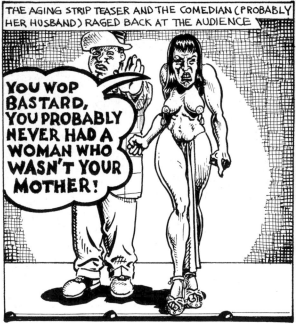

THE AGING STRIP TEASER AND THE COMEDIAN (PROBABLY HER HUSBAND) RAGED BACK AT THE AUDIENCE

YOU WOP BASTARD, YOU PROBABLY NEVER HAD A WOMAN WHO WASN'T YOUR MOTHER!

MY MOTHER'S DEAD BUT I'M SURE SHE LOOKS BETTER THAN YOU!

THE ARGUMENT RAGED BACK AND FORTH FOR A WHILE. THEN THE TWO PERFORMERS LEFT THE STAGE. THERE WOULD BE FEW BOXES OF AUNT MARTHA'S TOFFEE WITH THE RISQUÉ DICE SOLD AFTER THAT PERFORMANCE

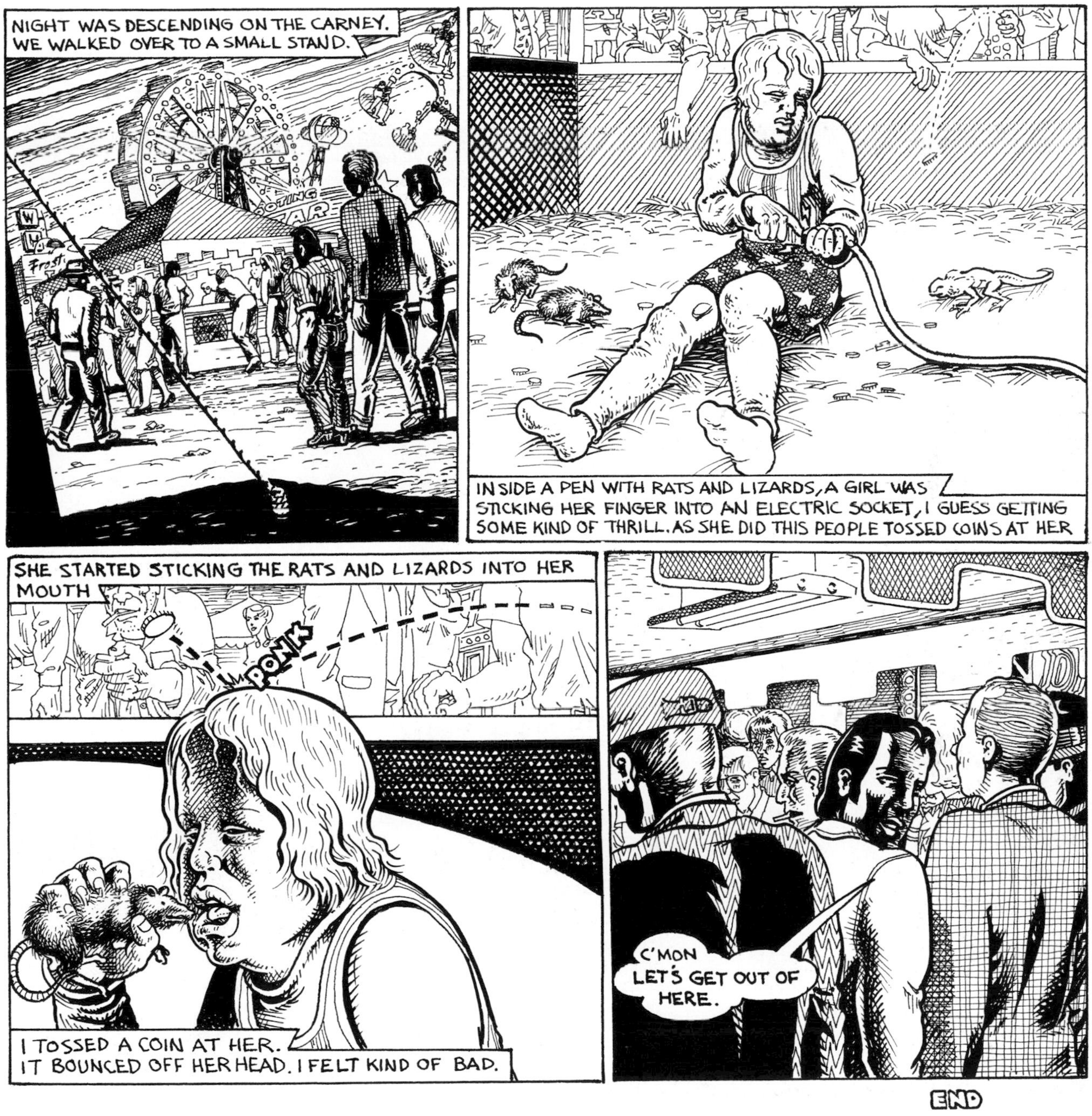
NIGHT WAS DESCENDING ON THE CARNEY. WE WALKED OVER TO A SMALL STAND.
INSIDE A PEN WITH RATS AND LIZARDS, A GIRL WAS STICKING HER FINGER INTO AN ELECTRIC SOCKET, I GUESS GETTING SOME KIND OF THRILL. AS SHE DID THIS PEOPLE TOSSED COINS AT HER
SHE STARTED STICKING THE RATS AND LIZARDS INTO HER MOUTH
PONK
I TOSSED A COIN AT HER. IT BOUNCED OFF HER HEAD. I FELT KIND OF BAD.
C'MON LET'S GET OUT OF HERE.
END

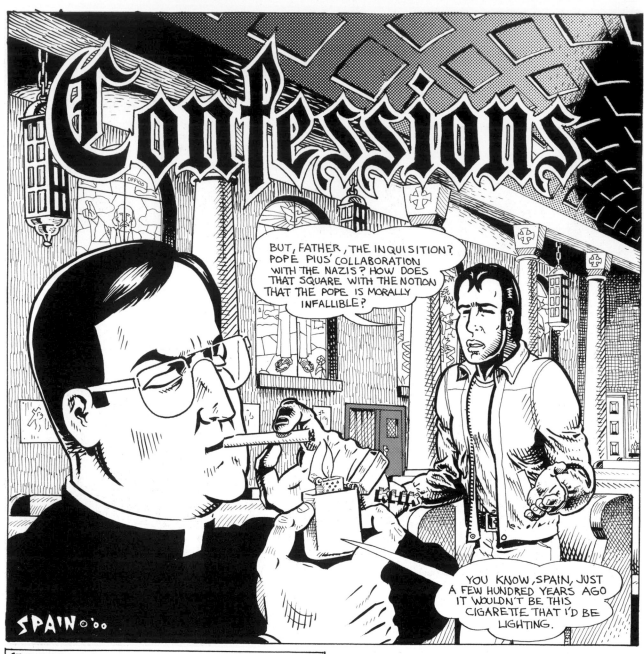

BUT, FATHER, THE INQUISITION? POPE PIUS' COLLABORATION WITH THE NAZIS? HOW DOES THAT SQUARE WITH THE NOTION THAT THE POPE IS MORALLY INFALLIBLE?

YOU KNOW, SPAIN, JUST A FEW HUNDRED YEARS AGO IT WOULDN'T BE THIS CIGARETTE THAT I'D BE LIGHTING.

SPAIN ©'00

ST. FRANCIS DE SALES CATHOLIC CHURCH, BUILT IN ROMANESQUE STYLE, STOOD AT THE CORNER OF NORTHLAND AND HUMBOLDT PARKWAY.

AS A KID, I WATCHED PEOPLE GOING TO MASS ON SUNDAYS. I WAS CURIOUS AND DECIDED TO GO SEE FOR MYSELF.

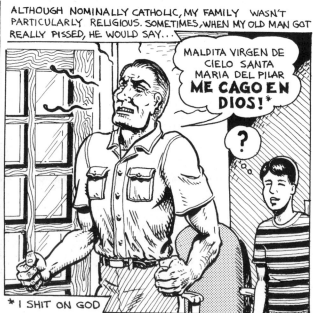

ALTHOUGH NOMINALLY CATHOLIC, MY FAMILY WASN'T PARTICULARLY RELIGIOUS. SOMETIMES, WHEN MY OLD MAN GOT REALLY PISSED, HE WOULD SAY...

MALDITA VIRGEN DE CIELO SANTA MARIA DEL PILAR **ME CAGO EN DIOS!***

?

* I SHIT ON GOD

P. 208–213 from *Blab!* #11, 2000

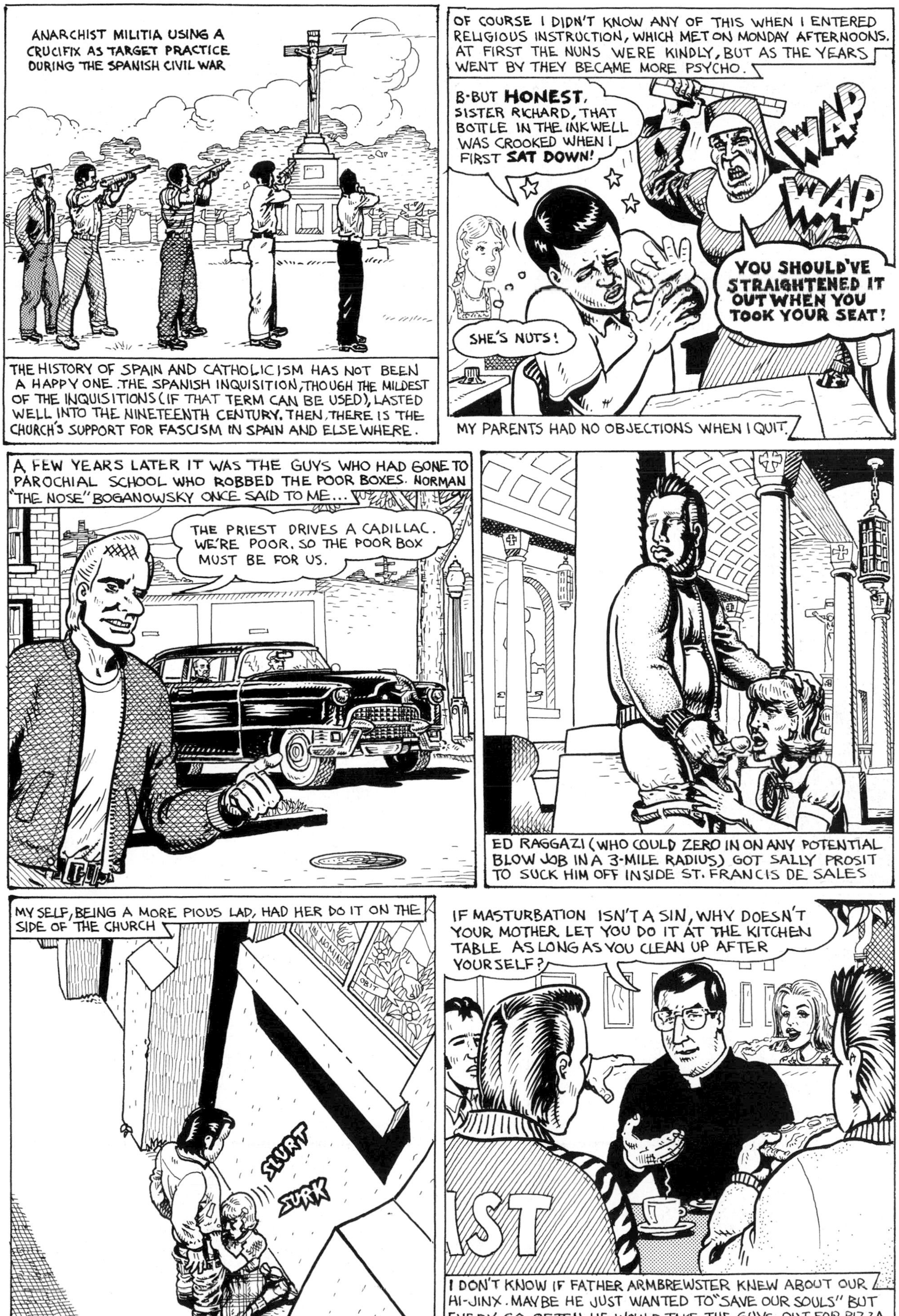
ANARCHIST MILITIA USING A CRUCIFIX AS TARGET PRACTICE DURING THE SPANISH CIVIL WAR
THE HISTORY OF SPAIN AND CATHOLICISM HAS NOT BEEN A HAPPY ONE. THE SPANISH INQUISITION, THOUGH THE MILDEST OF THE INQUISITIONS (IF THAT TERM CAN BE USED), LASTED WELL INTO THE NINETEENTH CENTURY. THEN, THERE IS THE CHURCH'S SUPPORT FOR FASCISM IN SPAIN AND ELSE WHERE.
OF COURSE I DIDN'T KNOW ANY OF THIS WHEN I ENTERED RELIGIOUS INSTRUCTION, WHICH MET ON MONDAY AFTERNOONS. AT FIRST THE NUNS WERE KINDLY, BUT AS THE YEARS WENT BY THEY BECAME MORE PSYCHO.
B-BUT **HONEST**, SISTER RICHARD, THAT BOTTLE IN THE INK WELL WAS CROOKED WHEN I FIRST **SAT DOWN**!
WAP
WAP
YOU SHOULD'VE STRAIGHTENED IT OUT WHEN YOU TOOK YOUR SEAT!
SHE'S NUTS!
MY PARENTS HAD NO OBJECTIONS WHEN I QUIT.
A FEW YEARS LATER IT WAS THE GUYS WHO HAD GONE TO PAROCHIAL SCHOOL WHO ROBBED THE POOR BOXES. NORMAN "THE NOSE" BOGANOWSKY ONCE SAID TO ME...
THE PRIEST DRIVES A CADILLAC. WE'RE POOR, SO THE POOR BOX MUST BE FOR US.
ED RAGGAZI (WHO COULD ZERO IN ON ANY POTENTIAL BLOW JOB IN A 3-MILE RADIUS) GOT SALLY PROSIT TO SUCK HIM OFF INSIDE ST. FRANCIS DE SALES
MYSELF, BEING A MORE PIOUS LAD, HAD HER DO IT ON THE SIDE OF THE CHURCH
SLURT
SURK
IF MASTURBATION ISN'T A SIN, WHY DOESN'T YOUR MOTHER LET YOU DO IT AT THE KITCHEN TABLE AS LONG AS YOU CLEAN UP AFTER YOURSELF?
I DON'T KNOW IF FATHER ARMBREWSTER KNEW ABOUT OUR HI-JINX. MAYBE HE JUST WANTED TO "SAVE OUR SOULS" BUT EVERY SO OFTEN HE WOULD TAKE THE GUYS OUT FOR PIZZA.

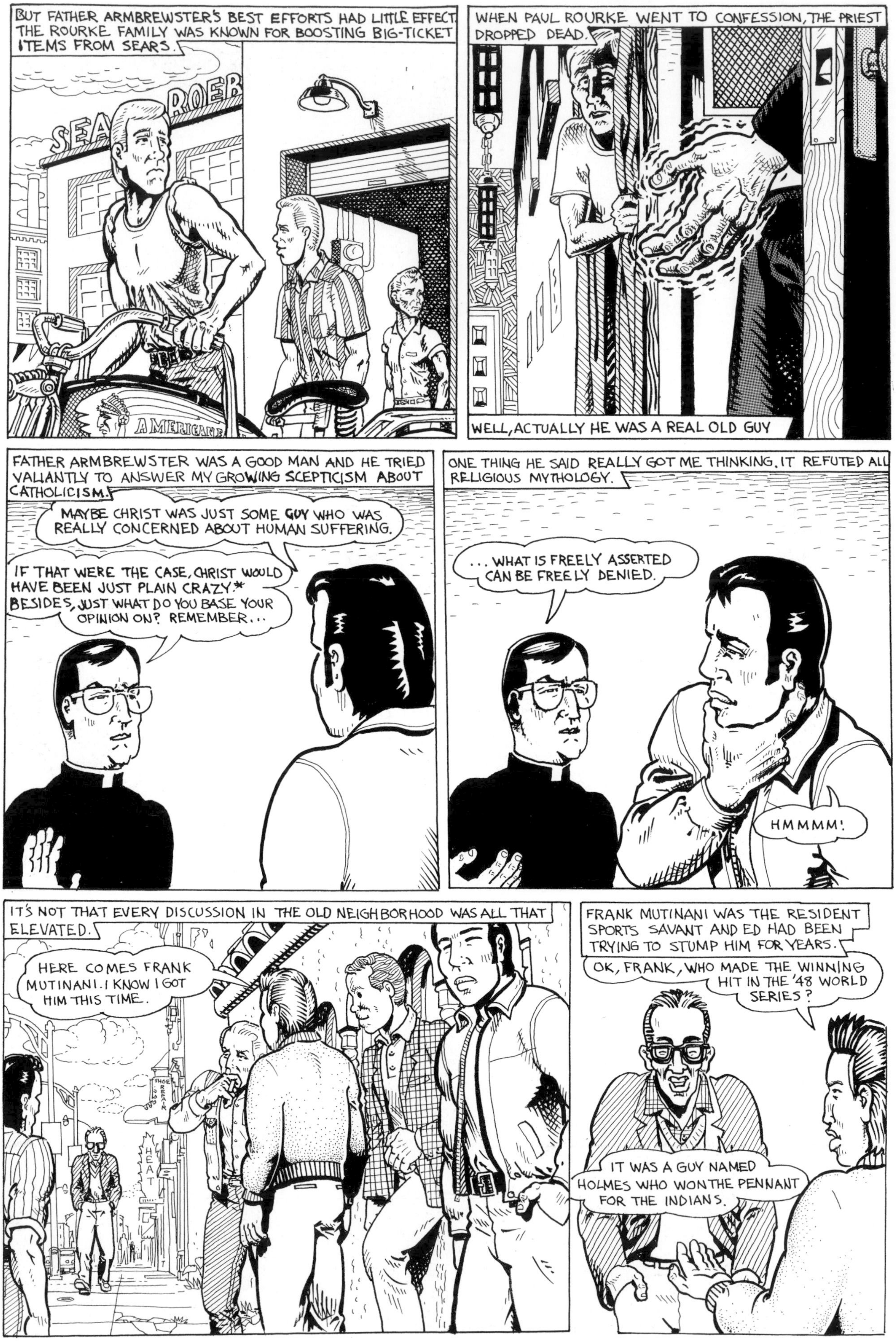
BUT FATHER ARMBREWSTER'S BEST EFFORTS HAD LITTLE EFFECT. THE ROURKE FAMILY WAS KNOWN FOR BOOSTING BIG-TICKET ITEMS FROM SEARS.
SEARS ROEB
AMERICAN
WHEN PAUL ROURKE WENT TO CONFESSION, THE PRIEST DROPPED DEAD.
WELL, ACTUALLY HE WAS A REAL OLD GUY
FATHER ARMBREWSTER WAS A GOOD MAN AND HE TRIED VALIANTLY TO ANSWER MY GROWING SCEPTICISM ABOUT CATHOLICISM.
MAYBE CHRIST WAS JUST SOME GUY WHO WAS REALLY CONCERNED ABOUT HUMAN SUFFERING.
IF THAT WERE THE CASE, CHRIST WOULD HAVE BEEN JUST PLAIN CRAZY.* BESIDES, JUST WHAT DO YOU BASE YOUR OPINION ON? REMEMBER...
ONE THING HE SAID REALLY GOT ME THINKING. IT REFUTED ALL RELIGIOUS MYTHOLOGY.
...WHAT IS FREELY ASSERTED CAN BE FREELY DENIED.
HMMMM!
IT'S NOT THAT EVERY DISCUSSION IN THE OLD NEIGHBORHOOD WAS ALL THAT ELEVATED.
HERE COMES FRANK MUTINANI. I KNOW I GOT HIM THIS TIME.
SHOE REPAIR
HEAT
FRANK MUTINANI WAS THE RESIDENT SPORTS SAVANT AND ED HAD BEEN TRYING TO STUMP HIM FOR YEARS.
OK, FRANK, WHO MADE THE WINNING HIT IN THE '48 WORLD SERIES?
IT WAS A GUY NAMED HOLMES WHO WON THE PENNANT FOR THE INDIANS.

* I NEVER QUITE UNDERSTOOD THIS ONE.

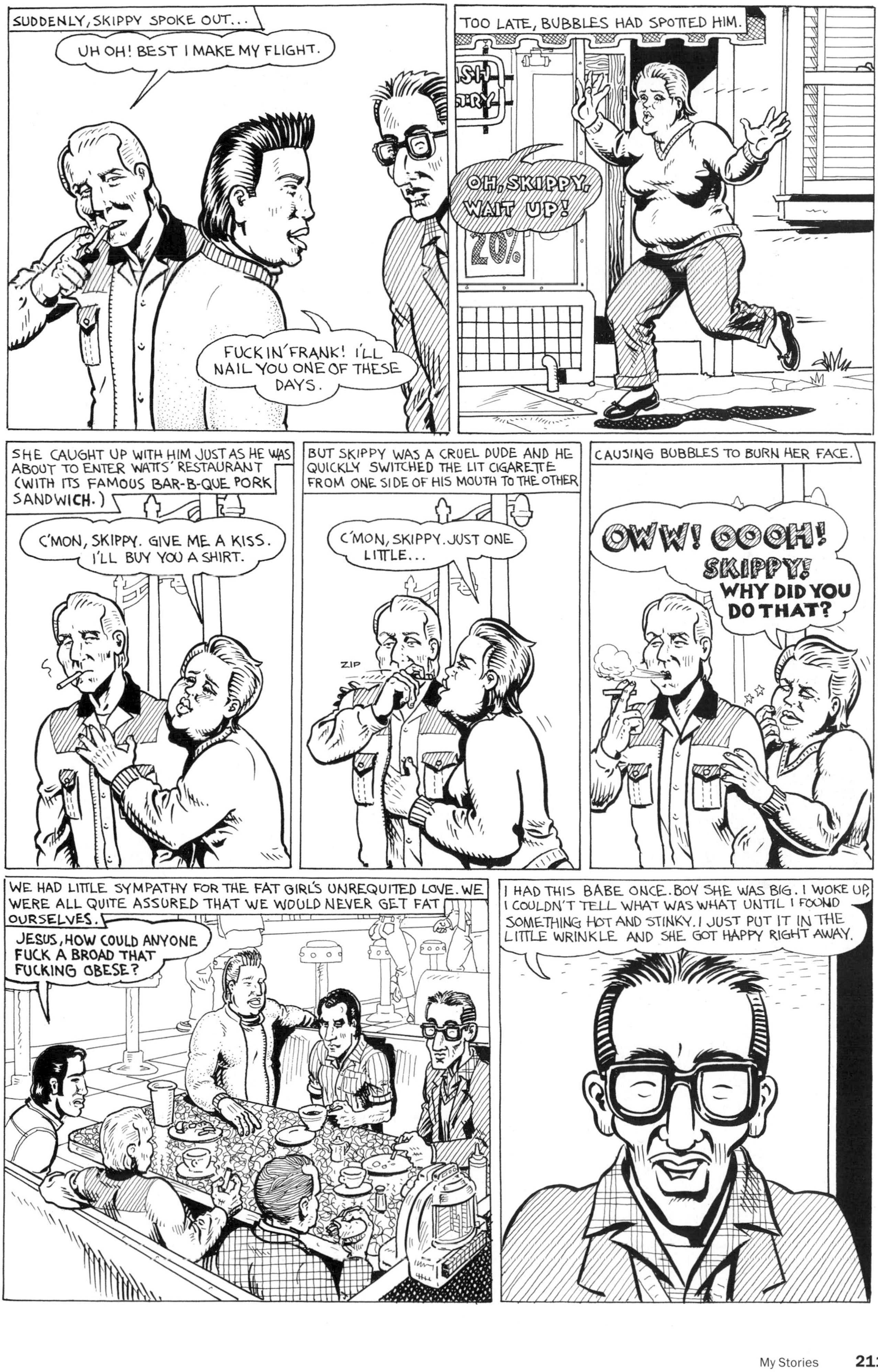
SUDDENLY, SKIPPY SPOKE OUT...
UH OH! BEST I MAKE MY FLIGHT.
FUCKIN' FRANK! I'LL NAIL YOU ONE OF THESE DAYS.
TOO LATE, BUBBLES HAD SPOTTED HIM.
OH, SKIPPY, WAIT UP!
20%
SHE CAUGHT UP WITH HIM JUST AS HE WAS ABOUT TO ENTER WATTS' RESTAURANT (WITH ITS FAMOUS BAR-B-QUE PORK SANDWICH.)
C'MON, SKIPPY. GIVE ME A KISS. I'LL BUY YOU A SHIRT.
BUT SKIPPY WAS A CRUEL DUDE AND HE QUICKLY SWITCHED THE LIT CIGARETTE FROM ONE SIDE OF HIS MOUTH TO THE OTHER
C'MON, SKIPPY. JUST ONE LITTLE...
ZIP
CAUSING BUBBLES TO BURN HER FACE.
OWW! OOOH! SKIPPY! WHY DID YOU DO THAT?
WE HAD LITTLE SYMPATHY FOR THE FAT GIRL'S UNREQUITED LOVE. WE WERE ALL QUITE ASSURED THAT WE WOULD NEVER GET FAT OURSELVES.
JESUS, HOW COULD ANYONE FUCK A BROAD THAT FUCKING OBESE?
I HAD THIS BABE ONCE. BOY SHE WAS BIG. I WOKE UP, I COULDN'T TELL WHAT WAS WHAT UNTIL I FOUND SOMETHING HOT AND STINKY. I JUST PUT IT IN THE LITTLE WRINKLE AND SHE GOT HAPPY RIGHT AWAY.

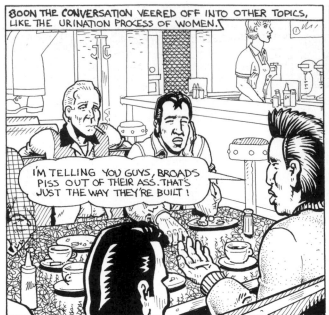

SOON THE CONVERSATION VEERED OFF INTO OTHER TOPICS, LIKE THE URINATION PROCESS OF WOMEN.

I'M TELLING YOU GUYS, BROADS PISS OUT OF THEIR ASS. THAT'S JUST THE WAY THEY'RE BUILT!

I, MYSELF, WASN'T QUITE SURE. BUT FRED WASN'T BUYING IT.

YOU BUNCH OF YOKELS. WOMEN PEE THROUGH A TUBE IN THEIR PUSSY.

BOX ST.

I GOTTA ADMIT, ED CRACKED ME UP WITH THAT STORY ABOUT WHEN HE WAS A KID, SEEING THE WOMAN PISSING IN THE PARK AND HIS MOM TELLS HIM, "EDWARD, TURN YOUR HEAD."

MIDLA

WE ALL WENT UP TO FRED'S PLACE (HE HAD TO GET SOME BREAD OR SOMETHING). HE WENT INTO ANOTHER ROOM AND AFTER A FEW MINUTES CALLED US IN.

AY, GUYS! DAH DAAH

IT'S FAKE. VEZAY FORGOT TO LOCK HIS TRUNK.

FRED'S BROTHER VEZAY HAD A DOCTORATE OF DIVINITY AND A TRUNK FULL OF GOODIES LIKE A REALISTICALLY COLORED 15-INCH DILDO

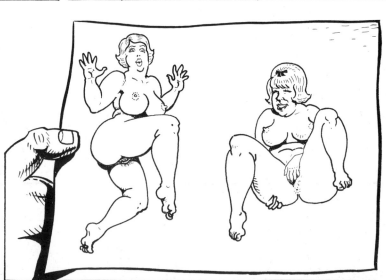

VEZAY, SOMETIMES REFERRED TO BY FRED AS "THE DALAI LAMA OF NORTH FILLMORE," ALSO DID BEAUTIFULLY RENDERED DRAWINGS OF FAT WOMEN. BUBBLES HAD TRULY FOCUSED HER ATTENTION ON THE WRONG GUY.

WHEN HE WAS SMALL, FRED WAS TERRORIZED BY HIS OLDER BROTHER. (BUT FRED HAD GROWN BIGGER IN THE INTERVENING YEARS AND NOW IT WAS FRED WHO ENJOYED TORMENTING VEZAY).

KEEP YOUR EYES OPEN, YOU LITTLE FUCK, OR I'LL LOCK YOU IN THE CLOSET AGAIN WHEN WE GET HOME.

BUT I'M SCARED!

CURIOUS AND BRIGHT, VEZAY HAD HIS OWN WAY OF SEEING THINGS.

BUT, VEZAY, WHY SHOULD ANYONE BELIEVE THAT STUFF WRITTEN THOUSANDS OF YEARS AGO? IF CHRIST WAS TRAVELING AT THE SPEED OF LIGHT AFTER HE WAS SUPPOSEDLY RESURRECTED, HE STILL WOULDN'T HAVE MADE IT OUT OF THE GALAXY.

PERHAPS GOD EXISTS IN ANOTHER DIMENSION AND HE'S JUST CREATED THIS ILLUSORY DIMENSION TO TEST OUR FAITH. THOSE WHO KEEP FAITH IN HIS WORD GET TO GO TO THE HEAVEN PLANET,

SO THE UNIVERSE IS JUST ONE BIG HOAX?

THAT VEZAY'S WORLD VIEW WAS A WACKED-OUT COMBINATION OF CHRISTIAN FUNDAMENTALISM AND SCIENCE FICTION SHOULDN'T HAVE COME AS A BIG SURPRISE. IN THE MIDDLE OF THEIR LIVING ROOM WAS A BIG CARDBOARD BARREL CONTAINING AN ASSORTMENT OF MEN'S MAGAZINES, SCIENCE FICTION BOOKS AND VARIOUS UNUSUAL PUBLICATIONS (INCLUDING ANYTHING PUT OUT BY HARVEY KURTZMAN).

ONE DAY, WHILE GOING THROUGH THE BARREL, I FOUND A COPY OF "SEXUS" BY HENRY MILLER. THE BOOK HAD BEEN STIRRING UP QUITE A FUSS IN THE NEWS RECENTLY. IT HAD JUST BEEN RELEASED AFTER DECADES OF SUPPRESSION.

"...TO GET THEM TO DRAPE A LEG OVER AN ARMCHAIR AND EXPOSE A LITTLE SALMON COLORED MEAT."

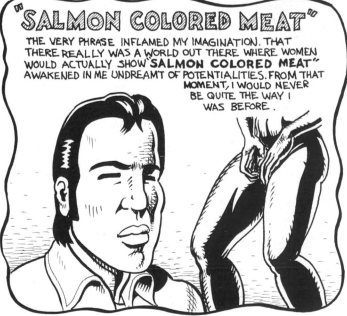

"SALMON COLORED MEAT"

THE VERY PHRASE INFLAMED MY IMAGINATION. THAT THERE REALLY WAS A WORLD OUT THERE WHERE WOMEN WOULD ACTUALLY SHOW "SALMON COLORED MEAT" AWAKENED IN ME UNDREAMT OF POTENTIALITIES. FROM THAT MOMENT, I WOULD NEVER BE QUITE THE WAY I WAS BEFORE.

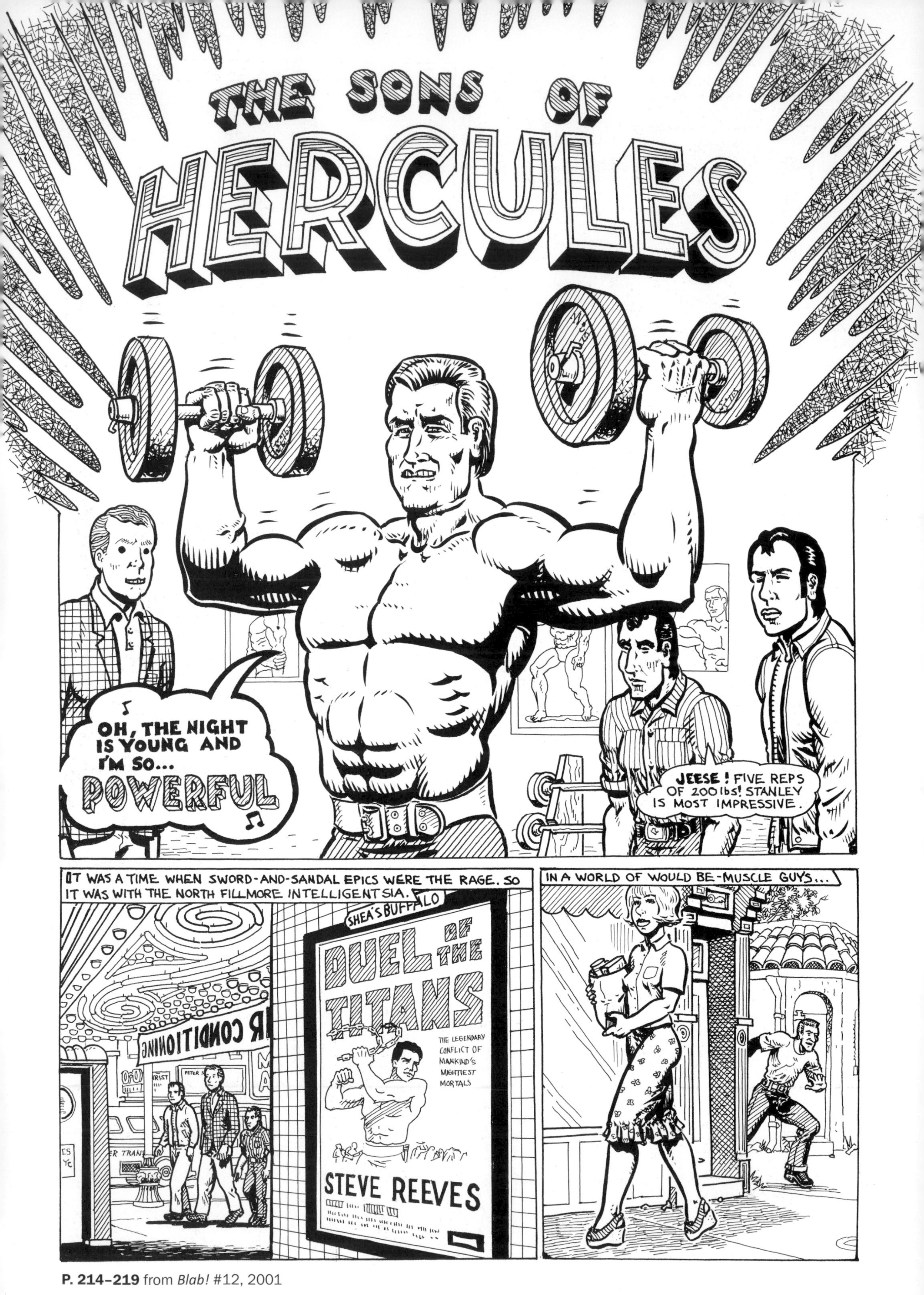

THE SONS OF HERCULES
OH, THE NIGHT IS YOUNG AND I'M SO... POWERFUL
JEESE! FIVE REPS OF 200 lbs! STANLEY IS MOST IMPRESSIVE.
IT WAS A TIME WHEN SWORD-AND-SANDAL EPICS WERE THE RAGE. SO IT WAS WITH THE NORTH FILLMORE INTELLIGENTSIA.
SHEA'S BUFFALO
AIR CONDITIONING
DUEL OF THE TITANS
THE LEGENDARY CONFLICT OF MANKIND'S MIGHTIEST MORTALS
STEVE REEVES
IN A WORLD OF WOULD BE-MUSCLE GUYS...

P. 214–219 from *Blab!* #12, 2001

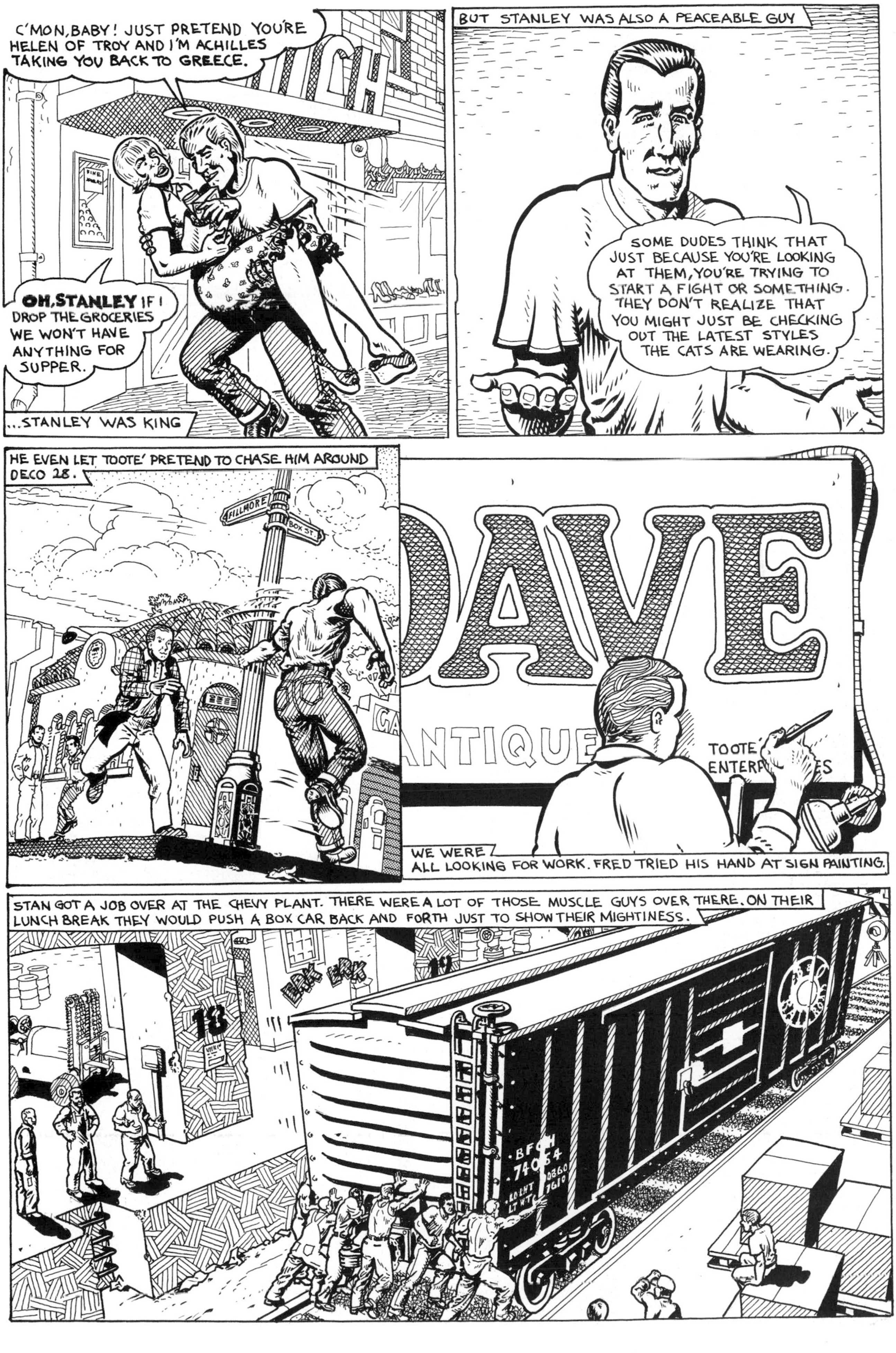
C'MON, BABY! JUST PRETEND YOU'RE HELEN OF TROY AND I'M ACHILLES TAKING YOU BACK TO GREECE.
OH, STANLEY IF I DROP THE GROCERIES WE WON'T HAVE ANYTHING FOR SUPPER.
...STANLEY WAS KING
BUT STANLEY WAS ALSO A PEACEABLE GUY
SOME DUDES THINK THAT JUST BECAUSE YOU'RE LOOKING AT THEM, YOU'RE TRYING TO START A FIGHT OR SOMETHING. THEY DON'T REALIZE THAT YOU MIGHT JUST BE CHECKING OUT THE LATEST STYLES THE CATS ARE WEARING.
HE EVEN LET TOOTE' PRETEND TO CHASE HIM AROUND DECO 28.
FILLMORE
BOX ST.
DAVE
ANTIQUE
TOOTE' ENTERP
WE WERE ALL LOOKING FOR WORK. FRED TRIED HIS HAND AT SIGN PAINTING.
STAN GOT A JOB OVER AT THE CHEVY PLANT. THERE WERE A LOT OF THOSE MUSCLE GUYS OVER THERE. ON THEIR LUNCH BREAK THEY WOULD PUSH A BOX CAR BACK AND FORTH JUST TO SHOW THEIR MIGHTINESS.
18
BFCH

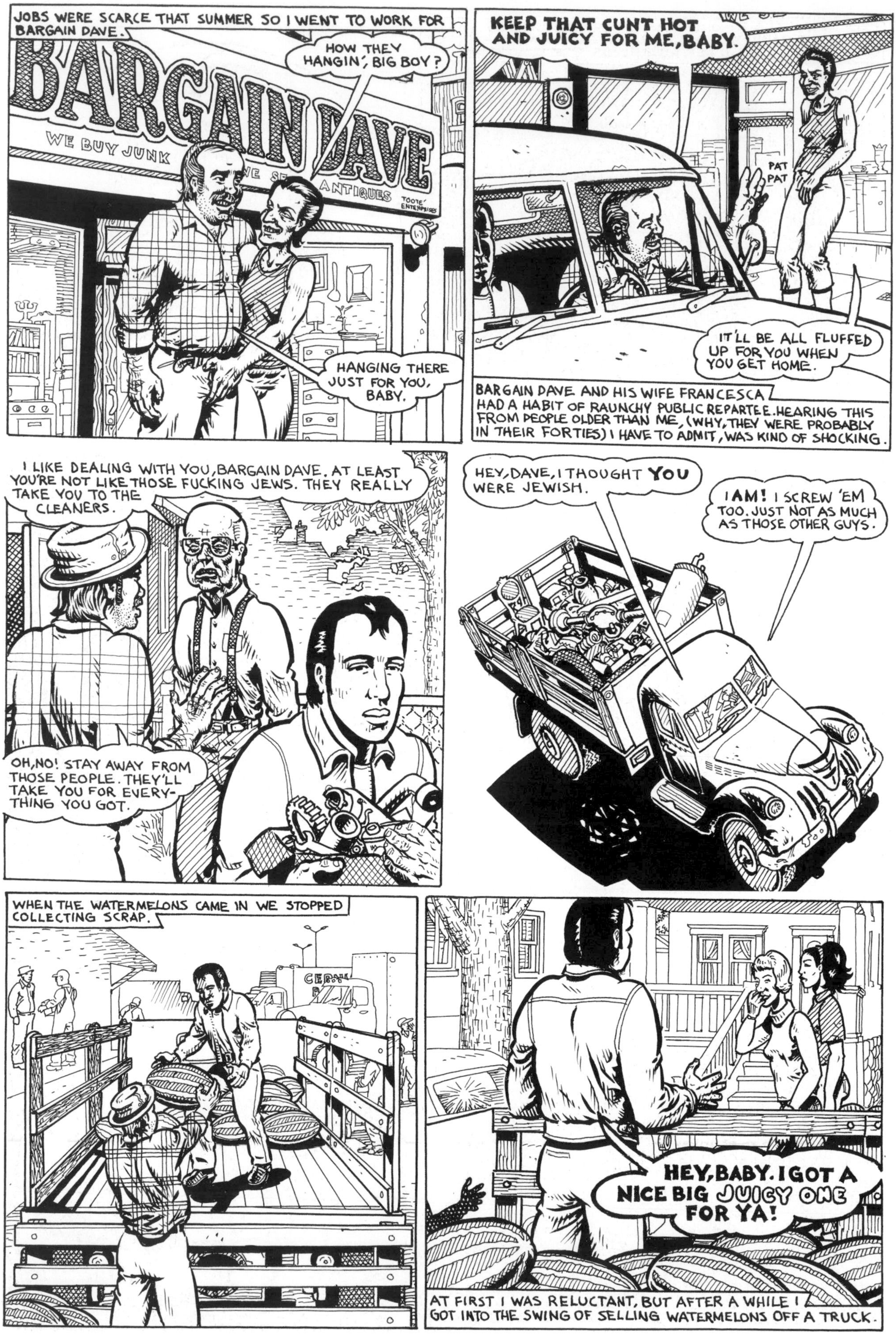

JOBS WERE SCARCE THAT SUMMER SO I WENT TO WORK FOR BARGAIN DAVE.
BARGAIN DAVE
WE BUY JUNK
ANTIQUES
TOOTE' ENTERPRISES
HOW THEY HANGIN', BIG BOY?
HANGING THERE JUST FOR YOU, BABY.
KEEP THAT CUNT HOT AND JUICY FOR ME, BABY.
PAT PAT
IT'LL BE ALL FLUFFED UP FOR YOU WHEN YOU GET HOME.
BARGAIN DAVE AND HIS WIFE FRANCESCA HAD A HABIT OF RAUNCHY PUBLIC REPARTEE. HEARING THIS FROM PEOPLE OLDER THAN ME, (WHY, THEY WERE PROBABLY IN THEIR FORTIES) I HAVE TO ADMIT, WAS KIND OF SHOCKING.
I LIKE DEALING WITH YOU, BARGAIN DAVE. AT LEAST YOU'RE NOT LIKE THOSE FUCKING JEWS. THEY REALLY TAKE YOU TO THE CLEANERS.
OH, NO! STAY AWAY FROM THOSE PEOPLE. THEY'LL TAKE YOU FOR EVERYTHING YOU GOT.
HEY, DAVE, I THOUGHT YOU WERE JEWISH.
I AM! I SCREW 'EM TOO. JUST NOT AS MUCH AS THOSE OTHER GUYS.
WHEN THE WATERMELONS CAME IN WE STOPPED COLLECTING SCRAP.
HEY, BABY. I GOT A NICE BIG JUICY ONE FOR YA!
AT FIRST I WAS RELUCTANT, BUT AFTER A WHILE I GOT INTO THE SWING OF SELLING WATERMELONS OFF A TRUCK.

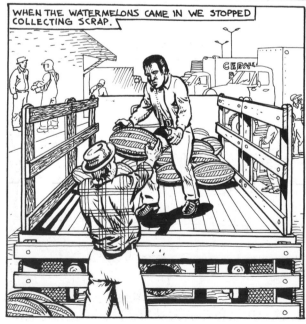

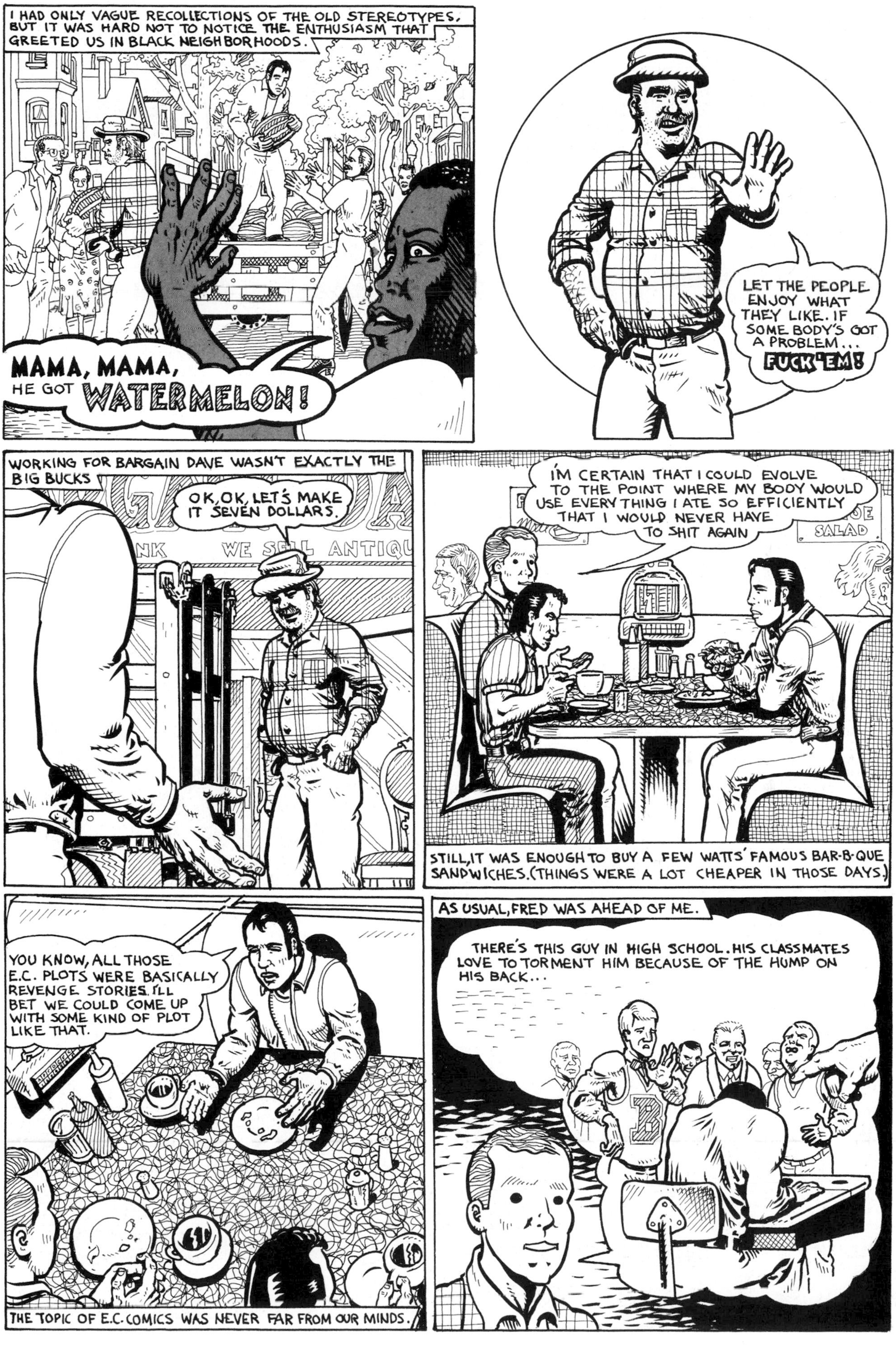

I HAD ONLY VAGUE RECOLLECTIONS OF THE OLD STEREOTYPES, BUT IT WAS HARD NOT TO NOTICE THE ENTHUSIASM THAT GREETED US IN BLACK NEIGHBORHOODS.
MAMA, MAMA, HE GOT WATERMELON!
LET THE PEOPLE ENJOY WHAT THEY LIKE. IF SOME BODY'S GOT A PROBLEM... FUCK 'EM!
WORKING FOR BARGAIN DAVE WASN'T EXACTLY THE BIG BUCKS
OK, OK, LET'S MAKE IT SEVEN DOLLARS.
WE SELL ANTIQU
I'M CERTAIN THAT I COULD EVOLVE TO THE POINT WHERE MY BODY WOULD USE EVERYTHING I ATE SO EFFICIENTLY THAT I WOULD NEVER HAVE TO SHIT AGAIN
SALAD
STILL, IT WAS ENOUGH TO BUY A FEW WATTS' FAMOUS BAR-B-QUE SANDWICHES. (THINGS WERE A LOT CHEAPER IN THOSE DAYS.)
YOU KNOW, ALL THOSE E.C. PLOTS WERE BASICALLY REVENGE STORIES. I'LL BET WE COULD COME UP WITH SOME KIND OF PLOT LIKE THAT.
THE TOPIC OF E.C. COMICS WAS NEVER FAR FROM OUR MINDS.
AS USUAL, FRED WAS AHEAD OF ME.
THERE'S THIS GUY IN HIGH SCHOOL. HIS CLASSMATES LOVE TO TORMENT HIM BECAUSE OF THE HUMP ON HIS BACK...

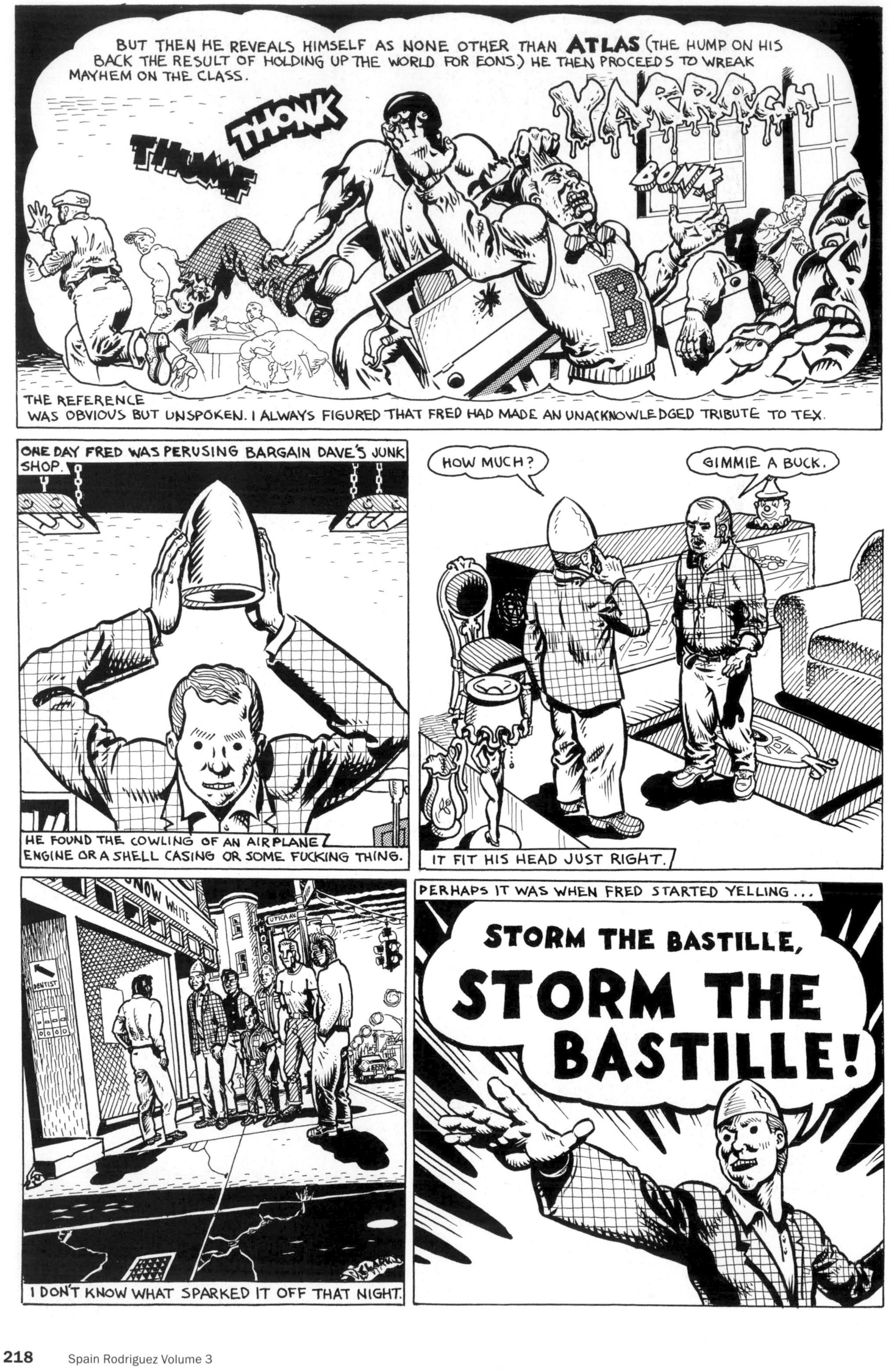
BUT THEN HE REVEALS HIMSELF AS NONE OTHER THAN ATLAS (THE HUMP ON HIS BACK THE RESULT OF HOLDING UP THE WORLD FOR EONS) HE THEN PROCEEDS TO WREAK MAYHEM ON THE CLASS.
THUMP
THONK
YARRRGH
BONK
THE REFERENCE WAS OBVIOUS BUT UNSPOKEN. I ALWAYS FIGURED THAT FRED HAD MADE AN UNACKNOWLEDGED TRIBUTE TO TEX.
ONE DAY FRED WAS PERUSING BARGAIN DAVE'S JUNK SHOP.
HE FOUND THE COWLING OF AN AIRPLANE ENGINE OR A SHELL CASING OR SOME FUCKING THING.
HOW MUCH?
GIMMIE A BUCK.
IT FIT HIS HEAD JUST RIGHT.
SNOW WHITE
DENTIST
I DON'T KNOW WHAT SPARKED IT OFF THAT NIGHT.
PERHAPS IT WAS WHEN FRED STARTED YELLING...
STORM THE BASTILLE,
STORM THE BASTILLE!

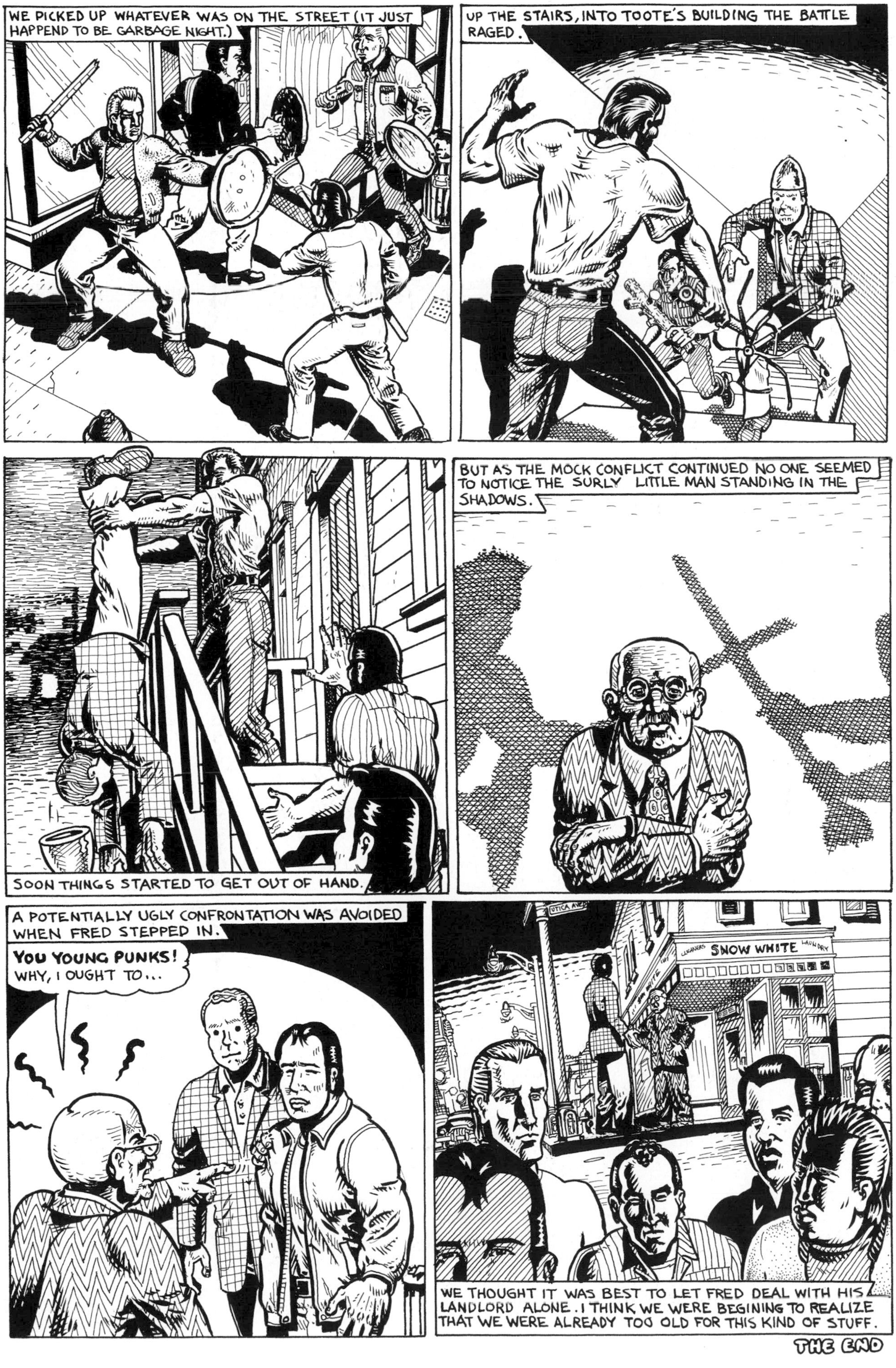
WE PICKED UP WHATEVER WAS ON THE STREET (IT JUST HAPPEND TO BE GARBAGE NIGHT.)
UP THE STAIRS, INTO TOOTE'S BUILDING THE BATTLE RAGED.
SOON THINGS STARTED TO GET OUT OF HAND.
BUT AS THE MOCK CONFLICT CONTINUED NO ONE SEEMED TO NOTICE THE SURLY LITTLE MAN STANDING IN THE SHADOWS.
A POTENTIALLY UGLY CONFRONTATION WAS AVOIDED WHEN FRED STEPPED IN.
YOU YOUNG PUNKS! WHY, I OUGHT TO...
UTICA AVE
CLEANERS SNOW WHITE LAUNDRY
WE THOUGHT IT WAS BEST TO LET FRED DEAL WITH HIS LANDLORD ALONE. I THINK WE WERE BEGINING TO REALIZE THAT WE WERE ALREADY TOO OLD FOR THIS KIND OF STUFF.
THE END

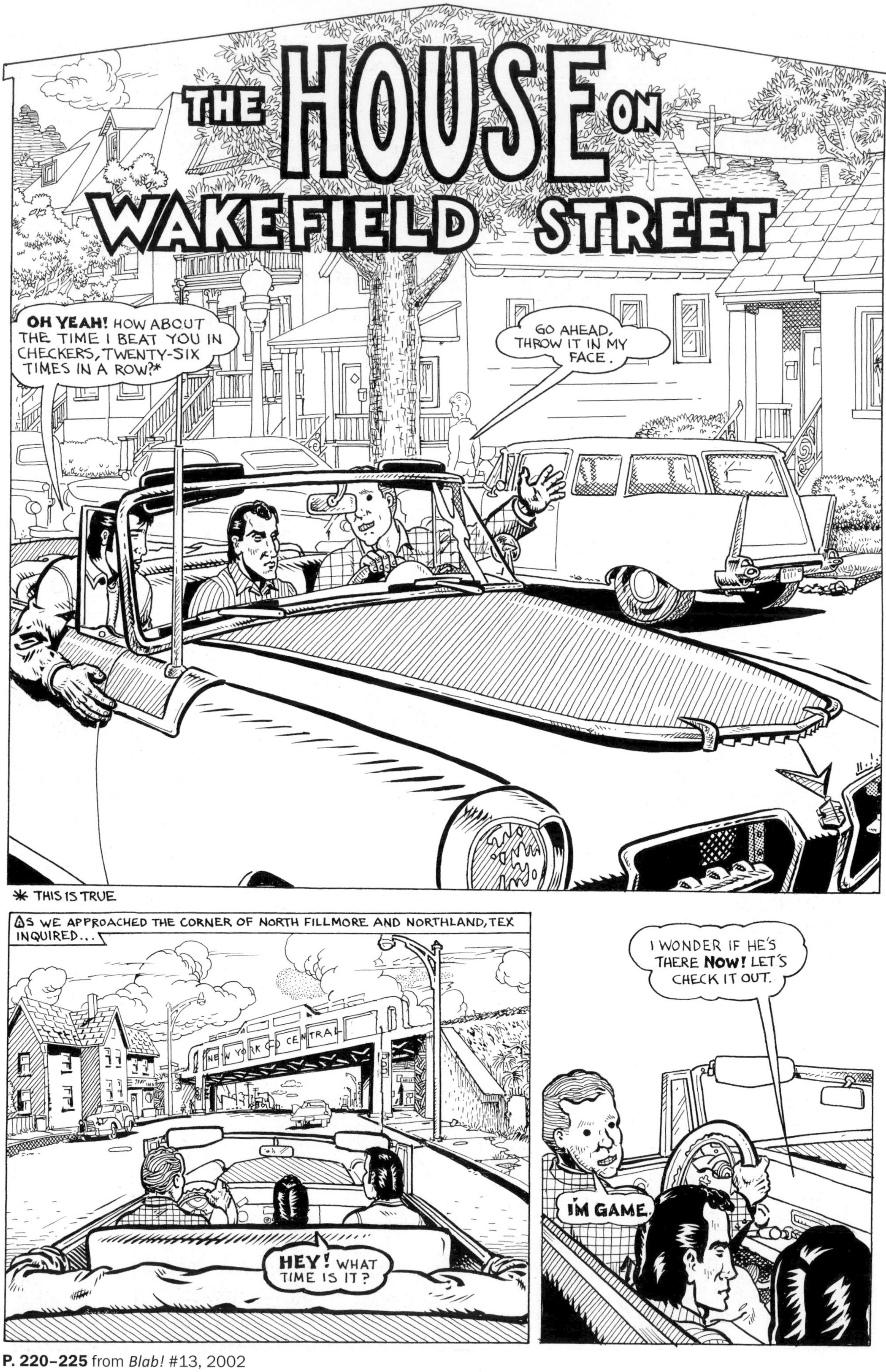
THE HOUSE ON WAKEFIELD STREET
OH YEAH! HOW ABOUT THE TIME I BEAT YOU IN CHECKERS, TWENTY-SIX TIMES IN A ROW?*
GO AHEAD, THROW IT IN MY FACE.
* THIS IS TRUE
AS WE APPROACHED THE CORNER OF NORTH FILLMORE AND NORTHLAND, TEX INQUIRED...
NEW YORK CENTRAL
HEY! WHAT TIME IS IT?
I WONDER IF HE'S THERE NOW! LET'S CHECK IT OUT.
I'M GAME.

P. 220–225 from *Blab!* #13, 2002

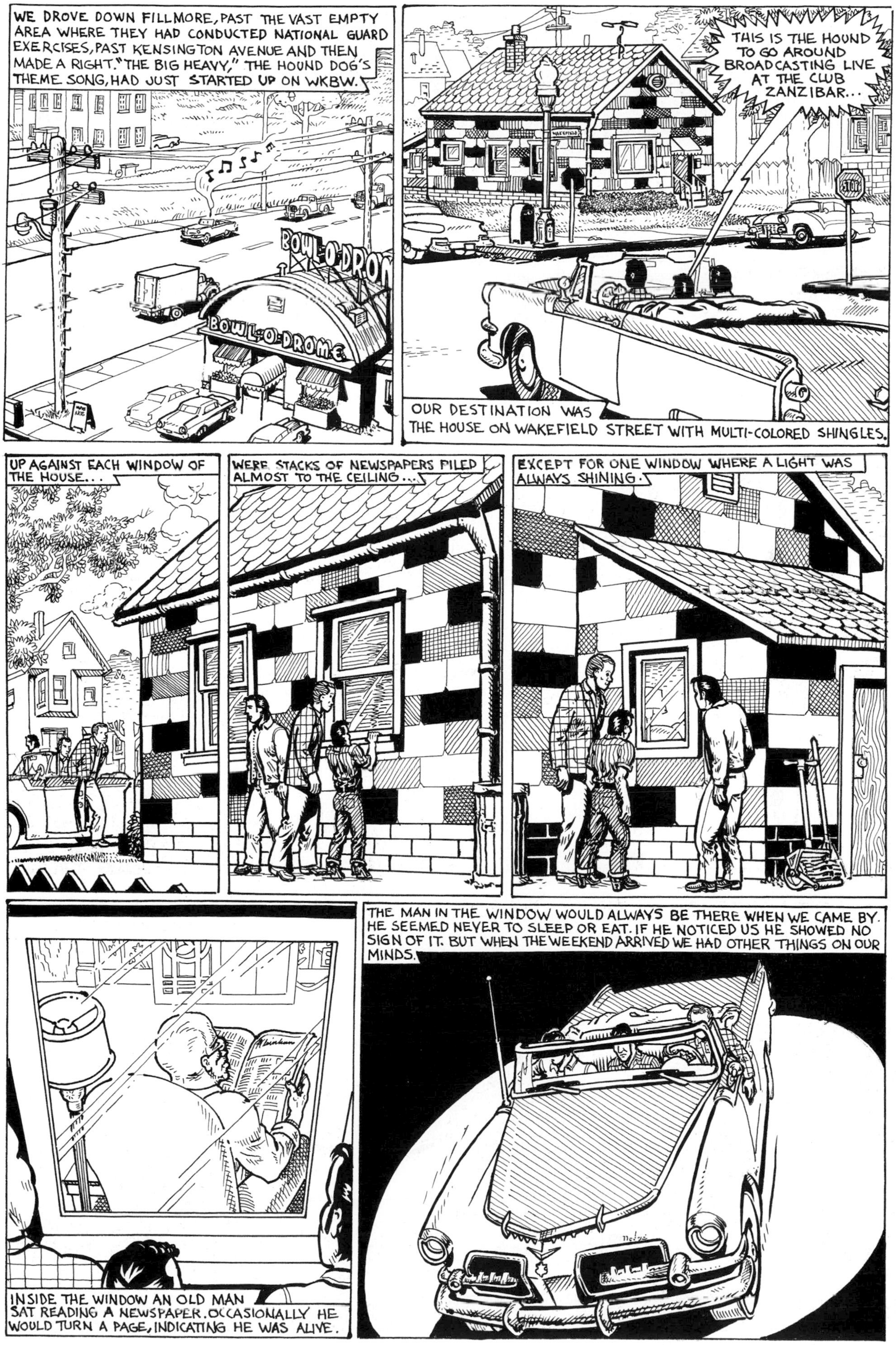

WE DROVE DOWN FILLMORE, PAST THE VAST EMPTY AREA WHERE THEY HAD CONDUCTED NATIONAL GUARD EXERCISES, PAST KENSINGTON AVENUE AND THEN MADE A RIGHT. "THE BIG HEAVY," THE HOUND DOG'S THEME SONG, HAD JUST STARTED UP ON WKBW.
BOWL-O-DROME
BOWL-O-DROME
THIS IS THE HOUND TO GO AROUND BROADCASTING LIVE AT THE CLUB ZANZIBAR...
STOP
OUR DESTINATION WAS THE HOUSE ON WAKEFIELD STREET WITH MULTI-COLORED SHINGLES.
UP AGAINST EACH WINDOW OF THE HOUSE...
WERE STACKS OF NEWSPAPERS PILED ALMOST TO THE CEILING...
EXCEPT FOR ONE WINDOW WHERE A LIGHT WAS ALWAYS SHINING.
INSIDE THE WINDOW AN OLD MAN SAT READING A NEWSPAPER. OCCASIONALLY HE WOULD TURN A PAGE, INDICATING HE WAS ALIVE.
THE MAN IN THE WINDOW WOULD ALWAYS BE THERE WHEN WE CAME BY. HE SEEMED NEVER TO SLEEP OR EAT. IF HE NOTICED US HE SHOWED NO SIGN OF IT. BUT WHEN THE WEEKEND ARRIVED WE HAD OTHER THINGS ON OUR MINDS.

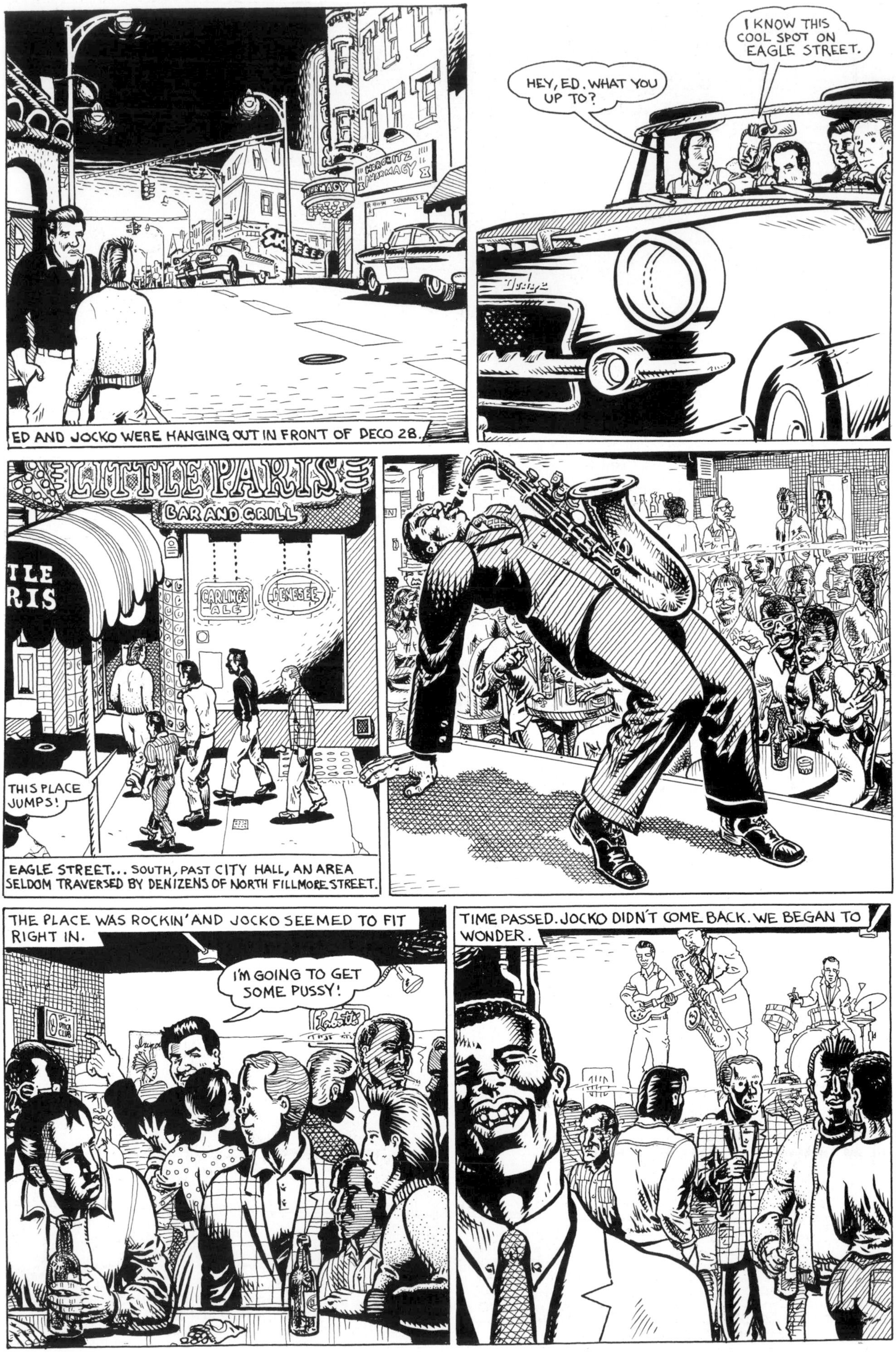

ED AND JOCKO WERE HANGING OUT IN FRONT OF DECO 28.
HOROWITZ PHARMACY
HEY, ED. WHAT YOU UP TO?
I KNOW THIS COOL SPOT ON EAGLE STREET.
LITTLE PARIS
BAR AND GRILL
CARLING'S ALE
GENESEE
THIS PLACE JUMPS!
EAGLE STREET... SOUTH, PAST CITY HALL, AN AREA SELDOM TRAVERSED BY DENIZENS OF NORTH FILLMORE STREET.
THE PLACE WAS ROCKIN' AND JOCKO SEEMED TO FIT RIGHT IN.
I'M GOING TO GET SOME PUSSY!
TIME PASSED. JOCKO DIDN'T COME BACK. WE BEGAN TO WONDER.

WE FOUND JOCKO AROUND THE CORNER, STANDING BETWEEN TWO HOUSES. HE HAD BEEN THERE FOR A LONG TIME.

HEY, JOCKO. WHAT'S HAPPENING?

I DON'T KNOW, I GAVE THE GUY $40 AND HE SAID TO WAIT RIGHT HERE AND HE WOULD BE BACK WITH A BOTTLE OF SCOTCH AND A WOMAN.

AFTER WE DROPPED OFF ED AND JOCKO WE WENT TO CHECK ON THE MAN IN THE HOUSE ON WAKEFIELD STREET. IT WAS ABOUT 4:00 A.M.

HE'S STILL THERE!

MAYBE HE'S DEAD!

NO, I SAW HIM MOVE!

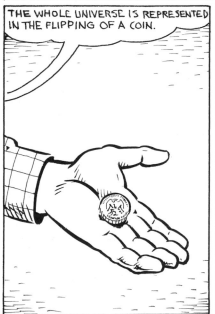

THE WHOLE UNIVERSE IS REPRESENTED IN THE FLIPPING OF A COIN.

WE KNOW THAT BECAUSE OF GRAVITY THE COIN WILL ALWAYS COME DOWN.

WE KNOW IT WILL EITHER BE HEADS OR TAILS. BECAUSE OF THE WAY THE COIN IS STRUCTURED IT WON'T BE ABLE TO LAND ON ITS SIDE.

FLIP

BUT ONCE THE COIN LEAVES THE HAND, IT'S SUBJECTED TO MANY FORCES WE CANNOT COMPREHEND. THIS IS **GOD**!

VEZAY DIDN'T RECEIVE A DOCTORATE OF DIVINITY FOR NOTHING.

THIS IS **BALONEY**, IT'S JUST A SET OF CAUSES THAT ARE TOO COMPLICATED FOR US TO FIGURE OUT. IF WE COULD OBSERVE ALL THOSE LITTLE THINGS THAT MAKE THE COIN FLIP, WE COULD FIGURE OUT JUST WHAT SIDE THE COIN WOULD END UP ON.

FATHER ARMBREWSTER HAD INTRODUCED ME TO THE IDEA OF CAUSALITY BUT I DOUBT HE WOULD HAVE APPROVED OF THE USE I PUT IT TO.

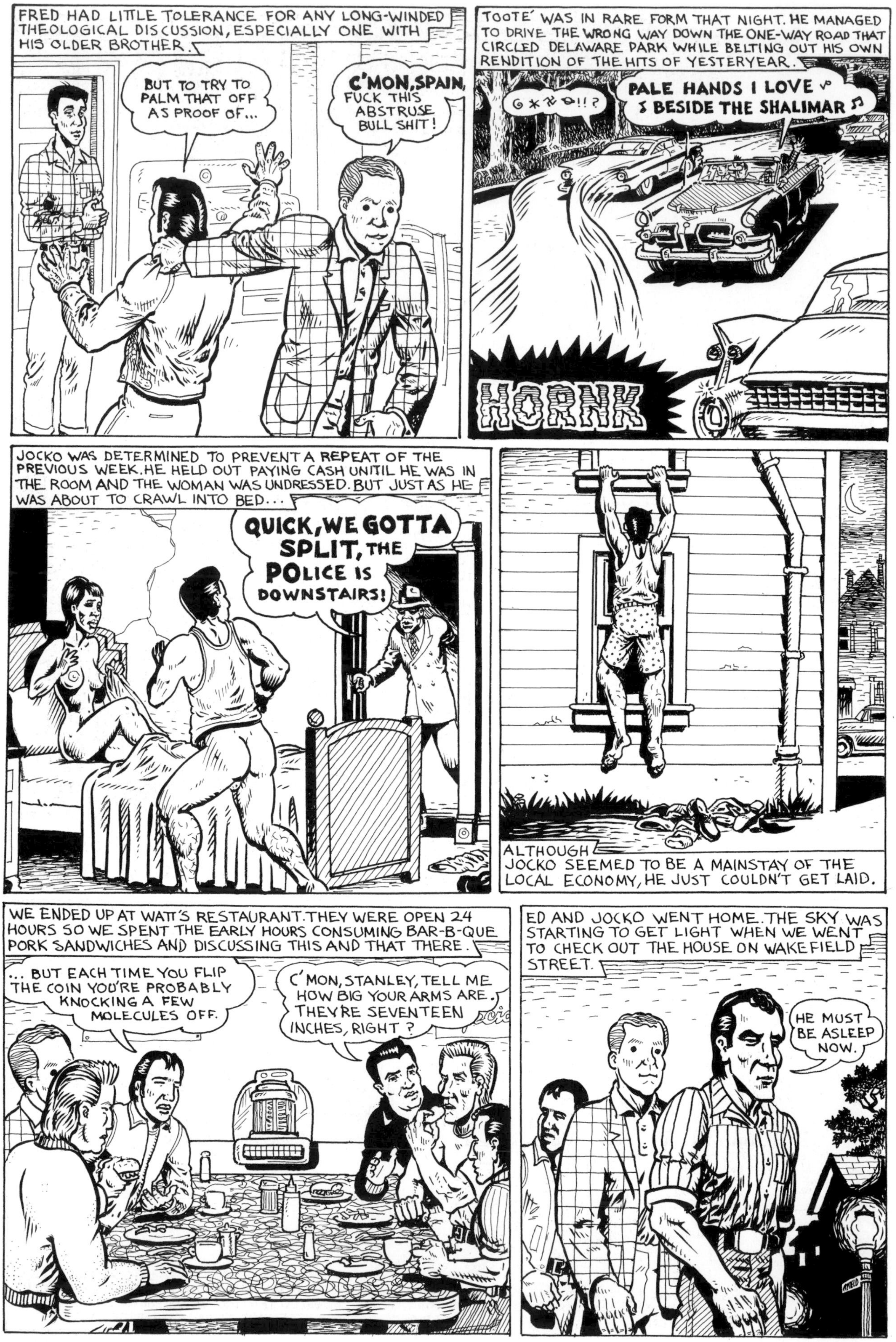
FRED HAD LITTLE TOLERANCE FOR ANY LONG-WINDED THEOLOGICAL DISCUSSION, ESPECIALLY ONE WITH HIS OLDER BROTHER.
BUT TO TRY TO PALM THAT OFF AS PROOF OF...
C'MON, SPAIN, FUCK THIS ABSTRUSE BULL SHIT!
TOOTE' WAS IN RARE FORM THAT NIGHT. HE MANAGED TO DRIVE THE WRONG WAY DOWN THE ONE-WAY ROAD THAT CIRCLED DELAWARE PARK WHILE BELTING OUT HIS OWN RENDITION OF THE HITS OF YESTERYEAR.
PALE HANDS I LOVE BESIDE THE SHALIMAR
HORNK
JOCKO WAS DETERMINED TO PREVENT A REPEAT OF THE PREVIOUS WEEK. HE HELD OUT PAYING CASH UNTIL HE WAS IN THE ROOM AND THE WOMAN WAS UNDRESSED. BUT JUST AS HE WAS ABOUT TO CRAWL INTO BED...
QUICK, WE GOTTA SPLIT, THE POLICE IS DOWNSTAIRS!
ALTHOUGH JOCKO SEEMED TO BE A MAINSTAY OF THE LOCAL ECONOMY, HE JUST COULDN'T GET LAID.
WE ENDED UP AT WATT'S RESTAURANT. THEY WERE OPEN 24 HOURS SO WE SPENT THE EARLY HOURS CONSUMING BAR-B-QUE PORK SANDWICHES AND DISCUSSING THIS AND THAT THERE.
... BUT EACH TIME YOU FLIP THE COIN YOU'RE PROBABLY KNOCKING A FEW MOLECULES OFF.
C'MON, STANLEY, TELL ME HOW BIG YOUR ARMS ARE. THEY'RE SEVENTEEN INCHES, RIGHT?
ED AND JOCKO WENT HOME. THE SKY WAS STARTING TO GET LIGHT WHEN WE WENT TO CHECK OUT THE HOUSE ON WAKEFIELD STREET.
HE MUST BE ASLEEP NOW.

BUT THERE HE WAS AS ALWAYS.
GRANT'S SALE
SUDDENLY...
NGGGGH!
GRANT'S SALE
PLUMF
WE TRIED ALL THE WINDOWS. THEY WERE LOCKED. WE FOUND ONE THAT WOULD OPEN JUST A LITTLE BIT AND TEX WAS ABLE TO SQUEEZE IN.
THERE WAS AN OLD 78 RPM RECORD PLAYING ON THE CONSOLE. THE RECORD KEPT SKIPPING OVER THE SAME PART.
MARTHA, MARTHA SKITCH MARTHA, MARTHA
THE OLD GUY WAS STILL ALIVE. FORTUNATELY THE HOSPITAL WAS JUST DOWN THE ROAD.
HELLO, MEYER MEMORIAL? WE HAVE AN EMERGENCY HERE.
GEEZE, I FEEL LIKE KID KINDYOUTH
WE FIGURED IT WAS BEST TO GET OUT OF THERE BEFORE WE HAD TO ANSWER ANY UNCOMFORTABLE QUESTIONS. BUT AS WE DROVE DOWN HUMBOLDT PARKWAY, I WONDERED IF I TOO WOULD END UP AS AN OLD GUY, ALONE LISTENING TO MY FAVORITE OLDIES.
THE END

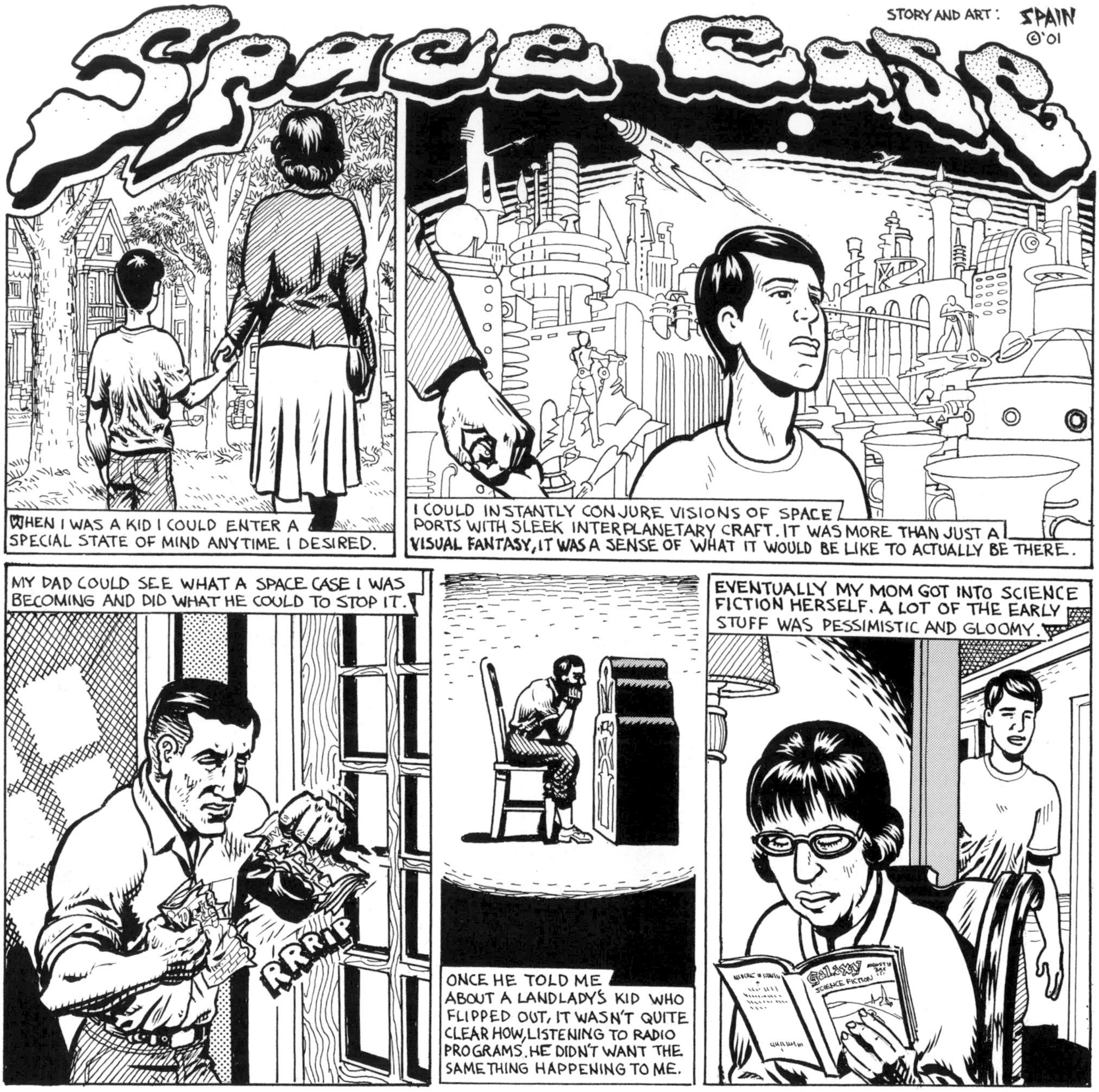
SPACE CASE
STORY AND ART: SPAIN ©'01
WHEN I WAS A KID I COULD ENTER A SPECIAL STATE OF MIND ANYTIME I DESIRED.
I COULD INSTANTLY CONJURE VISIONS OF SPACE PORTS WITH SLEEK INTERPLANETARY CRAFT. IT WAS MORE THAN JUST A VISUAL FANTASY, IT WAS A SENSE OF WHAT IT WOULD BE LIKE TO ACTUALLY BE THERE.
MY DAD COULD SEE WHAT A SPACE CASE I WAS BECOMING AND DID WHAT HE COULD TO STOP IT.
RRRIP
ONCE HE TOLD ME ABOUT A LANDLADY'S KID WHO FLIPPED OUT, IT WASN'T QUITE CLEAR HOW, LISTENING TO RADIO PROGRAMS. HE DIDN'T WANT THE SAME THING HAPPENING TO ME.
EVENTUALLY MY MOM GOT INTO SCIENCE FICTION HERSELF. A LOT OF THE EARLY STUFF WAS PESSIMISTIC AND GLOOMY.
Galaxy
SCIENCE FICTION

P. 226–227 from *The Comics Journal Special Edition* Volume 1, 2002

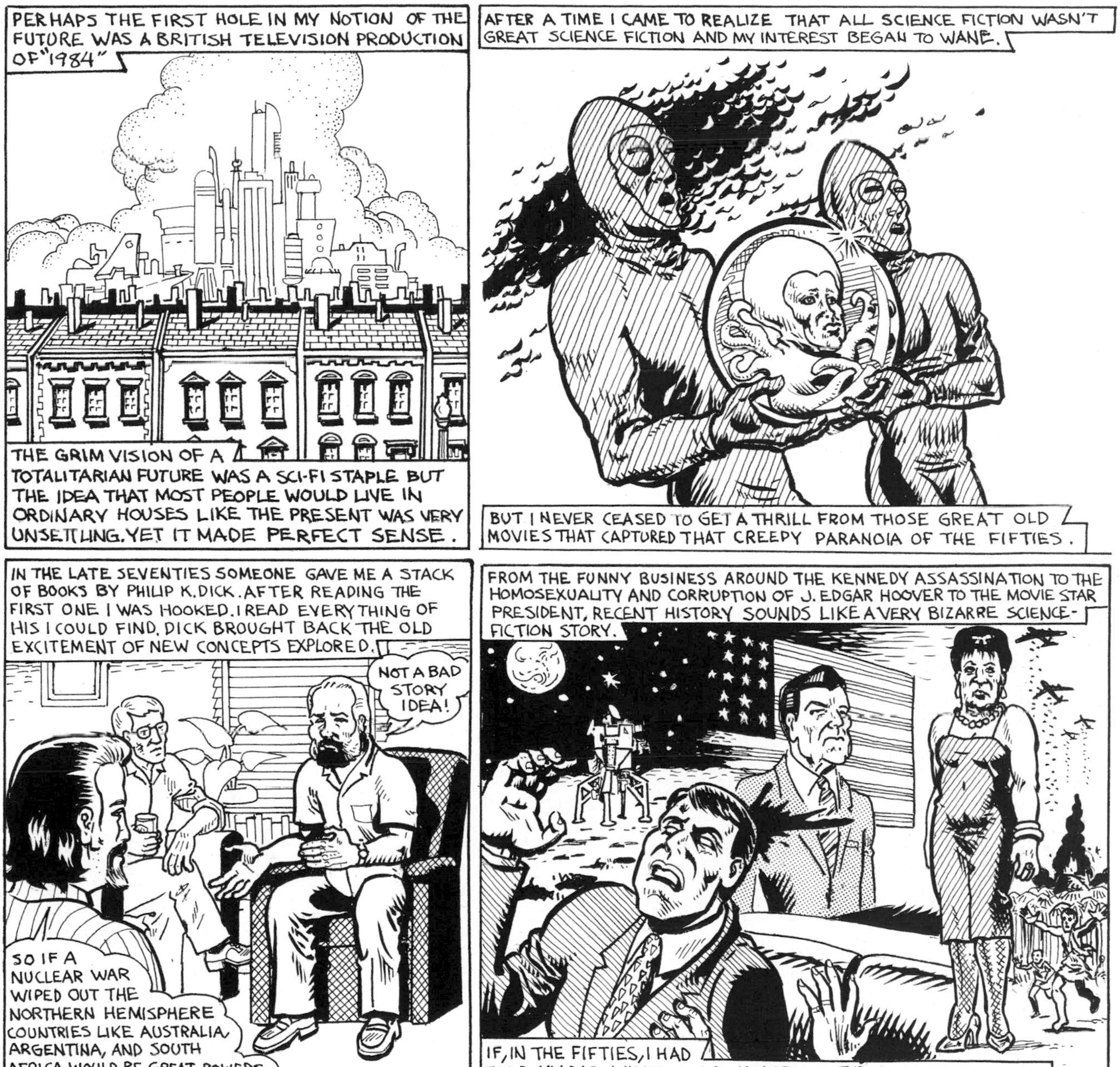
PERHAPS THE FIRST HOLE IN MY NOTION OF THE FUTURE WAS A BRITISH TELEVISION PRODUCTION OF "1984"
THE GRIM VISION OF A TOTALITARIAN FUTURE WAS A SCI-FI STAPLE BUT THE IDEA THAT MOST PEOPLE WOULD LIVE IN ORDINARY HOUSES LIKE THE PRESENT WAS VERY UNSETTLING. YET IT MADE PERFECT SENSE.
AFTER A TIME I CAME TO REALIZE THAT ALL SCIENCE FICTION WASN'T GREAT SCIENCE FICTION AND MY INTEREST BEGAN TO WANE.
BUT I NEVER CEASED TO GET A THRILL FROM THOSE GREAT OLD MOVIES THAT CAPTURED THAT CREEPY PARANOIA OF THE FIFTIES.
IN THE LATE SEVENTIES SOMEONE GAVE ME A STACK OF BOOKS BY PHILIP K. DICK. AFTER READING THE FIRST ONE I WAS HOOKED. I READ EVERYTHING OF HIS I COULD FIND. DICK BROUGHT BACK THE OLD EXCITEMENT OF NEW CONCEPTS EXPLORED.
NOT A BAD STORY IDEA!
SO IF A NUCLEAR WAR WIPED OUT THE NORTHERN HEMISPHERE COUNTRIES LIKE AUSTRALIA, ARGENTINA, AND SOUTH AFRICA WOULD BE GREAT POWERS.
I EVEN GOT TO HANG OUT WITH HIM FOR AN AFTERNOON.
FROM THE FUNNY BUSINESS AROUND THE KENNEDY ASSASSINATION TO THE HOMOSEXUALITY AND CORRUPTION OF J. EDGAR HOOVER TO THE MOVIE STAR PRESIDENT, RECENT HISTORY SOUNDS LIKE A VERY BIZARRE SCIENCE-FICTION STORY.
IF, IN THE FIFTIES, I HAD TOLD MY DAD WHAT WOULD HAPPEN IN THE LAST HALF OF THE 20th CENTURY HE WOULD HAVE REALLY THOUGHT I WAS NUTS.
END

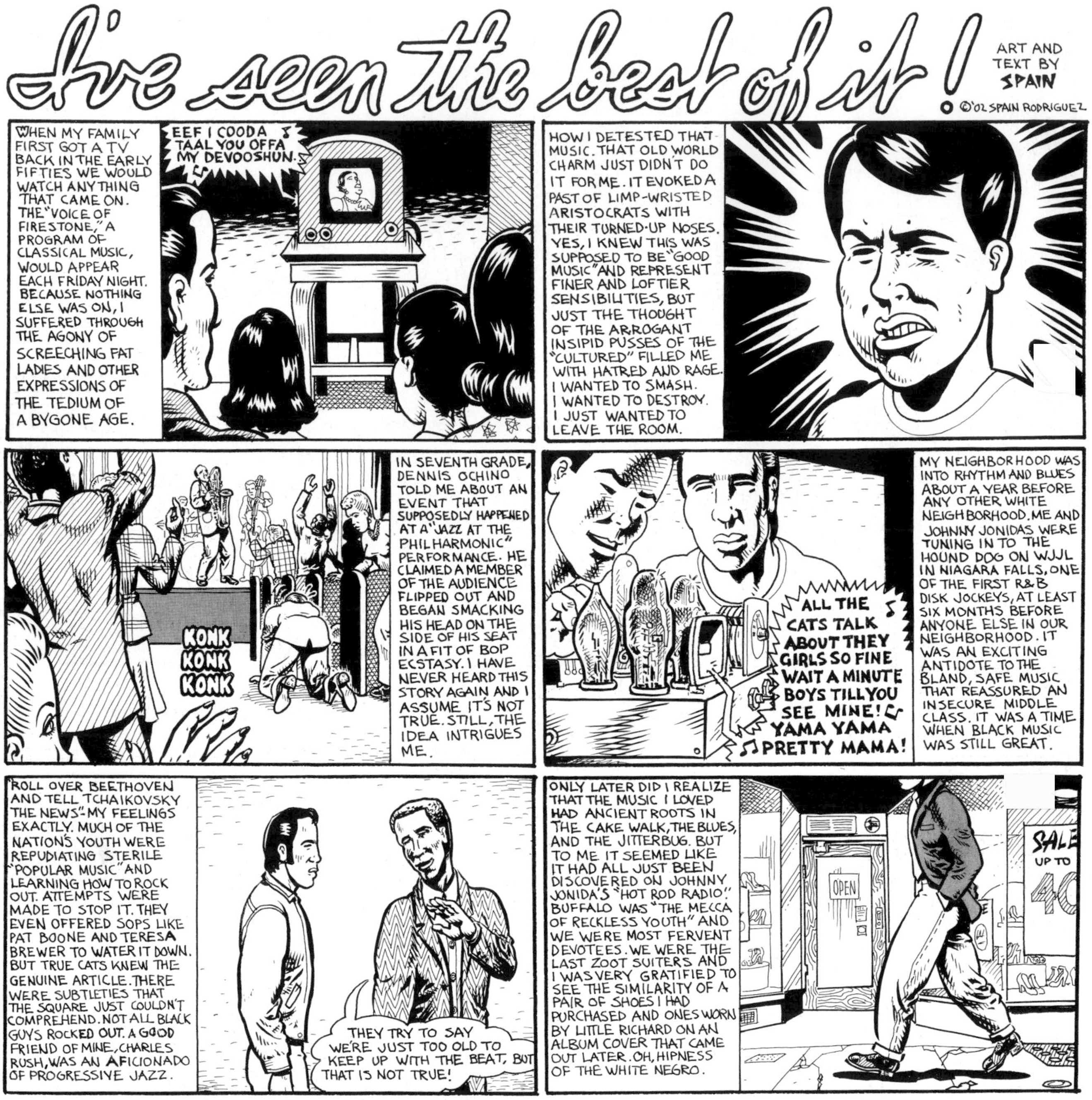
I've seen the best of it!
ART AND TEXT BY SPAIN
©'02 SPAIN RODRIGUEZ
WHEN MY FAMILY FIRST GOT A TV BACK IN THE EARLY FIFTIES WE WOULD WATCH ANYTHING THAT CAME ON. THE "VOICE OF FIRESTONE," A PROGRAM OF CLASSICAL MUSIC, WOULD APPEAR EACH FRIDAY NIGHT. BECAUSE NOTHING ELSE WAS ON, I SUFFERED THROUGH THE AGONY OF SCREECHING FAT LADIES AND OTHER EXPRESSIONS OF THE TEDIUM OF A BYGONE AGE.
EEF I COODA TAAL YOU OFFA MY DEVOOSHUN.
HOW I DETESTED THAT MUSIC. THAT OLD WORLD CHARM JUST DIDN'T DO IT FOR ME. IT EVOKED A PAST OF LIMP-WRISTED ARISTOCRATS WITH THEIR TURNED-UP NOSES. YES, I KNEW THIS WAS SUPPOSED TO BE "GOOD MUSIC" AND REPRESENT FINER AND LOFTIER SENSIBILITIES, BUT JUST THE THOUGHT OF THE ARROGANT INSIPID PUSSES OF THE "CULTURED" FILLED ME WITH HATRED AND RAGE. I WANTED TO SMASH. I WANTED TO DESTROY. I JUST WANTED TO LEAVE THE ROOM.
KONK KONK KONK
IN SEVENTH GRADE, DENNIS OCHINO TOLD ME ABOUT AN EVENT THAT SUPPOSEDLY HAPPENED AT A "JAZZ AT THE PHILHARMONIC" PERFORMANCE. HE CLAIMED A MEMBER OF THE AUDIENCE FLIPPED OUT AND BEGAN SMACKING HIS HEAD ON THE SIDE OF HIS SEAT IN A FIT OF BOP ECSTASY. I HAVE NEVER HEARD THIS STORY AGAIN AND I ASSUME IT'S NOT TRUE. STILL, THE IDEA INTRIGUES ME.
ALL THE CATS TALK ABOUT THEY GIRLS SO FINE WAIT A MINUTE BOYS TILL YOU SEE MINE! YAMA YAMA PRETTY MAMA!
MY NEIGHBORHOOD WAS INTO RHYTHM AND BLUES ABOUT A YEAR BEFORE ANY OTHER WHITE NEIGHBORHOOD. ME AND JOHNNY JONIDAS WERE TUNING IN TO THE HOUND DOG ON WJJL IN NIAGARA FALLS, ONE OF THE FIRST R&B DISK JOCKEYS, AT LEAST SIX MONTHS BEFORE ANYONE ELSE IN OUR NEIGHBORHOOD. IT WAS AN EXCITING ANTIDOTE TO THE BLAND, SAFE MUSIC THAT REASSURED AN INSECURE MIDDLE CLASS. IT WAS A TIME WHEN BLACK MUSIC WAS STILL GREAT.
"ROLL OVER BEETHOVEN AND TELL TCHAIKOVSKY THE NEWS"- MY FEELINGS EXACTLY. MUCH OF THE NATION'S YOUTH WERE REPUDIATING STERILE "POPULAR MUSIC" AND LEARNING HOW TO ROCK OUT. ATTEMPTS WERE MADE TO STOP IT. THEY EVEN OFFERED SOPS LIKE PAT BOONE AND TERESA BREWER TO WATER IT DOWN. BUT TRUE CATS KNEW THE GENUINE ARTICLE. THERE WERE SUBTLETIES THAT THE SQUARE JUST COULDN'T COMPREHEND. NOT ALL BLACK GUYS ROCKED OUT. A GOOD FRIEND OF MINE, CHARLES RUSH, WAS AN AFICIONADO OF PROGRESSIVE JAZZ.
THEY TRY TO SAY WE'RE JUST TOO OLD TO KEEP UP WITH THE BEAT, BUT THAT IS NOT TRUE!
ONLY LATER DID I REALIZE THAT THE MUSIC I LOVED HAD ANCIENT ROOTS IN THE CAKE WALK, THE BLUES, AND THE JITTERBUG. BUT TO ME IT SEEMED LIKE IT HAD ALL JUST BEEN DISCOVERED ON JOHNNY JONIDA'S "HOT ROD RADIO." BUFFALO WAS "THE MECCA OF RECKLESS YOUTH" AND WE WERE MOST FERVENT DEVOTEES. WE WERE THE LAST ZOOT SUITERS AND I WAS VERY GRATIFIED TO SEE THE SIMILARITY OF A PAIR OF SHOES I HAD PURCHASED AND ONES WORN BY LITTLE RICHARD ON AN ALBUM COVER THAT CAME OUT LATER. OH, HIPNESS OF THE WHITE NEGRO.
OPEN
SALE UP TO 40

P. 228–229 from *The Comics Journal Special Edition* Volume 2, 2002

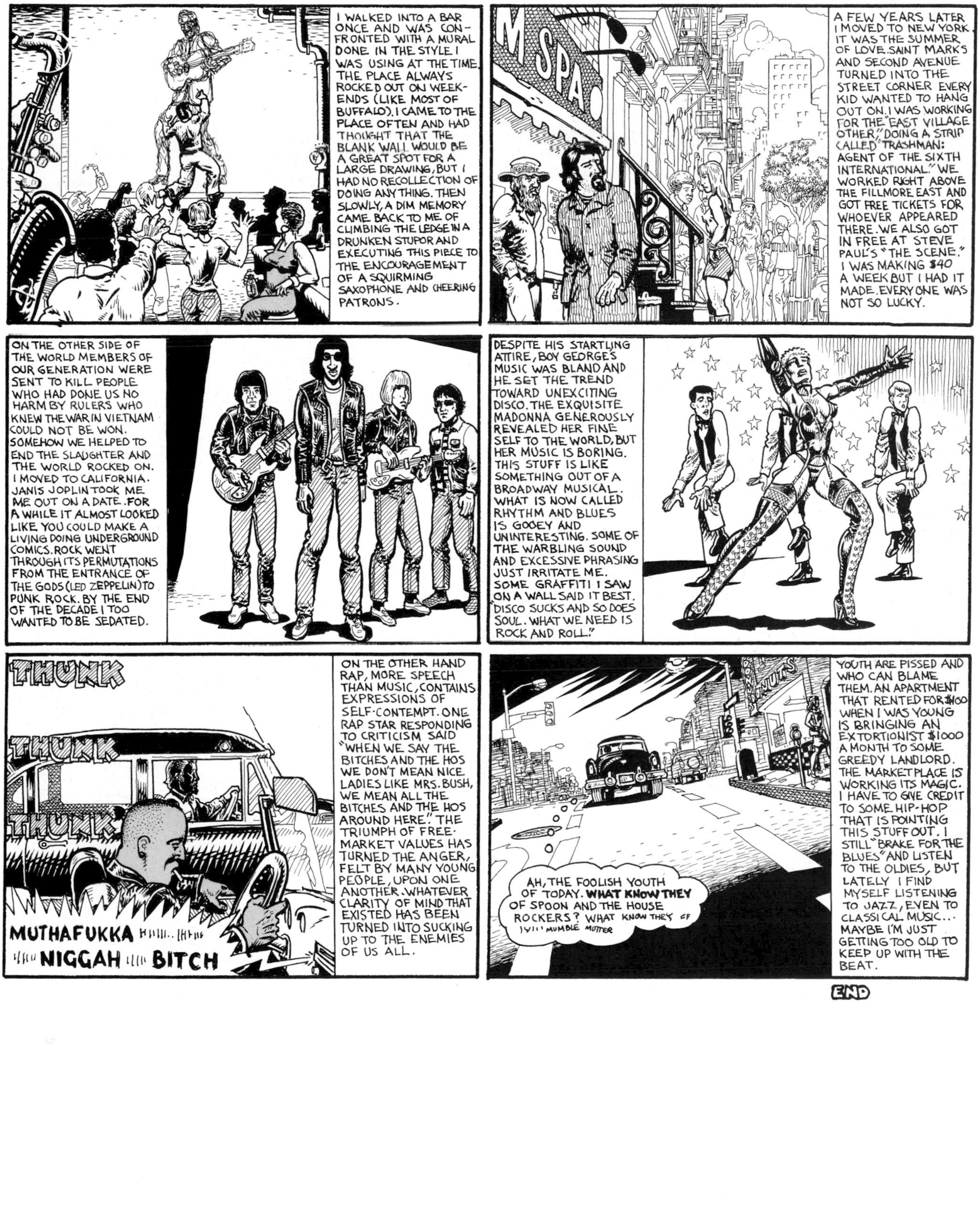
I WALKED INTO A BAR ONCE AND WAS CONFRONTED WITH A MURAL DONE IN THE STYLE I WAS USING AT THE TIME. THE PLACE ALWAYS ROCKED OUT ON WEEKENDS (LIKE MOST OF BUFFALO). I CAME TO THE PLACE OFTEN AND HAD THOUGHT THAT THE BLANK WALL WOULD BE A GREAT SPOT FOR A LARGE DRAWING, BUT I HAD NO RECOLLECTION OF DOING ANYTHING. THEN SLOWLY, A DIM MEMORY CAME BACK TO ME OF CLIMBING THE LEDGE IN A DRUNKEN STUPOR AND EXECUTING THIS PIECE TO THE ENCOURAGEMENT OF A SQUIRMING SAXOPHONE AND CHEERING PATRONS.
A FEW YEARS LATER I MOVED TO NEW YORK. IT WAS THE SUMMER OF LOVE. SAINT MARKS AND SECOND AVENUE TURNED INTO THE STREET CORNER EVERY KID WANTED TO HANG OUT ON. I WAS WORKING FOR THE "EAST VILLAGE OTHER," DOING A STRIP CALLED "TRASHMAN: AGENT OF THE SIXTH INTERNATIONAL." WE WORKED RIGHT ABOVE THE FILLMORE EAST AND GOT FREE TICKETS FOR WHOEVER APPEARED THERE. WE ALSO GOT IN FREE AT STEVE PAUL'S "THE SCENE." I WAS MAKING $40 A WEEK BUT I HAD IT MADE. EVERYONE WAS NOT SO LUCKY.
ON THE OTHER SIDE OF THE WORLD MEMBERS OF OUR GENERATION WERE SENT TO KILL PEOPLE WHO HAD DONE US NO HARM BY RULERS WHO KNEW THE WAR IN VIETNAM COULD NOT BE WON. SOMEHOW WE HELPED TO END THE SLAUGHTER AND THE WORLD ROCKED ON. I MOVED TO CALIFORNIA. JANIS JOPLIN TOOK ME ME OUT ON A DATE. FOR A WHILE IT ALMOST LOOKED LIKE YOU COULD MAKE A LIVING DOING UNDERGROUND COMICS. ROCK WENT THROUGH ITS PERMUTATIONS FROM THE ENTRANCE OF THE GODS (LED ZEPPELIN) TO PUNK ROCK. BY THE END OF THE DECADE I TOO WANTED TO BE SEDATED.
DESPITE HIS STARTLING ATTIRE, BOY GEORGE'S MUSIC WAS BLAND AND HE SET THE TREND TOWARD UNEXCITING DISCO. THE EXQUISITE MADONNA GENEROUSLY REVEALED HER FINE SELF TO THE WORLD, BUT HER MUSIC IS BORING. THIS STUFF IS LIKE SOMETHING OUT OF A BROADWAY MUSICAL. WHAT IS NOW CALLED RHYTHM AND BLUES IS GOOEY AND UNINTERESTING. SOME OF THE WARBLING SOUND AND EXCESSIVE PHRASING JUST IRRITATE ME. SOME GRAFFITI I SAW ON A WALL SAID IT BEST. "DISCO SUCKS AND SO DOES SOUL. WHAT WE NEED IS ROCK AND ROLL."
THUNK
THUNK
THUNK
MUTHAFUKKA
NIGGAH BITCH
ON THE OTHER HAND RAP, MORE SPEECH THAN MUSIC, CONTAINS EXPRESSIONS OF SELF-CONTEMPT. ONE RAP STAR RESPONDING TO CRITICISM SAID "WHEN WE SAY THE BITCHES AND THE HOS WE DON'T MEAN NICE LADIES LIKE MRS. BUSH, WE MEAN ALL THE BITCHES AND THE HOS AROUND HERE." THE TRIUMPH OF FREE-MARKET VALUES HAS TURNED THE ANGER, FELT BY MANY YOUNG PEOPLE, UPON ONE ANOTHER. WHATEVER CLARITY OF MIND THAT EXISTED HAS BEEN TURNED INTO SUCKING UP TO THE ENEMIES OF US ALL.
DONUTS
AH, THE FOOLISH YOUTH OF TODAY. **WHAT KNOW THEY** OF SPOON AND THE HOUSE ROCKERS? WHAT KNOW THEY OF MUMBLE MUTTER
YOUTH ARE PISSED AND WHO CAN BLAME THEM. AN APARTMENT THAT RENTED FOR $100 WHEN I WAS YOUNG IS BRINGING AN EXTORTIONIST $1000 A MONTH TO SOME GREEDY LANDLORD. THE MARKETPLACE IS WORKING ITS MAGIC. I HAVE TO GIVE CREDIT TO SOME HIP-HOP THAT IS POINTING THIS STUFF OUT. I STILL "BRAKE FOR THE BLUES" AND LISTEN TO THE OLDIES, BUT LATELY I FIND MYSELF LISTENING TO JAZZ, EVEN TO CLASSICAL MUSIC... MAYBE I'M JUST GETTING TOO OLD TO KEEP UP WITH THE BEAT.
END

THE BIRTH of PORN
© SPAIN '03
THE FIRST PORN I EVER SAW WAS A PHOTO FOUND IN A DRAWER IN HIS MOM'S ROOM BY A KID IN GRAMMAR SCHOOL.
HE, HE, HE!
MY FIRST VIEW OF A WOMAN'S PRIVATE PARTS WAS DISTURBING. IT TOOK ME A WHILE TO GET OVER IT.
PENDOWSKY'S AUTO REPAIR 725 GENESSE
B&G AUTO PARTS
LUBE TUNE-UP
SPECIAL OFFER
SAM'S TIRE SERVICE
TA-1496
FULL BRAKE AND LUBE SERVICE
ONCE I WENT BY A GARAGE ON GRIDER STREET. YOU COULD SEE THE OPPOSITE WALL COVERED WITH CALENDARS OF BARE-BREASTED WOMEN WITH ROUGED NIPPLES. NEXT TIME I WENT BY, THE CALENDARS WERE GONE.
THE ONLY THING HOT AVAILABLE TO A KID IN THE EARLY 50'S WERE "JOKE BOOKS". I REMEMBER A PICTURE OF EVE MEYER (RUSS MEYER'S FIRST WIFE) HOLDING HER BARE BREASTS.
OH, HOW FERVENTLY I IMAGINED THAT THE GRAY SMUDGE UNDER HER HAND WAS A NAKED NIPPLE.
AFTER THEY BANNED E.C. COMICS, I HAUNTED USED BOOK STORES LOOKING FOR THEM. IN ONE PLACE I OVERHEARD THE STORE OWNER TALKING TO A CUSTOMER...
HEY! HERE'S A "SHOCK SUSPENSTORIES"
TAKE A LOOK AT THIS NEW MAGAZINE FROM CHICAGO. IT'S CALLED "PLAYBOY."

P. 230–231 from *Blab!* #14, 2003

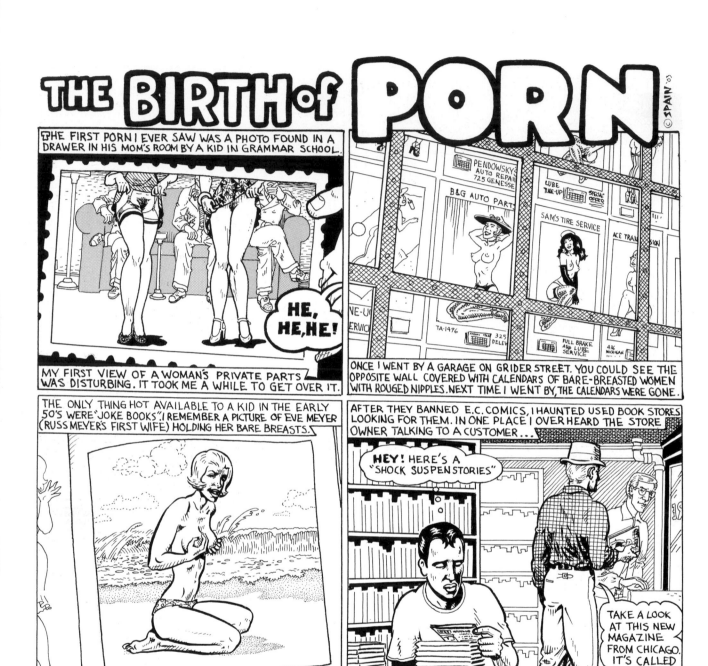

IN A FEW YEARS "PLAYBOY" WOULD BE EVERYWHERE.

I REMEMBER THIS BLACK CHICK WALKING DOWN THE ISLE OF OUR HIGH SCHOOL CAFETERIA WITH A PLAYBOY CENTERFOLD.

MY ACTUAL EXPERIENCE WITH A NAKED WOMAN WAS SEVERELY LIMITED.

THE CLOSEST REAL ENCOUNTER I HAD WITH A NUDE BABE WAS WHEN SKIPPY PULLED OUT A GIRL'S TIT AT KENSINGTON POOL.

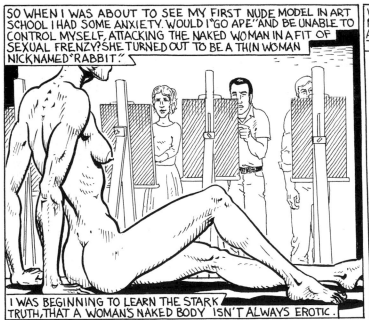

SO WHEN I WAS ABOUT TO SEE MY FIRST NUDE MODEL IN ART SCHOOL I HAD SOME ANXIETY. WOULD I "GO APE" AND BE UNABLE TO CONTROL MYSELF, ATTACKING THE NAKED WOMAN IN A FIT OF SEXUAL FRENZY? SHE TURNED OUT TO BE A THIN WOMAN NICKNAMED "RABBIT."

I WAS BEGINNING TO LEARN THE STARK TRUTH, THAT A WOMAN'S NAKED BODY ISN'T ALWAYS EROTIC.

WITH THE ADVENT OF EXPOSED PUSSIES IN MEN'S MAGAZINES, A NEW TREND HAS EMERGED: WOMEN ARE SHAVING THEIR PUBIC HAIR INTO NEAT LITTLE HITLER-TYPE MUSTACHES.

DESPITE THE EFFORTS OF AGENTS OF JOYLESSNESS, IT'S GREAT TO LIVE IN A TIME WHEN WOMEN CAN REVEAL THEMSELVES WITHOUT FEAR.

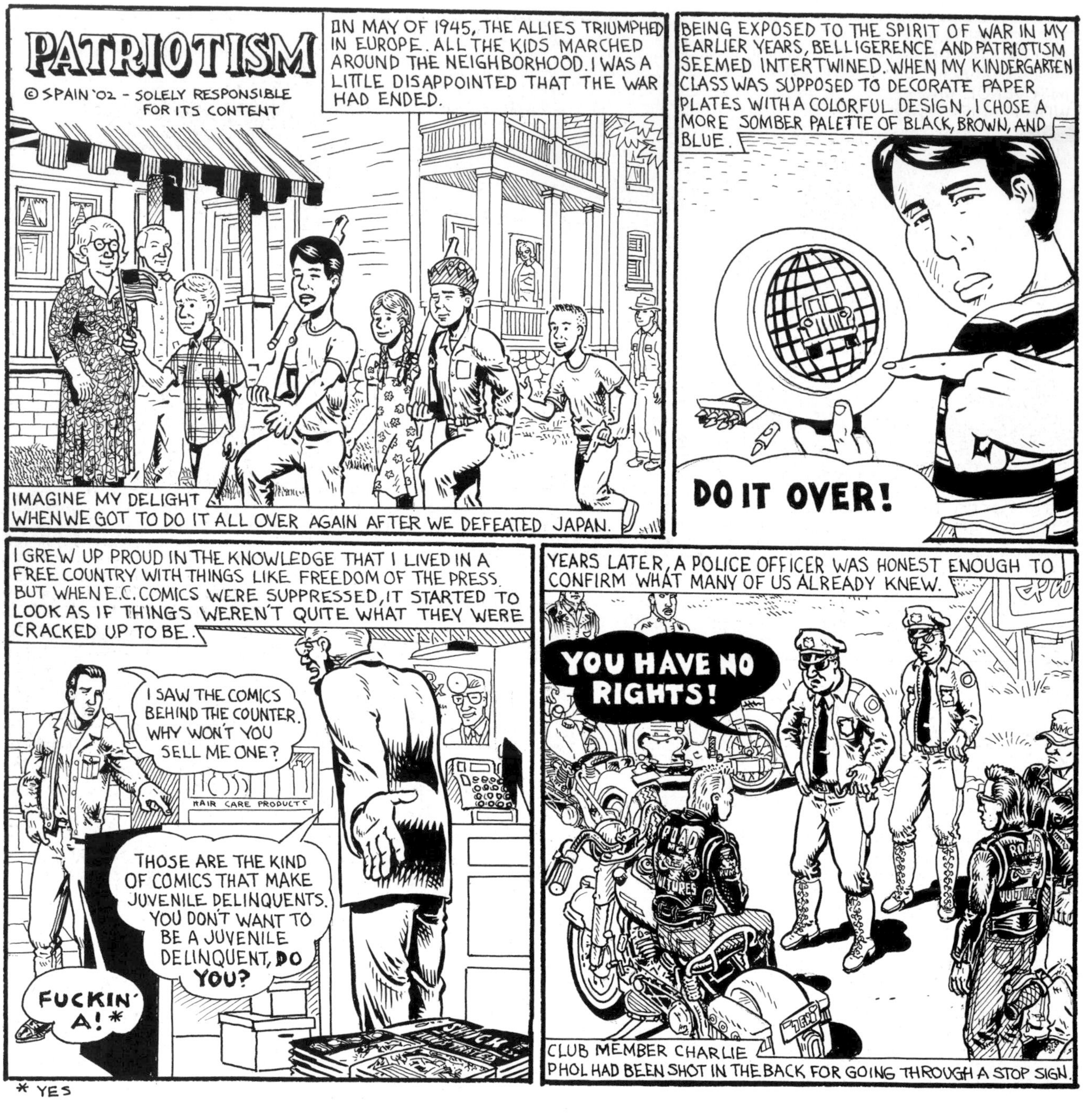
PATRIOTISM
© SPAIN '02 - SOLELY RESPONSIBLE FOR ITS CONTENT
IN MAY OF 1945, THE ALLIES TRIUMPHED IN EUROPE. ALL THE KIDS MARCHED AROUND THE NEIGHBORHOOD. I WAS A LITTLE DISAPPOINTED THAT THE WAR HAD ENDED.
IMAGINE MY DELIGHT WHEN WE GOT TO DO IT ALL OVER AGAIN AFTER WE DEFEATED JAPAN.
BEING EXPOSED TO THE SPIRIT OF WAR IN MY EARLIER YEARS, BELLIGERENCE AND PATRIOTISM SEEMED INTERTWINED. WHEN MY KINDERGARTEN CLASS WAS SUPPOSED TO DECORATE PAPER PLATES WITH A COLORFUL DESIGN, I CHOSE A MORE SOMBER PALETTE OF BLACK, BROWN, AND BLUE.
DO IT OVER!
I GREW UP PROUD IN THE KNOWLEDGE THAT I LIVED IN A FREE COUNTRY WITH THINGS LIKE FREEDOM OF THE PRESS. BUT WHEN E.C. COMICS WERE SUPPRESSED, IT STARTED TO LOOK AS IF THINGS WEREN'T QUITE WHAT THEY WERE CRACKED UP TO BE.
I SAW THE COMICS BEHIND THE COUNTER. WHY WON'T YOU SELL ME ONE?
HAIR CARE PRODUCTS
THOSE ARE THE KIND OF COMICS THAT MAKE JUVENILE DELINQUENTS. YOU DON'T WANT TO BE A JUVENILE DELINQUENT, DO YOU?
FUCKIN' A!*
* YES
YEARS LATER, A POLICE OFFICER WAS HONEST ENOUGH TO CONFIRM WHAT MANY OF US ALREADY KNEW.
YOU HAVE NO RIGHTS!
CLUB MEMBER CHARLIE PHOL HAD BEEN SHOT IN THE BACK FOR GOING THROUGH A STOP SIGN.

P. 232–233 from *The Comics Journal Special Edition* Volume 3, 2003

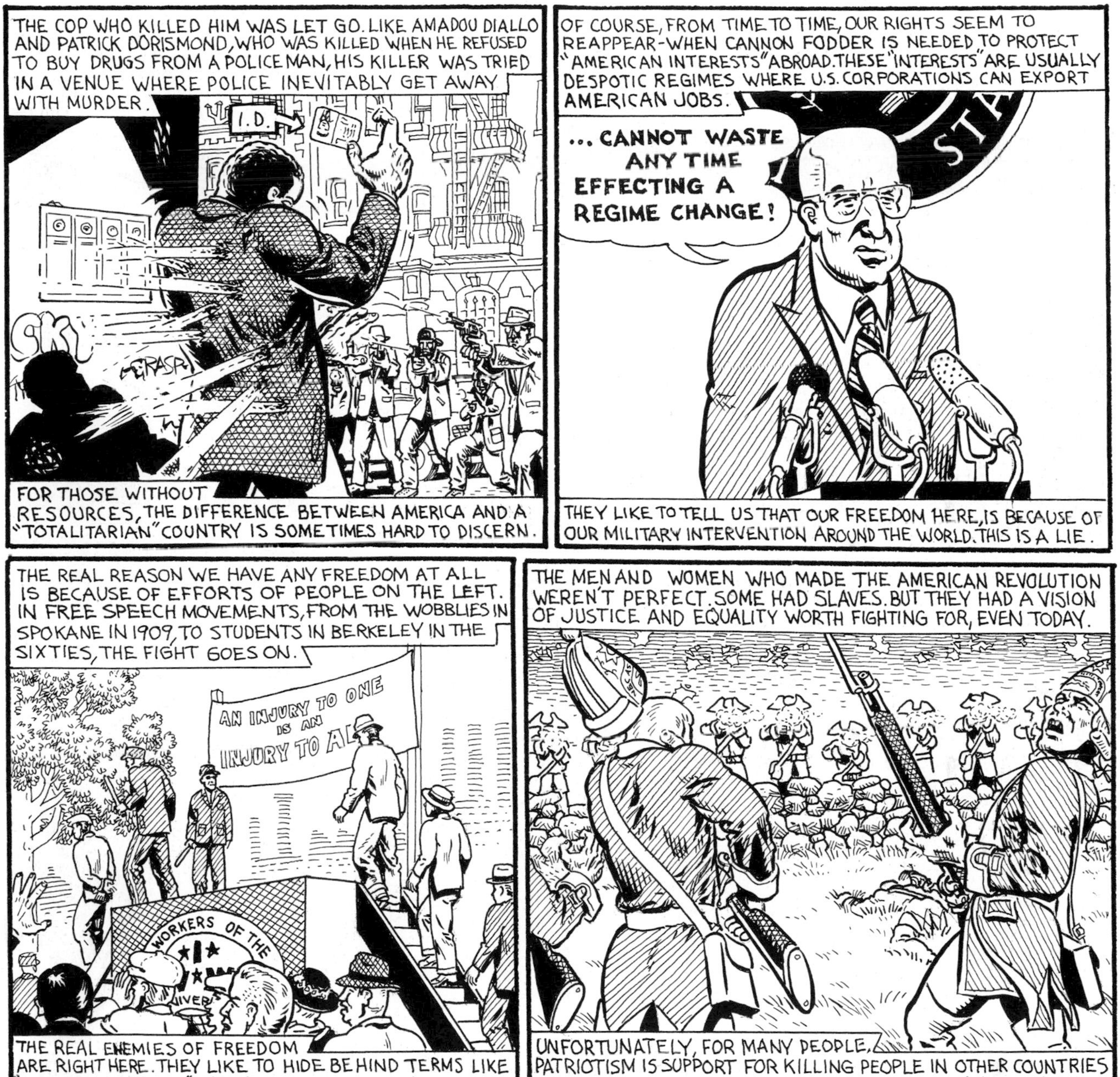
THE COP WHO KILLED HIM WAS LET GO. LIKE AMADOU DIALLO AND PATRICK DORISMOND, WHO WAS KILLED WHEN HE REFUSED TO BUY DRUGS FROM A POLICEMAN, HIS KILLER WAS TRIED IN A VENUE WHERE POLICE INEVITABLY GET AWAY WITH MURDER.
I.D.
GASP!
FOR THOSE WITHOUT RESOURCES, THE DIFFERENCE BETWEEN AMERICA AND A "TOTALITARIAN" COUNTRY IS SOMETIMES HARD TO DISCERN.
OF COURSE, FROM TIME TO TIME, OUR RIGHTS SEEM TO REAPPEAR-WHEN CANNON FODDER IS NEEDED TO PROTECT "AMERICAN INTERESTS" ABROAD. THESE "INTERESTS" ARE USUALLY DESPOTIC REGIMES WHERE U.S. CORPORATIONS CAN EXPORT AMERICAN JOBS.
... CANNOT WASTE ANY TIME EFFECTING A REGIME CHANGE!
THEY LIKE TO TELL US THAT OUR FREEDOM HERE, IS BECAUSE OF OUR MILITARY INTERVENTION AROUND THE WORLD. THIS IS A LIE.
THE REAL REASON WE HAVE ANY FREEDOM AT ALL IS BECAUSE OF EFFORTS OF PEOPLE ON THE LEFT. IN FREE SPEECH MOVEMENTS, FROM THE WOBBLIES IN SPOKANE IN 1909, TO STUDENTS IN BERKELEY IN THE SIXTIES, THE FIGHT GOES ON.
AN INJURY TO ONE IS AN INJURY TO AL
WORKERS OF THE
THE REAL ENEMIES OF FREEDOM ARE RIGHT HERE. THEY LIKE TO HIDE BEHIND TERMS LIKE "NATIONAL SECURITY" AND WRAP THEMSELVES IN THE FLAG.
THE MEN AND WOMEN WHO MADE THE AMERICAN REVOLUTION WEREN'T PERFECT. SOME HAD SLAVES. BUT THEY HAD A VISION OF JUSTICE AND EQUALITY WORTH FIGHTING FOR, EVEN TODAY.
UNFORTUNATELY, FOR MANY PEOPLE, PATRIOTISM IS SUPPORT FOR KILLING PEOPLE IN OTHER COUNTRIES INSTEAD OF SECURING THE BLESSINGS OF LIBERTY RIGHT HERE.
END

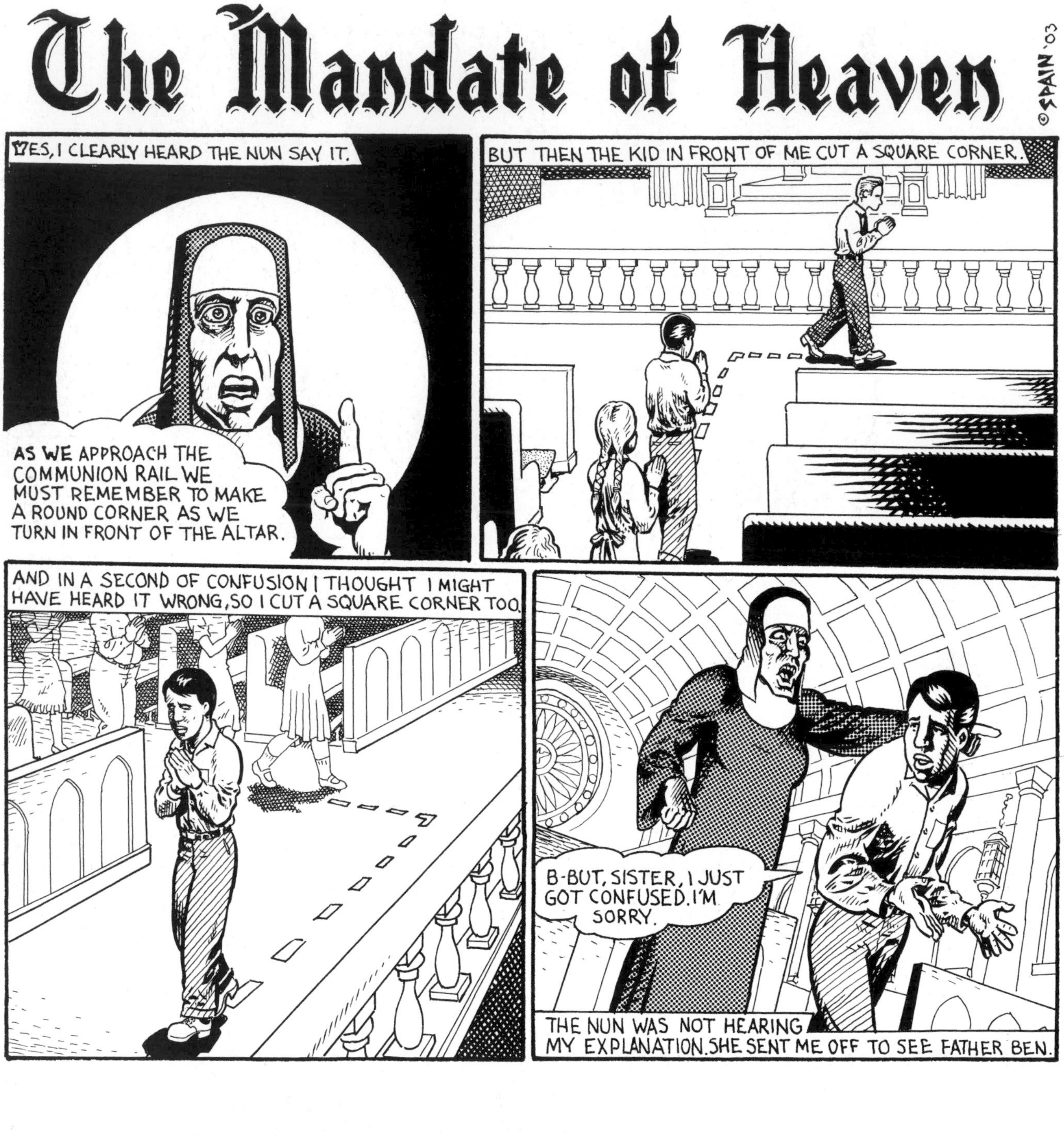
The Mandate of Heaven
©SPAIN '03
YES, I CLEARLY HEARD THE NUN SAY IT.
AS WE APPROACH THE COMMUNION RAIL WE MUST REMEMBER TO MAKE A ROUND CORNER AS WE TURN IN FRONT OF THE ALTAR.
BUT THEN THE KID IN FRONT OF ME CUT A SQUARE CORNER.
AND IN A SECOND OF CONFUSION I THOUGHT I MIGHT HAVE HEARD IT WRONG, SO I CUT A SQUARE CORNER TOO.
B-BUT, SISTER, I JUST GOT CONFUSED. I'M SORRY.
THE NUN WAS NOT HEARING MY EXPLANATION. SHE SENT ME OFF TO SEE FATHER BEN.

P. 234–235 from *The Comics Journal Special Edition* Volume 4, 2004

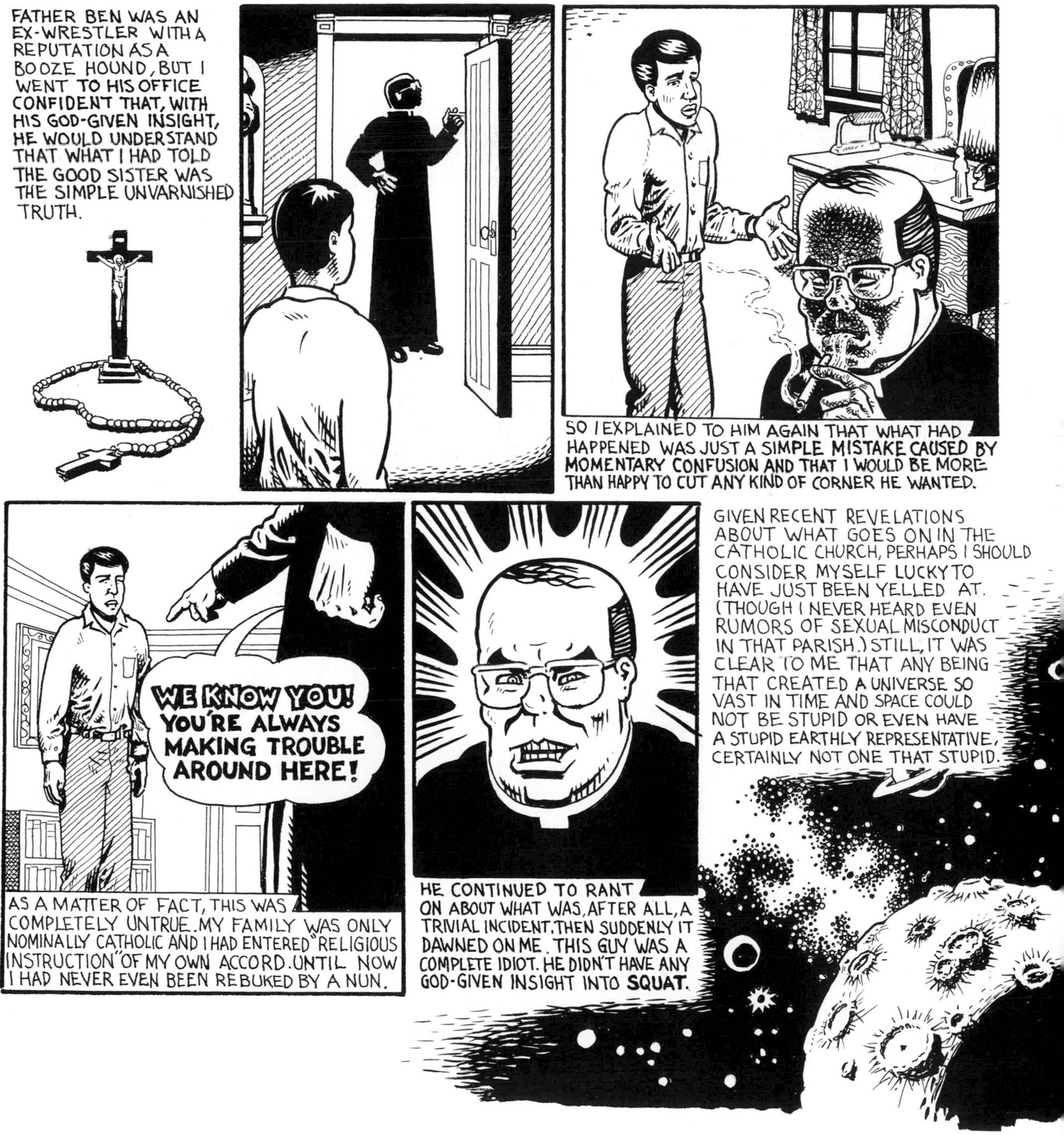
FATHER BEN WAS AN EX-WRESTLER WITH A REPUTATION AS A BOOZE HOUND, BUT I WENT TO HIS OFFICE CONFIDENT THAT, WITH HIS GOD-GIVEN INSIGHT, HE WOULD UNDERSTAND THAT WHAT I HAD TOLD THE GOOD SISTER WAS THE SIMPLE UNVARNISHED TRUTH.
SO I EXPLAINED TO HIM AGAIN THAT WHAT HAD HAPPENED WAS JUST A SIMPLE MISTAKE CAUSED BY MOMENTARY CONFUSION AND THAT I WOULD BE MORE THAN HAPPY TO CUT ANY KIND OF CORNER HE WANTED.
WE KNOW YOU! YOU'RE ALWAYS MAKING TROUBLE AROUND HERE!
AS A MATTER OF FACT, THIS WAS COMPLETELY UNTRUE. MY FAMILY WAS ONLY NOMINALLY CATHOLIC AND I HAD ENTERED "RELIGIOUS INSTRUCTION" OF MY OWN ACCORD. UNTIL NOW I HAD NEVER EVEN BEEN REBUKED BY A NUN.
HE CONTINUED TO RANT ON ABOUT WHAT WAS, AFTER ALL, A TRIVIAL INCIDENT. THEN SUDDENLY IT DAWNED ON ME. THIS GUY WAS A COMPLETE IDIOT. HE DIDN'T HAVE ANY GOD-GIVEN INSIGHT INTO SQUAT.
GIVEN RECENT REVELATIONS ABOUT WHAT GOES ON IN THE CATHOLIC CHURCH, PERHAPS I SHOULD CONSIDER MYSELF LUCKY TO HAVE JUST BEEN YELLED AT. (THOUGH I NEVER HEARD EVEN RUMORS OF SEXUAL MISCONDUCT IN THAT PARISH.) STILL, IT WAS CLEAR TO ME THAT ANY BEING THAT CREATED A UNIVERSE SO VAST IN TIME AND SPACE COULD NOT BE STUPID OR EVEN HAVE A STUPID EARTHLY REPRESENTATIVE, CERTAINLY NOT ONE THAT STUPID.

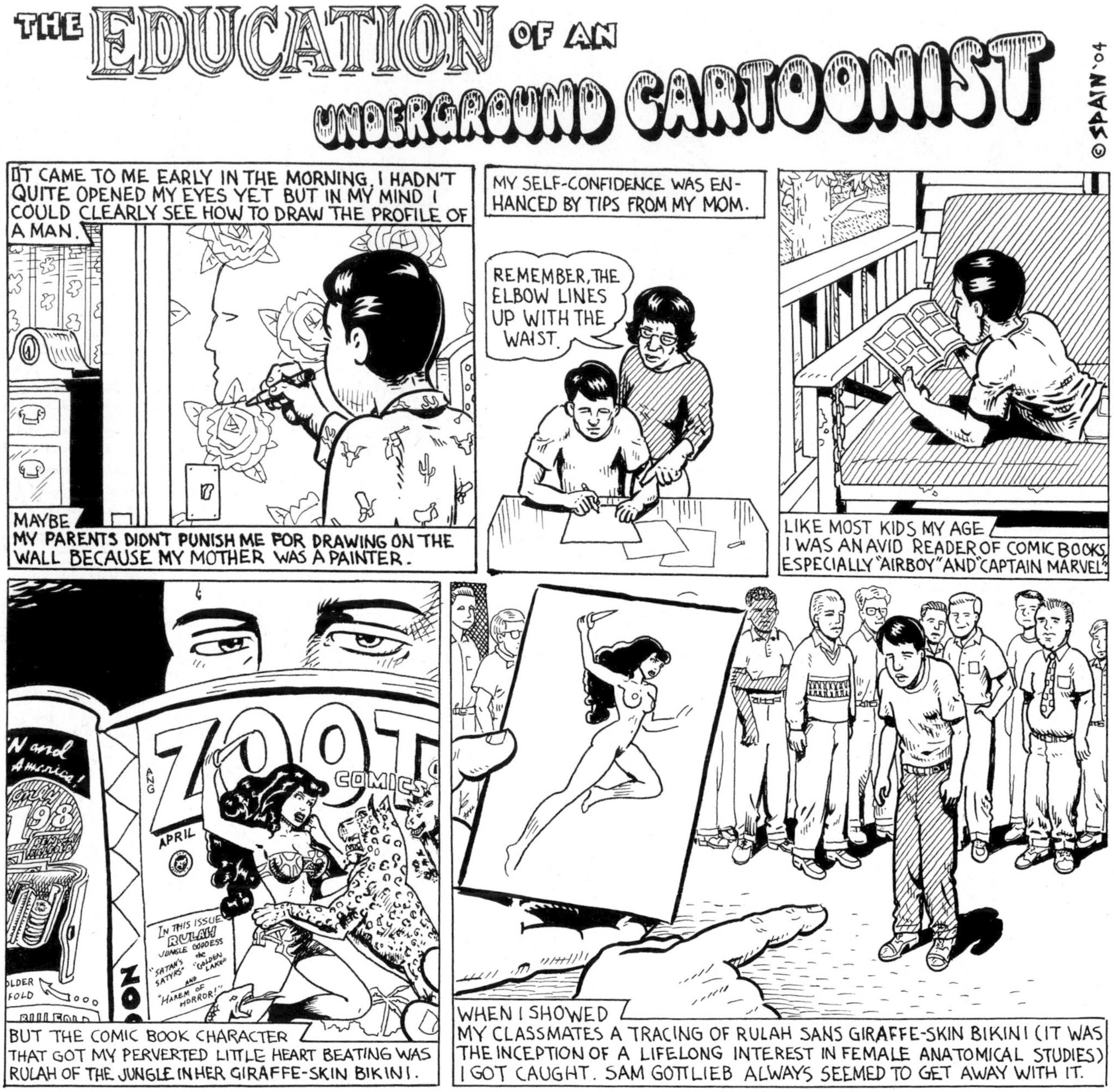
THE EDUCATION OF AN UNDERGROUND CARTOONIST
© SPAIN '04
IT CAME TO ME EARLY IN THE MORNING. I HADN'T QUITE OPENED MY EYES YET BUT IN MY MIND I COULD CLEARLY SEE HOW TO DRAW THE PROFILE OF A MAN.
MAYBE MY PARENTS DIDN'T PUNISH ME FOR DRAWING ON THE WALL BECAUSE MY MOTHER WAS A PAINTER.
MY SELF-CONFIDENCE WAS ENHANCED BY TIPS FROM MY MOM.
REMEMBER, THE ELBOW LINES UP WITH THE WAIST.
LIKE MOST KIDS MY AGE I WAS AN AVID READER OF COMIC BOOKS, ESPECIALLY "AIRBOY" AND "CAPTAIN MARVEL".
ZOOT
COMICS
APRIL
IN THIS ISSUE
RULAH
BUT THE COMIC BOOK CHARACTER THAT GOT MY PERVERTED LITTLE HEART BEATING WAS RULAH OF THE JUNGLE IN HER GIRAFFE-SKIN BIKINI.
WHEN I SHOWED MY CLASSMATES A TRACING OF RULAH SANS GIRAFFE-SKIN BIKINI (IT WAS THE INCEPTION OF A LIFELONG INTEREST IN FEMALE ANATOMICAL STUDIES) I GOT CAUGHT. SAM GOTTLIEB ALWAYS SEEMED TO GET AWAY WITH IT.

P. 236–239 from *Blab!* #15, 2004

RETURNING FROM A TRIP TO SPAIN IN THE EARLY FIFTIES, THE SHIP STOPPED IN HALIFAX. I FOUND A COMIC BOOK WITHOUT A COVER IN A USED BOOK STORE.

THE END!

NO MORE "STRANGE ADVENTURES" OR "MYSTERY IN SPACE". FROM THAT POINT ON, I WAS HOOKED ON E.C. COMICS.

MY YOUTHFUL CYNICISM WAS STOKED BY THE SUPRESSION OF E.C. COMICS, BUT BEFORE THEY WENT DOWN THEY LEFT US WITH AN INTRIGUING CONCEPT.

TALES ⊕ CALCU
LATED TO DRIVE YOU
10¢

MAD

Humor In A Jugular Vein

Comic Book Raid

Comics Go Underground

Comics Go Underground
In this remarkable photo (→) we see a comic book publisher whose books have been banned from newsstands, secretly peddling his comics on a busy street corner. It is rumored that this is only one that desperate comic-book publishers are in order to sell their books ...anoth

THE IDEA OF COMICS GOING UNDERGROUND MUST HAVE RESONATED IN YOUNG MINDS ACROSS THE COUNTRY.

TEMA

INSPIRED BY "THE HEAP" FROM "AIR BOY COMICS"

HEH, HEH, HEH ... HEH, HEH, HEH.

TEMA SELIGMAN WAS A GIRL IN OUR CLASS. WHAT BETTER USE OF OUR TALENT THAN TO TORMENT A SAD OVERWEIGHT CLASSMATE. IT WAS A CHEAP SHOT TO BE SURE, BUT IT WAS PROBABLY ONE OF THE EARLIEST ATTEMPTS AT AN UNDERGROUND COMIC. SOMETIME LATER I MET FRED TOOTE', ANOTHER AVID E.C. FANADDICT WHO COULD SPOT PEOPLE WHO COULD HAVE BEEN DRAWN BY VARIOUS E.C. ARTISTS. HE WAS SELDOM WRONG.

JACK DAVIS

YA, RIGHT!

AFTER HIGH SCHOOL MY MOM GOT ME A WORK SCHOLARSHIP AT SILVERMINE GUILD SCHOOL OF ART. IN OUR FIRST DRAWING CLASS OUR MODEL WAS A CEMENT BLOCK.

WHAT ELSE YA GOT?

I DREW THE CEMENT BLOCK AND EVERY THING BEHIND IT, INCLUDING THE RAFTERS. IT WAS A GESTURE OF ARROGANCE I WOULD PAY FOR LATER.

ART SCHOOL OPENED UP NEW VISTAS FOR ME. I LEARNED TO BROADEN MY APPRECIATION OF WHAT WAS WORTH SEEING, BUT AS MUCH AS I LIKED TO LOOK AT ABSTRACT ART I GOT NO PLEASURE DOING IT.

I CAN DIG IT!

FOR ME THE MAIN KICK OF MAKING IMAGES WAS WHAT IT HAD ALWAYS BEEN; TO MAKE A FLAT SURFACE APPEAR THREE DIMENSIONAL.

I HAD IMAGINED MYSELF TO BE SOMETHING OF A HOT SHOT. BUT FOR ALL MY BRAVADO, THE MOTHERFUCKERS HAD A WAY OF GETTING TO YOU.

BUT IT'S SNIF ILLUSTRATION

AFTER ALMOST THREE YEARS, WHAT LITTLE OUTPUT I PRODUCED HAD TAKEN A TURN FOR THE WEIRD.

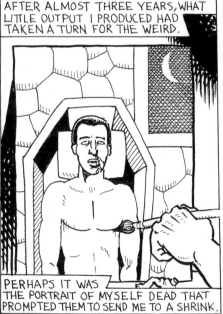

PERHAPS IT WAS THE PORTRAIT OF MYSELF DEAD THAT PROMPTED THEM TO SEND ME TO A SHRINK.

HER ANALYSIS WAS QUICK AND TO THE POINT.

YOU HATE IT HERE, DON'T YOU?

BLAH, BLAH BLAH... UNH YAH!

I LEFT SCHOOL IMMEDIATELY. TO THIS DAY, THE DAY I LEFT ART SCHOOL WAS THE HAPPIEST DAY OF MY LIFE.

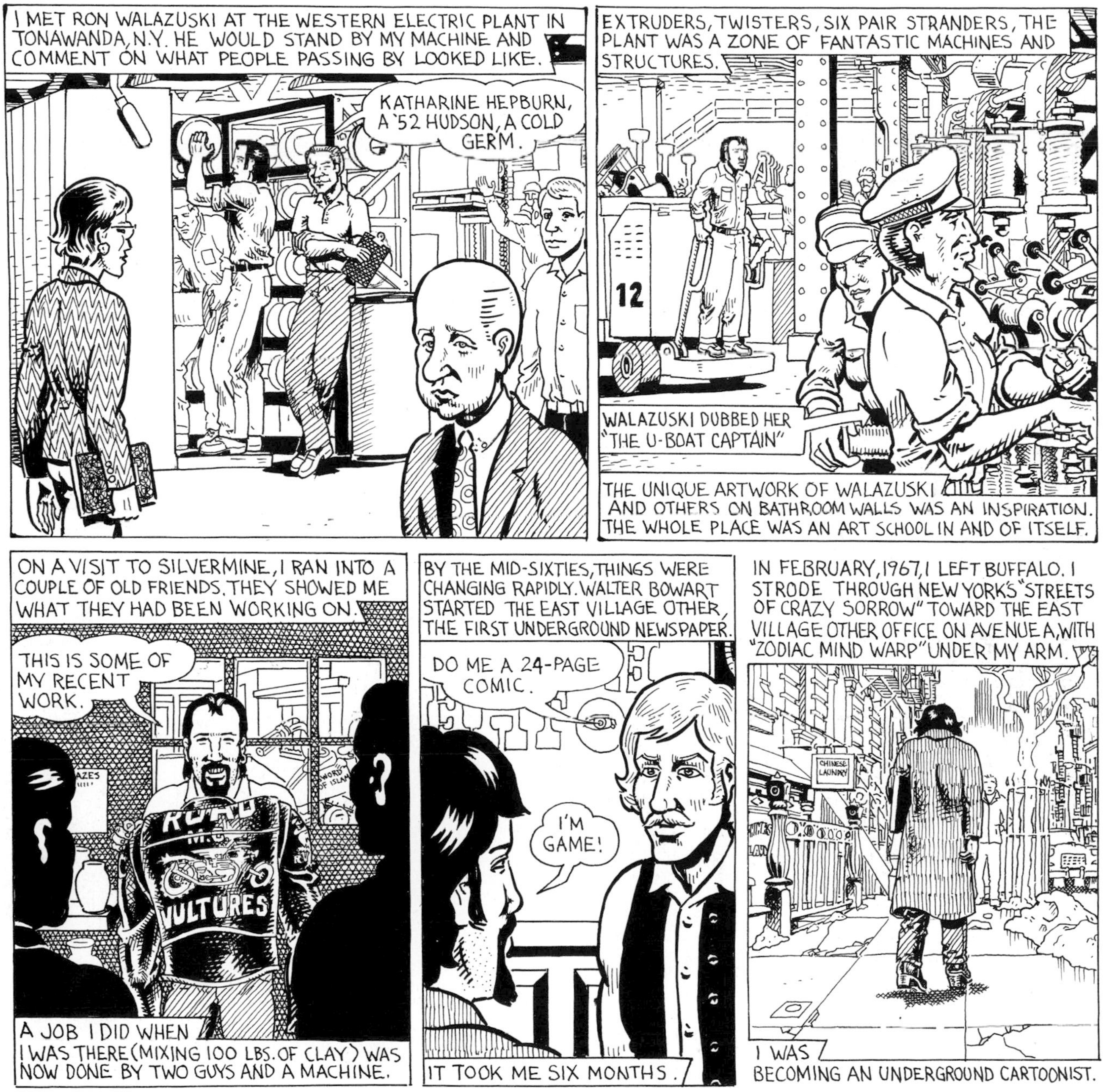
I MET RON WALAZUSKI AT THE WESTERN ELECTRIC PLANT IN TONAWANDA, N.Y. HE WOULD STAND BY MY MACHINE AND COMMENT ON WHAT PEOPLE PASSING BY LOOKED LIKE.
KATHARINE HEPBURN, A '52 HUDSON, A COLD GERM.
EXTRUDERS, TWISTERS, SIX PAIR STRANDERS, THE PLANT WAS A ZONE OF FANTASTIC MACHINES AND STRUCTURES.
12
WALAZUSKI DUBBED HER "THE U-BOAT CAPTAIN"
THE UNIQUE ARTWORK OF WALAZUSKI AND OTHERS ON BATHROOM WALLS WAS AN INSPIRATION. THE WHOLE PLACE WAS AN ART SCHOOL IN AND OF ITSELF.
ON A VISIT TO SILVERMINE, I RAN INTO A COUPLE OF OLD FRIENDS. THEY SHOWED ME WHAT THEY HAD BEEN WORKING ON.
THIS IS SOME OF MY RECENT WORK.
VULTURES
A JOB I DID WHEN I WAS THERE (MIXING 100 LBS. OF CLAY) WAS NOW DONE BY TWO GUYS AND A MACHINE.
BY THE MID-SIXTIES, THINGS WERE CHANGING RAPIDLY. WALTER BOWART STARTED THE EAST VILLAGE OTHER, THE FIRST UNDERGROUND NEWSPAPER.
DO ME A 24-PAGE COMIC.
I'M GAME!
IT TOOK ME SIX MONTHS.
IN FEBRUARY, 1967, I LEFT BUFFALO. I STRODE THROUGH NEW YORK'S "STREETS OF CRAZY SORROW" TOWARD THE EAST VILLAGE OTHER OFFICE ON AVENUE A, WITH "ZODIAC MIND WARP" UNDER MY ARM.
CHINESE LAUNDRY
I WAS BECOMING AN UNDERGROUND CARTOONIST.

THE RETURN OF JAMES

DAT BE SOME FUCKEIN BOOLSHIT!

NAH, LOOKY HEAH! AH AIN'T JES' BUMPIN' MAH GUMS, JACK!

THIS CAN MEAN ONLY ONE THING...

© SPAIN '05 CONSULTANT: GEORGE BRYCE.

WHEN ALL THE WHITE GUYS IN THE NEIGHBORHOOD STARTED TALKING LIKE BLACK PEOPLE IT MEANT THAT JAMES WAS GETTING OUT OF "THE JOINT."

THIS WAS NOT INTENDED AS A PARODY OF AFRICAN-AMERICAN SPEECH. WHITE GUYS IN THE NEIGHBORHOOD TALKED THAT WAY BECAUSE THAT'S THE WAY JAMES TALKED.

AH' DONE PAID MAH DEBT TO SO-SIE-YA-TEE. NAH, AHM OTTA THE CLUTCHES O' THESE FUNKY MUTHAFUKKAHS.

P. 240–245 from *Blab!* #16, 2005

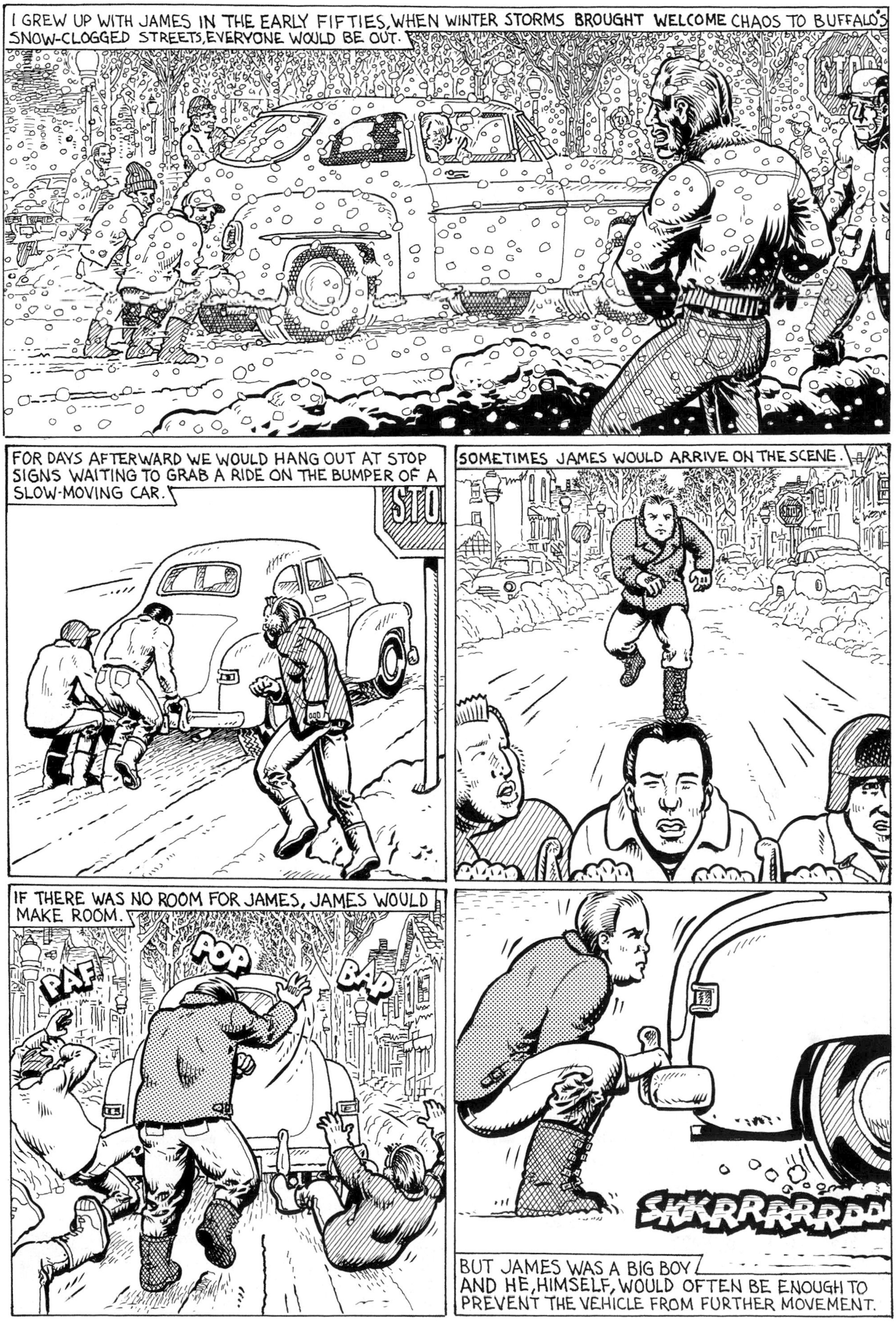
I GREW UP WITH JAMES IN THE EARLY FIFTIES, WHEN WINTER STORMS BROUGHT WELCOME CHAOS TO BUFFALO'S SNOW-CLOGGED STREETS, EVERYONE WOULD BE OUT.
FOR DAYS AFTERWARD WE WOULD HANG OUT AT STOP SIGNS WAITING TO GRAB A RIDE ON THE BUMPER OF A SLOW-MOVING CAR.
SOMETIMES JAMES WOULD ARRIVE ON THE SCENE.
IF THERE WAS NO ROOM FOR JAMES, JAMES WOULD MAKE ROOM.
PAF
POP
BAP
SKKRRRRRRDD
BUT JAMES WAS A BIG BOY
AND HE, HIMSELF, WOULD OFTEN BE ENOUGH TO PREVENT THE VEHICLE FROM FURTHER MOVEMENT.

JAMES WAS DESTINED FOR BADNESS. WHEN HE WAS FOURTEEN HE ROBBED $500 FROM A DOCTOR'S OFFICE.

HE BOUGHT HIS GOOD PALS BRAND NEW BICYCLES. $500 WAS A LOT OF MONEY IN THOSE DAYS, ESPECIALLY FOR TEENAGERS.

BUT HE FELL INTO THE POND WHILE HORSING AROUND AT DELAWARE PARK.

THEY TOOK THE REST OF THE MONEY AND LAID IT OUT BY THE SIDE OF THE POND TO DRY.

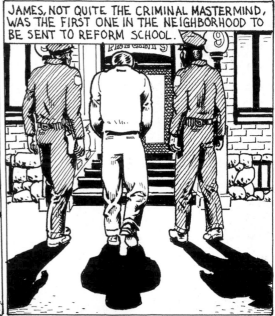

JAMES, NOT QUITE THE CRIMINAL MASTERMIND, WAS THE FIRST ONE IN THE NEIGHBORHOOD TO BE SENT TO REFORM SCHOOL.

AFTER JAMES WENT TO THE CAN THE "DISCIPLES OF JAMES" WENT ON A VANDALISM SPREE.

POK

THE BATHROOM! IT'S SHRUNK I CAN'T GET IN!

THE HOME LIFE OF JAMES AND HIS BROTHER, SKIPPY, WAS NOT A HAPPY ONE.

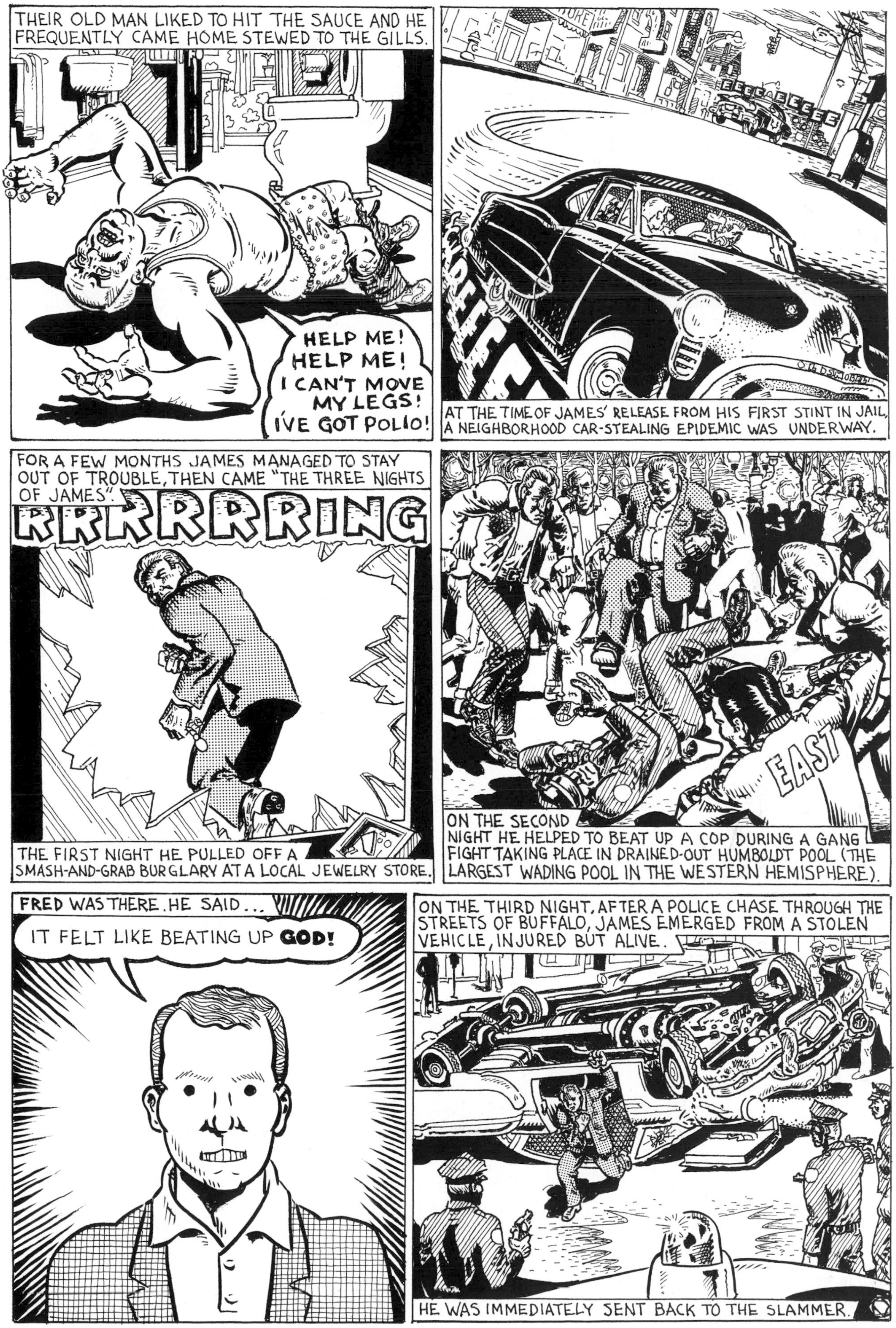
THEIR OLD MAN LIKED TO HIT THE SAUCE AND HE FREQUENTLY CAME HOME STEWED TO THE GILLS.
HELP ME! HELP ME! I CAN'T MOVE MY LEGS! I'VE GOT POLIO!
AT THE TIME OF JAMES' RELEASE FROM HIS FIRST STINT IN JAIL, A NEIGHBORHOOD CAR-STEALING EPIDEMIC WAS UNDERWAY.
FOR A FEW MONTHS JAMES MANAGED TO STAY OUT OF TROUBLE, THEN CAME "THE THREE NIGHTS OF JAMES".
RRRRRRING
THE FIRST NIGHT HE PULLED OFF A SMASH-AND-GRAB BURGLARY AT A LOCAL JEWELRY STORE.
EAST
ON THE SECOND NIGHT HE HELPED TO BEAT UP A COP DURING A GANG FIGHT TAKING PLACE IN DRAINED-OUT HUMBOLDT POOL (THE LARGEST WADING POOL IN THE WESTERN HEMISPHERE).
FRED WAS THERE. HE SAID...
IT FELT LIKE BEATING UP GOD!
ON THE THIRD NIGHT, AFTER A POLICE CHASE THROUGH THE STREETS OF BUFFALO, JAMES EMERGED FROM A STOLEN VEHICLE, INJURED BUT ALIVE.
HE WAS IMMEDIATELY SENT BACK TO THE SLAMMER.

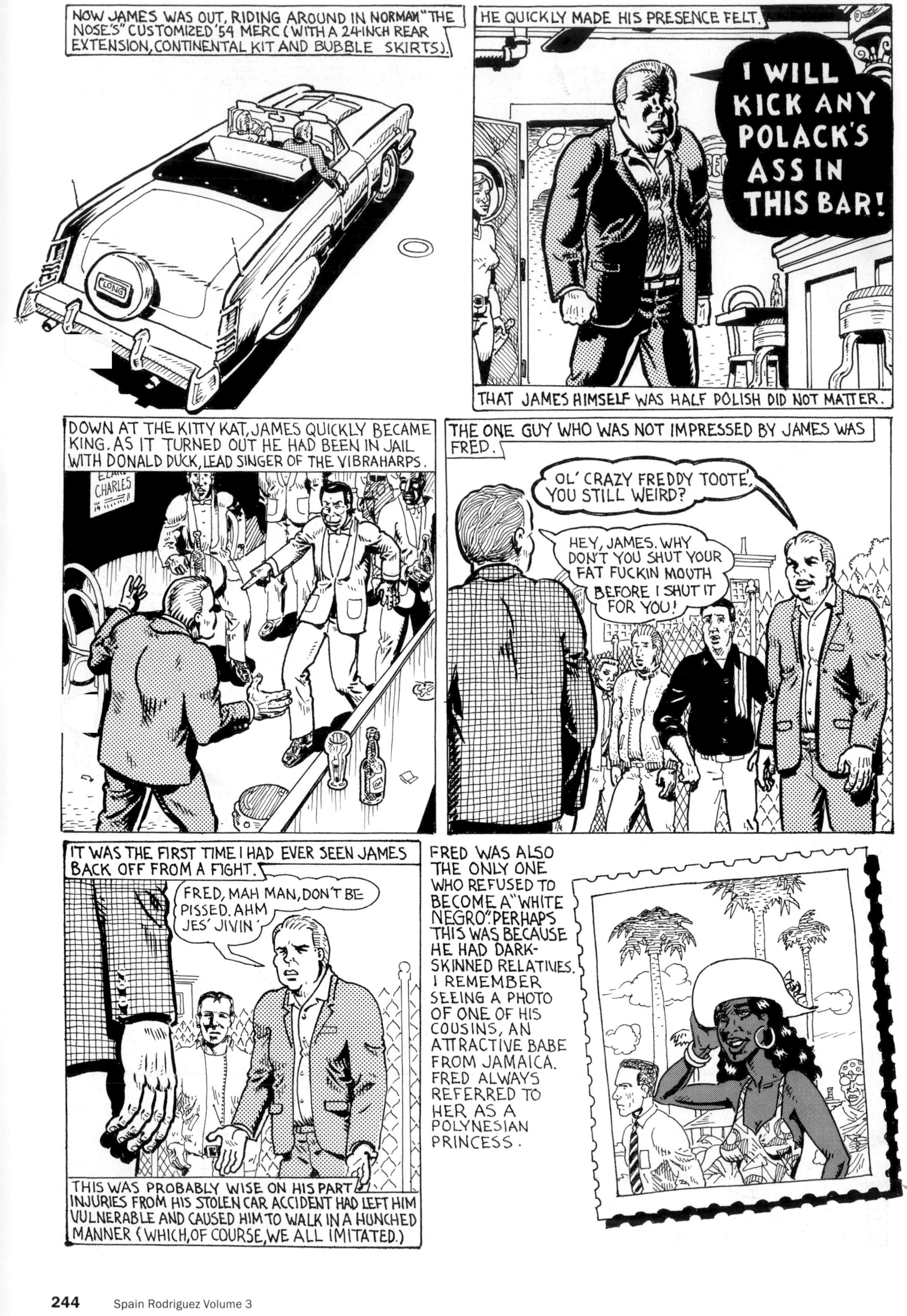
NOW JAMES WAS OUT, RIDING AROUND IN NORMAN "THE NOSE'S" CUSTOMIZED '54 MERC (WITH A 24-INCH REAR EXTENSION, CONTINENTAL KIT AND BUBBLE SKIRTS).
LONG
HE QUICKLY MADE HIS PRESENCE FELT.
I WILL KICK ANY POLACK'S ASS IN THIS BAR!
THAT JAMES HIMSELF WAS HALF POLISH DID NOT MATTER.
DOWN AT THE KITTY KAT, JAMES QUICKLY BECAME KING. AS IT TURNED OUT HE HAD BEEN IN JAIL WITH DONALD DUCK, LEAD SINGER OF THE VIBRAHARPS.
CHARLES
THE ONE GUY WHO WAS NOT IMPRESSED BY JAMES WAS FRED.
OL' CRAZY FREDDY TOOTE, YOU STILL WEIRD?
HEY, JAMES. WHY DON'T YOU SHUT YOUR FAT FUCKIN MOUTH BEFORE I SHUT IT FOR YOU!
IT WAS THE FIRST TIME I HAD EVER SEEN JAMES BACK OFF FROM A FIGHT.
FRED, MAH MAN, DON'T BE PISSED. AHM JES' JIVIN'.
THIS WAS PROBABLY WISE ON HIS PART. INJURIES FROM HIS STOLEN CAR ACCIDENT HAD LEFT HIM VULNERABLE AND CAUSED HIM TO WALK IN A HUNCHED MANNER (WHICH, OF COURSE, WE ALL IMITATED.)
FRED WAS ALSO THE ONLY ONE WHO REFUSED TO BECOME A "WHITE NEGRO". PERHAPS THIS WAS BECAUSE HE HAD DARK-SKINNED RELATIVES. I REMEMBER SEEING A PHOTO OF ONE OF HIS COUSINS, AN ATTRACTIVE BABE FROM JAMAICA. FRED ALWAYS REFERRED TO HER AS A POLYNESIAN PRINCESS.

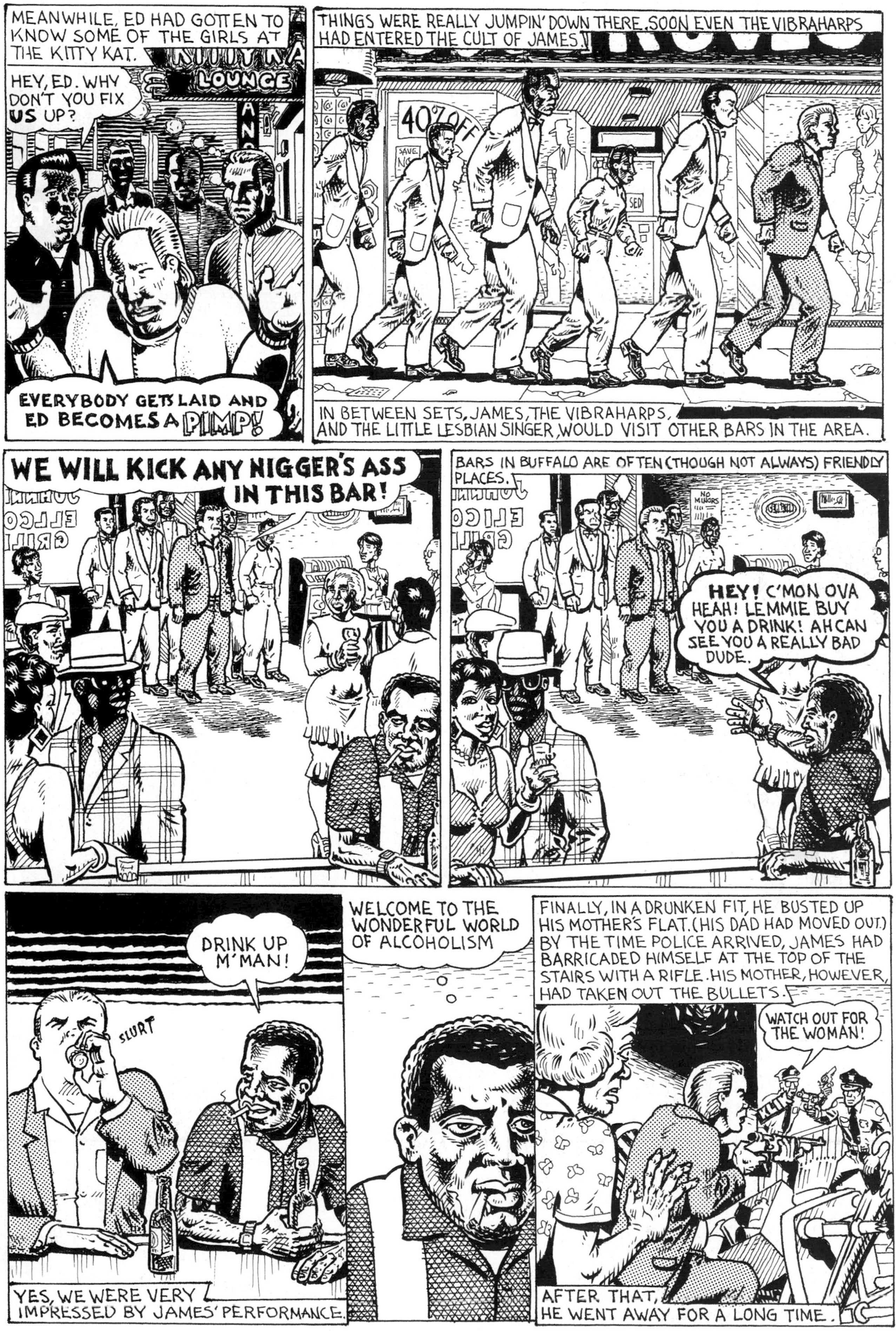
MEANWHILE, ED HAD GOTTEN TO KNOW SOME OF THE GIRLS AT THE KITTY KAT.
LOUNGE
HEY, ED. WHY DON'T YOU FIX US UP?
EVERYBODY GETS LAID AND ED BECOMES A PIMP!
THINGS WERE REALLY JUMPIN' DOWN THERE. SOON EVEN THE VIBRAHARPS HAD ENTERED THE CULT OF JAMES.
40% OFF
IN BETWEEN SETS, JAMES, THE VIBRAHARPS, AND THE LITTLE LESBIAN SINGER, WOULD VISIT OTHER BARS IN THE AREA.
WE WILL KICK ANY NIGGER'S ASS IN THIS BAR!
BARS IN BUFFALO ARE OFTEN (THOUGH NOT ALWAYS) FRIENDLY PLACES.
NO MINORS
HEY! C'MON OVA HEAH! LEMMIE BUY YOU A DRINK! AH CAN SEE YOU A REALLY BAD DUDE.
DRINK UP M'MAN!
SLURT
YES, WE WERE VERY IMPRESSED BY JAMES' PERFORMANCE.
WELCOME TO THE WONDERFUL WORLD OF ALCOHOLISM
FINALLY, IN A DRUNKEN FIT, HE BUSTED UP HIS MOTHER'S FLAT. (HIS DAD HAD MOVED OUT.) BY THE TIME POLICE ARRIVED, JAMES HAD BARRICADED HIMSELF AT THE TOP OF THE STAIRS WITH A RIFLE. HIS MOTHER, HOWEVER, HAD TAKEN OUT THE BULLETS.
WATCH OUT FOR THE WOMAN!
AFTER THAT, HE WENT AWAY FOR A LONG TIME.

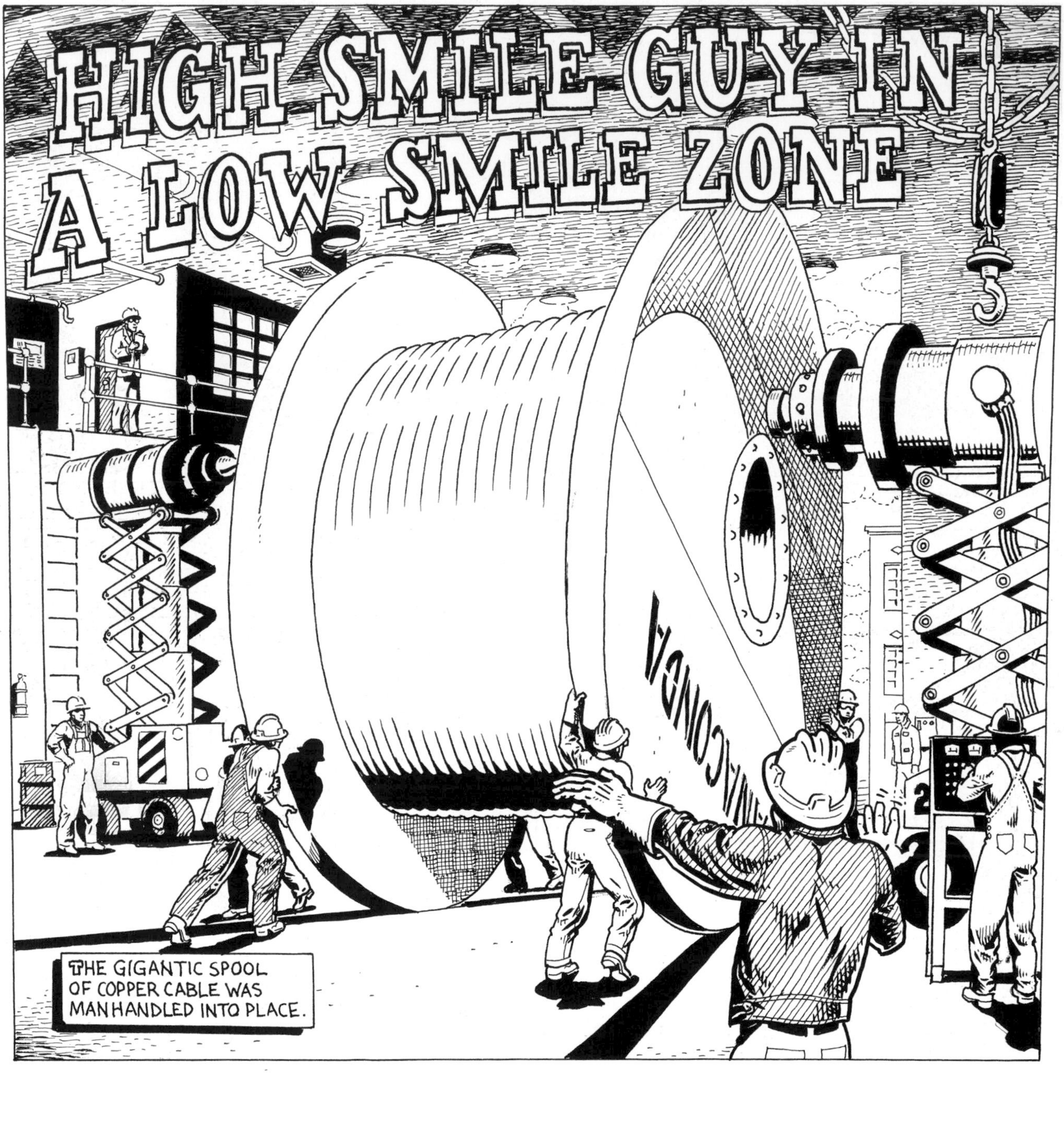
HIGH SMILE GUY IN A LOW SMILE ZONE
THE GIGANTIC SPOOL OF COPPER CABLE WAS MANHANDLED INTO PLACE.

P. 246–253 from *Blab!* #17, 2006

ONCE HOOKED UP TO ITS SPINDLE, THE FAT COPPER CABLE PROCEEDED TO PAINFULLY CRAWL THROUGH A SERIES OF DIES, EACH ONE SHRINKING ITS CIRCUMFERENCE TILL IT WAS TRANSFORMED INTO THIN WIRE RAPIDLY CAREENING OUT ONTO WAITING SPOOLS.

THE SPOOLS WERE THEN TAKEN INTO A MAZE OF BIZARRE MACHINES TO BE TURNED EVENTUALLY INTO TELEPHONE WIRE.

THUS I FOUND MYSELF THRUST INTO THIS SURREAL PALACE WHEN I BECAME EMPLOYED AS A JANITOR AT THE TONAWANDA PLANT OF WESTERN ELECTRIC.

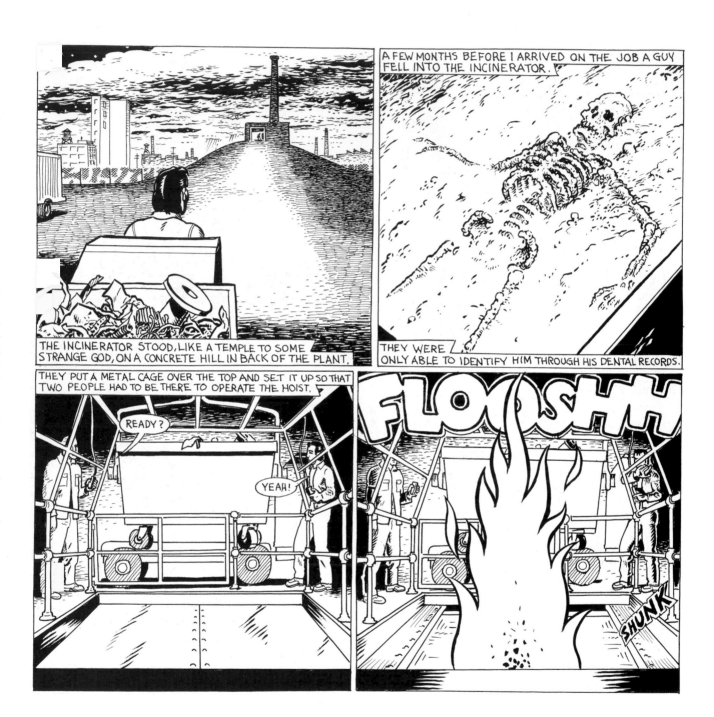

THE INCINERATOR STOOD, LIKE A TEMPLE TO SOME STRANGE GOD, ON A CONCRETE HILL IN BACK OF THE PLANT.

A FEW MONTHS BEFORE I ARRIVED ON THE JOB A GUY FELL INTO THE INCINERATOR.

THEY WERE ONLY ABLE TO IDENTIFY HIM THROUGH HIS DENTAL RECORDS.

THEY PUT A METAL CAGE OVER THE TOP AND SET IT UP SO THAT TWO PEOPLE HAD TO BE THERE TO OPERATE THE HOIST,

READY?

YEAH!

FLOOOSHH

SHUNK

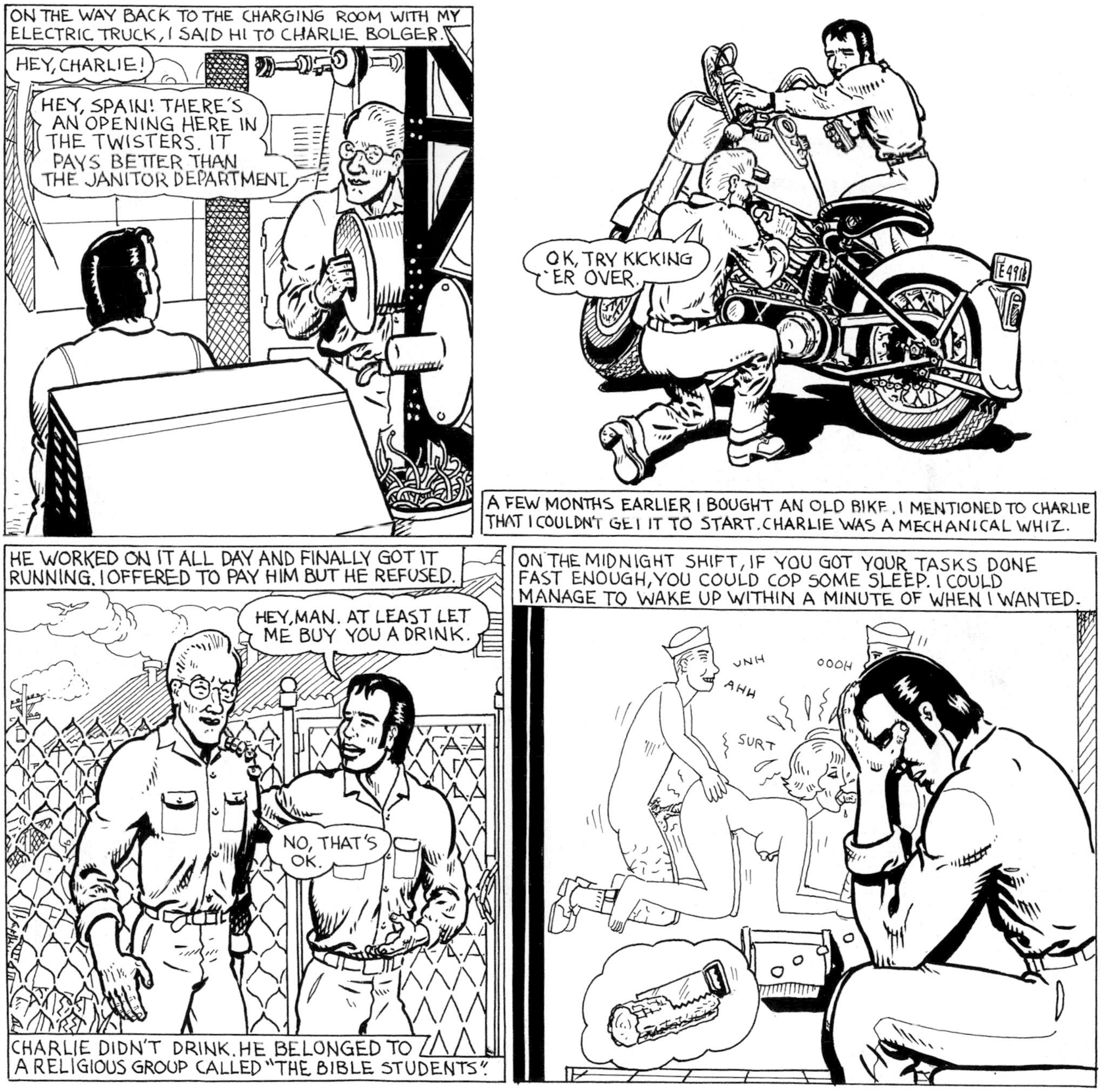
ON THE WAY BACK TO THE CHARGING ROOM WITH MY ELECTRIC TRUCK, I SAID HI TO CHARLIE BOLGER.
HEY, CHARLIE!
HEY, SPAIN! THERE'S AN OPENING HERE IN THE TWISTERS. IT PAYS BETTER THAN THE JANITOR DEPARTMENT.
OK, TRY KICKING 'ER OVER.
A FEW MONTHS EARLIER I BOUGHT AN OLD BIKE. I MENTIONED TO CHARLIE THAT I COULDN'T GET IT TO START. CHARLIE WAS A MECHANICAL WHIZ.
HE WORKED ON IT ALL DAY AND FINALLY GOT IT RUNNING. I OFFERED TO PAY HIM BUT HE REFUSED.
HEY, MAN. AT LEAST LET ME BUY YOU A DRINK.
NO, THAT'S OK.
CHARLIE DIDN'T DRINK. HE BELONGED TO A RELIGIOUS GROUP CALLED "THE BIBLE STUDENTS".
ON THE MIDNIGHT SHIFT, IF YOU GOT YOUR TASKS DONE FAST ENOUGH, YOU COULD COP SOME SLEEP. I COULD MANAGE TO WAKE UP WITHIN A MINUTE OF WHEN I WANTED.
UNH
OOOH
AHH
SURT

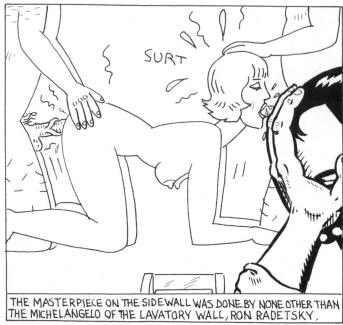

SURT
THE MASTERPIECE ON THE SIDEWALL WAS DONE BY NONE OTHER THAN THE MICHELANGELO OF THE LAVATORY WALL, RON RADETSKY.
BUT ONE MAN TOOK PARTICULAR UMBRAGE TO RON'S DISPLAY OF ARTISTRY. THAT MAN WAS CUSTODIAN ELMER DEDSEL.
SURT
SUCK
WIPE WIPE WIPE
ELMER DEDSEL WAS DETERMINED TO MAKE THE WALLS OF THE BATHROOM STALLS A PLACE OF NOT ONLY PHYSICAL BUT MORAL CLEANLINESS AS WELL.
THE PROBLEM WITH SLEEPING ON THE JOHN FOR ANY LENGTH OF TIME WAS THE RED MARKS FROM YOUR HANDS RESTING ON YOUR FOREHEAD.

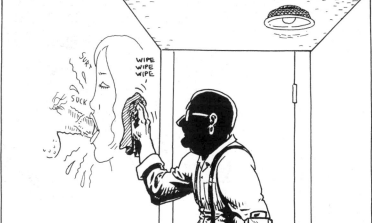

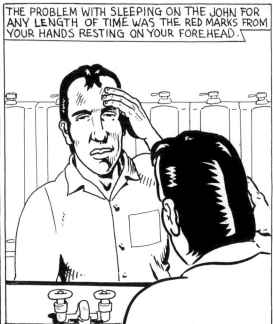

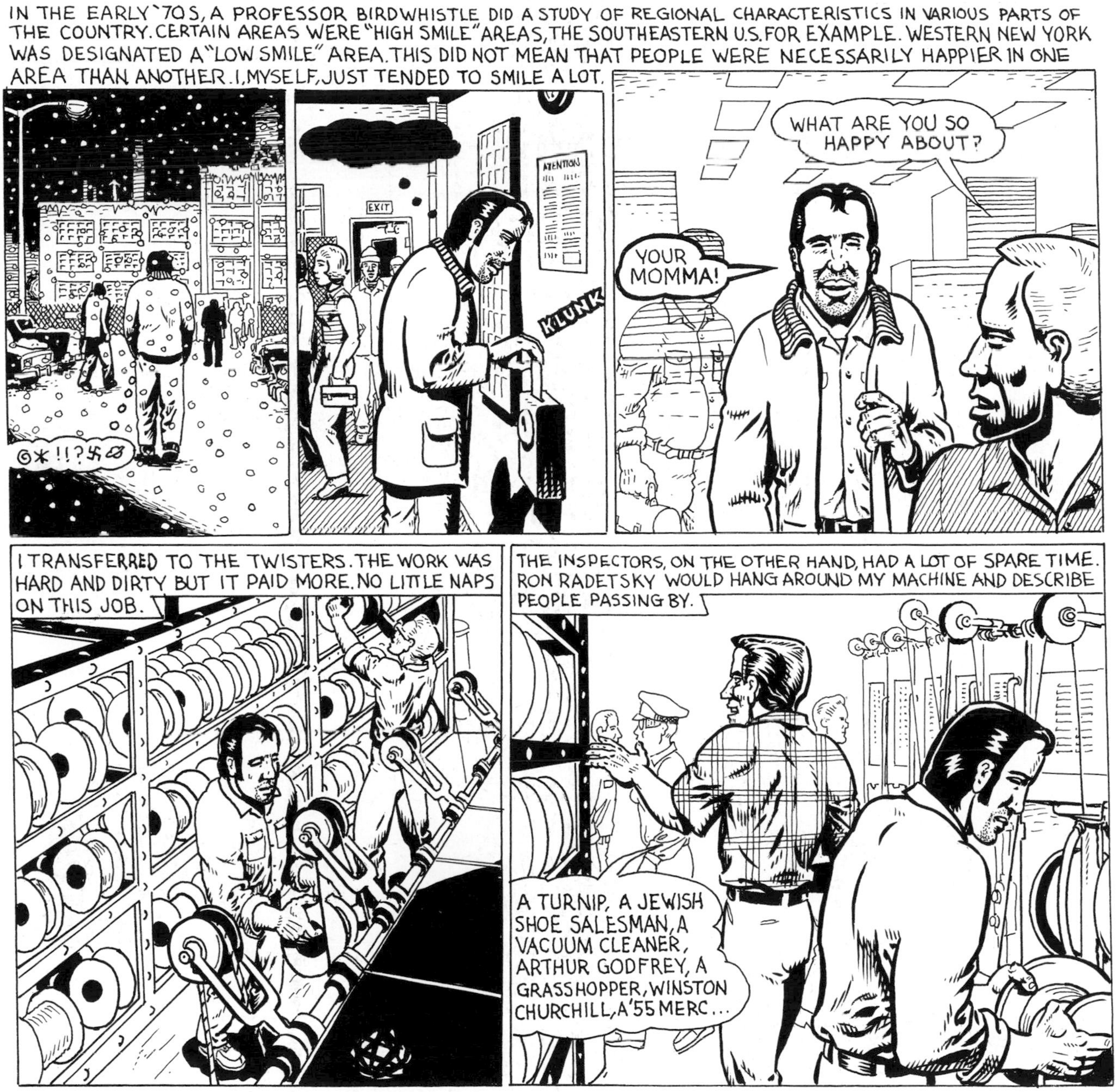
IN THE EARLY '70S, A PROFESSOR BIRDWHISTLE DID A STUDY OF REGIONAL CHARACTERISTICS IN VARIOUS PARTS OF THE COUNTRY. CERTAIN AREAS WERE "HIGH SMILE" AREAS, THE SOUTHEASTERN U.S. FOR EXAMPLE. WESTERN NEW YORK WAS DESIGNATED A "LOW SMILE" AREA. THIS DID NOT MEAN THAT PEOPLE WERE NECESSARILY HAPPIER IN ONE AREA THAN ANOTHER. I, MYSELF, JUST TENDED TO SMILE A LOT.
EXIT
ATTENTION
KLUNK
WHAT ARE YOU SO HAPPY ABOUT?
YOUR MOMMA!
I TRANSFERRED TO THE TWISTERS. THE WORK WAS HARD AND DIRTY BUT IT PAID MORE. NO LITTLE NAPS ON THIS JOB.
THE INSPECTORS, ON THE OTHER HAND, HAD A LOT OF SPARE TIME. RON RADETSKY WOULD HANG AROUND MY MACHINE AND DESCRIBE PEOPLE PASSING BY.
A TURNIP, A JEWISH SHOE SALESMAN, A VACUUM CLEANER, ARTHUR GODFREY, A GRASSHOPPER, WINSTON CHURCHILL, A '55 MERC...

ACTUALLY THE WHOLE DEPARTMENT HAD A REPUTATION FOR BEING A BIT STRANGE.

YA KNOW SOMETHING? YOU GUYS ARE REALLY WEIRD!

I DON'T KNOW IF IT WAS THE CHEMICALS OR THE SOCIOLOGY,

BUT AFTER A FEW MONTHS...

EVERYONE GOT WEIRD.

THEY SOON BEGAN TO STUDY US FOR "PIECE WORK." PIECE WORK IS A WAGE CUT DISGUISED AS A RAISE. FIRST THEY STUDIED YOU TO SEE WHAT YOUR AVERAGE OUTPUT WAS. THEN, IN ORDER TO GET YOUR PRESENT PAY YOU HAD TO EXCEED YOUR AVERAGE OUTPUT, YOU WOULD GET PAID MORE FOR ANYTHING ABOVE A PREDETERMINED LEVEL.

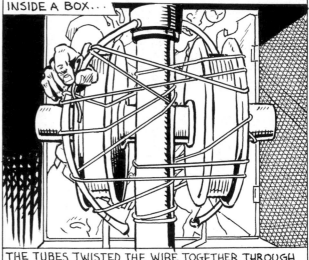

BUT WE HAD A SECRET WEAPON...CHARLIE! HE PUT HIS MECHANICAL WIZARDRY TO GOOD USE. THE WIRE RAN FROM TWO SPOOLS THROUGH TWO SPINNING TUBES INSIDE A BOX...

THE TUBES TWISTED THE WIRE TOGETHER THROUGH TO A LARGER SPOOL AT THE BOTTOM OF THE MACHINE.

THE MACHINES TENDED TO BREAK DOWN ANYWAY, BUT IF THEY STARTED RUNNING TOO GOOD, CHARLIE WOULD FIX THEM SO THE TUBES BROKE IN MID-SPIN, WRECKING EVERYTHING INSIDE THE BOX.
POP
THE ENGINEERS WHO OBSERVED US KNEW WE WERE DOING SOMETHING, THEY JUST COULD NEVER QUITE FIGURE OUT WHAT IT WAS.
BUT EVEN THOUGH EVERYONE WAS SLOWING DOWN, ONE GUY ON THE LAST BANK OF MACHINES CONTINUED TO BUST HIS HUMP.
WHAT A LITTLE JERK. WE SHOULD SLASH HIS TIRES OR SOMETHING!
NAW, THE UNION SAYS TO LEAVE HIM ALONE.
SOON AFTER THEY PUT US ON PIECE WORK THEY TRANSFERRED ME TO THE SIX PAIR STRANDER. IT BROKE DOWN EVEN MORE THAN THE TWISTERS AND THAT WAS ALL RIGHT WITH ME.
SCRAPE
SLURP
LICK
THE WAR BETWEEN ELMER DEDSEL AND THE GREAT RADETSKY ESCALATED. HE WAS NOW SCRAPING HIS MURALS IN TO BATHROOM WALLS WITH A CHURCH KEY.
THE END

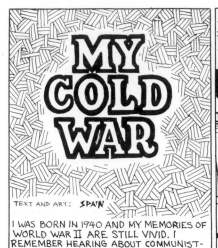

MY COLD WAR

TEXT AND ART: SPAIN

I WAS BORN IN 1940 AND MY MEMORIES OF WORLD WAR II ARE STILL VIVID. I REMEMBER HEARING ABOUT COMMUNIST-LED STRIKES AND ALTHOUGH THE REDS WERE ALWAYS SPOKEN OF IN OMINOUS TONES I FORMED AN OPINION OF THEM, SEEMINGLY ON MY OWN, AS GOOD GUYS FIGHTING FOR THE COMMON PEOPLE

© SPAIN RODRIGUEZ '02

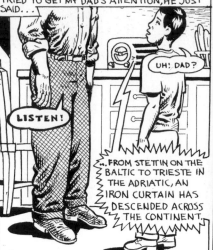

THE WAR HAD BEEN OVER FOR LESS THAN A YEAR WHEN WINSTON CHURCHILL GAVE HIS SPEECH IN FULTON, MISSOURI, ATTACKING OUR FORMER ALLY, THE SOVIET UNION. WHEN I TRIED TO GET MY DAD'S ATTENTION, HE JUST SAID...

LISTEN!

UH! DAD?

...FROM STETTIN ON THE BALTIC TO TRIESTE IN THE ADRIATIC, AN IRON CURTAIN HAS DESCENDED ACROSS THE CONTINENT.

OF COURSE I DIDN'T KNOW THAT CHURCHILL HAD STOLEN THE TERM "IRON CURTAIN" FROM NAZI PROPAGANDA MINISTER JOSEF GOEBBELS. I STILL HAD A CHILD'S COMPLETE FAITH IN THE ADULT WORLD, BUT STILL I WONDERED...

HOW COULD ANYONE BUILD AN IRON WALL ALL THE WAY ACROSS EUROPE?

MY DAD HAD DISMISSED CHURCHILL'S SPEECH AS "POLITICS", BUT IN THE NEXT FEW YEARS THINGS BEGAN TO HEAT UP. I REMEMBER HIM AND MY COUSIN, WHO HAD BEEN IN THE AIR FORCE IN WW II, LOOKING AT ONE OF MY BLACKHAWK COMICS.

THEY REALLY WANT A WAR. YOU CAN EVEN SEE IT IN THESE COMIC BOOKS.

ONE OF THE STORIES WAS ABOUT A SMALL NATION BEING INVADED BY A LARGER COUNTRY NAMED "RUSHAGA".

ABOUT THIS TIME A CHANGE IN ATTITUDE CAME OVER ME. I HAD COMPLETELY FORGOTTEN MY EARLIER IMPRESSIONS OF COMMUNISTS. (MY ATTENTION SPAN ON THESE ISSUES WAS ABOUT 35 SECONDS.)

WHY DO WORKERS THINK THEY HAVE A RIGHT TO STRIKE? IT'S CLEAR THAT FACTORY OWNERS SHOULD BE FREE TO DO WHATEVER THEY WANT WITH THEIR OWN PROPERTY.

LIKE MY EARLIER ATTITUDES, I HAVE NO MEMORY OF ANY ADULT INFLUENCE. TO MYSELF THEY SEEMED LIKE ORIGINAL IDEAS. THE FACT THAT I WOULD SOON BE ONE OF THE WORKERS THAT I LOOKED DOWN ON NEVER OCCURRED TO ME.

THE PROPAGANDA WAR GREW IN INTENSITY. IN ONE ANTICOMMUNIST SHORT, A MAN WAKES UP ONE SUNDAY MORNING TO FIND HIS KIDS RADICALLY CHANGED.

C'MON, KIDS. TIME FOR MASS!

RELIGION IS THE OPIATE OF THE PEOPLE, DAD.

BETTER THAN MASS, THE MASSES FREE OF SUPERSTITION.

FEAR OF AN ACTUAL SOVIET INVASION WAS IN THE AIR AND I HAD DREAMS OF THE RUSSIANS LANDING ON LAKE ERIE AND INVADING BUFFALO.

AFTER THE WAR WE HAD SEEMED INVINCIBLE. WHEN I ASKED MY DAD HOW THE RUSSIANS COULD JUST COME IN AND TAKE US OVER, HE DIDN'T ANSWER.

P. 254–255 from *Cruisin' with the Hound: The Life and Times of Fred Tooté*, 2012

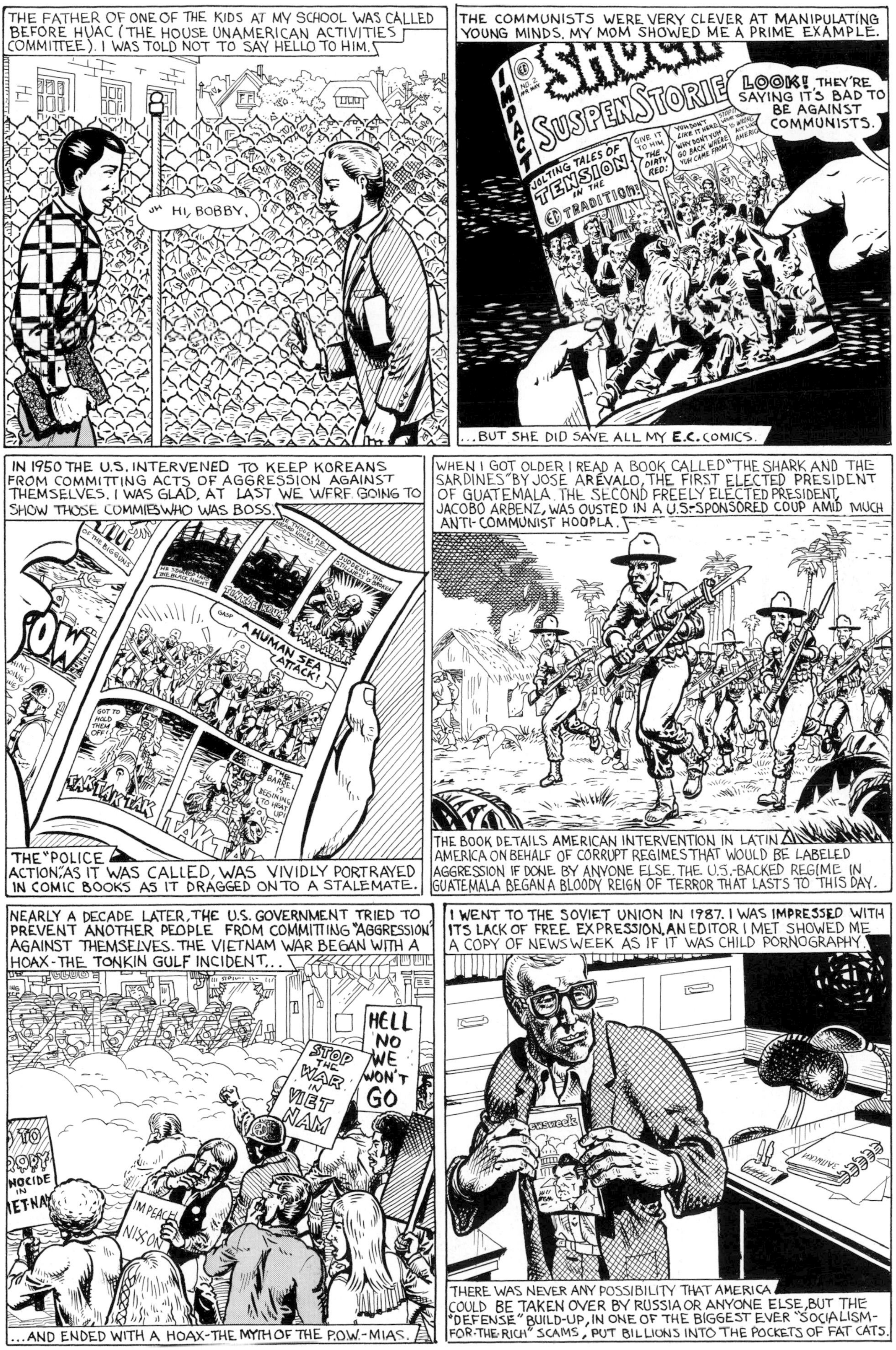
THE FATHER OF ONE OF THE KIDS AT MY SCHOOL WAS CALLED BEFORE HUAC (THE HOUSE UNAMERICAN ACTIVITIES COMMITTEE). I WAS TOLD NOT TO SAY HELLO TO HIM.
UH HI, BOBBY.
THE COMMUNISTS WERE VERY CLEVER AT MANIPULATING YOUNG MINDS. MY MOM SHOWED ME A PRIME EXAMPLE.
IMPACT
SUSPENSTORIES
JOLTING TALES OF TENSION IN THE EC TRADITION!
GIVE IT TO HIM, THE DIRTY RED!
YUH DON'T LIKE IT HERE. WHY DON'T YUH GO BACK WHERE YUH CAME FROM?
LOOK! THEY'RE SAYING IT'S BAD TO BE AGAINST COMMUNISTS.
...BUT SHE DID SAVE ALL MY E.C. COMICS.
IN 1950 THE U.S. INTERVENED TO KEEP KOREANS FROM COMMITTING ACTS OF AGGRESSION AGAINST THEMSELVES. I WAS GLAD, AT LAST WE WERE GOING TO SHOW THOSE COMMIES WHO WAS BOSS.
POW
HE STARED INTO THE BLACK NIGHT
SUDDENLY THE STILLNESS IS BROKEN
GASP
A HUMAN SEA ATTACK!
GOT TO HOLD THEM OFF!
TAK TAK TAK
THE BARREL IS BEGINING TO HEAT UP!
THE "POLICE ACTION," AS IT WAS CALLED, WAS VIVIDLY PORTRAYED IN COMIC BOOKS AS IT DRAGGED ON TO A STALEMATE.
WHEN I GOT OLDER I READ A BOOK CALLED "THE SHARK AND THE SARDINES" BY JOSE ARÉVALO, THE FIRST ELECTED PRESIDENT OF GUATEMALA. THE SECOND FREELY ELECTED PRESIDENT, JACOBO ARBENZ, WAS OUSTED IN A U.S.-SPONSORED COUP AMID MUCH ANTI-COMMUNIST HOOPLA.
THE BOOK DETAILS AMERICAN INTERVENTION IN LATIN AMERICA ON BEHALF OF CORRUPT REGIMES THAT WOULD BE LABELED AGGRESSION IF DONE BY ANYONE ELSE. THE U.S.-BACKED REGIME IN GUATEMALA BEGAN A BLOODY REIGN OF TERROR THAT LASTS TO THIS DAY.
NEARLY A DECADE LATER, THE U.S. GOVERNMENT TRIED TO PREVENT ANOTHER PEOPLE FROM COMMITTING "AGGRESSION" AGAINST THEMSELVES. THE VIETNAM WAR BEGAN WITH A HOAX - THE TONKIN GULF INCIDENT...
HELL NO WE WON'T GO
STOP THE WAR IN VIET NAM
IMPEACH NIXON
...AND ENDED WITH A HOAX - THE MYTH OF THE P.O.W.-MIAS.
I WENT TO THE SOVIET UNION IN 1987. I WAS IMPRESSED WITH ITS LACK OF FREE EXPRESSION. AN EDITOR I MET SHOWED ME A COPY OF NEWSWEEK AS IF IT WAS CHILD PORNOGRAPHY.
Newsweek
THERE WAS NEVER ANY POSSIBILITY THAT AMERICA COULD BE TAKEN OVER BY RUSSIA OR ANYONE ELSE, BUT THE "DEFENSE" BUILD-UP, IN ONE OF THE BIGGEST EVER "SOCIALISM-FOR-THE-RICH" SCAMS, PUT BILLIONS INTO THE POCKETS OF FAT CATS.

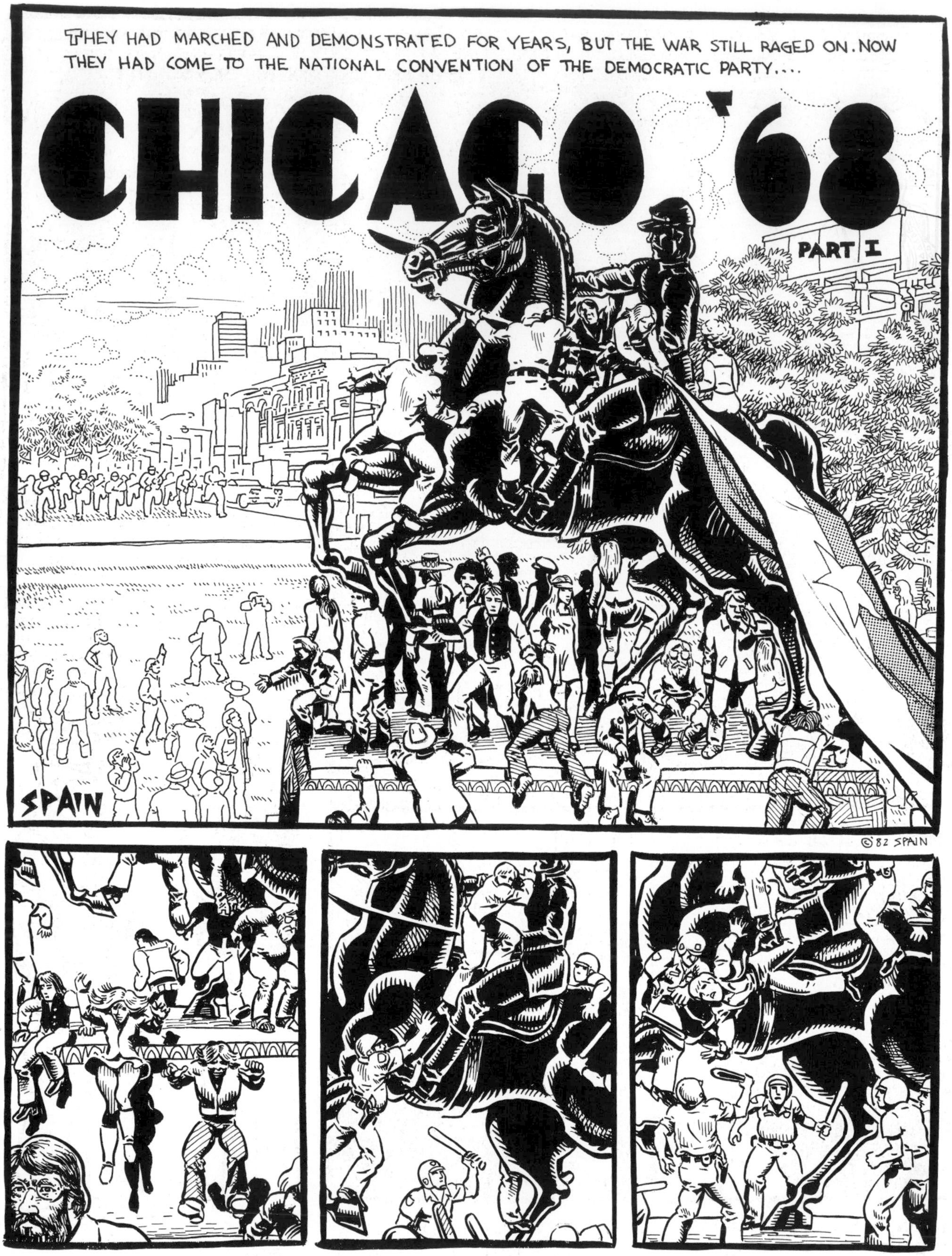
THEY HAD MARCHED AND DEMONSTRATED FOR YEARS, BUT THE WAR STILL RAGED ON. NOW THEY HAD COME TO THE NATIONAL CONVENTION OF THE DEMOCRATIC PARTY....
CHICAGO '68
PART I
SPAIN
©'82 SPAIN

P. 256–260 from *Gates of Eden* #1, 1982

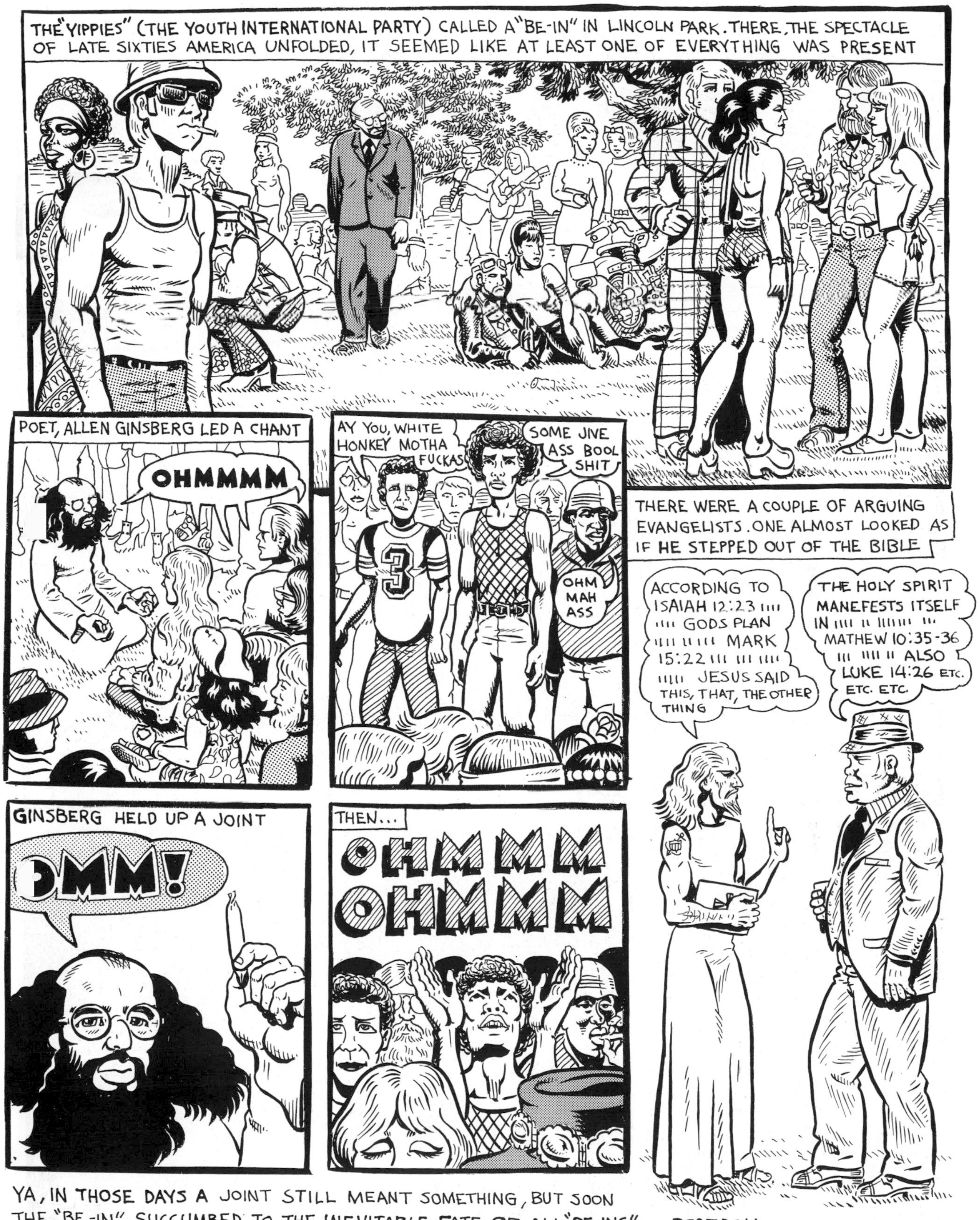
THE "YIPPIES" (THE YOUTH INTERNATIONAL PARTY) CALLED A "BE-IN" IN LINCOLN PARK. THERE, THE SPECTACLE OF LATE SIXTIES AMERICA UNFOLDED, IT SEEMED LIKE AT LEAST ONE OF EVERYTHING WAS PRESENT
POET, ALLEN GINSBERG LED A CHANT
OHMMMM
AY YOU, WHITE HONKEY MOTHA FUCKAS
SOME JIVE ASS BOOL SHIT
OHM MAH ASS
THERE WERE A COUPLE OF ARGUING EVANGELISTS. ONE ALMOST LOOKED AS IF HE STEPPED OUT OF THE BIBLE
ACCORDING TO ISAIAH 12:23 GODS PLAN MARK 15:22 JESUS SAID THIS, THAT, THE OTHER THING
THE HOLY SPIRIT MANEFESTS ITSELF IN MATHEW 10:35-36 ALSO LUKE 14:26 ETC. ETC. ETC.
GINSBERG HELD UP A JOINT
OMM!
THEN...
OHMMMM OHMMMM
YA, IN THOSE DAYS A JOINT STILL MEANT SOMETHING, BUT SOON THE "BE-IN" SUCCUMBED TO THE INEVITABLE FATE OF ALL "BE-INS".... BOREDOM

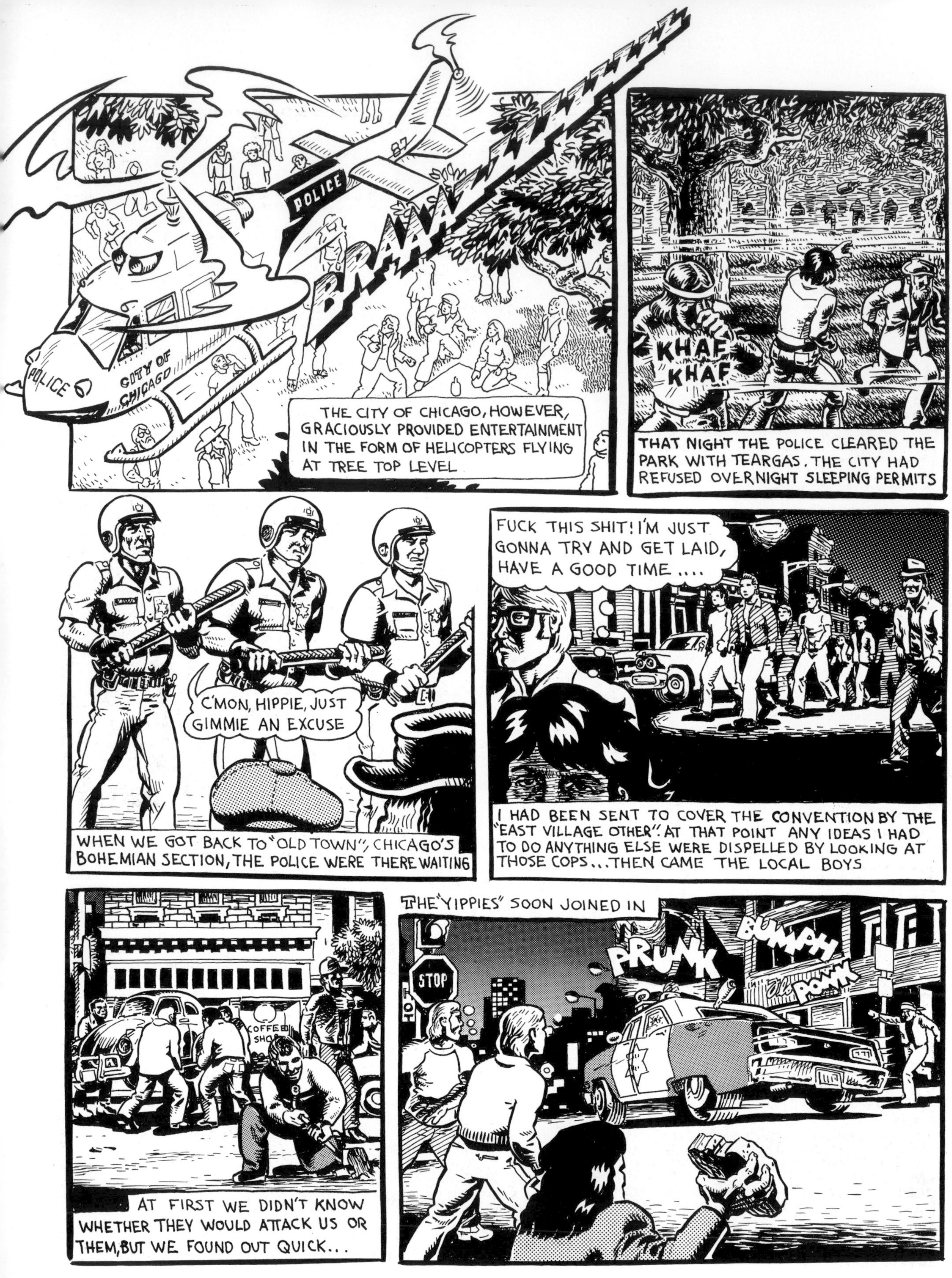
BRAAAAZZZZZZZZ
POLICE
CITY OF CHICAGO
POLICE
THE CITY OF CHICAGO, HOWEVER, GRACIOUSLY PROVIDED ENTERTAINMENT IN THE FORM OF HELICOPTERS FLYING AT TREE TOP LEVEL
KHAF KHAF
THAT NIGHT THE POLICE CLEARED THE PARK WITH TEARGAS. THE CITY HAD REFUSED OVERNIGHT SLEEPING PERMITS
C'MON, HIPPIE, JUST GIMMIE AN EXCUSE
WHEN WE GOT BACK TO "OLD TOWN", CHICAGO'S BOHEMIAN SECTION, THE POLICE WERE THERE WAITING
FUCK THIS SHIT! I'M JUST GONNA TRY AND GET LAID, HAVE A GOOD TIME....
I HAD BEEN SENT TO COVER THE CONVENTION BY THE "EAST VILLAGE OTHER". AT THAT POINT ANY IDEAS I HAD TO DO ANYTHING ELSE WERE DISPELLED BY LOOKING AT THOSE COPS... THEN CAME THE LOCAL BOYS
COFFEE SHO
AT FIRST WE DIDN'T KNOW WHETHER THEY WOULD ATTACK US OR THEM, BUT WE FOUND OUT QUICK...
THE "YIPPIES" SOON JOINED IN
STOP
PRUNK
BUMPH
POWK

YA, THE CHICAGO POLICE DEPT. WAS IN FOR A SURPRISE THAT NIGHT

LATER ON, AT A PARTY

SURE, IT'S ALL P.R., MAN. EVERYONE KNOWS THAT DRUGS MAKE YOU ALTRUISTIC, SO THE MORE KIDS GET LOADED THE MORE ALTRUISTIC THEY'LL BE

AND THAT'S THE REVOLUTION

I ..UNH.. DON'T THINK SO!

AS STONED AS I WAS, HIS ARGUMENT SEEMED PRETTY BIZARRE

U.S. OUT OF VIETNAM N

THE NEXT DAY WE TRIED TO GET AROUND THE ROADBLOCKS TO THE CONVENTION. AS WE PASSED MARINA CITY, I SAW A WOMAN WATCHING US FROM THE UPPER FLOORS. I WONDERED WHAT SHE WAS THINKING.

OUR WAY WAS BLOCKED OFF ON A SIDE STREET BY JEEPS WITH BARBED WIRE RACKS. WE WENT BACK

AS WE RETREATED, WE RAN INTO A POLICE CAR COMING THE OTHER WAY. THEY WERE OBVIOUSLY SURPRISED TO SEE US.

IN RESPONSE TO CRITICISM OF HIS POLICE DEPARTMENT'S HANDLING OF DEMONSTRATORS, THE MAYOR ISSUED A STATEMENT

THE POLICE ARE NOT HERE TO CREATE DISORDER, THEY ARE HERE TO PRESERVE DIS ORDER

ONE EVENING, A VIETCONG FLAG WAS PULLED DOWN BY A GEORGE WALLACE* SUPPORTER. IT WAS PICKED UP BY THE SWIRLING CROWD AND CARRIED THROUGH THE PARK

IN THE MIDDLE OF THIS CONFUSION ED SANDERS INTRODUCED ME TO JEAN GENET

THERE WERE AREAS THAT WERE DANGEROUS FOR DEMONSTRATORS

OTHER AREAS THAT WERE PERILOUS FOR "PIGS"

POMF

THEN THERE WERE EVEN PLACES THAT SEEMED LIKE NEUTRAL ZONES

AT THIS POINT THE POLICE WERE CLEARLY SHOWING SIGNS OF BEING OUT OF CONTROL

IMPROFESSIONAL BEHAVIOR

COMING NEXT PART III "THE REAL ACTION"

DEDICATED TO JOEL FABRICANT

* GEORGE WALLACE - RIGHTWING PRESIDENTIAL CANDIDATE

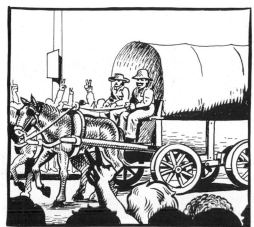

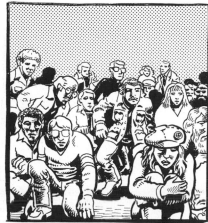

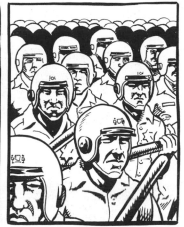

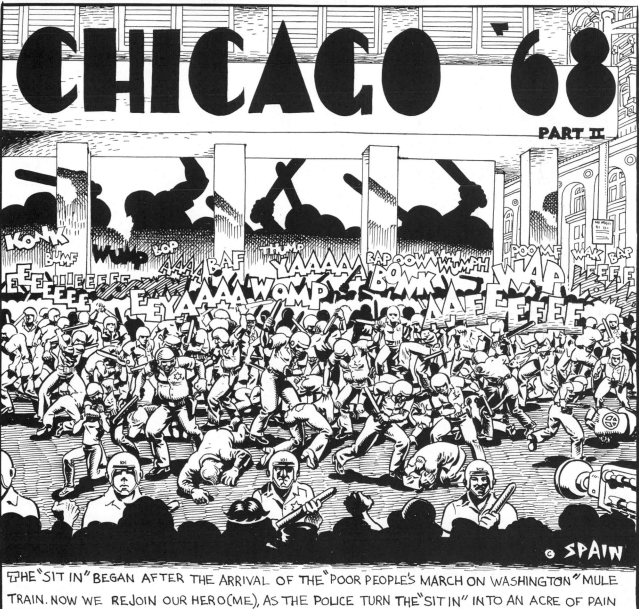

CHICAGO '68
PART II
KONK
BUMF
WUMP
BOP
THUMP
BAF
YAAAAA
BAP
OOW
WUMPH
POOMF
WAK
BAP
WAP
BONK
WOMP
EEYAAAA
AAEEEEE
© SPAIN
THE "SIT IN" BEGAN AFTER THE ARRIVAL OF THE "POOR PEOPLE'S MARCH ON WASHINGTON" MULE TRAIN. NOW WE REJOIN OUR HERO (ME), AS THE POLICE TURN THE "SIT IN" INTO AN ACRE OF PAIN
© SPAIN 1982

P. 261–264 from *Prime Cuts* #6, 1988

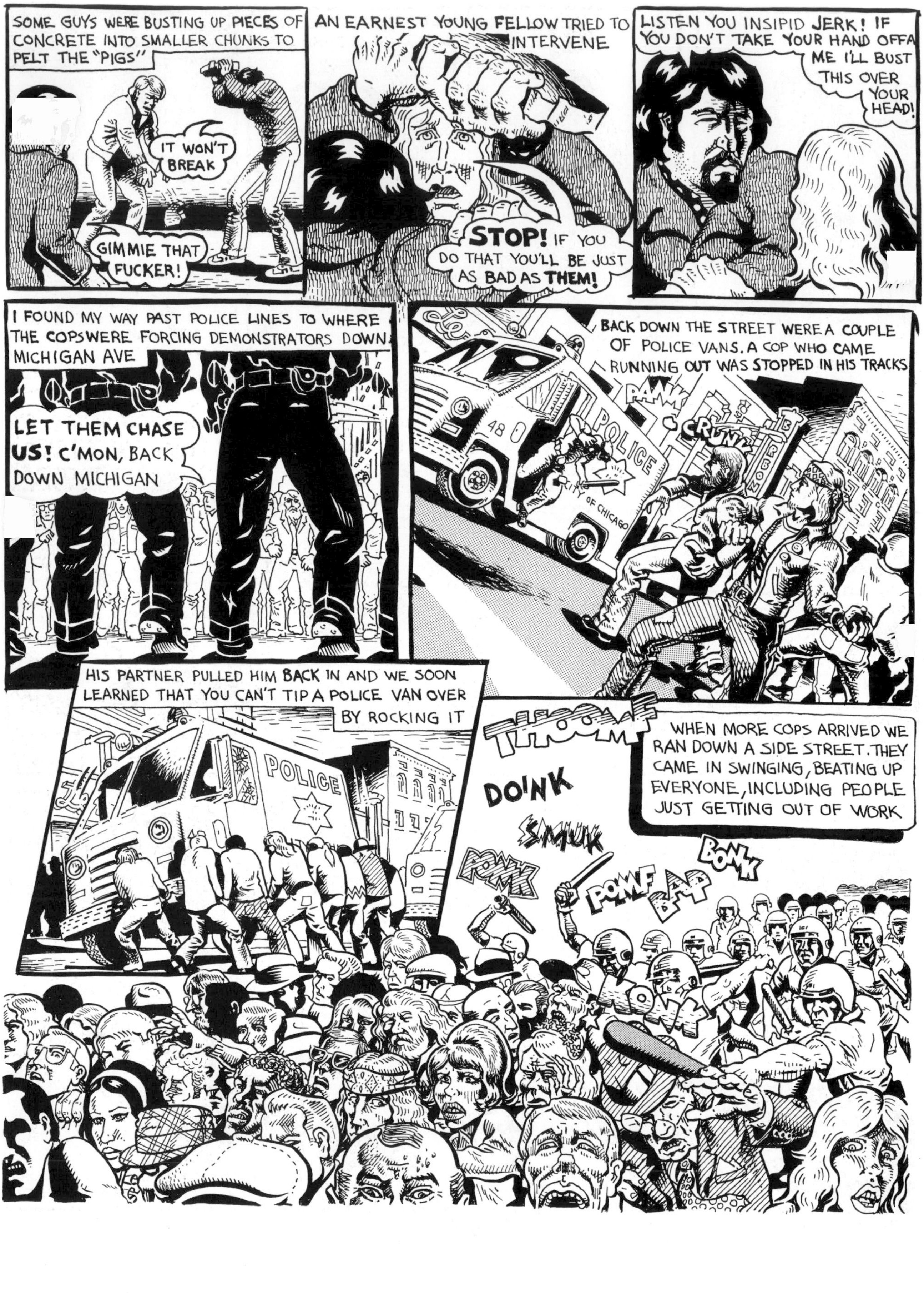
SOME GUYS WERE BUSTING UP PIECES OF CONCRETE INTO SMALLER CHUNKS TO PELT THE "PIGS"
IT WON'T BREAK
GIMMIE THAT FUCKER!
AN EARNEST YOUNG FELLOW TRIED TO INTERVENE
STOP! IF YOU DO THAT YOU'LL BE JUST AS BAD AS THEM!
LISTEN YOU INSIPID JERK! IF YOU DON'T TAKE YOUR HAND OFFA ME I'LL BUST THIS OVER YOUR HEAD!
I FOUND MY WAY PAST POLICE LINES TO WHERE THE COPS WERE FORCING DEMONSTRATORS DOWN MICHIGAN AVE
LET THEM CHASE US! C'MON, BACK DOWN MICHIGAN
BACK DOWN THE STREET WERE A COUPLE OF POLICE VANS. A COP WHO CAME RUNNING OUT WAS STOPPED IN HIS TRACKS
PANK
CRUNK
POLICE
CITY OF CHICAGO
HIS PARTNER PULLED HIM BACK IN AND WE SOON LEARNED THAT YOU CAN'T TIP A POLICE VAN OVER BY ROCKING IT
POLICE
THOOMP
WHEN MORE COPS ARRIVED WE RAN DOWN A SIDE STREET. THEY CAME IN SWINGING, BEATING UP EVERYONE, INCLUDING PEOPLE JUST GETTING OUT OF WORK
DOINK
SMUK
PONK
BONK
POMF
BAP
HONK

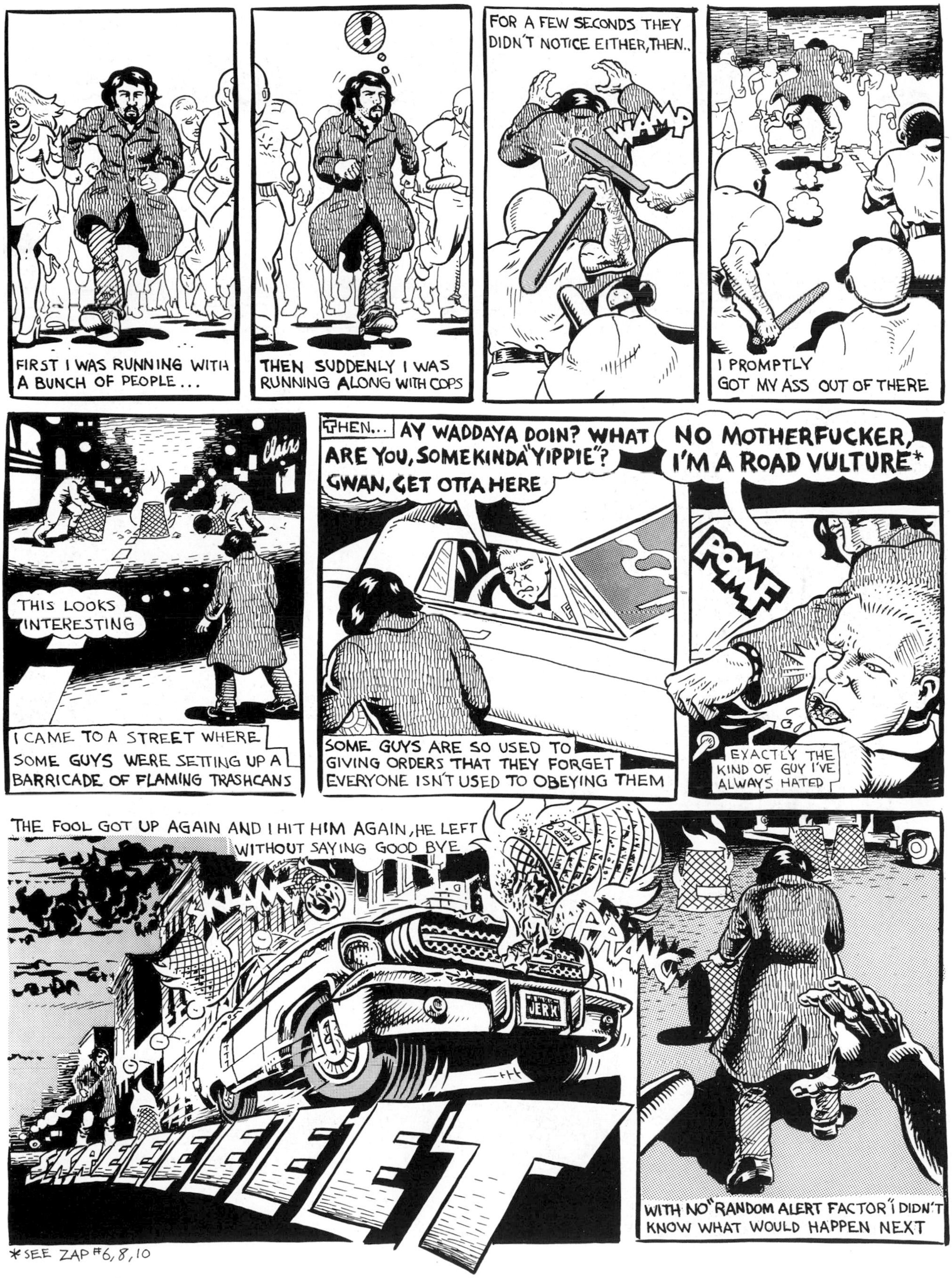

FIRST I WAS RUNNING WITH A BUNCH OF PEOPLE...
!
THEN SUDDENLY I WAS RUNNING ALONG WITH COPS
FOR A FEW SECONDS THEY DIDN'T NOTICE EITHER, THEN..
WAMP
I PROMPTLY GOT MY ASS OUT OF THERE
THIS LOOKS INTERESTING
I CAME TO A STREET WHERE SOME GUYS WERE SETTING UP A BARRICADE OF FLAMING TRASHCANS
THEN... AY WADDAYA DOIN? WHAT ARE YOU, SOMEKINDA "YIPPIE"? GWAN, GET OTTA HERE
SOME GUYS ARE SO USED TO GIVING ORDERS THAT THEY FORGET EVERYONE ISN'T USED TO OBEYING THEM
NO MOTHERFUCKER, I'M A ROAD VULTURE*
POMF
EXACTLY THE KIND OF GUY I'VE ALWAYS HATED
THE FOOL GOT UP AGAIN AND I HIT HIM AGAIN, HE LEFT WITHOUT SAYING GOOD BYE
KLAM
PRANG
JERK
SKREEEEEEET
WITH NO "RANDOM ALERT FACTOR" I DIDN'T KNOW WHAT WOULD HAPPEN NEXT
*SEE ZAP #6, 8, 10

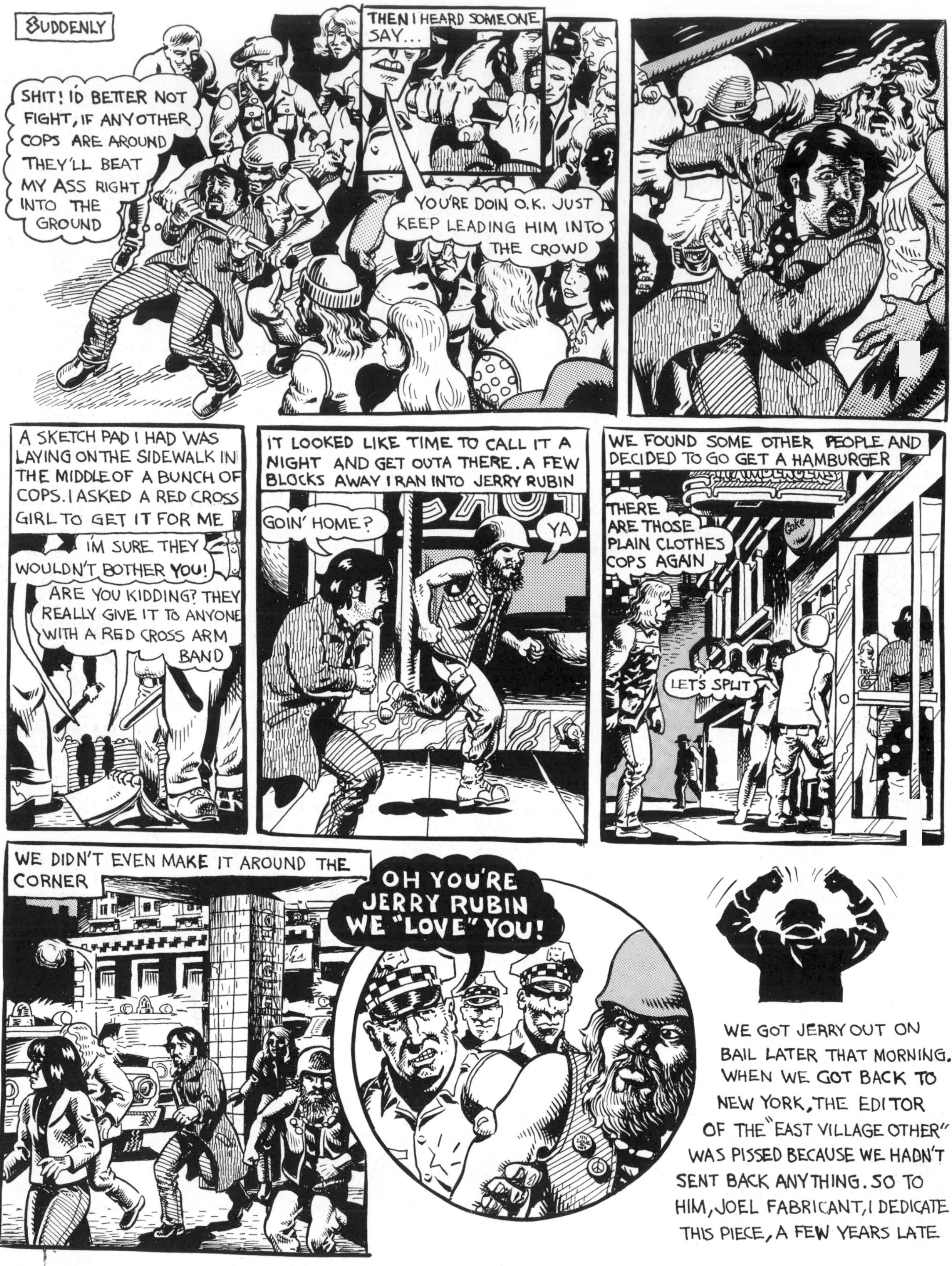
SUDDENLY
SHIT! I'D BETTER NOT FIGHT, IF ANY OTHER COPS ARE AROUND THEY'LL BEAT MY ASS RIGHT INTO THE GROUND
THEN I HEARD SOMEONE SAY...
YOU'RE DOIN O.K. JUST KEEP LEADING HIM INTO THE CROWD
A SKETCH PAD I HAD WAS LAYING ON THE SIDEWALK IN THE MIDDLE OF A BUNCH OF COPS. I ASKED A RED CROSS GIRL TO GET IT FOR ME
I'M SURE THEY WOULDN'T BOTHER YOU!
ARE YOU KIDDING? THEY REALLY GIVE IT TO ANYONE WITH A RED CROSS ARM BAND
IT LOOKED LIKE TIME TO CALL IT A NIGHT AND GET OUTA THERE. A FEW BLOCKS AWAY I RAN INTO JERRY RUBIN
GOIN' HOME?
YA
WE FOUND SOME OTHER PEOPLE AND DECIDED TO GO GET A HAMBURGER
THERE ARE THOSE PLAIN CLOTHES COPS AGAIN
LET'S SPLIT
WE DIDN'T EVEN MAKE IT AROUND THE CORNER
OH YOU'RE JERRY RUBIN WE "LOVE" YOU!
WE GOT JERRY OUT ON BAIL LATER THAT MORNING. WHEN WE GOT BACK TO NEW YORK, THE EDITOR OF THE "EAST VILLAGE OTHER" WAS PISSED BECAUSE WE HADN'T SENT BACK ANYTHING. SO TO HIM, JOEL FABRICANT, I DEDICATE THIS PIECE, A FEW YEARS LATE

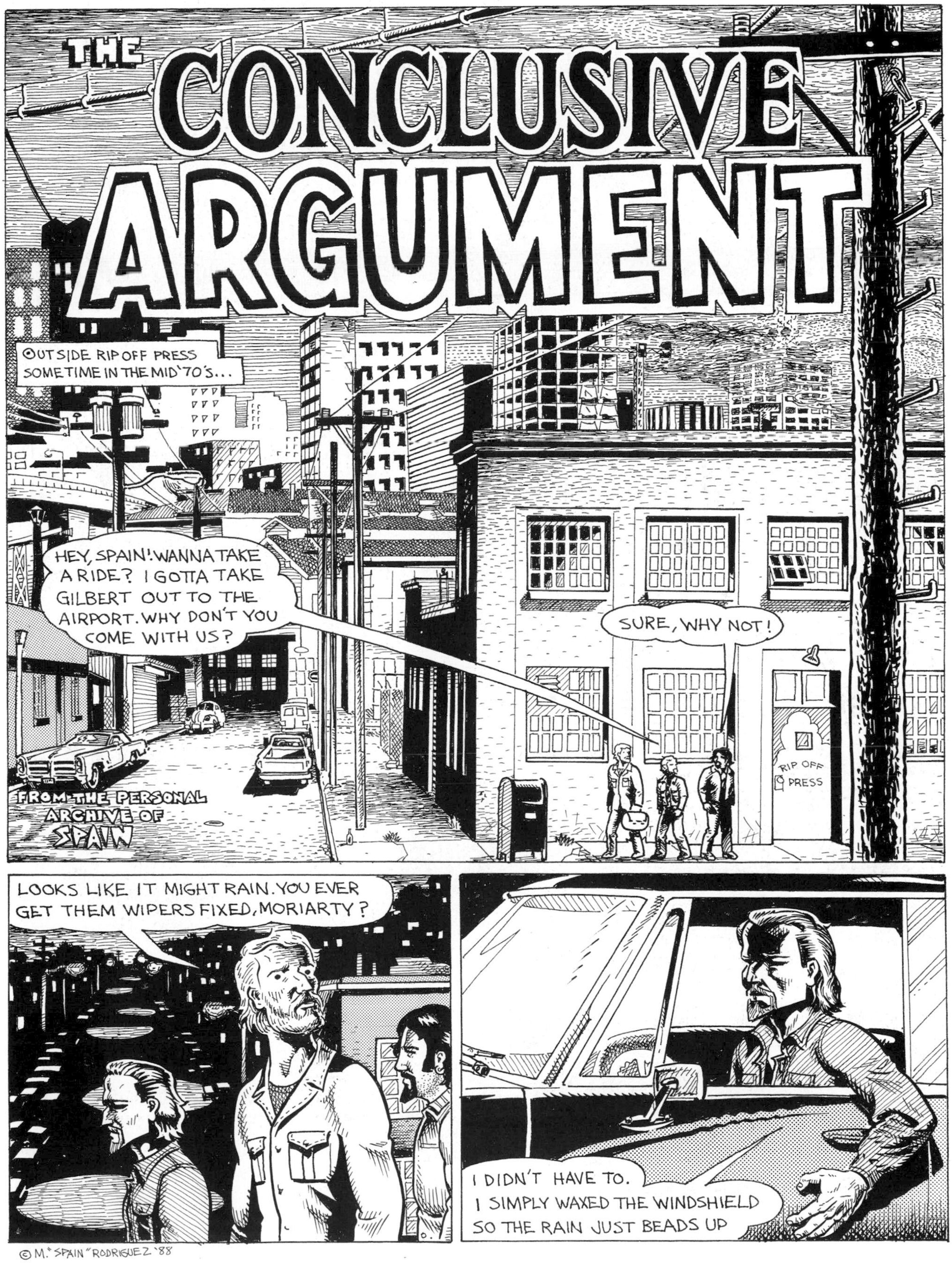
THE CONCLUSIVE ARGUMENT
OUTSIDE RIP OFF PRESS SOMETIME IN THE MID '70'S...
HEY, SPAIN! WANNA TAKE A RIDE? I GOTTA TAKE GILBERT OUT TO THE AIRPORT. WHY DON'T YOU COME WITH US?
SURE, WHY NOT!
RIP OFF PRESS
FROM THE PERSONAL ARCHIVE OF SPAIN
LOOKS LIKE IT MIGHT RAIN. YOU EVER GET THEM WIPERS FIXED, MORIARTY?
I DIDN'T HAVE TO. I SIMPLY WAXED THE WINDSHIELD SO THE RAIN JUST BEADS UP
© M. "SPAIN" RODRIGUEZ '88

P. 265–267 from *Rip Off Comix* #21, 1988

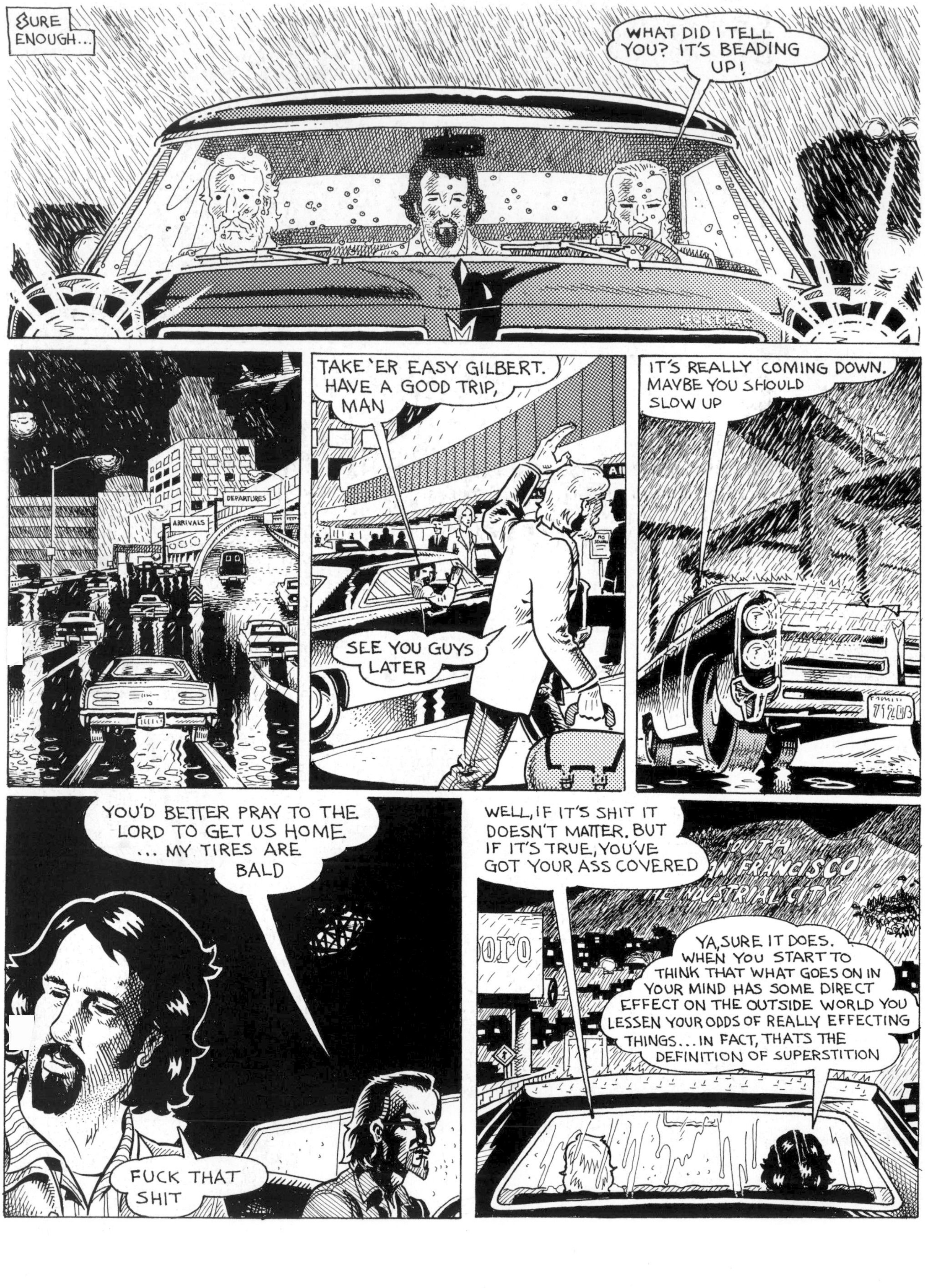
SURE ENOUGH...
WHAT DID I TELL YOU? IT'S BEADING UP!
DEPARTURES
ARRIVALS
TAKE 'ER EASY GILBERT. HAVE A GOOD TRIP, MAN
SEE YOU GUYS LATER
IT'S REALLY COMING DOWN. MAYBE YOU SHOULD SLOW UP
YOU'D BETTER PRAY TO THE LORD TO GET US HOME ... MY TIRES ARE BALD
FUCK THAT SHIT
WELL, IF IT'S SHIT IT DOESN'T MATTER. BUT IF IT'S TRUE, YOU'VE GOT YOUR ASS COVERED
YA, SURE IT DOES. WHEN YOU START TO THINK THAT WHAT GOES ON IN YOUR MIND HAS SOME DIRECT EFFECT ON THE OUTSIDE WORLD YOU LESSEN YOUR ODDS OF REALLY EFFECTING THINGS... IN FACT, THATS THE DEFINITION OF SUPERSTITION

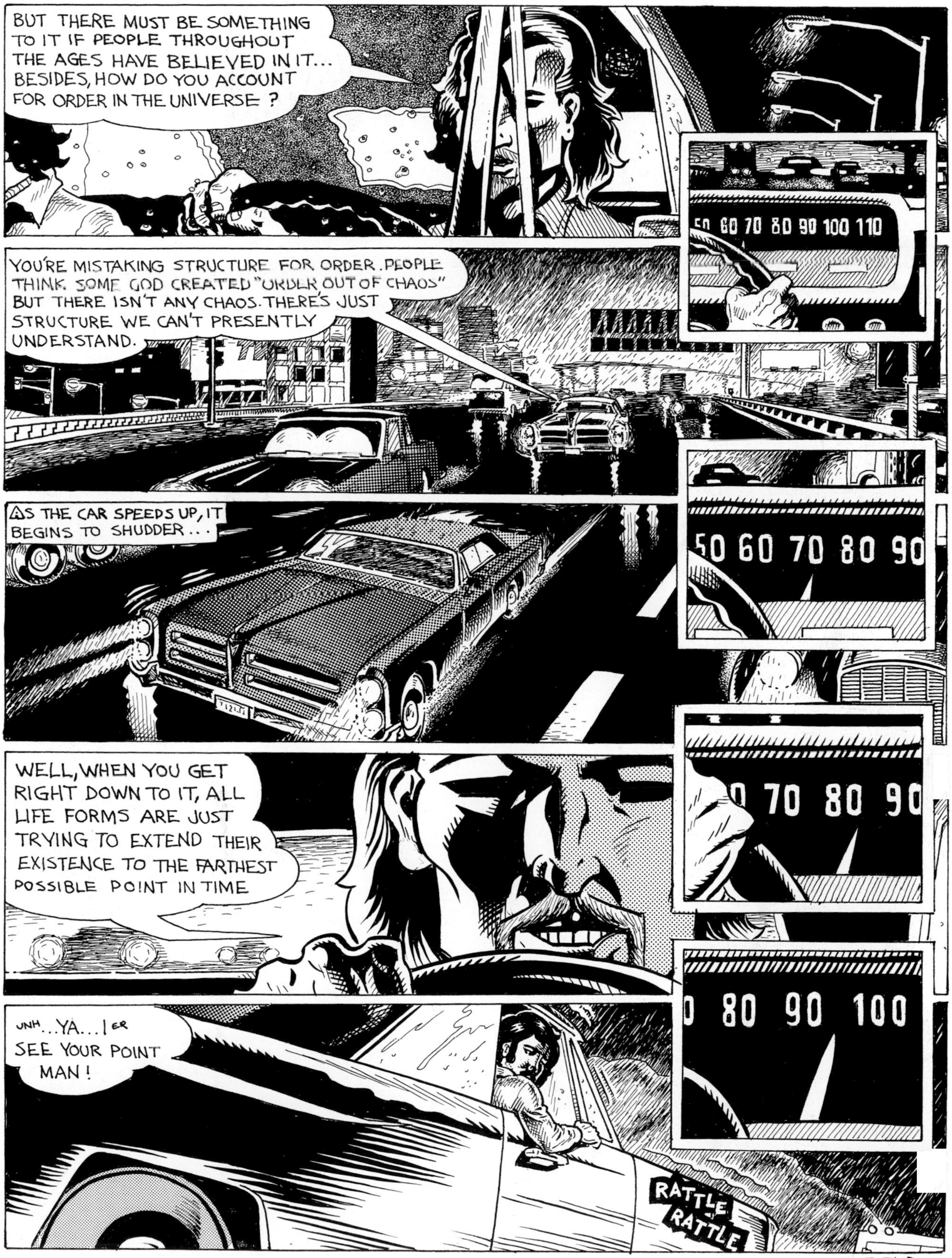
BUT THERE MUST BE SOMETHING TO IT IF PEOPLE THROUGHOUT THE AGES HAVE BELIEVED IN IT... BESIDES, HOW DO YOU ACCOUNT FOR ORDER IN THE UNIVERSE ?
50 60 70 80 90 100 110
YOU'RE MISTAKING STRUCTURE FOR ORDER. PEOPLE THINK SOME GOD CREATED "ORDER OUT OF CHAOS" BUT THERE ISN'T ANY CHAOS. THERE'S JUST STRUCTURE WE CAN'T PRESENTLY UNDERSTAND.
AS THE CAR SPEEDS UP, IT BEGINS TO SHUDDER...
50 60 70 80 90
WELL, WHEN YOU GET RIGHT DOWN TO IT, ALL LIFE FORMS ARE JUST TRYING TO EXTEND THEIR EXISTENCE TO THE FARTHEST POSSIBLE POINT IN TIME
0 70 80 90
UNH...YA...I ER SEE YOUR POINT MAN!
0 80 90 100
RATTLE RATTLE

THE END

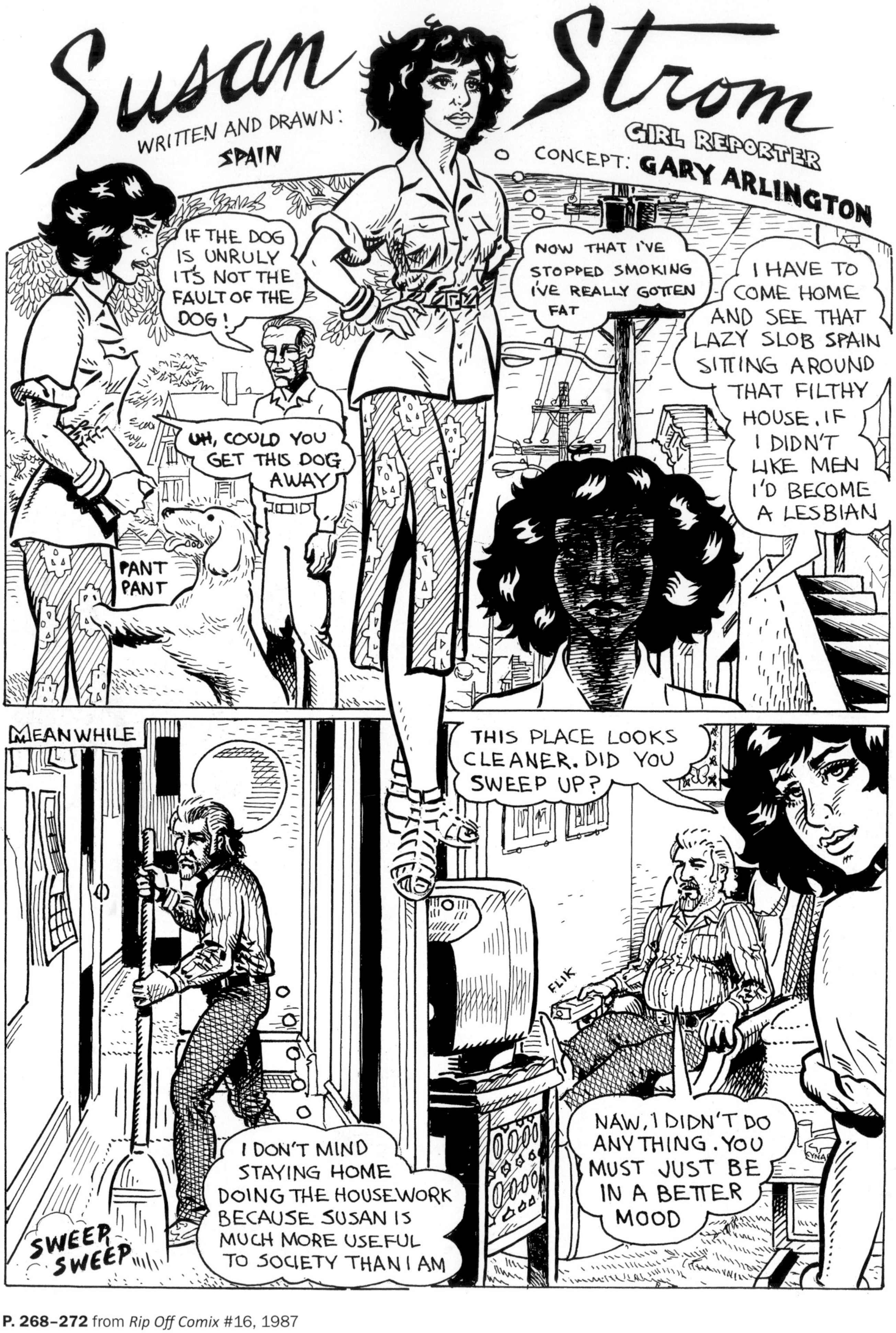
Susan Strom
WRITTEN AND DRAWN: SPAIN
GIRL REPORTER
CONCEPT: GARY ARLINGTON
IF THE DOG IS UNRULY IT'S NOT THE FAULT OF THE DOG!
UH, COULD YOU GET THIS DOG AWAY
PANT PANT
NOW THAT I'VE STOPPED SMOKING I'VE REALLY GOTTEN FAT
I HAVE TO COME HOME AND SEE THAT LAZY SLOB SPAIN SITTING AROUND THAT FILTHY HOUSE. IF I DIDN'T LIKE MEN I'D BECOME A LESBIAN
MEANWHILE
I DON'T MIND STAYING HOME DOING THE HOUSEWORK BECAUSE SUSAN IS MUCH MORE USEFUL TO SOCIETY THAN I AM
SWEEP SWEEP
THIS PLACE LOOKS CLEANER. DID YOU SWEEP UP?
FLIK
NAW, I DIDN'T DO ANYTHING. YOU MUST JUST BE IN A BETTER MOOD

P. 268–272 from *Rip Off Comix* #16, 1987

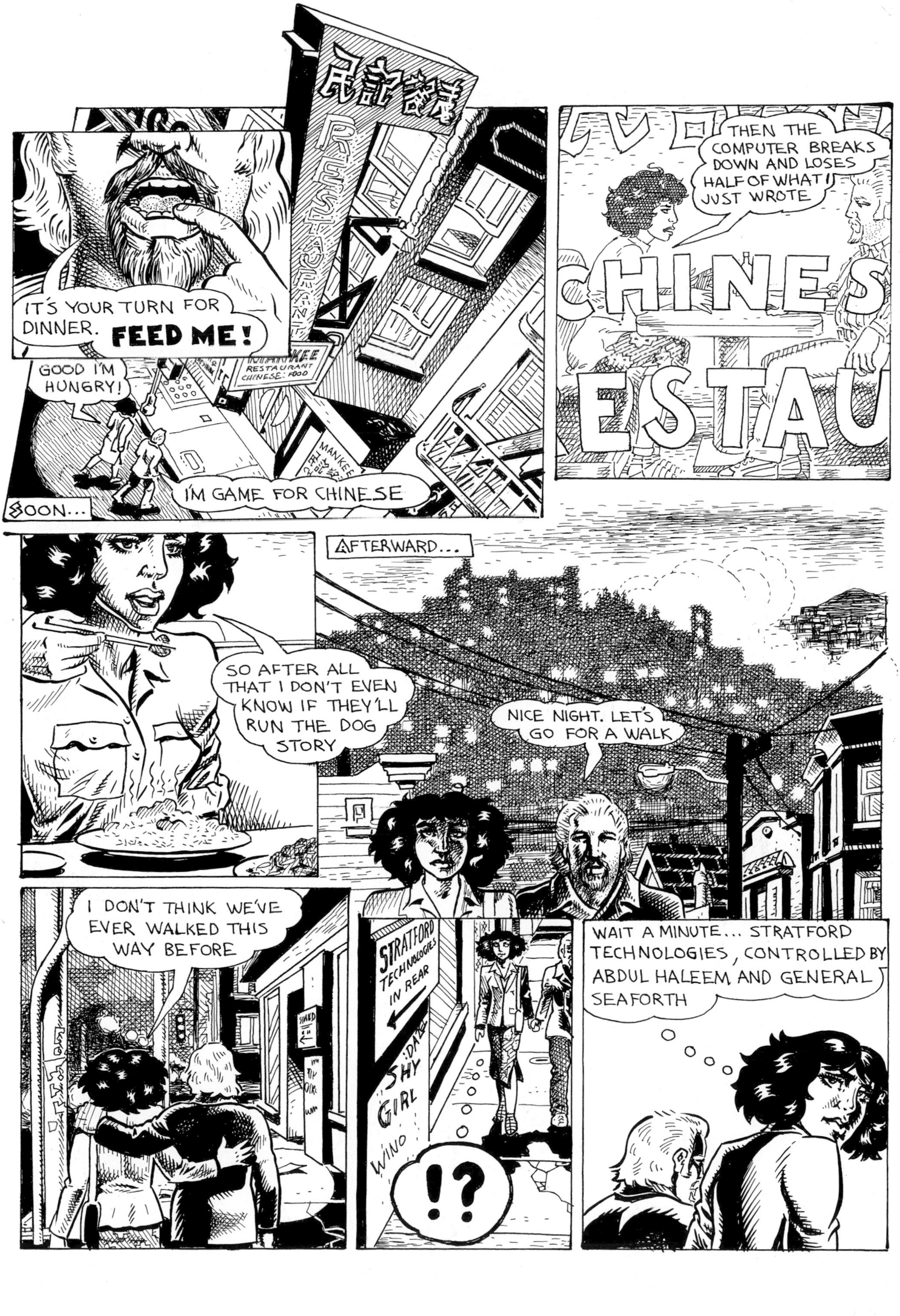
IT'S YOUR TURN FOR DINNER. FEED ME!
SOON...
GOOD I'M HUNGRY!
I'M GAME FOR CHINESE
RESTAURANT CHINESE FOOD
THEN THE COMPUTER BREAKS DOWN AND LOSES HALF OF WHAT I JUST WROTE
CHINES
ESTAU
SO AFTER ALL THAT I DON'T EVEN KNOW IF THEY'LL RUN THE DOG STORY
AFTERWARD...
NICE NIGHT. LET'S GO FOR A WALK
I DON'T THINK WE'VE EVER WALKED THIS WAY BEFORE
STRATFORD TECHNOLOGIES IN REAR
SHY GIRL
WINO
!?
WAIT A MINUTE... STRATFORD TECHNOLOGIES, CONTROLLED BY ABDUL HALEEM AND GENERAL SEAFORTH

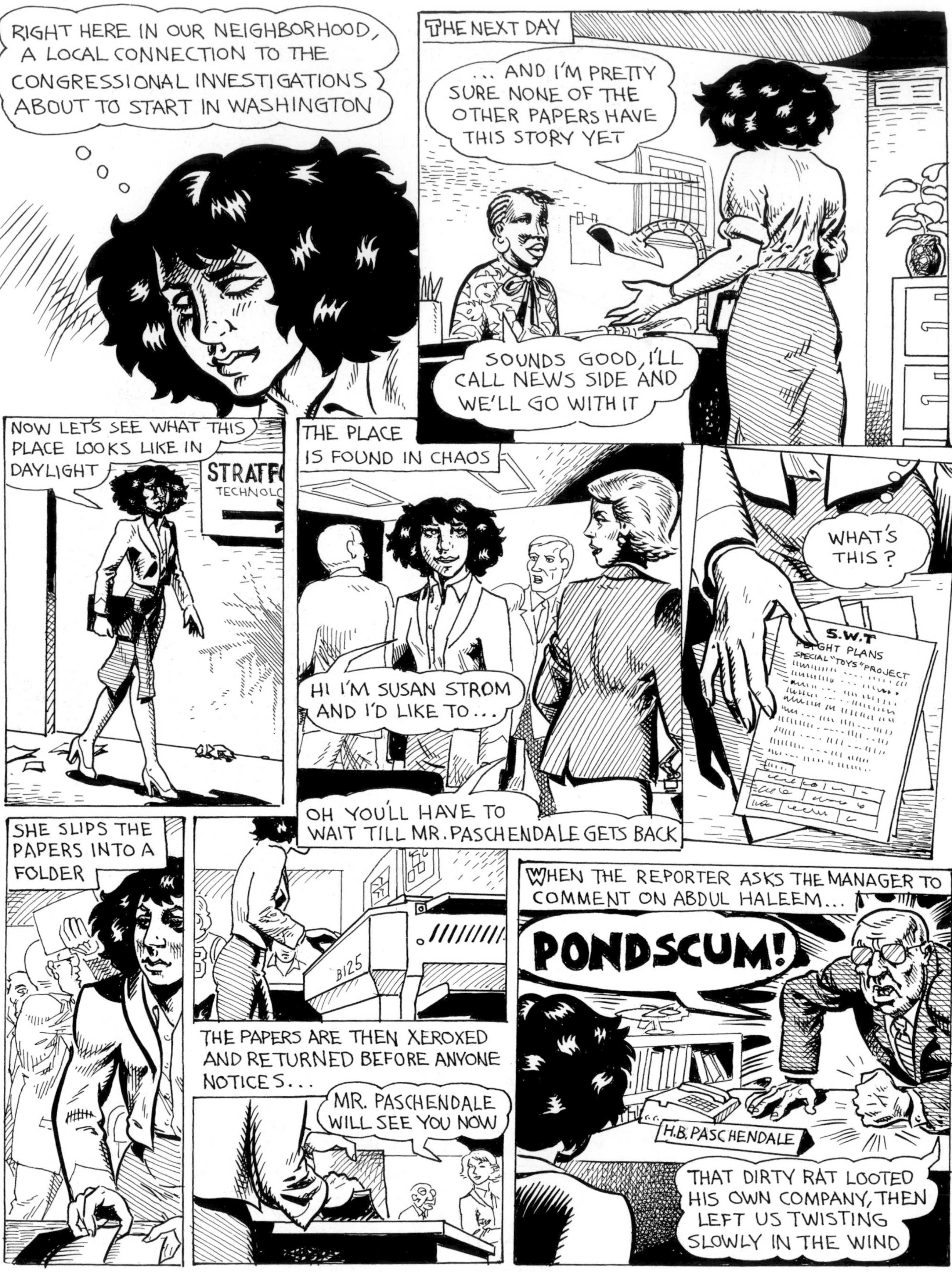
RIGHT HERE IN OUR NEIGHBORHOOD, A LOCAL CONNECTION TO THE CONGRESSIONAL INVESTIGATIONS ABOUT TO START IN WASHINGTON
THE NEXT DAY
... AND I'M PRETTY SURE NONE OF THE OTHER PAPERS HAVE THIS STORY YET
SOUNDS GOOD, I'LL CALL NEWS SIDE AND WE'LL GO WITH IT
NOW LET'S SEE WHAT THIS PLACE LOOKS LIKE IN DAYLIGHT
STRATF
TECHNOLO
THE PLACE IS FOUND IN CHAOS
HI I'M SUSAN STROM AND I'D LIKE TO...
OH YOU'LL HAVE TO WAIT TILL MR. PASCHENDALE GETS BACK
WHAT'S THIS?
S.W.T
SPECIAL "TOYS" PROJECT
SHE SLIPS THE PAPERS INTO A FOLDER
B125
THE PAPERS ARE THEN XEROXED AND RETURNED BEFORE ANYONE NOTICES...
MR. PASCHENDALE WILL SEE YOU NOW
WHEN THE REPORTER ASKS THE MANAGER TO COMMENT ON ABDUL HALEEM...
PONDSCUM!
H.B. PASCHENDALE
THAT DIRTY RAT LOOTED HIS OWN COMPANY, THEN LEFT US TWISTING SLOWLY IN THE WIND

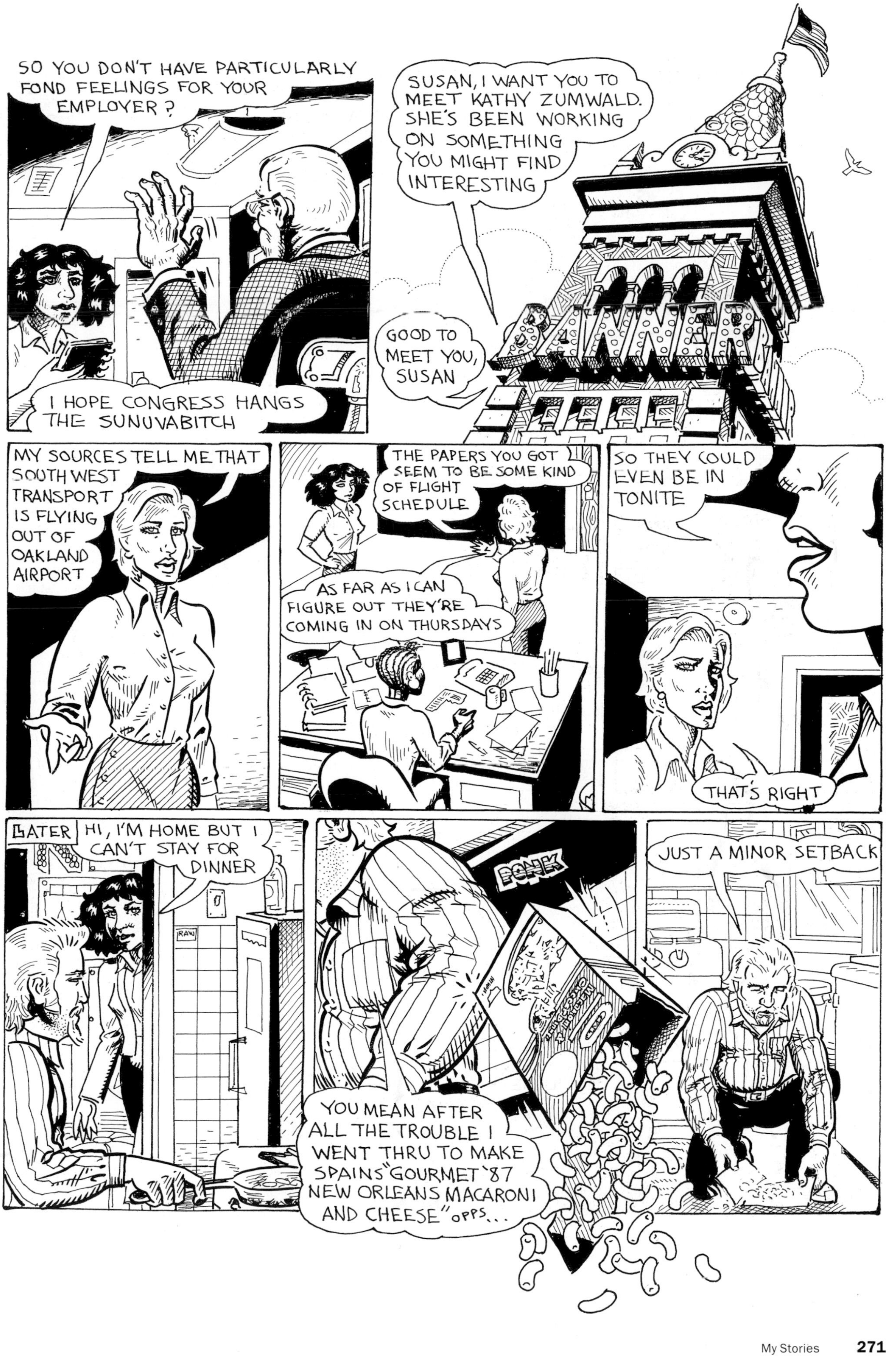
SO YOU DON'T HAVE PARTICULARLY FOND FEELINGS FOR YOUR EMPLOYER?
I HOPE CONGRESS HANGS THE SUNUVABITCH
SUSAN, I WANT YOU TO MEET KATHY ZUMWALD. SHE'S BEEN WORKING ON SOMETHING YOU MIGHT FIND INTERESTING
GOOD TO MEET YOU, SUSAN
BANNER
MY SOURCES TELL ME THAT SOUTH WEST TRANSPORT IS FLYING OUT OF OAKLAND AIRPORT
THE PAPERS YOU GOT SEEM TO BE SOME KIND OF FLIGHT SCHEDULE
AS FAR AS I CAN FIGURE OUT THEY'RE COMING IN ON THURSDAYS
SO THEY COULD EVEN BE IN TONITE
THAT'S RIGHT
LATER
HI, I'M HOME BUT I CAN'T STAY FOR DINNER
PONK
JUST A MINOR SETBACK
YOU MEAN AFTER ALL THE TROUBLE I WENT THRU TO MAKE SPAINS "GOURMET '87 NEW ORLEANS MACARONI AND CHEESE" OPPS...

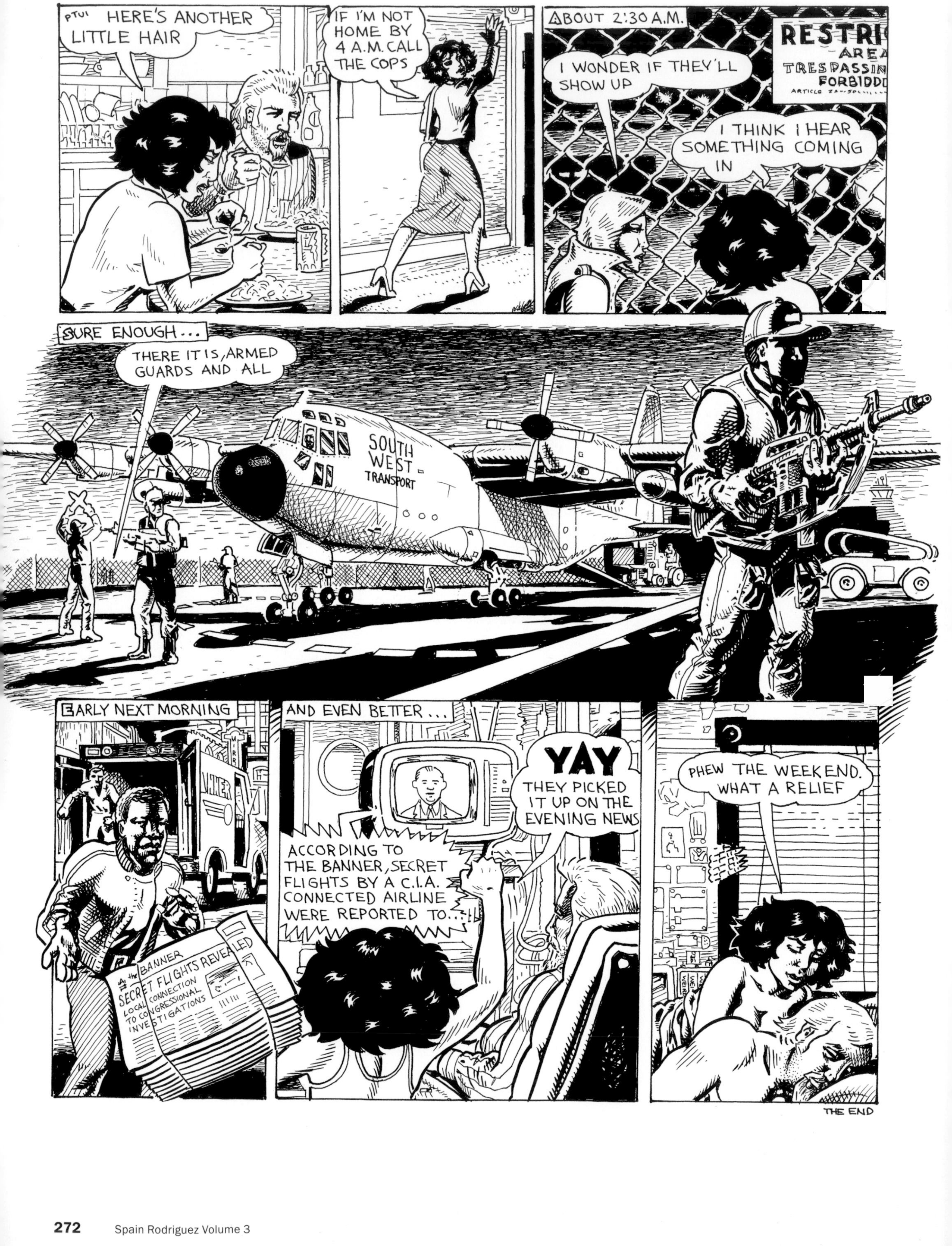
PTUI HERE'S ANOTHER LITTLE HAIR
IF I'M NOT HOME BY 4 A.M. CALL THE COPS
ABOUT 2:30 A.M.
RESTRIC
AREA
TRESPASSIN
FORBIDD
I WONDER IF THEY'LL SHOW UP
I THINK I HEAR SOMETHING COMING IN
SURE ENOUGH...
THERE IT IS, ARMED GUARDS AND ALL
SOUTH WEST TRANSPORT
EARLY NEXT MORNING
BANNER
SECRET FLIGHTS REVEALED
LOCAL CONNECTION TO CONGRESSIONAL INVESTIGATIONS
AND EVEN BETTER...
ACCORDING TO THE BANNER, SECRET FLIGHTS BY A C.I.A. CONNECTED AIRLINE WERE REPORTED TO...
YAY
THEY PICKED IT UP ON THE EVENING NEWS
PHEW THE WEEKEND. WHAT A RELIEF
THE END

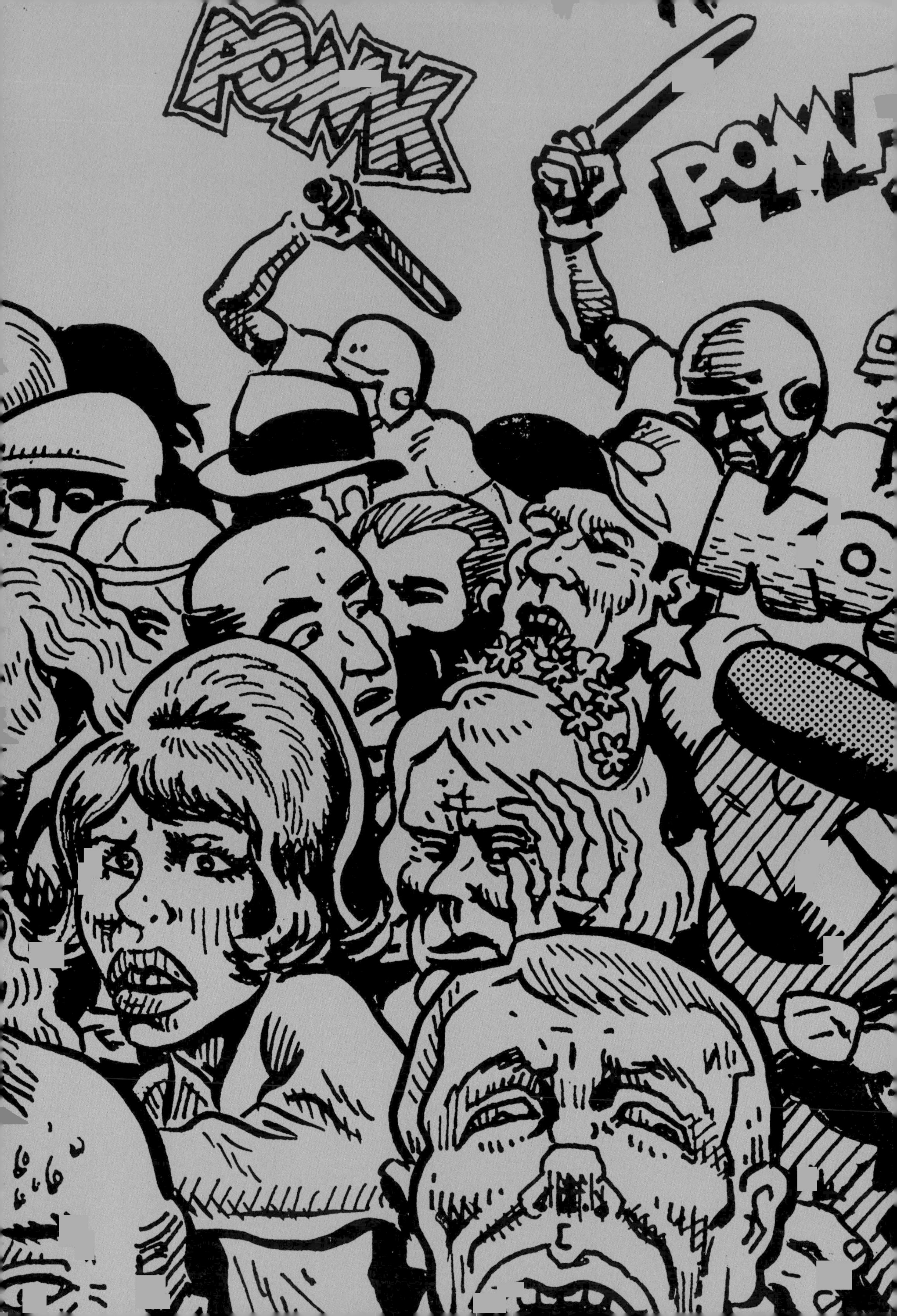
POWK